Give Your CPA Exam Score a Boost with these Essential Study Tools

Cram Course
Boost your score by 8-10 points!

- Get a final review with this condensed CPA Exam Review supplement – the perfect complement to your full review course
- Reinforce your understanding of the most heavily tested topics on the CPA Exam
- Take the Cram Course leading up to Exam Day to refresh your mind on important topics

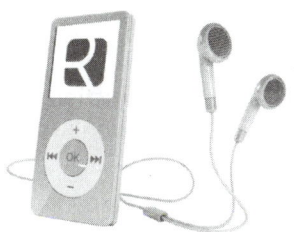

Audio Lectures
Maximize every minute leading up to the exam!

- Easy MP3 download – ideal for Apple or Android devices
- Turn any moment into a study opportunity! Listen to lectures on your commute, at the gym, or even as you nod off to sleep
- Immerse yourself in the most important CPA Exam topics

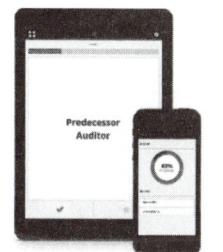

Digital Flashcards
Review on-the-go with the convenience of mobile flashcards!

- Solidify important CPA Exam concepts within each section
- Assess your strengths by flagging cards as *Mastered* or *Unmastered* for later review
- Customize your study session by breaking down your deck by topic and shuffle your card deck to encourage full understanding of each concept

CPA Exam Flashcards
Make studying portable, accessible, and fun!

- Harness overarching CPA Exam concepts
- Create important connections to actual CPA Exam usage and application
- Make studying more exciting by involving family & friends – pull out your flashcards for a quick & interactive study method.

CPA Exam MC Questions App
Quiz yourself anytime, anywhere!

- Quiz yourself with over 3,500 Multiple Choice Questions and AICPA-Released exam questions with expert-written solutions
- Assess your strengths & weaknesses with intuitive score reporting - then re-quiz on problem areas
- Bookmark specific questions, utilize built-in calculator, and hide or display time clock

FAR

Financial Accounting and Reporting

Written By:

Roger Philipp, CPA, CGMA

Roger CPA Review
2261 Market St. #333
San Francisco, California 94114
www.RogerCPAreview.com
(877) 764-4272
(415) 346-4272

Permissions

The following items are utilized in this volume, and are copyright property of the American Institute of Certified Public Accountants, Inc. (AICPA), all rights reserved:

- Uniform CPA Examination and Questions and Unofficial Answers, Copyright © 1991, 1992, 1993, 1994, 1995, 1996, 1997, 1998, 1999, 2000, 2001, 2002, 2003, 2004, 2005, 2006, 2007, 2008, 2009, 2010, 2011, 2012, 2013, 2014, 2015 and 2016
- Audit and Accounting Guides, Auditing Procedure Studies, Risk Alerts, Statements of Position, and code of Professional Conduct
- Statements on Auditing Standards, Statements on Standards for Consulting Services, Statements on Responsibilities in Personal Financial Planning Practice, Statements on Standards for Accounting and Review Services, Statements on Quality Control Standards, Statements on Standards for Attestation Engagements, and Statements on Responsibilities in Tax Practice
- Accounting Research Bulletins, APB Opinions, Audit and Accounting Guides, Auditing Procedure Studies, Risk Alerts, Statements of Position, and Code of Professional Conduct
- Uniform CPA Examination Blueprints
- Independent Standard Board (ISB) Standards

Portions of various FASB and GASB documents, copyright property of the Financial Accounting Foundation, 401 Merritt 7, PO Box 5116, Norwalk, CT 06856-5116, are utilized with permission. Complete copies of these documents are available from the Financial Accounting Foundation. These selections include the following:

Financial Accounting Standards Board (FASB)
- The FASB Accounting Standards Codification ™ and Statements of Financial Accounting Concepts
- FASB Statements, Interpretations, Technical Bulletins, and Statements of Financial Accounting Concepts

Governmental Accounting Standards Board (GASB)
- GASB Codification of Governmental Accounting and Financial Reporting Standards, GASB Statements, GASB Concepts Statements, and GASB Interpretations
- GASB Statements, Interpretations, and Technical Bulletins

The following items are utilized in this volume, and are copyright property of the International Financial Reporting Standards (IFRS) Foundation and the International Accounting Standards Board (IASB), all rights reserved:
- IASB International Reporting Standards (IFRS), International Accounting Standards (IAS) and Interpretations

Acknowledgement

This book includes contributions by members of the Roger CPA Review Editorial Team.

Copyright © 2017
By Roger Philipp CPA, CGMA
On behalf of Roger CPA Review
San Francisco, CA
USA

All rights reserved.
Reproduction or translation of any part of this work beyond that permitted by sections 107 and 108 of the United States Copyright Act without the permission of the copyright owner is unlawful.

Printed in English, in the United States of America.

ABOUT THE AUTHOR

Roger S. Philipp, CPA, CGMA
CEO and Instructor, Roger CPA Review

For over 28 years, Roger Philipp, CPA, CGMA has motivated aspiring accountants to pass the CPA Exam. As the lead instructor for Roger CPA Review, Roger connects multiple content specifications from differing areas within the discipline to deliver a comprehensive understanding of the Audit, Business Environment & Concepts, Financial Accounting & Reporting, and Regulation sections of the CPA Exam.

Throughout the program, Roger breaks down difficult accounting topics into simplified concepts. His renowned memory aids and exam hacks include creative mnemonics and humorous anecdotes that help students retain vital information in a fun and interesting way—improving students' recall on exam day. Leading a team of CPA Exam experts, Roger is the lead author of the Roger CPA Review course textbooks, ensuring lectures and texts are cohesive, and focus only on what students need to know to pass the CPA Exam. Many faculty across the country have adopted Roger's motivational instructional method, known as The Roger Method™. This effective teaching practice has helped to increase university students' knowledge of and interest in the CPA designation.

Roger attended California State University – Northridge, and went on to work for Deloitte and Touche until he decided to follow his passion for educational instruction. Working as a lead instructor for well-known review courses, Roger later branched off to spearhead a new review course, founding Roger CPA Review in 2001.

In 2014, Roger was honored in Accounting Today's Top 100 Most Influential People in Public Accounting.

When Roger is not helping thousands of CPA hopefuls pass the CPA Exam, he enjoys spending time with his wife and children at home in San Francisco, CA.

ABOUT THE EDITOR

Mark E. Dauberman, CPA, EMBA
Senior Editor, Roger CPA Review

Mark Dauberman brings over 40 years of experience in the accounting profession, including a strong foundation in CPA review, to the Roger CPA Review team. In 1975 he founded the Mark Dauberman CPA Review course, which grew to become the largest CPA review course in Southern California. The program prepared over 2,500 candidates per year in 12 Southern California locations. Mark's business later expanded to dominate several major US markets, offer courses throughout Asia and the Middle East, and was one of the first pioneers of an online course format.

Mark has been involved in accounting education since teaching his first university class in 1969. Additionally, he has spent many years teaching CPE, and provided technical staff training for CPA firms, private industry employers of accountants, and government organizations. He also authors CCH's "Knowledge-Based Compilations and Reviews."

Prior to joining the Roger CPA Review team, Mark enjoyed many years in public accounting and technical training, which included employment with Kenneth Leventhal & Company and NSBN. At NSBN, he served as a partner and director of the audit practice and was responsible for recruiting and training for the firm. His experience in the private sector includes working as a Controller, VP of Finance and Administration, and serving on several professional committees.

Mark earned his Executive MBA at the Peter Drucker and Masatoshi Ito School of Management at Claremont Graduate University, where he previously had been a student of Dr. Drucker's. He lives in Los Angeles, CA and spends his personal time cruising the country, traveling abroad, and visiting with his children, grandchildren, and great grandchildren.

FAR

Table of Contents

Introduction		Intro-1
Section 1	Conceptual Framework and IFRS	1-1
Section 2	Cash & Cash Equivalents, Balance Sheet	2-1
Section 3	Cost & Equity Method	3-1
Section 4	Marketable Securities	4-1
Section 5	Financial Instruments & Derivatives	5-1
Section 6	Foreign Operations	6-1
Section 7	Inventory	7-1
Section 8	Property, Plant & Equipment (Fixed Assets)	8-1
Section 9	Intangibles	9-1
Section 10	Receivables	10-1
Section 11	Bonds & Present Value Tables	11-1
Section 12	Accounting for Leases	12-1
Section 13	Liabilities	13-1
Section 14	Pensions & Postemployment Benefits	14-1
Section 15	Stockholders' Equity	15-1
Section 16	Earnings Per Share (EPS)	16-1
Section 17	Reporting the Results of Operations, and IFRS Financial Statements	17-1
Section 18	Accounting Changes and Error Corrections	18-1
Section 19	Accounting for Income Taxes (Deferred Taxes)	19-1
Section 20	Interim Financial Reporting	20-1
Section 21	Segment Reporting	21-1
Section 22	Installment Sales & Cost Recovery Method	22-1
Section 23	Long-Term Construction Contracts	23-1

Section 24	Going Concern Issues	24-1
Section 25	Statement of Cash Flows	25-1
Section 26	Financial Statement Analysis	26-1
Section 27	Inflation Accounting	27-1
Section 28	Partnerships	28-1
Section 29	Governmental Accounting	29-1
Section 30	Nonprofit Accounting	30-1
Section 31	Business Combinations and Consolidations	31-1
Section 32	FAR Final Review	32-1
Section 33	Document Review Simulations (DRS) Appendix	33-1

Introduction

Table of Contents

Welcome to your Roger CPA Review Course 1

Application, Scheduling and Taking the Exam 3

The CPA Exam 21

Uniform CPA Examination Blueprints 28

State Board Contact Information 41

Section - Introduction

Corresponding Lectures

Watch the following course lectures with this section:

Lecture 0.01 – Course Introduction
Lecture 0.02 – FAR Introduction

Lecture 0.01

Welcome to your Roger CPA Review Course!

Greetings Student,

As you begin your journey with Roger CPA Review, you will quickly learn why our students experience an 88% pass rate. Your motivating and engaging instructor, Roger Philipp, CPA, CGMA, focuses you on the information you need to know to pass the CPA Exam. Our course is structured for a variety of student types. Each topic is broken down from the beginning and taught as if the student has little to no prior knowledge of the particular topic at hand. Whether you are a first-time review student who has never attempted an exam part, or a seasoned professional returning to the exam after an earlier attempt, you will be prepared. Using the proven *Roger Method*™, you will learn and retain the necessary information rather than simply memorizing terms. Furthermore, all of your course materials and online study tools are part of a fully integrated system to help you reach your goal with as little pain as possible.

Ultimately, you control your destiny. As Roger always says, "The CPA Exam is not an IQ test. It is a test of discipline. If you study, you will pass!" With 300-400 hours of minimum preparation time recommended by the AICPA, the ability to manage your studies is essential. For this reason, your course includes Study Planners and adaptive course diagnostic tools to help you keep your eye on the ball throughout the process. To get the most out of your course, please **read through this Introduction** to understand more about the exam, course content, and study strategies. This book serves as a guide to course lectures; everything covered in the lectures is covered in the book. Within you will find our recommended approach to using your course and its support features, including these following overarching key steps of the *Roger Method*™:

- **Plan** your studies
- **Learn** with your course lectures and textbooks
- **Practice** your skills and understanding
- **Review** for exam day

This course is designed to prepare you to PASS the CPA Exam. The lectures and materials are comprehensive and focus on the most frequently tested topics, saving you time and effort by streamlining your study process. You will learn the topics tested on the exam without wasting time delving into topics not historically emphasized on the exam. All exam question types are taken apart piece-by-piece and presented from scratch to demonstrate the logical progression. Task-Based Simulations (TBSs, including Document Review Simulations or DRSs) and multiple choice questions are also covered during the lecture and reinforced with the Interactive Practice Questions (IPQ) software provided within your course.

Best,

Roger CPA Review Team

FOLLOW ROGER CPA REVIEW ON TWITTER **FOR CPA EXAM TIPS AND TRICKS** AT **@ROGERCPAREVIEW** AND SUBSCRIBE TO OUR BLOG TO GET THE MOST UP-TO-DATE EXAM INFO AS WELL AS PLENTY OF ADVICE ON CAREERS, EDUCATION AND THE CPA EXAM AT **ROGERCPAREVIEW.COM/BLOG**.

USING THE COURSE

A step-by-step guide to successfully studying with your Roger CPA Review course

I. PLAN

Step 1. Start with a plan and stick to it! In your student account, choose between the 3, 6, 9, or 12-month "Study Planner," whichever best suits your projected timeline for exam completion. Then, customize your planner to help build a personalized agenda that meets your individual study needs.

II. LEARN

Courses are broken into sections and topics. Work sequentially through the course and start with the first section. Cover all topics within the first section before moving on to the second section.

Step 2: Watch one lecture at a time in full, without frequent stops, and simultaneously follow along in your course textbook.

Step 3: As you proceed through all topics in a section, also watch the *Class Question* lectures and follow along with the Class Questions covered at the end of each section of your course textbook. Make sure to read the solution descriptions in order to understand why each answer option is correct or incorrect.

Step 4: After watching the lectures for the section, go back to your course textbook and thoroughly read all corresponding pages, making notes as needed. Helpful Note-taking and Video Bookmark functions are available in your course online. You can also follow along, highlight, and take notes in the physical textbooks if you prefer.

III. PRACTICE

Step 5: Use your Interactive Practice Questions (IPQ) software to reinforce and practice applying the concepts in each section of your course. As you complete every 2-3 sections in your textbooks and lectures, log into the IPQ to quiz yourself on what you've learned. Carefully work through each question, and read answer explanations to understand why you've answered each question correctly or incorrectly. Make sure to flag difficult questions for later review. Keep in mind that repeated exposure to the same questions will help you fully understand the concepts taught.

IV. REVIEW

Step 6: Revisit any lectures and rework any questions that you have bookmarked or noted for final review. This is also a great time to take a Roger CPA Review Cram Course, which will focus you only on the most heavily tested topics.

Step 7: To prepare for exam day, take full-length practice exams using the CPA Exam Simulator tool in your IPQ. This will help you hone your test taking strategy, time management and self-discipline under exam-like conditions, while continuing to expose you to the material.

Need help as you study? *Not sure why a question solution is either correct or incorrect, even after double checking in your course textbook and watching the lecture video? Visit the Homework Help Center in your student account for expert support.*

Application, Scheduling, & Taking the Exam

** All information regarding AICPA, NASBA and Prometric rules and regulations in this introduction are up to date as of September 2016. Please see aicpa.org and nasba.org for the most current information.

To ensure that the Uniform CPA Examination keeps pace with the evolution of the accounting and business worlds, the examination is a computer-based test (CBT). The computerized exam:
- Enables testing of higher-level cognitive skills.
- Permits integration of real-world entry-level requirements.
- Provides flexibility and convenience to candidates.
- Offers greater consistency in evaluation.
- Helps save time in administration, grading, and reporting.
- Provides added exam security.

The next version of the CPA Exam was launched on April 1, 2017. To see the latest information about the 2017 exam, please visit rogercpareview.com/cpa-exam/changes.

A tutorial that reviews the examination's format and navigation functions is available at aicpa.org. Choose the "Become a CPA" tab and then pick "CPA Exam" from the options in the list. From there, candidates can find the tutorial and sample tests. All exam candidates are encouraged to review this prior to sitting. The tutorial is intended to familiarize candidates with the functionality and types of questions and responses used in the examination format. The tutorial does not focus on examination content and is not intended as a replacement for study materials.

EXAM APPLICATION

State boards strongly urge candidates to apply online as the processing time is reduced. The applications for the CPA Exam are available online, and the link for the individual states can be found on our website at RogerCPAreview.com. Qualified candidates who have met all of the educational requirements may apply at any time. See individual state boards or NASBA.org for their specific application process. It is the candidate's responsibility to understand their jurisdiction's requirements to sit for the CPA exam and applicants are encouraged to familiarize themselves with licensure requirements prior to applying for the CPA exam.

Depending on the jurisdiction, candidates will apply directly through either their state board of accountancy or CPAES (CPA Examination Services, a division of NASBA). Some states have specific rules regarding coursework, applications and transcripts so candidates should contact their board if they are unsure on or unclear about any requirements. If candidates do not follow instructions and forget to submit required information with their application (fingerprint cards, photographs, etc.), the candidate will be rejected to sit in their state, forfeit application fee(s) and must re-apply.

Candidates in the following states must apply through **NASBA's CPA Examination Services** and may call **800-CPA-EXAM** for further information on application requirements and procedures:

Alaska, Colorado, Connecticut, Delaware, Florida, Georgia, Hawaii, Indiana, Iowa, Kansas, Louisiana, Maine, Massachusetts, Michigan, Minnesota, Missouri, Montana, Nebraska, New Hampshire, New Jersey, New Mexico, New York, Ohio, Pennsylvania, Puerto Rico, Rhode Island, South Carolina, Tennessee, Utah, Vermont, Washington, or Wisconsin.

Candidates in the following states must apply with their **Board of Accountancy**. See a full list of boards of accountancy and contact information at the end of this section:

Alabama, Arizona, Arkansas, California, District of Columbia, Guam, Idaho, Illinois, Kentucky, Maryland, Mississippi, Nevada, North Carolina, North Dakota, Oklahoma, Oregon, South Dakota, Texas, U.S. Virgin Islands, Virginia, West Virginia, or Wyoming.

Application Steps

STATE BOARD OF ACCOUNTANCY

1. Meet requirements and submit educational documents to Board
2. Create client account and obtain password from Board
3. Complete application using client account (print Application Remittance Form)
4. Submit signed Application Remittance Form and fee
5. Receive Board approval and select exam section(s)

NASBA

6. Receive Payment Coupon from NASBA
   - If you do not receive the Payment Coupon within 10 business days after section selection, visit NASBA's Web site at *nasba.org* to pay online.
7. Pay NASBA Exam Section Fee(s)
   - NASBA's Online Credit Card Payment Form: Answer only the required fields when paying online. In accordance with the Board's Privacy Policy, NASBA does not collect or require exam applicants to fill in the Mother's Maiden Name field on NASBA's form. Please enter the word UNKNOWN in the Mother's Maiden Name field. This will allow you to continue processing your online payment. For additional payment information, telephone 1-866-696-2722.
8. Receive Notice to Schedule (NTS) from NASBA
   - If you do not receive the NTS within 10 business days after you pay the section fee(s), notify the Board or NASBA. Your NTS is valid in most states for 6 months, in others it can be good for 3, 6, 9, or 12 months.

PROMETRIC

9. Schedule with Prometric
10. Take CPA Exam at a Prometric Testing Center
    - You MUST bring your NTS with you to the testing center. You will be denied entry to the CPA Exam if you do not present the NTS.

BOARD

11. Receive Score Report from Board

Additional Information

For additional information on how to get answers to common questions, consult this table.

For questions about:	Contact:
<ul><li>Eligibility to take the examination</li><li>Special testing accommodations</li><li>Completing application forms</li><li>Name and/or address changes</li><li>Examination scores</li><li>Your Board of Accountancy's fees</li></ul>	Write, call or send an e-mail to the appropriate Board of Accountancy. A complete list of Boards of Accountancy may be found at end of this section.
<ul><li>Receiving your Notice to Schedule (NTS)</li><li>Replacing a lost NTS</li><li>Payments to NASBA</li><li>General comments about the test center where you took your examination</li></ul>	Call NASBA at 1-800-CPA-EXAM (1-800-272-3926) or send an e-mail to cbtcpa@nasba.org
For questions about:	**Contact:**
<ul><li>Scheduling, rescheduling or canceling your examination appointment</li><li>Directions to your test center</li></ul>	All information and instant scheduling is available at prometric.com/cpa Additionally, candidates may contact the Prometric Candidate Services Call Center at 1-800-580-9648
<ul><li>Content of the examination</li><li>Specific multiple-choice questions and/or task-based simulations on the examination</li><li>Questions about rescore requests</li></ul>	Visit the AICPA's CPA Page: aicpa.org/BecomeACPA/CPAExam Or send an e-mail to cpaexam@aicpa.org

Test Centers

Test centers move, new ones are opened, and some close from time-to-time. The most current list of test centers may be found on the Prometric website at prometric.com/cpa.

Testing Windows

The Uniform CPA Examination is offered the first two months plus 10 days of each calendar quarter. These months of testing are known as the "testing windows." The examination is given in these testing windows to allow for systems and database maintenance. The exam is not available during the following times: March 11-March 31, June 11-June 30, September 11-September 31, and December 11-December 31. It is important to plan accordingly; it is the candidate's responsibility to schedule the remaining un-passed sections of the examination or the candidate may risk losing credit for previously passed sections. Candidates will be able to take any or all sections of the examination during any testing window and in any order but will not be allowed to take the same section more than once during any testing window. If a section is failed, the candidate must wait for the next available testing window and submit a re-application to receive a new NTS.

For Q2 2017, the exam window does not include the 10-day extension. That window is only April 1 – May 31, 2017. All subsequent windows will include the 10-day extension.

Testing is Available	Testing is NOT Available
January, February, March 1-10	March 11 to end of month
April, May, June 1-10	June 11 to end of month
July, August, September 1-10	September 11 to end of month
October, November, December 1-10	December 11 to end of month

EXAM SCHEDULING

Eligibility to Test

In order to make appointments at test centers, candidates must have a valid Notice to Schedule (NTS). Candidates receive an NTS after they apply to take an examination and are deemed eligible by their state boards of accountancy. An NTS is provided for every section a candidate has been approved to take. The NTS is valid only for a specified period of time and cannot be used once it expires. Therefore, **it is important that candidates schedule their test appointments as soon as they receive the NTS.** The NTS is good for **6 months** in most jurisdictions except the following:

- Texas — 90 days from date of application
- California — 9 months from date NTS is issued
- Hawaii — 9 months from date NTS is issued
- Louisiana — 9 months from date NTS is issued
- Utah — 9 months from date NTS is issued
- North Dakota — 12 months from date NTS is issued
- South Dakota — 12 months from date NTS is issued
- Virginia — 12 months from date NTS is issued

Testing Centers

Prometric will administer the exam at authorized CPA Exam testing sites throughout the United States, Guam, Puerto Rico, the Virgin Islands, and the District of Columbia, as well as at international sites in Japan, Bahrain, Kuwait, Lebanon, the United Arab Emirates, and Brazil. Other international locations are on the horizon. Special citizenship requirements and fees apply to testing internationally.

Candidates are not required to take the CPA Exam at a Prometric site located in the state where they applied and may schedule their exams at any authorized Prometric site regardless of location.

After submitting an application, receiving approval by the State Board of Accountancy (Board), and submitting the required fees to NASBA, the candidate will be authorized to contact Prometric to schedule a specific testing date and time. The test sites are normally open six days each week. Candidates are encouraged to check Prometric's Web site at *prometric.com* to locate a testing site near them.

Schedule Early

Scheduling is available throughout the year, but candidates should schedule examination appointments as soon as possible after receiving their NTS. Being proactive about scheduling will help to secure the candidate's first choice of date and location of test centers. Tests are scheduled on a first come, first served basis. To ensure that candidates are able to take their examination section(s) on the first desired date and time, candidates should make their appointment(s) at least 65 days before the date they want to take the examination. **The earlier candidates schedule appointments, the better their chances are of obtaining the location, date, and time of their choice.** Test appointments **cannot** be scheduled fewer than five days in advance of the desired test date. Walk-in testing is **not** allowed. The last two weeks of an exam window tend to fill up early, so candidates should plan ahead and schedule as early as possible.

Candidates may schedule examination sessions at *prometric.com/CPA* or by calling Prometric's Call Center at 1-800-580-9648. Candidates must have their Notice to Schedule available when making test appointments. Examination section(s) must be taken within the time period for which an NTS is valid (3-12 months depending on jurisdiction) and may not be rescheduled after the NTS has expired. Boards of Accountancy, NASBA and Prometric are not responsible if a candidate cannot schedule an appointment before deadlines in your jurisdiction; it is imperative to plan ahead.

Candidates have three scheduling options:

1. Visit prometric.com/cpa on the Internet

Candidates will find that the easiest and quickest way to schedule an examination appointment (as well as reschedule and cancel an appointment if necessary) is on the Internet. Using the Internet provides 24-hour access to scheduling and avoids any "on hold" waiting time. Because of this, candidates have the quickest and most direct access to preferred dates and test center locations. Additionally, they will quickly receive a detailed confirmation of exam appointments (on screen and via e-mail). Before making any appointments, candidates must have received a valid NTS and should have this available before beginning the scheduling process. Additionally, candidates must be ready to identify the dates, times and locations where they want to take each section. It is not necessary to make all appointments at one time and candidates may schedule one exam at a time even if they have paid for more than one on any particular NTS. During the scheduling process, candidates will be required to provide various pieces of information from the NTS. Online scheduling is done by completing the following easy steps:

1. Go to prometric.com/cpa. Select SCHEDULE APPOINTMENT.
2. Select CPA Exam and Country/State.
3. Read all the information on the Information Review screen, and click NEXT.
4. After viewing welcome screen, click NEXT, read all of the policy information and click "I Agree" to proceed.
5. On the Program Identifier Screen, enter your examination section identification number from your NTS (you have one identification number for each section of the examination—be sure to use the correct examination identification number for the section you are scheduling). Click "Next."
6. Confirm proper section and click NEXT.
7. Follow on-screen instructions to select the date and location you would like to schedule your section.
8. Select COMPLETE REGISTRATION to finalize your scheduling. Print the confirmation number for your appointment and keep it for your records.

2. Call 1-800-580-9648 (Candidate Services Call Center)

Prometric's Candidate Services Call Center is open Monday through Friday from 8:00 a.m. to 8:00 p.m. Eastern time. (Hearing-impaired candidates using teletypewriter (TTY) may call 1-800-529-3590 to schedule appointments.) Candidates must schedule a separate appointment for each section of the examination that they are planning to take. If calling to schedule two or more sections, candidates should be prepared to identify the dates, times and locations they want to take each section. It is not necessary to make all appointments in one call and candidates may make one appointment at a time. Before calling, the candidate must have an NTS and should have access to it during the call as they will be required to provide the customer service representative with various pieces of information from the NTS.

Candidates will NOT receive written confirmation of their appointment so must write down the date, time, location, and confirmation number for each appointment. Candidates may also visit prometric.com/cpa to confirm their appointment(s). If the candidate is not familiar with the test center location they should ask the customer service representative for directions while they are making the appointment over the phone. There are multiple test centers in some metropolitan areas, so it is important for candidates to be certain of the correct test center location where they are scheduled to take their examination(s).

Those interested in a test run of the Prometric system may also use the telephone call center to schedule a 15-minute generic sample test at the facility prior to examination so they can familiarize themselves with the location and Prometric. There is a $30 fee for this *Test Drive* service.

3. Call the Local Test Center

Some candidates prefer to speak to a customer service representative at the local test center; if this is the case, candidates may call the center directly to make an exam appointment. Calls will only be accepted during business hours, which vary for each test center. Leaving a voicemail message at the local test center is NOT an acceptable method of scheduling. If calling to take two or more sections, candidates should be prepared to identify the dates and times they want to take each section. It is not necessary to make all appointments in one call and the candidate may schedule one appointment at a time. Before calling, the candidate must have an NTS and should have access to it during the call as they will be required to provide the customer service representative with various pieces of information from the NTS.

Candidates will NOT receive written confirmation of their appointment so must write down the date, time, location, and confirmation number for each appointment. Candidates may also visit prometric.com/cpa to confirm their appointment(s). If the candidate is not familiar with the test center location they should ask the customer service representative for directions while they are making the appointment over the phone. There are multiple test centers in some metropolitan areas, so it is important for candidates to be certain of the correct test center location where they are scheduled to take their examination(s).

TESTING INTERNATIONALLY

The international testing format follows the same state board licensure process and the current examination structure. The exam is still only offered in English and is available during the same four testing windows per calendar year as offered to US candidates. There are additional fees that applicants must pay if they wish to take the exam internationally.

Who is eligible?

U.S. citizens and permanent residents living abroad, and citizens and long-term residents of the countries in which the exam is being administered. In some cases, permanent residents or citizens of neighboring countries may test at international testing centers. The only form of identification that an applicant can use to test internationally is a passport.

Non-US Countries Offering CPA Exam Testing

Japan, Brazil, the United Arab Emirates, Lebanon, Kuwait, and Bahrain

Citizenship Status C = Citizen PR = legal permanent or long term resident	Eligibility to Test in These Countries						
	U.S.	Japan	Brazil	UAE	Lebanon	Kuwait	Bahrain
U.S. C/PR	X	X	X	X	X	X	X
Japan C/PR	X	X					
Antigua/Barbuda C/PR			X				
Argentina C/PR	X		X				
Bahamas C/PR			X				
Barbados C/PR			X				
Belize C/PR			X				
Bolivia C/PR	X		X				
Brazil C/PR	X		X				
Cayman Islands C/PR			X				
Chile C/PR	X		X				
Colombia C/PR	X		X				
Costa Rica C/PR			X				
Dominica C/PR			X				
Dominican Republic C/PR			X				
Ecuador C/PR	X		X				
El Salvador C/PR			X				
French Guiana C/PR	X		X				
Grenada C/PR			X				
Guatemala C/PR			X				
Guyana C/PR	X		X				
Haiti C/PR			X				
Honduras C/PR			X				
Jamaica C/PR			X				
Mexico C/PR			X				
Nicaragua C/PR			X				
Panama C/PR			X				
Paraguay C/PR	X		X				
Peru C/PR	X		X				
St. Kitts/Nevis C/PR			X				
St. Lucia C/PR			X				
St. Vincent/Grenadines C/PR			X				
Suriname C/PR	X		X				
Trinidad & Tobago C/PR			X				
Uruguay C/PR	X		X				
Venezuela C/PR	X		X				
Bahrain C/PR	X			X	X	X	X
Egypt C/PR	X			X	X	X	X
Jordan C/PR	X			X	X	X	X
Kuwait C/PR	X			X	X	X	X
Lebanon C/PR	X			X	X	X	X
Oman C/PR	X			X	X	X	X
Qatar C/PR	X			X	X	X	X
Saudi Arabia C/PR	X			X	X	X	X
UAE C/PR	X			X	X	X	X
Yemen C/PR	X			X	X	X	X
India C/PR	X			X	X	X	X
Any other country in the world C/PR	X						

STEPS FOR APPLYING INTERNATIONALLY*

1. Students must first meet eligibility requirements and apply to a US 'State Board' as long as that state board is one that allows international testing. For states that allow this, please see the list on the next page.
2. Applicant receives their Notice to Schedule.
3. Once approved, the student would then need to complete a separate international registration process on the NASBA website.
4. The applicant must make a commitment to seek CPA licensure upon passing the CPA Exam, and thereafter maintain their status as licensees.
5. Meet citizenship/residency requirements in the jurisdiction in which they are sitting for their exams.
6. Pay additional fees (see below).

*For more on how to apply to sit for the CPA Exam in your non-US country please visit nasba.org/international/international-exam/.

Additional Exam Fees for Testing Internationally

Subject	Additional Amount
Auditing and Attestation (AUD)	$ 356.55
Business Environment and Concepts (BEC)	$ 356.55
Financial Accounting and Reporting (FAR)	$ 356.55
Regulation (REG)	$ 356.55

Changes for the International Exam

Scores for international candidates will be released on the same timeline as domestic scores.

You cannot take your test internationally without a passport. This is most relevant for people living within a testing country or area – in which they must STILL have a passport to demonstrate citizenship and nationality.

Students who are not eligible to test within an approved country's jurisdiction, but are still international (non-US applicant), must report to the United States only and cannot go to a different country to test.

US State Boards that Accept International Applicant Test-takers			
Alaska	Indiana	Nevada	South Carolina
Arizona	Iowa	New Hampshire	South Dakota
Arkansas	Kansas	New Mexico	Tennessee
Colorado	Louisiana	New York	Texas
Connecticut	Maine	North Dakota	Utah
District of Columbia	Massachusetts	Ohio	Vermont
Florida	Michigan	Oklahoma	Virginia
Georgia	Minnesota	Oregon	Washington
Guam	Missouri	Pennsylvania	West Virginia
Hawaii	Montana	Puerto Rico	Wisconsin
Illinois	Nebraska	Rhode Island	Wyoming

TAKING THE EXAMINATION IN GUAM

Regardless of which Board of Accountancy has declared a candidate eligible for the examination, if the candidate intends to take their examination in Guam, they must pay an additional $140 surcharge for each examination section. Residents of Guam who are able to pay at the Guam Computer Testing Center, will incur a reduced surcharge fee of $70. All Guam test-takers must schedule his/her appointments by either of the following two options:

1. Visit nasba.org/exams/cpaexam/guam/ on the Internet

NASBA operates the Guam computer testing center in cooperation with the Guam Board of Accountancy and Prometric. Before visiting this Web site, candidates should have an NTS and credit card readily available. Once at the website, candidates will be asked to provide information from their NTS and will pay the surcharge using a credit card. After paying the additional surcharge for each examination section, the candidate will need to wait at least 24 hours before scheduling an appointment following the instructions described above.

2. Call the Guam Computer Testing Center: 855-CPA-GUAM or 671-300-7441

The Guam computer testing center is open Monday through Friday from 7:00 a.m. to 4:00 p.m. Guam time. Have your NTS and credit card in front of you when you call. Candidates will be asked to provide information from their NTS and will pay the surcharge using a credit card. After paying the additional surcharge for each examination section, the candidate will need to wait at least 24 hours before scheduling an appointment following the instructions described above.

For Pre-approved Special Testing Accommodations, Call 1-800-967-1139

International Locations Accommodations Phone Numbers:
Japan 0120-34-7737
Latin America 1-443-751-4990
Middle East 31-320-239-530

DO NOT CALL ANY OF THESE NUMBER UNLESS YOU HAVE BEEN PRE-APPROVED FOR SPECIAL TESTING ACCOMMODATIONS BY YOUR BOARD OF ACCOUNTANCY.

If the Board of Accountancy has approved a candidate for special testing accommodations, the information regarding the nature of the accommodation will be sent to NASBA. The type of accommodation will be shown on the candidate's NTS and will be sent to Prometric. Neither the candidate nor the customer service representative may make any changes to the accommodations that have been approved. A candidate requiring special testing accommodations should contact their Board of Accountancy before proceeding if they believe there are any errors on the NTS. If you call to take two or more sections, be prepared to identify the dates, times and locations for each section you wish to take. It is not necessary to make all appointments in one call. If you prefer, you may make one appointment at a time.

Before calling, the candidate must have an NTS and should have access to it during the call as they will be required to provide the customer service representative with various pieces of information from the NTS.

Candidates may visit prometric.com/cpa to confirm their appointment(s). If the candidate is not familiar with the test center location they should ask the customer service representative for directions while they are making the appointment over the phone. There are multiple test centers in some metropolitan areas, so it is important for candidates to be certain of the correct test center location where they are scheduled to take their examination(s).

CHANGES TO APPOINTMENTS

After making an appointment for an examination section, the candidate may find it necessary to change or cancel an appointment. Candidates should be aware that they may be required to pay a penalty or forfeit examination fees, depending on when they notify Prometric of the change or cancellation.

Change the Date, Time or Location of an Appointment

There are three methods to reschedule or change an existing exam appointment:

- Use Prometric's Web scheduling tool located at prometric.com/cpa. The system is available 24 hours a day, seven days a week.
- Call the Prometric Candidate Services Call Center at 1-800-580-9648. The Center is open Monday through Friday from 8:00 a.m. to 8:00 p.m. Eastern time.
- Call the local test center where your appointment is scheduled. If you need to reschedule your appointment, review the table below to determine deadlines and associated fees. Please note that Saturday is considered a business day.

If calling to change an exam date, time or location, the candidate must speak with a staff member and cannot leave a message to reschedule. Candidates testing with special testing accommodations should call 1-800-967-1139 to reschedule. Candidates using a teletypewriter (TTY) should call 1-800-529-3590.

Some types of accommodations are only available at a limited number of test centers. A candidate's Board of Accountancy will have already notified the candidate of this before sending an NTS to a candidate who has requested special accommodations.

Ineligibility

If a candidate's Board of Accountancy informs NASBA that they are no longer eligible to take the Uniform CPA Examination for any reason, the NTS will be cancelled. The candidate will receive a copy of a canceled NTS by United States mail, fax or e-mail, depending on the method identified as the candidate's preferred method for receipt of information.

If the candidate has NOT scheduled an appointment, they do not need to take any other action. If they have scheduled an appointment, NASBA will contact Prometric to cancel the appointment and rescind eligibility. In the event that a candidate is determined to be no longer eligible to take the examination by their Board of Accountancy, examination fees will NOT be refunded.

Refunds

Under most circumstances, NASBA **will not** refund section fees. Additional information on payment of section fees can be found on NASBA's Web site at nasba.org.

Test Center Closings

If severe weather or other local emergency requires a test center to be closed, every attempt will be made to contact candidates scheduled to sit for the exam on that day. If a candidate is unsure of whether or not the test center will be open on their exam day due to inclement weather or other unforeseeable circumstance, the candidate may call their test center directly. If the center is open, it is the candidate's responsibility to keep the appointment. If the center is closed, the candidate will be given the opportunity to reschedule without penalty. If unable to contact the local test center, the candidate may check on the Web at prometric.com/cpa, or call the Candidate Services Call Center at 1-800-580-9648, Monday through Friday, from 8:00 a.m. to 8:00 p.m. Eastern time.

Fees

Fees for the 2016 Exam are as follows (fees for the 2017 Exam, starting April 1, 2017, were not available at the time of this printing; the 2017 fees will likely be consistent for all four parts of the exam):

Application/Qualification Fee paid	(Varies by State)
First time Qualifying and Sitting	Approx. $50-$200
Previously Qualified and Sat (Repeat)	Approx. $25-$75
Section Fees to be Paid Directly to NASBA	**(Uniform)**
Auditing and Attestation	$193.45
Financial Accounting and Reporting	$193.45
Regulation	$193.45
Business Environment and Concepts	$193.45
Total fees paid to NASBA for all four sections	**$773.80**

Credit Status

The Exam utilizes a "rolling" 18-month credit status system. This replaced the conditional credit system of the paper-and-pencil exam. Credit status is established by passing one section of the examination. Once a candidate passes a section of the examination, the candidate will be allowed a maximum of 18 months to pass all remaining sections in order to retain credit on the passed section. If the candidate does not pass all four sections within that 18-month period, the candidate will lose credit for the first section of the exam passed. A new 18-month period will commence with a start date of the next section that was passed. There are state boards that offer exceptions to the above-described 18-month credit status period but for the majority of jurisdictions the 18-month rolling period applies and begins from the date the candidate sits for their first passed exam.

TAKE YOUR EXAMINATION

Arrive Early

Candidates must arrive at the test center at least 30 minutes before the scheduled appointment time for their examination. This allows time to sign in, have a digital photograph taken, be fingerprinted, review the security and test center policies and be seated at the workstation. If a candidate arrives for their scheduled testing appointment any time after the scheduled start time, they may be denied permission to test and will not receive a refund. Therefore, candidates should be sure to arrive at least 30 minutes before their scheduled appointment time to avoid forfeiting all fees for the examination section.

YOU MUST BRING YOUR NOTICE TO SCHEDULE (NTS) WITH YOU

The NTS contains an "Examination Password" that will be entered on the computer before starting the exam as a part of the log-in process. It is important to bring the correct NTS to the testing center as it is possible for a candidate to have more than one active NTS at a time. A candidate will not be admitted into the test center without the correct NTS and will forfeit all examination fees for that section if denied entry for this reason.

Personal Identification

The Uniform CPA Examination employs very strict security measures. One level of security involves identification. **The same form of the candidate's name must appear on the candidate's application, NTS, and on the primary identification presented at the test center.** It is important for candidates to spell and present their names correctly during the application process to assure the correct information is reflected on their Notice to Schedule. If the candidate's name is different from identifications presented at check-in, the candidate will not be permitted to test. Candidates must present two forms of identification, one of which must contain a recent photograph, to test center staff before being allowed into the examination. Each form of identification must bear the candidate's signature and must not be expired. Candidates who do not present valid ID will be barred entry to the exam and exam fees will not be refunded.

You must present *one* of the following primary forms of identification:
- A valid (not expired) state- or territory-issued driver's license with photograph and signature
- A valid (not expired) state- or territory-issued identification card with a recent photograph and signature (Candidates who do not drive may have an identification card issued by the agency which also issues driver's licenses.)
- A valid (not expired) government-issued passport with a recent photograph and signature.
- A United States military identification card with a recent photograph and signature

Your secondary form of identification may be one of the following (or another item from the list above):
- An identification card issued by your Board of Accountancy which includes the same name that appears on the NTS (if applicable to your jurisdiction)
- A valid (not expired) credit card
- A bank ATM card
- A debit card

The following are *UNACCEPTABLE* forms of identification:
- A draft classification card
- A Social Security card
- A student identification card
- A United States permanent residency card (green card)

The secondary form of identification **does not** have to match the information on a candidate's NTS exactly. For example, if a candidate's middle name is printed on their driver's license and NTS but not unexpired ATM card, the driver's license may be used as primary identification while the debit card can serve as secondary identification without issue. It is important to keep this in mind when applying to the state board so that the candidate's name is printed correctly on the NTS.

If the test center staff have questions about the identification presented, the candidate may be asked for additional proof of identity and, if staff are unable to verify identity, the candidate may be refused admission to the exam and will forfeit the examination fee for that section. Admittance to the test center and examination does not imply that the identification presented is valid or that the candidate's scores will be reported if subsequent investigations reveal impersonation or forgery.

Fingerprint Requirement

All CPA exam candidates are required to have a digital fingerprint taken at Prometric that is used as primary identification for subsequent exam appearances as well as for re-admission to the test center after a break.

Digital fingerprint images will be encrypted and stored electronically together with candidate identification information. Fingerprint images will also be used to detect any attempt to impersonate CPA candidates.

Fingerprinting will be required every time a candidate reports to the test center. In addition, candidates returning to test rooms after breaks will be asked to have their fingerprints taken again for comparison with the fingerprints captured at the beginning of the session. Candidates should keep this in mind if they choose to take breaks during the exam.

At the Test Center

The staff at each test center have been trained in the procedures specific to the Uniform CPA Examination. The staff are there to guide candidates through the guidelines that have been developed by the Boards of Accountancy, NASBA and the AICPA.

1. You must arrive at the test center at least 30 minutes before your scheduled appointment. If you arrive after your scheduled appointment time, you may forfeit your appointment and will not be eligible to have your examination fees refunded.

2. Your examination should begin within 30 minutes of the scheduled start time. If circumstances arise that delay your session more than 30 minutes, you will be given the choice of continuing to wait or rescheduling your appointment.

3. You must place personal belongings, such as a purse or cell phone, in the storage lockers provided by the test center. You will be given the key to your locker which must be returned to the test center staff when you leave. The lockers are very small and are not intended to hold large items. Do not bring anything to the test center unless it is absolutely necessary. Test center personnel will not be responsible for lost or stolen items.

4. You will submit a digital fingerprint that will be used for identification purposes for future Prometric visits or to verify your identity if you leave the testing room for any reason during the exam (like a break or to put your sweater in your locker). Keep your photo ID on you at all times as well but expect your fingerprint to be used as your primary identification within the testing center.

5. You will have a digital photograph taken of your face. (If the digital camera equipment is not working, a Polaroid picture will be taken.)
6. You will be required to sign the test center log book. Each time you exit and re-enter the testing room, you will be required to sign the log book and present your identification.

7. You will be escorted to a workstation by test center staff. You must remain in your seat during the examination, except when authorized to get up and leave the testing room. Except for a

standard break at the halfway point of the Exam, any breaks taken (e.g. to use the restroom) will count against the clock.

8. Candidates will be provided with two double-sided, laminated, colored sheets called "noteboards," as well as a fine point marker for making notations. This has replaced the paper and pencil scratch paper provided in the past. You will be directed to write your examination Launch Code (from your NTS) on your noteboards. You will be required to return the noteboards to the test center staff when your exam is complete. If more writing space is required, you may request additional noteboards from the test center staff once you have turned in the original noteboards you received. You must not bring any paper or pencils to the workstation in the testing room.

9. Notify the test center staff if:
   a. You experience a problem with your computer
   b. An error message appears on the computer screen (do not clear the message)
   c. You need additional scratch paper or pencils
   d. You need the test center staff for any other reason

10. When you finish the examination, leave the testing room quietly, turn in your noteboard and sign the test center log book. The test center staff will dismiss you after completing all necessary procedures.

Test Center Regulations

A standardized environment is necessary to ensure that candidates take equivalent but different exams. For this reason, all candidates must follow the same regulations.
- Papers, books, food or purses are not allowed in the testing room.
- Eating, drinking or use of tobacco is not allowed in the testing room.
- Talking or communicating with other candidates is not allowed in the testing room
- Calculators, personal digital assistants or other computer devices are not allowed in the testing room.
- Communication devices (e.g., cell phones, pagers, two-way radios, wireless internet connections to personal digital assistants devices) are not allowed in the testing room.
- Recording devices (audio and video) are not allowed in the testing room.
- You must not leave the testing room without the permission of the test center staff.
- You must be fingerprinted to re-enter the room after any breaks.

A complete list of prohibited items can be found on the AICPA website.

Breaks

Each examination section contains units known as testlets. Each testlet is comprised of either a group of multiple-choice questions or several task-based problems known as simulations. After each testlet, the candidate will be asked if he or she would like to take a non-standardized break (see below for information about the new standardized break). Those who do choose a break will be asked to leave the testing room quietly and sign the test center log book. Test center staff will confirm that the candidate has completed a testlet before allowing a break. Remember: you do not have to take a break and the clock will keep running if you do (for a non-standardized break)! Therefore, it is recommended that you use break time wisely. Leaving the testing room at any time without exiting the testlet and selecting the break option will result in the candidate being barred from reentry into the testing room and information regarding the candidate's absence will be reported to their Board of Accountancy.

Beginning with the April 1, 2017, Exam candidates are given a standardized break after the third (of five) testlets. This standardized break is up to 15 minutes and will NOT count against the candidate's time in the Exam. **We recommend that you take this break** to refresh before continuing with the exam.

The standardized break will not count against a candidate's time on the exam, but any other break will count against the time on the exam.

Examination Confidentiality and Break Policy

All candidates must accept the terms of the confidentiality and break policy statement before beginning their examination. The statement must be accepted or the test will be terminated and any exam fees will be forfeited.

Candidate Misconduct, Cheating, Copyright Infringement

The Boards of Accountancy, NASBA and the AICPA take candidate misconduct, including cheating on the Uniform CPA Examination, very seriously. If a Board of Accountancy determines that a candidate is culpable of misconduct or has cheated, the candidate will be subject to a variety of penalties including, but not limited to: invalidation of grades, disqualification from subsequent examination administrations, and civil and criminal penalties. In cases where candidate misconduct or cheating is discovered after a candidate has obtained a CPA license or certificate, a Board of Accountancy may rescind the license or certificate. If the test center staff suspects misconduct, a warning will be given to the candidate for any of the following situations:

- Communicating, orally or otherwise, with another candidate or person
- Copying from or looking at another candidate's materials or workstation
- Allowing another candidate to copy from or look at materials or workstation
- Giving or receiving assistance in answering examination questions or problems
- Reading examination questions or simulations aloud
- Engaging in conduct that interferes with the administration of the examination or unnecessarily disturbing staff or other candidates
- Grounds for confiscation of a prohibited item and warning the candidate include: Possession of any prohibited item (whether or not in use) inside, or while entering or exiting the testing room. This includes use of any prohibited item during a break in a manner that could result in cheating or the removal of examination questions or simulations

Prohibited items include, but are not limited to:
- Books
- Briefcase
- Calculator/Portable Computer
- Calculator Watch
- Camera, Photographic or Scanning Device (still or video)
- Cellular Phone
- Cigarette/Tobacco Product
- Container of any kind
- Dictionary
- Earphone
- Earplug (not provided by Test Center)
- Eraser
- Eyeglass Case
- Food or Beverage
- Handbag/Backpack/Hip Pack

- Hat or Visor (except head coverings worn for religious reasons)
- Headset or Audio Earmuffs (if not provided by Testing Center). You may bring soft, foam earplugs with no strings attached for your use. TCAs will inspect the earplugs
- Jewelry – Pendant Necklace or Large Earrings
- Newspaper or Magazine
- Non-Prescription Sunglasses
- Notebook
- Notes in any written form
- Organizer / Day Planner
- Outline
- Pager / Beeper
- Paper (if not provided by Test Center)
- Pen / Pencil (if not provided by Test Center)
- Pencil Sharpener
- Personal Digital Assistant or Other Electronic Device
- Plastic Bag
- Purse/Wallet
- Radio/Transmitter/Receiver
- Ruler/Slide Ruler
- Study Material
- Tape/Disk Recorder or Player
- Umbrella
- Watch
- Weapon of any kind

In addition, jackets, coats, and sweaters are also prohibited; however, if you require a separate sweater or a jacket due to room temperature, it must be worn at all times.

The Boards of Accountancy, NASBA, the AICPA and Prometric use a variety of procedures to prevent candidate misconduct and cheating on the examination. Test center staff are trained to watch for unusual behavior and incidents during the examination. In addition, all examination sessions are audio/videotaped to document the occurrence of any unusual activity and candidate misconduct is reported to Boards of Accountancy on a daily basis.

All examination materials are owned and copyrighted by the AICPA. Any reproduction and/or distribution of examination materials, including memorization, without the express written authorization of the AICPA, is prohibited. This behavior infringes on the legal rights of the AICPA and, in addition to the penalties listed above, the AICPA will take appropriate legal action when any copyright infringements have occurred.

Please see the AICPA's website at *aicpa.org* for a complete list of prohibited items and current information on examination policies.

Grounds for Dismissal

Test center staff may dismiss candidates from the examination or may have scores canceled by the candidate's Board of Accountancy for engaging in misconduct or not following the test center regulations. The following are examples of behavior that will not be tolerated during the examination:
- Repeating acts of misconduct after receiving prior warning(s)
- Attempting to remove or removing examination questions from the testing room by any means
- Copying, writing or summarizing examination questions on any material other than the scratch paper issued to you

- Tampering with computer software or hardware, or attempting to use a computer for any reason other than completing the examination session
- Intentional refusal or failure to comply with instructions of the test center staff
- Attempting to have an impersonator gain admission to the testing room or to substitute for you after a break
- Conduct that may threaten bodily harm or damage to property

RECEIVE YOUR SCORE(S)

Generally, Boards of Accountancy will report scores on a numeric scale of 0-99, with 75 as a passing score. This scale does NOT represent "percent correct." A score of 75 reflects examination performance that represents the knowledge and skills needed to protect the public. A few Boards of Accountancy have elected to report a pass or fail status instead of numeric scores. All questions contained in the examination, including BEC written communication task-based simulations, are formatted to allow responses to be scored electronically. Human graders score selected written communication responses. Candidates receive points for each correct answer to a multiple-choice question.

Similarly, responses to the questions asked in the simulations receive points based on correct answers or correct completion of the presented task. Points are not subtracted for incorrect responses. The points are accumulated according to the relative contributions of each question, which are weighted (see the Uniform CPA Examination Blueprints and skills definition documents for specific content areas and weights, or go to aicpa.org). Overall scores are then adjusted to ensure scores for all candidates (even those who test in different administrations with different examinations) are comparable and equivalent.

When You Should Expect Your Scores

The AICPA sends candidate scores to NASBA. The AICPA will release scores for the exams taken in a window on a specific target date according to the schedule on the following page. However, distribution of scores to the exam takers is the responsibility of the Boards of Accountancy. Each Board of Accountancy sets its own schedule regarding the frequency with which it will approve and release scores.

The AICPA target dates are not guaranteed and may be pushed back due to unforeseen issues. Additionally, BEC scores may be subject to longer delays due to the scoring of Written Communication. Candidates who do not receive their scores should call NASBA at 866-MY-NASBA.

Day of Exam in Testing Window*	Target Release Date Timeline
Day 1-20	11 business days following day 20 of the testing window
Day 21-45	6 business days following day 45 of the testing window
Day 46-Close of Window	6 business days following the close of the testing window
After Close of Window	6 business days after receiving all scoring data for the window

*date the records are received by the AICPA

The Score Review and Appeal Processes

Score Review

Score Review is an independent verification of a candidate's Uniform CPA Examination score, and NOT a re-grading or reconsideration of the candidate's responses on the examination. Because all scores undergo several quality control checks before they are reported, the likelihood of a score change following score review is exceedingly small, **or less than 1%** of all requested score reviews since the inception of the computer-based test. However, the score review option is available to candidates who would like to have their scores checked one more time. Fees apply.

Appeals

If allowed in a candidate's jurisdiction, an option to appeal a failing score may exist. This option enables the candidate to view the questions that he or she answered incorrectly as well as their responses. Such viewing takes place only in an authorized location, under secure conditions, and in the presence of a representative of the candidate's Board of Accountancy. In order to qualify for a score appeal, the candidate must submit a formal request to their Board of Accountancy within 30 days of the date printed on the score report, obtain the Board of Accountancy's approval, and pay the required fee. Contact your Board of Accountancy for specific instructions on the score appeal process. If a candidate is allowed a score appeal, they will be given the opportunity to view the questions they answered incorrectly as well as their responses to those questions. The AICPA will respond to any comments made by the candidate, rescore appealed responses and forward the results to NASBA. NASBA will then forward the scores to the candidate's Board of Accountancy.

RETAKING THE EXAMINATION

Candidates who fail any section of the CPA exam may retake that section in a future testing window but are not allowed to repeat a failed section within the same two-month testing window. Information on how to retake a failed examination section will be sent to the candidate from their Board of Accountancy with a score report detailing the candidate's performance in each area of that particular exam section. This information may be helpful when preparing to retake any examination sections or in planning for near-term continuing professional education needs. For any questions on retake policies and fees, contact your Board of Accountancy.

ETHICS EXAM

Some jurisdictions require CPA exam candidates to successfully complete an ethics examination as a requirement of CPA licensure, generally after the candidate has passed all four sections of the exam. The ethics portion is either administered through the AICPA or through continuing education (CPE) provided by your state society of CPAs. Check with your state board for more information on ethics requirements for your jurisdiction.

The CPA Exam

STRUCTURE

Beginning April 1, 2017, the Uniform CPA Examination spans 16 hours and consists of four separate exam parts.

The Uniform CPA Exam
Auditing & Attestation (AUD - 4 hours)
Financial Accounting & Reporting (FAR - 4 hours)
Regulation (REG - 4 hours)
Business Environment & Concepts (BEC - 4 hours)

Examination Content

The content areas for each exam part, along with skills tested, are outlined in the Uniform CPA Examination Blueprints published by the AICPA. For more information about the examination blueprints, visit aicpa.org and choose the "Become a CPA" tab.

Uniform CPA Examination Blueprints

With the 2017 exam the AICPA introduced a set of Uniform CPA Examination Blueprints, which document the minimum level of knowledge and skills needed for initial licensure in content areas and in representative tasks. The blueprints are organized by content AREA, content GROUP, and content TOPIC. Each topic includes one or more representative TASK(s) that a newly licensed CPA may be expected to complete. Each representative task is linked to a SKILL tested in the exam.

Skills are based on Bloom's Taxonomy of Educational Objectives. Critical thinking skills range from the lowest level (Remembering and Understanding) to the highest level (Evaluation), as summarized in the following table.

Skill Levels (beginning with the highest)	
Evaluation	The examination or assessment of problems and use of judgment to draw conclusions.
Analysis	The examination and study of the interrelationships of separate areas in order to identify causes and find evidence to support inferences.
Application	The use or demonstration of knowledge, concepts or techniques.
Remembering and Understanding	The perception and comprehension of the significance of an area utilizing knowledge gained.

The AICPA conducted a Practice Analysis from 2014-2015 in which one main finding was clear: firms expect newly licensed CPAs on their staff to perform at a higher level. The AICPA raised the bar with the revamped 2017 CPA Exam that more authentically tests candidates on the tasks and skill levels that will be required of them as newly licensed CPAs.

Types of Questions

Your score on each exam part is determined by the sum of points assigned to individual questions and simulation parts. Thus, you must attempt to maximize your points on each individual item. To familiarize yourself with the examination's format, functions, and question and response types, review the examination tutorial at aicpa.org. A sample test that contains a few sample multiple-choice questions and simulations for each applicable section is currently available. Neither the tutorial nor the sample test will be available at the test centers and candidates are encouraged to familiarize themselves with the test format prior to taking their first examination.

Multiple Choice Questions

A format is considered objective when it can be graded without subjectivity. Grading objective examinations is a mechanical process that requires little judgment. Any format that can be graded by machine is generally considered objective. Objective formats result in very consistent scores because the acceptability of particular responses is determined before grading begins. The most widely used objective format is multiple-choice (i.e., 4-option questions) because it has a restricted set of alternatives from which the correct answer must be selected. Multiple-choice questions (MCQs) make up 50% of FAR, AUD, REG and BEC.

The multiple-choice questions within each exam part are organized into two groups which are referred to as testlets. The first two testlets of each exam section will contain 31-38 multiple-choice questions per testlet, which are together worth up 50 percent of the exam part. The multiple-choice testlets vary in overall difficulty. A testlet is labeled either 'moderate' or 'difficult' based on its makeup. The questions in a 'difficult' testlet have a higher average level of difficulty than those in a 'moderate' testlet; however, questions of higher difficulty carry a higher point percentage rate therefore fewer must be answered correctly to pass. Every candidate's first multiple-choice testlet in each section will be a 'moderate' testlet. If a candidate scores well on the first testlet, he or she will receive a 'difficult' second testlet. Candidates that do not perform well on the first testlet receive a second 'moderate' testlet. Because the scoring procedure takes the difficulty of the testlet into account, candidates are scored fairly regardless of the type of testlets they receive.

Each multiple-choice testlet contains "operational" and "pretest" questions. The operational questions are the only ones that are used to determine your score. Pretest questions are not scored; they are being tested for future use as operational questions. However, you have no way of knowing which questions are operational and which questions are pretest questions. Therefore, you must approach each question as if it will be used to determine your grade. Of the multiple-choice questions, there are 72 operational and 12 pretest questions in the AUD exam, 66 operational and 11 pretest questions in the FAR exam, 76 operational and 12 pretest questions in the REG exam, and 62 operational and 10 pretest questions in the BEC exam.

Task-Based Simulations

Task-based simulations (TBSs) make up 50% of the FAR, AUD, and REG exams, but only 35% of the BEC exam (with written communications problems taking up the remaining 15%). Each operational TBS in the FAR, AUD, and REG exams is worth approximately 7.1% of the exam score. Each operational TBS in the BEC exam is worth approximately 11.7% of the exam score. In the 2017 exam, the FAR, AUD, and REG sections of the exam each contain 8 task-based simulations. The BEC section includes 4 simulation problems as well as 3 written communication problems, of which 2 are graded. Each of these 2 graded written communications problems is worth approximately 7.5% of the exam score. The actual percentage of total score assigned to each requirement will vary according to its difficulty. Each TBS should be allotted about 10 to 25 minutes to complete, depending on difficulty. Candidates will be required to demonstrate their ability to apply certain skills (application, analysis, or evaluation) in each part of the CPA Exam using task-based simulations. These skills will be tested in a variety of methods such as simulation, or relational case studies, which will test candidates' knowledge and skills using work-related situations. Simulations will require candidates to have basic computer skills, knowledge of common spreadsheet and word processing functions, the ability to use a financial calculator or a spreadsheet to perform standard financial calculations, and the ability to use electronic tools such as databases for research. Therefore, you need to become proficient in the use of these tools to maximize your score on the task-based simulation component of each applicable exam section.

Each TBS contains three distinct tabs: the work tab, labeled according to the TBS, e.g. Research, Journal Entry, or Form 1065, the information tab, usually labeled Authoritative Literature, and the help tab, labeled Help. The work tab (identified by a pencil icon) is the part of the question that will be graded and contains directions for completion of the task. The information tab(s) may contain authoritative literature or other relevant information to assist in completing the task presented in the work tab. Some task-based simulations may contain more than one information tab while others may not have any information tabs at all. The help tab provides assistance with the exam software such as instructions on using the provided word processor for written communication problems. While the exam environment closely mirrors common software programs that candidates are likely familiar with, it is recommended that candidates view the help tab for specific instructions on using the exam's provided software.

Document Review Simulations

A new type of simulation was introduced in the July 2016 exam and is known as the Document Review Simulation, or DRS. DRSs are designed to simulate tasks that the candidate will be required to perform as a newly licensed CPA (based on up to two years' experience as a CPA). Each DRS presents a document that has a series of highlighted phrases or sentences that the candidate will need to determine are correct or incorrect. To help make these conclusions, numerous supporting documents, or resources, such as legal letters, phone transcripts, financial statements, trial balances and authoritative literature will be included. The candidate will need to sort through these documents to determine what is, and what is not important to solving the problem. Please see the Appendix at the end of this book for more information about DRSs.

Written Communication – BEC

Written communication will be assessed through the use of responses to essay questions, which will be based upon the content topics as outlined in the Blueprints. Candidates will have access to a word processor, which includes a spell check feature. Candidates are encouraged to use the "Help" tab for more information on the word processor functionality as it is similar to but not exactly like popular word processor programs the candidate may already be familiar with.

Research Task Format

FAR, AUD and REG will each contain at least one research problem. If a candidate's exam contains two research problems, it is likely that one of them is a problem being pre-tested.

Candidates will be asked to search through the database to find an appropriate reference that addresses the issue presented in the research problem. A scenario is presented in which the candidate must find his or her answer in the authoritative literature using a pre-determined list of codes (such as Professional Standards or federal taxation code). The candidate will choose the appropriate code title from the drop-down list and then enter a specific reference number applicable to their given scenario.

Authoritative literature for each section appears as follows:

FAR: Candidates will search the FASB ASC (Accounting Standards Codification) for their responses; this section does not have a dropdown menu to select from.

REG: IRC - Internal Revenue Code

AUD: AU-C - Clarified U.S. Auditing Standards
PCAOB – AS - PCAOB Auditing Standards
AT-C - Attestation Services
AR-C - Statements on Standards for Accounting and Review Services
ET - Code of Professional Conduct
BL - Bylaws
VS - Statements on Standards for Valuation Services
CS - Statement on Standards for Consulting Services
PFP - Personal Financial Planning
CPE - Continuing Professional Education
TS – Tax Services
PR – Peer Review Standards
QC - Quality Control

For example, a candidate may be asked the following question:

> A company appropriates retained earnings for a loss contingency. How should this be disclosed in the financial statements?

Using the Authoritative Literature tab, the candidate will search for keywords associated with the question using the search box, which will pull up all references within the literature to those keywords. From there, the candidate should use the "search within" function to find specific instances of keywords within each subsection. Keywords will be highlighted in the text and the candidate can go through them to find the relevant text that answers the research problem.

In this case, a search for "appropriation of retained earnings" and a more detailed search within all references to that topic using the *search within* button would likely bring up FAS 5 (ASC 450), paragraph 15 which reads:

> Some enterprises have classified a portion of retained earnings as "appropriated" for loss contingencies. In some cases, the appropriation has been shown outside the stockholders' equity section of the balance sheet. Appropriation of retained earnings is not prohibited by this Statement provided that it is shown within the stockholders' equity section of the balance sheet and is clearly identified as an appropriation of retained earnings. Costs or losses shall not be

charged to an appropriation of retained earnings, and no part of the appropriation shall be transferred to income.

Using the provided drop-down menu, the candidate would then select the appropriate literature reference from the list (in this case, FASB codification) and enter the pronouncement and paragraph numbers in the two blank boxes. It will look something like this:

> A company appropriates retained earnings for a loss contingency. How should this be disclosed in the financial statements? Research the Professional Standards for the section that provides guidance on appropriating retained earnings. Enter your response in the answer fields below.

ASC	450	5	15

Research questions will also alert the candidate if they have correctly formatted their answer by displaying "Your response is correctly formatted" in a box below the candidate response if the candidate has entered reference numbers correctly. For example, single-digit reference numbers (such as "paragraph 3") may be formatted as a two-digit response (such as "paragraph "03").

To master research type questions, you can either practice at the below NASBA website, or you can use the Interactive Practice Questions software included in your course.

CPA Exam Candidates: Free Online Access to Professional Literature Package

CPA Exam candidates can get a free six-month subscription to professional literature used in the CPA Examination. This online package includes AICPA Professional Standards, FASB Current Text and FASB Original Pronouncements. Only candidates who have applied to take the CPA exam and have been deemed eligible by state boards of accountancy will receive access to this package of professional literature. NASBA will verify that a candidate has a valid NTS (Notice to Schedule). A candidate must be in receipt of a valid NTS prior to receiving authorization to the professional literature.

To subscribe visit: **https://nasba.org/NASBAWeb.nsf/ENCD**

Another good source for Researching Tax Codes for the **Regulation Exam**:

irs.gov/taxpros/article/0,,id=98137,00.html

Testlets

Each section of the exam is presented in 5 testlets. The first 2 testlets contain multiple-choice questions (MCQs) and the last 3 testlets contain task-based simulations. (In the BEC exam, 2 of the last 3 testlets contain task-based simulations and 1 contains written communication problems.) Candidates can go back and forth between different questions within a testlet but cannot go back to previous testlets or review their questions once they have submitted their exam as complete.

Additional facts about the Exam

- You may take 1 part at a time.
- Results are released at various times throughout the exam window.
- In most jurisdictions, candidates must pass all four parts of the Uniform CPA Examination within a "rolling" eighteen-month period, which begins on the date that the first section(s) passed is taken.
- Generally, any credit for any exam part(s) passed outside the eighteen-month period will expire and that section(s) must be retaken.
- Candidates will not be allowed to retake a failed exam part(s) within the same quarter (examination window)
- Candidates will take different, equivalent exams.

Effective Date of Pronouncements (AICPA, 07/12/2015)

Accounting and auditing pronouncements are eligible to be tested on the Uniform CPA Examination in the later of: (1) the first testing window beginning after the pronouncement's earliest mandatory effective date or (2) the first testing window beginning six (6) months after the pronouncement's issuance date. In either case, there is a simultaneous introduction of content related to the new pronouncement and removal of content related to the previous pronouncement.

For the federal taxation area, the Internal Revenue Code and federal tax regulations in effect six months after the enactment date or the change's effective date, whichever is later, are eligible for testing.

For all other subjects covered in the Regulation (REG) and Business Environment and Concepts (BEC) sections, materials eligible to be tested include federal laws in the window beginning six months after their effective date, and uniform acts in the window beginning one year after their adoption by a simple majority of the jurisdictions.

Lecture 0.02

Financial Accounting and Reporting- 4 Hours

Content Allocation

The content areas tested in the FAR section of the exam, as well as the weight given to each content area, are summarized in the following table.

Content Area		Weight
Area I	Conceptual Framework, Standard-Setting and Financial Reporting	25-35%
Area II	Select Financial Statement Accounts	30-40%
Area III	Select Transactions	20-30%
Area IV	State and Local Governments	5-15%

Skill Allocation

The skills tested in the FAR exam, as well as the weight given to each skill, are summarized in the following table.

Skill	Weight
Evaluation	-
Analysis	25-35%
Application	50-60%
Remembering and Understanding	10-20%

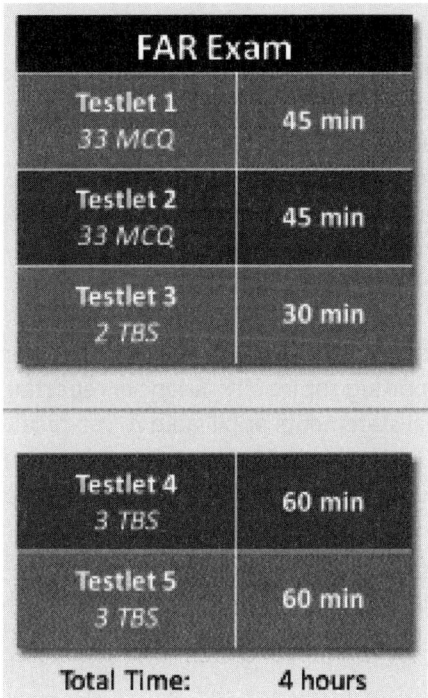

Things to consider:
- **FAR includes calculations**
- **Allocate 80 seconds per multiple choice question as a benchmark**
- **Allocate 15-25 minutes per task-based simulation, depending on complexity**
- **Plan to use no more than 10 minutes per research question**
- **Take the standard 15-minute break after the 3rd testlet – it doesn't count against your time**

Uniform CPA Examination Blueprints
Effective April 1, 2017

FINANCIAL ACCOUNTING AND REPORTING (FAR)

According to the AICPA, the Financial Accounting and Reporting (FAR) exam assesses the knowledge and skills that a newly licensed CPA must demonstrate in the financial accounting and reporting frameworks used by business entities (public and nonpublic), not-for-profit entities and state and local government entities.

The financial accounting and reporting frameworks that are eligible for assessment within the FAR exam include the standards and regulations issued by the:
- Financial Accounting Standards Board (FASB)
- U.S. Securities and Exchange Commission (U.S. SEC)
- American Institute of Certified Public Accountants (AICPA)
- Governmental Accounting Standards Board (GASB)
- International Accounting Standards Board (IASB)

Area I of the FAR exam blueprint covers FASB's Conceptual Framework, FASB's standard-setting process and several different financial reporting topics. The financial reporting topics include the following:
- General-purpose financial statements applicable to for-profit entities, not-for-profit entities and employee benefit plans under the FASB Accounting Standards Codification
- Disclosures specific to public companies including earnings per share and segment reporting under the FASB Accounting Standards Codification and the interim, annual and periodic filing requirements for U.S. registrants in accordance with the rules of the U.S. SEC
- Financial statements prepared under special purpose frameworks as described in AU-C Section 800 of the Codification of Statements on Auditing Standards

Area II of the FAR exam blueprint covers the financial accounting and reporting requirements in the FASB Accounting Standards Codification that are applicable to select financial statement accounts.
- To the extent applicable, each group and topic in the area is eligible for testing within the context of both for-profit and not-for-profit entities
    - If significant accounting or reporting differences exist between for-profit and not-for-profit entities for a given group or topic, such differences are in representative not-for-profit tasks in the blueprint

Area III of the FAR exam blueprint covers the financial accounting and reporting requirements for select transactions that are applicable to entities under the FASB
Accounting Standards Codification and the IASB standards.
- The testing of content under the IASB standards is limited to a separate group titled, "Differences between IFRS and U.S. GAAP"
- To the extent applicable, the remaining groups in the area are eligible for testing within the context of both for-profit and not-for-profit entities
    - If significant accounting or reporting differences exist between for-profit and not-for-profit entities, such differences are in representative not-for-profit tasks in the blueprint

Area IV of the FAR exam blueprint covers GASB's conceptual framework as well the financial accounting and reporting requirements for state and local governments under the GASB standards and interpretations.

References – Financial Accounting and Reporting

Financial Accounting Standards Board (FASB) Accounting Standards Codification

FASB Concepts Statements

U.S. Securities and Exchange Commission References:
- Securities Exchange Act of 1934
- Regulation S-X of the Code of Federal Regulations (17 CFR Part 210)
- Regulation S-K of the Code of Federal Regulations (17 CFR Part 229)

Codification of Statements on Auditing Standards: AU-C Section 800, Special Considerations – Audits of Financial Statements Prepared in Accordance with Special Purpose Frameworks

AICPA Accounting and Auditing Guides

International Financial Reporting Standards (IFRS) References:
- International Financial Reporting Standards
- International Accounting Standards
- Interpretations issued by the IFRS Interpretations Committee
- Interpretations issued by the Standing Interpretations Committee

State and Local Government References:
- Governmental Accounting Standards Board (GASB) Codification of
- Governmental Accounting and Financial Reporting Standards
- GASB Statements, Interpretations, Technical Bulletins and Concepts Statements
- National Council on Governmental Accounting (NCGA) Statements and Interpretation

Current textbooks on accounting for business entities, not-for-profit entities, and state and local government entities

FINANCIAL ACCOUNTING AND REPORTING

Area I — Conceptual Framework, Standard-Setting and Financial Reporting (25–35%)

Content Group/Topic	Skill				Representative Task
	Remembering and Understanding	Application	Analysis	Evaluation	
A. CONCEPTUAL FRAMEWORK AND STANDARD-SETTING FOR BUSINESS AND NONBUSINESS ENTITIES					
1. Conceptual framework	✓				Recall the purpose and characteristics in the conceptual framework for business and nonbusiness entities.
2. Standard-setting process	✓				Recall the due process steps followed by the FASB to establish financial accounting and reporting standards.
B. GENERAL-PURPOSE FINANCIAL STATEMENTS: FOR-PROFIT BUSINESS ENTITIES					
1. Balance sheet/ statement of financial position		✓			Prepare a classified balance sheet from a trial balance and supporting documentation.
		✓			Adjust the balance sheet to correct identified errors.
			✓		Detect, investigate and correct discrepancies while agreeing the balance sheet amounts to supporting documentation.
			✓		Calculate fluctuations and ratios and interpret the results while reviewing comparative balance sheets.
2. Income statement/ statement of profit or loss		✓			Prepare a multiple-step income statement from a trial balance and supporting documentation.
		✓			Prepare a single-step income statement from a trial balance and supporting documentation.
		✓			Adjust the income statement to correct identified errors.
			✓		Detect, investigate and correct discrepancies while agreeing the income statement amounts to supporting documentation.
			✓		Calculate fluctuations and ratios and interpret the results while reviewing comparative income statements.

FINANCIAL ACCOUNTING AND REPORTING

Area I — Conceptual Framework, Standard-Setting and Financial Reporting (25–35%) Continued

Content Group/Topic	Skill				Representative Task
	Remembering and Understanding	Application	Analysis	Evaluation	
B. GENERAL-PURPOSE FINANCIAL STATEMENTS: FOR-PROFIT BUSINESS ENTITIES, continued					
3. Statement of comprehensive income		✓			Prepare a statement of comprehensive income from a trial balance and supporting documentation.
		✓			Calculate reclassification adjustments for items of other comprehensive income.
		✓			Adjust the statement of comprehensive income to correct identified errors.
			✓		Detect, investigate and correct discrepancies while agreeing the statement of comprehensive income amounts to supporting documentation.
4. Statement of changes in equity		✓			Prepare a statement of changes in equity from a trial balance and supporting documentation.
		✓			Adjust the statement of changes in equity to correct identified errors.
			✓		Detect, investigate and correct discrepancies while agreeing the statement of changes in equity amounts to supporting documentation.
5. Statement of cash flows		✓			Prepare a statement of cash flows using the direct method and required disclosures from supporting documentation.
		✓			Prepare a statement of cash flows using the indirect method and required disclosures from supporting documentation.
		✓			Adjust a statement of cash flows to correct identified errors.
			✓		Detect, investigate and correct discrepancies while agreeing the statement of cash flows amounts to supporting documentation.
			✓		Derive the impact of transactions on the statement of cash flows.

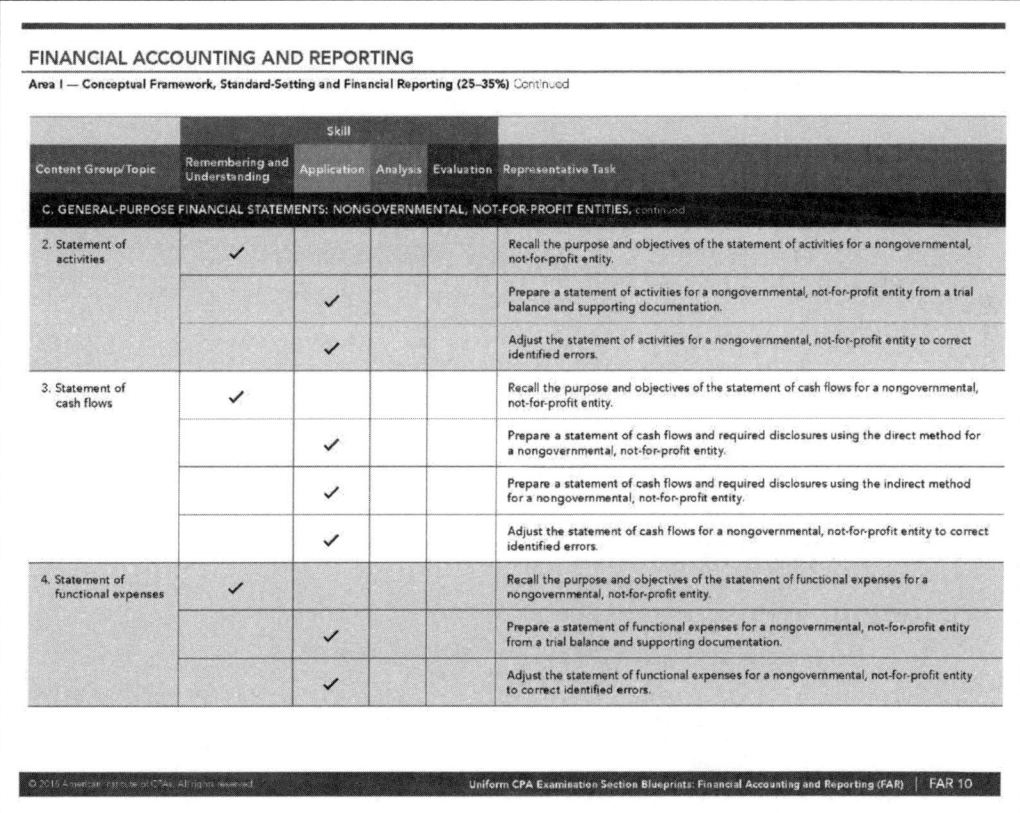

FINANCIAL ACCOUNTING AND REPORTING

Area I — Conceptual Framework, Standard-Setting and Financial Reporting (25–35%) Continued

Content Group/Topic	Remembering and Understanding	Application	Analysis	Evaluation	Representative Task
D. PUBLIC COMPANY REPORTING TOPICS (U.S. SEC REPORTING REQUIREMENTS, EARNINGS PER SHARE AND SEGMENT REPORTING)					
	✓				Recall the purpose of forms 10-Q, 10-K and 8-K that a U.S. registrant is required to file with the U.S. Securities and Exchange Commission under the Securities Exchange Act of 1934.
	✓				Identify the significant components of Form 10-Q and Form 10-K filed with the U.S. Securities and Exchange Commission.
		✓			Prepare financial statement note disclosures for reportable segments.
		✓			Calculate basic earnings per share.
		✓			Calculate diluted earnings per share.
E. FINANCIAL STATEMENTS OF EMPLOYEE BENEFIT PLANS					
	✓				Identify the required financial statements for a defined benefit pension plan and a defined contribution pension plan.
		✓			Prepare a statement of changes in net assets available for benefits for a defined benefit pension plan and a defined contribution pension plan.
		✓			Prepare a statement of net assets available for benefits for a defined benefit pension plan and a defined contribution pension plan.

FINANCIAL ACCOUNTING AND REPORTING

Area I — Conceptual Framework, Standard-Setting and Financial Reporting (25–35%) Continued

Content Group/Topic	Remembering and Understanding	Application	Analysis	Evaluation	Representative Task
F. SPECIAL PURPOSE FRAMEWORKS					
	✓				Recall appropriate financial statement titles to be used for the financial statements prepared under a special purpose framework.
		✓			Perform calculations to convert cash basis or modified cash basis financial statements to accrual basis financial statements.
		✓			Prepare financial statements using the cash basis of accounting.
		✓			Prepare financial statements using a modified cash basis of accounting.
		✓			Prepare financial statements using the income tax basis of accounting.

FINANCIAL ACCOUNTING AND REPORTING
Area II — Select Financial Statement Accounts (30–40%)

Content Group/Topic	Skill				Representative Task
	Remembering and Understanding	Application	Analysis	Evaluation	
A. CASH AND CASH EQUIVALENTS					
		✓			Calculate cash and cash equivalents balances to be reported in the financial statements.
			✓		Reconcile the cash balance per the bank statement to the general ledger.
			✓		Investigate unreconciled cash balances to determine whether an adjustment to the general ledger is necessary.
B. TRADE RECEIVABLES					
		✓			Calculate trade accounts receivable and allowances and prepare journal entries.
		✓			Prepare any required journal entries to record the transfer of trade receivables (secured borrowings, factoring, assignment, pledging).
			✓		Prepare a rollforward of the trade receivables account balance using various sources of information.
			✓		Reconcile and investigate differences between the subledger and general ledger for trade receivables to determine whether an adjustment is necessary.
C. INVENTORY					
		✓			Calculate the carrying amount of inventory and prepare journal entries using various costing methods.
		✓			Measure impairment losses on inventory.
			✓		Reconcile and investigate differences between the subledger and general ledger for inventory to determine whether an adjustment is necessary.
			✓		Prepare a rollforward of the inventory account balance using various sources of information.

Uniform CPA Examination Section Blueprints: Financial Accounting and Reporting (FAR) | FAR 13

FINANCIAL ACCOUNTING AND REPORTING
Area II — Select Financial Statement Accounts (30–40%) Continued

Content Group/Topic	Skill				Representative Task
	Remembering and Understanding	Application	Analysis	Evaluation	
D. PROPERTY, PLANT AND EQUIPMENT					
		✓			Calculate the gross and net property, plant and equipment balances and prepare journal entries.
		✓			Calculate gains or losses on the disposal of long-lived assets to be recognized in the financial statements.
		✓			Measure impairment losses on long-lived assets to be recognized in the financial statements.
		✓			Calculate the amounts necessary to prepare journal entries to record a nonmonetary exchange.
		✓			Determine whether an asset qualifies to be reported as held for sale in the financial statements.
		✓			Adjust the carrying amount of assets held for sale and calculate the loss to be recognized in the financial statements.
			✓		Prepare a rollforward of the property, plant and equipment account balance using various sources of information.
			✓		Reconcile and investigate differences between the subledger and general ledger for property, plant and equipment to determine whether an adjustment is necessary.
E. INVESTMENTS					
1. Financial assets at fair value	✓				Identify investments that are eligible or required to be reported at fair value in the financial statements.
		✓			Calculate the carrying amount of investments measured at fair value and prepare journal entries (excluding impairment).

Uniform CPA Examination Section Blueprints: Financial Accounting and Reporting (FAR) | FAR 14

FINANCIAL ACCOUNTING AND REPORTING
Area II — Select Financial Statement Accounts (30–40%) Continued

Content Group/Topic	Remembering and Understanding	Application	Analysis	Evaluation	Representative Task
E. INVESTMENTS, continued					
1. Financial assets at fair value, continued		✓			Calculate gains and losses to be recognized in net income or other comprehensive income for investments measured at fair value and prepare journal entries.
		✓			Calculate investment income to be recognized in net income for investments measured at fair value and prepare journal entries.
		✓			Measure impairment losses to be recognized on applicable investments reported at fair value in the financial statements.
2. Financial assets at amortized cost	✓				Identify investments that are eligible to be reported at amortized cost in the financial statements.
		✓			Calculate the carrying amount of investments measured at amortized cost and prepare journal entries (excluding impairment).
		✓			Measure impairment losses to be recognized on investments reported at amortized cost in the financial statements.
3. Equity method investments	✓				Identify when the equity method of accounting can be applied to an investment.
		✓			Calculate the carrying amount of equity method investments and prepare journal entries (excluding impairment).
		✓			Measure impairment losses to be recognized in the financial statements on equity method investments.

FINANCIAL ACCOUNTING AND REPORTING
Area II — Select Financial Statement Accounts (30–40%) Continued

Content Group/Topic	Remembering and Understanding	Application	Analysis	Evaluation	Representative Task
F. INTANGIBLE ASSETS – GOODWILL AND OTHER					
	✓				Identify the criteria for recognizing intangible assets in the statement of financial position and classify intangible assets as either finite-lived or indefinite-lived.
	✓				Identify impairment indicators for goodwill and other indefinite-lived intangible assets.
		✓			Calculate the carrying amount of finite-lived intangible assets reported in the financial statements (initial measurement, amortization and impairment) and prepare journal entries.
		✓			Calculate the carrying amount of goodwill and other indefinite-lived intangible assets reported in the financial statements (includes initial measurement and impairment) and prepare journal entries.
G. PAYABLES AND ACCRUED LIABILITIES					
		✓			Calculate the carrying amount of payables and accrued liabilities and prepare journal entries.
		✓			Identify and calculate liabilities arising from exit or disposal activities and determine the timing of recognition in the financial statements.
		✓			Calculate the liabilities and assets resulting from asset retirement obligations and prepare journal entries.
			✓		Reconcile and investigate differences between the subledger and general ledger for accounts payable and accrued liabilities to determine whether an adjustment is necessary.
H. LONG-TERM DEBT (FINANCIAL LIABILITIES)					
1. Notes and bonds payable	✓				Classify a change to a debt instrument as either a modification of terms or an extinguishment of debt.
	✓				Understand when a change to the terms of a debt instrument qualifies as a troubled debt restructuring.
	✓				Classify a financial instrument as either debt or equity, based on its characteristics.

FINANCIAL ACCOUNTING AND REPORTING
Area II — Select Financial Statement Accounts (30–40%) Continued

Content Group/Topic	Remembering and Understanding	Application	Analysis	Evaluation	Representative Task
H. LONG-TERM DEBT (FINANCIAL LIABILITIES), continued					
1. Notes and bonds payable, continued		✓			Calculate the interest expense attributable to notes and bonds payable reported in the financial statements (including discounts, premiums or debt issuance costs).
		✓			Calculate the carrying amount of notes and bonds payable and prepare journal entries.
2. Debt covenant compliance		✓			Calculate debt covenants as stipulated in a debt agreement to ascertain compliance.
I. EQUITY					
		✓			Prepare journal entries to recognize equity transactions in the financial statements.
		✓			Calculate unrestricted, temporarily restricted and permanently restricted net asset balances for a nongovernmental, not-for-profit entity and prepare journal entries.
J. REVENUE RECOGNITION					
	✓				Recall concepts of accounting for revenue.
		✓			Determine the amount and timing of revenue to be recognized under an arrangement with multiple goods and/or services and prepare journal entries.
		✓			Determine the amount and timing of revenue to be recognized under an arrangement for a single good or service and prepare journal entries.
		✓			Determine the amount and timing of revenue to be recognized under an arrangement where delivery is continuous and prepare journal entries.
		✓			Determine revenue to be recognized by a nongovernmental, not-for-profit entity for contributed services received and prepare journal entries.

Uniform CPA Examination Section Blueprints: Financial Accounting and Reporting (FAR) | FAR 17

FINANCIAL ACCOUNTING AND REPORTING
Area II — Select Financial Statement Accounts (30–40%) Continued

Content Group/Topic	Remembering and Understanding	Application	Analysis	Evaluation	Representative Task
J. REVENUE RECOGNITION, continued					
			✓		Interpret agreements, contracts and/or other supporting documentation to determine the amount and timing of revenue to be recognized in the financial statements.
			✓		Reconcile and investigate differences between the sales subledger and the general ledger to determine whether an adjustment is necessary.
K. COMPENSATION AND BENEFITS					
1. Compensated absences		✓			Calculate the carrying amount of the liability for compensated absences and prepare journal entries.
2. Retirement benefits		✓			Use actuarial outputs to calculate the costs and the funded status for a defined benefit pension plan or a defined benefit postretirement plan and prepare journal entries.
3. Stock compensation (share-based payments)	✓				Recall concepts associated with share-based payment arrangements (grant date, vesting conditions, inputs to valuation techniques, valuation models).
		✓			Calculate compensation costs to be recognized for a share-based payment arrangement classified as an equity award and prepare journal entries.
		✓			Calculate compensation costs to be recognized for a share-based payment arrangement classified as a liability award and prepare journal entries.
L. INCOME TAXES					
	✓				Recall the criteria for recognizing uncertain tax positions in the financial statements.
	✓				Recall the criteria for recognizing or adjusting a valuation allowance for a deferred tax asset in the financial statements.
		✓			Calculate the income tax expense, current taxes payable/receivable and deferred tax liabilities/assets to be reported in the financial statements.
		✓			Prepare journal entries to record the tax provision in the financial statements.

Uniform CPA Examination Section Blueprints: Financial Accounting and Reporting (FAR) | FAR 18

FINANCIAL ACCOUNTING AND REPORTING

Area III — Select Transactions (20–30%)

Content Group/Topic	Remembering and Understanding	Application	Analysis	Evaluation	Representative Task
A. ACCOUNTING CHANGES AND ERROR CORRECTIONS					
		✓			Calculate a required adjustment to the financial statements due to an accounting change or error correction and determine whether it requires prospective or retrospective application.
			✓		Derive the impact to the financial statements and related note disclosures of an accounting change or an error correction.
B. BUSINESS COMBINATIONS					
		✓			Prepare journal entries to record the identifiable net assets acquired in a business combination that results in the recognition of goodwill.
		✓			Prepare journal entries to record the identifiable net assets acquired in a business combination that includes a noncontrolling interest.
		✓			Prepare journal entries to record the identifiable net assets acquired in a business combination that results in the recognition of a bargain purchase gain.
		✓			Adjust the financial statements to properly reflect changes in contingent consideration related to a business combination.
		✓			Calculate the consideration transferred in a business combination.
		✓			Adjust the financial statements to properly reflect measurement period adjustments related to a business combination.

FINANCIAL ACCOUNTING AND REPORTING

Area III — Select Transactions (20–30%) Continued

Content Group/Topic	Remembering and Understanding	Application	Analysis	Evaluation	Representative Task
C. CONTINGENCIES AND COMMITMENTS					
	✓				Recall the recognition and disclosure criteria used to identify commitments and contingencies.
		✓			Calculate amounts of contingencies and prepare journal entries.
			✓		Review supporting documentation to determine whether a commitment or contingency requires recognition or disclosure in the financial statements.
D. DERIVATIVES AND HEDGE ACCOUNTING (E.G. SWAPS, OPTIONS, FORWARDS)					
	✓				Identify the characteristics of a freestanding and/or embedded derivative financial instrument to be recognized in the financial statements.
	✓				Identify the criteria necessary to qualify for hedge accounting.
		✓			Prepare journal entries for hedging transactions.
		✓			Prepare journal entries for derivative financial instruments (swaps, options and forwards).
E. FOREIGN CURRENCY TRANSACTIONS AND TRANSLATION					
	✓				Recall the basic functional currency concepts including the indicators to be considered when determining an entity's functional currency.
		✓			Calculate transaction gains or losses recognized from monetary transactions denominated in a foreign currency.
		✓			Adjust an entity's financial statements (local currency to functional currency or functional currency to reporting currency) and recognize the effect on equity through net income or other comprehensive income.

FINANCIAL ACCOUNTING AND REPORTING

Area III — Select Transactions (20–30%) Continued

Content Group/Topic	Remembering and Understanding	Application	Analysis	Evaluation	Representative Task
F. LEASES					
	✓				Recall the appropriate accounting treatment for residual value guarantees, bargain purchase options and variable lease payments included in leasing arrangements.
	✓				Identify the criteria for classifying a lease arrangement.
		✓			Calculate the carrying amount of lease-related assets and liabilities and prepare journal entries that a lessee should record.
		✓			Calculate the carrying amount of lease-related assets and prepare journal entries that a lessor should record.
		✓			Calculate the lease costs that a lessee should recognize in the income statement.
		✓			Prepare journal entries that the seller/lessee should record for a sale-leaseback transaction.
		✓			Calculate the amount of lease income that a lessor should recognize in the income statement.
			✓		Interpret agreements, contracts and/or other supporting documentation to determine the appropriate accounting treatment of a leasing arrangement and prepare the journal entries that the lessee should record.
G. NONRECIPROCAL TRANSFERS					
	✓				Recall the recognition requirements associated with conditional and unconditional promises to give (pledges) for a nongovernmental, not-for-profit entity.
	✓				Identify transfers to a nongovernmental, not-for-profit entity acting as an agent or intermediary that are not recognized as contributions in the statement of activities.

FINANCIAL ACCOUNTING AND REPORTING

Area III — Select Transactions (20–30%) Continued

Content Group/Topic	Remembering and Understanding	Application	Analysis	Evaluation	Representative Task
G. NONRECIPROCAL TRANSFERS, continued					
		✓			Calculate the carrying amount of donated assets (financial assets or long-lived assets) to be reported in the statement of financial position.
		✓			Calculate increases in unrestricted, temporarily restricted or permanently restricted net assets attributable to contributions for a nongovernmental, not-for-profit entity.
H. RESEARCH AND DEVELOPMENT COSTS					
	✓				Identify research and development costs and classify the costs as an expense in the financial statements.
		✓			Calculate the research and development costs to be reported as an expense in the financial statements.
I. SOFTWARE COSTS					
	✓				Identify the criteria necessary to capitalize software costs (software for internal use or sale) in the financial statements.
		✓			Calculate capitalized software costs (software for internal use or sale) to be reported in the financial statements and the related amortization expense.
J. SUBSEQUENT EVENTS					
	✓				Identify a subsequent event and recall its appropriate accounting treatment.
		✓			Calculate required adjustments to financial statements and/or note disclosures based on identified subsequent events.
			✓		Derive the impact to the financial statements and required note disclosures due to identified subsequent events.

FINANCIAL ACCOUNTING AND REPORTING
Area III — Select Transactions (20–30%) Continued

Content Group/Topic	Remembering and Understanding	Application	Analysis	Evaluation	Representative Task
K. FAIR VALUE MEASUREMENTS					
	✓				Identify the valuation techniques used to measure fair value.
		✓			Use the fair value hierarchy to determine the classification of a fair value measurement.
		✓			Use the fair value guidance (e.g. highest and best use, market participant assumptions, unit of account) to measure the fair value of assets and liabilities.
L. DIFFERENCES BETWEEN IFRS AND U.S. GAAP					
	✓				Identify accounting and reporting differences between IFRS and U.S. GAAP.
		✓			Determine the impact of the differences between IFRS and U.S. GAAP on the financial statements.

FINANCIAL ACCOUNTING AND REPORTING
Area IV — State and Local Governments (5–15%)

Content Group/Topic	Remembering and Understanding	Application	Analysis	Evaluation	Representative Task
A. STATE AND LOCAL GOVERNMENT CONCEPTS					
1. Conceptual framework	✓				Recall the purpose and characteristics of the conceptual framework for state and local governments.
2. Measurement focus and basis of accounting	✓				Recall the measurement focus and basis of accounting used by state and local governments for fund and government-wide financial reporting.
3. Purpose of funds		✓			Determine the appropriate fund(s) that a state or local government should use to record its activities.
B. FORMAT AND CONTENT OF THE FINANCIAL SECTION OF THE COMPREHENSIVE ANNUAL FINANCIAL REPORT (CAFR)					
1. Government-wide financial statements	✓				Identify and recall basic concepts and principles associated with government-wide financial statements (e.g., required activities, financial statements and financial statement components).
		✓			Prepare the government-wide statement of net position for a state or local government from trial balances and supporting documentation.
		✓			Prepare the government-wide statement of activities for a state or local government from trial balances and supporting documentation.
2. Governmental funds financial statements	✓				Identify and recall basic concepts and principles associated with governmental fund financial statements (e.g., required funds, financial statements and financial statement components).
		✓			Prepare the statement of revenues, expenditures and changes in fund balances for the governmental funds of a state or local government from trial balances and supporting documentation.
		✓			Prepare the balance sheet for the governmental funds of a state or local government from trial balances and supporting documentation.

FINANCIAL ACCOUNTING AND REPORTING

Area IV — State and Local Governments (5–15%) Continued

Content Group/Topic	Remembering and Understanding	Application	Analysis	Evaluation	Representative Task
B. FORMAT AND CONTENT OF THE FINANCIAL SECTION OF THE COMPREHENSIVE ANNUAL FINANCIAL REPORT (CAFR) continued					
3. Proprietary funds financial statements	✓				Identify and recall basic concepts and principles associated with proprietary fund financial statements (e.g., required funds, financial statements and financial statement components).
		✓			Prepare the statement of revenues, expenses and changes in fund net position for the proprietary funds of a state or local government from trial balances and supporting documentation.
		✓			Prepare the statement of net position for the proprietary funds of a state or local government from trial balances and supporting documentation.
		✓			Prepare the statement of cash flows for the proprietary funds of a state or local government.
4. Fiduciary funds financial statements	✓				Identify and recall basic concepts and principles associated with fiduciary fund financial statements (e.g., required funds, financial statements and financial statement components).
		✓			Prepare the statement of changes in fiduciary net position for the fiduciary funds of a state or local government from trial balances and supporting documentation.
		✓			Prepare the statement of net position for the fiduciary funds of a state or local government from trial balances and supporting documentation.
5. Notes to financial statements	✓				Recall the disclosure requirements for the notes to the basic financial statements of state and local governments.
6. Management's discussion and analysis	✓				Recall the objectives and components of management's discussion and analysis in the comprehensive annual financial report for state and local governments.
7. Budgetary comparison reporting	✓				Recall the objectives and components of budgetary comparison reporting in the comprehensive annual financial report for state and local governments.

FINANCIAL ACCOUNTING AND REPORTING

Area IV — State and Local Governments (5–15%) Continued

Content Group/Topic	Remembering and Understanding	Application	Analysis	Evaluation	Representative Task
B. FORMAT AND CONTENT OF THE FINANCIAL SECTION OF THE COMPREHENSIVE ANNUAL FINANCIAL REPORT (CAFR) continued					
8. Required supplementary information (RSI) other than management's discussion and analysis	✓				Recall the objectives and components of required supplementary information other than management's discussion and analysis in the comprehensive annual financial report for state and local governments.
9. Financial reporting entity, including blended and discrete component units	✓				Recall the criteria for classifying an entity as a component unit of a state or local government and the financial statement presentation requirements (discrete or blended).
C. DERIVING GOVERNMENT-WIDE FINANCIAL STATEMENTS AND RECONCILIATION REQUIREMENTS					
		✓			Prepare worksheets to convert the governmental fund financial statements to the governmental activities reported in the government-wide financial statements.
		✓			Prepare the schedule to reconcile the total fund balances and the net change in fund balances reported in the governmental fund financial statements to the net position and change in net position reported in the government-wide financial statements.

FINANCIAL ACCOUNTING AND REPORTING

Area IV — State and Local Governments (5–15%) Continued

Content Group/Topic	Remembering and Understanding	Application	Analysis	Evaluation	Representative Task
D. TYPICAL ITEMS AND SPECIFIC TYPES OF TRANSACTIONS AND EVENTS: MEASUREMENT, VALUATION, CALCULATION AND PRESENTATION IN GOVERNMENTAL ENTITY FINANCIAL STATEMENTS					
1. Net position and components thereof		✓			Calculate the net position balances (unrestricted, restricted and net investment in capital assets) for state and local governments and prepare journal entries.
2. Fund balances and components thereof		✓			Calculate the fund balances (assigned, unassigned, nonspendable, committed and restricted) for state and local governments and prepare journal entries.
3. Capital assets and infrastructure assets	✓				Identify capital assets reported in the government-wide financial statements of state and local governments.
		✓			Calculate the net general capital assets balance for state and local governments and prepare journal entries (initial measurement and subsequent depreciation and amortization).
4. General and proprietary long-term liabilities	✓				Identify general and proprietary long-term liabilities reported in the government-wide financial statements of state and local governments.
		✓			Calculate the total indebtedness to be reported in the government-wide financial statements of a state or local government.
		✓			Calculate the net general long-term debt balance for state and local governments and prepare journal entries (debt issuance, interest payments, issue premiums or issue discounts).
5. Interfund activity, including transfers		✓			Prepare eliminations of interfund activity in the government-wide financial statements of state and local governments.
		✓			Prepare journal entries to recognize interfund activity within state and local governments.

FINANCIAL ACCOUNTING AND REPORTING

Area IV — State and Local Governments (5–15%) Continued

Content Group/Topic	Remembering and Understanding	Application	Analysis	Evaluation	Representative Task
D. TYPICAL ITEMS AND SPECIFIC TYPES OF TRANSACTIONS AND EVENTS: MEASUREMENT, VALUATION, CALCULATION AND PRESENTATION IN GOVERNMENTAL ENTITY FINANCIAL STATEMENTS, continued					
6. Nonexchange revenue transactions		✓			Calculate the amount of nonexchange revenue to be recognized by state and local governments using the modified accrual basis of accounting and prepare journal entries.
		✓			Calculate the amount of nonexchange revenue to be recognized by state and local governments using the accrual basis of accounting and prepare journal entries.
7. Expenditures and expenses		✓			Calculate expenditures to be recognized under the modified accrual basis of accounting (paid from available fund financial resources) for state and local governments and prepare journal entries.
		✓			Calculate expenses to be recognized under the accrual basis of accounting for state and local governments and prepare journal entries.
8. Special items	✓				Identify transactions that require presentation as special items in government-wide financial statements for state and local governments.
9. Budgetary accounting and encumbrances	✓				Recall and explain the types of budgets used by state and local governments.
		✓			Prepare journal entries to record budgets (original and final) of state and local governments.
		✓			Prepare journal entries to record encumbrances of state and local governments.
10. Other financing sources and uses		✓			Calculate the amount to be reported as other financing sources and other financing uses in the governmental funds financial statements.

State	State Board Web Address	Telephone #
AK	commerce.state.ak.us/occ/pcpa.htm	(907) 465-3811
AL	asbpa.alabama.gov	(334) 242-5700
AR	state.ar.us/asbpa	(501) 682-1520
AZ	azaccountancy.gov	(602) 364-0804
CA	dca.ca.gov/cba	(916) 263-3680
CO	dora.state.co.us/accountants	(303) 894-7800
CT	ct.gov/sboa	(860) 509-6179
DC	pearsonvue.com/dc/accountancy/	(202) 442-4320
DE	dpr.delaware.gov/boards/accountancy/index.shtml	(302) 744-4500
FL	myfloridalicense.com/dbpr/cpa/	(850) 487-1395
GA	sos.state.ga.us/plb/accountancy/	(478) 207-1400
GU	guamboa.org	(671) 647-0813
HI	hawaii.gov/dcca/areas/pvl/boards/accountancy	(808) 586-2696
IA	state.ia.us/iacc	(515) 281-5910
ID	isba.idaho.gov	(208) 334-2490
IL	ilboa.org	(217) 531-0950
IN	in.gov/pla/accountancy.htm	(317) 234-3040
KS	ksboa.org	(785) 296-2162
KY	cpa.ky.gov	(502) 595-3037
LA	cpaboard.state.la.us	(504) 566-1244
MA	mass.gov/reg/boards/pa	(617) 727-1806
MD	dllr.state.md.us/license/occprof/account.html	(410) 230-6322
ME	maine.gov/pfr/professionallicensing/professions/accountants/index.htm	(207) 624-8603
MI	michigan.gov/accountancy	(517) 241-9249
MN	boa.state.mn.us	(651) 296-7938
MO	pr.mo.gov/accountancy.asp	(573) 751-0012
MS	msbpa.state.ms.us	(601) 354-7320
MT	publicaccountant.mt.gov	(406) 841-2389
NC	nccpaboard.gov	(919) 733-4222
ND	state.nd.us/ndsba	(800) 532-5904
NE	nol.org/home/BPA	(402) 471-3595
NH	nh.gov/accountancy	(603) 271-3286
NJ	state.nj.us/lps/ca/accountancy/	(973) 504-6380
NM	rld.state.nm.us/accountancy/index.html	(505) 841-9108
NV	nvaccountancy.com/	(775) 786-0231
NY	op.nysed.gov/cpa.htm	(518) 474-3817
OH	acc.ohio.gov/	(614) 466-4135
OK	oab.state.ok.us	(405) 521-2397
OR	egov.oregon.gov/BOA/	(503) 378-4181
PA	dos.state.pa.us/account	(717) 783-1404
PR	estado.gobierno.pr/	(787) 722-4816
RI	dbr.ri.gov/divisions/accountancy/	(401) 222-3185
SC	llr.state.sc.us/POL/Accountancy	(803) 896-4770
SD	state.sd.us/dol/Boards/accountancy/acc-home.htm	(605) 367-5770
TN	tn.gov/commerce/boards/tnsba/index.shtml	(615) 741-2550
TX	tsbpa.state.tx.us	(512) 305-7800
UT	dopl.utah.gov	(801) 530-6396
VA	boa.virginia.gov	(804) 367-8505
VI	dlca.gov.vi	(340) 773-4305
VT	vtprofessionals.org/opr1/accountants	(802) 828-2837
WA	cpaboard.wa.gov	(360) 753-2585
WI	drl.wi.gov/profession.asp?profid=60&locid=0	(608) 266-5511
WV	boa.wv.gov/Pages/default.aspx	(304) 558-3557
WY	cpaboard.state.wy.us	(307) 777-7551

Section 1 - Conceptual Framework & IFRS Corresponding Lectures

Watch the following course lectures with this section:

Lecture 1.01 – Generally Accepted Accounting Principles (GAAP)
Lecture 1.02 – Conceptual Framework – Class Questions
Lecture 1.03 – Elements of Financial Statements
Lecture 1.04 – Fair Value Option Accounting
Lecture 1.05 – Revenue and Expense Recognition
Lecture 1.06 – Elements of Financial Statements – Class Questions
Lecture 1.07 – International Financial Reporting Standards
Lecture 1.08 – Major Differences between US GAAP and IFRS
Lecture 1.09 – IFRS – Class Questions
Lecture 1.10 – Research Task Format

EXAM NOTE: Please refer to the AICPA FAR Blueprint in the Introduction to find a listing of the representative tasks (and their associated skill levels—i.e., Remembering and Understanding, Application, and Analysis) that the candidate should be able to perform based on the knowledge obtained in this section.

Conceptual Framework & IFRS

Lecture 1.01

GENERALLY ACCEPTED ACCOUNTING PRINCIPLES (GAAP)

The Financial Accounting and Reporting (FAR) exam tests the CPA candidate's knowledge of how transactions, events, and circumstances are accounted for and how they are reported upon. Most FAR questions are based on Generally Accepted Accounting Principles (GAAP), referred to as a **General Purpose Financial Reporting Framework**, consists of a set of principles and guidelines that were developed by the Financial Accounting Standards Board (FASB), who is authorized to establish accounting standards by the Securities and Exchange Commission (SEC).

A financial reporting framework (FRF) includes
- *Recognition criteria*, which determine what will appear on financial statements and when it will appear;
- *Measurement criteria*, which determine the amount at which it will be reported;
- *Presentation criteria*, which determine where it will appear on the financial statements;
- *Disclosure criteria*, which determine what information and how much information must be provided to financial statement users.

Financial reporting frameworks may be general purpose frameworks or special purpose frameworks. There are currently two **general purpose frameworks**:
- **GAAP** – Accounting Principles Generally Accepted in the United States
- **IFRS** – International Financial Reporting Standards

Publicly-held entities are required to submit their financial statements to the SEC prepared in accordance with a general purpose framework, either GAAP or IFRS.

Nonpublic entities, however, have a greater number of choices and select a framework that fairly balances the needs of their financial statements users and the cost of providing information. Like public entities, nonpublic entities may prepare their financial statements under either GAAP or IFRS. In addition, however, they may prepare them in accordance with a special purpose framework, also referred to as an *Other Comprehensive Basis of Accounting* (OCBOA).

Special Purpose Frameworks

A special purpose framework, or OCBOA, is defined as "A definite set of criteria, other than accounting principles generally accepted in the United States of America or International Financial Reporting Standards (IFRSs), having substantial support underlying the preparation of financial statements prepared pursuant to that basis.[1]" Statements prepared under a special purpose framework must have modified titles showing the basis of accounting, e.g. "Consolidated Statements of Assets, Liabilities and Equity (FRF for SMEs Basis)."

There are numerous **special purpose frameworks**. These include:
- The **cash basis** of accounting under which revenues are recognized when they are received, regardless of when they are earned; and expenses are recognized when they are paid, regardless of when they are incurred. Fixed assets are expensed and not capitalized.

---

[1] AR 60.04

One could also use the **modified cash basis**, which is considered a sort of *hybrid* approach between cash and accrual, where assets could be capitalized and taxes and inventory could be accrued.
- The **tax basis** of accounting under which revenues and expenses are recognized for financial reporting purposes in the same periods and in the same amount as they are recognized when the entity is preparing its income tax return. The tax basis could be cash-basis or accrual-basis.
- A **contractual basis** of accounting is one that is required to be used by a party to a contract and is generally designed to assist users in determining whether or not terms of the contract, and other requirements related to it, are being adhered to.
- A **regulatory basis** of accounting is one that is one that is imposed by a governmental regulatory agency to which the entity is required to report.
- The Financial Reporting Framework for Small- and Medium-Sized Entities, abbreviated as **FRF for SMEs**.

With the exception of the cash basis of accounting and in some cases the tax basis, both general purpose frameworks and most special purpose frameworks apply the accrual basis of accounting. Under the accrual basis, revenues are recognized in the periods in which they are earned, regardless of when they are received; and expenses are recognized in the periods in which they are incurred, regardless of when they are paid.

The CPA exam periodically includes questions that require the candidate to determine the amount of revenue or expenses that should be recognized on the accrual basis when given the amount of cash received or paid and the opening and closing balances of various accrual accounts, or changes in them. This will be covered in detail later in the course.

A closely related topic is the statement of cash flows, a statement required to be presented along with every complete set of financial statements prepared in conformity with GAAP. In order to prepare a statement of cash flows, however, the amounts of revenue and expense items determined under the accrual basis are generally known and the amounts of cash received and paid must be determined, a common area of testing on the CPA exam.

The process to be applied, discussed in the chapter related to Statement of Cash Flows, is basically the reverse of the procedure used to convert from cash to accrual.

Alternative Accounting Approaches for Nonpublic Entities

In order to reduce the cost of financial reporting for nonpublic entities, and to bring the cost more in line with the benefits derived by users of financial statements, the FASB created the ***Private Company Council***, or **PCC**. The PCC is charged with evaluating existing GAAP to determine if there are requirements, including disclosures, from which **nonpublic entities** should be exempt; or simplified accounting approaches that may be applied to transactions or financial statement elements that will reduce the cost of reporting without diminishing the relative value of the information provided.

The PCC has developed alternative accounting approaches for goodwill; certain interest rate swaps, a common form of derivative; and for potential variable interest entities (VIE's) involving leases in which the lessor and lessee are under common control. These alternative accounting approaches may only be applied by a nonpublic entity. In order to do so, the entity will elect the

Conceptual Framework & IFRS

alternative accounting treatment by including information in its *Summary of Significant Accounting Policies*.
- In the period of adoption, the entity will indicate that it is adopting the alternative treatment and the primary differences between it and the previous requirements.
- It will also be disclosed in subsequent periods, since it represents a choice among acceptable alternative accounting treatments.

An entity electing to adopt the alternative accounting approaches is still preparing its financial statements in accordance with GAAP since the pronouncements of the PCC are incorporated into the FASB Accounting Standards Codification. As indicated, they apply to nonpublic entities which are all of those entities that are not considered public entities. The FASB defines *public entities* as those:
- That submit financial statements to the SEC, either as a result of a requirement to do so or who do so voluntarily
- That are regulated under the 1934 Securities Exchange Act
- Issuing securities that are traded or have securities that are listed on an exchange
- Required to apply GAAP and has securities that are not restricted as to transfer

FASB CONCEPTUAL FRAMEWORK FOR ACCOUNTING

The conceptual framework for accounting was established by the FASB in order to define the objectives and concepts that underlie Financial Reporting (Per SFAC 8).

The **Objectives** of financial reporting (which focuses on the **USERS** of F/S) are:
1. To provide information that is useful to existing and potential **investors, lenders, and other creditors** in making decisions about providing resources to the entity.
2. Information about a reporting entity's **economic resources** and claims against the entity (Financial Position-B/S).
3. **Changes** in economic resources and claims.
4. Financial performance reflected by **accrual accounting** (provides a better basis for assessing the entity's past and future performance than does cash basis – Income Statement).
5. Financial performance reflected by past **cash flow** (Cash Flows)
6. Changes in economic resources and claims, **NOT** resulting from financial performance (ex: issuing additional Stock).

We can achieve our objectives if F/S have certain **Primary Qualitative Characteristics** that makes information **USEFUL**. In order to be useful, information must have **BOTH** Relevance & Faithful Representation.
- **Relevance** (Roger is *PC*) – Capable of making a difference in a User's decision making process.
  The 2 Ingredients are:
    - *Predictive value* – Helps decision makers predict or forecast future results.
    - *Confirmatory value* (Feedback value) – Confirm or correct prior predictions.
    - Or Both
        - **Materiality** – Capable of making a difference in the User's decision making process if omitted or misstated (auditor's judgment). Considered an entity-specific aspect of *Relevance* that applies at the individual entity level.
- **Faithful Representation** – (Roger is never on the *FENC*e) The information depicts what it purports to represent. The 3 ingredients are:

- o *Free from **E**rror* – No errors or omissions in the info
- o *Neutrality* (w/o bias) – The info is free from bias.
- o *Completeness* – Info is presented in a way that users can understand

Enhancing Qualitative Characteristics that relate to both Relevance and Faithful Representation (Roger is **CUT** like a **V**).

- **C**omparability (Consistency) – Same *principles* being used with business enterprises in similar Industry / (Consistency – Same accounting *methods* in different periods).
- **U**nderstandability – Classifying, characterizing and presenting info clearly and concisely.
- **T**imeliness – Info is available to a decision maker when it is useful to make the decision.
- **V**erifiability – Different sources agree on an amount through either direct or indirect verification.

One pervasive **constraint** that overrides the usefulness of Info.
- **Cost/benefit** – cost of obtaining and presenting the information shouldn't exceed the benefit.

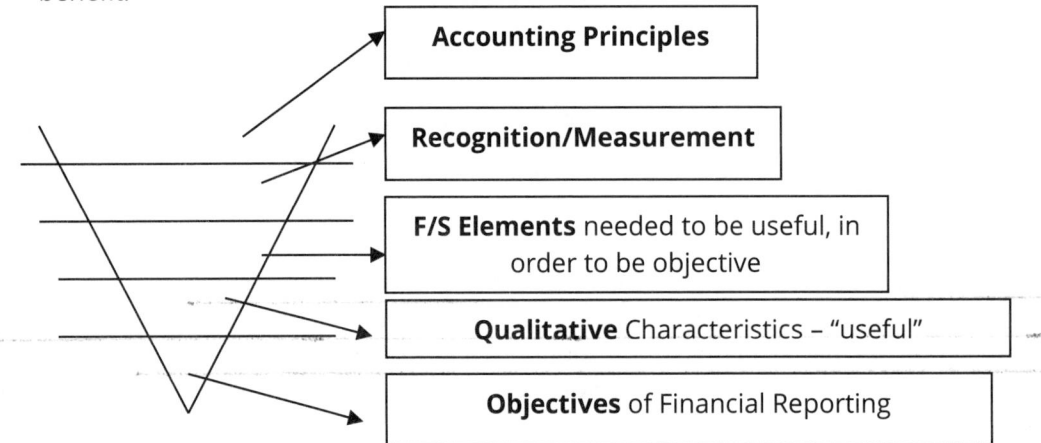

Accounting Principles

Recognition/Measurement

F/S Elements needed to be useful, in order to be objective

Qualitative Characteristics – "useful"

Objectives of Financial Reporting

USEFUL (2 Primary Qualitative Characteristics SFAC-8)

Relevance (Roger is PC)
- **P**redictive value
- **C**onfirmatory value
  (feedback – confirm or changes)

Faithful Representation (FENCe)
- Free from **E**rror
- **N**eutral (w/o Bias)
- **C**ompleteness

- Or *Both*

Material (an entity-specific aspect of *Relevance* that applies at the individual entity level – it's omission or misstatement could influence a user's decision)

Enhancing Qualitative Characteristics (CUT like a V) (enhance the Usefulness of the info – Very desirable, but not required)
- o **C**omparability (Consistency)
- o **U**nderstandability (classified/characterized & presented clearly)
- o **T**imeliness
- o **V**erifiability

Constraint:
- *Cost/benefit*

Conceptual Framework & IFRS   Section 1

Lecture 1.02

CLASS QUESTIONS

Please see the Class Questions and Class Solutions for this Lecture at the end of this Section.

Lecture 1.03

Elements of Financial Statements

A full set of financial statements includes:
- Statement of Position (Balance sheet)
- Statement of Earnings Financial & Comprehensive Income (Income statement)
- Statement of Cash Flows
- Statement of Changes in Owners' Equity (statement of Investments by and Distributions to Owners)

The Financial statement elements need to be Useful. There are **10 key elements** that make up all the financial statements. They include Assets, Liabilities, Equity, Investments by owners, Distributions to owners, Comprehensive Income, Revenue, Expenses, Gains and Losses.

The 3 Basic elements are:
- **Assets** – an economic resource that has a probable future benefit, one can obtain the benefit, and the transaction creating the benefit has already occurred.
- **Liabilities** – an economic obligation in which one needs to use or transfer an asset, it can't be avoided and the transaction has already occurred.
- **Equity or Net Assets** – assets left over after deducting liabilities.

    Equity consists of 3 elements:
    - Contributions/ investments by owners
    - Distributions to owners – (dividends)
    - **Comprehensive income** – all changes in equity other than "owner" sources. These items affect Comp. Income, but not net income (**DENT**):
        - **D**erivative cash flow hedges
        - **E**xcess adjustment of Pension PBO and FV of plan assets at year end
        - **N**et unrealized gains or losses on "available-for-sale" securities
        - **T**ranslation adjustments for foreign currency

    When deciding what will be included in income (comprehensive or net income), the capital maintenance concept being used needs to be known.
    - **Physical capital maintenance concept** – only recognize an event when an asset is sold or a liability is settled (measures the effects of price changes in nominal or constant dollars).
    - **Financial capital maintenance concept** – recognize an event as a change in the value of an asset or liability occurs. (recognize holding gains and losses – current GAAP).

    Current accounting methods emphasize the physical capital approach with fixed assets, which are not adjusted to market value, but emphasize the financial capital approach with most marketable securities, which are reported at market value, except in limited cases. Part of the reason relates to the Enhancing Qualitative Characteristics of Verifiability: market values of fixed assets are difficult to verify and adjustments based on management estimates subject to biases, while the active market for investment securities provides numbers that are verifiable and not subject to management bias, hence meeting the Enhancing Qualitative Characteristic of Verifiability.

Comprehensive income consists of four elements:
- Revenues – inflows from an entity's primary operations
- Expenses – outflows due to an entity's primary operations.
- Gains – increases in equity from incidental transactions.
- Losses – decreases in equity from incidental transactions.

Accounting rules and concepts that go along with the key elements:
- **Consistency** – same principle each year
- **Conservatism** – considering all risks inherent in the business (accruing a contingent loss)
- **Cost/Benefit** – costs don't exceed benefits to be derived.
- **Matching** – recognize a cost as an expense in the same period as the benefit (usually a revenue) is recognized
- **Allocation** – spreading a cost over more than one period.
- **Full Disclosure** – providing all useful info in the financial statements
- **Recognition** – booking an item in the financial statements
- **Realization** – converting non-cash resources into cash or a claim to cash

Recognition and Measurement

When to **recognize** a financial statement element and how to **measure** it.
- Meets the definition of an element (asset, liability, etc.)
- Element is capable of being measured in monetary terms
- The item is Relevant and Faithful Representation (useful)

To measure in **Monetary terms**
- **Historical cost** – amount you paid for it (PP&E)
- **Replacement cost** – what it would cost to replace an item (inventory)
- **Fair Market Value** (FMV) – Per **ASC 820**, "the price that would be received to sell an asset or paid to transfer a liability in an orderly transaction between market participants at the measurement date" (see below).
- **Net realizable value** (NRV) – amount expected to be converted into (A/R)
- **Present Value** (PV) – discounted cash flows due to the time value of money (Notes/Receivable, Bonds/Payable, Leases)

Lecture 1.04

Fair Value and the Option to Report Financial Assets and Financial Liabilities at Fair Value

ASC 820 does not allow, nor require, assets or liabilities be reported at fair value unless there is another requirement to do so. An entity is **required to recognize various items at fair value**, including the following:
- Investments in marketable debt or equity securities that are classified as either ***trading securities or available for sale*** securities are reported at fair value (***mark-to-market***) as of each balance sheet date.
    - Unrealized gains and losses on trading securities are recognized in the statement of income.

- - Unrealized gains and losses on available for sale securities are recognized in other comprehensive income.
- With very few exceptions, *assets acquired and liabilities* assumed in a business combination are initially recognized at fair value, but are not adjusted to fair value in subsequent periods for presentation on the balance sheet.
- **Impairment losses** result in the reduction in the carrying value of an asset to its fair value in the period of the impairment.
  - Impairment of a receivable is recognized when it is expected that some or all payments will either not be received or not received as scheduled.
    - The receivable is generally written down to its fair value, usually the present value of the expected future cash flows.
    - In certain circumstances, it is written down to the net realizable value of collateral.
  - Goodwill and intangibles other than goodwill that also have indefinite useful lives are tested for impairment at least annually and written down to their fair values when impaired.
  - Depreciable assets and amortizable intangibles are evaluated for impairment when there is an indication that they have been impaired and, when that is the case, they are written down to their fair values.
- **All derivatives** are always reported at fair value.
  - Unrealized gains and losses are generally reported in income.
  - Unrealized gains and losses on derivatives that are designated as cash flow hedges accumulate in other comprehensive income until recognized at the same time as the gain or loss on the hedged items.

In addition to those items that are required to be measured at fair value, ASC 825, Financial Instruments, allows an entity to elect to report some or all of its financial assets and liabilities at their fair values. The election may be made regarding individual financial instruments without being required to be made for other financial instruments, even if similar in nature.

Although certain specific items may involve measurements at fair value, they **do not qualify for the fair value election.** These items have their own established accounting principles, which are required to be followed
- Pension plan, post-retirement, and other post-employment benefits (ASC 712 and 715)
- Leases (ASC 840)
- Financial instruments that are components of equity (ASC 505)
- Share based payments and stock options (ASC 718)

A financial instrument is defined as "cash, evidence of an ownership interest in an entity, or a contract that both:
- Imposes on one entity a contractual obligation that either:
  - To deliver cash or another financial instrument to a second entity.
  - To exchange other financial instruments on potentially unfavorable terms with the second entity.
- Conveys to that second entity a contractual right either:
  - To receive cash or another financial instrument from the first entity.
  - To exchange other financial instruments on potentially favorable terms with the first entity.

Examples of financial assets and liabilities that would *qualify for the fair value election* include:
- Most investments
    - Available for sale securities would be reported at fair value with unrealized gains or losses being reported on the income statement rather than as a component of comprehensive income.
    - Held to maturity securities would be reported at fair value and any adjustments from the amortized cost would be reported in income.
    - Investments accounted for under the equity method would be reported at fair value with increases or decreases reported in income.
- Firm commitments involving financial instruments, such as forward exchange contracts to purchase or sell a foreign currency.

If an entity decides to elect the fair value option, it may apply it to any qualifying financial instrument, without being required to apply it to others, including those that are similar. An election may only be made when a financial asset or liability is acquired or in other limited circumstances, referred to as election dates. Likewise, once elected, the fair value option is permanent and may only be discontinued on a subsequent election date.

When the fair value option is elected, **unrealized gains and losses are reported in income.**

The accounting literature defines fair value for certain items. In a business combination, for example:
- The fair value of cash is its face amount.
- The fair value of an investment in marketable securities is its market value.
- The fair value of accounts receivable is its net realizable value (NRV).
- The fair value of inventory is its replacement cost, subject to floor and ceiling limitations.

For many items, however, there is nothing in the authoritative literature that can be used to determine fair value. This section defines fair value for those purposes as *"the price that would be received to sell an asset or paid to transfer a liability in an orderly transaction between market participants at the measurement date".* For a transaction to be orderly, it cannot be a forced transaction. Instead, the asset or liability is assumed to be exposed to the market for a time period that is customary for that type of asset or liability. *Market participants* are parties that are:
- Independent of the entity.
- Reasonably knowledgeable about the asset or liability.
- In a position to acquire the asset or assume the liability.
- Voluntarily willing to acquire the asset or assume the liability.

The definition of fair value retains the **exchange price** notion, but the focus is on the price that would be received to sell the asset or paid to transfer the liability, which is the *exit price*, not the price that would be paid to acquire the asset or received to assume the liability, the *entry price.*

Fair value measurements are not intended to be an application of conservatism. Assets, other than financial assets, are measured on the basis of their "highest and best use". Some assets are more valuable *in exchange* and are measured at what would be received upon sale. Others are more valuable *in use* and are measured at the value represented in the form of some combination of potential revenues earned and costs saved that result from their use.
- It is assumed that a transaction will occur in the **principal market** in which the asset or liability would most frequently be traded.

- When there is no principal market, values are based on the assumption that a transaction would occur in the **most advantageous** market.

This is intended as a measure of an asset's or liability's fair value without assuming that the asset will actually be disposed of or the liability transferred. As a result, the value is determined without taking into consideration costs of the transaction, such as costs to transfer the asset or liability. If an asset needs to be transported to its principal market, however, the cost of doing so is taken into account when measuring the asset's fair value.

When measuring an item at fair value, the entity will apply one of **three valuation techniques**, the market approach, the income approach, or the cost approach (**MIC**).
- The **market approach** involves using information generated by market transactions that involve identical or comparable assets or liabilities.
- The **income approach** involves analyzing future amounts in the form of revenues, cost savings, earnings, or some other item. *(present value technique)*
- The **cost approach** involves measuring the cost that would be incurred to replace the benefit derived from an asset.

The fair values of various items are not necessarily readily determinable. As a result, an entity reporting an item at fair value may use different types of inputs to determine the appropriate measurement. These inputs are not equally reliable, which will affect how users interpret the information. As a result, an entity reporting an item at fair value is also required to disclose the nature of inputs that were used for measurement purposes.

There are **three levels of inputs** that might be applied: *quoted prices in active market.*
- **Level I**, the most reliable, involves the use of observable data from actual market transactions, occurring in an active market, for identical assets or liabilities.
- **Level II** also involves the use of observable data from actual market transactions but either: *quoted prices for similar assets in active market.*
  - The **transactions did not occur in an active market**, or
  - The **transactions** relate to similar, but not identical, assets or liabilities.
- **Level III** involves the use of unobservable data and are largely based on management's judgment. *(financial forecast).* *unobservable inputs for the asset.*

In some cases, an entity will have an equity interest in an entity that reports its net asset value per share. As a practical expedient, such an investment may be reported at the published net asset value per share.
- Since the fair value is not determined using a technique designated by standards for doing so, the fair value measurement does not fit into the hierarchy.
- As a result, an entity applying the practical expedient is not required to disclose the level of inputs that were used to determine fair value.

Fair value measurement may be applied using the following approach:
1. Identify the asset or liability to be measured.
2. Determine the principal or most advantageous market (*highest and best use*).
3. Determine the valuation premise (*in-use or in-exchange*).
4. Determine the appropriate valuation technique (*market, income, or cost approach*).
5. Obtain inputs for valuation (*Level 1, Level 2, or Level 3*).
   - Fair value hierarchy must be used to prioritize the inputs to valuation techniques.
6. Calculate the fair value of the asset.

Disclosures about the use of fair value to measure assets and liabilities should provide users of financial statements with better information about the extent to which fair value is used to measure recognized assets and liabilities, the inputs used to develop the measurements, and the effect of certain measurements on earnings (or changes in net assets) for the period.

In developing ASC 820, the Board considered the need for increased **consistency** and **comparability** in fair value measurements and for expanded disclosures about fair value measurements. Some of the required disclosures include:
- Identification of which items are reported at fair value and where they can be found on the financial statements.
- The level of inputs (I, II, or III) that were applied in measuring fair value.
- The valuation technique applied (market, income, or cost).
- The disposition of changes in fair value (income or comprehensive income).

Using cash flow info and present value in accounting measurements (SFAC #7)

When assets or services are exchanged for future cash, the most appropriate means of measuring the transaction may be the present value of future cash flows. SFAC 7 provides a framework for using future cash flows as the basis for accounting measurements at initial recognition or fresh-start measurements and for the interest method of amortization. FASB limited SFAC 7 to measurement issues (how to measure) and chose not to address recognition questions (when to measure). SFAC 7 introduces the expected cash flow approach, which differs from the traditional approach by focusing on explicit assumptions about the range of possible estimated cash flows and their respective probabilities. The factors that must be considered are:
- **Risk** – the probability that the cash will actually be paid or received
- **Timing** – the periods in which the payments are expected to be received
- **Interest** – the interest rates that would be appropriate taking into consideration market rates and the credit standing of the parties involved.
- **Amount of cash flows**
    - **Traditional approach** – use most likely cash flow amounts
    - **Expected approach** – use weighted average of different possibilities
    Example - Cash flow has a 10% chance of being $100, 60% chance of $200, 30% chance of $300
        - **Traditional** – $200 (since it is most likely)
        - **Expected** – $220 (10% x $100 + 60% x $200 + 30% x $300)
    - When measuring a liability, one must look at the credit standing of the entity who owes you the money.

Lecture 1.05

Revenue and Expense Recognition

Under the accrual basis of accounting, revenues are recognized in the period earned, regardless of when they are collected and expenses are recognized in the period incurred, regardless of when they are paid.
- Under **accrual accounting**, *revenue or gains* are recognized when they are:
    - **Earned** – earnings process is complete (goods delivered)
    - **Realizable (realized)** – collect cash or a claim to cash

    Based on **Revenue Recognition**, a revenue is recognized when:
    - A binding arrangement exists (signed contract)
    - Services rendered or delivery has occurred

- Fixed or determinable price exists
- Collection is reasonably assured

Sales may be made in which the buyer has a **right of return:**
- If returns are *reasonably estimable*, revenue is recognized in the period of sale with an allowance for returns
- If returns *cannot be* reasonably estimated, revenue is not recognized until the right of return has expired

- Recognize *EXPENSES or losses* as **Incurred**:
  - Economic benefit is used up (**consumed**) or assets lose future benefit (as **incurred**)
    - *Cause and effect* – expenses that produce revenue at identifiable points in time can be matched directly to revenues (e.g. cost of goods sold).
    - *Systematic and rational allocation* – expenses that produce revenue over long periods of time are matched to those periods using a reasonable means of allocation (e.g. depreciation).
    - *Immediate recognition* - some expenses cannot be directly related to specific benefits and are expensed as incurred (e.g. monthly salaries of selling, general & administrative employees).

Note: The revenue recognition changes brought about by Accounting Standards Updates 2014-09 and 2016-11 will not be testable on the exam until 1 January 2018.

Risks and Uncertainties

ASC Topic 275, Risks and Uncertainties, requires disclosure in financial statements of risks and uncertainties existing as of the date of those statements. **The four areas of disclosure are:**
- Nature of operations
- Use of estimates
- Certain significant estimates
- Current vulnerability associated with certain concentrations

Disclosure of the **nature of operations** will include a description of how the entity generates revenue such as major products and services and principal markets served.
- Entities providing multiple products and service will include an indication of their relative importance.
- Not-for-profit entities will include a description of the principal services provided and the entity's revenue sources.

Disclosure related to the **use of estimates** should indicate that the preparation of financial statements in accordance with GAAP, as well as other applicable financial reporting frameworks, requires the use of estimates. Users are also cautioned that actual results may differ from those estimates.

Certain significant estimates include those for which it is at least reasonably possible that a material change in the estimate will occur in the near term. For these items, the entity will disclose the nature of the uncertainty and that a change in the estimate is at least reasonably possible. When appropriate, disclosure will include an estimate of a possible loss or the fact that an estimate cannot be made.

Current vulnerability due to certain concentrations occur when an entity does not diversify. These may result from doing large amounts of business with a limited number of customers; relying on a limited number of products or services; providing goods or services to customers in limited geographical areas or with limited demographics; or relying on few suppliers for materials, labor, or services. An entity will disclose information about such concentrations that exist at the balance sheet date if:
- The entity is vulnerable to a possible severe impact in the near term; and
- Events that would cause the severe impact are at least reasonably possible in the near term.

FASB ACCOUNTING STANDARDS CODIFICATION (ASC)

FASB ASC is the single source of authoritative US GAAP for nongovernmental entities. This replaces all previously issued non-SEC accounting literature. GAAP hasn't changed, but the goal was to create one cohesive set of accounting standards. The Codification reorganized thousands of GAAP pronouncements into approximately 90 accounting topics. This is expected to improve the ease of researching US GAAP issues.

GAAP hierarchy will now consist of two levels: one that is authoritative (in FASB ASC) and one that is nonauthoritative (not in FASB ASC).

FASB Accounting Standards Codification Topics

Topic	Numbered
Presentation	200-299
Assets	300-399
Liabilities	400-499
Equity	500-599
Revenues	600-699
Expenses	700-799
Broad Transactions	800-899
Industry	900-999

The FASB periodically issues **Statements on Financial Accounting Concepts (SFAC)** which, unlike Statements on Financial Accounting Standards (SFAS), are not applications of GAAP to specific situations, but instead represent the ideas of the FASB as to the theoretical framework which it believes should guide financial accounting and reporting. SFAC 8 replaced SFAC 1 & 2 as previously discussed.

Emerging Issues Task Force (EITF) was created in 1984 by the FASB to reach a consensus on how to account for new and unusual financial transactions that have the potential for creating differing financial reporting practices. The FASB works on long-term problems, while the EITF deals with short-term emerging issues.

Notes

The notes to the financial statements are used to ensure that all disclosures that are required under GAAP are made.
- *Summary of significant accounting policies* – this is usually either the first or second footnote and describes the selection of significant accounting principles and methods used in the financial statements (e.g. inventory costing method).

Conceptual Framework & IFRS — Section 1

- *Summary of significant assumptions* – for **prospective** financial statements (those that present forecasted or projected future results), this describes the assumptions used to estimate future amounts (e.g. anticipated rate of inflation).
- *Other Notes to the financial statements* – the other footnotes contain all the other relevant information that investors and creditors may find interesting such as information regarding contingent liabilities, contractual obligations, amount coming due for bonds and leases in the next 5 years and the aggregate beyond 5 years, significant changes in account balances.

Lecture 1.06

CLASS QUESTIONS
Please see the Class Questions and Class Solutions for this Lecture at the end of this Section.

Lecture 1.07

INTERNATIONAL FINANCIAL REPORTING STANDARDS (IFRS)

As a result of an agreement entered into among various bodies regulating or overseeing accounting in the United States and 8 other jurisdictions, the International Accounting Standards Committee (IASC) was formed and developed a series of International Accounting Standards (IAS). This body was replaced by the International Accounting Standards Board (IASB), which issues International Financial Reporting Standards (IFRS). In addition, the International Financial Reporting Interpretations Committee (IFRIC) issues interpretations.

Many consider IFRS to be **principle-based** or concept-based, indicating that they provide general guidelines but provide a great deal of latitude in the recognition, measurement, and presentation of information on the financial statements, leaving a great deal up to the **judgment** of this issuers of the financial statements.

GAAP, on the other hand, is considered to be more **rules-based**, indicating that more specific guidelines are established and, based on the terms of an arrangement and the surrounding circumstances, the accounting treatment is prescribed.

This comparison may largely be due to the fact that US GAAP has been in existence much longer than IFRS and has evolved further. Unfortunately, as pronouncements are issued, entities will often seek opportunities to structure their transactions to avoid accounting treatments that may be considered unfavorable. To avoid abusive reporting practices, the standard setting bodies create rules to "close these potential loopholes". As a result, as standards evolve, more rules tend to be added.
- There are many who believe that, given a little time, IFRS will be just as rules-based as US GAAP.
- In addition, as part of a project to converge US GAAP and IFRS, US standard setters are "scaling back" some of the rules-based approaches and incorporating approaches that are more principles-based.

In recent years, the FASB and IASB have been involved in a **convergence** project in which the most significant differences between GAAP and IFRS are being eliminated when possible and otherwise minimized. As a result, there are relatively few substantive differences between GAAP and IFRS. Most differences fall into one of these basic categories:
- **Terminology and definitions**.

- **Recognition** – Different criteria used to determine when an item will appear on the financial statements.
- **Measurement** – Different approaches for measuring a financial statement element resulting in different amounts being reported.
- **Presentation** – Differences in where certain items will appear on the financial statements and how they will be identified.
- **Disclosure** – Differences in the amount and nature of disclosures.

Similar to the FASB, the IASB uses a conceptual framework as a basis for the development of IFRS. The focus of their conceptual framework is:
- Reporting entity.
- Elements of financial statements, including recognition and derecognition.
- Measurement, presentation, and disclosure.

IASB Framework

Like the FASB, the IASB develops IFRS using principles that are established in a conceptual framework, referred to as "The Conceptual Framework for Financial Reporting". The IASB is in the process of revising its conceptual framework and, so far, has completed the revisions of Chapter 1, The objective of general purpose financial reporting; and Chapter 3, Qualitative characteristics of useful financial information. Chapter 2, a new chapter entitled The reporting entity, is not complete. These revisions, completed as part of a joint project with the FASB, has essentially eliminated any significant differences in the frameworks.

The remainder of the already existing conceptual framework will remain in effect as Chapter 4 until it is replaced. This section, in the process of being revised, includes:
- The definitions, criteria for recognition, and means of measurement of elements of financial reporting from which financial statements are constructed.
- Concepts of capital and capital maintenance.

Unlike that of the FASB, the IASB conceptual framework is authoritative but is lower in the hierarchy of standards than IFRSs. An IFRS that addresses a transaction, event, or element of financial reporting is authoritative. An entity that is seeking guidance in the accounting for a transaction, event, or element that is not addressed in an IFRS will refer to the conceptual framework.

The Objective of General Purpose Financial Reporting

The IASB conceptual framework indicates that "the objective of general purpose financial reporting is to provide financial information about the reporting entity that is useful to existing and potential investors, lenders and other creditors (*referred to below as users*) in making decisions about providing resources to the entity." Under IFRS the financial statements are prepared on the **accrual basis** based on the **going concern** concept.
- Existing and potential users need information to assess amounts, timing, and uncertainty of future cash inflows to evaluate potential returns in the form of dividends to investors and principal and interest payments to creditors.
- Prospects for future cash inflows are largely dependent on the resources available to the entity and claims against those resources.

Conceptual Framework & IFRS — Section 1

- They are also largely dependent on how efficiently and effectively management and governance have discharged their responsibilities in relation to the use of those resources.
    - It will entail information about how management responded to economic and business factors.
    - This information is also useful to investors who may have the ability to influence, through voting or otherwise, the activities of management.

To meet the objectives, general purpose financial reporting will provide information about the entities financial position, identifying economic resources and claims against those resources.

General purpose financial reporting will also provide information about the effects of events and transactions on the entity's economic resources and claims against them, distinguishing between those that result from the entity's financial performance and those that result from other events or transactions, such as issuing debt or equity.
- Financial performance reflected under accrual accounting depicts effects in the periods in which they occur, enabling assessment of past and future performance.
- Financial performance reflected under cash accounting indicates how an entity obtains and spends cash and provides information about its ability to generate future cash inflows.

Qualitative Characteristics of Useful Financial Information

In order to be useful, financial information must be **relevant** and it must **faithfully represent** that which it purports to represent.

To be **relevant**, financial information must be capable of making a difference to users in making decisions related to the entity, which will be the case if it has one or both of the following (PC-MAT):
- **Predictive value** allows information to be used to predict future outcomes.
- **Confirmatory value** provides feedback about events or transactions that have occurred.

Materiality is a consideration in determining the relevance of certain information. Information is material if omitting it would influence users' decisions. Materiality:
- Is entity-specific.
- Considers both nature and magnitude.

Faithful representation implies that the information does report resources, claims against those resources, and effects of transactions and events factually and in appropriate amounts. The characteristics of faithful representation are (FENC):
- **Freedom from Error**
- **Neutrality**
- **Completeness**

Other characteristics that **enhance** the usefulness of financial information include (CUT-V):
- **C**omparability
- **U**nderstandability
- **T**imeliness
- **V**erifiability

In applying the conceptual framework, the **benefits** of reporting particular items of information should be weighed against the **cost** of collecting, processing, verifying, and disseminating that information (Cost/Benefit).

In addition, financial information is prepared under the assumption that the entity is a *going concern*.

USEFUL (2 Primary Qualitative Characteristics IASB)

Relevance (Roger is PC)
- **P**redictive value
- **C**onfirmatory value
  (feedback – confirm
   or changes)

- Or *Both*

Faithful Representation (FENCe)
- **F**ree from **E**rror
- **N**eutral (w/o Bias)
- **C**ompleteness

Material (an entity-specific aspect of *Relevance* that applies at the individual entity level – it's omission or misstatement could influence a user's decision)

Enhancing Qualitative Characteristics (CUT like a V) (enhance the Usefulness of the info – Very desirable, but not required)
- **C**omparability (Consistency)
- **U**nderstandability (classified/characterized & presented clearly)
- **T**imeliness
- **V**erifiability

   Constraint:
   o Cost/benefit
   o Going Concern - assumption

---

5 Basic F/S Elements

The IASB *Framework* defines **five elements of financial reporting**. There are 3 elements of financial position: Assets, Liabilities, and Equity. There are 2 elements of performance: Income and Expenses. The FASB conceptual framework defines 10 elements.

Depending on an entity definition of capital maintenance, the elements of income and expenses may include **capital maintenance adjustments**.
- Under the ***financial capital*** definition, gains and losses in relation to assets and liabilities are only recognized when they affect the amount of financial net assets, such as when assets or liabilities change in value.
- Under the ***physical capital*** definition, gains and losses in relation to assets and liabilities are recognized when the productive capacity of the entity is affected, such as when assets are disposed of or liabilities are settled.

Under the IASB conceptual framework, increase or decreases in assets or liabilities meet the definitions of revenues and expenses. Under the physical capital definition, these increases or decreases are not recognized until they are realized. Under the financial capital definition, assets and liabilities may be revalued or restated, resulting in the recognition of income or expenses.

Conceptual Framework & IFRS

Elements of Financial Position

These are defined in the conceptual framework as follows:
- **Asset** – "a *resource* controlled by the entity as a result of *past events* and from which *future* economic benefits are expected to flow to the entity".
- **Liability** – "a present *obligation* of the entity arising from *past* events, the settlement of which is expected to result in an outflow from the entity of resources embodying economic benefits".
- **Equity** – "the *residual interest* in the assets of the entity after deducting all its liabilities".

Elements of Performance

These are defined in the conceptual framework as follows:
- **Income** – "*increases in economic benefits* during the accounting period in the form of inflows or enhancements of assets or decreases of liabilities that result in *increases in equity*, other than those relating to contributions from equity participants".
  - Income includes both **revenues** (ordinary activities – sales, interest, rent) and **gains.** Gains are not treated as a separate element since they may also arise due to ordinary activities. Income may be realized or unrealized.

- **Expenses** – "expenses are *decreases in economic benefits* during the accounting period in the form of outflows or depletions of assets or incurrence of liabilities that result in decreases in equity, other than those relating to distributions to equity participants".
  - **Expenses** result from ordinary activities. Similar to gains, **losses** may also result from ordinary activities so are not treated as separate elements. Expenses may be realized or not realized.
  - **Capital Maintenance Adjustments** – result from the revaluation or restatement of assets and liabilities that cause an increase or decrease in equity (Fixed assets), but not from income or expenses.

As you can see, there are vocabulary differences regarding the elements of financial statements as well. Under GAAP, "income" is not a financial statement element; and it is used to describe a calculation of some type (e.g., income from continuing operations, net income) or to designate a specific type of income such as interest income. However, with IFRS, the term income is a financial statement element, and the items that are considered "income" are revenues and gains. As such, IFRS uses the term **"profit"** whereas US GAAP uses the term **"net income."**

Recognition and Measurement

Recognition describes when an item that fits the definition of an element of financial reporting will be incorporated in the balance sheet or income statement, which will be when 2 criteria have been met: *[Recognize probable and measurement must be reliable under IFRS, but not GAAP.]*
- **Probability** of occurrence
- **Reliable measurement**

An asset is recognized on the balance sheet when it is probable that an economic benefit that can be reliably measured will flow to the entity.

A liability is recognized on the balance sheet when it is probable that an outflow of resources that can be reliably measured will result from settlement of a present obligation.

Income is recognized on the income statement when an increase in future economic benefits that can be reliably measured relates to an increase in an asset or decrease of a liability.

Expense is recognized on the income statement when a decrease in future economic benefits that can be reliably measured relates to a decrease in an asset or increase of a liability.

The reliability with which an item can be measured is a matter of professional judgment. The different **measurement approaches** that are used to measure items recognized on the financial statements include:
- **Historical cost**
- **Current cost** – the amount it would currently cost to replace the same or an equivalent asset.
- **Realizable, or settlement, value** – the amount that would be realized upon sale or other disposal of an asset or the amount that would be required to settle a liability.
- **Present value** – the discounted net amount of future cash inflows and outflows.

Asset	An asset is a *resource* controlled by the entity as a result of past events and from which future economic benefits are expected to flow to the entity.
Liability	A liability is a present *obligation* of the entity arising from past events, the settlement of which is expected to result in an outflow from the entity of resources embodying economic benefits.
Equity	Equity is the *residual interest* in the assets of the entity after deducting all its liabilities.
Income	Income is increases in economic benefits during the accounting period in the form of inflows or enhancements of assets or decreases of liabilities that result in *increases in equity*, other than those relating to contributions from equity participants.
Expenses	Expenses are decreases in economic benefits during the accounting period in the form of outflows or depletions of assets or incurrences of liabilities that result in *decreases in equity*, other than those relating to distributions to equity participants.
Capital Maintenance Adjustments	Result from the revaluation or restatement of assets and liabilities that cause an increase or decrease in equity, but not based on the definition of Income or expense items.

Since revenues result from increases in equity, or capital, and expenses result from decreases in equity, or capital, an entity must establish a concept of capital so that it can determine when increases or decreases occur. There are **two basic concepts of capital**, which can be used to determine when revenue is earned and when expenses are incurred.
- Most entities apply the **financial capital** concept in preparing their financial statements under which capital is the net assets of the entity. Under the *financial capital maintenance* theory, income is earned when the amount of net assets has increased during the period after eliminating the effects of transactions with owners.
- An alternative is the **physical capital** concept under which capital is considered the productive capacity of the entity. Under the *physical capital maintenance* theory, income is earned when the operating capacity of the entity increases during the period after eliminating the effects of transactions with owners.

Conceptual Framework & IFRS

Differences in the FASB Concept Statements and the IASB *Framework*:

FASB Conceptual Framework	IASB *Framework*
10 elements of Financial Statements	**5 elements of Financial Statements**

3 basic elements
• Assets
• Liabilities
• Equity or Net Assets
 	
3 elements of Equity
• Contributions/investments by owners
• Distributions to owners
• Comprehensive income (DENT)
 	
4 elements of comprehensive income
• Revenues
• Expenses
• Gains
• Losses
	3 elements of financial position
	• Assets
	• Liabilities
	• Equity
	
	2 elements of performance
	• Income
	• Expenses
	    Capital maintenance
	    adjustments
	    (Revaluation
	    adjustments)

• Net Income	• Profit

Revenue Recognition

Under IFRS, requirements for recognizing revenue were established in IAS 18. These requirements were modified by IFRS 15, issued in May of 2014, and effective on the CPA Exam January 1, 2018. Under IAS 18, the requirements apply to all transactions involving revenue from:
- The sale of goods
- The rendering of services
- The use of assets to earn interest, royalties, and dividends

Revenue is measured at the **fair value of consideration received** or receivable.

Revenues from the **sale of goods** occur when 5 criteria have been met:
- Significant risks and rewards of ownership transferred to the buyer.
- The selling entity does not retain managerial involvement associated with ownership of the asset.
- The amount can be reliably measured.
- Economic benefits are likely to flow to the entity.
- Costs incurred and to be incurred in relation to the transaction can be reliably measured.

For transactions involving r**endering of services**:
- When the outcome can be reliably estimated, revenue is recognized based on the stage of completion (percentage-of-completion).
- When the outcome cannot be reliably estimated, revenue is recognized to the extent of recoverable expenses recognized (cost recovery).

Revenues from **interest, royalties, and dividends** are recognized when the amounts can be reliably estimated and economic benefits are likely to flow to the entity.

- Interest is recognized applying the effective interest method.
- Royalties are recognized on the accrual basis.
- Dividends are recognized when the shareholders' right to receive payment is established.

Disclosures will include:
- Accounting policies adopted for recognizing revenues.
- Amount of revenue recognized in each significant category
    - Sale of goods
    - Rendering of services
    - Interest
    - Royalties
    - Dividends
- Amount of revenue from exchange of goods and services in each category

Lecture 1.08

SUMMARY OF SIGNIFICANT DIFFERENCES BETWEEN US GAAP & IFRS

As a result of the joint efforts of the FASB and the IASB to converge US GAAP with IFRS, the significant differences between the two financial reporting frameworks is not extensive. This list shows only items that are different.

IAS 1 – Presentation of Financial Statements

IFRS requires:
- **Comparative financial statements**, presenting information from the prior period.
- Assets and liabilities distinguished between **current and noncurrent** or listed in order of liquidity.
- Requires a separate statement of comprehensive income and statement of changes in equity.

IFRS allows:
- Classification of expenses by nature or function.

GAAP
- No specific requirement regarding comparative info
- Comprehensive income may either be a separate statement or combined with a statement of net income

IAS 2 – Inventories

IFRS requires:
- Reporting inventory at the **lower of cost or net realizable value (LCNRV)**.
- Items that are not interchangeable to be accounted for using **specific identification**.
- All other items to be accounted for under **FIFO or weighted average**.

IFRS allows:
- Measurement under standard costing or the retail method if the amount approximates cost.
- Recognition of recoveries of losses due to previous declines in value (may reverse impairment loss).

IFRS does not allow:
- Reporting inventory using **LIFO.**

GAAP
- Inventory reported at LCM
- LIFO is allowed
- Impairment losses may NOT be reversed

IAS 7 – Statement of Cash Flows

IFRS requires:
- Reporting cash overdrafts as negative cash equivalents.

IFRS allows:
- Direct, Indirect or the Modified indirect method (which shows revenues and expenses in operating activities, and then reports the changes in working capital accounts).
- Interest and dividends RECEIVED as either operating or investing activities
- Interest and dividends PAID as either operating or financing activities

GAAP
- No modified indirect method
- Interest received and paid and dividends received are operating
- Negative cash balance is a current liability

IAS 8 – Accounting Policies, Changes in Accounting Estimates and Errors
- Change in Reporting Entity doesn't exist under IFRS
- Remainder, no significant differences

IAS 10 – Events After the Reporting Period (Subsequent Events)
- No significant differences.

IAS 11 – Construction Contracts (Revenue Recognition)

When the International Accounting Standards Board issued IFRS 15, Revenue from Contracts with Customers, it provided revenue recognition standards that superseded those of IAS 11. IFRS 15 is scheduled to be eligible for exam testing in January 2018, making IAS 11 relevant until then. Under IAS 11:

IFRS requires:
- **Stage of completion** (percentage of completion) accounting when the outcome can be reasonably estimated.
- **Zero profit** (cost recovery) accounting when the outcome cannot be reasonably estimated.

IFRS does not allow:
- Use of the **completed contract** method.

GAAP
- Percentage of completion is used if certain criteria are met, otherwise use completed contract method

IAS 12 – Income Taxes

IFRS requires:
- Measuring deferred tax assets and liabilities at the **future tax rate that is enacted or substantially enacted** as of the end of the period.
- All deferred tax assets & liabilities to be classified as **noncurrent**.

IFRS does not allow:
- Recognition of deferred tax assets unless except to the extent that it is probable that taxable profit will be available against which to utilize deductible temporary differences.
    - Includes benefit of unused tax loss and tax credit carryforwards.
    - Unrecognized deferred tax assets are reassessed each reporting period.

GAAP
- Deferred tax asset valuation allowances are used to reduce benefits to amount "more likely than not" to be realized.
- On B/S deferred tax assets and liabilities may be current or non-current
- Use future enacted tax rate

IAS 16 – Property, Plant and Equipment (PP&E)

IFRS requires:
- Use of **component depreciation** with each significant cost depreciated separately (ex: land and building, furniture, fixtures, equipment).

IFRS allows:
- Recognition subsequent to acquisition based on a revaluation model applied to the entire class of property, plant, and equipment.
    - The **cost model (CM)** recognizes the asset at cost net of accumulated depreciation and impairments.
    - The **revaluation model (RM)** recognizes the asset at fair value at the date of revaluation less subsequent accumulated depreciation and impairments.
- Recognition of **recovery of impairments**.
- Biological assets are a separate category and not included in PP&E (agricultural assets – animals or plants).
- Revaluation gains are reported in OCI as revaluation surplus, revaluation losses are reported on the income statement.
    - Impairment loss is recorded by first reducing any revaluation surplus to zero and any additional loss is reported on the income statement.

IFRS does not allow:
- Recognition subsequent to acquisition based on a cost model applied to the entire class of property, plant, and equipment.

- The cost model recognizes the asset at cost net of accumulated depreciation and impairments.
- The revaluation model recognizes the asset at fair value at the date of revaluation less subsequent accumulated depreciation and impairments.

GAAP
- Revaluation method is not permitted
- Assets are generally valued using the Cost Model (CM)
- Biological assets are not a separate category
- Impairment losses, which are calculated using a 2 step test are NOT reversed.
- Component depreciation is NOT required

IAS 17 – Leases
IFRS requires:
- Classification based on transfer of **risks and rewards of ownership**.
    - **Finance lease** if transferred (called a Capital lease under GAAP)
    - **Operating lease** if not transferred.
- Impairment loss may be recovered
- To record as a finance lease, TT, BPO, "major part" of life or P.V equal to "substantially all" of F.V.
- Initial direct costs are capitalized when a Finance lease.

GAAP
- Classified as either an Operating or a Capital lease
- TT, BPO, ≥75 or ≥90
- Operating leases are never recorded on the balance sheet
- Initial direct costs are expenses by Lessee as incurred

IAS 18 – Revenue Recognition
Under IFRS, requirements for recognizing revenue were established in IAS 18. The requirements apply to all transactions involving revenue from:
- The sale of goods
- The rendering of services
- The use of assets to earn interest, royalties, and dividends

Effective in 2017, and earlier for those entities so choosing, IFRS 15, Revenue from Contracts with Customers, will supersede this pronouncement. IFRS 15 becomes effective on the CPA Exam in January 2018.

Revenue is measured at the **fair value of consideration received** or receivable.

Revenues from the **sale of goods** occur when 5 criteria have been met:
- Significant risks and rewards of ownership transferred to the buyer.
- The selling entity does not retain managerial involvement associated with ownership of the asset.
- The amount can be reliably measured.
- Economic benefits are likely to flow to the entity.
- Costs incurred and to be incurred in relation to the transaction can be reliably measured.

For transactions involving **rendering of services**:
- When the outcome can be reliably estimated, revenue is recognized based on the stage of completion (percentage-of-completion).
- When the outcome cannot be reliably estimated, revenue is recognized to the extent of recoverable expenses recognized (cost recovery).

Revenues from **interest, royalties, and dividends** are recognized when the amounts can be reliably estimated and economic benefits are likely to flow to the entity.
- Interest is recognized applying the effective interest method.
- Royalties are recognized on the accrual basis.
- Dividends are recognized when the shareholders' right to receive payment is established.

Disclosures will include:
- Accounting policies adopted for recognizing revenues.
- Amount of revenue recognized in each significant category
    - Sale of goods
    - Rendering of services
    - Interest
    - Royalties
    - Dividends
- Amount of revenue from exchange of goods and services in each category

IAS 36 – Impairment of Assets

IFRS requires:
- Application of a **single approach** to goodwill, intangible assets, and tangible assets.
- Defining an impairment loss as the excess the **carrying value over its recoverable amount**.
    - Recoverable amount is defined as **lesser of net selling price or value in use**.
    - Both are measured at **discounted amounts**.

IFRS allows:
- Recognition of **impairment recoveries**.

GAAP
- Impairment losses, which are calculated using a 2 step test (first test for recoverability and then calculate the impairment loss) are NOT reversed.

IAS 37 – Provisions, Contingent Liabilities and Contingent Assets

IFRS requires:
- Recognition of **PROVISIONS when three conditions** apply:
    - Entity has **present obligation** resulting from a past event.
    - An outflow of resources will **probably** be required to settle the obligation.
    - The amount can be **reliably estimated (measurable).**
        - Else just disclose

IFRS does not allow:
- Recognition of **contingent assets or liabilities.**

Conceptual Framework & IFRS — Section 1

GAAP
- Contingencies that are *probable* and can be reasonably *estimated* are accrued
- If *intent and ability* to refinance a S/T obligation exists, can reclassify to L/T (IFRS only if agreement entered into)

IAS 38 – Intangible Assets

IFRS requires:
- Amortization of intangibles with finite useful lives over estimate, not generally greater than 20 years.
- Research must be expensed (Development costs may be capitalized if 6 criteria are met).
- Reported using either the Cost Model (CM) or the Revaluation Model (RM).

IFRS allows:
- Recognition of intangible assets for advertising, training, start-up costs, research and development, and other items
    - Recognized at cost if controlled by the entity; distinguishable from goodwill; probable that an economic benefit will flow to the entity; and reliably measurable.
    - Subsequently measured at cost less accumulated amortization and accumulated impairment losses.
    - Intangibles reported using either the cost model or the revaluation model.
    - Impairment loss may be reversed.

GAAP
- Research and Development costs must be expensed
- Assets reported using Cost Model (CM)
- Impairment loss may NOT be reversed

IFRS 3 – Business Combinations

IFRS allows:
- **Noncontrolling interest** to be recognized either at:
    - **Fair value** at the acquisition date
    - Noncontrolling interest's **proportionate share** of net assets

GAAP
- Requires that noncontrolling interests be initially measured at fair value

IFRS 9 – Financial Instruments

IFRS requires:
- **Financial** assets generally measured at **fair value** with unrealized gains and losses recognized in income unless two conditions apply:
    - The entity's business model entails holding the instrument to collect cash flows
    - The asset provides for cash flows limited to principle and interest at specified dates
- **Financial liabilities** to be measured at **amortized cost** with few exceptions
- Allowance for credit losses recognized on financial assets measured at amortized cost or at fair value through other comprehensive income
    - If credit losses have not increased significantly since initial recognition, allowance equal to 12 months expected credit losses

- o If credit losses have increased significantly since initial recognition, allowance equal to lifetime expected credit losses

IFRS allows:
- Financial assets to be measured at **amortized cost** when both conditions are met:
  - o Business model may involve both holding the instrument to collect cash flows and **selling the financial instrument**
  - o When that is the case, the instrument is measured at **fair value** with unrealized gains and losses recognized in **other comprehensive income**
- Designation of a **financial liability** as measured at fair value with unrealized gains or losses recognized in income
- Irrevocable election to report certain financial assets at fair value through profit and loss to avoid inconsistency resulting from applying different bases to the measurement of financial assets and financial liabilities or recognizing gains or losses on them
- Derivative and non-derivative financial assets or liabilities involving contracts with parties external to the reporting entity to be designated as **hedges**

IFRS does not allow:
- Reclassification of financial assets unless the entity changes its business model
- Reclassification of any financial liabilities

GAAP
- Financial instruments accounted for based on their nature
- Irrevocable election to selectively report financial assets or liabilities at fair value

IFRS 10 – Consolidated Financial Statements
IFRS requires:
- Consolidated financial statements that include all entities under control of parent
  - o Three elements of control:
    - Power over investee
    - Exposure, or rights, to variable returns resulting from involvement with entity
    - Ability to use power to affect returns
  - o Reassessed only upon changes in one of elements

GAAP
- Consolidation required when controlling financial interest obtained through either equity ownership or relationship
- Controlling financial interest (primary beneficiary status) reassessed on a regular basis

IFRS 12 – Disclosures of Interests in Other Entities
IFRS requires:
- Disclosures related to unconsolidated subsidiaries and interests in other entities
- Enable users to evaluate:
  - o The nature of the interests and associated risks
  - o How interests affect financial position, financial performance, and cash flows

GAAP
- Different disclosure requirements related to interests in other entities based on various methods of accounting being applied
- Disclosures related to variable interest in variable interest entity when entity is not primary beneficiary and does not consolidate

IFRS 13 – Fair Value Measurement

IFRS 13 requires:
- Defines fair value as the price received to sell an asset or paid to transfer a liability in an orderly transaction between market participants at the measurement date.
- Requires measurement of fair value using a single framework consisting of determining the specific asset or liability being measured, the highest or best use for nonfinancial assets, the market in which an orderly transaction would take place, and the appropriate valuation technique to measure fair value resulting in the maximum use of observable inputs.
- Requires disclosure about the fair value measurement and its relative reliability.

GAAP
- Only slight differences due to the convergence of ASC 820 and IFRS 13

IFRS 15 – Revenue from Contracts with Customers

IFRS requires that revenue be recognized applying a 5-step process, which will be effective for CPA Exam testing in January 2018.

1. Identify the contracts with customers
2. Identify all performance obligations within each contract
3. Determine the total consideration from the contract
4. Allocate the total consideration among all performance obligations
5. Recognize revenues when each performance obligation is satisfied or, in some cases, while performance obligations are being satisfied.

GAAP
- Revenue recognition should be similar under GAAP in 2018 for public entities and later for nonpublic entities, although the FASB has indicated that the effective dates will be postponed for 1 year.

Significant Difference Between US GAAP and IFRS	
US GAAP	**IFRS**
Financial Statement Presentation	
No requirement for comparative financial statements.	Comparative financial statements required, including immediately prior period.
Comprehensive income may either be a separate statement or combined with a statement of net income.	Requires a separate statement of comprehensive income and statement of changes in equity.
Inventory	
Market considered replacement cost with floor & ceiling limits for LCM evaluation (NRV).	Market considered net realizable value for LCM evaluation (LCNRV).
Allows FIFO, LIFO, or average.	Allows FIFO or average, *not* LIFO.
Does not allow reversal of impairment losses.	Allows reversal of impairment losses.
Statement of Cash Flows	
Allows direct method or indirect method of reporting operating activities.	Allows direct, indirect, or *modified direct method* showing rev & exp & changes in working capital accounts in operating activities.
Interest & div received reported as operating activities.	Int & div rec'd investing activities unless lending is normal business activity (operating).
Interest paid is operating.	Interest paid is financing.
Negative cash balance reported as current liability.	Negative cash balance reported as negative cash equivalent.
Accounting Changes	
Change in reporting entity recognized with retroactive restatement.	No provision for change in reporting entity.
Long-term Construction Contracts	
Requires completed contract method when outcome not reasonably estimable, else use percentage of completion method (stage of completion).	Requires zero profit (cost recovery) method, recognizing rev equal to expense when outcome not estimable under IAS 18.
	Completed contract not allowed under IFRS.

Income Taxes	
Applies enacted future tax rate.	Allows enacted or substantially enacted future tax rate.
Deferred tax assets & liabilities classified as current or noncurrent depending on source.	All deferred taxes classified as noncurrent
All deferred tax assets recognized subject to valuation allowance.	Deferred tax assets only recognized when reasonably assured of realization.
Property, Plant, & Equipment (PP&E)	
Requires recognition at cost subject to depreciation and impairment.	Allows revaluation method (RM) when fair value can be determined, else use cost model (CM).
Biological assets (agricultural assets, animals, plants) not a separate category.	Biological assets in separate category
Impairment testing using 2 step method only required when impairment suspected.	Impairment testing using 1 step method required at f/s date.
Impairment recoveries not recognized.	Impairment recoveries recognized to extent of losses previously recognition.
Leases	
Lessee reports as capital lease if one of certain criteria (TT, BPO, 75, 90) are met and otherwise as operating lease.	Lessee reports as *finance* lease if risks & rewards of ownership transferred & otherwise as operating.
Lessee recognizes initial direct costs as expense when incurred.	Lessee capitalizes initial direct costs for a finance lease.
Lessor reports as sales-type, direct financing, or leveraged if certain criteria met & otherwise as operating.	Lessor reports as finance lease if risks & rewards of ownership transferred & otherwise operating.
Impairments	
Applies different approaches (2 *step test*) for depreciable and amortizable assets, goodwill, and intangibles with indefinite lives other than goodwill.	Applies same *single step* approach to tangible assets, goodwill, and all other intangible assets with finite or indefinite lives (CV over recoverable amount).
Impairment recoveries not recognized.	Impairment recoveries recognized in income to extent losses previously recognized.
Provisions and Contingencies	
Contingent losses recognized if probable and reasonably estimable.	No contingencies are recognized.
No separate category for provisions.	Loss that is probable & estimable, resulting from past event recognized as *provision*, all recognized.

Provisions and Contingencies (continued)	
Contingent gains may be disclosed but never required.	Contingent gains required to be disclosed if probable.
Short-term obligations classified as long-term if entity can demonstrate *intent & ability* to refinance on long-term basis	Short-term obligations classified as long-term if entity has entered into agreement to refinance on long-term basis.
Intangibles	
All research & development costs expensed as incurred.	Research expensed, but development costs capitalized if certain criteria are met.
All intangibles accounted for using cost model (CM).	Revaluation model (RM) allowed if fair value reasonably estimable.
Impairment recoveries NOT recognized.	Impairment reversals recognized to extent of previous losses.
Business Combinations	
Noncontrolling interest initially recognized at fair value.	Noncontrolling interest recognized either at fair value or proportionate amount of net assets.
Financial Instruments	
Financial assets accounted for based on their nature.	Financial assets recognized at fair value unless certain criteria are met, requiring amortized cost.
Provides irrevocable option to elect to selectively report financial assets or liabilities at fair value.	Allows financial liabilities to be reported at fair value through profit or loss (FVTPL).
Consolidated Financial Statements	
Consolidation required when entity has controlling financial interest in other entity through equity or relationship.	Consolidation required when entity has control evidenced by power over investee, exposure to variable returns, and power to affect returns.
Control through relationship (VIE) reassessed on regular basis.	Consolidation reassessed only if change in circumstances.

Lecture 1.09

CLASS QUESTIONS

Please see the Class Questions and Class Solutions for this Lecture at the end of this Section.

Lecture 1.10

RESEARCH TASK FORMAT FOR FAR

Research is tested in its own independent task-based simulation problem. Each FAR exam will include at least one Research type TBS. The Candidate will be asked to search through the database to find an appropriate reference that addresses the issue presented in the research problem. A scenario is presented in which the candidate must find the answer in the authoritative literature using a pre-determined list of codes. You will be provided with a searchable database containing the FASB Accounting Standards Codification™ (ASC) for this purpose. The candidate will choose the appropriate code title from the drop-down list and then enter a specific reference number applicable to their given scenario.

Using the Authoritative Literature tab, the candidate will search for keywords associated with the question using the search box, which will pull up all references within the literature to those keywords. From there, the candidate should use the "search within" function to find specific instances of keywords within each subsection. Keywords will be highlighted in the text and the candidate can go through them to find the relevant text that answers the research problem.

Research questions will also alert the candidate if they have correctly formatted their answer by displaying "Your response is correctly formatted" in a box below the candidate response if the candidate has entered reference numbers correctly. For example, single-digit reference numbers (such as "paragraph 3") may be formatted as a two-digit response (such as "paragraph "03"). A good tool is to also use the "Research" tab to look up answers to other TBS in the exam; for example, if a TBS asks you about a particular Financial Statement, use the Research tab to assist you in solving this TBS.

The FASB Accounting Standards Codification™ (FASB ASC) is a complete reorganization of all of the separate US Generally Accepted Accounting Principles (GAAP) standards into one topically structured body of authoritative guidance.

FASB ASC is the sole source of authoritative U.S. accounting and reporting standards for all nongovernmental entities, superseding all existing non-SEC accounting and reporting standards. The FASB ASC did not materially change any existing principles, but it will require financial professionals to familiarize themselves with the new organization and numbering system of the new codified standards.

Suggested Approach

When performing a research question on FAR, the first step will be to determine the area from the FASB Codification in which the item is most likely covered. The areas to choose from are:

100s - General Principles – It is very unlikely that this area will be selected. There is only one topic in this area, Generally Accepted Accounting Principles, which designates the ASC as the only authoritative source of GAAP.

200s – Presentation – This area will be selected if the question relates to the actual presentation of information on one of the financial statements. It does not address how items are to be accounted for or how amounts are to be determined. Within the area, a specific topic will be selected.

Within that topic, a subtopic is also to be chosen. For some topics, the only subtopic will be subtopic 10, "Overall". Other topics will have two or more subtopics, the first of which will be subtopic 10, "Overall". Determine if one of the subtopics other than "Overall" appears to more directly relate to the question being asked or the issue being raised. If not, select subtopic 10, "Overall".

Topics and subtopics, excluding "Overall" within the Presentation area include the following:
- 205 Presentation of Financial Statements
  205-20 Discontinued Operations
  205-30 Liquidation Basis of Accounting
  205-40 Going Concern
- 210 Balance Sheet
  210-20 Offsetting
- 215 Statement of Shareholder Equity
- 220 Comprehensive Income
- 225 Income Statement
  225-20 Unusual Items
  225-30 Business Interruption Insurance
- 230 Statement of Cash Flows
- 235 Notes to Financial Statements
- 250 Accounting Changes and Error Corrections
- 255 Changing Prices
- 260 Earnings per Share
- 270 Interim Reporting
- 272 Limited Liability Entities
- 274 Personal Financial Statements
- 275 Risks and Uncertainties
- 280 Segment Reporting

300s – Assets – This area will be selected if the question relates to the reporting of an asset. It may involve determining whether or not it will be reported on the financial statements, the amount at which it will be reported, the accounting for the asset while it is being held or for its disposal, or related disclosures. Within the area, a specific topic will be selected.

Within that topic, a subtopic is also to be chosen. For some topics, the only subtopic will be subtopic 10, "Overall". Other topics will have two or more subtopics, the first of which will be subtopic 10, "Overall". Determine if one of the subtopics, other than "Overall" appears to more directly relate to the question being asked or the issue being raised. If not, select subtopic 10, "Overall".

Topics and subtopics, excluding "Overall" within the Assets area include the following:
- 305 Cash and Cash Equivalents
- 310 Receivables
  310-20 Nonrefundable Fees and Other Costs
  310-30 Loans and Debt Securities Acquired with Deteriorated Credit Quality
  310-40 Troubled Debt Restructurings by Creditors

Conceptual Framework & IFRS — Section 1

- 320 Investments – Debt and Equity Securities
- 323 Investments – Equity Method and Joint Ventures
  323-30 Partnerships, Joint Ventures, and Limited Liability Entities
- 325 Investments – Other
  325-20 Cost Method Investments
  325-30 Investments in Insurance Contracts
  325-40 Beneficial Interests in Securitized Financial Assets
- 330 Inventories
- 340 Other Assets and Deferred Costs
  340-20 Capitalized Advertising Costs
  340-30 Insurance Contracts That Do Not Transfer Insurance Risk
  340-40 Contracts with Customers
- 350 Intangibles – Goodwill and Other
  350-20 Goodwill
  350-30 General Intangibles Other Than Goodwill
  350-40 Internal Use Software
  350-50 Website Development Costs
- 360 Property, Plant, and Equipment
  360-20 Real Estate Sales

400s – Liabilities – This area will be selected if the question relates to the reporting of a liability. It may involve determining whether or not it will be reported on the financial statements, the amount at which it will be reported, the accounting for it while it is owed, its settlement, or related disclosures. Within the area, a specific topic will be selected.

Within that topic, a subtopic is also to be chosen. For some topics, the only subtopic will be subtopic 10, "Overall". Other topics will have two or more subtopics, the first of which will be subtopic 10, "Overall". Determine if one of the subtopics, other than "Overall" appears to more directly relate to the question being asked or the issue being raised. If not, select subtopic 10, "Overall".

Topics and subtopics, excluding "Overall" within the Liabilities area include the following:
- 405 Liabilities
  405-20 Extinguishment of Liabilities
  405-30 Insurance Related Assessments
  405-40 Obligations Resulting from Joint and Several Liability Arrangements
- 410 Asset Retirement and Environmental Obligations
  410-20 Asset Retirement Obligations
  410-30 Environmental Obligations
- 420 Exit or Disposal Cost Obligations
- 430 Deferred Revenue
- 440 Commitments
- 450 Contingencies
  450-20 Loss Contingencies
  450-30 Gain Contingencies
- 460 Guarantees
- 470 Debt
  470-20 Debt with Conversion and Other Options
  470-30 Participating Mortgage Loans
  470-40 Product Financing Arrangements

- 470-50 Modifications and Extinguishments
- 470-60 Troubled Debt Restructurings by Debtors
- 480 Distinguishing Liabilities from Equity

500s – Equity – This area will be selected if the question relates to the reporting of equity. It may involve determining whether or not it will be reported on the financial statements, the amount at which it will be reported, the accounting for equity transactions, distributions, or related disclosures. Within the area, a specific topic will be selected.

Within that topic, a subtopic is also to be chosen. For some topics, the only subtopic will be subtopic 10, "Overall". Other topics will have two or more subtopics, the first of which will be subtopic 10, "Overall". Determine if one of the subtopics, other than "Overall" appears to more directly relate to the question being asked or the issue being raised. If not, select subtopic 10, "Overall".

Topics and subtopics, excluding "Overall" within the Equity area include the following:
- 505 Equity
  - 505-20 Stock Dividends and Stock Splits
  - 505-30 Treasury Stock
  - 505-50 Equity-Based Payments to Non-Employees
  - 505-60 Spinoffs and Reverse Spinoffs

600s – Revenue – This area will be selected if the question relates to the recognition of revenue. It may involve determining whether or not it will be reported on the financial statements in a given period, the amount that will be recognized, the accounting for deferred revenue, accounting for revenue recognized over time, or related disclosures. Within the area, a specific topic will be selected.

Within that topic, a subtopic is also to be chosen. For some topics, the only subtopic will be subtopic 10, "Overall". Other topics will have two or more subtopics, the first of which will be subtopic 10, "Overall". Determine if one of the subtopics, other than "Overall" appears to more directly relate to the question being asked or the issue being raised. If not, select subtopic 10, "Overall".

Topics and subtopics, excluding "Overall" within the Revenue area include the following:
- 605 Revenue Recognition
  - 605-15 Products
  - 605-20 Services
  - 605-25 Multiple-Element Arrangements
  - 605-28 Milestone Method
  - 605-30 Rights to Use
  - 605-35 Construction-Type and Production-Type Contracts
  - 605-40 Gains and Losses
  - 605-45 Principal Agent Considerations
  - 605-50 Customer Payments and Incentives
- 606 Revenue from Contracts with Customers
- 610 Other Income
  - 610-20 Gains and Losses from the Derecognition of Nonfinancial Assets
  - 610-30 Gains and Losses on Involuntary Conversions

Conceptual Framework & IFRS Section 1

700s – Expenses – This area will be selected if the question relates to the reporting of expenses. It may involve determining whether or not an expense will be recognized, the period in which it will be recognized, the amount that will be reported, the classification of the expense, or related disclosures. Within the area, a specific topic will be selected.

Within that topic, a subtopic is also to be chosen. For some topics, the only subtopic will be subtopic 10, "Overall". Other topics will have two or more subtopics, the first of which will be subtopic 10, "Overall". Determine if one of the subtopics, other than "Overall" appears to more directly relate to the question being asked or the issue being raised. If not, select subtopic 10, "Overall".

Topics and subtopics, excluding "Overall" within the Expenses area include the following:
- 705 Cost of Sales and Services
  - 705-20 Accounting for Consideration
- 710 Compensation - General
- 712 Compensation – Nonretirement Postemployment Benefits
- 715 Compensation – Retirement Benefits
  - 715-20 Defined Benefit Plans – General
  - 715-30 Defined Benefit Plans Pension
  - 715-60 Defined Benefit Plans – Other Postretirement
  - 715-70 Defined Contribution Plans
  - 715-80 Multiemployer Plans
- 718 Compensation – Stock Compensation
  - 718-20 Awards Classified as Equity
  - 718-30 Awards Classified as Liabilities
  - 718-40 Employee Stock Ownership Plans
  - 718-50 Employer Share Purchase Plans
- 720 Other Expenses
  - 720-15 Start-up Costs
  - 720-20 Insurance Costs
  - 720-25 Contributions Made
  - 720-30 Real and Personal Property Taxes
  - 720-35 Advertising Costs
  - 720-40 Electronic Equipment Waste Obligations
  - 720-50 Fees Paid to the Federal Government by Pharmaceutical Manufacturers and Health Insurers
- 730 Research and Development
  - 730-20 Research and Development Arrangements
- 740 Income Taxes
  - 740-20 Intraperiod Tax Allocation
  - 740-30 Other Considerations or Special Areas

800s – Broad Transactions – This area will be selected if the question relates to an area that affects more than one financial statement, more than one asset, liability, equity, revenue, or expense account, or some combination. When transactions affect more than one area, such as leases, business combinations, or nonmonetary transactions, it is treated as a separate topic with its effects on other topics referenced. Within the area, a specific topic will be selected.

Within that topic, a subtopic is also to be chosen. For some topics, the only subtopic will be subtopic 10, "Overall". Other topics will have two or more subtopics, the first of which will be subtopic 10, "Overall". Determine if one of the subtopics, other than "Overall" appears to more directly relate to the question being asked or the issue being raised. If not, select subtopic 10, "Overall".

Topics and subtopics, excluding "Overall" within the Broad Transactions area include the following:
- 805 Business Combinations
  805-20 Identifiable Assets and Liabilities, and Any Noncontrolling Interest
  805-30 Goodwill or Gain from Bargain Purchase, Including Consideration Transferred
  805-40 Reverse Acquisitions
  805-50 Related Issues
- 808 Collaborative Arrangements
- 810 Consolidation
  810-20 Control of Partnerships and Similar Entities
  810-30 Research and Development Arrangements
- 815 Derivatives and Hedging
  815-15 Embedded Derivatives
  815-20 Hedging – General
  815-25 Fair Value Hedges
  815-30 Cash Flow Hedges
  815-35 New Investment Hedges
  815-40 Contracts in entity's Own Equity
  815-45 Weather Derivatives
- 820 Fair Value Measurement
- 825 Financial Instruments
  825-20 Registration Payment Arrangements
- 830 Foreign Currency Matters
  830-20 Foreign Currency Transactions
  830-30 Translation of Financial Statements
- 835 Interest
  835-20 Capitalization of Interest
  835-30 Imputation of Interest
- 840 Leases
  840-20 Operating Leases
  840-30 Capital Leases
  840-40 Sale-Leaseback Transactions
- 845 Nonmonetary Transactions
- 850 Related Party Disclosures
- 852 Reorganizations
  852-20 Quasi-Reorganizations
- 853 Service Concession Arrangements
- 855 Subsequent Events
- 860 Transfers and Servicing
  860-20 Sales of Financial Assets
  860-30 Secured Borrowing and Collateral
  860-40 Transfers to Qualifying Special Purpose Entities
  860-50 Servicing Assets and Liabilities

900s – Industry – This area will be selected if the question relates how an accounting area is treated in a particular industry. When an industry has special principles for the presentation of its financial statements, the accounting for an asset, liability, equity, revenue, or expense, the accounting for a broad transaction, or special disclosures, the topic will be selected from within that industry. Within the industry, a specific topic will be selected.

Within that topic, a subtopic is also to be chosen. For some topics, the only subtopic will be subtopic 10, "Overall". Other topics will have two or more subtopics, the first of which will be subtopic 10, "Overall". Determine if one of the subtopics, other than "Overall" appears to more directly relate to the question being asked or the issue being raised. If not, select subtopic 10, "Overall".

Topics and subtopics, excluding "Overall" within the Industry area include the following:
- 905 Agriculture
- 908 Airlines
- 910 Contractors – Construction
  - 910-20 Contract costs
- 912 Contractors – Federal Government
  - 912-20 Contract Costs
- 915 Development Stage Entities
- 920 Entertainment – Broadcasters
- 922 Entertainment – Cable Television
- 924 Entertainment – Casinos
- 926 Entertainment – Films
  - 926-20 Other Assets – Film Costs
- 928 Entertainment – Music
- 930 Extractive Industries – Mining
- 932 Extractive Industries – Oil and Gas
- 940 Financial Services – Brokers and Dealers
  - 940-20 Broker-Dealer Activities
- 942 Financial Services – Depository and Lending
- 944 Financial Services –Insurance
  - 944-20 Insurance Activities
  - 944-30 Acquisition Costs
  - 944-40 Claim Costs and Liabilities for Future Policy Benefits
  - 944-50 Policyholder Dividends
  - 944-60 Premium Deficiency and Loss Recognition
  - 944-80 Separate Accounts
- 946 Financial Services – Investment Companies
  - 946-20 Investment Company Activities
- 948 Financial Services – Mortgage Banking
- 950 Financial Services – Plant Title
- 952 Franchisors
- 954 HealthCare Entities
- 958 Not-for-Profit Entities
  - 958-20 Financially Interrelated entities
  - 958-30 Split-Interest Agreements
- 960 Plan Accounting – Defined Benefit Pension Plans
  - 960-20 Accumulated Plan Benefits

- 960-30 Net Assets Available for Plan Benefits
- 960-40 Terminating Plans
- 962 Plan Accounting – Defined Contribution Pension Plans
- 962-40 Terminating Plans
- 965 Plan Accounting – Health and Welfare Benefit Plans
- 965-20 Net Assets Available for Plan Benefits
- 965-30 Plan Benefit Obligations
- 965-40 Terminating Plans
- 970 Real Estate – General
- 972 Real Estate – Common Interest Realty Associations
- 974 Real Estate – Real Estate Investment Trusts
- 976 Real Estate – Retail Land
- 978 Real Estate – Time-Sharing Activities
- 980 Regulated Operations
- 980-20 Discontinuation of Rate Regulated Accounting
- 985 Software
- 985-20 Costs of Software to Be Sold, Leased, or Marketed
- 994 U.S. Steamship Entities

Once the specific topic and subtopic have been selected, the appropriate section should be determined. The sections, which are uniformly numbered within each subtopic, including the "Overall" subtopic, each address a specific aspect to the accounting for the topic, when the subtopic is "Overall" or the subtopic for any other. A section will only appear within a subtopic when it is relevant and, as a result, all sections will not be listed under every subtopic.

The sections are:

00 Status – This section provides information about the changes that were made to the subtopic, which paragraphs were affected, the source of the change, and the date on which the change was put into the Codification.

05 Overview and Background – This section provides a general overview and background of the subtopic without summarizing the requirements. It often contains material to enable a user to understand the situations that are typically covered by the standard.

10 Objectives – This section indicates the high-level objective of the standard, although it does not provide guidance as to the main principle of the standard.

15 Scope and Scope Exceptions – This section indicates when the guidance does or does not apply including, perhaps, a description of the entities that must or are not required to apply the principles, or the transactions to which it does or does not apply.

20 Glossary – This section includes definitions of terms that are unique to the principle.

25 Recognition – This section indicates the circumstances under which an item will appear on the financial statements, including the criteria for an item to be recognized, the time at which or period in which it will be recognized, and the location within the financial statements where it will appear.

30 Initial Measurement – This section indicates the amount at which the item will appear on the financial statements when it is first recognized.

35 Subsequent Measurement – This section indicates how a balance sheet item will be accounted for once it is recognized on the financial statements. It may indicate, for example, that an item should be amortized or depreciated, adjusted to fair value, adjusted to amortized cost, or tested for impairment.

40 Derecognition – This section indicates how a balance sheet item will be removed from the financial statements once it has been recognized and provides a basis for gain or loss recognition.

45 Other Presentation Matters – This section provides information about the specific placement or handling of an item on the financial statements. Examples may include whether an item is required to be reported as current or noncurrent, the section of the income statement or the statement of cash flows in which it will appear, requirements for a specific description to be used to identify the item on the financial statements, or where an item may not appear on the financial statements.

50 Disclosure – This section describes the disclosure requirements for the topic other than those that would be included due to the general disclosure requirements indicated in ASC Topic 235, Notes to Financial Statements.

55 Implementation Guidance and Illustrations – This section provides guidance as to how to apply the standard in simple and general situations and, when appropriate, provides illustrations. Illustrations may be of financial statements or sections thereof, schedules, footnotes, or a description of the methodology for applying the standard.

60 Relationships – This section provides references to other subtopics that are related to this subtopic and may provide more information that is relevant to it.

65 Transition and Open Effective Date Information – This section indicates when changes in principles go into effect and how an entity makes the transition from the outdated standard to the new one.

70 Grandfathered Guidance – This section includes principles that do not apply to current transactions but may still apply to the preparation of financial statements due to historical transactions, such as the pooling-of-interests method for preparing consolidated financial statements.

75 XBRL Elements – This section provides coding information required by XBRL, which stands for the Extensible Business Related Language, so that financial information can be appropriately tagged to facilitate financial analysis.

Once the appropriate section has been identified, scroll through that section to find the particular paragraph that provides the information sought.

TASK-BASED SIMULATION: A SAMPLE RESEARCH QUESTION

 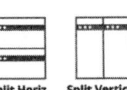 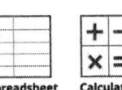

Sample Research Question:

Identify the section of professional standards that specifies where cash received from selling available-for-sale securities should be disclosed on the statement of cash flows.

Answer: ASC 320-10-45-11
The question applies to the sale of investment securities, indicating that the topic will be Topic 320, Investments – Debt and Equity Securities. The question does not specify a particular industry and the only subtopic under topic 320 is subtopic 10, Overall. The question specifically asks where, on the statement of cash flows, the proceeds from the sale of the securities will appear, which relates to the presentation on the financial statements, indicating section 45, Other Presentation Matters.

Upon scrolling through that section, there is a heading before paragraphs 11-13 indicating "Cash Flow Presentation". Scanning those paragraphs will reveal that in paragraph 11 it states in the first sentence "Cash flows from purchases, sales, and maturities of available-for-sale securities and held-to-maturity securities shall be classified as cash flows from investing activities and reported gross for each security classification in the statement of cash flows."

Task-Based Simulation Solution

FASB ASC	320	10	45	11

Conceptual Framework & IFRS   Section 1

CLASS QUESTIONS

Work through the below Class Questions while following along with the respective lectures. Once this is complete, you can begin independently practicing what you've learned by quizzing yourself on this course section in your Interactive Practice Questions (IPQ), which can be found in your online Student Dashboard. Your IPQ simulates the computer-based testing experience, and will also help you understand how concepts are applied to the exam. Each question includes answer explanations from expert CPAs that will help you determine why you answered a question correctly or incorrectly. This is key to your success on the CPA Exam.

Lecture 1.02

1. The enhancing qualitative characteristics of financial reporting are

    a. Relevance, reliability, and faithful representation.
    b. Cost-benefit and materiality.
    c. Comparability, understandability, timeliness, and verifiability.
    d. Completeness, neutrality, and free from error.

2. According to Statements of Financial Accounting Concepts, neutrality is an ingredient of

	Faithful Representation	Relevance
a.	Yes	Yes
b.	Yes	No
c.	No	Yes
d.	No	No

3. According to the FASB conceptual framework, which of the following is an enhancing quality that relates to both relevance and faithful representation?

    a. Comparability.
    b. Confirmatory value.
    c. Predictive value.
    d. Neutrality.

Lecture 1.06

4. According to the FASB conceptual framework, the process of reporting an item in the financial statements of an entity is

    a. Allocation.
    b. Matching.
    c. Realization.
    d. Recognition.

5. According to the FASB conceptual framework, which of the following is an essential characteristic of an asset?

    a. The asset is tangible.
    b. An asset is obtained at a cost.
    c. The claims to an asset's benefit are legally enforceable.
    d. An asset provides a future benefit.

6. Crossroads Co. chooses to report a financial asset at its fair value. The asset trades in two different markets; however, neither market is the principal market for the financial asset. In the first market, sales proceeds are $76, which is net of transaction costs of $6. In the second market, the sales proceeds are $80, which is net of transaction costs of $1. What amount should Crossroads report as the fair value of the asset?

   a. $76
   b. $80
   c. $81
   d. $82

Lecture 1.09

7. According to the IASB Framework, the qualitative characteristic of relevance includes

   a. Confirmatory value, Predictive value, and Comparability.
   b. Free from Error, Neutrality, and Completeness.
   c. Predictive value, Confirmatory value, and Materiality.
   d. Neutrality, Completeness and Comparability.

8. According to the IASB Framework, the financial statement element that is defined as "a present obligation of the entity arising from past events, the settlement of which is expected to result in an outflow from the entity", is which of the following?

   a. Equity.
   b. Liability.
   c. Expense.
   d. Cost.

CLASS SOLUTIONS

1. (c) The enhancing qualitative characteristics of financial reporting are (Roger is CUT-V – CUT like a V) comparability, understandability, timeliness, and verifiability. Answer (a) is incorrect because relevance and faithful representation are the primary qualitative characteristics of financial information. Answer (b) is incorrect because cost – benefit is an overall constraint to the usefulness of information and materiality relates to the relevance of information. Answer (d) is incorrect because completeness, neutrality, and free from error are the ingredients that make up faithful representation.

2. (b) Faithful representation consists of the ingredients of Free from Error, Neutrality and Completeness. Remember that Roger is never on the FENC. Relevance consists of Predictive value and confirmatory value, or both. (Roger is P.C.)

3. (a) The enhancing qualitative characteristics of financial reporting relate to both relevance and faithful representation. They are (Roger is CUT-V – CUT like a V) comparability, understandability, timeliness, and verifiability. Answers (b), (c), and (d) are incorrect because confirmatory value and predictive value relate to Relevance, and Neutrality relates to Faithful representation.

4. (d) Recognition is the process of reporting an item on the financial statements. Answer (a) is incorrect because allocation is the process of spreading a cost over more than one period. Answer (b) is incorrect because matching is the process of recognizing an expense in the same period in which a related benefit is recognized. Answer (c) is incorrect because realization is the conversion of an item or service into cash or a claim to cash.

5. (d) An asset is an economic resource that has (1) a probable future benefit, (2) one can obtain that benefit and (3) the transaction creating the benefit has already occurred. Therefore, (d) is correct as it has a future benefit. Answer (a) is incorrect because assets may be tangible or intangible (copyright). Answer (b) is incorrect because assets may be acquired at a cost or without any cost. An asset may be obtained at a cost, but may also result from the sale of goods or the performance of some revenue producing activities. Answer (c) is incorrect because the legal enforceability of an asset is not a prerequisite for a benefit to qualify as an asset. Although many assets are associated with legal rights, such as the right of ownership, it is not essential as long as the entity controls the benefits.

6. (c) When there is no principal market, fair values are based on the assumption that a transaction would occur in the most **advantageous** market. Therefore the second market, which would result in net sales proceeds of $80, is assumed. Though transaction costs are considered in determining the most advantageous market, they are ignored for the purpose of the fair value measurement. Therefore, the transaction cost of $1 is added back to net sales proceeds of $80, for a fair value measurement of $81, which is the answer. Answer choices a) and d) are wrong because they assume the first market is the most advantageous market. Answer choice b) is wrong because it does not add back the transaction costs.

7. (c) The qualitative characteristics for Relevance under the IASB Framework are Predictive value, Confirmatory value and Materiality, which is very similar under the FASB conceptual framework. Remember that Roger is PC, but also very Materialistic. Answer (a) is incorrect because comparability is an enhancing qualitative characteristic. Answer (b) is incorrect because completeness, neutrality, and free from error are the ingredients that make up faithful representation. Answer (d) is incorrect because completeness and neutrality are ingredients that make up faithful representation.

8. (b) According to the IASB Framework, there are 5 elements that make up the financial statements, they include: asset, liability, equity, income, and expense. The definition given is that of a Liability, which is a present obligation arising from past events. Answer (a) is incorrect because equity is the residual interest in assets after deducting liabilities. Answer (c) is incorrect because an expense is an outflow or decrease in assets or an increase in liabilities that result in decreases in equity but that do not result from distributions to equity holders. Answer (d) is incorrect because a cost is not a financial statement element.

TASK-BASED SIMULATION

Task-Based Simulation 1

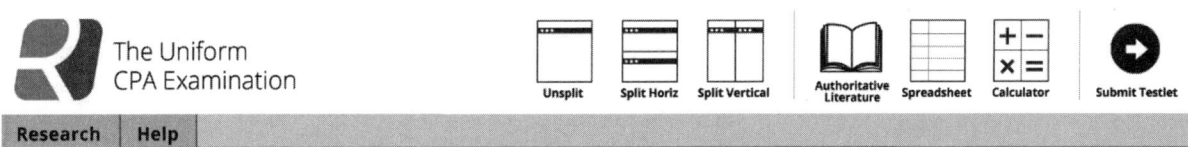

An entity is determining the fair value of a machine acquired in a business combination. Although its sales value is very low, it is expected to make a significant contribution to future revenues. Identify the location in the professional standards that indicates that the fair value measurement of a nonfinancial asset takes into account the asset's highest and best use.

Task-Based Simulation 2

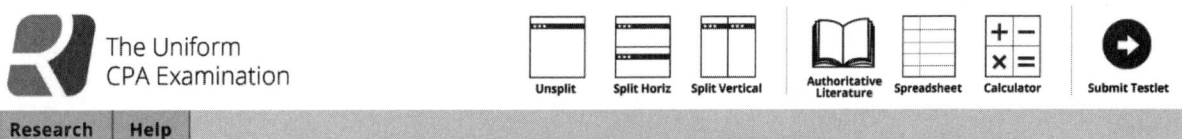

While preparing its financial statements, an entity is trying to determine what they are required to disclose in relation to certain assets recently acquired that may become very valuable or may decline in value, depending on future events and circumstances. Identify the location in professional standards that indicates the disclosures a reporting entity is required to make about risks and uncertainties existing as of the date of the financial statements.

TASK-BASED SIMULATION SOLUTION

Task-Based Simulation Solution 1

FASB ASC	820	10	35	10A

Task-Based Simulation Solution 2

FASB ASC	275	10	50	1

Section 2 - Cash & Cash Equivalents, Balance Sheet

Section 2 - Cash & Cash Equivalents, Balance Sheet

Corresponding Lectures

Watch the following course lectures with this section:

Lecture 2.01 – Balance Sheet
Lecture 2.02 – Cash and Cash Equivalents – Class Questions
Lecture 2.03 – GAAP Income Statement
Lecture 2.04 – Monetary Current Assets under IFRS

EXAM NOTE: Please refer to the AICPA FAR Blueprint in the Introduction to find a listing of the representative tasks (and their associated skill levels—i.e., Remembering and Understanding, Application, and Analysis) that the candidate should be able to perform based on the knowledge obtained in this section.

Cash & Cash Equivalents, Balance Sheet
(Statement of Financial Position)

Lecture 2.01

BALANCE SHEET (STMT OF FINANCIAL POSITION)(ASC 210)

The balance sheet, also called the Statement of Financial Position, reports the effect of transactions at a point in time. It consists of assets, liabilities and stockholders' equity. The items are broken down into *current* and *non-current*.

Current Assets are assets that will be used up or converted into cash within one year or the operating cycle, whichever is Longer.
- Cash, temporary trading securities, A/R, N/R, inventories and prepaid expenses.

Current Liabilities are liabilities that will be settled within one year or the operating cycle, whichever is Longer.
- Accounts payable, accrued expenses, dividends payable, income taxes payable, current portion of L/T debt.

Cash (ASC 305) is the most liquid asset of an enterprise, thus it is usually the first item presented in the current assets section of the balance sheet.

A **Cash Equivalent** is a security that is easily converted into cash with an **original maturity of 90 days or less**. A cash equivalent is a financial instrument that is **both**:
- Easily convertible into a known amount of cash (**highly liquid**), and
- **Original maturity of 3 months or less** from the date of purchase. Since it is so close to maturity, this presents very little risk of change in value, due to changes in interest rates.
    (e.g. Treasury bills, commercial paper & money market funds)

Examples of **cash and cash equivalents**
- Coin and currency on hand (petty cash)
- Money market accounts
- Unmailed checks
- Savings accounts
- CDs with an original maturity of 3 months or less
- Negotiable paper (bank checks, travelers checks, money orders)

An investment which has a total term exceeding 3 months, such as a 5-year U.S. Treasury Note, will not be considered a cash equivalent unless the investor acquires the investment on the open market when its remaining time to maturity is under 3 months. An investment that has been excluded from cash equivalents because of a term exceeding 3 months will NOT be reclassified to cash equivalents as it approaches the maturity date, since there is no transaction or event occurring 3 months before maturity that would justify the preparation of a journal entry.

Items **excluded** from cash
- **Compensating balances** – *legally restricted* deposits that are either a current asset or a non-current asset, but not considered part of cash. If funds are *NOT legally restricted*, present them along with cash.
- **Postdated checks or NSF** (non-sufficient funds) are receivables.
- **Overdraft protection**
    - If in same bank, net them, if positive then show it as cash, if negative, show it as a current liability.
    - If in different banks, show the positive as an asset, and the negative as a current liability.
- **Restricted cash**
    - Current – restricted for a current asset or liability (segregated from cash)
    - Non-current – restricted for a noncurrent asset or liability (either other assets or Investments)
- **Postage stamps** are considered supplies (prepaid expense)

Bank Reconciliation

Bank reconciliations are used to reconcile differences between cash balances per bank and per book to arrive at a corrected balance between the two. Several factors can cause a differential between bank and book cash balances such as deposits in transit, outstanding checks, errors or bank service charges. A simple bank reconciliation looks something like this:

Balance on bank statement		**Checkbook balance**
+	Deposits in transit	+ Amounts collected by bank
-	Outstanding checks	- Unrecorded bank charges
±	Errors made by bank	± Errors made in recording transactions
=	Corrected balance	= Corrected balance

Roger Company
GAAP BALANCE SHEET/Statement of Financial Position
December 31, 20X7

Assets

Current Assets
- Cash and cash equivalents (unrestricted and restricted)
- Temporary term investments (trading securities)
- Receivables (NRV)
    - Tax and other refunds
    - Receivables from affiliates and employees and overpayments to creditors
    - Accounts receivable, net of allowance for bad debts
    - Current portions of installments receivable and notes receivable
- Inventories (LCM)
    - Raw materials
    - Work-in-process
    - Finished goods
- Prepaid expenses (such as insurance and rent)
- Current deferred tax asset

Total Current Assets

Noncurrent Investments
- Nonmarketable securities (cost or equity method)
- Long-term investments in marketable securities
    - Available for sale
    - Held to maturity (Bonds)

Property, Plant, and Equipment (Fixed Assets)
- Land, buildings, and improvements
- Machinery and equipment, leased assets
- Less accumulated depreciation

Intangible Assets (net of amortization)
- Goodwill
- Other identifiable intangibles (such as patents, trademarks, and copyrights)

Other Assets
- Deposits, unamortized BIC
- Noncurrent receivables (including noncurrent portions of installments receivable and notes receivable)
- Noncurrent deferred tax asset
- Equipment to be disposed of

Total Noncurrent Assets

Total Assets

Liabilities and Stockholders' Equity

Current liabilities
- Short-term notes payable
- Accounts payable
- Accrued expenses (such as salaries and wages, interest, and utilities)
- Estimated current liabilities (such as warranty expense)
- Taxes payable (such as income taxes, collected sales taxes, and withheld payroll taxes)
- Current deferred tax liability
- Unearned revenues (including rents or fees collected in advance)
- Dividends payable
- Current portion of long-term debt (such as noncurrent portions of capital lease obligations and notes and loans payable)

Total Current Liabilities

Noncurrent Liabilities
- Notes payable (net of current portion)
- Bonds payable
- Noncurrent deferred tax liability
- Other noncurrent liabilities (such as noncurrent portions of capital lease obligations and warranty obligations)
- Deferred liabilities (such as liabilities under pension plans, post employment plans, and post retirement plans)

Total Noncurrent Liabilities

Stockholders' Equity
- Contributed capital (APIC)
    - Preferred stock
    - Common stock (net of T/S at par)
    - Additional paid-in capital (APIC)
- Noncontrolling interest
- Earned capital
    - Retained earnings (appropriated and unappropriated)
    - Accumulated other comprehensive income (**OCI**) - (**DENT**)

Subtract
- Treasury stock at cost

Total Liabilities & Equity

Section 2   Cash and Cash Equivalents & Balance Sheet

Lecture 2.02

CLASS QUESTIONS

Please see the Class Questions and Class Solutions for this Lecture at the end of this Section.

Lecture 2.03

Multiple Step GAAP Income Statement (ON-TIDe-N-OC)

Roger Company
Statement of Earnings and Comprehensive Income
(Statement of Profit and Loss)
For the Year Ended December 31, 20X7

Sales		$2,000,000
Cost of sales		600,000
Gross profit		1,400,000
Less:		
Selling expenses	$340,000	
General & administrative expenses	260,000	
Depreciation Expense (impairment loss – public co)	100,000	700,000
Operating income (O)		700,000
Other income and (expense): (**Non-operating**)		
Interest/Dividend income	10,000	
Interest expense/unusual and/or infrequent items	(20,000)	
Loss due to earthquake	(72,000)	
Gain on sale of equipment/Investments (imp loss –non public)	30,000	(52000)
Income before income tax		648,000
Provision for income Tax (T):		
Current	150,000	
Deferred	40,000	190,000
Income from continuing operations **(I)**		$ 458,000
Gain (loss) from operations of **Discontinued component unit, (FASB ASC 205)**		
net of tax of $30,000 **(De)**		45,000
Net income (N)		$503,000
Other Comprehensive income **(OCI) (DENT)** (net of tax) **(O)**		
Derivative Cash Flow Hedge Gain/Loss		xxx
Excess adjustment of Pension PBO and FV of Plan assets at year end		(xxx)
Net Unrealized holding gains (AFS) arising during period		xxx
Translation adjustment of Foreign currency		xxx
Other comprehensive income		xxx
Comprehensive Income (C)		$xxx,xxx
Earnings per share:		
Income from continuing operations		$2.29
Income from Discontinued operations		.23
Net Income per share		$2.52

As part of a simplification initiative, the concept of extraordinary gains and losses was eliminated. This change was made in order to align GAAP more closely to IAS 1, Presentation of Financial Statements.

Lecture 2.04

MONETARY CURRENT ASSETS AND CURRENT LIABILITIES UNDER IFRS

Normally, assets are reported as current and noncurrent, and liabilities are reported as current and noncurrent on the Statement of Financial Position (balance sheet). If a liquidity presentation provides more relevant and reliable information, then balance sheet items may be reported based on their liquidity without segregation.

In a balance sheet segregated between current and noncurrent items, an **asset** is classified as **current** when:
1. The entity expects to realize the asset or to consume or sell it within 12 months or the normal operating cycle, or
2. The entity holds the asset primarily for the purpose of trading.

A liability is classified as current when:
1. The entity expects to settle the liability within the normal operating cycle
2. The liability will be settled within 12 months after the reporting period, or
3. The entity holds the liability for the purpose of trading

IFRS defines a **financial instrument** as any contract that gives results in a financial asset of one entity and a financial liability or equity instrument of another entity.

A **financial asset** is:
- Cash
- An equity instrument of another entity
- A contractual right:
    o To receive cash or another financial asset from another entity; or
    o To exchange financial assets or financial liabilities with another entity on potentially favorable terms
- A contract that will be settled in the entity's own equity instruments

A **financial liability** is:
- A contractual obligation:
    o To deliver cash or another financial asset to another entity; or
    o To exchange financial assets or financial liabilities with another entity on potentially unfavorable terms
- A contract that will be settle in the entity's own equity instruments

Financial assets are measured at amortized cost only if two conditions are met:
- The entity's business model is to hold the asset to collect scheduled cash flows
- The terms of the instrument call for cash flows that are exclusively payments of principal and interest on specified dates

All other financial assets are measured at fair value. In general, unrealized gains and losses are reported in profit or loss.

- Business model may involve both holding the instrument to collect cash flows and **selling the financial instrument**.
- When that is the case, the instrument is measured at **fair value** with unrealized gains and losses recognized in **other comprehensive income**.

In general, financial liabilities are measured at amortized cost, but may be measured at fair value, with unrealized gains or losses recognized in income, when it will result in more relevant information.

IFRS Statement of Financial Position

Assets	Notes	20X2	20X1
Noncurrent assets			
Goodwill	i	x,xxx	x,xxx
Other intangible assets	j	x,xxx	x,xxx
Property, plant, and equipment	k	x,xxx	x,xxx
Investments (such as equity method investments)	g	x,xxx	x,xxx
Investment property			
Biological Assets	m	x,xxx	x,xxx
Deferred tax assets	o	x,xxx	x,xxx
Loans and other receivables (trade and other)			
Employee benefits	n	x,xxx	x,xxx
Noncurrent assets		xx,xxx	xx,xxx
Current assets			
Inventories			
Biological Assets	p	x,xxx	x,xxx
Loans and other Receivables (trade and other)	q	x,xxx	x,xxx
Prepayments		x,xxx	x,xxx
Current tax assets		x,xxx	x,xxx
Short-term financial assets and investments (derivatives)	n	x,xxx	x,xxx
Cash and cash equivalents	r	x,xxx	x,xxx
Current assets		xx,xxx	xx,xxx
Assets classified as held for sale	s	x,xxx	- - - -
Total assets		xxx,xxx	xxx,xxx
Equity and liabilities			
Equity			
Equity attributable to parent owners			
Share capital	t	x,xxx	x,xxx
Share premium	t	x,xxx	x,xxx
Retained earnings		x,xxx	x,xxx
Reserves	u	x,xxx	x,xxx
Accumulated other comprehensive income (**DENT-R**)		x,xxx	x,xxx
		xx,xxx	xx,xxx
Noncontrolling interest		x,xxx	x,xxx
Total equity		xx,xxx	xx,xxx
Noncurrent Liabilities			
Pension and other benefit obligations	v	x,xxx	x,xxx
Loans and borrowings	n	x,xxx	x,xxx
Deferred tax liabilities	o	x,xxx	x,xxx
Other liabilities & provisions	w	x,xxx	x,xxx
Noncurrent liabilities		xx,xxx	xx,xxx

IFRS Statement of Financial Position (Con't)

Assets	Notes	20X2	20X1
Current Liabilities			
Bank overdraft			
Trade and other payables	v	x,xxx	x,xxx
Current tax liabilities		x,xxx	x,xxx
Short-term loans and borrowings	n	x,xxx	x,xxx
Provisions	u	x,xxx	x,xxx
Current liabilities		xx,xxx	xx,xxx
Liabilities associated with assets held for sale	s	x,xxx	- - - -
Total liabilities		xx,xxx	xx,xxx
Total equity and liabilities		xxx,xxx	xxx,xxx

Section 2   Cash and Cash Equivalents & Balance Sheet

CLASS QUESTIONS

Work through the below Class Questions while following along with the respective lectures. Once this is complete, you can begin independently practicing what you've learned by quizzing yourself on this course section in your Interactive Practice Questions (IPQ), which can be found in your online Student Dashboard. Your IPQ simulates the computer-based testing experience, and will also help you understand how concepts are applied to the exam. Each question includes answer explanations from expert CPAs that will help you determine why you answered a question correctly or incorrectly. This is key to your success on the CPA Exam.

Lecture 2.02

1. The following information pertains to Grey Co. at December 31, 20X3:

Checkbook balance	$12,000
Bank statement balance	16,000
Check drawn on Grey's account, payable to a vendor, dated and recorded 12/31/X3 but not mailed until 1/10/X4	1,800

    On Grey's December 31, 20X3, balance sheet, what amount should be reported as cash?

    a. $12,000
    b. $13,800
    c. $14,200
    d. $16,000

2. Bob Co. has a checking account at Home Bank and an interest-bearing savings account at Chasen Bank. On December 31, year 1, the bank reconciliations for Bob Co. are as follows:

<u>Chasen Bank</u>	
Bank Balance	$150,000
<u>Deposit in transit</u>	<u>5,000</u>
Book Balance	$155,000
<u>Home Bank</u>	
Bank balance	$1,500
<u>Outstanding checks</u>	<u>(8,500)</u>
Book balance	$(7,000)

    What amount should be classified as cash on Bob's balance sheet at December 31, year 1?

    a. $148,000
    b. $151,000
    c. $155,000
    d. $156,000

Page 2-8   ©Roger CPA Review

3. Philipp Co.'s monthly bank statement shows a balance of $54,200. Reconciliation of the statement with company books reveals the following information:

from Bank to Book

Bank Service Charge	$10	(Bank already knows)
Insufficient funds check	650	(Bank already knows)
Outstanding Checks	1,500	∴ these 2 #s
Deposits in transit	350	are part of $54,200 already.

Check deposited by Philipp and cleared by the bank for $125, but improperly recorded by Philipp as $152.

What is the net cash balance per books after the reconciliation?

a. $52,363
b. $53,023
c. $53,050
d. $53,077

∴ 54,200
 (1,500)
 + 350
 ─────
 53,023.

also, ∵ its from bank to book.
the bank did correctly. no need to do anything for
152 vs. 125.

CLASS SOLUTIONS

1. (b) In most cases the amount reported as cash will be the checkbook balance unless there are adjustments due to unrecorded transactions or errors that are revealed when preparing a bank reconciliation. When a check is written during a period but not mailed until after the end of the period, it is considered not to have been written and is added back to the checkbook balance. As a result, cash will be reported at the checkbook balance of $12,000 plus the check of $1,800 mailed after year-end for a total of $13,800.

2. (c) Normally, both checking accounts and interest-bearing savings accounts are included in cash and reported in amounts equal to their reconciled balances, the book balances in this case. When an account is overdrawn, however, it may not be offset against accounts with positive balances unless they are in the same institution with the right of offset. When that is not the case, as in this case, the overdraft is reported as a liability and only the positive balance of $155,000 will be reported as cash.

3. (c) The cash balance per books will equal the reconciled bank balance, which will consist of the bank balance of $54,200, increased by deposits in transit of $350, and decreased by outstanding checks of $1,500 for a net amount of $53,050. The bank service charge has already been deducted from the bank balance as has the insufficient funds check. These may require adjusting entries to correct the recorded book balance. In addition, the $125 check is properly included in the bank balance but will require an adjustment to the book balance to correct the misrecording. After the adjustments are made for the error, the bank charges, and the insufficient funds, the balance per books will equal the reconciled bank balance of $53,050.

TASK-BASED SIMULATIONS

Task-Based Simulation 1

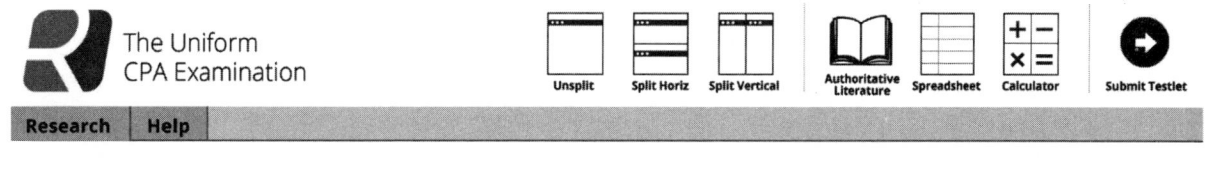

A client needs to calculate its working capital in order to determine if it is in compliance with certain loan covenants. Identify the location in professional standards that indicates what items would generally be included in current assets.

Task-Based Simulation 2

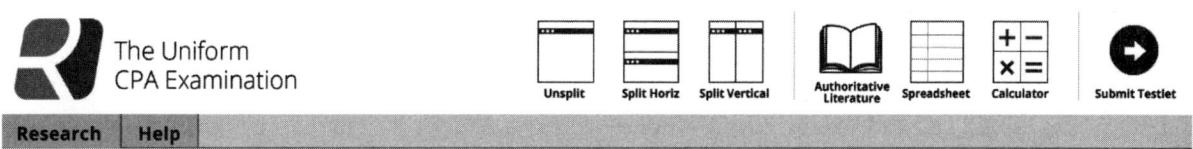

Your client thinks that an account like the allowance for doubtful accounts must be reported as a liability or equity account since it has a credit balance. Identify the location in professional standards that indicates how asset valuation accounts should be reported.

TASK-BASED SIMULATION SOLUTIONS

Task-Based Simulation Solution 1

FASB ASC	210	10	45	1

Task-Based Simulation Solution 2

FASB ASC	210	10	45	13

Section 3 - Cost and Equity Method Corresponding Lectures

Watch the following course lectures with this section:

Lecture 3.01 – Investments in the Stock of Other Entities
Lecture 3.02 – Cost Method, Changes in Ownership & Fair Value Accounting
Lecture 3.03 – Cost and Equity Method – Class Questions
Lecture 3.04 – Investments under IFRS – Cost and Equity Method
Lecture 3.05 – Cost and Equity Method TBS – Class Questions

EXAM NOTE: Please refer to the AICPA FAR Blueprint in the Introduction to find a listing of the representative tasks (and their associated skill levels—i.e., Remembering and Understanding, Application, and Analysis) that the candidate should be able to perform based on the knowledge obtained in this section.

Cost and Equity Method

Lecture 3.01

INVESTMENTS IN THE STOCK OF OTHER ENTITIES

An investor may acquire equity securities (common or preferred stock), debt securities (bonds) and derivatives (stock rights) in other companies. When a company acquires common stock, we need to determine the appropriate method of accounting for the investment, and this will depend primarily upon the amount of stock that is owned by the investor.

- **0 – 20% Cost method or Marketable securities**
    - The implication is that no influence over the investee company exists.
    - If the security isn't marketable, use the cost method

- **20 – 50% Equity method.** (one-line consolidation)
    - The implication is that the investor has significant voting influence over the investee.

- **50% + Consolidation (Section 31)**
    - The implication is that the investor has control over the investee.
    - Members of the investor company constitute a majority of the board of directors of the investee.

Equity Method (ASC 323)

The equity method is used when the investor has **significant influence** over the operating and financial policies of the investee. This method is more consistent with accrual accounting. Even if ownership is less than 20%, one must consider how much influence exists between the two entities. Some **factors** to consider are:
- Significant intercompany transactions, or technological dependency.
- Officers of the investor serving as officers or board members of the investee.
- The investor is a major customer or supplier of the investee
- The investor owns at least 20% of the voting stock of the investee (but not if another shareholder or small voting block owns a majority and exercises total control).
- The investor has definite plans to acquire additional stock in the future to bring their interest up to at least 20%.

Some points of interest **(equity method)**
- The investment is originally recorded at Cost
- As the investee earns money, this is recorded as an increase on the investor's books based on the % the investor owns. This is considered "**equity in earnings**" and is shown on the income statement as a component of continuing operations.
- Dividends received are considered a reduction of the investment account and do NOT show up on the income statement.
- Any difference paid between the purchase price paid for the investee and the book value of the investee's net assets must be accounted for.

- Those **differences are considered**:
  - FMV write up of assets (FMV increment)
    - **PP&E** -depreciated
    - **Inventory** -written off when sold
    - **Land** -not depreciated but written off when sold
    - **Goodwill** -not amortized but impairment losses recognized

Ownership of **preferred stock** cannot, by itself, give an investor significant influence, but the investor may have such influence due to other causes, and use the equity method of accounting for the preferred stock investment. Preferred stock income under the equity method is equal to the dividends allocated to it. For non-cumulative preferred stock, this will equal declared dividends only. For cumulative preferred stock, this will equal the annual dividend preference regardless of payments in that year.

The equity method of accounting, used when the investor has significant influence, is more consistent with accrual accounting. The investment is still recorded initially at purchase price, but subsequent income changes the account balance on a continuous basis. The investor reports its share of the investee's income as an increase in its investment account, with offsetting recognition of equity in earnings of investee on the income statement. Dividends reduce the investment carrying value and are not reported in income.

For example, let's assume the investor paid $300 on 1/1/X1 to acquire 30% of the stock of the investee, at a time when the investee's net assets (equity) equaled $1,000, so that the original investment equaled the investor's 30% share of equity. In 20X1, the investee reported net income of $400 and paid dividends totaling $100 to stockholders of record on 12/31/X1 with a payment date of 1/7/X2. The investment entry is:

1/1/X1	Investment	300	
	Cash		300

The entry to report the investor's share of income is:

12/31/X1	Investment	120	
	Equity in Investee Income		120

The entry to record the dividend:

12/31/X1	Dividends receivable	30	
	Investment		30

Cost and Equity Method

Of course, there is also an entry on 1/7/X2 for the collection of the receivable. Notice that the investor's investment account changes as the equity of the investee changes (this is one reason it is known as the equity method):

	S/E of Investee	Investment (30%)
Purchase Date, 1/1/X1	$1,000	$300
Net Income	400	120
Dividends	(100)	(30)
Balance, 12/31/X1	1,300	390

In the earlier example, the $300 purchase price equaled 30% of the equity of the investee. When the purchase price exceeds the investor's share of equity, the excess needs to be identified, and accounted for in an appropriate manner. First, any assets with fair values differing from carrying values are identified, and the investor determines their percentage share of that excess (or deficiency). Any remaining excess is assumed to represent goodwill on the purchase.

The excess of the cost of the investment over book value is not reported separately on the financial statement; it is included in the investment. Nevertheless, it will have an impact on the subsequent reporting of income by the investor that depends on the nature of the asset causing the difference:
- Depreciable and amortizable assets – differences will be amortized against the reported equity in investee income based on the appropriate life of the asset.
- Goodwill – amount initially recorded will later reduce reported income in periods that impairment losses are recognized.
- All assets – outstanding differences will be written off against reported income at the time the asset is sold.

Assume the investor's 30% investment in the previous example cost $380 instead of $300, that $10 of the excess was attributable to inventory, which was sold during 20X1, $30 was attributable to land, which was still owned by the investee at the end of 20X1, and the remaining $40 represented a building, with an estimated useful life of 40 years. The inventory excess should be written off in 20X1, the land excess should remain, and building depreciation of $40 / 40 = $1 should be recorded in 20X1. As a result, the equity in investee income reported by the investor is $109, computed as follows:

Net income of investee	400
Percentage	30%
Investor share	120
Inventory	(10)
Land	(0)
Building	(1)
Equity in investee income	109

Examine the changes in the investment account in 20X1, in comparison to the changes in the investor's share of the investee's equity:

	S/E of Investee	Investment (30%)	Equity (30%)	Excess
Purchase Date, 1/1/X1	$1,000	$380	$300	$80
Net Income	400	109	120	(11)
Dividends	(100)	(30)	(30)	-----
Balance, 12/31/X1	1,300	459	390	69

By including the adjustments for the sale of inventory and depreciation on the building in income, the excess of cost over book value in the initial investment is gradually being written off. After the land is sold by the investee and building is completely depreciated, the investment will equal equity, and further reported income will be at straight percentages.

Lecture 3.02

Cost Method (ASC 325)

When no significant influence exists, we then must determine if the investment has a readily determinable market value.
- If a market value exists
    - Use marketable securities rules (trading, avail-for-sale, held to maturity)
- If no market value exists
    - Use the Cost method

Some points of interest: **(COST METHOD)**
- The original investment is recorded at cost
- When the investee earns money, NO journal entry is recorded
- When a dividend is received it is recorded as **Dividend Income** on the income statement (not a reduction of the Investment)
    - In rare cases, if the dividend received is greater than the investor's proportionate share of the investee's income since acquisition, then it is recorded as a **reduction** of the investment (these usually are distributions of an investee's earnings that occurred BEFORE the investor made their purchase of the investee).

Cash	X	
Investment		X

- No difference between BV and purchase price is taken into consideration (no excess amortization or depreciation as in the equity method).

Example for Both Equity and Cost

On 1/1/X1, we acquire 30% of a company for $1,000. FV of investee is $3,000 and BV is $2,500. The difference is from PP&E with a FMV $500 higher than its BV. During the year, the investee reports income of $120 and pays dividends of $40. PP&E is depreciated over 10 years and 10% of initial goodwill is impaired that year.

Cost and Equity Method   Section 3

```
        Investee's balances    FMV  $3,000   /Investee's income = $120 / G/w impaired
            at 1/1/X1          B.V. $2,500   /Dividend paid     = $40      by $10
        ---------------------------------------------------------------
            Purchase price          $1,000

            FMV of investor's                        > $100 Goodwill – impaired by $10 = $10
            share of investee       $900 (3000 x 30%)

                                                      >$150 FMV increment
            B.V of investor's                                (PP&E)  /10yrs        = $15 yr
            share of investee       $750 (2500 x 30%)                                $25
```

The journal entries under the **Equity method** would be:

Acquisition of investment at cost

    Investment $1000   (B.V. $750 + PP&E $150 + G/W $100)

        Cash $1000

Investor records % of earnings ($120 annual income x 30% = 36)

    Investment $36

        Equity in earnings $36 (I/S account)

% of Cash dividend ($40 is dividend received x 30% = 12)

    Cash $12

        Investment $12

To record **Amortization/Depreciation/Impairment of excess** between BV and purchase price (1000-750)

    Equity in earnings $25   ($10 G.W + $15 PP&E)

        Investment $25

The **T-account** for the investment under the equity method would look as follows:

```
        Investment T-account
         1000   |
          +36   |  -12
                |  - 25
         ─────  |
          999   |
```

Note: The investment account changes as the investee's equity account changes, better accrual.

The same example for the **Cost method: (owns 30% but other investor owns 70%)**

Record at cost

Investment	1000	
Cash		1000

Record % of earnings
No entry

Record % of cash dividend (40 x 30%)

Cash	12	
Dividend income		12 (Income statement account)

Amortization/Depreciation of excess
No entry

Note: the investment at the end of the year is still at COST

Investment T-account

```
     1000  |
           |
    -------|-------
     1000  |
```

Notice that, while the investor's share of the investee net income is $120 x 30% = $36, only the dividend received of $40 x 30% = $12 is recorded in income. Although this is not consistent with the accrual principle of recognizing revenue when earned, investments using this method are generally relatively small in amount, so the differences are usually not material.

Dividends received under the cost method are not always distributions of income to the investor. If the investee declares dividends which exceed the cumulative income it has earned since the date of the investment, the excess distribution is a **return of capital** to the investor, and is accounted for as a reduction in the carrying value of the investment.

For example, if the investee declares a dividend of $450, and the income earned since the investment date is only $400, the entry on the dividend record date by a 10% investor would have been:

Dividends receivable	45	
Dividend income		40
Investment		5

If an investee declares a **stock dividend or issues stock rights** or other classes of stock to existing shareholders, no income is reported. Instead, the carrying value of the investment is simply allocated over the increased quantity of securities. If the securities are all of the same class, no entry is needed (the number of shares is disclosed in the notes to the financial statements, if material). If the new securities are in a different class, an entry is made to transfer part of the carrying value, using the relative FMV approach.

For example, assume a client purchased 100 shares of stock at a price of $22 per share, or a total cost of $2,200:

Investment in stock	2,200	
Cash		2200

If the investee declares a **10% stock dividend**, then the number of shares held by the investor will increase to 110, but no entry is made. Instead, the $2,200 is allocated over 110 shares, so that the cost basis of each share becomes $20.

If, instead, the investee issues a **stock right** for each existing share, and the FMV of the stock and the stock rights on the record date are $24 per share and $6 per right, respectively, then the rights will be allocated 6 / (24+6) = 20% of the carrying value of the securities:

Investment in rights	440	
Investment in stock		440

No income is reported on dividends in arrears on cumulative preferred stock under the cost method, since this represents dividends that have not been declared. Only once they are declared and the date of record is reached can they be reported in the investor's records as dividend income.

The purchase of **life insurance** on an officer can be a form of investment, when it builds up a cash value (**cash surrender value**). The portion of the premium that increases the cash value is accumulated as an asset (non-current asset) on the balance sheet, and the rest of the premium is recognized as life insurance expense. If the officer dies, the proceeds from the policy are recognized as income only to the extent they exceed the cash value. Dividends on life insurance are treated as reductions of the net premium cost, and are not reported as dividend income.

EQUITY	COST
1) Buy	**1) Buy**

Investment   1000 (Includes 750 BV; 150 FMV>BV; 100 Goodwill)
    Cash   1000
	Investment 1000
	    Cash 1000

2) Investee Earns Money	**2) Investee Earns Money**
Investment 36 (120 x 30%) Equity in Earnings 36 EIE = I/S (N) section – Not cash $\Rightarrow$ back out in Cash Flow	No Journal Entry
3) Pay a Dividend	**3) Pay a Dividend**

Cash   12 (40 x 30%)
    Investment   12
	Cash 12
	    Dividend Income 12
	              DI = I/S (N) section

4) Amortize/Depreciation/Impairment of Excess	**4) Amortize/Depreciation of Excess**

Purchase $1000   Goodwill   =   1000 – 900
FMV   900   =   100
BV   750   Impairment = $ 10
 	
Depreciation = 900 – 750 =   150/10 = $ 15
                                                     $ 25
Equity in Earnings   25
    Investment   25
 	
Taking out Amortization/Depreciation/Impairment
	No Journal Entry

Investment follows Equity Balance of Investee, better Accrual	**No change to Investment**

Changes in Ownership Percentages

An entity may change its percentage of ownership in another entity by selling some shares, in which case the entity may lose the ability to exercise significant influence, requiring a change from the equity to the cost method, or by acquiring additional shares, in which case the entity may obtain the ability to exercise significant influence, requiring a change from the cost to the equity method. The ownership percentage may also change if the investee issues additional shares, which will decrease the percentage, or reacquires shares, which will increase it.

- **Equity to Cost** – (e.g. ownership changes from 40% to 10%) use the cost method going forward (**prospective**).
- **Cost to Equity** – (e.g. ownership changes from 10% to 40%) **prospectively** apply the equity method after increasing the carrying value of the investment by the cost of any additional investment made to obtain significant influence.

When an investment that has been accounted for as an available for sale security becomes eligible for the equity method of accounting, any unrealized holding gain or loss that is in accumulated other comprehensive income will be recognized in earnings.

For example, assume an investor has an investment in a marketable equity security that is accounted for as an available for sale (AFS) security. The investment was obtained at a cost of $1,200,000 in 20X1 and had a fair value of $1,350,000 as of the end of 20X1. The increase in value of $150,000 represents an unrealized holding gain that will have been recognized with an increase or decrease to the investment and the recognition of a corresponding unrealized gain or loss in comprehensive income.

The entry to record the acquisition would be

20X1	Investment in available-for sale securities	1,200,000	
	Cash		1,200,000

At the end of 20X1, the investment was worth $1,350,000. The entry is:

12/31/X1	Investment in available for sale securities	150,000	
	Unrealized gain due to increase in value of available for sale securities		150,000

The unrealized gain would be reported as a component of other comprehensive income (OCI) and closed into the equity account entitled accumulated other comprehensive income (AOCI).

Assume that in 20X2, the investor became a member of the board of directors and determined that the ability to significantly influence the investee had been achieved, qualifying the investment for the equity method of accounting. Since no additional investment had been made, the investment would be reclassified from an available for sale security to an equity investment. In addition, the unrealized gain that had been recognized in the previous period will be reclassified from accumulated other comprehensive income and reported in the current period's earnings.

20X2	Accumulated other comprehensive income	150,000	
	Gain due to increase in value of investment		150,000

FAIR VALUE ACCOUNTING OPTION (ASC 825)

FASB ASC 825, Financial Instruments, includes a provision that allows an entity to choose to report almost any of its financial instruments, including both its financial assets and financial liabilities, at fair value. This is referred to as the fair value option and may be applied to **eligible financial instruments** on specified **election dates** on a **security by security basis** and may be applied to some or all of a group of securities.

Under GAAP, a financial instrument is defined as "cash, evidence of an ownership interest in an entity, or a contract that both:
  a. Imposes on one entity a contractual obligation (**financial liability**) either:
     1. To deliver cash or another financial instrument to a second entity.
     2. To exchange other financial instruments on potentially unfavorable terms with the second entity.
  b. Conveys to that second entity a contractual right (financial asset) either:
     1. To receive cash or another financial instrument from the first entity.
     2. To exchange other financial instruments on potentially favorable terms with the first entity."

As a result, all receivables and payables are financial instruments as are derivatives and investments in debt and equity securities. **Eligible financial instruments** include:
- Recognized financial assets and liabilities.
- Firm commitments that involve only financial instruments or written loan commitment.

The **election dates** on which an entity may elect the fair value option include:
- When the eligible item is first recognized.
- When an eligible firm commitment is entered into.
- When items previously presented at fair value due to specialized accounting principles, with unrealized gains or losses recognized in earnings, no longer qualify for the specialized accounting principles.
- When there is a change in the method of accounting for an equity investment, such as to or from the equity method or ceasing to consolidate an investee.
- When an item is required to be measured at fair value on a one-time basis but is not required to be adjusted to fair value on subsequent financial statement dates.

On a given election date, the entity may elect to report the item or items at fair value or may apply the election to only some of the items, with the decision being made on a *security by security basis*.
- An entity with numerous firm commitments may elect to report some, all, or none of them at fair value.
- An entity with several investments accounted for under the equity method may elect to report some, all, or none of them at fair value.

Once made, a fair value election is irrevocable. It may, however, be changed on a subsequent election date. When the fair value election is made, the eligible item will be measured at its **fair value on each balance sheet date**. Any unrealized gains or losses will be recognized as a component of **income**. If the fair value election were applied to:
- An equity method investment, it would be measured at fair value on each balance sheet date and any changes, net of dividends received, will be recognized as a gain or loss.
- An available for sale (AFS) investment, will be reported at the same value as before the election but the unrealized gains and losses will be reported as a component of income rather than other comprehensive income.

- A held to maturity (HTM) investment, it would continue to be accounted for under the amortized cost method, applying the effective interest method, but after amortization of discount or premium, the carrying value will be increased or reduced to fair value at the balance sheet date and the unrealized gain or loss will be recognized in income.
- A firm commitment, such as a foreign currency forward exchange contract, an asset or liability would be recognized at fair value as the subject of the commitment, such as the foreign currency exchange rate, changes.

Lecture 3.03

CLASS QUESTIONS

Please see the Class Questions and Class Solutions for this Lecture at the end of this Section.

Lecture 3.04

INVESTMENTS IN FINANCIAL INSTRUMENTS UNDER IFRS

When an entity acquires the debt or equity securities of another entity, it is considered an investment in financial assets. In addition, financial assets may be originated by the entity, such as when it makes a loan to another entity. IFRS provides for different methods of accounting for various investments, based on their natures. There are **three general approaches** applied to investments in financial instruments.

When certain conditions are met, an investment in a financial instrument is reported at **amortized cost**. Under the amortized cost approach, any difference between the original cost and the face amount is treated as a discount or premium and the effective interest method of amortization is applied. The conditions are:
- The instrument calls for scheduled payments that consist exclusively of principal and interest.
- The entity's business model has, as an objective, to *hold until maturity* such instruments in order to collect the contractual cash flows.

A second type of investment in financial instrument is accounted for at *fair value* with unrealized gains and losses recognized in *other comprehensive income (OCI)*. This approach is referred to as **fair value through other comprehensive income** or **FVTOCI**. It is applied to financial assets when two conditions are met.

These conditions are similar to those for using the amortized cost approach except the FVTOCI approach is required if the entity, as a business model, may either hold the financial asset to maturity or dispose of it, whereas the amortized cost approach is only applied when the entity, as a business model, holds the financial asset to maturity.

The applicable requirements for FVTOCI are:
- The instrument calls for scheduled payments that consist exclusively of principal and interest.
- The entity's business model has, as an objective, to either hold such instruments in order to collect the contractual cash flows or to sell them.

Under this approach, such items as interest income, foreign exchange gains and losses, and impairment losses are recognized in income. After recognizing those items and adjusting the investment to its fair value, the net difference is recognized as an adjustment to other comprehensive income.

The amortized cost and the FVTOCI approaches would generally *not be appropriate for investments in the equity securities* of another entity since they do not generally call for scheduled payments of principal and interest. Therefore they only deal with debt securities.
- FVTOCI may only be applied only to those equity securities that are neither held for trading nor as contingent consideration recognized by an acquirer in a business combination.
- The entity must make an irrevocable election when the investment is initially recognized.
- While changes in fair value are recognized in OCI, dividends are recognized in profit or loss.

When an equity investment is measured at FVTOCI, impairment losses are recognized in profit or loss. Subsequent to an impairment loss, recoveries in fair value, to the extent of previously recognized impairment losses, are recognized in income. Increases in fair value in excess of previously recognized impairment losses are recognized in OCI. All other investments in financial instruments (all equity and some debt) are reported at **fair value.** They are remeasured to fair value at the end of each accounting period, with unrealized gains and losses recognized in *income*. This is often referred to as the **fair value through profit or loss method** or **FVTPL**.

Under IFRS, accounting for **impairment** depends on the nature of the financial asset.

For ***financial assets accounted for using the FVTPL*** approach, any impairment is included in the adjustment of the instrument to its fair value and is recognized in *income*.

For purchased financial assets and those that are credit impaired at inception, expected credit losses are taken into account when the financial asset is originally recognized, increasing or decreasing the effective interest rate. Changes in expected losses identified after initial recognition of these financial assets are recognized in income and accumulated in an allowance account.

For financial assets accounted for at **amortized cost** and for those measured at **FVTOCI**, expected credit losses are recognized using a *loss allowance*.

In certain circumstances, the amount will be the expected credit losses for all credit related circumstances over the life of the instrument. This measurement is required to be used when either:
- The credit risk of the financial asset has increased significantly, or
- The financial asset is either a contract asset or trade receivable.

For all other financial assets, the amount will be based on the credit losses expected to result from defaults within a 12-month period.

When an investment is made in an entity over which it has significant influence, it is considered an investment in an **associate** (affiliate). An investment in an associate is accounted for under the **equity method** of accounting. Significant influence indicates that the investor has the authority and power to participate in policy decisions of the investee without having or sharing control of the entity.
- If the investor has control, consolidated financial statements are appropriate.
- If the investor shares control in a joint arrangement, the investment will be considered either a joint operation or a joint venture, which will determine the accounting.

A joint arrangement is considered a **joint venture** if those who share control also have rights to the net assets of the arrangement. Such an arrangement is referred to as a joint venture and is accounted for under the **equity method** of accounting.

When those with joint control do not also have rights to the net assets, the joint arrangement is referred to as a **joint operation** and is accounted for using a **proportionate consolidation** approach.
- The investor measures and recognizes a proportionate amount of the operation's assets, liabilities, revenues, and expenses for inclusion on its financial statements.
- Measurement and recognition is in accordance with the IFRS relevant to the particular assets, liabilities, revenues, or expenses.

Lecture 3.05

CLASS QUESTIONS

Please see the Class Questions and Class Solutions for this Lecture at the end of this Section.

CLASS QUESTIONS

Work through the below Class Questions while following along with the respective lectures. Once this is complete, you can begin independently practicing what you've learned by quizzing yourself on this course section in your Interactive Practice Questions (IPQ), which can be found in your online Student Dashboard. Your IPQ simulates the computer-based testing experience, and will also help you understand how concepts are applied to the exam. Each question includes answer explanations from expert CPAs that will help you determine why you answered a question correctly or incorrectly. This is key to your success on the CPA Exam.

Lecture 3.03

1. Sage, Inc. bought 40% of Adams Corp.'s outstanding common stock on January 2, 20X3, for $400,000. The carrying amount of Adams' net assets at the purchase date totaled $900,000. Fair values and carrying amounts were the same for all items except for plant and inventory, for which fair values exceeded their carrying amounts by $90,000 and $10,000, respectively. The plant has an eighteen-year life. All inventory was sold during 20X3. During 20X3, Adams reported net income of $120,000 and paid a $20,000 cash dividend. Assume that Sage uses the equity method to account for this investment. What amount should Sage report in its income statement from its investment in Adams for the year ended December 31, 20X3?

    a. $48,000
    b. $42,000
    c. $36,000
    d. $32,000

2. Park Co. uses the equity method to account for its January 1, 20X3 purchase of Tun Inc.'s common stock. On January 1, 20X3, the fair values of Tun's FIFO inventory and land exceeded their carrying amounts. How do these excesses of fair values over carrying amounts affect Park's reported equity in Tun's 20X3 earnings?

	Inventory Excess	Land Excess
a.	Decrease	Decrease
b.	Decrease	No effect
c.	Increase	Increase
d.	Increase	No effect

3. On January 1, 20X3, Point, Inc. purchased 10% of Iona Co.'s common stock. Point purchased additional shares bringing its ownership up to 40% of Iona's common stock outstanding on August 1, 20X3. During October 20X3, Iona declared and paid a cash dividend on all of its outstanding common stock. Point uses the equity method to account for its investment in Iona. How much income from the Iona investment should Point's 20X3 income statement report?

    a. 10% of Iona's income for January 1 to July 31, 20X3, plus 40% of Iona's income for August 1 to December 31, 20X3.
    b. 40% of Iona's income for August 1 to December 31, 20X3 only.
    c. 40% of Iona's 20X3 income.
    d. Amount equal to dividends received from Iona.

Cost and Equity Method — Section 3

4. On January 2, 20X3, Well Co. purchased 10% of Rea, Inc.'s outstanding common shares for $400,000. Well is the largest single shareholder in Rea, and Well's officers are a majority on Rea's board of directors. Rea reported net income of $500,000 for 20X3, and paid dividends of $150,000. Well does not elect the fair value option to report its investment in Rea. In its December 31, 20X3 balance sheet, what amount should Well report as investment in Rea?

    a. $450,000
    b. $435,000
    c. $400,000
    d. $385,000

5. Under IFRS an equity investment is considered an investment in an associate if the investor has significant influence over the investee. Significant influence is indicated by

    a. Ownership of at least 10%.
    b. Ownership of at least 20% but no more than 50%.
    c. Having the power to participate in the decisions of the investee.
    d. Having the power to direct the activities of the investee.

CLASS SOLUTIONS

1. (b) Sage's unadjusted equity in Adams' earnings is 40% x $120,000, or $48,000. This amount must be adjusted for any differences between the book and fair values of Adams' total assets at the time of Sage's investment, prorated by Sage's ownership percentage. Since the fair values of Adams' plant and inventory exceeded their book values by $90,000 and $10,000, respectively, these differences will be prorated by Sage's ownership percentage and either expensed in the year(s) sold, which is the case with inventory, or amortized over the depreciable life of the asset, which is the case with plant. Therefore, Sage will reduce equity in earnings by $2,000 as an adjustment for plant (($90,000 / 18) x 40% = $2,000) and will reduce equity in earnings by $4,000 as an adjustment for inventory, which was all sold during the year ($10,000 x 40% = $4,000). Sage will report equity in earnings from its investment in Adams of $48,000 - $2,000 - $4,000, or $42,000.

2. (b) Similar to consolidation, under the equity method, when assets or liabilities of the investee are under- or over-valued at the acquisition date, the investor's share of the investee's net income is adjusted to reflect income as if the items had been reported at their fair values on the acquisition date. If the inventory had been adjusted, since the investee uses FIFO, those goods would have been sold in the following year, increasing cost of sales and decreasing earnings. Land is not depreciated and has no income statement effect unless it is impaired or disposed of.

3. (b) When an investor obtains the ability to exercise significant influence over an investee during the period, often as a result of an increase in ownership, the investor applies the equity method to the investment on a prospective basis only. Therefore, the equity method only becomes effective August 1, when Point became a 40% owner of Iona. With 40% ownership, Point records equity in earnings of 40% of Iona's income from August 1 onward.

4. (b) Although an owner of less than 20% of the equity of another entity does not generally have the ability to exercise significant influence over the investee, other factors, such as being the largest single shareholder and occupying the majority of the seats on the board of directors, when combined with a smaller ownership percentage, will generally result in that ability. As a result, in this case, Well will apply the equity method and will recognize 10% of Rea's income as an increase in the investment and 10% of the dividends paid by Rea as a reduction.

Initial investment	$400,000
Income (10% of $500,000)	50,000
Dividends (10% of $150,000)	(15,000)
Ending balance	$435,000

5. (c) Under both GAAP and IFRS, the equity method is applied when an entity has the ability to exercise significant influence over the investee. Under IFRS, that is considered to be the case when the investor has the power to participate in the decisions of the investee. Answer (a) is incorrect because ownership of 10% would not give an investor significant influence over an investee under either GAAP or IFRS unless other factors contributed to that influence. Answer (b) is incorrect because under US GAAP, not IFRS, ownership of at least 20% but no more than 50% would be an indication of significant influence unless other factors indicated otherwise. Answer (d) is incorrect because the power to direct activities of an investee is an indication of control, which would require consolidation, not significant influence.

Lecture 3.05

TASK-BASED SIMULATIONS

Task-Based Simulation 1

Scenario

Johnson, an investor in Acme Co., asked Smith, CPA for advice on the propriety of Acme's financial reporting for two of its investments. Smith obtained the following information related to the investments from Acme's December 31, 20X7, financial statements:

- 20% ownership interest in Kern Co., represented by 200,000 shares of outstanding common stock purchased on January 2, 20X7, for $600,000.
- 20% ownership interest in Wand Co., represented by 20,000 shares of outstanding common stock purchased on January 2, 20X7, for $300,000.
- On January 2, 20X7, the carrying values of the acquired shares of both investments equaled their purchase price.
- Kern reported earnings of $400,000 for the year ended December 31, 20X7, and declared and paid dividends of $100,000 during 20X7.
- Wand reported earnings of $350,000 for the year ended December 31, 20X7, and declared and paid dividends of $60,000 during 20X7.
- On December 31, 20X7, Kern's and Wand's common stock were trading over-the counter at $18 and $20 per share, respectively.
- The investment in Kern is accounted for using the *equity method*.
- The investment in Wand is accounted for as *available-for-sale securities*.

Smith recalculated the amounts reported in Acme's December 31, 20X7, financial statements, and determined that they were correct. Stressing that the information available in the financial statements was limited, Smith advised Johnson that, assuming Acme properly applied generally accepted accounting principles, Acme may have appropriately used two different methods to account for its investments in Kern and Wand, even though the investments represent equal ownership interests.

Required:

Complete the schedule indicating the amounts Acme should report for the two investments in its December 31, 20X7, balance sheet (1a & 2a) and statement of income (1b & 2b) and comprehensive income (1c & 2c). Show all calculations. Ignore income taxes.

Items to be answered:

Carrying Value on Balance Sheet	Answers:
Kern investment on B/S	**1a.**
Wand investment on B/S	**2a.**
Income on Income Statement (I/S)	
Kern investment	**1b.**
Wand investment	**2b.**
Other comprehensive income (OCI)	
Kern investment	**1c.**
Wand investment	**2c.**

Cost and Equity Method — Section 3

Task-Based Simulation 2

Required:

On January 2, 20X4, Bing Co. purchased 39,000 shares of Latt Co.'s 200,000 shares of outstanding common stock for $585,000. On that date, the carrying amount of the acquired shares on Latt's books was $405,000. Bing attributed the excess of cost over carrying amount to goodwill. Bing's policy is to evaluate goodwill each period for impairment. As of December 31, 20X4, goodwill has not been impaired.

During 20X4, Bing's president gained a seat on Latt's board of directors. Latt reported earnings of $400,000 for the year ended December 31, 20X4, and declared and paid dividends of $100,000 during 20X4. On December 31, 20X4, Latt's common stock was trading over-the-counter at $15 per share.

Items to be answered:

1. What criteria should Bing consider in determining whether to account for its investment in Latt under the equity method? Is the equity method consistent with accrual accounting? Explain.

2. Assuming Bing accounts for the investment using the equity method, prepare a schedule of the amounts related to this investment to be reported on Bing's income statement for the year ended 20X4 and the amount in the investment in Latt account in the balance sheet at December 31, 20X4. Show all computations. Disregard income taxes.

Task-Based Simulation 3

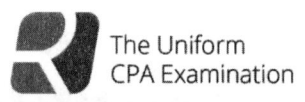   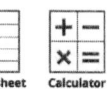

A company accounting for an equity investment under the equity method is preparing its income statement and is trying to determine what amount should be included as income from the investee. Identify the location in professional standards that indicates that, under the equity method, the investor recognizes its share of the earnings or loss of the investee.

Task-Based Simulation 4

 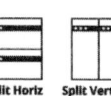

A company's investment in an unaffiliated non-public entity is being accounted for under the cost method. The company is aware of the entity's earnings, a portion of which was received as a dividend. Identify the location in professional standards that indicates that, under the cost method, dividends are the basis for recognizing earnings from an investee.

TASK-BASED SIMULATION SOLUTIONS

Task-Based Simulation Solution 1

Carrying Value on Balance Sheet	Answers:
Kern investment on B/S	1a. $660,000
Wand investment on B/S	2a. $400,000
Income on Income Statement (I/S)	
Kern investment	1b. $80,000
Wand investment	2b. $12,000
Other comprehensive income (OCI)	
Kern investment	1c. $0
Wand investment	2c. $100,000

1. Under the equity method of accounting, Acme would account for the investment in **KERN** as follows:

    - The initial investment would be recorded at cost of $600,000.
    - Acme would recognize 20% of Kern's $400,000 in income, or $80,000 as an increase in the investment and on the income statement as "equity in earnings of Kern".
    - Acme would recognize 20% of Kern's $100,000 in dividends, or $20,000, as a decrease in the investment.

    Carrying amount = $600,000 + $80.000 -$20,000 = $660,000

As a result, your solution should indicate:
Acme's **Balance Sheet** would report an investment in Kern of $660,000.

Acquisition of investment in KERN at cost:

Investment	$600	
Cash		$600

Investor records % of earnings ($400,000 annual income x 20% = $80,000)

Investment	$80	
Equity in earnings		$80 (I/S account) (1b.)

% of Cash dividend ($100,000 is dividend received x 20% = 20)

Cash	$20	
Investment		$20

The **T-account** for the investment under the equity method would look as follows:

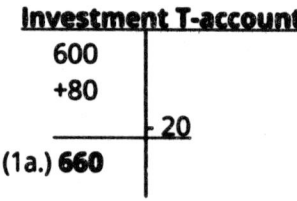

So for KERN,
    1a. $660,000
    1b. $80,000
    1c. $0 (no effect on comprehensive income)

2. Under the Available for Sale (AFS) method of accounting, Acme would account for the investment in **WAND** as follows:

To purchase:

Investment in Wand	**300**	
Cash		300

At 12/x7 the FMV is now 400 (20,000 x $20). Since we want to keep the security at FMV, we can either increase the investment account, or set up a valuation allowance account.

Market adjustment	**300**	
AFS security (B/S)	100	
Unrealized gain **(B/S)**		100 (OCI) (2)

The market adjustment account is on the B/S and increases the carrying value of the available-for-sale security in the asset section from $300 to $400 (2a); the unrealized gain is ALSO on the B/S as part of other comprehensive income in the equity section of $100 (2c).

The dividends received would be recorded as cash and dividend income on the income statement of $60,000 x 20% = $12,000 (2b)

Cash **(B/S)**	12	
Dividend Income **(I/S)**		12 (2b)

As an investment is available for sale securities, Acme would account for the investment in Wand as follows:
- The initial investment would be recorded at cost of $300,000.
- Acme would not recognize any portion of Wand's $350,000 in income.
- Acme would recognize 20% of Wand's $60,000 in dividends, or $12,000, as dividend income on the income statement.
- Since Wand's shares were trading for $20 per share at 12/31/x7, the investment would be adjusted to its market value of 20,000 x $20 or $400,000. The adjustment of $100,000 would be an unrealized gain reported after net income as a component of other comprehensive income.

As a result, your solution should indicate:

2a. - Acme's **Balance Sheet** would report an investment in Kern of $400,000.

2b, 2c, - Acme's **Statement of Income and Comprehensive Income** would report dividend income of $12,000 as a component of net income and an unrealized gain on Wand of $100,000 as a component of other comprehensive income (OCI).

Task-Based Simulation Solution 2

1. The primary criterion that Bing should consider in determining whether or not to use the equity method of accounting for its investment in Latt is whether or not Bing has the ability to exercise significant influence over the operating and financing policies of Latt. It is normally assumed that an investor has the ability to exercise significant influence when ownership is 20% or more. Despite the fact that Bing owns only 19 ½% of Latt's stock, the fact that Bing's president gained a seat on Latt's board of directors makes it likely that Bing will have the ability to exercise significant influence indicating the equity method of accounting.

The equity method of accounting is consistent with the accrual method of accounting since the investor recognizes its proportionate share of the investee's earnings in the period in which they are earned by the investee regardless of the period in which they are distributed.

2. Bing will report its proportionate share of Latt's earnings as Equity in income of Latt Co. on its income statement. It will be reported as a component of income from continuing operations.

Since Bing invested $585,000 for shares that had an underlying book value of $405,000, the difference of $180,000 will be attributed to goodwill, which has not been impaired. As a result, Bing's share of Latt's income will be:

Latt's reported income	$400,000
Bing's ownership percentage	19 ½ %
Bing's share of Latt's reported income	$ 78,000

Bing will report the investment as a long-term investment in the noncurrent asset section of its balance sheet. Under the equity method, the investment is initially recorded at its cost. It is increased by the investor's share of the investee's income and decreased by its share of dividends.

Initial investment	$585,000
Equity in earnings of Latt Co. (above)	78,000
	663,000
Dividends - $100,000 x 19 ½%	19,500
Investment at 12/31/X4	$643,500

Task-Based Simulation Solution 3

| FASB ASC | 323 | 10 | 35 | 4 |

Task-Based Simulation Solution 4

| FASB ASC | 325 | 20 | 35 | 1 |

Section 4 - Marketable Securities
Corresponding Lectures

Watch the following course lectures with this section:

Lecture 4.01 – Marketable Securities - Trading
Lecture 4.02 – Marketable Securities – Available For Sale
Lecture 4.03 – Trading vs. Available For Sale – Class Questions
Lecture 4.04 – Sale of AFS and Impairment Loss
Lecture 4.05 – Held to Maturity and Fair Value Accounting
Lecture 4.06 – Marketable Securities – Class Questions
Lecture 4.07 – Investments under IFRS – Marketable Securities

EXAM NOTE: *Please refer to the AICPA FAR Blueprint in the Introduction to find a listing of the representative tasks (and their associated skill levels—i.e., Remembering and Understanding, Application, and Analysis) that the candidate should be able to perform based on the knowledge obtained in this section.*

Marketable Securities

Lecture 4.01

TYPES OF MARKETABLE SECURITIES

When an investment is made in securities (debt or equity) that are **publicly traded**, and the investment is not large enough to provide the investor with any significant influence over the investee, the accounting for the investment will depend on the classification (**ASC 320**):
- Trading securities
- Available-for-sale securities
- Held-to-maturity securities

Trading Securities (HFT – Held For Trading) are investments in equity instruments, such as stocks, options, rights warrants or debt instruments, such as bonds, which the investor has acquired in an attempt to make profits by buying and selling within a short period of time. These are normally classified as current assets.

Available-For-Sale (AFS/AVS) securities are all investments in marketable equity or debt instruments that do not fit the definitions of HTM or trading securities. These may be classified as current or noncurrent assets, depending on the expected date of sale. If the holding period of the securities is indefinite, they should be classified as noncurrent assets.

Held-To-Maturity (HTM) securities are investments in bonds and other debt instruments which the investor has the ability and intent to hold until the due date for repayment. These are classified as noncurrent assets (unless the maturity date is less than one year from the balance sheet date).

As a result, there are two different categories for equity securities (these cannot be HTM securities), and three categories for debt securities. They are categorized based on **management's intentions.**

Trading Securities (HFT)

When trading securities are acquired, they are recorded at cost. Since they are being purchased for the purpose of generating *profits from resale*, they are a *form of inventory*, and transactions are normally reported in the *operating activities* section of the statement of cash flows.

Due to the marketable nature of these securities, and the intention to sell them in the near future, fluctuations in market price are taken into account in reported net income each period, even for securities that have not been sold during the period. The carrying values of the securities are adjusted to market price on a continuous basis.

Trading securities are purchased for the purpose of selling in the near term. They are:
- Current asset on the balance sheet if operating and noncurrent if investing.
- Include both debt and equity securities (bonds & stocks)
- Initially recorded at cost, but carried at FMV (ASC 320)
- Any **unrealized gains and losses** (temporary) appear on the **income statement**
- Realized gains and losses are always on the Income statement along with Interest and dividend income.

- The acquisition and disposal of trading securities is normally an **operating activity** on the statement of cash flows
    - According to FASB ASC 320, trading securities can be classified as either *operating* cash flows or *investing* cash flows based on the nature and purpose for which the securities were acquired. If current, normally operating.

CLASS EXAMPLE:

Purchase price, 1/1/X1	$100
FMV, 12/31/X1	$140
FMV, 12/31/X2	$ 90

To purchase:

Investment in trading securities	100	
Cash		100

At 12/X1 the FMV is now 140. Since we want to keep the security at FMV, we can either increase the investment account, or set up a valuation allowance account.

Market Adjustment - Trading Security (B/S)	40	
Unrealized gain **(I/S)**		40

The market adjustment account is on the B/S and increases the carrying value of the trading security in the current asset section; the unrealized gain is on the income statement as part of income from continuing operations.

At 12/X2 the FMV is now 90. **We have a loss of 50 (140 – 90)**

Unrealized Loss **(I/S)**	50	
Market Adjustment – Trading Security (B/S)		50

Note: the income statement effect in X1 is $40, and in X2 is ($50). These amounts represent the current year effects only since they are both Income statement items.

Lecture 4.02

Available For Sale Securities (AFS/AVS)

AFS securities are similar to trading securities in that they are likely to be sold some day, and since they are marketable, changes in market price are reflected on the balance sheet on a continuous basis. Since they were not, however, purchased primarily to gain short-term profits from resale, they are not considered to be inventory, and purchases and sales are reported in investing activities. Also, fluctuations in price are not reported in net income until the securities are sold. Instead, they are considered part of other comprehensive income, and are reported directly in stockholders' equity immediately below retained earnings in a section called "accumulated other comprehensive income."

Marketable Securities
Section 4

Available for sale securities are either debt or equity securities that don't fall into the other two categories.
- Current or noncurrent (if holding period is indefinite, assume noncurrent)
- Include both debt and equity securities
- Initially recorded at cost, but carried at FMV (ASC 320)
- Any **unrealized gains and losses** appear on the **balance sheet** as part of **Comprehensive income** in the stockholders' equity section. The cumulative amount is called "accumulated other comprehensive income."
- Realized gains and losses are always on the income statement as well as interest and dividend income
- The acquisition and disposal of AFS investments is an **investing activity** on the statement of cash flows.

Same example as above, except for the treatment of the unrealized gain and loss.

To purchase:

Investment in AFS security	100	
Cash		100

At 12/X1 the FMV is now 140. Since we want to keep the security at FMV, we can either increase the investment account, or set up a valuation allowance account.

Market Adjustment - AFS Security (B/S)	40	
Unrealized gain **(B/S)**		40

The market adjustment account is on the B/S and increases the carrying value of the available-for-sale security in the asset section; the unrealized gain is ALSO on the B/S as part of comprehensive income in the equity section.

At 12/X2 the FMV is now 90. We have a loss of 50 (140 – 90).

Unrealized Loss **(B/S)**	50	
Market Adjustment – AFS Security **(B/S)**		50

Note: The unrealized gain in X1 is $40 called "other comprehensive income" (OCI), and in X2 $(50), however, the net unrealized loss in X2 on the B/S is only $10. Since it is a B/S account, we are concerned with the *cumulative balance*; this amount is called "accumulated other comprehensive income".

GAAP Statement of Comprehensive Income (ON-TIDe-N-OC)	20X1	20X2	
Operating Income			
Non-operating	40	(50)	If Trading, goes here
Taxes			
Income continuing operations			
Discontinued Operations			
Net Income	100	200	300 to RE
Other Comprehensive Income (OCI)	**40**	**(50)**	**(10) Accumulated OCI**
Comprehensive Income	140	150	290 net effect on B/S

This may be presented as a single statement of comprehensive income, as above, or in two separate statements.

- The first statement is the **income statement**, or 'statement of earnings' or 'statement of operations.' It includes all components leading to net income or 'earnings.'

- The second statement is the **statement of comprehensive income**. It is required to immediately follow the income statement when both statements are presented. It includes net income, components of other comprehensive income, a total for other comprehensive income, and the grand total of both net income and other comprehensive income. This grand total is comprehensive income.

Lecture 4.03

CLASS QUESTIONS

Please see the Class Questions and Class Solutions for this Lecture at the end of this Section.

Lecture 4.04

Sale of Available For Sale (AFS) Security

When the investment in **AFS is sold**, the difference between the cost and the proceeds is treated as a **realized gain/loss**. **Ignore** the allowance account and adjust to the new target balance without the security that was just sold, unless it is the last investment, then the allowance and the unrealized gain/loss must both be eliminated.

Impairment Loss – "Other Than Temporary"

Investment in marketable securities that are accounted for as trading securities would not be subject to impairment loss. Since they are reported at market value and unrealized gains and losses are already recognized in income, any impairment would be recognized in the ordinary course of accounting for them.

Investments in marketable debt securities that are accounted for as held-to-maturity would be subject to an impairment loss if the investor had reason to believe that the issuer of the debt security would not make all principal and interest payments as scheduled. Since the investor intends to hold the securities until they mature, fluctuations in the market value of the securities would not affect the cash flows that the investor will receive and, as a result, not affect the carrying value of the investment.

Investments in marketable securities that are accounted for as available for sale securities are subject to impairment loss. They are impaired when there is a decline in value that is considered "other than temporary". Although the investment will already be written down to its market value at the balance sheet date, the portion of the unrealized loss that represents the nontemporary decline will be recognized in income.
- The **amount** will be the difference between the investment's original cost and the declined value from which it is not expected to recover.
- That amount will be reclassified out of other comprehensive income and recognized as a **loss** in calculating **net income**.
- Once written down, recoveries will **not be recognized.**
    - The security is written down to **FMV**
    - The loss is treated as a **realized loss** on the income statement, and the remaining balance is considered to be the new cost.

```
Loss                              X (I/S)
    Investment in AFS                         X
```

A 2 step process is applied to determine if a decline in value is other than temporary, requiring an adjustment:
- **Step 1 – Determine whether an investment is impaired**
    - If the Fair value is less than its Cost, the investment is considered to be impaired.
- **Step 2 – Evaluate whether an impairment is Other-Than-Temporary**

Different approaches are used for investments in equity securities and investments in debt securities when determining if an impairment is other than temporary.
- For investments in equity securities, indications that an impairment is other than temporary include a series of operating losses, or the inability of an investee to maintain an earnings capacity that is sufficient to justify the carrying value.
    - If the investor intends to sell the investment before it recovers in value, an impairment is considered nontemporary and recognized in the period in which the decision is made to sell the investment.
    - If the investor does not intend to sell the investment, the loss is recognized in the period in which the loss that is considered nontemporary occurs.
- For debt securities;
    - If the entity intends to sell the security, a nontemporary loss is considered to have occurred.
    - If the entity does not intend to sell the security, a nontemporary loss will be recognized if it is more likely than not that the entity will be required to sell the security before the value is recovered or if the present value of the amount expected to be recovered is less than the carrying value.

If a decline is determined to be other than temporary, **the amount of loss will be:**
- For *equity securities*, the difference between the fair value at the balance sheet date and the cost of the investment.
- For *debt securities*:

- If the investor expects to sell, or to be required to sell the security before recovery, the difference between the fair value at the balance sheet date and the amortized cost.
- If the investor does not expect to sell, or be required to sell the security before recovery, a portion of the loss attributable to credit factors will be recognized in earnings and the remainder, attributable to other factors, will be recognized in other comprehensive income.

Reclassifications

Reclassifications between *Trading and AFS* may sometimes occur as a result of changes in management's intentions (ASC 320).

Securities may be reclassified from one of the categories to another, and the accounting approaches vary depending on the old and new classifications. Exam testing has been on reclassifications between trading securities and AFS securities. The approach is to treat the securities as if they are being sold from the portfolio they are leaving, then repurchased at the current market price into the portfolio they are entering. In other words, current market price is used to determine the transfer.
- Reclassify at **FMV**
- The difference is treated as a **realized** gain/loss on the income statement.
- Eliminate any related valuation allowance accounts.

Reclassifications between *Held to Maturity and AFS*
- Reclassify at **FMV**
- If HTM to AFS then record in Other Comprehensive Income (OCI)
- If AFS to HTM then the unrealized holding gain/loss is reported on the **B/S** as part of Comprehensive income and amortized over the remaining life of the security.

In some circumstances, an investment that may have been accounted for as AFS will qualify for accounting under the equity method.

For example, assume an investor has an investment in a marketable equity security that is accounted for as an available for sale security. The investment was obtained at a cost of $1,200,000 in 20X1 and had a fair value of $1,350,000 as of the end of 20X1. The increase in value of $150,000 represents an unrealized holding gain that will have been recognized with an increase or decrease to the investment and the recognition of a corresponding unrealized gain or loss in comprehensive income.

The entry to record the acquisition would be

20X1	Investment in available-for sale securities	1,200,000	
	Cash		1,200,000

At the end of 20X1, the investment was worth $1,350,000. The entry is:

12/31/X1	Investment in available for sale securities	150,000	
	Unrealized gain due to increase in value of available for sale securities		150,000

Marketable Securities — Section 4

The unrealized gain would be reported as a component of other comprehensive income and closed into the equity account entitled accumulated other comprehensive income.

12/31/X1	Unrealized gain due to increase in value of available for sale securities	150,000	
	Accumulated other comprehensive income (B/S)		150,000

Assume that in 20X2, the investor became a member of the board of directors and determined that the ability to significantly influence the investee had been achieved, qualifying the investment for the equity method of accounting. Since no additional investment had been made, the investment would be reclassified from an available for sale security to an equity investment. In addition, the unrealized gain that had been recognized in the previous period will be reclassified from accumulated other comprehensive income and reported in the current period's earnings.

20X2	Accumulated other comprehensive income	150,000	
	Gain due to increase in value of investment		150,000 (I/S)

Lecture 4.05

Held to Maturity (HTM)
Bonds the company has both the intent and ability to hold until maturity.

An HTM security is initially recorded at cost, and the difference between the cost and maturity value is amortized over the life of the security, using the effective rate method discussed in the bond section. The straight-line method may be used if it doesn't materially differ. Interest income is recognized in each period.

Since HTM securities are not going to be sold, fluctuations in market price are ignored, and they are always carried at the amortized cost. In the rare cases where these securities are not held to maturity (such as when the issuer exercises a call provision compelling the investor to redeem them early), an ordinary gain or loss on disposal results. Purchases and sales (redemptions) of these securities are investing activities on the statement of cash flows.
- Non-current, unless maturity date is less than one year from the balance sheet date.
- Bonds only (no stocks)
- Record at cost
- Carry at **Amortized cost** (face net of unamortized discount or premium)
- Unrealized gains/losses – not applicable
- Realized gains/losses shouldn't happen, but could
- Report interest income net of amortization on the Income Statement
- Investing activity on the statement of cash flows
- Considered held to maturity if sale occurs after at least 85% of principle has been collected.

Marketable Securities Overview

	Trading securities (HFT)	**Available for sale (AFS)**	**Held to maturity (HTM)**
B/S	Current only Debt/equity FMV	Current/non-current Debt/equity FMV *Unrealized gains/losses on B/S as part of comprehensive income	Non-current (current) Debt only Amortized cost
I/S	*Unrealized gains/losses Realized gain/loss Interest & dividend income	Realized gain/loss Interest & dividend income	Realized gain/loss Interest income
Cash Flows	Operating activity	Investing activity	Investing Activity

FAIR VALUE ACCOUNTING OPTION (ASC 825)

FASB ASC Topic 825, Financial Instruments, allows an entity to value various **eligible items** at **fair value** at certain dates, referred to as **election dates**.

Eligible items include:
- Most recognized **financial instruments**
    - Applies to both financial assets and financial liabilities
    - Does not apply to certain instruments
        - Subsidiaries or VIEs required to be consolidated
        - Deferred compensation arrangements including pension or other postretirement or post-employment obligations and stock option or stock purchase plans
        - Assets or liabilities recognized under leases
        - Deposit liabilities of depository institutions
        - Financial instruments classified as a component of stockholders' equity
- Firm commitments involving only financial instruments that would not be recognized at inception
- If a reporting entity has an equity interest in an entity that reports net asset value per share, ASC 820 allows the reporting entity, as a practical expedient, to report the investment at its published net asset value per share.
- Written loan commitments
- Rights and obligations under insurance contracts or warranties when certain requirements are met:
    - The insurance contract or warranty is not a financial instrument
    - The insurer or warrantor is allowed by the terms to pay a third party to provide goods or services to settle the obligation

A **financial instrument** can be cash, a security representing an ownership interest in another entity, or a contract that has two components:
- It represents a potential financial liability for one party by imposing an obligation to do one of the following:
    - Deliver cash or another financial instrument to another entity
    - Exchange other financial instruments with the other entity on potentially unfavorable terms
- It represents a potential financial asset for the other party by conveying a right to one of the following:
    - Receive cash or another financial instrument from the other entity
    - Exchange other financial instruments with the other entity on potentially favorable terms

The fair value option may be elected for eligible items only on election dates. In addition to when the entity first recognizes an item, **election dates** include:
- The date on which the entity enters into an eligible firm commitment
- When an item that was reported at fair value due to specialized accounting principles, with unrealized gains or losses reported in earnings, no longer qualify for the specialized accounting treatment
- An investment that becomes subject to the equity method or a retained interest in a subsidiary or VIE that no longer qualifies for consolidation
- A circumstance requiring the item to be reported at fair value at a point in time but not at each reporting date, other than an impairment

An election date also occurs when *an event* requires an eligible item to be reported at fair value or to be recognized initially, such as:
- Business combinations
- Consolidation or deconsolidation of a VIE
- Significant debt modifications

The fair value option can be elected on an instrument-by-instrument basis. Electing the fair value option for a particular instrument does not require election for a similar instrument held by the same entity.

Some of the specific applications of the fair value option include the following:
- An investment accounted for under the **equity method** would be reported at fair value on each balance sheet date, increases or decreases will be recognized as unrealized gains or losses on the income statement, and dividends received will be recognized as income.
- **Available for sale securities** will be reported at fair value on each balance sheet date, as already required. Unrealized gains or losses are reported as a component of net income, however, instead of other comprehensive income.
- **Trading securities** are not affected.
- **Held to maturity** securities continue to be accounted for at amortized cost, recognizing interest income under the effective interest method. In addition, the carrying value is adjusted to fair value on each balance sheet date with the increase or decrease recognized as a component of net income.

Once the fair value option is elected, it is **irrevocable** until a subsequent election date.

Disclosures under Fair Value Accounting Option

When an entity elects the *fair value option*, certain disclosures are required as of each balance sheet date.
- Management's reasons for electing the fair value option for each item for which the election was made
- If elected for some, but not all, items within a group of similar items, a description of the similar items, the reasons for a partial election, and how the similar items affect line items on the statement of financial position
- The differences between fair value amounts and principal balances of receivables or payables with contractual principal amounts
- Disclosures required when applying the fair value option for investments that would have been accounted for under the equity method if the fair value election had not been made

Disclosures are also required for each period for which an income statement is presented:
- Amounts of each gain or loss recognized in earnings as a result of changes in fair values
- An indication as to where interest and dividends are reported on the income statement and how they are measured
- For receivables held as assets, the gains or losses resulting from changes in the instrument's credit risk, including how it is measured
- For liabilities affected by changes in the instrument's credit risk during the period, the gains or losses resulting from changes in the instruments credit risk, reasons for the change, and how the gains or losses are measured

Lecture 4.06

CLASS QUESTIONS

Please see the Class Questions and Class Solutions for this Lecture at the end of this Section.

Lecture 4.07

INVESTMENTS IN FINANCIAL INSTRUMENTS OF OTHER ENTITIES UNDER IFRS

IFRS defines a **financial instrument** as any contract that results in a financial asset of one entity and a financial liability or equity instrument of another entity.

A **financial asset** is:
- Cash
- An equity instrument of another entity
- A contractual right:
    - To receive cash or another financial asset from another entity; or
    - To exchange financial assets or financial liabilities with another entity on potentially favorable terms
- A contract that will be settled in the entity's own equity instruments

A **financial liability** is:
- A contractual obligation:
    - To deliver cash or another financial asset to another entity; or

- To exchange financial assets or financial liabilities with another entity on potentially unfavorable terms
- A contract that will be settled in the entity's own equity instruments

Financial assets and liabilities are not **recognized** until an entity becomes a party to the contract that results in them.

Financial assets are generally measured at **fair value through profit or loss (FVTPL)**. When measured at FVTPL, increases or decreases in fair value are reported as gains or losses on the statement of operations (**Income Statement**).

Under certain circumstances, financial assets are measured at **amortized cost**. This is only the case if two conditions are met:
- The entity's business model is to hold the asset to collect scheduled cash flows
- The terms of the instrument call for cash flows that are exclusively payments of principal and interest on specified dates

When a financial asset is recognized under the amortized cost method, the entity is required to evaluate the asset for impairment at the end of each reporting period. The initial assessment is done by determining if there is objective evidence indicating that the financial asset has been impaired, which will be in the form of a loss event or events occurring since acquisition of the financial asset. *Examples of loss events* include those that normally surround significant financial difficulty on the part of the other party, including:
- Breach of contract, such as a default or delinquency
- Granting a concession to the borrower for economic or legal reasons related to the debtor's financial circumstances
- Likelihood of the debtor going into bankruptcy
- Inactivity of the market for the instrument due to the financial difficulty
- Observable data indicating an expected decrease in future cash flows
- Economic conditions contributing to defaults

When a financial asset recognized at amortized cost is impaired, the present value of the expected future cash flows will be measured.
- The asset is written down to that amount
- The difference is recognized as an impairment loss

An **impairment loss may be reversed** if the asset recovers in value. The recovery must be the result of an event occurring after the impairment and may not increase the asset above the amount that would have been recorded at its amortized cost if the impairment had not been recognized.

An entity may also **elect** to report financial assets at FVTPL that would otherwise be measured at amortized cost.
- The election must be made when the financial asset is first recognized.
- The election is irrevocable
- Fair value measurement must eliminate or reduce an inconsistency that would result from recognizing gains or losses on a different basis

In general, financial liabilities are measured at amortized cost. Certain liabilities may be measured under an alternate approach when it will result in more relevant information.
- Derivatives that are liabilities, and similar liabilities, are measured at FVTPL
- Financial guarantee contracts are measured at the higher of their original amount less accumulated amortization or amounts that would be recognized under the requirements for contingent liabilities

Similar to financial assets, an entity may elect to report financial liabilities at FVTPL.
- The election must be made when the financial liability is first recognized.
- The election is irrevocable.
- Doing so provides more relevant information.

Financial assets and liabilities that are **not** reported at FVTPL are initially recognized at their fair values adjusted for transaction costs directly attributable to the acquisition of a financial asset or issuance of a financial liability.

Gains and losses on financial assets or liabilities measured at fair value are generally recognized in profit or loss. That is not the case, however, when:
- The instrument is part of a hedging relationship, in which case hedge accounting would apply
- It is an investment in an equity instrument and the entity has elected to report gains and losses in other comprehensive income (OCI)
- It is a financial liability designated as FVTPL
    - Increases or decreases in value resulting from changes in credit risk are recognized in other comprehensive income
    - Remaining increases or decreases in value are recognized in profit or loss

Gains and losses on financial assets measured at amortized cost, other than that amount recognized as a result of amortization, are recognized when the financial asset is impaired, reclassified, or derecognized.

When an **investment in an equity instrument** is not held for trading, the entity may elect to recognize changes in **fair value** in other comprehensive income (FVTOCI) rather than in profit or loss.
- The election must be made at initial recognition
- The election is irrevocable
- Dividends are recognized in profit or loss

When an equity investment is measured at FVTOCI, impairment losses are recognized in profit or loss. Subsequent to an impairment loss, recoveries in fair value, to the extent of previously recognized impairment losses, are recognized in income. Increases in fair value in excess of previously recognized impairment losses are recognized in OCI.

Financial Investments

US GAAP	IFRS
• Marketable equity securities are classified as either Trading or Available for sale and marketable debt securities are classified as Trading, Available for sale, or Held to maturity.	• Marketable securities are reported at Fair value through profit or loss (FVTPL) or at amortized cost if the security consists of principal and interest and is expected to be held for the purpose of collecting the cash flows.
• For debt securities that are not held to maturity, a change in interest rate may cause a decline in fair value that will result in an impairment loss.	• Generally, only as a result of a loss event resulting from significant financial difficulty of other party to instrument is reported at amortized cost
• The cost basis of the investment is reduced as a result of an impairment loss and recoveries are not recognized	• Impairment losses in securities reported at amortized cost may be reversed upon occurrence of a recovery event.
• Loans, notes, and other receivables are measured at amortized cost if held for investment and lower of cost or fair value if held for sale. Either will be recognized at fair value if the fair value option is elected.	• Financial assets normally measured at *Fair Value* Through Profit or Loss (FVTPL) by electing the fair value option
• Compound (hybrid) financial instruments may be bifurcated, dividing them into debt and derivative components, but are not divided into debt and equity components.	• Compound (hybrid) financial interests (e.g., convertible bonds) are treated as a single contract and accounted for at amortized cost, as appropriate.

CLASS QUESTIONS

Work through the below Class Questions while following along with the respective lectures. Once this is complete, you can begin independently practicing what you've learned by quizzing yourself on this course section in your Interactive Practice Questions (IPQ), which can be found in your online Student Dashboard. Your IPQ simulates the computer-based testing experience, and will also help you understand how concepts are applied to the exam. Each question includes answer explanations from expert CPAs that will help you determine why you answered a question correctly or incorrectly. This is key to your success on the CPA Exam.

Lecture 4.03

1. Nola has a portfolio of marketable equity securities that it does not intend to sell in the near term. Assume Nola does not elect the fair value option to report these securities. How should Nola classify these securities, and how should it report unrealized gains and losses from these securities?

	Classify as	**Report as a**
a.	Trading securities	Component of income from continuing operations
b.	Available-for-sale securities	Separate component of other comprehensive income
c.	Trading securities	Separate component of other comprehensive income
d.	Available-for-sale securities	Component of income from continuing operations

2. Data regarding Ball Corp.'s available-for-sale securities follow:

	Cost	**Market Value**
December 31, 20X2	$150,000	$130,000
December 31, 20X3	150,000	160,000

    Differences between cost and market values are considered temporary. Ball does not elect the fair value option to account for available-for-sale securities. Ball's 20X3 other comprehensive income would be

    a. $30,000
    b. $20,000
    c. $10,000
    d. $ 0

Marketable Securities
Section 4

Lecture 4.06

Items 3 and 4 are based on the following:

Sun Corp. had investments in marketable debt securities costing $650,000 that were classified as available-for sale. On June 30, 20X3, Sun decided to hold the investments to maturity and accordingly reclassified them to the held-to-maturity category on that date. The investments' market value was $575,000 at December 31, 20X2, $530,000 at June 30, 20X3, and $490,000 at December 31, 20X3. Sun does not elect the fair value option to account for these investments.

3. What amount of loss from investments should Sun report in its 20X3 income statement?

   a. $ 45,000
   b. $ 85,000
   c. $120,000
   d. $0

4. What amount should Sun report as net unrealized loss on marketable debt securities in its 20X3 statement of stockholders' equity?

   a. $ 40,000
   b. $ 45,000
   c. $160,000
   d. $120,000

5. Alton Co. began operations on January 1, 20X8. The following information pertains to Alton's December 31, 20X8 portfolio of marketable equity securities:

	Trading Securities	Available-for-Sale Securities
Aggregate cost	$360,000	$550,000
Aggregate market value	320,000	450,000
Aggregate lower of cost or market value applied to each security in the portfolio	304,000	420,000

Alton uses the provisions of ASC 825 and elects the fair value option for all financial instruments. If the market declines are judged to be temporary, what amounts should Alton report as a loss on these securities in its December 31, 20X8 income statement?

	Trading Securities	Available-for-Sale Securities
a.	$40,000	$0
b.	$0	$100,000
c.	$40,000	$100,000
d.	$56,000	$130,000

6. Antonio Corp. has a portfolio of marketable equity securities that it does not intend to sell in the near term. Antonio elects the fair value option for reporting its financial assets in accordance with ASC 825. How should Antonio classify these securities, and how should it report unrealized gains and losses?

	Classify as	**Report as a**
a.	Trading securities	Component of income from continuing operations
b.	Available-for-sale securities	Separate component of other comprehensive income
c.	Trading securities	Separate component of other comprehensive income
d.	Available-for-sale securities	Component of income from continuing operations

7. In 20X2, Gem Corp, which prepares its financial statements in accordance with IFRS, made a $125,000 investment in marketable equity securities. The securities are not held for trading and Gem has elected to recognize changes in fair value in other comprehensive income rather than profit or loss. At December 31, 20X2, the investment had a fair value of only $95,000 and it was determined that it was required to recognize an impairment loss in income. At December 31, 20X3, the investment had a market value of $140,000. At what amount will the investment be reported on the balance sheet and how will the change be recognized by Gem?

    a. The investment will be reported at $125,000 and $30,000 will be reported in other comprehensive income.
    b. The investment will be reported at $140,000 and $45,000 will be reported in other comprehensive income.
    c. The investment will be reported at $140,000 and $30,000 will be recognized in profit or loss; $15,000 will be reported in other comprehensive income.
    d. The investment will be reported at $125,000 and $30,000 will be recognized in profit or loss.

CLASS SOLUTIONS

1. (b) Investments in marketable equity securities that an entity does not intend to sell in the near future are accounted for as available for sale. They are reported at their balance sheet market values and any decreases that are nontemporary and any increases are recognized in other comprehensive income until the investments are disposed of or reclassified. Trading securities, which are investments the entity does intend to sell in the near future, are also reported at their balance sheet market values but differences are recognized in income.

2. (a) The amount reported in other comprehensive for available for sale (AFS) investments is the increase or decrease in market value during the period. Since the AFS were reported at their market value of $130,000 at 12/31/X2, they would be increased to their 12/31/X3 market value of $160,000 with an increase to the investment and a credit (increase) to other comprehensive income for the difference of $30,000. However, the accumulated OCI would be $10,000, but that wasn't asked in this problem.

3. (d) When an investment in a debt security is reclassified from available for sale (AFS) to held to maturity (HTM), the transfer occurs at its market value on the date of transfer. Any unrealized holding gain or loss is recognized in other comprehensive income (OCI) and amortized as an adjustment to the effective interest rate on the HTM security. On the date of transfer, the market value of $530,000 is $120,000 lower than its $650,000 cost, which is recognized in OCI, but no portion is recognized in income.

4. (d) When an investment in a debt security is reclassified from available for sale (AFS) to held to maturity (HTM), the transfer occurs at its market value on the date of transfer. Any unrealized holding gain or loss is recognized in other comprehensive income (OCI) and amortized as an adjustment to the effective interest rate on the HTM security. On the date of transfer, the market value of $530,000 is $120,000 lower than its $650,000 cost, which is recognized in OCI, but no portion is recognized in income.

5. (c) When an entity elects the fair value option for all financial instruments, all changes in fair value are recognized in income regardless of whether the securities are classified as trading, available for sale (AFS), held to maturity, or otherwise. The trading securities had a cost of $360,000 and a fair value of $320,000, resulting in a loss of $40,000, which would be recognized in income regardless of whether or not the fair value option had been elected. The AFS securities had a cost of $550,000 and a fair value of $450,000 resulting in an unrealized loss of $100,000, which would also be reported in income.

6. (d) Electing the fair value option does not have any effect on how securities are classified. Since Antonio does not intend to sell the investment in the near term, they are considered available for sale (AFS) securities. Unrealized gains and losses on AFS securities are normally recognized as a component of other comprehensive income.

7. (c) When an entity elects to recognize changes in fair value of an equity instrument in other comprehensive income (OCI) rather than profit or loss, the investment is reported at its fair value on the balance sheet and any increases or decreases are recognized in OCI. This is not the case with impairments, which are recognized in profit or loss. When an investment for which changes are recognized in OCI increases in fair value, any previously recorded impairment losses are reversed. Any remaining increase is reported in OCI. Gem would have recognized an impairment loss of $30,000 in 20X2. In 20X3, the investment would be increased to its fair value of $140,000, representing a $45,000 increase. The loss of $30,000 would be reversed, resulting in a $30,000 gain in profit or loss. The remaining $15,000 is recognized in OCI.

Lecture 4.03

TASK-BASED SIMULATIONS

Task-Based Simulation 1

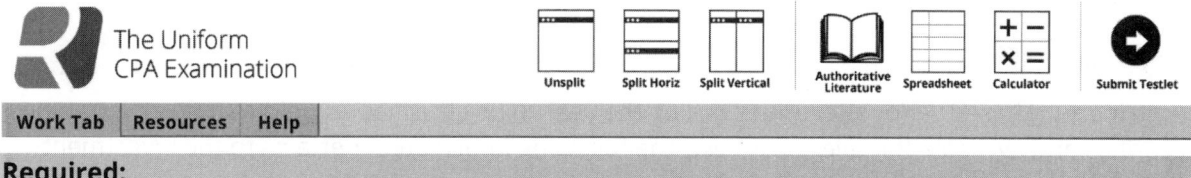

Required:

Items 1 through 4 are based on the following:

Camp Co. purchased various securities during 20X4 to be classified as held-to-maturity securities, trading securities, or available-for-sale securities.

Items to be answered:

Items 1 through 4 describe various securities purchased by Camp. For each item, select from the following list the appropriate category for each security.

- **H.** Held-to-maturity.
- **T.** Trading.
- **A.** Available-for sale.

1. Debt securities bought and held for the purpose of selling in the near term.

2. U.S. Treasury bonds that Camp has both the positive intent and the ability to hold to maturity.

3. $3 million debt security bought and held for the purpose of selling in three years to finance payment of Camp's $2 million long-term note payable when it matures.

4. Convertible preferred stock that Camp does not intend to sell in the near term.

Section 4   Marketable Securities

Lecture 4.06

Task-Based Simulation 2

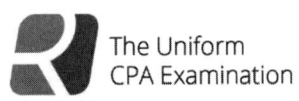

Required:

Dayle inc. purchased various securities during the year to be classified as held-to maturity, trading securities and available-for-sale securities. The following information pertains to the investment portfolio of marketable investments for the year ended December 31, 20X2:

	Cost	Fair value 12/31/X1	20X2 activity Purchases	Sales	Fair value 12/31/X2
Held-to-maturity securities					
Security ABC			$100,000		$95,000
Trading securities					
Security DEF	$150,000	$160,000			155,000
Available-for-sale securities					
Security GHI	190,000	165,000		$175,000	
Security JKL	170,000	175,000			160,000

Security ABC was purchased at par. All declines in fair value are considered to be temporary. Dayle, Inc. does not elect the fair value option for any of its financial assets.

For the following questions, choose from the answer list below.

Answer List

- A. $0
- B. $5,000
- C. $10,000
- D. $15,000
- E. $25,000
- F. $95,000
- G. $100,000
- H. $150,000
- I. $155,000
- J. $160,000
- K. $170,000

Marketable Securities   Section 4

Items to be answered:

Items 1 through 6 describe amounts to be reported in Dayle, Inc. 20X2 financial statements. For each item, select from the following list the correct numerical response. An amount may be selected once, more than once, or not at all. Ignore income tax considerations.

	Amount										
	(A)	(B)	(C)	(D)	(E)	(F)	(G)	(H)	(I)	(J)	(K)
1. Carrying amount of security ABC at December 31, 20X2.	○	○	○	○	○	○	○	○	○	○	○
2. Carrying amount of security DEF at December 31, 20X2.	○	○	○	○	○	○	○	○	○	○	○
3. Carrying amount of security JKL at December 31, 20X2.	○	○	○	○	○	○	○	○	○	○	○

Items 4 through 6 require a second response. For each item, indicate whether a gain or a loss is to be reported.

	Amount											Gain	Loss
	(A)	(B)	(C)	(D)	(E)	(F)	(G)	(H)	(I)	(J)	(K)		
4. Recognized gain or loss on sale of security GHI.	○	○	○	○	○	○	○	○	○	○	○	○	○
5. Unrealized gain or loss to be reported in 20X2 net income.	○	○	○	○	○	○	○	○	○	○	○	○	○
6. Unrealized gain or loss to be reported at December 31, 20X2, as a separate component of stockholders' equity entitled "accumulated other comprehensive income."	○	○	○	○	○	○	○	○	○	○	○	○	○

Task-Based Simulation 3

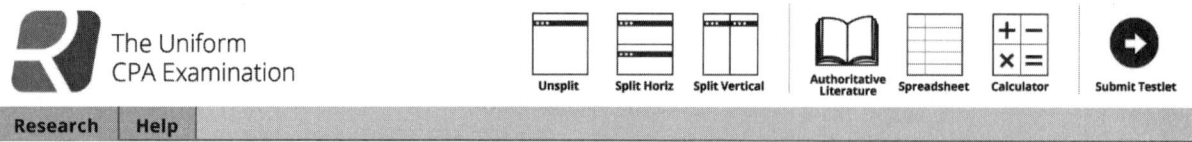
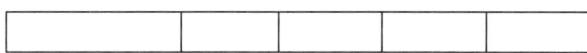

A company is accumulating funds for future expansion and has begun investing in debt and equity securities of other entities. Identify the location in professional standards that indicates how investments in debt and equity securities should be measured for balance sheets prepared subsequent to their acquisition.

Task-Based Simulation 4

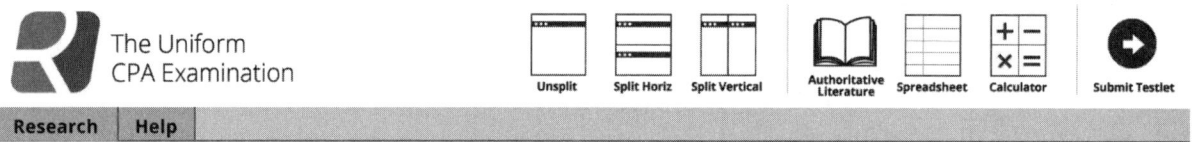
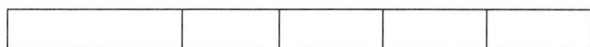

An entity has a note receivable from an unrelated entity that bears interest at a relatively high rate. They think it has increased in value due to a decline in market rates. Identify the location in professional standards that indicates when an entity may choose to elect the fair value option for an eligible item.

TASK-BASED SIMULATION SOLUTIONS

Task-Based Simulation Solution 1

1. **T** — Securities, whether debt or equity, that are acquired with the intention of selling them in the near term, are classified as trading securities.

2. **H** — When a company acquires debt securities, including U.S. Treasury bonds, that it has the intent and the ability to hold until maturity, they are classified as held-to-maturity.

3. **A** — Securities, whether debt or equity, that are acquired with the intent of holding them for a while, but ultimately selling them, are classified as securities available for sale.

4. **A** — An investment in equity securities cannot be classified as held-to-maturity. If they are expected to be sold in the near term, they will be classified as trading securities. If they are not intended to be sold in the near term, they are classified as securities available for sale.

Task-Based Simulation Solution 2

	Amount										
	(A)	(B)	(C)	(D)	(E)	(F)	(G)	(H)	(I)	(J)	(K)
1. Carrying amount of security ABC at December 31, 20X2.	○	○	○	○	○	○	●	○	○	○	○
2. Carrying amount of security DEF at December 31, 20X2.	○	○	○	○	○	○	○	○	●	○	○
3. Carrying amount of security JKL at December 31, 20X2.	○	○	○	○	○	○	○	○	○	●	○

	Amount											Gain	Loss
	(A)	(B)	(C)	(D)	(E)	(F)	(G)	(H)	(I)	(J)	(K)		
4. Recognized gain or loss on sale of security GHI.	○	○	○	●	○	○	○	○	○	○	○	○	●
5. Unrealized gain or loss to be reported in 20X2 net income.	○	●	○	○	○	○	○	○	○	○	○	○	●
6. Unrealized gain or loss to be reported at December 31, 20X2, as a separate component of stockholders' equity entitled "accumulated other comprehensive income."	○	○	●	○	○	○	○	○	○	○	○	○	●

Explanation of solutions

1. **(G; $100,000)** Debt securities classified as held-to-maturity are originally recorded at cost. Any discount or premium is then amortized using the effective interest method resulting in a carrying value at amortized cost. Since Security ABC was acquired at par, there is no discount or premium to amortize and the carrying amount will be the cost of $100,000.

2. **(I; $155,000)** Trading securities are reported at their fair market values as of the balance sheet date. Security DEF will be reported at its 12/31/X2 market value of $155,000.

3. **(J; $160,000)** Securities classifies as available for sale are reported at their fair market values as of the balance sheet date. Security JKL will be reported at its 12/31/X2 market value of $160,000.

4. **(D, L)** The amount of gain or loss recognized on the sale of a security classified as available for sale will be the realized gain or loss, equal to the difference between the sales price and the original cost. Security GHI had a sales price of $175,000 compared to an original cost of $190,000 resulting in a realized loss to be reported in the amount of $15,000.

    The journal entry to record the sale would be

Cash	175,000	
Realized loss on sale of AFS	15,000	
A-F-S securities		165,000
Unrealized loss on AFS (OCI)		25,000

5. **(B, L)** Unrealized gains or losses on trading securities are reported on the income statement. Security DEF, the only trading security, was adjusted to its market value of $160,000 at 12/31/X1. As of 12/31/X2, it will be reduced to its market value of $155,000 resulting in an unrealized loss of $5,000 to be reported in the income statement.

6. **(C, L)** The amount reported as a separate component of stockholders' equity is the cumulative amount of unrealized gain or loss on securities available for sale. As of 12/31/X2, the only security available for sale is security JKL with a cost of $170,000 and a carrying value equal to its market value of $160,000. The difference is an unrealized loss of $10,000 would be reported as both a valuation allowance reducing the investment account and as a separate component of stockholders' equity (accumulated other comprehensive income).

Task-Based Simulation Solution 3

| FASB ASC | 320 | 10 | 35 | 1 |

Task-Based Simulation Solution 4

| FASB ASC | 825 | 10 | 25 | 4 |

Section 5 - Financial Instruments & Derivatives

Section 5 – Financial Instruments & Derivatives

Corresponding Lectures

Watch the following course lectures with this section:

Lecture 5.01 – Financial Instruments and Derivatives
Lecture 5.02 – Fair Value vs. Cash Flow Hedge
Lecture 5.03 – Embedded Derivatives
Lecture 5.04 – Financial Instruments and Derivatives – Class Questions
Lecture 5.05 – Derivatives and Hedging Instruments under IFRS

EXAM NOTE: Please refer to the AICPA FAR Blueprint in the Introduction to find a listing of the representative tasks (and their associated skill levels—i.e., Remembering and Understanding, Application, and Analysis) that the candidate should be able to perform based on the knowledge obtained in this section.

Financial Instruments & Derivatives

Lecture 5.01

FINANCIAL INSTRUMENTS

Financial instruments include the following:
- **C**ash
- **O**wnership interests in an entity (e.g. stock)
- **D**erivative contracts that create a right and obligation to transfer other financial instruments (e.g. stock options).

Some financial instruments, including notes and loans receivable or payable, are generally reported at amortized cost. Investments in the equity securities of nonpublic companies are accounted for at cost or under a valuation approach, such as the equity method. Many financial instruments, including investments in certain marketable securities and all derivatives, should be reported on the financial statements at fair market value. Notice that, in the case of a contract that creates an obligation, the instrument may be a liability rather than an asset.

Investments in Derivatives (ASC 815)

Entities acquire derivatives for *three reasons.* They acquire them as investments, for arbitrage, or as hedges.

1. Investments – An entity may invest its excess working capital, or amounts set aside in sinking funds, in derivatives such as stock options to increase its return on investment. When an entity's stock options are publicly traded, they generally sell for substantially less than the security they provide the option to acquire. An increase in the value of the stock will result in a comparable increase in the value of the stock option.
- Based on a lower investment amount, the return is greater.
- If the value of the stock decreases, of course, there is a comparably disproportionate decrease in the value of the derivative, making it a relatively high risk investment.

2. Arbitrage – Arbitrage is the ability to take advantage of price differentials in separate markets allowing the entity to enter into transactions that are potentially profitable without significant risk of loss. If, for example, the 6 month future price of a commodity was $1, the entity may enter into a futures contract requiring it to buy 100,000 units at $1 at the end of six months. In another market, the 6 month future price may be $1.05 and the entity may enter into a futures contract requiring it to sell 100,000 units at $1.05 after six months. In reality, they will neither buy nor sell the commodity. Instead:
- If the market price is below $1, the entity will pay the difference between $1 and the market price to the counterparty in the buy contract. At the same time, the entity will receive the difference between $1.05 and the market price from the counterparty to the sell contract. As a result, the entity will earn the difference, $.05 per unit.
- If the market price is above $1.05, the entity will receive the difference between $1 and the market price from the counterparty in the buy contract. At the same time, the entity will pay the difference between $1.05 and the market price to the counterparty to the sell contract. As a result, the entity will earn the difference, $.05 per unit.

- If the market price is between $1 and $1.05, the entity will receive the difference between $1 and the market price from the counterparty in the buy contract. At the same time, the entity will receive the difference between $1.05 and the market price from the counterparty to the sell contract. As a result, the entity will earn the difference, $.05 per unit.

3. Hedge – A hedge is the use of a derivative to reduce or eliminate a risk that the entity is subject to either as a result of an asset or liability recognized on its financial statements or a future transaction. If, for example, an entity has a commitment for an asset being manufactured for it that is expected to be delivered in 6 months at a cost of 100,000 Foreign Currency Units or FCU (such as Euros or Pesos), which has an exchange rate of $1.25. In other words, 1 FCU will cost $1.25 and the cost of the machine is $125,000.

If the exchange rate of the FCU increases to $1.30, the asset will cost the entity $130,000 instead of $125,000, which may be more than the entity has budgeted for the acquisition. The entity may enter into a derivative such as a forward exchange contract under which it is required to acquire 100,000 FCUs at the end of 6 months at the exchange rate of $1.25 per FCU.
- If the exchange rate increases above $1.25, the entity will pay more for the asset but will receive the difference from the counterparty.
- If the exchange rate decreases below $1.25, the entity will pay less for the asset, but will be required to pay the difference to the counterparty.

As indicated, derivatives are acquired to increase potential gains when used as investments but may also produce losses. Derivatives are used as hedges to reduce or eliminate the risk of an adverse change in circumstances, but also eliminate the opportunity to take advantage of a favorable change.
- Derivatives may be assets or liabilities
- Derivatives are always reported at their *fair values*
- Unrealized gains and losses are generally recognized in income
    - Unrealized gains and losses on cash flow hedges are temporarily recognized in other comprehensive income instead of income
    - Unrealized gains and losses on fair value hedges are recognized in income along with offsetting losses or gains on the hedged item
    - All other unrealized gains and losses on hedges are recognized in income in the period of the increase or decrease in value

Derivatives are financial instruments that have the following three characteristics: (**NUNS**)
- **No net investment** – To be considered a derivative, there must either be no initial net investment or an initial net investment that is smaller than would normally be required for an instrument that would respond similarly in the market. Derivatives such as interest rate swaps, futures contracts, and forward exchange contracts often require no initial net investment or an investment that is limited to fees paid to attorneys and others to establish the derivative. Derivatives such as stock options require a smaller investment than the shares underlying the derivative yet will respond similarly to the shares as the value of the shares increase or decrease.
- **An Underlying and a Notional amount** – The notional amount is basically the number of units (units, bushels, pounds) and the underlying is the factor that affects the derivative's value (specified price, interest rate, exchange rate). In a forward exchange contract, for example, the notional amount would be the number of FCUs and the underlying would be the future exchange rate.

- **Net Settlement** – The derivative can be settled in a net amount. In the case of a forward exchange contract, for example, the entity does not actually buy or sell the FCUs but, instead, receives or pays the difference between the agreed upon exchange rate and the market rate. In the case of an interest rate swap, the parties don't pay each other the contractual interest amounts but the difference is paid from one party to the other.

Since one of the characteristics of a derivative is the requirement that it can be settled on a net basis, a derivative will always be settled by the transfer of a financial instrument. As a result, a derivative is always considered a financial instrument for financial reporting purposes.

- **Examples of Derivatives include:**
    - **Option contract** (has *right* but *not obligation* to purchase/sell in the future. Put-option, right to sell shares, Call-option, right to acquire shares in the future)
    - **Futures contract** (has *right and obligation* to deliver/purchase foreign currency or goods in the future at a price set today. Similar to a Forward contract normally traded on a national exchange)
    - **Forward contract** (has *right and obligation* to buy or sell a commodity at a future date for an agreed-upon price)
    - **Interest rate or foreign currency swap** (a forward-based contract or agreement between two counterparties to exchange streams of cash flows over a specified period in the future).

- Note: these instruments create **off-balance sheet risk**, due to the possible changes in amounts owed.
    - Disclose the **credit risk** – risk that a loss occurs because another party fails to perform according to the terms of a contract.
    - Required disclosures about each significant concentration
        - Activity, region, or economic characteristic
    - The maximum amount of loss due to credit risk
    - The entity's policy of requiring collateral or other security
    - The entity's policy arrangements to mitigate the credit risk.
    - Optional to disclose **market risk** – Risk a loss may occur as a result of changes in the market value of financial instruments due to economic circumstances.

Some examples:
Someone who wants to make a large investment in the stock market can do so without buying any stocks through the use of **stock index futures**. Let's select a popular index of stock market prices, the Standard and Poor's 500 index based on the market value of 500 large U.S. corporations (commonly known as the S&P index). Assume for the moment that a corporation wants to make a $10,000,000 investment in the U.S. stock market on October 1 at a time the S&P index is 1000. The company can buy a stock index futures contract for 10,000 units of the S&P index. With an underlying of 1000 and a notional amount of 10,000, this is the equivalent of making an investment of 1000 x 10,000 = $10,000,000. The company does not, however, put up any cash. Let's assume that the futures contract has a settlement date on January 2 of the following year, and that the S&P index has risen to 1200 as of the end of the current year. The increase of 200 in the underlying multiplied by the 10,000 notional amount means that the company expects to receive a check for 200 x 10,000 = $2,000,000 from the party that took the other side of the futures contract.

There is no entry on October 1, since no exchange of cash took place. At the end of the year, the expectation of receiving a settlement of $2,000,000 in a couple of days is reported as follows:

12/31	Receivable on derivative	2,000,000	
	Gain on derivative		2,000,000

This is a gain on the **speculative** use of derivatives, since the company acquired the derivative purely as an attempt to profit from stock market increases.

If, instead, the S&P dropped to 800 during that time period, the company would have to pay $2,000,000 to the other side. A payable and loss would be recorded for the cash expected to be paid at settlement. Notice that no actual stock needs to be involved: the derivative is settled by a transfer of cash from one side to the other.

Popular derivatives such as stock index futures are easily available through public securities markets, but derivatives can also be created privately. One common example of a private derivative is an **interest rate swap agreement**. A bank that has made a large number of loans with variable interest rates might contract with a bank that has made a large number of loans with fixed interest rates. The former bank is concerned about a drop in interest rates that would reduce its interest income, and the latter bank is concerned about a rise in interest rates that it couldn't benefit from with fixed rate loans. The parties sign a contract agreeing that each party will pay the other amounts based on the interest rates of the loans each bank has outstanding with customers. In the specific case of the interest rate swap, there are two risks that cannot be reflected on the financial statements (**off-balance sheet risk**) but need to be disclosed in connection with such an agreement:
- The risk of exchanging a lower interest rate for a higher one.
- The risk that the other bank might default on the agreement (**credit risk**).

In general, any financial instrument with off-balance sheet risks requires disclosures in the notes to the financial statements. In addition, for all financial instruments, the client must disclose **concentration of credit risk**, which is a special risk of multiple defaults when a client is depending on the performance of a large number of different parties who are affected by common issues. For example, a bank which lends only to farmers in a certain area has a concentration of credit risk associated with the possibility of weather-related crop failures or general declines in agricultural prices affecting all of the bank's customers at once.

Finally, the client may hold investments whose fair value cannot be reasonably estimated. When this is the case, disclosure must be made of any information that might assist the user of the financial statements in determining the value of the investments, and an explanation is needed of the reason the value cannot be estimated.

As indicated, all derivatives are required to be reported at fair value. When accounted for as a cash flow hedge, unrealized gains and losses are initially reported in other comprehensive income. Unrealized gains and losses on fair value hedges and derivatives that are not designated as hedges are reported in net income.

In many cases, the fair value of a derivative is readily determinable. When it is not, the intrinsic value of the instrument is often used. An option to purchase a share of stock for $30 when its market value is $30 has no intrinsic value because it provides no benefit to the holder. An option to purchase a share at $30 when its market value is $35, however, has an intrinsic value of $5. In

Financial Instruments & Derivatives

addition, depending on the length of the exercise period remaining, there may be a time value, which would be added to the intrinsic value in determining the value of the option.

Lecture 5.02

Fair Value vs. Cash Flow Hedges

When a derivative contract has been made in order to **hedge** against the risk associated with another contract or planned activity, the method of accounting for changes in the fair value of the derivative depends on the type of hedge involved:

- **Fair value hedge** - If the derivative is hedging against a recognized asset or liability on the balance sheet or a firm purchase commitment, then changes in the value of the derivative are reported in **income from continuing operations**. An example is the purchase of put options to protect against a possible decline in the market price of a stock portfolio. Should the market decline, the losses on the stock should be offset by gains on the puts. Fair value hedges can be used to hedge against the value of inventories, the value of a fixed-income investment, the value of a fixed-rate debt obligation, and a firm commitment.

- **Cash flow hedge** - If the derivative is hedging against a forecasted transaction that is expected to take place in the future, but which is not yet a legal commitment, then changes in the value of the derivative are reported as direct adjustments to stockholders' equity and included in **other comprehensive income** until the transaction is complete and the cash flows have actually occurred. An example is the purchase of a futures contract on steel by a company that believes it will need to make large steel purchases in the near future. An increase in the price of steel will cause the value of the futures contract to rise, helping the company pay the increased costs. Since those costs aren't yet reflected in income, the increase in the futures contract is not reflected either.

For example: Assume the client is an oil distributor, and has purchased 100 million gallons of gasoline from its supplier refinery on October 1 at a cost of 70 cents per gallon. They plan to sell the oil to various airlines in early January, but are concerned that, in the meantime, the price of oil might drop considerably from the current selling price of 80 cents. To protect the inventory, the client sells a gasoline futures contract based on a wholesale gasoline price index per gallon (the underlying) times 100,000,000 gallons (the notional amount), with a settlement date of January 2. Assume the price of the index drops 4 cents per gallon by the end of the year.

The purchase of the inventory by the distributor from the refinery is recorded as follows (assume immediate payment and entries in millions of dollars):

10/1	Inventory	70	
	Cash		70

When the futures contract is established, there is no entry, since no cash is involved. This is a **fair value hedge**, since the distributor is hedging against an existing asset.

As of the end of the year, the decline of 4 cents per share in the price of oil results in a loss on the inventory of $4,000,000. The futures contract, however, is now expected to result in a collection of $4,000,000 upon settlement. The entries are:

12/31	Loss on market decline in inventory	4	
	Inventory		4
	Receivable on derivative	4	
	Gain on fair value hedge		4

Both the loss on inventory and gain on the fair value hedge are included in the computation of net income, so there is no net income effect. This, of course, was the goal of the hedge.

Let's now go back to October 1 and look at the side of the airline that is planning on purchasing the gasoline in early January. This client might enter the very same contract to hedge against a price increase, but it would be a **cash flow hedge**, since there is no asset, liability, or fixed commitment as yet for the purchase.

On October 1, the airline enters into a derivative based on the gasoline index with the same notional amount of 100,000,000 gallons. There is **no entry** on that date.

On December 31, the price decline of 4 cents per gallon in the index means that the airline expects to have to pay $4,000,000 on the settlement date. The entry is:

12/31	Other comprehensive income – loss on cash flow hedge	4	
	Payable on derivative		4

Note that the loss is **not** included in the calculation of net income. The reason is that the decline in gasoline is expected to reduce the cost of inventory in the next period, so this loss will be offset by reduction of cost of sales in the next period. Since the offsetting event is not yet reflected in net income, neither can the hedge.

Some hedges do not entirely protect a company against the risk that the hedge is intended to mitigate. A fair value hedge, for example, may not offset all changes in the fair value of the hedged item. Likewise, a cash flow hedge may not offset all changes in the cash flows associated with the hedged item. The degree to which a change in the value of a fair value hedge offsets the change in the value of the hedged item, and the degree to which a change in the cash flows of a cash flow hedge offset changes in the cash flows of the hedged item is called the hedge's **effectiveness**.
- A hedge is **perfectly effective** if all changes in the fair value or cash flows of the hedged item are offset by corresponding changes in the hedge.
- A hedge is **highly effective** if most changes in the fair value or cash flows of the hedged item are offset by corresponding changes in the hedge. The portion not offset is the degree to which the hedge is **ineffective**.
- A hedge is considered **ineffective** if relatively few or none of the changes in the fair value or cash flows of the hedged item are offset by changes in the hedge.

When a hedge is not perfectly effective, hedge reporting only applies to the effective portion. Changes to the hedge that do not offset changes in the hedged item, the degree to which it is **ineffective**, are reported in income in the period of the change. The **effective** portion:
- Is recognized in income for a fair value hedge, causing the corresponding gain or loss on the hedged item to be reported in income.

Financial Instruments & Derivatives — Section 5

- Is recognized in other comprehensive income for a cash flow hedge, to be taken into income in the same period in which changes to the hedged item affect income.

To summarize, when derivatives are used as speculation or fair value hedges, gains and losses are reported in net income (in the case of a fair value hedge, there will be offsetting amounts on the asset or commitment being hedged). When derivatives are used as cash flow hedges, gains and losses are reported in other comprehensive income (they are transferred to net income when the expected events occur and offsetting amounts are reported in net income).

Derivatives Summary

Speculation (non-hedge)
- Acquired to take on risk in the hopes of profit.
- Gain or loss in income from continuing operations. **(I/S)**

Fair value hedge
- Acquired to hedge against a recognized asset or liability or a firm purchase commitment.
- Gain or loss in income from continuing operations. **(I/S)** Should be offset by loss or gain on hedged item.

Cash flow hedge
- Acquired to hedge against a forecasted future transaction.
- Gain or loss in other comprehensive income (OCI) **(B/S)**
- Nothing included in net income until forecasted activity occurs.

Foreign currency hedge against an investment in foreign operations
- Acquired to hedge against currency risk from a major investment in a company with a functional currency (currency in which books are maintained) other than the U.S. dollar.
- Gain or loss in other comprehensive income (OCI) **(B/S)**
- Offsets translation losses or gains from investment in foreign operations.

Alternative Accounting Approach for Nonpublic Entities (Interest Rate Swaps)

The Private Company Council (PCC) of the FASB established an alternative accounting approach that is available to nonpublic entities when accounting for certain interest rate swaps, often referred to as "plain vanilla" interest rate swaps, and which have become very common among large and small entities.

This Simplified Hedge Accounting Approach gives nonpublic companies the option to use this simpler approach to account for certain types of interest rate swaps that are entered into for the purpose of economically converting variable-rate interest payments to fixed-rate payments.

An interest rate swap to which the alternative accounting approach applies is one related to the following circumstances:
- The entity has an obligation that bears interest at a variable rate.
- The entity enters into a derivative contract known as an interest rate swap under which:
  - The entity will receive payments from the other party at a variable rate
  - The entity will make payments to the other party at a fixed rate
- As a result of the swap, the net interest paid by the entity is equivalent to what would have been paid if the obligation had interest at a fixed rate.

In order to qualify for the alternative treatment, the variable rate in the swap must vary according to changes in the same index that causes changes in the rate on the related obligation. In addition:
- The terms must be virtually identical such that they mirror the terms of the underlying obligation.
- The settlement date on which payments are exchanged for the swap are very close to the dates on which payments are made on the underlying obligation.
- The initial fair value of the swap is zero, indicating that the interest rates are comparable on the date it is entered into and that the parties have different views on anticipated future changes in the index rate.
- The notional amount of the swap, the amount on which the swapped interest rates are calculated, must be equal to, or lower than the principal balance of the hedged instrument.
- All interest payments must be designated as hedged, in proportion to the ratio of the notional amount of the hedge and the principal balance of the underlying obligation.

If all conditions are met and the entity elects to apply the alternative accounting approach, there are several differences in the requirements. First, *documentation* and other elements are not required to be completed in advance. They may be completed any time until the first set of financial statements on which the alternative accounting approach is applied are either issued or available to be issued, whichever is earlier.

The remaining differences are included in the *alternative accounting approach* which will be applied as follows:
- It is assumed that the swap is perfectly effective and the debt obligation is accounted for as if it bore interest at a fixed rate.
- The hedge, the interest rate swap, is reported at its *settlement amount* rather than its fair value.
- Any difference between reported amounts and payments made or received are reported in *other comprehensive income*.

The accounting for an interest rate swap under the alternative approach will result in the following:
- Interest expense will be debited for an amount calculated by applying the fixed rate to the principal balance, adjusted for the amount of time elapsed since the previous calculation.
- Principal will be debited for the amount by which it is reduced as a result of applying the terms of the obligation to any payments made.
- An asset or liability will be debited or credited to adjust the amount reported as the balance of the derivative to the settlement value of the interest rate swap.
- Cash will be credited for the net amount paid, including the payment on the underlying obligation adjusted for the net amount received from the counterparty or paid to the counterparty to the swap, depending on whether the index rate has increased or decreased, respectively.

- The amount required to balance the entry will be reported as a debit or credit to *other comprehensive income*.

Lecture 5.03

Embedded Derivatives and Bifurcation

Some instruments are not derivatives but include features that have the characteristics of a derivative. An investment in bonds has two inherent risks:
- There is credit risk because the issuer of bonds may or may not perform, which will affect the interest rate.
- There is market risk because the bonds will bear interest at a fixed rate and market interest rates may change, making the bonds more or less desirable and causing increases or decreases in their fair values.

Convertible bonds have an added feature in that they can be converted into common stock. As a result, increases in the stock price mitigate market risk as the bondholders can convert their bonds into shares of stock if the value of the stock exceeds that of the bonds. As a result, the value of the bonds will fluctuate as interest rates fluctuate and as the value of the stock fluctuates.
- The convertible bond would be considered a compound or **hybrid** instrument.
- The bond is the **host instrument**.
- The conversion feature would be considered an **embedded derivative**.

Since all derivatives are required to be reported at fair value, the entity will account for a hybrid instrument in one of two manners:
- If the host instrument is reported at fair value, the derivative is also reported at fair value.
- If the host instrument is not reported at fair value, the derivative will be separated or **bifurcated** from the host instrument and accounted for separately.
    - This would only be appropriate if the features have the characteristics of a derivative.
    - The derivative should have characteristics that respond to market influences differently from the host instrument

An example of an embedded derivative that can be separated from its host is a detachable stock purchase warrant that was acquired with an investment in bonds to be held to maturity. An example of an embedded derivative that **cannot** be separated from its host is the convertibility provision obtained with an investment in convertible bonds.

FASB ASC 815 was issued to improve the financial reporting of certain hybrid financial instruments by requiring more consistent accounting that eliminates exemptions and provides a means to simplify the accounting for these instruments. Specifically, it allows financial instruments that have embedded derivatives to be accounted for as a whole if the holder elects to account for the whole instrument on a fair value basis.

The following qualitative **disclosures** are required, regarding:
- How and why an entity uses derivative instruments
- How derivative instruments and related hedge items are accounted for
- How derivative instruments and related hedge items affect an entity's financial position, financial performance, and cash flows.
    - **Additional Disclosures:**
        - Objectives for holding or issuing such instruments, and strategies for achieving those objectives.

- Context to understand the instrument.
- Risk management policies
- A list of hedged instruments.
- Disclosure of fair value of financial instruments required when practicable to estimate fair value.

Transfer and Servicing of Financial Assets

Entities, particularly financial institutions, will often dispose of financial instruments by transferring them to another entity. In many cases, these instruments are relatively favorable investments and the transferring entity may desire the ability to reacquire it. In other cases, the instrument may entail certain risks and the acquiring entity may desire the ability to dispose of it.

- A transfer of financial assets in which the transferor retains either the right or the obligation to reacquire the instrument, prior to its maturity, for an amount determined at the transfer date, is accounted for as a financing transaction, rather than a sale.
- In order to recognize the transfer as a sale, allowing the transferor to derecognize the instrument and recognize a gain or loss on disposal, three conditions must be satisfied:
  - The asset must be beyond the reach of the transferor and its creditors.
  - The transferor cannot place any restrictions on what the transferee can do with the asset.
  - There is no repurchase or redemption agreement that might allow the transferor to force a return of the asset.

Fair Value Option for Reporting Financial Assets and Financial Liabilities

FASB ASC 820 defines fair value as "the price that would be received to sell an asset or paid to transfer a liability in an orderly transaction between market participants at the measurement date (at exit price)". An orderly transaction is a transaction that allows for normal marketing activities that are usual and customary, so they are NOT a forced transaction or sale.

Fair value measurements are required in very few circumstances:
- Derivatives are always reported at fair value
- Identifiable assets acquired and liabilities assumed in a business combination are originally measured at fair value
- Investments in marketable securities other than debt securities accounted for as held to maturity are reported at market value on each balance sheet date
- Impaired assets are written down due to their fair values
- Nonmonetary transactions are measured at the fair value of the consideration exchanged

In addition, there is a fair value option that allows an entity to elect to report virtually any or all of its financial assets and liabilities at fair value. When this irrevocable election is made, the item is remeasured at fair value on each balance sheet date and unrealized gains and losses are recognized in income.

Lecture 5.04

CLASS QUESTIONS

Please see the Class Questions and Class Solutions for this Lecture at the end of this Section.

Financial Instruments & Derivatives

Lecture 5.05

DERIVATIVES AND HEDGING INSTRUMENTS UNDER IFRS

As is true under US GAAP, derivatives that are not designated as hedges are recognized as assets or liabilities in the statement of financial position, they are reported at fair value, and remeasured each balance sheet date with unrealized gains and losses included in income. Also, as is true under US GAAP, derivatives can be designated as hedges. Under IFRS, however, there are three types of hedges:

- **Cash flow hedges** reduce or eliminate the risk of changes in cash flows that results from a specific risk associated with a recognized asset or liability or a forecast transaction that is highly probable. A debtor with a variable rate loan, for example may mitigate the risk of changes in payment amounts by entering into an interest rate swap essentially fixing the loans rate and, therefore, its cash flows. Similar to US GAAP, unrealized gains or losses are temporarily recognized in other comprehensive income.
- **Fair value hedges** reduce or eliminate the risk of changes in the fair value of a recognized asset or liability or an unrecognized firm commitment. An entity with an inventory consisting of agricultural products may enter into a futures contract to mitigate the risk of changes in the fair value of the inventory. Similar to US GAAP, unrealized gains and losses are recognized in earnings.
- **Hedges of net investments in foreign operations** are accounted for as cash flow hedges.

Compound financial interests are non-derivative financial instruments that have both liability and equity components (e.g., convertible bonds). They are split into debt, equity and, if applicable, derivative components, whereas under GAAP, they are only split if certain requirements are met. Some contracts that include debt and equity components also have a component that causes the cash flows from the combined instrument to occur in a manner that is similar to a derivative, indicating an embedded derivative.

- When the host contract is a financial asset, it is reported as a single instrument and is accounted for under the amortized cost method or at FVTPL, as appropriate.
- When the host contract is not an asset, the embedded derivative is separated, or bifurcated, from the host instrument and accounted for separately.

Financial Investments	
US GAAP	**IFRS**
• Financial instruments that have an embedded derivative (compound or hybrid instruments) are only divided into debt and equity components when certain requirements are met. Bifurcation (separation into debt and derivative components may be required.	• Compound financial interests are treated as a single instrument that is either accounted for at FVTPL or at amortized cost, as appropriate, if the host is an asset. Otherwise, bifurcation is required.

©Roger CPA Review

CLASS QUESTIONS

Work through the below Class Questions while following along with the respective lectures. Once this is complete, you can begin independently practicing what you've learned by quizzing yourself on this course section in your Interactive Practice Questions (IPQ), which can be found in your online Student Dashboard. Your IPQ simulates the computer-based testing experience, and will also help you understand how concepts are applied to the exam. Each question includes answer explanations from expert CPAs that will help you determine why you answered a question correctly or incorrectly. This is key to your success on the CPA Exam.

Lecture 5.04

1. A hedge of the exposure to changes in the fair value of a recognized asset or liability, or an unrecognized firm commitment, is classified as a

    a. Fair value hedge.
    b. Cash flow hedge.
    c. Foreign currency hedge.
    d. Underlying.

2. Gains and losses of the effective portion of a hedging instrument will be recognized in current earnings in each reporting period for which of the following?

	Fair value Hedge	Cash Flow Hedge
a.	Yes	No
b.	Yes	Yes
c.	No	No
d.	No	Yes

3. James Corp entered into an interest rate swap with another entity in which it will be paying interest monthly at the annual rate of prime plus 1% based on a principal amount of $1,000,000 and will receive 7% per year based on the same principal amount. James paid a small fee to an entity that facilitated the arrangement, the terms of which call for a payment by one party or the other based on the difference between the interest amounts. What is the underlying in this transaction?

    a. It is the prime rate.
    b. It is the underlying agreement between James and the other entity.
    c. It is the annual interest at 7% or $70,000.
    d. It is principal balance of $1,000,000.

4. A company has invested in a financial instrument and is trying to determine whether or not it is a derivative. Which of the following is not a requirement for reporting a financial instrument as a derivative?

    a. There must be at least one underlying.
    b. There must be a notional amount.
    c. The amount invested must be material.
    d. The contract may be settled on a net basis.

Financial Instruments & Derivatives

5. Which of the following cannot be a derivative?

   a. A contract requiring the company to buy Euros at some time in the future at a fixed price.
   b. An option to buy shares of another company's stock for a fixed price for a set period of time.
   c. An agreement to pay interest at a fixed rate on a specific amount in exchange for the right to receive interest on the same specific amount at a variable rate.
   d. An option to buy another company's land for a fixed price for a set period of time.

6. Under IFRS, a cash flow hedge and a hedge of a net investment in foreign operations are accounted for by

   a. Not recognizing gains and losses.
   b. Recognizing gains and losses in other comprehensive income.
   c. Recognizing gains and losses in profit and loss.
   d. Recognizing gains and losses when the hedge is closed out.

CLASS SOLUTIONS

1. (a) A hedge designed to mitigate or eliminate a risk associated with an exposure to changes in the fair value of a recognized asset or liability or firm commitment is a fair value hedge. Answer (b) is incorrect because a hedge designed to mitigate or eliminate a risk associated with an exposure to changes in future cash flows as a result of a transaction that has occurred or an anticipated transaction is a cash flow hedge. Answer (c) is incorrect because a foreign currency is a hedge designed to mitigate or eliminate a risk associated with an exposure to changes in the fair value of an investment in a foreign entity or of a recognized asset or liability or firm commitment denominated in a foreign currency, making it a foreign currency fair value hedge. It may also mitigate or eliminate a risk associated with an exposure to changes in future cash flows that will be denominated in a foreign currency, making it a foreign currency cash flow hedge. Answer (d) is incorrect because an underlying is a factor, such as an interest rate, a foreign currency exchange rate, a commodity or stock price, or some other factor that, as it changes, will affect the value of a derivative.

2. (a) Changes in the fair value of all derivatives that are not recognized as hedges and on the ineffective portion of derivatives designated as hedges are recognized in income. Gains or losses on the effective portion of fair value hedges are also recognized in income in the period in which the fair value changes. Gains or losses on the effective portion of cash flow hedges are reported in other comprehensive until such time as the corresponding gain or loss on the hedged item is recognized in income.

3. (a) The underlying is the factor that is used in the formula applied to the notional amount to determine that amount that will be exchanged between the parties. In this case, the amount to be paid will be the prime rate of interest, which is the underlying, plus 1% multiplied by the $1,000,000 principal balance, which is the notional amount.

4. (c) For a financial instrument to be a derivative, it must have at least one underlying and at least one notional amount, it must allow for net settlement, and must require no net initial investment, or one that is much lower than would ordinarily be necessary for the same response to changes in market conditions. If the amount invested is material, the financial instrument is not a derivative.

5. (d) A derivative is a financial instrument that meets certain requirements. An option to buy land is not a financial instrument and, therefore, cannot be a derivative. Answer (a) is incorrect because a contract to buy Euros, which is a forward exchange contract, is an agreement to exchange one currency, dollars, for another, Euros, making it an agreement to exchange one financial instrument for another. The contract is a financial instrument and may be a derivative. Answer (b) is incorrect because an option to buy another company's shares for a fixed price for a set period is a stock option, which is a form of derivative. Answer (c) is incorrect because an agreement to pay interest at a fixed rate on a specific amount in exchange for the right to receive interest on the same specific amount at a variable rate is an interest rate swap, which is a form of derivative.

6. (b) Under IFRS, cash flow hedges are accounted for similarly to US GAAP in that they are reported at fair value and gains or losses are recognized in other comprehensive income (OCI). The same is true, under IFRS, for hedges of net investments in foreign operations.

TASK-BASED SIMULATIONS

Task-Based Simulation 1

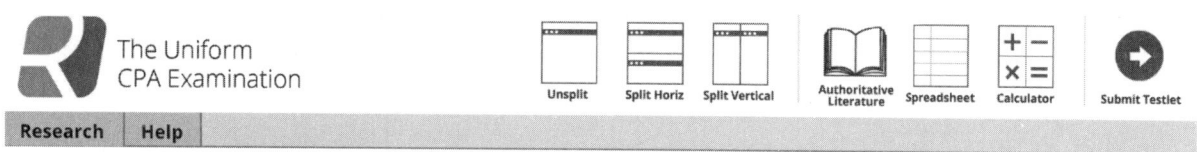

A client has entered into an interest rate swap and just learned that it is considered a derivative. The cost was negligible and the entity is trying to determine at what amount to report it on its balance sheet. Identify the location in professional standards that indicates how derivatives should initially be measured.

Task-Based Simulation 2

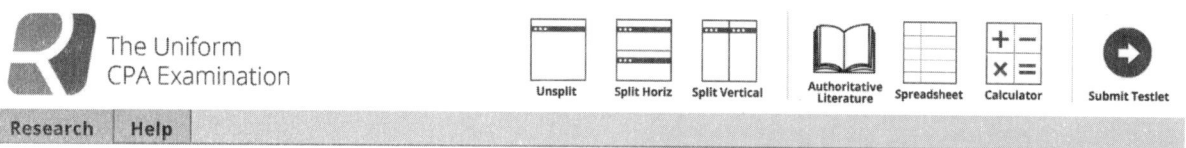

An entity has entered into a contract to purchase goods from another entity with an understanding that the price will be modified based on changes in the exchange rate between the US dollar and the Euro. The entity believes this is an embedded derivative. Identify the location in professional standards that indicates when an embedded derivative should be separated from the host contract.

TASK-BASED SIMULATION SOLUTIONS

Task-Based Simulation Solution 1

| FASB ASC | 815 | 10 | 30 | 1 |

Task-Based Simulation Solution 2

| FASB ASC | 815 | 15 | 25 | 1 |

Section 6 – Foreign Operations
Corresponding Lectures

Watch the following course lectures with this section:

Lecture 6.01 – Foreign Currency
Lecture 6.02 – Foreign Currency Exchange Transactions
Lecture 6.03 – Foreign Currency Exchange Transaction – Hedging – Fair Value Hedge
Lecture 6.04 – Foreign Currency Exchange Transaction – Hedging – Cash Flow Hedge
Lecture 6.05 – Foreign Investees
Lecture 6.06 – Foreign operations – Class Questions
Lecture 6.07 – Foreign operations under IFRS

EXAM NOTE: *Please refer to the AICPA FAR Blueprint in the Introduction to find a listing of the representative tasks (and their associated skill levels—i.e., Remembering and Understanding, Application, and Analysis) that the candidate should be able to perform based on the knowledge obtained in this section.*

Foreign Operations

Lecture 6.01

FOREIGN CURRENCY (ASC 830)

There are a number of ways in which an entity may be involved in foreign operations:
1. The may enter into **foreign currency transactions** with an entity in a foreign country that involves a receipt or payment in a foreign currency. The entity must determine how that transaction will be reported in US dollars.
2. An entity may have a **receivable or payable** on its financial statements that is **denominated** in a foreign currency, meaning it will be settled by the receipt or payment of some amount of foreign currency. The amount of the receivable or payable must be converted into US dollars for inclusion on the reporting entity's financial statements.
3. An entity may get involved in **foreign currency exchange transactions**, such as forward exchange contracts. These transactions may be entered into for a variety of reasons but, regardless, often result in a net amount being paid or received to settle the contract, representing a liability or asset.
4. An entity may have a **foreign division or subsidiary** that maintains books and records in a foreign currency but will be included in the reporting entity's consolidated financial statements. The financial statements must be converted into US dollars in order to include them.

1. Foreign Currency Transactions

When an entity enters into a transaction that will be settled through the payment or receipt of foreign currency, it is initially recognized in the **functional currency** of the entity using the exchange rate in effect on the *date of the transaction*. The exchange rate that is effective on a particular date is referred to as a *spot rate*.

An entity's functional currency is the currency that has the greatest economic impact on the entity's financial performance. A company based in the northern part of the state of Washington, for example, may obtain all of its raw materials from Canadian suppliers, may assemble its product in the United States, and then sells all of its output to Canadian customers. Even though the company might maintain its books and records in US dollars, its functional currency would be the Canadian dollar.

Various factors will be considered when identifying the functional currency. Some may be more important than others, depending on the circumstances and not all will necessarily apply.

These factors may include, for example, which currency may have the greatest influence on:
- Cash flows
- Sales prices
- Demand for the company's products or services
- Expense
- Financing and financing costs
- Intra-entity arrangements

In general, an entity's functional currency is its local currency, which is the one in which it maintains its books and records. That is not, however, always the case.
- When a transaction occurs in some currency other than the functional currency, it is **remeasured** as if the transaction had originally occurred at the functional currency.
- When the functional currency is not the same as the currency used for reporting, amounts are **translated** from the functional currency into the reporting currency.

- **Transactional Currency** = Local ("recording currency") → the currency of a particular country. Usually Books & Records are kept

- **Functional Currency** = Greatest economic impact on company
  (Currency in which entity generates and expends cash)

- **Reporting Currency** = Currency in which the enterprise prepares
  Its financial statements ($US)

Remeasurement → I/S

Translation → B/S
(Comprehensive Income)

For example, a company's functional currency, the US dollar, is also its reporting currency.

> On December 15 of the current year, the company enters into a transaction in which it purchases a printing press from X Company in Heidelberg, Germany at a cost of €250,000 at the time when the exchange rate was 1.30 (€1.00 = $1.30). The balance is due on January 15 of the following year.
>
> The transaction would be remeasured into US dollars by determining the US dollar equivalent of €250,000, which is (€250,000 x 1.30) $325,000 and the transaction would be recorded as follows:

    Equipment   325,000
        Due to X Company   325,000

2. Financial Instruments Denominated in a Foreign Currency

When an entity has financial instruments, such as accounts receivable or payable, or notes and loans receivable or payable, that are denominated in a foreign currency, they are adjusted for changes in exchange rates as of each balance sheet date.
- The carrying value of the financial instrument will be remeasured based on the *spot rate* on the balance sheet date.
- Any increase or decrease is generally recognized in *income or loss* as a foreign currency transaction gain or loss.

> **For example,** when the company prepares its financial statements as of December 31, the exchange rate has increased to 1.35. It will now require (€250,000 x 1.35) $337,500 to settle the obligation. The liability will be increased to that amount as of the balance sheet date and a loss will be recognized.

Foreign currency exchange loss	12,500	
Due to X Company		12,500

Note that the loss can also be calculated by multiplying the amount of the payable in Euros by the change in the exchange rate (€250,000 x .05 = $12,500).

When the instrument is settled, an additional gain or loss may be recognized if the exchange rate has changed since the last balance sheet date. When it is settled, the entity will pay or receive some amount of money and will either convert dollars into a foreign currency to make a payment or receive a foreign currency and convert it into dollars to deposit it into its US bank account.

For example, when the company remits payment on January 15 of the following period, the exchange rate has decreased to 1.20. It will now only require (€250,000 x 1.20) $300,000 to settle the obligation. The entity will buy 250,000 Euros for $300,000 and repay the liability, resulting in the recognition of a gain.

Due to X Company	337,500	
Foreign Currency Exchange Gain		37,500
Cash		300,000

Lecture 6.02

3. Foreign Currency Exchange Transactions

An entity may enter into a transaction in which they agree to exchange one currency for another at a specific exchange rate at a specific future point in time. These foreign currency exchange transactions are often referred to as **forward exchange contracts**. There are many reasons an entity may enter into a forward exchange contract.

Some companies enter into forward exchange contracts as **hedges**. This would be the case if the entity has an "exposure" that is denominated in a foreign currency and it desires protection from fluctuations in exchange rates.

Using the same example, the company may have budgeted exactly $325,000 to purchase the printing press based on the exchange rate at December 15. Although it would be to its benefit if the exchange rate decreases, resulting in a gain, it may create financial difficulties for the entity if the exchange rate increases, requiring a larger payment.

To avoid this risk, the company may enter into a forward exchange contract with another entity, referred to as a counterparty. The company will agree to buy 250,000 Euros at the exchange rate of 1.30 on January 15 of the following year.
- If the exchange rate increases above 1.30, the company will benefit from the transaction by being able to purchase the Euros for $1.30 per Euro, which is below market, and realize a gain.
- If the exchange rate decreases below 1.30, the company will be adversely affected as it will have to purchase the Euros for $1.30 per Euro, which is above the market price, and incur a loss.

- Regardless of whether the exchange rate increases, decreases, or remains unchanged, the company will buy 250,000 Euros for $325,000 and give them to Company X in exchange for the press. In essence, the company has eliminated the market risk associated with changes in the exchange rate.

The fact that an entity enters into a transaction for the purposes of mitigating some risk, using a hedge, does not necessarily mean that they will report the transaction using hedge accounting. FASB ASC 815 establishes strict requirements that must be met in order for a transaction to be accounted for as a hedge.

Other companies may enter into forward exchange contracts for **speculation** purposes. If a company has some reason to believe, for example, that an exchange rate is going to change in the future, it may enter into a forward exchange contract:
- To *buy* that currency at a future date at a predetermined exchange rate if they believe that rate will be higher on that date.
- To *sell* that currency at a future date at a predetermined exchange rate if they believe that rate will be lower on that date.

Another reason companies may enter into forward exchange contracts is to **"protect"** the reported value of an investment on their financial statements. A company, for example, may have an investment in a foreign entity that is reported as a single amount on its balance sheet. In addition to the effects of the entity's performance, the carrying amount of the investment may be affected by changes in exchange rates. To isolate the effects of performance and eliminate the effects of a change in exchange rates, the company may enter into a forward exchange contract in which they would be the seller.
- If the reported value of the investee decreases due to a decrease in the exchange rate, the forward exchange contract would increase in value due to the company's ability to sell the foreign currency at the higher contract exchange rate.
- If the reported value of the investee increases due to an increase in the exchange rate, the forward exchange contract would decrease in value, resulting in a liability, since the company will be required to sell the foreign currency at the lower contract exchange rate.

Speculation

Unless an entity qualifies for and chooses to account for its forward exchange contracts as hedges, they will all be accounted for as if entered into for speculation purposes. Forward exchange contracts are forms of **derivatives** and all derivatives that are not designated as hedges are required to be reported at their fair values, with gains or losses resulting from fluctuations of those values reported in profit or loss (I/S).

The fair value of a forward exchange contract is determined by the exchange rate that is used to value it. The types of exchange rates that might be used are:
- The **spot rate**, which is the actual exchange rate on a particular date; or
- The **forward rate**, which is what the exchange rate is expected to be at some point in the future.
    - There might be, for example, 30-day, 60-day, or 90-day forward rates.
    - A 60-day forward rate would indicate the exchange rate that is expected to be in effect 60-days from that date.

A forward exchange contract is generally entered into at the appropriate forward rate as of the date of the contract.

For example, on June 1 of the current period, a company enters into a forward exchange contract in which they agree to buy 100,000 Euros 90 days in the future. They prepare quarterly financial statements and, as a result, their next financial statements will be prepared as of June 30. The contract will be settled with a net payment on August 29, at the end of 90 days.

Applicable exchange rates are:

	June 1	June 30	August 29
Spot rate	1.30	1.33	1.29
60-day forward rate	1.35	1.39	1.28
90-day forward rate	1.37	1.42	1.30

On June 1, when the contract is entered into, it will be based on the 90-day forward rate, since that is the rate that is expected to apply when the contract will be settled at the end of 90 days. In essence, the company is agreeing to buy 100,000 Euros for $137,000 ($1.37) on August 29, and the counter party is agreeing to sell 100,000 Euros for $137,000.

Since each party is basically required to exchange currencies that are expected to be equal in value and as a result, the forward exchange contract would have no value at that time. *No entry would be recorded*, although both parties would have disclosures to make.

On June 30, the forward exchange contract will be adjusted to at its fair value for financial statement purposes. Although the actual fair value may differ due to the time value of money, volatility, and other factors, the fair value would approximate the difference between the expected values of the currencies that will be exchanged as of the balance sheet date.

As of June 30, the contract will now be settled at the end of 60 days. On June 30, the 60-day forward rate is 1.39 indicating:
- The buying party will be paying $137,000 for Euros that are expected to be worth $139,000. The fair value of the forward exchange contract would be approximately $2,000.
- The selling party will be receiving $137,000 for Euros that are expected to be worth $139,000. The forward exchange contract represents an obligation to be reported as a liability for approximately $2,000.
- *The buying party will recognize a gain and the selling party will recognize a loss.*

The buying party's entry may be:

Forward exchange contract	2,000	
Gain on forward exchange contract		2,000

The seller's entry may be:

Loss on forward exchange contract	2,000	
Forward exchange contract		2,000

The contract will be settled on August 29, when the spot rate is 1.29. The buyer would theoretically pay $137,000 to the seller for Euros that are actually only worth $129,000. In reality, however, the buyer will pay the seller the difference of $8,000. Since the exchange rate has gone from 1.39 at June 30 to 1.29 at August 31, the buyer will incur a loss, and the seller will have a gain, of 100,000 x the difference of $.10 or $10,000. The buying party's entry may be:

Loss on forward exchange contract	10,000	
Forward exchange contract		2,000
Cash		8,000

The seller's entry may be:

Cash	8,000	
Forward exchange contract	2,000	
Gain on forward exchange contract		10,000

Lecture 6.03

Hedging

When a forward exchange contract is entered into for the purposes of mitigating or eliminating a risk, it is referred to as a hedge. In order to account for a derivative such as a forward exchange contract as a hedge, it must designate the derivative as a hedge and must meet certain requirements including documentation regarding the relationship between the hedge and the hedged risk and an indication that the hedge is expected to be highly effective, with an explanation as to how the entity measures the hedge's effectiveness.

Assuming a forward exchange contract does qualify as a hedge and hedge reporting is elected, the entity will have to determine if it is a fair value hedge or a cash flow hedge.

Fair Value Hedges

As the name implies, a fair value hedge protects a company against risks associated with changes in fair values, such as the fair value of a reported asset or liability (*hedging against a **recognized asset or liability on the balance sheet or a firm purchase commitment***). Since all derivatives are required to be reported at fair value, on each balance sheet date, the carrying value would be increased or decreased, as appropriate.
- The increase or decrease will be recognized as a **gain or loss in the income statement**.
- A corresponding loss or gain will be recognized on the hedged item in the same period.

The corresponding loss or gain on the hedged item will be recognized, regardless of the normal accounting for the item.

> **For example,** a company is doing business with an unrelated entity that is located in Europe. To enhance the relationship, the company has purchased 100,000 shares of the European Company's stock, which is publicly held but not actively traded. The market price of the stock, which has not changed for many years and is not expected to change any time in the future, is €20. The spot rate on the date of the investment was 1.30 and the total cost of $2,600,000 was recorded as an available for sale investment (100,000 x €20 x 1.3 = $2,600,000).

The company wishes to protect itself from fluctuations in the fair value of the investment that result from changes in the exchange rate. If, for example, the exchange rate was to drop to 1.20, even though the shares are still selling for €20, their carrying value would be reduced to $2,400,000. Since these are available-for-sale securities, the loss would be an unrealized loss that would be reported, net of tax, in other comprehensive income.

To protect itself, the company enters into a forward exchange contract to sell 2,000,000 Euros (100,000 shares at €20) in the future for $2,600,000. When the company enters into the contract, the exchange rate is 1.30 and the contract has no value.

On the next balance sheet date, the stock is still selling for €20, but the forward exchange rate has dropped to 1.25. The following would occur as a result:
- The forward exchange contract would now have a fair value of approximately $100,000 since the company has the ability to sell Euros worth $2,500,000 for $2,600,000.
- The fair value of the available for sale investment would be reduced to $2,500,000, which is the fair value of the investment in dollars. The entries would be:

Forward exchange contract (B/S)	100,000	
Gain on forward exchange contract (I/S)		100,000
Loss due to decline in value resulting from change in exchange rate (I/S)	100,000	
Investment in AFS securities (B/S)		100,000

Even though the loss due to decline in value of the available for sale securities would ordinarily go into other comprehensive income, it is reported on the income statement due to the use of hedge reporting.

If, as an alternative, the stock had changed in value due to both a change in the stock price and a change in the exchange rate, only the portion related to the change in the exchange rate would be reported using hedge accounting. The residual gain or loss would receive the accounting treatment that was normal for the hedged item. If, for example, in addition to the exchange rate dropping to 1.25, the share price increased to €21, the stock would now have a value of (100,000 x 21 x 1.25) $2,625,000.

The entries would be:

Forward exchange contract (B/S)	100,000	
Gain on forward exchange contract (I/S)		100,000
Loss due to decline in value resulting from change in exchange rate (I/S)	100,000	
Investment in AFS securities (B/S)	25,000	
Unrealized gain due to increase in value of AFS securities (OCI)		125,000

Lecture 6.04

Cash Flow Hedges

As the name implies, a cash flow hedge protects an entity from fluctuations in cash flows. If an entity enters into a contract involving a receivable or payable that will be settled in a foreign currency at some point in the future (**forecasted transaction** *that is expected to take place in the future - **anticipated transaction**), the entity may enter into a forward exchange contract to make certain that the number of dollars required to settle the contract do not fluctuate as the exchange rate changes.

When a derivative such as a forward exchange contract is accounted for as a cash flow hedge, it too, like all derivatives, must be adjusted to its fair value on each balance sheet date. The change in value, however, is not reported in profit or loss but, rather, it is reported in **other comprehensive income (OCI)**. The amount in other comprehensive income is reversed when the effect is recognized on the hedged transaction.

> **For example,** in performing its analysis of capital budgeting for the next few years, a company decides it will be purchasing an expensive piece of equipment from a European supplier in 6 months. The cost is €200,000 and the 6-month forward exchange rate is 1.30. As a result, the company budgets $260,000 for the purchase.
>
> To avoid changes in the dollar amount of the purchase price due to changes in the exchange rate, the company enters into a forward exchange contract to purchase 200,000 Euros at the 6-month forward exchange rate of 1.30.
>
> After 2 months, when the company is preparing its year-end financial statements, the 4-month forward exchange rate is 1.35. As a result of an increase in the exchange rate of .05, the fair value of the forward exchange contract will be approximately $10,000.
>
> Since the company has not contracted to purchase the equipment, it has nothing to report on its balance sheet in relation to it. The gain on the forward exchange contract would be reported in other comprehensive income and reclassified when the hedged transaction is affected.
>
> The entry on the balance sheet date would be:
> | | | |
> |---|---:|---:|
> | Forward exchange contract | 10,000 | |
> | Unrealized **gain** due to Increase in value of forward exchange contract (**OCI**) | | 10,000 |

Assume the exchange rate remains at 1.35 when the company purchases the equipment.

> The combined entry would be:
> | | | |
> |---|---:|---:|
> | Equipment | 260,000 | |
> | Unrealized **gain** due to Increase in value of forward exchange contract (OCI) | 10,000 | |
> | Cash (received from counterparty) | 10,000 | |
> | Forward exchange contract | | 10,000 |
> | Cash (paid to equipment vendor) | | 270,000 |

Foreign Operations　　　　　　　　　　　　　　　　　　　　　　　　Section 6

Lecture 6.05

4. Foreign Investees

When a company has an investment in a foreign division or subsidiary that will be included in the company's consolidated financial statements, it must convert the foreign entity's financial information from its local currency, the currency in which it maintains its books and records, into the parent's reporting currency, presumably the US dollar.

The process by which the entity will convert the financial statements from the local currency into US dollars will depend on the functional currency.
- If the functional currency is the local currency, the process is referred to as **translation**.
- If the functional currency is the US dollar, the process is referred to as **remeasurement**.

It is also possible that there will be three currencies involved.
- The subsidiary or division may be maintaining its books and records in its local currency.
- Because of the nature of its operations, its functional currency is a different one, but not the US dollar.
- The company is included in the parent's financial statements prepared in the reporting currency, the US dollar.

As a result:
- The entity will **remeasure** its financial information from the local currency to the functional currency.
- The entity will then **translate** its financial information from the functional currency to the reporting currency.

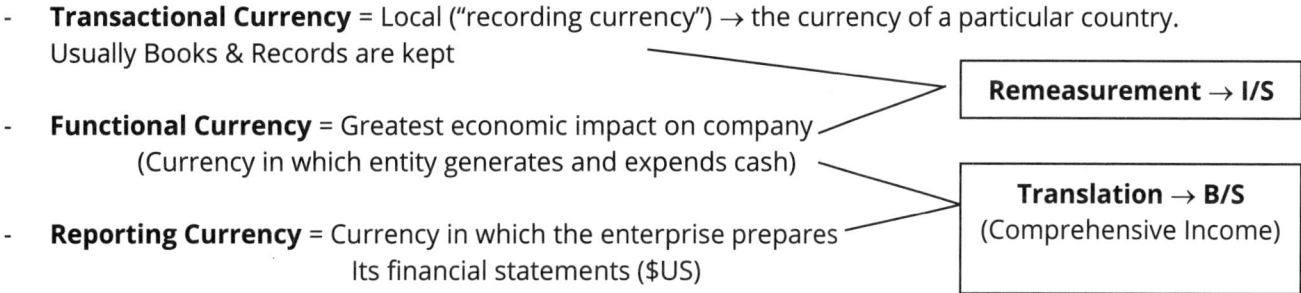

- **Transactional Currency** = Local ("recording currency") → the currency of a particular country. Usually Books & Records are kept
- **Functional Currency** = Greatest economic impact on company (Currency in which entity generates and expends cash)
- **Reporting Currency** = Currency in which the enterprise prepares Its financial statements ($US)

Remeasurement → I/S

Translation → B/S (Comprehensive Income)

Translation of Financial Statements

When the local currency is the functional currency, in order to prepare consolidated financial statements that are expressed in dollars, the parent will translate the financial statements of the subsidiary into US dollars. The basic principles of translation are:
- **Assets and liabilities** are translated at the ***current exchange rate***, which is the exchange rate at the balance sheet date.
- **Income statement** items are translated at the *exchange rates **effective on the date that those items are recognized*** on the financial statements.
    - Sales that occurred uniformly throughout the year, for example, would be translated at the **weighted average** exchange rate.
    - A gain on the sale of a piece of equipment will be translated using the rate in effect on the **date the gain** was realized.

- o Intra entity income and expense items that are eliminated in consolidation are translated at the exchange rate in effect on the **date of the intra entity exchange**.
- The amount required to balance the entry is referred to as a **translation adjustment**.
  - o The translation adjustment occurs because items are being translated at different exchange rates and the result is not likely to balance.
  - o The translation adjustment is not recognized in income but is included in **other comprehensive income (OCI)**.

The normal process for performing a **translation** involves the following steps:
1. Translate all income statement items (weighted average). This will provide a translated amount for net income.
2. Translate items on the balance sheet as follows:
   a. Assets and liabilities are translated using the rates at the **balance sheet date** (end).
   b. Contributed capital accounts (c/s & apic) are translated using **historical rates**.
   c. Retained earnings is "rolled forward". Net income derived from translating the income statement is added to the ending balance from the prior period. Dividends are translated using the rate in effect on the date of the dividend. The result is the current period's ending balance of retained earnings.
3. The difference will be the translation adjustment recognized in other comprehensive income on the balance sheet.

In general, the cumulative translation adjustment remains in accumulated other comprehensive income until such time as the investment in the foreign investee is either disposed of or substantially liquidated. The entity may, however, lose a controlling interest in a foreign investee without disposing of it or substantially liquidating it. This might be the case, for example, when an entity obtains a controlling financial interest in a foreign VIE and subsequently loses that controlling financial interest due to a change in the relationship or other circumstances.

When this is the case, it will be considered equivalent to a disposal and the cumulative translation adjustment is reclassified out of accumulated other comprehensive income and will be recognized in income.

Remeasurement of Financial Statements

When the functional currency is the reporting currency, presumably the US dollar, in order to prepare consolidated financial statements that are expressed in dollars, the parent will remeasure the financial statements of the subsidiary into US dollars. Remeasurement is intended to present financial information as if all transactions had originally been recorded in the functional currency.

The basic principles of remeasurement are:
- Certain **balance sheet** items (**non-monetary** assets/liabilities) are remeasured at **historical rates,** the rates that were in effect when the assets were acquired; the liabilities were incurred, or when contributed capital was actually contributed. This includes:
  - o Marketable securities and inventory carried at cost.
  - o Prepaid expenses
  - o Property, plant, and equipment and its accumulated depreciation
  - o Intangibles
  - o Deferred charges, credits, and deferred income
  - o Preferred stock carried at issuance price and common stock

- o Revenues and expenses that are nonmonetary in nature such as cost of sales, depreciation, and amortization
- **Monetary assets and liabilities** are remeasured using the exchange rate at the **balance sheet date**
- Remeasurement of revenues, expense, gains, or losses (**Income statement**) will be determined by their natures.
    - o Many revenues and expenses that are incurred throughout the period will be remeasured at the **weighted average** exchange rate.
    - o Gains and losses will be remeasured using the **rates in effect on the dates** of the transactions generating the gains and losses.
    - o Revenues and expenses that are nonmonetary in nature, such as cost of sales, depreciation, and amortization are remeasured using **historical rates**.
        - Depreciation and amortization are remeasured using the same rates that are applied to the items being depreciated and amortized.
        - Cost of sales is remeasured by remeasuring beginning and ending inventory at their historical rates and purchases at the weighted average rate.
- The amount required to balance the entry is referred to as a **remeasurement adjustment**.
    - o The remeasurement adjustment occurs because items are being remeasured at different exchange rates and the result is not likely to balance.
    - o The remeasurement adjustment is recognized in **income (I/S)**.

The normal process for performing a **remeasurement** involves the following steps:
1. Remeasure items on the balance sheet as follows:
    a. *Monetary assets and liabilities* are remeasured using the rates at the **balance sheet date.**
    b. *Nonmonetary assets and liabilities* and *contributed capital* are remeasured using **historical rates** based on when assets were acquired, liabilities were incurred, and capital was contributed.
    c. The difference is ending retained earnings. The beginning balance will be rolled forward from the previous period and dividends, remeasured using the rate in effect on the dividend date, are deducted. The difference between that amount and the ending balance is the current period's **net income or loss**.
2. Remeasure all income statement items.
3. The difference between net income or loss and the result of remeasuring all income statement items will be the **remeasurement adjustment recognized in income.**

When the functional currency is in a **highly inflationary economy**, which is defined as one that has cumulative inflation of 100% or more over a 3-year period, the reporting currency will be considered the functional currency and financial statements will be remeasured rather than translated.

Lecture 6.06

CLASS QUESTIONS

Please see the Class Questions and Class Solutions for this Lecture at the end of this Section.

Lecture 6.07

FOREIGN CURRENCY TRANSACTIONS AND TRANSLATIONS UNDER IFRS

IAS 21 describes two types of circumstances that may involve foreign currency as foreign currency transactions and foreign operations. It provides guidance on how to report foreign currency transactions in an entity's financial statements and how to translate the financial statements related to foreign operations from the currency in which books and records are maintained, referred to as a **foreign currency (local)**, into the currency in which the financial statements are being presented, referred to as the **presentation currency (reporting)**.

- **Foreign Currency** = Local ("recording currency") → the currency of a particular country. Usually Books & Records are kept

- **Functional Currency** = Greatest economic impact on company (Currency in which entity generates and expends cash)

- **Presentation Currency** = Currency in which the enterprise prepares its financial statements ($US)

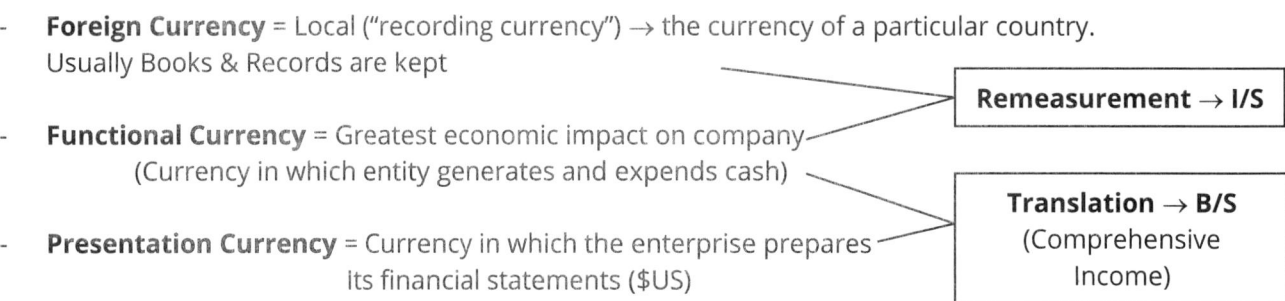

In most **foreign currency transactions**, the presentation currency is also the functional currency.
- The functional currency is the currency associated with the economy within which the entity predominantly operates.
- The transaction will initially be recorded in the functional currency using the spot exchange rate on the date of the transaction.
- At the balance sheet date, items that are measured in a foreign currency are translated into the functional currency:
    - Monetary items are translated using the rate at the balance sheet date.
    - Nonmonetary items reported at historical cost are translated using their historical rates.
    - Nonmonetary items reported at fair value are translated using the rates on the date the fair value measurement was made.
- Differences resulting from changes in monetary items are recognized in income.
- Differences resulting from changes in nonmonetary items:
    - Are recognized in other comprehensive income if gains or losses on exchanges would be recognized in other comprehensive income.
    - Are recognized in profit or loss if gains or losses on exchanges would be recognized in profit or loss.

When an entity is preparing financial statements that include **foreign operations**, first all information is translated into the functional currency if it is not the same as the currency in which the books and records are maintained. This is accomplished by applying the same approach that is used for foreign currency transactions with differences recognized in income or other comprehensive income, as appropriate.

If the functional currency is the same as the presentation currency, the information can be included in the consolidated financial statements. If it is not, once the financial statements have been translated into the functional currency, the entity's results and financial position are translated into the presentation currency.
- Assets and liabilities are translated at the rate on the balance sheet date.
- Income and expenses are translated at the rates in effect on the dates of the underlying transactions.
- Differences are recognized in other comprehensive income.

CLASS QUESTIONS

Work through the below Class Questions while following along with the respective lectures. Once this is complete, you can begin independently practicing what you've learned by quizzing yourself on this course section in your Interactive Practice Questions (IPQ), which can be found in your online Student Dashboard. Your IPQ simulates the computer-based testing experience, and will also help you understand how concepts are applied to the exam. Each question includes answer explanations from expert CPAs that will help you determine why you answered a question correctly or incorrectly. This is key to your success on the CPA Exam.

Lecture 6.06

1. A foreign subsidiary's functional currency is its local currency, which has not experienced significant inflation. The weighted-average exchange rate for the current year would be the appropriate exchange rate for translating

	Sales to Customers	Wages Expense
a.	No	No
b.	Yes	Yes
c.	No	Yes
d.	Yes	No

2. A balance arising from the translation or remeasurement of a subsidiary's foreign currency financial statements is reported in the consolidated income statement when the subsidiary's functional currency is the

	Foreign Currency	US Dollar
a.	No	No
b.	No	Yes
c.	Yes	No
d.	Yes	Yes

3. Park Co.'s wholly owned subsidiary, Schnell Corp., maintains its accounting records in Thai Baht. Because all of Schnell's branch offices are in Switzerland, its functional currency is the Swiss franc. Remeasurement of Schnell's 20X3 financial statements resulted in a $7,600 gain, and translation of its financial statements resulted in an $8,100 gain. What amount should Park report as a foreign exchange gain as net income in its income statement for the year ended December 31, 20X3?

   a. $0
   b. $ 7,600
   c. $ 8,100
   d. $15,700

4. On September 1, 20X3, Cano & Co., a US corporation, sold merchandise to a foreign firm for 250,000 Botswana pula. Terms of the sale require payment in pula on February 1, 20X4. On September 1, 20X3, the spot exchange rate was $.20 per pula. At December 31, 20X3, Cano's year end, the spot rate was $.19, but the rate increased to $.22 by February 1, 20X4, when payment was received. How much should Cano report as foreign exchange transaction gain or loss as part of 20X4 income?

   a. $0.
   b. $2,500 loss.
   c. $5,000 gain.
   d. $7,500 gain.

Questions 5, 6 and 7 all relate to the following information.

Three companies are doing business with a German entity and, as a result, each has entered into a forward exchange contract on December 18, 20X2, under which each will purchase 300,000 Euros on February 18, 20X3. Relevant exchange rates are as follows:

	Spot Rate	Forward Rate (for 2/18/X3)
November 18, 20X2	$ 1.27	$ 1.30
December 18, 20X2	1.32	1.25
December 31, 20X2	1.35	1.31
February 18, 20X3	1.37	

5. Company A entered into a contract to purchase a printing press for 300,000 Euros. The press will be ready, and the company is expected to pay for it, when it is completed on February 18, 20X3. The company entered into the forward exchange contract to avoid having to pay more for the printing press if the exchange rate should increase and is recognized as a cash flow hedge. What amount of foreign currency gain should be recognized in income on December 31, 20X2?

   a. $0
   b. $18,000 gain
   c. $18,000 loss
   d. $6,000 loss

6. Company B believes that the exchange rate is going to increase. As a result, they entered into the forward contract for speculation purposes. What amount of foreign currency gain should be recognized in income on December 31, 20X2?

   a. $0
   b. $18,000 gain
   c. $18,000 loss
   d. $6,000 loss

7. Company C purchased printing supplies from a German supplier on November 18, 20X2, on 90 day terms, and is required to pay 300,000 Euros on February 18, 20X3. When the exchange rate increased on December 18, the company decided to enter into the forward exchange contract, which was not designated as a hedge. What amount of foreign currency gain should be recognized in income on December 31, 20X2?

    a. $0
    b. $9,000 gain
    c $9,000 loss
    d. $6,000 loss

8. A U.S. company purchased inventory on account at a cost of 1,000 foreign currency units (FCU) from a non-U.S. company on November 15, to be paid on December 15. The FCU is valued at $0.85 on November 15 and at $0.90 on December 15. The journal entry to record payment on December 15 should include which of the following?

    a. Debit inventory and credit cash for $850.
    b. Debit exchange gains and losses and credit accounts payable for $50.
    c. Debit accounts payable and credit exchange gains and losses for $50.
    d. Debit accounts payable and credit cash for $850.

CLASS SOLUTIONS

1. (b) If a foreign subsidiary's local currency is its functional currency, its financial statements will be translated into the reporting currency. Revenue and expense items, including sales to customers and wages expense would be translated at the weighted average exchange rate for the period.

2. (b) When the subsidiary's functional currency is the foreign currency, financial statements will be translated into US dollars and the translation adjustment is reported in other comprehensive income, not on the income statement. When the functional currency is the US dollar, the financial statements are remeasured and the remeasurement adjustment is included in income.

3. (b) Remeasurement adjustments, such as the $7,600 gain, that result from converting financial statements from the local currency into the functional currency, are recognized in income. Translation adjustments, such as the $8,100 gain, that result from converting financial statements from the functional currency into the reporting currency, are recognized in other comprehensive income, not in the income statement.

4. (d) When the sale was made on 9/1/X3, the receivable would have been recorded at the spot rate of .20, or $50,000. On December 31, X3, the spot rate had declined to .19. The receivable would have been reduced to $47,500 and a foreign currency transaction loss of $2,500 would have been recognized in 20X3. When the receivable was settled in 20X4, the exchange rate was .22, and the amount received would be $55,000. Since the carrying value of the receivable was $47,500, the difference of $7,500 would be recognized as a gain in 20X4.

5. (a) Since the forward exchange contract is recognized as a cash flow hedge, no gain or loss will be recognized on the hedge until such time as it effects the hedged transaction. On December 18, 20X2, Company A enters into a contract to purchase 300,000 Euros at $1.25 on February 18, 20X3. As of December 31, it is expected that those Euros will be worth $1.31 each and, as a result, Company A will gain $.06 per Euro or a total of $18,000. Since it is a cash flow hedge, however, the gain is reported in other comprehensive income, not in earnings

6. (b) On December 18, 20X2, Company B enters into a contract to purchase 300,000 Euros at $1.25 on February 18, 20X3. As of December 31, it is expected that those Euros will be worth $1.31 each and, as a result, Company A will gain $.06 per Euro or a total of $18,000. Since the derivative was acquired on speculation, the gain will be recognized in earnings.

7. (d) When Company C incurred the liability on November 18, 20X2, it recorded the liability at the spot rate of $1.27 resulting in a liability of $381,000. On December 31, 20X2, when the spot rate was $1.35, the liability would be increased to $405,000, resulting in a loss of $24,000, which will be reported in earnings. In addition, the company entered into a contract to purchase 300,000 Euros at $1.25 on December 18, 20X3. As of December 31, it is expected that those Euros will be worth $1.31 each and, as a result, Company A will gain $.06 per Euro or a total of $18,000. Since the derivative was acquired on speculation, the gain will also be recognized in earnings. As a result, the net amount recognized in earnings will be a loss of $6,000.

8. (b) The journal entry on November 15 for the purchase of inventory on account would be:

15 Nov	Inventory	850	
	A/P (1,000 FCU x $0.85)		850

The summarizing journal entry on December 15 to record the payment for the inventory would be:

15 Dec	A/P	850	
	Foreign Exchange Loss	50	
	Cash (1,000 FCU x $0.90)		900

The above journal entry summarizes the following two journal entries:

15 Dec	Foreign Exchange Loss	50	
	A/P		50

To increase the payable by the loss.

15 Dec	A/P	900	
	Cash		900

To close out the payable.

Answer choice b) is the best of the available answer choices because it debits exchange gains and losses and credits A/P for $50, as shown in the journal entries above. Answer choice a) is wrong because inventory would have been debited at the time of purchase, plus $900 in cash is required to settle the account. Answer choice c) is wrong because it recognizes the change in the exchange rate as a gain, rather than a loss. Answer choice d) is wrong because $900 in cash is required to settle the account.

TASK-BASED SIMULATIONS

Task-Based Simulation 1

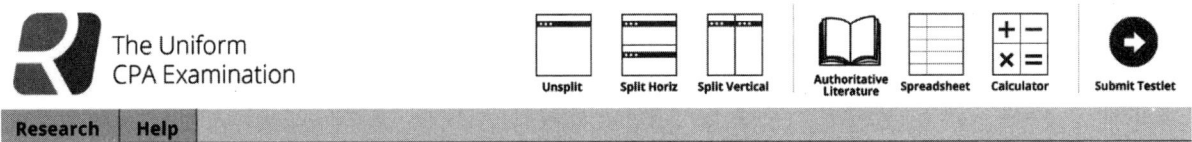

On its December 31 balance sheet, an entity has a receivable that is denominated in a foreign currency that is expected to be settled on March 15. The entity is uncertain as to whether to adjust the receivable based on changes in the exchange rate and whether to use the spot rate at December 31 or the forward rate for March 15. Identify the location in professional standards that indicates whether or not the receivable should be adjusted and the rate to use if it should.

Task-Based Simulation 2

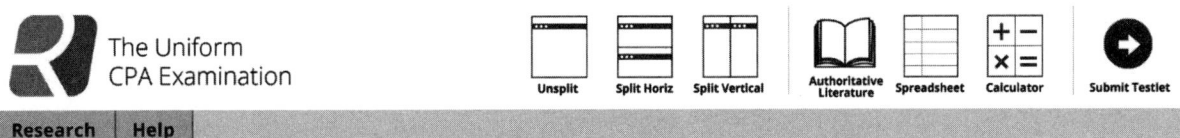

An entity has a foreign subsidiary for which the foreign currency is the functional currency. Upon translating the subsidiary's financial statements from the foreign currency into the reporting currency, the entity is trying to determine how to report the translation adjustment. Identify the location in professional standards that indicates how to account for a translation adjustment.

TASK-BASED SIMULATION SOLUTIONS

Task-Based Simulation Solution 1

| FASB ASC | 830 | 20 | 35 | 2 |

Task-Based Simulation Solution 2

| FASB ASC | 830 | 30 | 45 | 12 |

Section 7 - Inventory

Section 7 – Inventory
Corresponding Lectures

Watch the following course lectures with this section:

Lecture 7.01 – Accounting for Inventory
Lecture 7.02 – Inventory Costing Methods
Lecture 7.03 – Inventory Costing Methods – Class Questions
Lecture 7.04 – Dollar Value LIFO
Lecture 7.05 – Dollar Value LIFO – Class Questions & TBS
Lecture 7.06 – Lower of Cost or Market or Lower of Cost or NRV
Lecture 7.07 – Inventory Estimation Methods
Lecture 7.08 – Inventory Estimation Methods – Class Questions
Lecture 7.09 – Inventory under IFRS
Lecture 7.10 – Inventory under IFRS – Class Questions
Lecture 7.11 – Inventory – Class Questions & TBS
Lecture 7.12 – Inventory – Document Review Simulation

EXAM NOTE: *Please refer to the AICPA FAR Blueprint in the Introduction to find a listing of the representative tasks (and their associated skill levels—i.e., Remembering and Understanding, Application, and Analysis) that the candidate should be able to perform based on the knowledge obtained in this section.*

Inventory

Lecture 7.01

ACCOUNTING FOR INVENTORY

The Financial Accounting & Reporting exam normally deals with merchandise inventory only. Raw materials, work in process and finished goods inventory are usually tested in cost accounting, which is part of the Business Environment & Concepts exam **(ASC 330)**.

Cost of Inventory (Intended Use)
Includes all costs of acquisition and preparation for sale
- Warehousing costs prior to sale.
- Insurance, repackaging, modifications
- Freight-in paid by the buyer.
- Transportation costs paid by the seller on consignment arrangements.
- Do NOT include *abnormal costs* for idle factory expense, unallocated fixed overhead costs, excessive spoilage, double freight, and rehandling costs (these should be expensed immediately).

Goods in Transit

FOB shipping point
- Title passes to the buyer when the seller delivers the goods to a common carrier (shipped).
- Included in buyer's books at year end.

FOB destination
- Title passes to the buyer when the buyer receives the goods from the common carrier (received).
- Included in seller's books until received by buyer

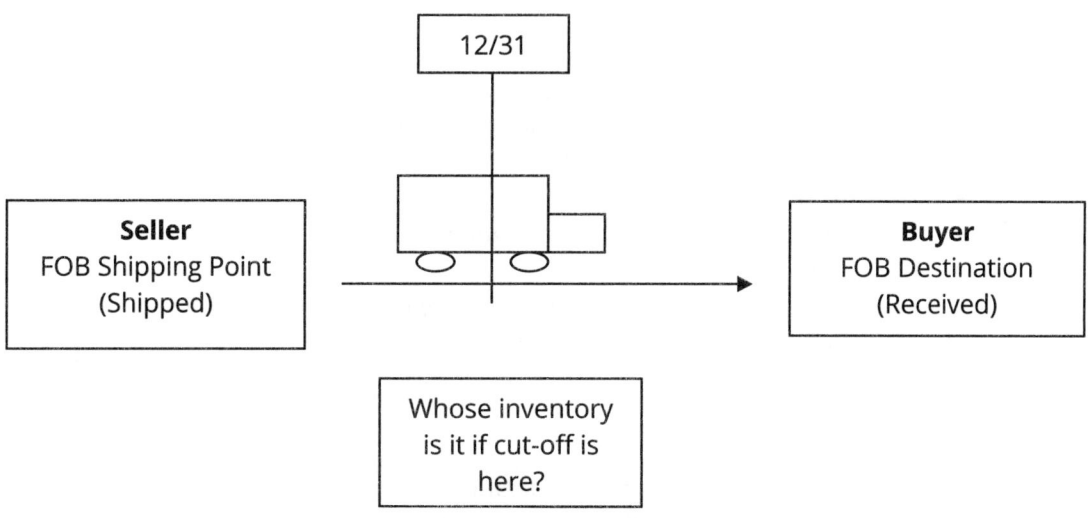

If goods that have been sold are returned, the seller should reduce net sales and add the cost of the items back to inventory. This should take place as soon as the seller has authorized the goods for return, so long as the actual return of the item is considered probable.

All of the costs associated with inventories will remain on the balance sheet until the point of sale, consistent with the matching principle. This means that the inventory account will include the purchase price of the goods as well as freight-in paid by the buyer and warehousing costs of goods prior to resale.

Financing costs are not, however, treated as part of the cost of inventory, and should be reported as interest expense. This will include interest on loans obtained in order to purchase inventory, as well as additional payments made to the seller of the goods as a result of interest on unpaid balances or early-payment discounts not taken. For example, if goods are purchased with a $100 invoice 2/10, net 30, then the client is entitled to a 2% discount if payment is made within 10 days, and records the inventory at $98 (net method). If payment is made more than 10 days after invoicing, the extra amounts paid will be recognized as financing expenses and not included in inventory.

Costs incurred at the time of sale, such as freight-out paid by the seller and sales commissions, are generally recognized as selling expenses at the time of sale, consistent with the matching principle.

Consignment Inventory   Consign**or** → Consign**ee**

Occasionally, a seller and buyer will enter into a consignment arrangement. This takes place when a buyer is acquiring goods for resale, but only wants to purchase those goods once they have been able to arrange the resale.

In these circumstances, the potential seller (consignor) arranges for the goods to be delivered to the potential buyer (consignee), but retains legal ownership of the goods. The consignor usually pays the transportation costs as well, and these are added to the consignor's inventory cost (notice these are not the same as freight-out costs, since no sale has occurred yet). Actually, the consignee never owns the goods, since their purchase only occurs at the time they are able to resell them, and will be reported immediately as cost of sales.

- **Consignor**
    - Includes inventory in his balance sheet.
    - Has ownership, but not possession of the goods.
    - Costs incurred by consignor in transferring goods to the consignee are considered inventory costs until sold. They include:
        - The cost of the goods
        - Freight paid on shipments to consignee
        - Warehousing costs
        - Advertising (but **not** included in inventory if paid for by consignee, reimbursable by consignor)
        - In-transit insurance

- **Consignee**
    - Items are not included in his inventory balance.
    - Has possession, but not ownership of the goods.
    - When sold, the sales price is given to the consignor after deducting any reimbursable costs and commissions earned by the consignee.

Cost of Goods Sold (COGS)

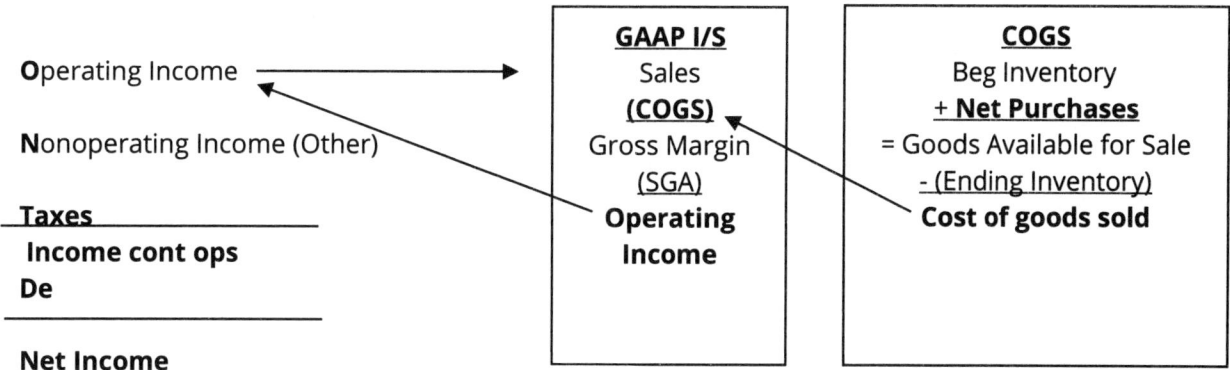

Operating Income

Nonoperating Income (Other)

Taxes
 Income cont ops
 De
_____

Net Income

Two Systems for Measuring Inventory Quantities

Periodic Inventory System (physical inventory count) Inventory quantity is determined by a physical count, usually done at year end.
- Inventory purchases are debited to purchases.
- No adjustment is made to inventory until the end of the period, when a physical inventory count is made and ending inventory is calculated.
- COGS is the plug and the exact amount of inventory shortages cannot be determined since it is buried in COGS.

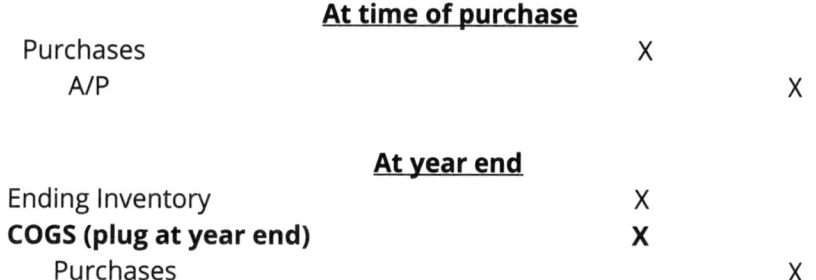

At time of purchase

Purchases	X	
A/P		X

At year end

Ending Inventory	X	
COGS (plug at year end)	**X**	
Purchases		X

Perpetual inventory system (ongoing, real-time count)
- Inventory purchases are debited to Inventory. The quantity on hand can be determined at any point in time.

At time of purchase

Inventory	80	
A/P		80

As sales occur

A/R	100	
Sales Rev		100
COGS	**80**	
Inventory		80

One advantage of a perpetual inventory system is that it enables the entity to determine how much inventory is on hand at any given point in time. Not only does this assist in the management of inventory but, by performing an inventory reconciliation, comparing the recorded amounts to physical counts, management will be able to identify errors in the recording of transactions involving inventory and find indicators of potential theft.

The exam has included problems and questions calling for an **inventory reconciliation** in which the candidate is expected to compare recorded amounts to physical counts and determine the reasons for differences and whether adjustments should be made to the recorded amount.

To reconcile from recorded amount to physical count:
1. Begin with recorded amount
2. Add goods held on consignment
3. Add goods sold fob shipping point and set aside but included in the count
4. (Subtract goods in transit that were sold fob destination)
5. (Subtract goods in transit that were purchased fob shipping point)

The result should be equal to the **physical count**.
(Any differences will be due to errors or fraud)

To reconcile from physical count to recorded amounts, the process will be reversed:
1. Begin with the physical count
2. Add goods in transit that were purchased fob shipping point
3. Add goods in transit that were sold fob destination
4. (Subtract goods sold fob shipping point that are set aside but included in the count)
5. (Subtract goods held on consignment)

The result should be equal to the **amount recorded**.
(Any differences will be due to errors or fraud)

Lecture 7.02

INVENTORY COSTING METHODS

Specific Identification
- Must be able to identify each unit sold. Used when inventory is few in number, very expensive and can be clearly identified, very heterogeneous items.

FIFO: First-in, First-out (LISH)

The inventory remaining on hand is presumed to consist of the most recent purchases. In periods of rising prices, FIFO results in the highest ending inventory, lowest cost of goods sold and the highest net income.
- FIFO assumes that goods are sold in the order of acquisition
- Closely relates to the actual physical flow of goods.
- First items acquired are the first items sold (FIFO).
- Last items acquired are still here in ending inventory (LISH)
- Perpetual and periodic inventory systems are the same.

Inventory

Section 7

LIFO: Last-in, First-out (FISH)

The most recent costs are expensed and matched with current revenues. The inventory remaining on hand is presumed to consist of the goods acquired first. In periods of rising prices LIFO results in the lowest ending inventory, highest cost of goods sold and the lowest net income.

- Better represents the flow of cash
- Last items acquired are the first items sold (LIFO)
- First items acquired are still here in ending inventory (FISH)
- Perpetual and periodic inventory systems are different.
- LIFO does not, however, assume goods are sold in the reverse order of acquisition. Instead, the use of the most recently acquired item as the cost of goods sold is an attempt to approximate the replacement cost of the item. This is based on an idea known as the *capital maintenance* concept, which presumes that a company that wishes to remain a going concern must maintain a basic level of investment in the assets that comprise the business. Thus, the true cost of an item that has been sold is the cost of replacing it in inventory. LIFO is as close as a company can get to replacement cost while still matching costs to the point of sale.
- If used for tax purposes, must also be used for financial reporting purposes. This is known as the LIFO conformity rule.

FIFO = COGS; (LISH = Ending Inventory)	**LIFO** = COGS; (FISH = Ending Inventory)
(Last In Still Here)	(First In Still Here)
If COSTS are going ↑ up	
COGS Understated	COGS Ok
NI Overstated	Profits Ok – I/S is Fair
Ending Inventory - Ok	Ending Inventory - Understated
Balance Sheet Ok (I/S not ok)	**Income statement Ok** (B/S not Ok)

Average Inventory methods

- Assign the same unit price to similar goods available during the period.
    - *Perpetual* (Moving Average) – This method computes the average after each purchase.
    - *Periodic* (Weighted Average) – This method takes total costs of all inventory purchases during the year and divides them by the total number of inventory units available during the year.

For example, assume a company had the following activity in the month of January:

Date	Units Purchased (Sold)
Beginning inventory, January 1	2
Purchase, January 5	2
Sale, January 12	(1)
Purchase, January 19	2
Sale, January 26	(1)
Ending inventory, January 31	4

©Roger CPA Review

To make it easier to follow, let's name the first two units in inventory, A and B, the two units purchased on 1/5, C and D, and the two units purchased on 1/19, E and F.

Assuming the **perpetual** approach is used, each transaction is processed as it happens. Let's see which units are left in inventory after each transaction, using FIFO and LIFO:

Units after transaction	FIFO	LIFO
Start of Month	A+B	A+B
January 5, Plus 2	A+B+C+D	A+B+C+D
January 12, Minus 1	B+C+D	A+B+C
January 19, Plus 2	B+C+D+E+F	A+B+C+E+F
January 26, Minus 1	C+D+E+F	A+B+C+E

If a **periodic** approach is used, all the purchases are recorded first, then the sales:

Units after transaction	FIFO	LIFO
Start of Month	A+B	A+B
Purchases, Plus 4	A+B+C+D+E+F	A+B+C+D+E+F
Sales, Minus 2	C+D+E+F	A+B+C+D

Lecture 7.03

CLASS QUESTIONS

Please see the Class Questions and Class Solutions for this Lecture at the end of this Section.

Lecture 7.04

Dollar Value LIFO

In certain industries, inventory is measured at current prices with increases added to the historical cost of beginning inventory, using current prices, and decreases measured on the basis of the most recent goods purchased, at their historical cost.
- Inventory is measured in terms of dollars, not units, and is adjusted for changing price levels.
- Inventory is combined into natural groups called "Inventory Pools" and each pool is valued separately. A price level index is used to convert the inventory value from LIFO to Dollar-value LIFO.

For most companies, the inventory method best matching their pricing policy is LIFO. Most companies price goods for sale based on replacement cost, and LIFO results in the most recent purchases being treated as cost of sales, coming closest to replacement cost of all GAAP methods.

Nevertheless, there are **two potential difficulties** that arise from the application of the LIFO method:
- The company needs to keep track of the different unit costs for items acquired on different dates, going all the way back to the date the company first adopted the method, which could be the date the company was founded. This need to keep cumulative accurate

records will result in increasing record-keeping costs over time. And when a client has several different types of products in its inventory, the **costs can be enormous**.

- When inventory levels decline temporarily, older costs previously inventoried will become a part of cost of goods sold, causing a distortion of that account if there have been substantial price changes over time. This is because the unit costs in inventory that are several years old are likely to be radically different from the approximation of replacement cost represented by the most recent purchases.

A useful solution is a method known as **Dollar-Value LIFO (DV LIFO)**. Under this approach, related inventory items are grouped in **pools**, and an overall price index is used to approximate changes in inventory costs. It addresses both of the difficulties mentioned above:

- It is only necessary to **keep track of annual layers** of inventory cost and price indexes for each inventory pool, instead of retaining detailed records of each unit cost of each item purchased over the life of the company. As a result, the record-keeping costs of this method are substantially lower than traditional LIFO.

- Since related items are grouped together and layers are computed annually, reductions in the level of a certain type of item in inventory that are offset by increases in the level of other items in the pool, or reductions at interim periods that are compensated by year-end, won't result in the use of older costs in the calculation of cost of goods sold. As a result, this method substantially reduces the probability that older inventory layers will be liquidated and reported in cost of goods sold.

To apply the DV LIFO method, **two figures are needed**:

- The **total current cost** of the inventory in the pool at the end of each year (this would usually be the replacement cost or the ending inventory under a FIFO approach).

- A **price index** indicating the overall price level compared to the base date (the date the method was first adopted).

Section 7   Inventory

Dollar Value LIFO EXAMPLE:

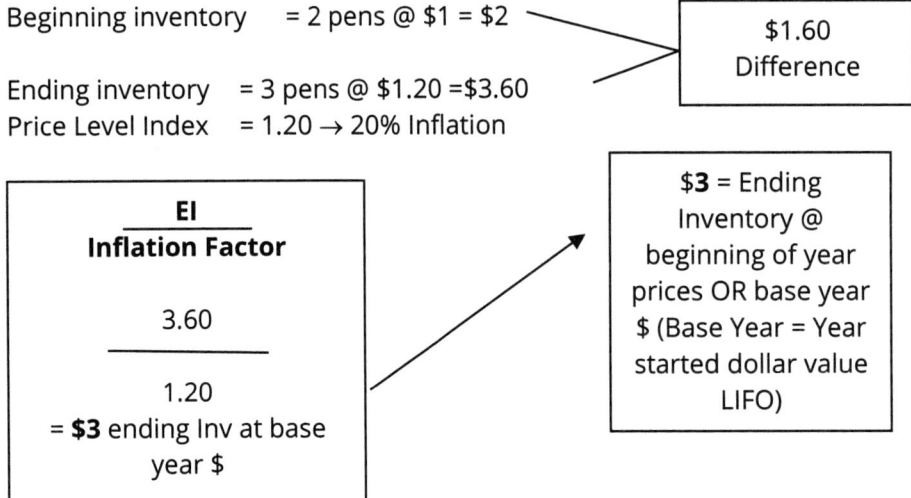

Beginning inventory = 2 pens @ $1 = $2

Ending inventory = 3 pens @ $1.20 = $3.60
Price Level Index = 1.20 → 20% Inflation

$1.60 Difference

$$\frac{EI}{\text{Inflation Factor}}$$

$$\frac{3.60}{1.20}$$

= **$3** ending Inv at base year $

$3 = Ending Inventory @ beginning of year prices OR base year $ (Base Year = Year started dollar value LIFO)

Adding Layers

LAYER
LAYER
BASE

$3 =	End Inv @ beginning of year prices OR Base Year $
(2) =	Subtract Base
$1 =	Increase in inventory @ base year $
x 1.20 =	Multiply by inflation factor
1.20 =	Layer @ current costs
+ 2.00 =	Still around (old inventory) @ base cost
3.20 =	End Inv. @ current cost

Year	Inventory @ Y/E $ ÷	Price level Index =	End Inv @ Base Year $	Addtl Layer	X2 (1.0)	X3 (1.2)	X4 (1.3)	X5 (1.4)	X6 (1.5)
X2	$2	1.0	2	$2					
X3	3.60	1.2	3	$1		$1 0.9			
X4	4.30	1.3	3.3	0.3			0.3		
X5	4.06	1.4	2.9	(0.4)				0 (0.4) Sold	
X6	5.25	1.5	3.5	0.6					0.6
					$2	$1.2	0.39		0.9

What you sold comes out of LIFO

- **Price level index (approaches)**
    o   Simplified (CPI for your industry – given)
    o   Link Chain (single cumulative index, compare with previous year)
    o   Double extension (extend back to base year)

- **Ending inventory**
  - X2 = $2   (2 x 1.0)
  - X3 = $3.2   (2 + 1.2 (1 x 1.2))
  - X4 = $3.59   (2 + 1.2 + .39 (.3 x 1.3))
  - X5 = $3.08   (2 + 1.08 (.9 x 1.2))
  - X6 = $3.98   (2 + 1.08 + .9 (.6 x 1.5))

For example, assume that the method was adopted on 12/31/X1, and the following facts applied to the first year in which the method was applied:

Date	Current Cost (CC)	Price Index (PI)
12/31/X1	$1,000	1.00
12/31/X2	$1,320	1.10

Notice that the price index is automatically set at 1.00 on the date the method is adopted, and the above information indicates that prices increased by 10% in 20X2.

Our first step is to determine if inventory rose or fell after eliminating the effects of price changes. We do this by factoring out inflation, which is accomplished by dividing the current cost by the price index each year:

Date	Current Cost	Price Index	Base Cost (BC)
12/31/X1	$1,000	1.00	$1,000
12/31/X2	$1,320	1.10	$1,200

In a sense, we can think of the price index as the unit cost of the items, not in physical units, but in units of base cost. Thus, at the end of 20X1 (beginning of 20X2), the company held 1,000 base units at $1.00 each, and at the end of 20X2, the company held 1,200 base units at $1.10 each, so that the inventory went up in real terms by 200 base units, or 20%. The rest of the increase in the dollar value of inventory was the result of inflation.

Once the increase at base cost is computed, it must be adjusted back to current prices, since the increase occurred in the current year. This results in different layers of inventory at different price indexes:

Date	CC	PI	BC	Layer	PI	DV LIFO
12/31/X1	$1,000	1.00	$1,000	$1,000	1.00	$1,000
12/31/X2	$1,320	1.10	$1,200	$200	1.10	$220
Total						$1,220

If inventory at current cost is $1,560 at 12/31/X3, and the price index has increased to 1.20, representing 20% of cumulative inflation since 12/31/X1, the next year's computation is as follows:

Date	CC	PI	BC	Layer	PI	DV LIFO
12/31/X1	$1,000	1.00	$1,000	$1,000	1.00	$1,000
12/31/X2	$1,320	1.10	$1,200	$200	1.10	$220
12/31/X3	$1,560	1.20	$1,300	$100	1.20	$120
Total						$1,340

Finally, if inventory declines in 12/31/X4 to a current cost of $1,430 while the index rises to 1.30, we will be removing some of the layers from the previous years as follows:

Date	CC	PI	BC	Layer	PI	DV LIFO
12/31/X1	$1,000	1.00	$1,000	$1,000	1.00	$1,000
12/31/X2	$1,320	1.10	$1,200	$100	1.10	$110
12/31/X3	$1,560	1.20	$1,300			
12/31/X4	$1,430	1.30	$1,100			
Total						$1,110

Compare this table to the previous one, and notice that, to account for the $200 decline at base cost from $1,300 to $1,100, we removed the 20X3 layer of $100 at 1.20, and then removed $100 from the 20X2 layer at 1.10, leaving the layers noted in the last chart.

In all of the examples so far, the price index has been provided. There are **3 different methods** for arriving at an index:
- **Simplified**
- **Double Extension** (extend back to base year)
- **Link-Chain** (cumulative index, compare with previous year)

The **Simplified** method refers to the use of a generally available index of prices, typically a government index such as the Consumer Price Index for Urban Consumers (**CPI**).

The **Double Extension method** requires the client to count the inventory and then extend inventory prices twice (which is the reason the term "double" is used). Then the two results are compared to determine a price index:
- Current Quantity x Current Unit Cost = Current Cost
- Current Quantity x Base Date Unit Cost = Base Cost
- Current Cost / Base Cost = Price Index

Notice that the 3 numbers calculated are the same three figures as in earlier examples. The difference is that the earlier examples used Current Cost / Price Index = Base Cost, but since division is transitive (if A / B = C then A / C = B), either approach is acceptable.

Let's look at an example of computing the index using the double extension method. Assume a company has two products, X and Y, with the following inventory quantities and unit costs at the end of each year:

Year	X Quantity	Y Quantity	X Unit Cost	Y Unit Cost
20X1 (base)	26	12	$20	$40
20X2	30	15	$26	$44
20X3	36	18	$28	$64

The 20X3 current cost and base cost amounts are computed as follows:

Product	Quantity	Unit Cost	Total Cost	Aggregate
X	36	$28	$1,008	
Y	18	$64	$1,152	
Current Cost				$2,160
X	36	$20	$720	
Y	18	$40	$720	
Base Cost				$1,440

The index for 20X3 is then $2,160 / $1,440 = 1.50

The **Link-Chain method** is similar to the Double Extension method, except that year-to-year price changes, rather than cumulative changes, are computed, then the annual changes are linked (multiplied) together to determine a price index. To determine the year-to-year changes, the calculation is:
- Current Quantity x End-of-year Unit Cost = Current Cost
- Current Quantity x Start-of-year Unit Cost = Prior Year Cost
- Current Cost / Prior Year Cost = Annual Cost Index

For example, use the same facts as in the previous example:

Year	X Quantity	Y Quantity	X Unit Cost	Y Unit Cost
20X1(base)	26	12	$20	$40
20X2	30	15	$26	$44
20X3	36	18	$28	$64

The 20X2 annual index calculation is:

Product	Quantity	Unit Cost	Total Cost	Aggregate
X	30	$26	$780	
Y	15	$44	$660	
Current Cost				$1,440
X	30	$20	$600	
Y	15	$40	$600	
Prior Cost				$1,200
Annual Index				1.20

Section 7   Inventory

The 20X3 annual index calculation is:

		36	$28	$1,008	
Y		18	$64	$1,152	
Current Cost					$2,160
X		36	$26	$936	
Y		18	$44	$792	
Prior Cost					$1,728
Annual Index					1.25

The price index for 20X3 is the result of linking these indexes together:

Year	Annual Cost Index	Overall Price Index
20X1		1.00
20X2	1.20	1.20
20X3	1.25	1.50

The overall price index at the end of 20X3 is the result of multiplying the annual cost indexes for 20X2 and 20X3 (1.20 x 1.25 = 1.50).

Lecture 7.05

CLASS QUESTIONS

Please see the Class Questions and Class Solutions for this Lecture at the end of this Section.

Lecture 7.06

Lower of Cost or Market or Lower of Cost or NRV Rule (LCM or LCNRV)

- **Conservatism & Matching principle.**
- Cost = Original Cost
- Market = middle of 3 numbers:
    - **Ceiling** = Net Realizable Value (NRV) = (selling price – disposal costs)
        - disposal costs (cost to complete, freight out, sales commissions)
    - **Floor** = NRV – normal Profit Margin
    - **Replacement cost** = Purchase or reproduction
        - Middle of these numbers is used as market, then compare market with cost and take the Lower (LCM).

Inventory   Section 7

UPDATE ALERT

As a result of ASU 2015-11, the Lower of Cost or Market rule (LCM) applies only to inventory accounted for under the LIFO or retail inventory methods. For all other inventory a simplified **Lower of Cost or NRV** rule will apply. This change became effective on the CPA Exam January 1, 2017.

To summarize, apply the Lower of Cost or Market rule only to inventory accounted for under the LIFO or retail inventory methods. For all other inventory, apply the simplified **Lower of Cost or NRV** rule (LCNRV).

- Inventory *valuation* may be based upon:
    - Individual items
    - Categories
    - Total inventory

- *Losses* are recognized immediately on the income statement.
    - Do NOT recover loss (once inventory is written down there is no recovery from the write down until the units are sold).

Loss on Inventory due to market decline	X
Inventory	X

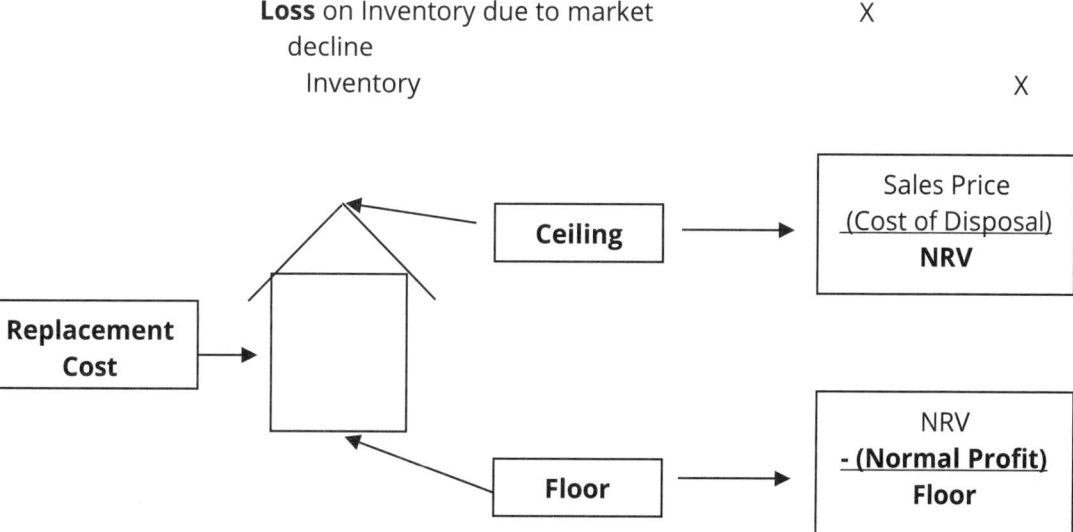

Lower of Cost or NRV (LCNRV)
Effective for periods beginning after December 15, 2016, ASC 330 requires that all inventory, other than inventory accounted for under the LIFO or retail inventory methods, be reported on the balance sheet at the lower of cost or net realizable value (LCNRV). This is due to the simplification initiative to align GAAP more closely with IFRS. This change became effective on the CPA Exam January 1, 2017.

Regardless of the choice of inventory costing method, a company must consider the need to account for declines in the market value of unsold inventories. Based on the **conservatism** principle, a company will normally carry inventories on the balance sheet at the lower of cost or market.

One problem to consider is that there are two different markets in which the company operates: the market in which the company purchases the inventories, and the market in which the company sells the inventories. Under normal circumstances, the company will use the market in which purchases occur, so that the term "market" is usually referring to the *replacement cost* of the inventories, or what it would cost the company if they were to purchase the items today.

If the prices of goods in inventory have been consistently rising, then the valuation under an LCM or LCNRV approach will usually be at cost, regardless of which costing method was used. If the prices of goods in inventory have been consistently falling, then the valuation under an LCM or LCNRV approach will usually be at market, regardless of which costing method was used.

For example, assume that a company in its first year of existence had the following transactions:

Date	Transaction	Units	Unit Cost
March	Purchase	1	$3
November	Purchase	1	$5
December	Sale	(1)	?

Assume the replacement cost of the remaining unit in inventory is $6 on December 31, and represents the appropriate number to use as market. Assume that NRV is also $6. On either a lower of cost or market or lower of cost or NRV basis, the ending inventory under FIFO and LIFO approaches is determined as follows:

Method	FIFO	LIFO
Cost	5	3
Market / NRV	6	6
LCM or LCNRV	5	3

Now let's look at a case of **falling prices**. For example, assume the following transactions took place in the first year of a company's operations:

Date	Transaction	Units	Unit Cost
March	Purchase	1	$7
November	Purchase	1	$5
December	Sale	(1)	?

Assume the replacement cost of the remaining unit in inventory is $4 on December 31, and represents the appropriate number to use as market. Assume that NRV is also $4. On a lower of cost or market or lower of cost or NRV basis, the ending inventory under FIFO and LIFO approaches is determined as follows:

Method	FIFO	LIFO
Cost	5	7
Market / NRV	4	4
LCM or LCNRV	4	4

Unfortunately, when the lower of cost or market rule is applied, the determination of market value is significantly more complicated than it might at first appear. Actually, there are three different numbers that need to be computed before market can be determined:
- **Replacement cost** – the estimated purchase price of the goods.
- **Net realizable value (NRV)** – the estimated selling price of the goods reduced by costs of disposal (such as necessary costs to complete the goods, freight-out, and sales commissions) (**Ceiling**).
- **NRV less normal profit margin (floor)** – the price at which the client would make no profit at all.

Under normal circumstances, the replacement cost is lower than the net realizable value and higher than the net realizable value less normal profit margin, and is used as market. The NRV is the ceiling on market, however, and when replacement cost is higher than NRV, the NRV is used as market. The NRV less normal profit margin is the floor on market, so replacement cost is not used if it is lower than that.

Assume the following facts:

Replacement cost	100
Estimated selling price	120
Estimated selling expenses	30
Normal profit margin	20

From the above information, we can determine the normal, ceiling, and floor amounts for market:

Normal: Replacement cost	100
Ceiling: Net realizable value	90
Floor: NRV less normal profit margin	70

Since the replacement cost of 100 exceeds the ceiling of 90, the market is 90, and that number will be compared with historical cost to determine the lower of cost or market.

These complications, of course, do not arise with inventory for which the simplified lower of cost or NRV rule applies. Effective on the exam January 1, 2017, this simplified rule applies for all inventory other than inventory accounted for under the LIFO or retail inventory methods.

Lecture 7.07

INVENTORY ESTIMATION METHODS
Gross Profit (Margin) Method
Gross profit can be used to prepare interim financial statements or as an estimate if ending inventory is missing or destroyed. First, calculate an estimate of COGS by using the *Historical Gross Profit Percentage,* then back into ending inventory.

Beginning Inventory	100
+ Purchases	300
Goods Available for Sale	400
(Ending Inventory) ??	**220 (plugged)**
Cost of Goods Sold	**180**

Gross Profit % = 40%   so if Sales = 300 (60%) = **180 COGS**
COGS % = 60% (estimated)

Retail Inventory Methods

These are rarely used and extremely complicated techniques for estimation of inventory.
- **Conventional Retail Inventory method**
    - The company keeps track of inventory costs at both cost and retail. Sales, theft losses and employee discounts during the year are recorded at retail and at the end of the year, the co. converts ending inventory from retail back to cost by using a cost/retail percentage. This method approximates the results that would be obtained by taking a physical inventory and pricing the goods at the lower of cost or market (LCM).
        - Net mark-ups are included in the cost to retail percentage calculation
        - Net mark-downs are not included in the cost to retail percentage calculation.

	Cost		Retail
Beginning Inventory	X		X
+ Purchases	X		X
+ Freight in	X		-
+Net Markups	-		X
Goods available for sale	X	/	X = C/R %
-Net Markdowns			(X)
Sales price of goods available for sale			X
- Losses			(X)
- Sales @ Retail			(X)
Ending Inventory @ **Retail**			X
Multiply ending inventory at Retail by C/R%			**C/R%**
Equals ending inventory at Cost			X

- **Net mark-ups** = mark-ups – mark-up cancellations
- **Net mark-downs** = mark-downs – mark-down cancellations

- **LIFO Retail Inventory method**
    - The LIFO Retail method approximates the **original cost** of the merchandise as opposed to the conventional retail method which approximates LCM.
        - The two differences are that:
            - Net mark-ups and net mark-downs are **both included** in the cost to retail percentage calculation.
            - Beginning inventory is **not** included in the cost to retail percentage calculation.

Inventory   Section 7

Firm Purchase Commitments

A non-cancelable agreement to buy inventory in the future. If it is expected that a loss will occur in the future, the loss is recognized at the time of the decline in price. The loss is the difference between the contract price and the market price of the minimum required amount of inventory that must be purchased in the future.

Estimated Loss (I/S)	X	
Estimated Liability		X

Note: For Inventory Ratio Homework see Financial Statement Analysis section.

Lecture 7.08

CLASS QUESTIONS

Please see the Class Questions and Class Solutions for this Lecture at the end of this Section.

Lecture 7.09

INVENTORY UNDER IFRS

Requirements related to accounting for inventories are very similar under IFRS to those under US GAAP. IFRS principles of accounting for inventories apply to most inventories, but do not apply to work-in-progress resulting from construction contracts, financial instruments, or the biological assets of an agricultural entity.

IFRS requires that inventory be reported at the **lower of cost or net realizable value (LCNRV)**. Cost includes:
- The cost of purchase
- Costs of conversion
  - This is calculated similarly to US GAAP
  - In limited circumstances, IFRS allows for the capitalization of borrowing costs
- Other costs incurred in bringing the inventory to its current location and condition

The method for determining cost depends on the nature of the inventory:
- The *specific identification* method is required for items that are not interchangeable and for items that are produced and segregated for specific projects
- Cost is determined using FIFO or weighted average for all other inventories
  - **LIFO is not allowed**
  - Standard cost or the retail methods are allowed if the results approximate cost under either FIFO or weighted average

- Effective for periods beginning after December 15, 2016, ASC 330 requires that under US GAAP all inventory, other than inventory accounted for under the LIFO or retail inventory methods, be reported on the balance sheet at the *lower of cost or net realizable value* (LCNRV). This is due to the simplification initiative to align GAAP more closely with IFRS. This change became effective on the CPA Exam January 1, 2017.

Inventories are charged to expense, generally in the form of cost of sales, in the same period as related revenues are recognized.

Losses and write-downs are recognized in the period of occurrence.
- This is the period in which the net realizable value falls below cost
- **Reversals** of write-downs are also recognized as a reduction of expense

The primary differences between US GAAP and IFRS in accounting for inventory are:
- IFRS does not allow LIFO.
- IFRS requires inventories to be reported at the lower of cost or net realizable value (LCNRV) rather than the lower of cost or market (LCM). Effective on the CPA Exam January 1, 2017, most inventories under GAAP are reported at LCNRV, but inventory accounted for under the LIFO or retail inventory methods are still reported at LCM.
- IFRS allows recoveries in the value of inventory when the net realizable value increases after inventory has been written down.

In addition, in limited circumstances, IFRS allows *borrowing costs* to be capitalized as part of the cost of conversion when measuring the cost of inventory. This is only allowed in circumstances where inventory requires a substantial period of time to get ready for sale.

As indicated, a key difference between GAAP and IFRS is that under IFRS, **a loss may be recovered.** If the LCNRV is $80 for inventory with a historical cost of $100 at the end of year, the inventory would be written down to $80 with a corresponding expense on the income statement. If the inventory value at the end of Year 2 was $90, a recovery of the loss of $10 would be recorded by debiting Inventory and crediting an income account (COGS).

```
Inventory                              xxx
     Recovery of inventory loss (I/S)              xxx
```

Inventory	
US GAAP	**IFRS**
• Allows FIFO, LIFO, or average cost flow assumption • Most inventories valued at lower of cost or net realizable value (LCNRV), but some still require lower of cost or market (LCM) – effective on the exam January 1, 2017. • Any impairment write-downs create a new cost basis; previously recognized impairment losses are *NOT reversed*.	• Allows FIFO or average, *not LIFO* • Inventories are valued at lower of cost or net realizable value (LCNRV) • Previously recognized impairment losses *may be reversed*.

Lecture 7.10

CLASS QUESTIONS

Please see the Class Questions and Class Solutions for this Lecture at the end of this Section.

Lecture 7.11

CLASS QUESTIONS

Please see the Class Questions and Class Solutions for this Lecture at the end of this Section.

Lecture 7.12
CLASS QUESTIONS
Please see the Class Questions and Class Solutions for this Lecture at the end of this Section.

Section 7   Inventory

CLASS QUESTIONS

Work through the below Class Questions while following along with the respective lectures. Once this is complete, you can begin independently practicing what you've learned by quizzing yourself on this course section in your Interactive Practice Questions (IPQ), which can be found in your online Student Dashboard. Your IPQ simulates the computer-based testing experience, and will also help you understand how concepts are applied to the exam. Each question includes answer explanations from expert CPAs that will help you determine why you answered a question correctly or incorrectly. This is key to your success on the CPA Exam.

Lecture 7.03

Questions 1 and 2 are based on the following information:

During January 20X3, Metro Co., which maintains a perpetual inventory system, recorded the following information pertaining to its inventory:

	Units	Unit cost	Total cost	Units on hand
Balance on 1/1/X3	1,000	$1	$1,000	1,000
Purchased on 1/7/X3	600	3	1,800	1,600
Sold on 1/20/X3	900			700
Purchased on 1/25/X3	400	5	2,000	1,100

1. Under the moving-average method, what amount should Metro report as inventory at January 31, 20X3?

    a. $2,640
    b. $3,225
    c. $3,300
    d. $3,900

2. Under the LIFO method, what amount should Metro report as inventory at January 31, 20X3?

    a. $1,300
    b. $2,700
    c. $3,900
    d. $4,100

3. During periods of rising prices, a perpetual inventory system would result in the same dollar amount of ending inventory as a periodic inventory system under which of the following inventory cost flow methods?

	FIFO	LIFO
a.	Yes	No
b.	Yes	Yes
c.	No	Yes
d.	No	No

Inventory   Section 7

4. Herc Co's inventory at December 31, 20X2 was $1,500,000 based on a physical count priced at cost, and before any necessary adjustment for the following:
   - Merchandise costing $90,000 shipped FOB shipping point from a vendor on December 30, 20X2 was received and recorded on January 5, 20X3.
   - Goods in the shipping area were excluded from inventory although shipment was not made until January 3, 20X3. The goods, billed to the customer FOB shipping point on December 30, 20X2, had a cost of $120,000.

   What amount should Herc report as Inventory in its December 31, 20X2 balance sheet?

   a. $1,500,000
   b. $1,590,000
   c. $1,620,000
   d. $1,710,000

Lecture 7.05

5. Brock Co. adopted the dollar-value LIFO inventory method as of January 1, 20X1. A single inventory pool and an internally computed price index are used to compute Brock's LIFO inventory layers. Information about Brock's dollar value inventory follows:

	Inventory		
Date	At base year cost	At current year cost	At dollar value LIFO
1/1/X1	$40,000	$40,000	$40,000
20X1 layer	5,000	14,000	6,000
12/31/X1	45,000	54,000	46,000
20X2 layer	15,000	26,000	?
12/31/X2	$60,000	$80,000	?

   What was Brock's dollar value LIFO inventory at December 31, 20X2?

   a. $80,000
   b. $74,000
   c. $66,000
   d. $60,000

Lecture 7.08

6. The original cost of an inventory item for which the lower of cost or market rule applies is below both replacement cost and net realizable value. The net realizable value less normal profit margin is below the original cost. Under the lower of cost or market method, the inventory item should be valued at

   a. Replacement cost.
   b. Net realizable value.
   c. Net realizable value less normal profit margin.
   d. Original cost.

Section 7   Inventory

7. Hutch, Inc. uses the conventional retail inventory method to account for inventory. The following information relates to 20X1 operations:

	Cost	Average Retail
Beginning inventory and purchases	$600,000	$920,000
Net markups		40,000
Net markdowns		60,000
Sales		780,000

What amount should be reported as cost of sales for 20X1?

- a. $480,000
- b. $487,500
- c. $520,000
- d. $525,000

Lecture 7.10

8. Alexes Co values its inventory at the lower of cost or net realizable value (LCNRV) as required by IFRS. Alexes has the following information regarding its inventory:

Historical cost	$1,000
Estimated selling price	900
Estimated costs to complete and sell	50
Replacement cost	800

What is the amount for inventory that Alexes Co should report on the balance sheet under the lower of cost or net realizable value method?

- a. $1,000
- b. $ 900
- c. $ 850
- d. $ 750

9. Even Steven Corp. has inventory that, at December 31, 20X2, consisted of 2,000,000 units. The value at December 31, 20X2 was as follows:

Original cost	$11.00 per unit
Replacement cost	$9.50 per unit
Normal sales price	$12.50 per unit
Costs of disposal	$2.00 per unit
Normal profit	$2.50 per unit

What amount will Even Steven report as inventory in its financial statements prepared under IFRS?

- a. $22,000,000.
- b. $19,000,000.
- c. $21,000,000.
- d. $16,000,000.

10. Conrad's Computers, a company that prepares its financial statements under IFRS, supplies computer equipment to various European governmental agencies on a cost plus basis. Although he sells the computers in the order in which he acquires them, Conrad wishes to apply the highest costs to computers sold, and the lowest costs to those remaining in inventory. In periods of rising prices, which of the following methods may Conrad use to minimize the amount reported in inventory and maximize the amount charged to cost of sales?

    a. FIFO.
    b. Weighted average.
    c. LIFO.
    d. Specific identification.

CLASS SOLUTIONS

1. (b) The moving-average method requires that a new unit cost be computed each time goods are purchased. The new unit cost is used to cost all sales of inventory until the next purchase. After the 1/7/x3 purchase, Metro owns 1,600 units (1,000 + 600) at a total cost of $2,800 ($1,000 + $1,800). Therefore, the moving-average unit cost at that time is $1.75 ($2,800 ÷ 1,600 units). After the 1/20/x3 sale of 900 units (at a unit of cost of $1.75), Metro owns 700 units at a unit cost of $1.75 (700 x $1.75 = $1,225). The 1/25/x3 purchase of 400 units at a total cost of $2,000 increases inventory to its 1/31/x3 balance of $3,225 ($1,225 + $2,000). The new unit cost (not required) is $2.93 ($3,225 ÷ 1,100).

2. (b) LIFO stands for last-in, first-out; this means that it is assumed that any units sold are the units most recently purchased. In a perpetual system, LIFO is applied at the time of each sale rather than once a year as in a periodic system. Using LIFO, the 900 units sold on 1/20/x3 would consist of the 600 units purchased on 1/7/x3 and 300 of the 1,000 units in the 1/1/x3 balance. This would leave in inventory 700 units from the 1/1/x3 balance. After the 1/25/x3 purchase, inventory included those 700 units plus the 400 units purchased on 1/25/x3. Therefore, ending inventory is $2,700 [(700 x $1) + (400 x $5)].

3. (a) Under FIFO, which is first-in, first-out, the earliest goods purchased are charged to cost of sales and the most recent purchases remain in inventory. As a result, FIFO inventory will be the same whether accounted for using a perpetual or a periodic system. Since LIFO, which is last-in, first out, charges the cost of the goods purchased most recently to cost of sales, when a sale was made will determine which goods were most recently purchased. Under periodic LIFO, the evaluation is made at the end of the period. As a result, ending inventory would consist of goods on hand at the beginning of the year with any increases in quantities coming from the most recent purchases. Under perpetual LIFO, however, the evaluation is made at the time of each sale. As a result, when goods were sold between or before purchases, inventory on hand at the beginning of the year may have been used for sales that occurred before additional inventory was purchased. Perpetual LIFO will provide different results than periodic LIFO.

4. (d) The merchandise in transit to Herc should be included in inventory since it was shipped FOB shipping point and therefore it belonged to Herc as soon as it was delivered to the common carrier. The merchandise in the shipping area that was excluded since it had not been delivered to a common carrier as of the end of the period. As a result, inventory would be ($1,500,000 + $90,000 + $120,000) $1,710,000.

5. (c) Since ending inventory at base year cost is $60,000 and at current year cost is $80,000, the 20X2 layer of $15,000 can be converted to current year costs by:

$15,000 x $80,000/$60,000 = $20,000

Ending inventory will consist of:		
Base year layer - $40,000 at base year prices	=	$40,000
20X1 layer - $5,000 x $54,000/$45,000	=	$6,000
20X2 layer - $15,000 x $80,000/$60,000	=	$20,000
Total ending inventory	=	$66,000

6. (d) Inventory accounted for under the LIFO or retail inventory methods is required to be reported at the lower of cost or market. Under the lower of cost or market rule, 'market' is defined as replacement cost subject to maximum, ceiling, and minimum, floor, limitations. First, the replacement cost is compared to the ceiling, which is the net realizable value. If replacement cost is higher than net realizable value, the net realizable value is considered market value. If replacement cost is lower than net realizable value, it is then compared to the floor, which is the net realizable value less a normal margin. If replacement cost is higher than the floor, and is between ceiling and floor, then replacement value is market value. If replacement cost is lower than the floor, the floor is considered market value, which would be the case here. This value for 'market' will then be compared to the original cost, the lower of which, the original cost in this case, would be the carrying value of the inventory.

7. (d) Under the conventional retail method, beginning inventory at cost of $600,000 is compared to beginning inventory at retail including the retail price of purchases and markups for a total of $960,000. The result is a cost to retail percentage of 62.5%. Ending inventory at retail will be $960,000 reduced by sales of $780,000 and markdowns of $60,000 for a net amount of $120,000. This will be multiplied by the cost to retail percentage to give ending inventory at the approximate lower of cost or market of $75,000. Based on purchases of $600,000, cost of goods sold must be the difference of $525,000.

8. (c) IFRS requires that inventory be reported at the lower of cost, which in this case is $1,000, or net realizable value (LCNRV). Net realizable value is the sales price of $900 reduced by costs to complete the units as well as costs required to sell the units. In this case, the estimated cost to complete is $50 and the net realizable value would be $850. Since it is lower than cost, it will be the carrying value of the inventory.

9. (c) IFRS requires that inventory be reported at the lower of cost, which in this case is $11.00 per unit, or net realizable value. Net realizable value is the sales price of $12.50 per unit reduced by costs to complete the units as well as costs required to sell the units. In this case, the costs of disposal are $2.00 per unit, making the net realizable value $10.50. Since this is lower than the original cost, it will be used to value inventory, which will be reported at (2,000,000 x $10.50) $21,000,000.

10. (b) Among FIFO, LIFO, and weighted average, in periods of rising prices, FIFO will result in the highest value of inventory, LIFO the lowest, with average somewhere between. When goods are sold in the order they are acquired, specific identification will give the same results as FIFO. Since LIFO is not an acceptable method under IFRS, weighted average will result in the lowest inventory value.

Lecture 7.05
TASK-BASED SIMULATIONS

Task-Based Simulation 1

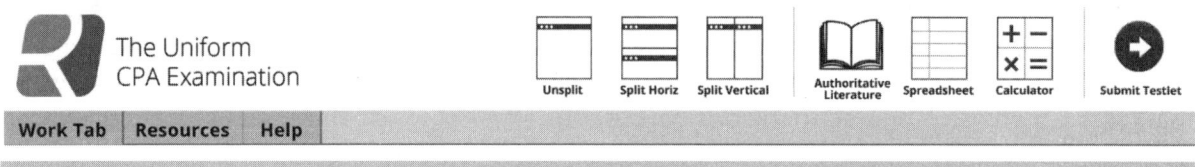

Required:

On January 1, 20X1, Silver Industries, Inc. adopted the dollar-value LIFO method of determining inventory costs for financial and income tax reporting. The following information relates to this change.

- Silver has continued to use the FIFO method, which approximates current costs, for internal reporting purposes. Silver's FIFO inventories at December 31, 20X1, 20X2, and 20X3 were $100,000, $137,500, and $195,000, respectively.
- The FIFO inventory amounts are converted to dollar-value LIFO amounts using a single inventory pool and cost indices developed using the simplified method. Silver estimated that the price level indices were 1.25 for 20X2 and 1.50 for 20X3.

Items to be answered:

Prepare a schedule showing the computation of Silver's dollar-value LIFO inventory at December 31, 20X2 and 20X3. Show all calculations.

Lecture 7.11
Task-Based Simulation 2

Required:

York Co. sells one product, which it purchases from various suppliers. York's trial balance at December 31, 20X2, included the following accounts:

Sales (33,000 units @ $16)	$528,000
Sales discounts	7,500
Purchases	368,900
Purchase discounts	18,000
Freight-in	5,000
Freight-out	11,000

York Co.'s inventory purchases during 20X2 were as follows:

	Units	Cost per unit	Total cost
Beginning inventory, January 1	8,000	$8.20	$ 65,600
Purchases, quarter ended March 31	12,000	8.25	99,000
Purchases, quarter ended June 30	15,000	7.90	118,500
Purchases, quarter ended September 30	13,000	7.50	97,500
Purchases, quarter ended December 31	7,000	7.70	53,900
	55,000		$434,500

Additional information

York's accounting policy is to report inventory in its financial statements at the lower of cost or market, applied to total inventory. Cost is determined under the last-in, first-out (LIFO) method.

York has determined that, at December 31, 20X2, the replacement cost of its inventory was $8 per unit and the net realizable value was $8.80 per unit. York's normal profit margin is $1.05 per unit.

Items to be answered:

Prepare York's schedule of cost of goods sold, with supporting schedule of ending inventory.

York Co.
SUPPORTING SCHEDULE OF ENDING INVENTORY
December 31, 20X2

Inventory at cost (LIFO):

	Units	Cost per unit	Total cost
Beginning inventory, January 1			
Purchases, quarter ended March 31			
Purchases, quarter ended June 30			
Totals			

York Co.
SCHEDULE OF COST OF GOODS SOLD
For the Year Ended December 31, 20X2

Beginning inventory	
Add: Purchases	
Less: Purchase discounts	
Add: Freight-in	
Goods available for sale	
Less: Ending inventory	
Cost of goods sold	

Task-Based Simulation 3

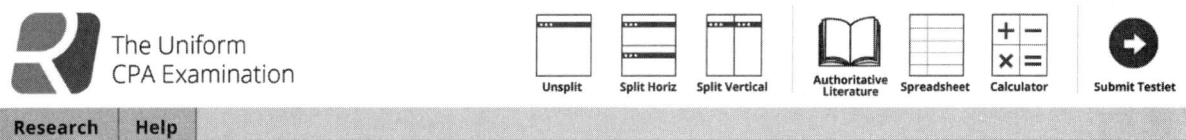

A company sells its inventory in the order in which it is acquired, but sets sales prices based on the most recent purchases. It is trying to determine how to report the inventory in its balance sheet. Identify the location in professional standards that indicates that the cost of inventory may be determined using one of several cost flow assumptions.

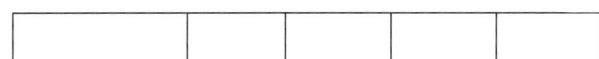

Task-Based Simulation 4

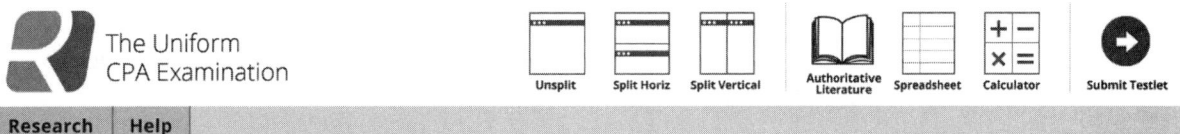

Your client does not understand why inventory is written down to the lower of cost or market or the lower of cost or net realizable value. Identify the location in professional standards that indicates the purpose of reducing the carrying amount of inventory.

TASK-BASED SIMULATION SOLUTIONS

Task-Based Simulation Solution 1

In applying dollar-value LIFO, Silver will consider the 20X1 inventory of $100,000 as the base layer at base year prices.

The 20X2 inventory of $137,500 is at 20X2 prices. It can be converted into base year prices by dividing the price level index of 1.25 resulting in 20X2 inventory, restated to base year prices of $137,500 ÷ 1.25 or $110,000. As a result, the 20X2 inventory will consist of the base layer of $100,000 and an incremental layer of $10,000 at base year prices. The incremental layer is converted back to 20X2 prices by multiplying by the 1.25 price level index.

Inventory at 12/31/X2 would be:

Base layer	$100,000 @ 1.00	$100,000
20X2 incremental layer	$10,000 @ 1.25	12,500
Inventory at 12/31/X2		**$112,500**

The 20X3 inventory of $195,000 is at 20X3 prices. The year end inventory can be converted into base year prices by dividing by the price level index of 1.50 resulting in 20X3 inventory, restated to base year prices of $195,000 ÷ 1.50 or $130,000. As a result, the 20X3 inventory will consist of the base layer of $100,000, the 20X2 incremental layer of $10,000 at base year prices, and a new 20X3 incremental layer of $20,000 at base year prices. The incremental layers are converted back to 20X2 and 20X3 prices by multiplying by the appropriate price level indices.

Inventory at 12/31/X3 would be:

Base layer	$100,000 @ 1.00	$100,000
20X2 incremental layer	$ 10,000 @ 1.25	12,500
20X3 incremental layer	$ 20,000 @ 1.50	30,000
Inventory at 12/31/X3		**$142,500**

Date	CC	PI	BC	Layer	PI	DV LIFO
12/31/X1	$100,000	1.00	$100,000	$100,000	1.00	$100,000
12/31/X2	$137,500	1.25	$110,000	$10,000	1.25	$12,500
Inventory @ 12/31/X2						**$112,500**
12/31/X3	$195,000	1.50	$130,000	$20,000	1.50	$30,000

Task-Based Simulation Solution 2

York Co.
SUPPORTING SCHEDULE OF ENDING INVENTORY
December 31, 20X2

Inventory at cost (LIFO):

	Units	Cost per unit	Total cost
Beginning inventory, January 1	8,000	$8.20	$ 65,600
Purchases, quarter ended March 31	12,000	8.25	99,000
Purchases, quarter ended June 30	2,000	7.90	15,800
	22,000		$180,400

York Co.
SCHEDULE OF COST OF GOODS SOLD
For the Year Ended December 31, 20X2

Beginning inventory	$ 65,600
Add: Purchases	368,900
Less: Purchase discounts	(18,000)
Add: Freight-in	5,000
Goods available for sale	421,500
Less: Ending inventory	(176,000) [1]
Cost of Goods Sold	$245,500

[1] Inventory at market value:
22,000 units @ $8 = $176,000

Solution:

Begin by setting up the schedule to compute cost of goods sold and filling in the appropriate information that is given. All aspects can be complete based on the information given with the exception of ending inventory.

York Co.
Cost of Goods Sold
For the Year Ended December 31, 20X2

Beginning inventory (given)		$65,600
Plus net purchases		
Purchases	$368,900	
Less purchase discounts	(18,000)	
Plus freight-in	5,000	
Net purchases		355,900
Cost of goods available for sale		421,500
Less ending inventory		?
Cost of goods sold		

Since York had a total of 55,000 units available, including beginning inventory and purchases, and sold a total of 33,000 units, ending inventory was 22,000 units. Under LIFO, ending inventory would consist of:

Beginning inventory - 8,000 units @ $8.20	$65,600
1st quarter purchases - 12,000 units @ $8.25	99,000
2nd quarter purchases - 2,000 units @ $7.90	15,800
Total	$180,400

Because York uses LIFO, the lower of cost or market rule applies. Note that the simplified lower of cost or NRV rule applies for all inventories other than those accounted for under the LIFO or retail inventory methods.

Applying the lower of cost or market rule involves comparing the cost of inventory to the market value and using the lower amount. Market value is the replacement cost of $8 per unit, subject to maximum (ceiling) and minimum (floor) limitations.
- Ceiling is net realizable value of $8.80 per unit.
- Floor is net realizable value minus a normal profit or $8.80 - $1.05 or $7.75 per unit.

Since the replacement cost is between the floor and the ceiling, market value will be $8 per unit. At $8 per unit, ending inventory would be 22,000 units @ $8 or $176,000. Since that is lower than the cost of $180,400, ending inventory will be reduced to **$176,000**.

Task-Based Simulation Solution 3

FASB ASC	330	10	30	9

Task-Based Simulation Solution 4

FASB ASC	330	10	35	9

DOCUMENT REVIEW SIMULATION

Document Review Simulation 1

 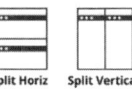 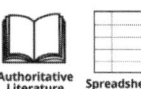

High Steppers, Inc. is a retailer of women's fitness shoes which began operations on January 2, 20X5. During a recent storm in 20X6, the warehouse was flooded and the entire inventory of shoes was either damaged or destroyed. The controller, Erin Whitehead, needs to determine the value of the inventory as of date of the flood, April 6, 20X6, in order to complete the insurance claim. She has asked Edward Stevens, one of the staff accountants, to prepare a memo regarding the valuation of the inventory and the estimated insurance claim.

Review the memo from the staff accountant to the controller and make any changes necessary to ensure it is accurate and consistent with the information and documents provided.

High Steppers, Inc.

To: Erin Whitehead, Controller
From: Edward Stevens, Staff Accountant
Date: May 1, 20X6
Re: Valuation of Inventory

Per your request, I have reviewed the records and documents in order to estimate the ending inventory on April 6, 20X6. Below are my findings.

In order to determine the ending inventory on the date of the flood, an estimate for cost of goods sold must first be calculated. In researching possible methods to estimate the cost of goods sold in this situation, I discovered that **1) <u>GAAP only allows the inventory valuation method normally used by the company for interim financial statements or to determine the value of inventory that is destroyed.</u>**

Using this method, **2) <u>the recomputed estimate for the cost of goods sold is $325,875 as of April 5.</u>**

Based on the reconstructed cost of goods sold, I have computed that High Steppers, Inc. **3) <u>should report an estimated ending inventory of $66,386 on its interim financial statements dated April 5, 20X6.</u>**

According to the accounting records, **4) <u>the estimated number of units destroyed or damaged by the flood is 10,200 units, which equals the beginning units plus units purchased less units sold as of April 5.</u>**

When determining the insurance claim, **5) <u>all the units purchased through April 5 are included</u>** since the shipping terms are FOB, shipping point.

Therefore, the insurance claim **6) <u>should be based on an inventory value of $33,016.</u>**

Sincerely,

Edward Stevens
Staff Accountant

Inventory   Section 7

Resources

Account Balances

Select general ledger account balances on April 5, 20X6

Per the general ledger on April 5, 20X6, the following accounts balances were reported:

- Sales returns: A debit balance of $18,520.
- Freight-in: A debit balance of $12,800.
- Freight-out: A debit balance of $985.
- Purchase returns: A credit balance of $1,320 that corresponds with February purchases.

Inventory Clerk Email

From:	knorman@highsteppers.com
Sent:	April 20, 20X6
To:	'estevens@highsteppers.com'
Subject:	Inventory questions

Edward:

Per your question regarding physical counts of inventory, a physical count is only conducted on December 31. As far as a recommendation of an accepted method to estimate the ending inventory on the day of the flood, I suggest the gross profit method. If I can be of any further assistance, please let me know.

Kipper

Kipper Norman, Inventory clerk
High-Steppers, Inc.
knorman@highsteppers.com

Warehouse Manager Email

From: sreynolds@highsteppers.com
Sent: April 14, 20X6
To: 'ewhitehead@highsteppers.com'
Subject: Inventory units

Erin:

In response to your question regarding the amount of inventory in the warehouse on December 31, 20X5, I can confirm we reported 9,500 units of inventory on hand. Please let me know if you have any questions.

Stanley

Stanley Reynolds, Warehouse Manager
High-Steppers, Inc.
sreynolds@highsteppers.com

Financial Statement Excerpts

Excerpts from the audited financial statements for the year-ended December 31, 20X5:

High Steppers, Inc.
Balance Sheet
December 31, 20X5

Assets

Cash and cash equivalents	$690,020
Accounts receivable (net)	245,300
Inventory	138,225
Property, plant and equipment (net)	1,768,000
Total Assets	**$2,841,545**

High Steppers, Inc.
Income Statement
For the Year Ended December 31, 20X5

Revenues

Sales (net)	$3,245,200
Cost of goods sold	1,784,860
Gross profit	$1,460,340

NOTE 1 SUMMARY OF SIGNIFICANT ACCOUNTING POLICIES

Merchandise Inventory – Inventory is stated at the lower of cost or net realizable value using the first-in, first-out method of inventory accounting. The cost of inventory also includes certain costs associated with the preparation of inventory for resale.

Section 7   Inventory

Purchase Recap

Report from the Purchasing Department

Below is a recap of the purchases before April 6, 20X6. All purchases are shipped, FOB, shipping point. If you have any questions regarding the recap, contact Jay Phillips at extension #4478.

Purchases for January 1 - April 1, 20X6				
Date Ordered and Shipped	Date Received	Number of Units	Unit Cost	Total Cost
January 11, 20X6	January 15, 20X6	7,000	$6.50	$45,500
February 5, 20X6	February 12, 20X6	10,000	$6.60	$66,000
March 3, 20X6	March 8, 20X6	12,500	$7.00	$87,500
April 1, 20X6	April 8, 20X6	6,500	$6.90	$44,850
Totals		36,000		$243,850

Sales Recap

Sales Report from the Accounting Department

Below is a recap of the sales transactions through April 5, 20X6. If you have any questions regarding the recap, contact Euclid Seibel at extension #4533.

Sales from January 1 - April 5, 20X6		
Date	Sales in Units	Net Sales in Dollars
January, 20X6	9,000	$119,000
February, 20X6	12,500	$234,000
March, 20X6	12,000	$218,500
April 1-5, 20X6	1,800	$21,000
Totals	35,300	$592,500

Inventory
Section 7

Items for Analysis

GAAP only allows the inventory valuation method normally used by the company for interim financial statements or to determine the value of inventory that is destroyed.

1. Choose an option below:

   - [Original text] GAAP only allows the inventory valuation method normally used by the company for interim financial statements or to determine the value of inventory that is destroyed.
   - [Delete text]
   - GAAP only allows the inventory valuation method normally used by the company for interim financial statements or to determine the value of inventory that is destroyed.
   - GAAP only allows the inventory valuation normally used by the company for interim financial statements but will allow the net realizable value method to determine the value of inventory that is destroyed.
   - GAAP allows the gross profit method for interim financial statements but only allows the inventory valuation method normally used by the company to determine the value of inventory that is destroyed.
   - GAAP allows the gross profit method for interim financial statements or to determine inventory that is destroyed.

The recomputed estimate for the cost of goods sold is $325,875 as of April 5.

2. Choose an option below:

   - [Original text] The recomputed estimate for the cost of goods sold is $325,875 as of April 5.
   - [Delete text]
   - the recomputed estimate for the cost of goods sold is $325,875 as of April 5.
   - the recomputed estimate for the cost of goods sold is $803,187 as of April 5.
   - the recomputed estimate for the cost of goods sold is $348,650 as of April 5.
   - the recomputed estimate for the cost of goods sold is $315,689 as of April 5.
   - the recomputed estimate for the cost of goods sold is $258,291 as of April 5.

Should report an estimated ending inventory of $66,386 on its interim financial statements dated April 5, 20X6.

3. Choose an option below:
   - [Original text] should report an estimated ending inventory of $66,386 on its interim financial statements dated April 5, 20X6.
   - [Delete text]
   - should report an estimated ending inventory of $66,386 on its interim financial statements dated April 5, 20X6.
   - should report an estimated ending inventory of $66,051 on its interim financial statements dated April 5, 20X6.

- should report an estimated ending inventory of $65,066 on its interim financial statements dated April 5, 20X6.
- should report an estimated ending inventory of $77,866 on its interim financial statements dated April 5, 20X6.

The estimated number of units destroyed or damaged by the flood is 10,200 units, which equals the beginning units plus units purchased less units sold as of April 5.

4. Choose an option below:
   - [Original text] The estimated number of units destroyed or damaged by the flood is 10,200 units, which equals the beginning units plus units purchased less units sold as of April 5.
   - [Delete text]
   - the estimated number of units destroyed or damaged by the flood is 10,200 units, which equals the beginning units plus units purchased less units sold as of April 5.
   - the estimated number of units destroyed or damaged by the flood is 700 units, which equals the units purchased less units sold as of April 5.
   - the estimated number of units destroyed or damaged by the flood is 3,700 units, which equals the beginning units plus units purchased and received less units sold as of April 5.
   - the estimated number of units destroyed or damaged by the flood is 8,800 units, which equals the beginning units less units purchased plus the units sold as of April 5.

All the units purchased through April 5 are included

5. Choose an option below:
   - [Original text] All the units purchased through April 5 are included
   - [Delete text]
   - only the 6,500 units purchased in April are included
   - all but the 6,500 units purchased April 1 are included
   - only the 12,500 units purchased in March plus the 6,500 units purchased in April are included

should be based on an inventory value of $33,016.

6. Choose an option below:
   - [Original text] should be based on an inventory value of $33,016.
   - [Delete text]
   - should be based on an inventory value of $31,696.
   - should be based on an inventory value of $32,366.
   - should be based on an inventory value of $77,866.

DOCUMENT REVIEW SIMULATION SOLUTION

Document Review Simulation Solution 1

1. <u>GAAP allows the gross profit method for interim financial statements or to determine inventory that is destroyed.</u>

   Because it is impractical for interim financial statements, and generally impossible in cases where inventory is missing or destroyed, for a company to use the inventory valuation method normally used for its year-end financial statements, GAAP allows for the use of gross profit method, which is an estimation method, in either situation.

2. <u>The recomputed estimate for the cost of goods sold is $315,689 as of April 5.</u>

   First, refer to the Financial Statement Excerpts to calculate the historical gross profit margin.

   - Net sales and gross profit in 20X5 amounted to $3,245,200 and $1,460,340, respectively. Since 1,460,340 / 3,245,200 = 45%, that is the gross profit margin we will use to estimate cost of goods sold as of April 5, 20X6.

   With a gross profit margin of 45%, we know the ratio of cost of goods sold (COGS) to sales will be 55%.

   Next, refer to the Sales Recap and Account Balances documents in order to calculate net sales through April 5, 20X6.

   - The Sales Recap shows gross sales of $592,500. The Account Balances file shows a debit balance of $18,520 for sales returns. Net sales, then, is $592,500 - $18,520, or $573,980.

   Now just apply the COGS percentage of 55% to net sales of $573,980.

   - $573,980 x 55% = **$315,689 estimated COGS.**

3. <u>Should report an estimated ending inventory of $77,866 on its interim financial statements dated April 5, 20X6.</u>

   Cost of goods available for sale minus estimated cost of goods sold (COGS) will equal estimated ending inventory.

   Cost of goods available for sale consists of beginning inventory + net purchases for the period.

   - Beginning inventory is $138,225 – it is the 20X5 ending inventory as shown in the Financial Statement Excerpts.

   - Net purchases consists of the $243,850 shown in the Purchases Recap, plus freight-in of $12,800 shown in the Account Balances file, minus purchase returns of $1,320 also shown in Account Balances. Net purchases is therefore $243,850 + $12,800 - $1,320 = $255,330.

   - Cost of goods available for sale = $138,225 + $255,330, or $393,555.

Estimated ending inventory is $393,555 - $315,689, or $77,866.

4. <u>the estimated number of units destroyed or damaged by the flood is 3,700 units, which equals the beginning units plus units purchased and received less units sold as of April 5.</u>

   Units physically present in the warehouse at 6 April 20X6, when the flood occurred, consist of beginning inventory plus units purchased **and received** minus units sold through 5 April.

   The email from the warehouse manager provides the beginning inventory of 9,500 units.

   The Purchase Recap provides units purchased through 1 April, totaling 36,000 units. The 1 April shipment of 6,500 units was not actually received until 8 April, so would be backed out of this purchased total for an adjusted total of 29,500.

   Units available for sale and physically present in the warehouse through the date of the flood, then, numbered 9,500 + 29,500, or 39,000.

   Sales were shipped to customers prior to the flood so must be subtracted from this physically available total. The Sales Recap provides a 20X6 sales figure of 35,300.

   The estimate for units physically present in the warehouse at the date of the flood, therefore, is 39,000 - 35,300, or **3,700**.

   Incidentally, sales returns are not mentioned in any of the answer choices.

5. <u>all but the 6,500 units purchased April 1 are included</u>

   The insurance claim would **exclude** the 6,500 units purchased and shipped FOB, shipping point on April 1. Although the title passed on the date shipped and the company "legally" owned the items, they could not have been damaged in the flood since the delivery date was after April 6, the day the flood damage occurred.

6. Keep original text: <u>should be based on an inventory value of $33,016.</u>

   The insurance claim will exclude the 6,500 units purchased April 1 and still in transit at the time of the flood. Therefore, the insurance claim should be based on $33,016, which is the $77,866 estimated inventory minus the $44,850 cost of the April 1 purchase.

Section 8 – Property, Plant & Equipment (PP&E - Fixed Assets)

Corresponding Lectures

Watch the following course lectures with this section:

Lecture 8.01 – Property Plant & Equipment - Fixed Assets
Lecture 8.02 – Asset Retirement Obligation
Lecture 8.03 – Capitalization of Interest
Lecture 8.04 – Costs Incurred After Acquisition
Lecture 8.05 – Property Plant & Equipment – Class Questions & TBS
Lecture 8.06 – Depreciation Methods
Lecture 8.07 – Depreciation Example and other Dep Methods
Lecture 8.08 – Depreciation – Class Questions & TBS
Lecture 8.09 – Impairments
Lecture 8.10 – Impairments – Class Questions
Lecture 8.11 – Non-Monetary Exchanges
Lecture 8.12 – Non-Monetary Exchanges – Class Questions
Lecture 8.13 – Fixed Assets under IFRS
Lecture 8.14 – IFRS Fixed Assets – Class Questions
Lecture 8.15 – PP&E Document Review Simulation

EXAM NOTE: *Please refer to the AICPA FAR Blueprint in the Introduction to find a listing of the representative tasks (and their associated skill levels—i.e., Remembering and Understanding, Application, and Analysis) that the candidate should be able to perform based on the knowledge obtained in this section.*

Property, Plant & Equipment (PP&E)
(Fixed Assets - ASC-360)

Lecture 8.01

FIXED ASSETS

PP&E are tangible assets acquired for long-term use in the normal course of business. They are not for resale and are generally subject to depreciation.

Asset	X	
Cash		X

Acquisition Costs (Intended Use)

Acquisition costs, which are capitalized as part of the cost of the asset, include not only the purchase price of the asset, but also costs associated with obtaining it and preparing the asset for its intended use.

- Include all costs of acquisition or construction as well as preparation for use.
    - Purchase price
    - Legal fees
    - Delinquent taxes
    - Title insurance
    - Transportation (freight in)
    - Installation
    - Test runs
    - Sales taxes

The cost of *land* includes:

- Purchase price (including any existing building that is to be demolished)
- Surveying
- Clearing, grading, and landscaping
- Costs of razing or demolishing an old building are added to the land cost.
- Proceeds from the sale of any scrap (old bricks) are subtracted from the land cost.

For example, assume that a piece of land with an existing building on it is acquired, with the following facts applying:

Purchase Price	$300,000
Cost of razing old building	50,000
Sale of scrap from clearing old building	8,000

The cost of the land is $300,000 + $50,000 - $8,000 = $342,000. Notice that nothing is allocated to the old building, since it is being demolished. No benefits are being derived from the old building, so the matching principle indicates that none of the costs should be allocated to it.

Lump Sum Purchases
- If acquire Land and Building for a lump sum, use the **Relative Fair Value method** to allocate the value between both assets.

For example, if property is acquired for $600,000, and the only available information to allocate is the tax appraisal, which allocates $100,000 to the land and $400,000 to the building, for a total of $500,000 tax value, then the cost of the property will be allocated 100,000 / 500,000, or 20%, to land, and 400,000 / 500,000, or 80%, to building. The entry to record acquisition of the property is:

Land	120,000	
Building	480,000	
Cash		600,000

If land is acquired along with a depleting asset, such as oil in the ground, then the land is normally allocated its estimated residual value assuming all oil had been removed, and the remainder is allocated to the oil itself. One complication, however, is that the cost of the property includes all costs of acquisition and preparation of the property for drilling, as well as any estimated restoration costs for the property following the completion of drilling.

Lecture 8.02

Asset Retirement Obligations

Pursuant to **ASC 410**, asset retirement obligations (ARO), such as estimated restoration costs, that are expected to be paid at the end of the period of usage, should be recorded as a liability at *fair market value*, which is the amount at which that obligation could be settled today. If this cannot be determined, estimates should be made based on the *present value of the expected future costs*. The liability will have to be increased each year based on the discount rate and reported as accretion expense (a form of interest expense). The liability is considered long term and is amortized using the effective interest method. Recognize at either:
- Fair value of liability
- **Present value** of estimated future restoration costs using credit adjusted risk-free rate.

For example, assume an oil field is acquired at a cash price of $100,000. It is estimated that, following the extraction of oil, it is expected to cost approximately $20,000 to restore the property to an acceptable condition when extraction is completed (estimated to be 12 years from now), and that the land will, at that point, have a $30,000 value. Assume further that the fair value of the restoration costs cannot be determined, but that a discount rate of 6% is considered appropriate.

The present value of 1 at 6% for 12 years is 0.50, so the restoration costs of $20,000 have a present value (estimated fair market value) of $20,000 x 0.50 = $10,000. The entry to record acquisition of the property is:

Land	30,000	
Oil reserves	80,000	
Cash		100,000
Est rest costs (asset retirement obligation - ARO)		10,000

Property, Plant and Equipment (PP&E) — Section 8

Estimated restoration costs are classified as **long-term liabilities**, since they won't be paid until drilling is completed, possibly decades from now (12 years in this example). The oil reserves, which result from a plug in the above entry, are depleted and inventoried as oil is removed from the ground, then expensed as oil is sold. The estimated restoration costs are increased each year by the incremental rate of 6%, so that the liability will be increased by a credit of $10,000 x 6% = $600 in the first year, with an offsetting debit to accretion expense. Accretion expense is the growth of the liability over time so that when the liability is satisfied, it is reported at its total non-discounted value.

Accretion Expense	600	
ARO Liability		600

Disclosures:
- Description of the obligation and related asset
- Description of how fair value was determined
- The funding policy
- A reconciliation of the beginning and ending carrying value

On occasion, a company will receive an **asset as a donation**. The receipt of the donated asset is generally treated as ordinary income for the fair market value of the asset.

For example, if an individual donates land worth $3,000,000 to the company, the entry is:

Land	3,000,000	
Other income		
(Contribution Revenue)		3,000,000

Lecture 8.03

Capitalization of Interest (ASC 835)

- Interest cost incurred during the construction period needs to be capitalized. The amount capitalized is considered the avoidable interest (could have avoided had you not built the building). This amount is added to the cost of building the asset.
- Include interest incurred on construction loans, but only to the extent the funds have been spent on construction:
    - Capitalize interest cost if asset is:
        - Constructed for company's **own use** (built by self or outsider).
        - Assets manufactured for resale resulting from a **special order** (ships).
    - Do **not** capitalize interest if:
        - Costs are incurred *after* completion of construction.
        - Inventory manufactured in the ordinary course of business.
    - Amount to be capitalized is:
        - **Weighted average accumulated expenditures** x interest rate = capitalized portion of interest.
        - Interest on other debt that could have been avoided by repayment of debt.
        - Never exceed actual interest cost.

For example, assume that a client takes out a 12% loan of $1,000,000 on 1/1/X1 to finance construction of a building for the company's own use. Construction begins immediately, and $600,000 is spent at an even pace during 20X1. The remaining $400,000 is spent at an even pace during 20X2, with construction completed on 12/31/X2. The capitalized interest is computed as follows:

	20X1	20X2
Annual expenditure	$600,000	$400,000
Prorated over year	50%	50%
Avg current expenditure	300,000	200,000
Prior year spending	---	600,000
Avg accumulated expend	300,000	800,000
Interest rate	12%	12%
Capitalized interest	36,000	96,000

The capitalized interest of $36,000 for 20X1 and $96,000 for 20X2 represent a portion of the total interest paid by the company each year. Let's assume that the $1,000,000 12% loan in the previous example required annual interest payments at the end of each year. The entries to record the interest payments are:

12/31/X1   Building WIP   36,000
               Interest expense   84,000
                  Cash   120,000

12/31/X2   Building WIP   96,000
               Interest expense   24,000
                  Cash   120,000

Once construction is finished, the building is no longer a work-in-process, but a completed asset, and the entire balance of Building WIP is transferred to Building. Any interest incurred after 12/31/X2 is expensed immediately, in accordance with the matching principle, since the building is now being used and providing benefits to the company. The capitalized interest will now be a part of the depreciation expense on the building over its useful life.

In the above example, there was an identifiable loan related to the building construction. In other cases, there might be borrowings by the company that would not have needed to take place had construction not occurred, and these may be capitalized as well. If, however, the total interest incurred by a company during a year is less than the interest on the accumulated construction expenditures, capitalization is limited to the actual interest incurred. In the case of a company with no loans outstanding, no interest will be capitalized, since the construction was entirely self-financed by the company.

Keep in mind that the pace of construction does not have to be even within a year. If the $600,000 spent in 20X1 in the earlier example involved the majority of work in the early part of the year, the average cumulative expenditures over the course of the year would have been greater than $300,000. If so, then this information would have been provided in the problem, and capitalized interest would have been calculated on the average accumulated expenditures rather than using the approach of taking half of spending for the year.

Property, Plant and Equipment (PP&E) — Section 8

Lecture 8.04

Costs Incurred After Acquisition

- **Repairs and maintenance expense** (*revenue expenditure*) – Costs incurred to keep or restore an asset to its normal operating condition. These costs are **expensed** as incurred. For example, repairing a damaged truck, routine maintenance (engine tune-ups, oil changes).
- If the cost makes the asset BIGGER, BETTER, or LONGER that's GOOD, since one would rather capitalize the cost than expense it (*capital expenditure*).
    - **BIGGER** – *additions*, new capacity, new functions. (hospital wing)

        Asset   X
            Cash   X

    - **BETTER** – improving efficiency (betterment/improvement), such as a rearrangement or improving a concrete floor in place of a wooden floor.

        Asset   X
            Cash   X

    - **LONGER** – extension of an asset's useful life (overhaul)
        - Costs that extend the useful life of the asset are subtracted from accumulated depreciation thereby increasing the carrying value.

        Accumulated Depreciation   X
            Cash   X

- **Refurbishment** - Replace a part of the asset.
    1. **Identifiable** - Account for as if sold the old part and are replacing it with a new part.

        Accumulated Depreciation   X
        Loss   X
            Asset   X

        Asset   X
            Cash   X

    2. **Not Identifiable**
        A) *Enhances the asset* (similar to an addition or betterment)

        Asset   X
            Cash   X

        B) *Increasing the asset's useful life* (similar to an Extension)

        Accumulated Depreciation   X
            Cash   X

©Roger CPA Review

Section 8   Property, Plant and Equipment (PP&E)

Lecture 8.05

CLASS QUESTIONS

Please see the Class Questions and Class Solutions for this Lecture at the end of this Section.

Lecture 8.06

DEPRECIATION METHODS

A systematic & rational method of allocating the cost of an asset to the periods benefited – **Matching** concept.

Straight-Line Method (S/L)

- Used when assets give equal benefits to the company throughout their useful lives. Ex. a building.
- Depreciation expense is the same amount each year.
- Depreciation rate = 1/useful life (1/5 years = 20%)
- (Cost – salvage value) / Useful life = Depreciation expense year 1,2,3,4...
- Considers depreciation a function of time instead of a function of usage.

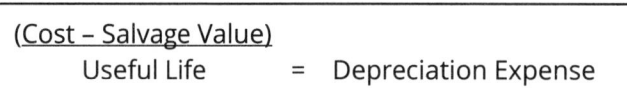

To record depreciation:

Depreciation Expense (I/S)   X
    Accumulated Depreciation   X

Accelerated Methods

Used when an asset gives greater benefits in earlier years than in later years. (Example: office equipment).

Sum of the Years Digits (SYD)

- An accelerated depreciation method that is considered less aggressive than the double-declining balance method.
    - Numerator = the number of years left in the asset's useful life. For example, if it were a 3-year asset, in the first year the numerator would be 3, then 2 then 1.
    - Denominator = The sum of the years in the asset's useful life. The formula is **N(N+1)/2.** For example, 3(3+1)/2 = 6.
        - So, in year 1 take the Basis and multiply it by 3/6, then 2/6 then 1/6.

Property, Plant and Equipment (PP&E) — Section 8

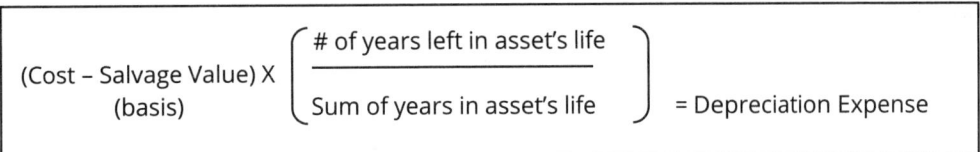

$$(\text{Cost} - \text{Salvage Value}) \times \left(\frac{\text{\# of years left in asset's life}}{\text{Sum of years in asset's life}} \right) = \text{Depreciation Expense}$$

(basis)

SYD Example – 3 year asset

Straight-Line	SYD	Y1	Y2	Y3
1/3 = Rate	3	3/6	2/6	1/6
	2			
	1			
	= **6**			

$$\frac{N(N+1)}{2}$$

Double Declining Balance (DDB)

- A depreciation rate that is twice the straight-line rate is applied against the book value of the asset. For example: 1/5 = 20% (S/L rate) x 2 = 40% (DDB rate)
- *Salvage value is ignored.*
- Depreciation expense should not be reduced below the salvage value. In the final year either:
    - Calculate depreciation expense in the last year as the amount to reduce the carrying value to the salvage value.
    - Switch from DDB to either SYD or S/L toward the end of the asset's useful life, depreciating the asset to its Salvage value.

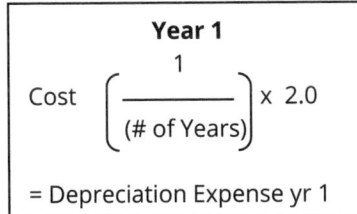

Year 1

$$\text{Cost} \left(\frac{1}{\text{\# of Years}} \right) \times 2.0 = \text{Depreciation Expense yr 1}$$

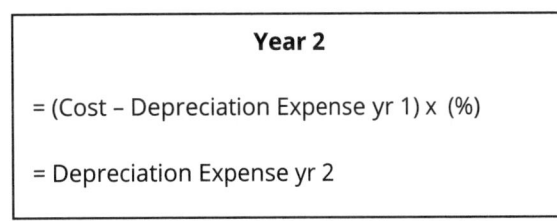

Year 2

= (Cost − Depreciation Expense yr 1) x (%)

= Depreciation Expense yr 2

- Balance declines, rate stays the same
- Never get to zero, so eventually must switch over to another method.

Units of Production (UOP) - Activity Method (Variable Charge approach or Physical usage depreciation)

- Assumes depreciation is a function of use (machine hours) or productivity (finished widgets) instead of the passage of time.

$$(\text{Cost} - \text{SV}) \times \frac{\text{(hours this year)}}{\text{(Total estimated hours)}} = \text{Depreciation expense}$$

- **Benefits of accelerated methods**
    - Better **matching** since asset is more productive in earlier years.
    - Minimize loss due to **obsolescence**. Since the asset was depreciated more quickly, the Carrying value is lower therefore the loss is smaller.

- **Helps to even out expenses.** Since Repairs and Maintenance in the earlier years is lower, if we take more depreciation earlier on, the total expenses would be more constant over time.

Lecture 8.07

Depreciation Class Example

To review the basic methods of depreciation, let's use the following example of a machine, and calculate depreciation expense for each of the **first 2 years**:

Purchase date	1/1/X1
Cost	$1,000
Estimated useful life	5 years
Estimated salvage value	$100
Estimated total output	1,000 units
20X1 output	250 units
20X2 output	300 units

SL depreciation allocates the depreciable basis (cost − salvage) over the useful life:

20X1 Cost 1,000 − Salvage 100 = Basis 900 / Life 5 years = $180

20X2 Cost 1,000 − Salvage 100 = Basis 900 / Life 5 years = $180

Units of Production depreciation multiplies the basis by a fraction whose numerator is the current output and whose denominator is the estimated total output.

20X1 Basis 900 x Current Output 250 / Total Output 1,000 = 225

20X2 Basis 900 x Current Output 300 / Total Output 1,000 = 270

SYD depreciation multiplies the basis by a fraction whose numerator is the number of the years left in the life of the asset as of the beginning of the year and whose denominator is the sum of the number of years in the life of the asset.

20X1 Basis 900 x Ratio 5 / (1+2+3+4+5) = 900 x 5 / 15 = 300

20X2 Basis 900 x Ratio 4 / (1+2+3+4+5) = 900 x 4 / 15 = 240

DDB depreciation multiplies the book value (cost − accumulated depreciation) at the beginning of each period by a fraction that is double the straight-line depreciation rate.

20X1 Cost 1,000 x Multiplier 2 / SL rate 5 = 1,000 x 2 / 5 = 400

20X2 Cost 1,000 − A/D 400 = Book value 600 x 2 / 5 = 240

Other declining balance approaches work the same way as the double-declining balance approach, except that the multiplier of the straight-line rate is different.

Property, Plant and Equipment (PP&E) — Section 8

Partial period depreciation – In computing depreciation expense for partial periods, it is necessary to determine the depreciation expense for the full year and then to prorate the depreciation expense between the two periods involved. Continue this process throughout the useful life of the asset.

When an asset is bought on some date other than the beginning of the fiscal year, depreciation in the year of acquisition needs to take into account the fractional time period for all methods except the UOP method (which is based on output rather than the passage of time). Assume the same facts applied as in the previous example, except that the purchase date was later in the year:

Purchase date	7/1/X1
Cost	$1,000
Estimated useful life	5 years
Estimated salvage value	$100
Estimated total output	1,000 units
20X1 output	250 units
20X2 output	300 units

Since the asset was purchased in the middle of the year, first year depreciation is based on one-half of a year, and the second year is affected as well:

SL depreciation:
20X1 Cost 1,000 – Salvage 100 = Basis 900 / Life 5 years x ½ = $90
20X2 Cost 1,000 – Salvage 100 = Basis 900 / Life 5 years = $180

UOP depreciation:
20X1 Basis 900 x Current Output 250 / Total Output 1,000 = 225
20X2 Basis 900 x Current Output 300 / Total Output 1,000 = 270

SYD depreciation:
20X1 Basis 900 x Ratio 5 / (1+2+3+4+5) x ½ = 900 x 5 / 15 x ½ = 150
20X2 Basis 900 x Ratio 4.5 / (1+2+3+4+5) = 900 x 4.5 / 15 = 270

Note: Using SYD, the numerator is the amount of life remaining at the start of the year. For a 5 year asset that is a 1/2 a year old, the remaining life is 4.5 years at the start of the second year.

DDB depreciation:
20X1 Cost 1,000 x Multiplier 2 / SL rate 5 x ½ = 1,000 x 2 / 5 x ½ = 200
20X2 Cost 1,000 – A/D 200 = Book value 800 x 2 / 5 = 320

Charting the Results

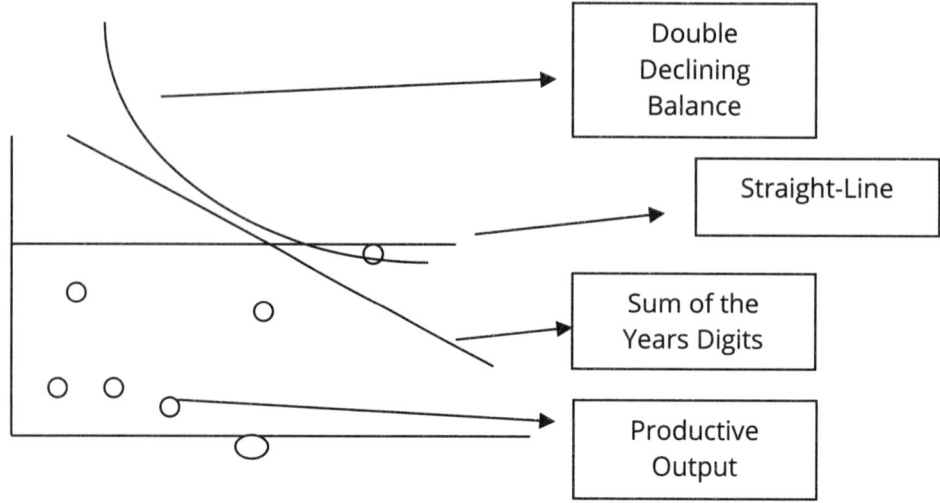

Group or Composite

- Depreciate as a group. (e.g. a fleet of trucks)
- *Group* refers to a collection of assets that are *similar* in nature, fairly homogeneous and have approximately the same useful lives.
- *Composite* refers to a collection of assets that are *dissimilar* in nature, fairly heterogeneous and have different lives.
- Problem occurs when you sell one of the assets in the group. Accumulated depreciation is not known.
    - Assume cash received = carrying value
    - Assume no Gain/Loss
    - Plug Accumulated Depreciation

```
Cash                         20
Accumulated Depreciation     80
Loss                         NONE
    Asset                           100
    Gain                            NONE
```

Under the *composite method* of depreciation, a building that is furnished with tables, chairs, and other items might elect to determine a weighted average life for all of the furnishings, and depreciate the total over this life. In the first year, the company determines the individual depreciation amounts for the items, totals them, and then divides this amount into the total cost to determine an average life that is then used from that point forward.

For example, assume a company acquires a desk, chair, and lamp to furnish an office and that these items will be of approximately equal usefulness each year, with no salvage at the end of their individual lives:

Item	Cost	Estimated life in years	Annual depreciation
Desk	$1,000	10	$100
Chair	$200	5	$40
Lamp	$100	4	$25
Total	$1,300	7.88	$165

Under the composite approach, the furnishings for the room are carried on the depreciation schedule at a single cost of $1,300, and depreciated over a life of 7.88 years ($1,300 / $165).

Of course, the above example doesn't show the value of the composite method, which often involves hundreds of items (not just 3) being depreciated together instead of separately. The savings in bookkeeping effort can be enormous. If this method seems strange, consider that it is actually being used in almost all depreciation already. An automobile, for example, actually includes an engine, transmission, axle, belts, and other parts that don't all have the exact same life, yet an automobile is depreciated as a single asset. This is a form of the composite approach.

Appraisal or Inventory Method of Depreciation

This method is rarely used. Under this approach, an estimate is made at the end of each year of the value of the assets, and sufficient depreciation expense is recorded to reduce the carrying value to that amount. Since this approach doesn't systematically match costs to benefits, it is only used when the loss in value is directly related to productivity, such as for property being rented to others.

Depletion

While assets like property, plant, and equipment have limited useful lives, some assets actually get used up. Mining companies and others in what are referred to as *extractive industries* will buy, or otherwise obtain rights to real property that is expected to have some natural resource, such as *oil, minerals, precious metals, or other commodities*.

When property with a natural resource is acquired, the cost is allocated to the property and the natural resource based on their relative estimated fair values. As the natural resource is extracted from the property, the cost is transferred from the natural resource to inventory and, ultimately, to cost of sales when the inventory is disposed of.

Depletion is recognized each period in a three-step process that is similar to the process used to calculate depreciation and is also often referred to as the **activity method**.
1. The total volume of the resource is estimated
    - The volume is measured in terms of number of units such as barrels of oil, tons of coal, or cubic feet of natural gas
    - In the initial period, the estimate will be the total of the estimated reserves
    - In subsequent periods, it will be the estimated amount remaining as of the beginning of the period, which includes the amount extracted during the period plus the amount estimated to be remaining at the end of the period.

2. The total volume is divided into the remaining cost, referred to as the **depletion base**, to get a cost per barrel, ton, cubic foot, or other unit.
   - In the initial period, this will be the total amount allocated to the resource (Cost + additional costs + restoration costs – Salvage/Residual value)
   - In subsequent periods, it will be the carrying value of the resource, which will be the original amount minus any depletion taken in previous periods.
3. The amount per unit is multiplied by the amount extracted during the period to determine the depletion for the period.

$$\text{Depletion} = \frac{\text{Depletion base}}{\text{Total volume at beginning of year}} \times \text{Units Extracted}$$

As the natural resource is extracted, the depletion represents the cost of the resource itself. The depletion, along with other direct costs such as labor and overhead, are reported as inventory. Once the inventory is sold, the cost is transferred from inventory to cost of sales.
- An entity in the oil and gas industry may incur costs when evaluating property to determine whether or not a sought natural resource is present and to develop an estimate of the volume. These costs, referred to as **exploration costs**, may be accounted for in one of two ways: Under the **full-cost approach**, all exploration costs are capitalized and become part of the cost of depleted resources that are found. As a result, depletion includes all of these costs.
- Under the **successful efforts approach**, exploration costs are attributed separately to each property and only those that yield an extractable resource are capitalized.
  - Exploration costs attributable to unsuccessful efforts are recognized as expense in the period.
  - Exploration costs attributable to successful efforts become part of the cost included in the depletion base.

Amortization, depreciation and depletion, like many areas of accounting, require the use of numerous estimates. These include estimates used in allocating costs when assets are acquired, estimates of salvage values and useful lives of property, plant, and equipment and certain intangibles, and estimates of volumes of remaining reserves of natural resources. These estimates are subject to scrutiny every period and, as they change, they are accounted for as changes in accounting estimates. As such:
- Prior period financial statements are not adjusted
- The new estimate is applied prospectively, in the current and future periods

When an entity **changes its method of depreciation, amortization, or depletion** of an asset, it is a change in accounting principle, but it is also a change in the estimate of how the entity is obtaining benefits from the use of that asset. As a result:
- A change in depreciation, amortization, or depletion method is accounted for **prospectively** like a change in estimate
- Since it involves a change in accounting principle, the entity must *justify the change* on the basis that the new method is preferable.

Property, Plant and Equipment (PP&E)   Section 8

Lecture 8.08

CLASS QUESTIONS

Please see the Class Questions and Class Solutions for this Lecture at the end of this Section.

Lecture 8.09

Impairments (ASC 360)

Impairment of Long-lived assets <u>Held for Use</u> occurs when the carrying amount of an asset is not recoverable and a write-off is needed. Examples of *impairments* include:
- A significant decrease in the market value of an asset.
- A significant change in an asset's physical condition or the extent or manner in which it is used.
- A significant adverse change in legal factors or in the business climate that affects the value of an asset.
- An accumulation of costs significantly in excess of the amount originally expected to acquire or construct the asset.
- A projection or forecast that demonstrates continuing losses associated with an asset.
- An expectation that it is more-likely-than-not that the asset will be disposed of before the end of its expected useful life.

The process of *determining an impairment loss* is as follows:
1. Review events or changes in circumstances for possible impairment (above), if none are identified, no further testing is required
2. If the review indicates impairment, apply the *recoverability test*. If the *sum of* **the expected future net cash flows** from the long-lived asset is less than the **carrying amount** of the asset, an impairment has occurred.
3. The **impairment loss** is the amount by which the **carrying amount** of the asset is *greater than* the **fair value** of the asset. The fair value is the market value or the present value.

> **Example:** Asset carrying value is $600, the expected future net cash flows is $580, and the market value is $525. Since 580 is less than 600, an impairment has occurred. The amount of the loss is 600 – 525 = 75. Now calculate future depreciation from the $525 value.
> - Do **NOT recover** the impairment for assets *Held for Use*.
> - Losses reported in income from continuing operations on Income statement.
>
> Loss on Impairment (I/S)   75 (oNt)
>   Accumulated Depreciation   75

Disclosures
- Description of impaired assets and circumstances which led to impairment
- Amount of impairment and manner in which fair value was determined
- Caption in income statement in which impairment loss is aggregated, if it is not presented separately

Note that estimated *future cash flows* are used to determine if impairment has occurred, but the asset is adjusted to its *estimated fair value*, **not** estimated future cash flows, once the determination has been made.

The impairment loss may **NOT be restored** for an asset *held for use*.

Occasionally, however, a company will use estimated values to record extra depreciation, and this occurs when there has been some *permanent impairment in value*. This, of course, is a normal business risk, and occurs regularly in certain industries. If, for example, technological change in an industry suddenly makes an asset obsolete, that asset may be written down to its estimated fair value. This should occur whenever the impairment has caused the **estimated future cash flows from the asset to be less than the carrying amount**. Assets should be tested for impairment whenever an event gives the company reason to believe such a situation exists.

Let's say a company purchases production machinery for $10,000, and is depreciating that full cost on a SL basis over 10 years, at $1,000 per year. After 3 years, the carrying value of the asset is $7,000. Early in the 4th year, however, the development of new products has caused the output of this machine to be less valued in the marketplace, and the client believes that it will only be able to generate future cash flows of $3,500 over the remaining life of the machinery. Since this is less than the carrying value, an impairment has occurred. If the asset has an estimated fair value of $3,000 and is expected to have a remaining useful life of only 2 years, after which the machine is expected to be worthless, immediate depreciation is recorded to bring the asset down to its $3,000 value, and this is depreciated over the next 2 years. At the end of the 4th year, the asset will have a remaining book value of $1,500, and accumulated depreciation of $8,500, reflecting:

1. $3,000 of depreciation recorded over the 1st 3 years,
2. $4,000 to write the asset down to its estimated recoverable amount at the beginning of the 4th year, and
3. $1,500 of depreciation during the 4th year on the remaining asset value.

Note that estimated future cash flows are used to determine if impairment has occurred, but that the asset is adjusted to its estimated fair value, **not** estimated future cash flows, once the determination has been made.
- When the carrying value of an asset exceeds the expected future cash flows resulting from the use and eventual disposition of the asset (fair value).
- Write asset down to the new fair value and record a loss for the difference between the fair value and the old carrying value.

Impairment Loss (I/S)	X	
Accumulated Depreciation		X

Impairment testing applies to asset groups as well as individual assets. The impairment is applied proportionately to all of the long-lived assets in the asset group (but no asset is reduced below its fair market value).

Impairment of Long Lived Assets to be *DISPOSED Of* (Held for Sale):

When assets are no longer being used in operations, they are reclassified on the balance sheet. They are taken out of property, plant, and equipment and are reported in **Other assets** and described as held for sale.

- When first transferred to the held-for-sale category, the amount is the *lower of* the asset's **carrying value** and its **net realizable value** (NRV), which is its estimated selling price less costs of disposal.
    - If NRV is lower, it becomes the new carrying value (CV) and a loss is recognized on the income statement in Continuing Operations.
    - If the old CV is lower, it remains as the CV and no loss is recognized.
- Assets held for sale are NOT depreciated.
- In subsequent periods, increases or decreases in the NRV are recognized:
    - The asset is increased or decreased to its NRV at the balance sheet date, provided it is not increased to an amount that exceeds its CV before the transfer.
    - The increases or decreases are recognized as gains or losses.
    - Thus an asset held for disposal **CAN be written up or down** in future periods as long as the write-up is never greater than the carrying amount of the asset before the impairment.

Loss on planned disposition	700	
Equipment to be disposed of (other assets)	1500 (NRV)	
Accumulated Depreciation	3800	
Equipment		6000

Disposal of Fixed Assets

When a company disposes of a fixed asset, they will normally remove the original cost and accumulated depreciation, record any amounts received or due to them as a result of disposal, and recognize a gain or loss for the difference. The gain or loss is reported in continuing operations as part of other items.

For example, if a client owns a machine with a cost of $10,000 and carrying amount of $3,000, and it is sold for $2,500 cash, the entry is:

Cash	2,500	
Loss on sale	500	
Accumulated depreciation	7,000	
Machinery & equipment		10,000

Involuntary Conversion

Disposals include *destruction of property* as well as seizure by government entities as a result of condemnation or eminent domain actions. The accounting for these events is identical to voluntary sales, and GAAP does not allow deferral of gains or losses as a result of subsequent replacement of such property.

As an example, assume that, on 9/15/X1, fire destroyed a client's warehouse with an original cost of $1,000,000 and accumulated depreciation on the date of destruction of $225,000. Removal of debris cost $20,000. On 1/20/X2, the insurance company issued a check to the client for $1,200,000, and a new warehouse was built and completed on 6/30/X2 at a cost of $1,300,000. In 20X1, entries to account for the effects of the fire will have the following effect:

Due from insurance	1,200,000	
Accumulated depreciation	225,000	
Involuntary conversion gain		405,000
Warehouse		1,000,000
Cash		20,000

In 20X2, the collection of the insurance payment and construction of the new warehouse result in the following:

Cash	1,200,000	
Due from insurance		1,200,000
Warehouse	1,300,000	
Cash		1,300,000

In determining the accumulated depreciation balance at the time of a disposal, the asset should reflect any depreciation in the current period prior to the time of the sale. Also, in determining the gain or loss, all costs associated with the sale should be included. Let's look at an example with the following facts on a piece of equipment:

Purchase date	1/1/X1
Cost	$50,000
Estimated useful life	5 years
Estimated salvage value	None
Depreciation method	Straight-line
Accumulated depreciation, 12/31/X3	$30,000
Sale date	7/1/X4
Sales price	$18,000
Commission owed to sales agent	$900

Before computing the sale, we need to update accumulated depreciation for the six months of depreciation in 20X4:

6/30/X4	Depreciation expense	5,000	
	Accumulated depreciation		5,000

Then the sale is recorded:

7/1/X4	Cash	18,000	
	Accumulated depreciation	35,000	
	Gain on sale		2,100
	Equipment		50,000
	Due to sales agent		900

If an asset that is part of a group being depreciated under the composite method is sold or removed from service before the entire group has been fully depreciated, determining the asset's cost and accumulated depreciation may be impossible. In such a case, the carrying value of the group is simply reduced by net proceeds (if any) resulting from disposal, and no gain or loss is recorded.

Property, Plant and Equipment (PP&E) Section 8

Lecture 8.10

CLASS QUESTIONS

Please see the Class Questions and Class Solutions for this Lecture at the end of this Section.

Lecture 8.11

Nonmonetary Exchanges (Trade an Asset for an Asset)

In some cases, there may be an exchange of assets between entities that does not involve cash or cash equivalents, receivables, or payables. These transactions, referred to as nonmonetary exchanges, are generally recognized at **fair value**:
- The sales price of the asset surrendered is considered its fair value:
  - If the fair value of the asset given is not readily determinable, the assumed sales price will be the fair value of the asset received plus any monetary consideration received or minus any monetary consideration given.
  - If neither fair value is readily determinable, the assumed sales price will be the carrying value of the asset surrendered.
- A gain or loss on disposal, equal to the difference between the sales price and the carrying value of the asset, will be recognized in income.
- The asset acquired will be recognized at the sales price amount minus any monetary consideration received or plus any monetary consideration given.

There are three circumstances in which a nonmonetary transaction has an assumed sales price that is equal to the carrying value of the asset given, with *losses but no gains recognized*. These are:
- Transactions in which neither the fair value of the asset given nor the fair value of the asset received can be readily determined
- Transactions that lack commercial substance.
- An exchange of assets sold in the ordinary course of business for assets sold in the same line of business (inventory for inventory) to facilitate sales to third party customers.

A nonmonetary exchange, unless it lacks commercial substance, is treated as if it were two unrelated events:

1. Sale of the asset relinquished
2. Purchase of the asset received

As a result, a gain or loss is recognized on the difference between the fair value and book value of the asset relinquished. If the fair value of the asset relinquished is not known, the fair value received is used. If neither fair value can be determined, then the book value of the asset relinquished will have to be used, with no gain or loss.

Exchanges with Commercial Substance:
- Recognize ALL gains and losses
- Record new asset at FMV. If know #1 below, use it as the debit to the new asset. If #1 not known, use #2, etc.
    1. FMV given up + cash paid (– cash received)
    2. FMV of asset received
    3. Book Value (BV) given up + cash paid (– cash received)

Exchanges *Lacking* Commercial Substance:

When an exchange lacks commercial substance, it is handled differently. ASC 845 considers an exchange to have commercial substance whenever the *risk, timing, and/or amount of cash flows* (these three elements together are called the "configuration") are affected by the exchange. Since nearly all exchanges will result in SOME change in future cash flows, assume commercial substance on all exam questions involving nonmonetary exchanges **unless**:
- The fair value of the assets received/relinquished cannot be determined within a reasonable limit.
- The exchange is made purely to facilitate the sale of the product to a party that is not a party of the exchange (usually such exchanges take place with a competitor or vendor merely to facilitate future sales to unrelated customers).
- The exchange lacks commercial substance. The question will state that the cash flows are expected to be substantially unchanged as a result of the exchange.

In all three of these exceptions, the *carryover basis* (book value or carrying amount, adjusted for the cash paid or received as a part of the transaction) is used to measure the transaction instead of the fair value.

To summarize: Per **ASC 845**, a nonmonetary exchange is recognized at fair value *unless* the fair value is not determinable, the exchange transaction is to facilitate sales to customers, or the exchange transactions lacks commercial substance.

If an exchange lacks commercial substance, then there has been no realization under GAAP, and it is inappropriate to recognize gains. Realization is not required under GAAP, however, to report losses, so these are reported in full, in the same manner as other exchanges.

- Recognize all losses
- Defer all gains, unless boot is RECEIVED

> LCM – Debit asset for lower of these three

- Record at Lower of:
    1. FMV given up + cash paid (– cash received)
    2. FMV of asset received
    3. Book Value (BV) given up + cash paid (– cash received)

- **FOUR EXAMPLES:** 2 examples with commercial substance and 2 lacking commercial substance. In example A cash paid out is $10 and in example B, $20 cash is paid out. The FMV given up is not known, the FMV of the asset received is $30 and the book value of the old asset is $15.
    - Book Value of old = $15
    - FMV of new = $30
    - Cash paying out = $10 (example A); $20 (example B)

Property, Plant and Equipment (PP&E) — Section 8

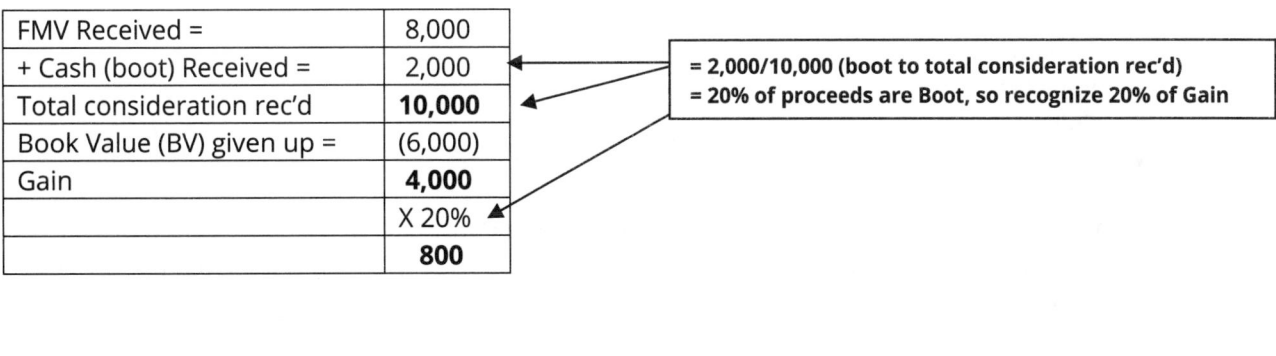

Substance A		Substance B	
JOURNAL ENTRIES		**JOURNAL ENTRIES**	
New	30	New	30
Old	15	Loss	5
Cash	10	Old	15
Gain	5	Cash	20
Lack Substance A		**Lack Substance B**	
New	25	New	30
Old	15	Loss	5
Cash	10	Old	15
		Cash	20

LCM – ex:A
1) ?
2) 30
3) **25**

LCM – ex:B
1) ?
2) **30**
3) 35

Lacks commercial substance – *BOOT Received*

There is one type of exchange lacking commercial substance in which gain IS recognized, however, and that is when boot is received by the client in the exchange. The reason for this exception to the general rule of deferral is that the cash received results in a small amount of commercial substance, and that part of the transaction must be reported differently from the portion of the exchange that lacks it.

- Defer all gains unless boot is received, then recognize the gain up to the proportionate share of boot received to total consideration received. The Ratio to use is: total boot received / total consideration received (boot + FV of asset received), multiplied by the gain.
- When the boot received is ≥ 25% of the total consideration received (including the boot), the transaction is viewed as a monetary exchange and all of the gain is recognized.

Example: Receive inventory with a FMV of $8000 and cash of $2000, by giving up similar inventory with a book value of $6000.

FMV Received =	8,000
+ Cash (boot) Received =	2,000
Total consideration rec'd	**10,000**
Book Value (BV) given up =	(6,000)
Gain	**4,000**
	X 20%
	800

= 2,000/10,000 (boot to total consideration rec'd)
= 20% of proceeds are Boot, so recognize 20% of Gain

```
New (plugged)        4,800
Cash                 2,000
     Old                        6,000
     Gain                         800
```

- Recognized gain based on portion of proceeds that are cash.

In all, there are six different situations that need to be distinguished in determining whether *gains* (FMV exceeds carrying amount) and *losses* (carrying amount exceeds FMV) are recognized:

Commercial Substance	**Yes**	**Yes**	**Yes**	**No**	**No**	**No**
Boot	None	Paid	Received	None	Paid	Received
Gain	Yes	Yes	Yes	No	No	Part
Loss	Yes	Yes	Yes	Yes	Yes	Yes

Lecture 8.12

CLASS QUESTIONS

Please see the Class Questions and Class Solutions for this Lecture at the end of this Section.

Lecture 8.13

FIXED ASSETS UNDER IFRS

There are many similarities in the accounting for fixed assets under US GAAP and IFRS, but the differences are fairly significant. In most cases, the initial carrying values of assets will be the same under both but the amounts at which they will be reported in subsequent periods may differ by substantial amounts. IFRS also uses different categories (Biological Assets) as compared with GAAP.

Plant, Property, and Equipment (PP&E)

PP&E are initially recorded at cost, which includes all the normal costs of acquisition and getting them to their intended location and ready for their "intended use." PP&E will initially be recorded in a category or class of assets based on its characteristics. Classes include:
- Land
- Buildings
- Equipment
- Furniture and fixtures
- Vehicles
- Ships
- Aircraft

Once categorized into the appropriate class of assets, the entity decides on the method by which the asset will be measured on subsequent balance sheets. The entity will choose to apply either the **cost model (CM)** or the **revaluation model (RM)**. The RM may only be used when the fair value of the asset is readily determinable.
- Under the **Cost Model (CM),** the asset is depreciated to its *residual value*
    - Each significant part of the asset is depreciated separately
    - The method should reflect the pattern based on the economic benefits the entity obtains from the use of the asset
    - Depreciation is recognized in income unless it is included in the cost of another asset such as manufactured inventory
- Under the **Revaluation Model (RM),** the asset is periodically adjusted to its estimated fair value

- o Revaluations to fair value must be made regularly to assure that the carrying amount is not significantly different from fair value
- o The asset is reported at its revalued amount less depreciation and any impairments from the date of revaluation to the balance sheet date
- o Changes in value are generally recognized in income:
    - Increases in value prior to any decreases are recognized in other comprehensive income (**OCI**).
    - Decreases in value first offset cumulative amounts of increases in other comprehensive income (**OCI**) with the excess reported in **income**
    - Increases in value occurring subsequent to decreases are first recognized in **income** to the extent they offset decreases previously recognized in income with the excess reported in other comprehensive income (**OCI**).

The residual value of an asset is the estimated amount that would be received upon disposal on the financial statement date:
- The amount is net of costs of disposal
- The asset is assumed to be of the age and in the condition that is expected when the asset is ready for disposal

IFRS requires the recognition of a decommissioning liability, similar to an asset retirement obligation. It represents the estimated amount it will cost an entity to put property into a usable or sellable condition when it is no longer going to be used by the entity for its original purpose. The liability is periodically adjusted to reflect changes in the estimated cost.
- Increases or decreases in the liability are generally recognized as increases or decreases to the carrying value of the related property.
- This will increase or decrease subsequent depreciation or amortization expense.
- Adjustments to the liability occurring after the property is fully depreciated are recognized in profit or loss.

Under IFRS, an asset may not be reported at an amount that exceeds its recoverable amount, which is the greater of the amount it will generate through use or the amount that will be generated through disposal, net of costs of disposal. When an asset's carrying value exceeds its recoverable amount, an **impairment** loss is recognized.
- If either an asset's disposal value or its value in use exceeds its carrying value, the asset is not impaired.
- The value in use takes into account the time value of money and the effects of uncertainty.
- If impaired, the loss will be the difference between the carrying amount and the greater amount.

An impairment loss is recognized in the period incurred:
- If the asset is accounted for under the CM, the impairment loss is recognized immediately in **profit or loss**.
- If the asset is accounted for under the RM, the impairment loss is a **revaluation decrease**

An impairment test in which the entity estimates the recoverable amount of an asset is only required for most assets when there is an indication that the asset has been impaired. Certain intangibles are required to be tested for impairment regardless of whether or not there is an indication of impairment:
- Intangibles with indefinite useful lives
- Intangibles not yet ready for use by the entity

On each financial statement date, the entity determines if there is an indication that assets have been impaired. In addition, it also assesses whether a previously recognized impairment no longer exists, in which case it is reversed.

Investment Property

IFRS considers property that is held for capital appreciation or to earn rentals to be investment property. Investment property is initially recognized at cost, including transaction costs. This entity may also include investment property held by a lessee in a lease classified as an operating lease provided the lease is accounted for as if it was a finance lease and the entity applies the fair value model to the asset.

An entity may apply the *fair value model* (**FVM**) to investment property under which the property is measured at fair value at each balance sheet date with changes recognized in profit or loss. Under FVM, **no depreciation is recorded**. As an alternative, an entity may apply the *cost model* (**CM**) to investment property under which the property is measured at initial cost less accumulated depreciation and accumulated impairment losses. Use of the CM requires the entity to disclose the asset's fair value.

Biological Assets

Biological assets are living things, including plants and animals. Biological assets are distinguished from agricultural products, which are the harvested product of an entity's biological assets. Under IFRS biological assets are recognized that are within their control when they can measure the fair value or cost reliably and it is probable that the entity will obtain future economic benefits from the asset.

- Biological assets and agricultural products are recognized at **fair value less costs to sell** at harvest (**NRV**)
- This treatment does not apply to biological assets for which the fair value cannot be reliably measured
- This treatment applies to biological assets on each balance sheet date but to agricultural products only at the point of harvest, at which time they become inventory and are accounted for accordingly.
- Gains and losses from changes in NRV are recognized in income

When the fair value of a biological asset cannot be measured reliably, it is measured at *cost less accumulated depreciation and accumulated impairment losses*. Once the fair value can be measured reliably, however, the carrying value will be the fair value less the cost to sell.

Borrowing Costs

Under IFRS, when an asset requires a substantial amount of time to get it ready for its intended use, borrowing costs are **capitalized** as part of the cost of that asset.

- Borrowing costs consist of interest and other costs associated with borrowing
- Capitalized costs include those borrowing costs directly attributable to the obtaining of the asset through acquisition, construction, or production
- All other borrowing costs are recognized as expense as incurred.

The period over which borrowing costs are capitalized:
- Begin when the entity incurs costs related to the asset, it incurs borrowing costs, and it begins to prepare the asset for its intended use or for sale.

Property, Plant and Equipment (PP&E) Section 8

- Ends when the entity is no longer preparing the asset for its intended use or for sale.

Fixed Assets	
GAAP	**IFRS**
• Fixed assets, other than those held for sale, are accounted for at using a cost model (CM) under which the asset is depreciated to its salvage value.	• Fixed assets may be accounted for under the cost model (CM) or, when fair value is readily determinable, the revaluation model (RM) in which the asset is reported at revalued amount (fair value) less depreciation and impairments since the most recent revaluation.
• Fixed assets not required to be depreciated using component deprecation.	• Fixed assets accounted for under cost model must use component depreciation, depreciating each significant part separately.

• Property held for investment or rental not treated differently than other fixed assets (no separate category exists)	• Property held for investment or rental considered investment property and may be measured using:
	  ○ The *revaluation or fair value model*, with changes recognized in profit or loss except revaluation gains in excess of previously recognized losses, which are in other comprehensive income, or
	  ○ The *cost model*, under which the asset is reported at initial cost less accumulated depreciation and impairment losses.

• Biological assets, consisting of living things, not accounted for in a separate category.	• Biological assets are recognized at fair value less disposal costs at harvest (net realizable value), unless fair value cannot be reliably measured (cost model applied), with gains and losses recognized in income.
• Impairment losses may Not be reversed	• Previously recognized impairment losses may be reversed if an impaired asset recovers its value, up to previously recognized losses.
• Impairment losses are calculated using a 2-step approach comparing the carrying value to undiscounted future cash flows and, if lower, writing the carrying value down to fair value.	• Impairment losses are calculated using a 1-step approach comparing the carrying value to the asset's recovery value, which is the higher of its net realizable value or its value in use.
• Depreciation factors, such as salvage value, useful life, and method, are NOT required to be reevaluated each period.	• Depreciation factors, such as salvage value, useful life, and method are required to be reevaluated each period.

©Roger CPA Review

Section 8   Property, Plant and Equipment (PP&E)

PP&E: Cost Model (CM) or Revaluation Model (RM)

PP&E is initially recognized at cost

    PP&E   100,000

        Cash   100,000

Choose one of the following measurement models by class
- Cost model (CM)
- Revaluation model (RM)

Cost Model (CM) (record depreciation (S/L, DB or Units dep method) and Impairment loss, like normal)

    Depreciation Expense   5,000

        Accumulated depreciation   5,000

Impairment loss CM [CV > recoverable amt (> net selling price or value in use)]

    Impairment Loss (I/S) or Dep exp   2,000

        Accumulated depreciation
            (Impairment)   2,000

(CV of asset = Cost – Accumulated Depreciation – Accumulated Impairment Loss)

Reversal of Impairment loss CM (NEW) (up to previously recognized Imp loss)

    Accumulated depreciation   2,000

        Impairment recovery (I/S)   2,000

Revaluation Model (RM) (CV = revalued amount = Fair Value at Revaluation date)

    PP&E   30,000

        Revaluation Surplus (OCI)   30,000

(Accumulated Depreciation can be adjusted proportionately or accumulated depreciation can be eliminated and the asset is shown at net)

Now depreciate and test for impairment as normal at new value

If carrying amount is *decreased* due to revaluation

    Revaluation Surplus (to 0)   30,000

    Revaluation Loss (I/S)   10,000

        PP&E   40,000

Property, Plant and Equipment (PP&E) — Section 8

<u>When dispose of asset (derecognize), JE like normal</u>

Cash	25,000	
Accumulated depreciation	60,000	
Loss on Sale (I/S)	5,000	
Gain on sale of equip		XXX
PP&E		90,000

<u>If remainder exists in Revaluation Surplus, transfer to Retained Earnings</u>

Revaluation Surplus	XXX	
Retained Earnings		XXX

Impairment loss RM [CV > recoverable amt (> net selling price or value in use)]

Revaluation Surplus (OCI to 0)	2,000	
Impairment Loss (I/S –balance)	XXX	
Accumulated depreciation (Impairment)		2,000 + XXX

<u>Reversal of Impairment loss RM (in income up to previously recognized Imp loss)</u>

Accumulated depreciation	XXX	
Gain due to impairment recovery (IS)		XXX
Revaluation Surplus (OCI)		XXX

Investment Property: Cost Method (CM) or Fair Value Model (FVM)

FVM measure at fair value, changes are recognized in Income Statement profit or loss (NOT OCI)

Investment property	30,000	
Revaluation Gain (I/S)		30,000

Intangible Assets: Cost Model (CM) or Revaluation Model (RM)
(like PP&E to OCI)

(RM requires that FV be determined in an active market)

Intangible Asset	30,000	
Revaluation Surplus (OCI)		30,000

Non-Monetary Exchanges under IFRS

Accounting for Non-monetary exchanges under IFRS are similar, however the terminology is different (similar to the old GAAP rules). Under IFRS exchanges are characterized as Similar (lacking commercial substance) and Dissimilar (having commercial substance). The other difference is that under Similar exchanges, losses are recognized and gains are not.

Non-Monetary Exchanges	
GAAP	**IFRS**
• Exchanges are characterized as having Commercial Substance and Lacking Commercial Substance	• Exchanges are characterized as Similar assets and Dissimilar assets.
• Exchanges with Commercial Substance are accounted for at F.V. and all gains and losses are recognized.	• Exchanges that are Dissimilar are accounted for the same way as exchanges with commercial substance; both gains and losses are recognized.
• Exchanges Lacking Commercial Substance are recognized at the lower of the 3 choices, and losses are always recognized, gains are only recognized if "boot" is received.	• In all exchanges of Similar assets, losses are recognized and gains are not.

Lecture 8.14

CLASS QUESTIONS

Please see the Class Questions and Class Solutions for this Lecture at the end of this Section.

Lecture 8.15

CLASS QUESTIONS

Please see the Class Questions and Class Solutions for this Lecture at the end of this Section.

Property, Plant and Equipment (PP&E) — Section 8

CLASS QUESTIONS

Work through the below Class Questions while following along with the respective lectures. Once this is complete, you can begin independently practicing what you've learned by quizzing yourself on this course section in your Interactive Practice Questions (IPQ), which can be found in your online Student Dashboard. Your IPQ simulates the computer-based testing experience, and will also help you understand how concepts are applied to the exam. Each question includes answer explanations from expert CPAs that will help you determine why you answered a question correctly or incorrectly. This is key to your success on the CPA Exam.

Lecture 8.05

1. During 20X0, Burr Co. had the following transactions pertaining to its new office building:

Purchase price of land	$ 60,000
Legal fees for contracts to purchase land	2,000
Architects' fees	8,000
Demolition of old building on site	5,000
Sale of scrap from old building	3,000
Construction cost of new building (fully completed)	350,000

   In Burr's December 31, 20X0, balance sheet, what amounts should be reported as the cost of land and cost of building?

	Land	Building
a.	$60,000	$360,000
b.	$62,000	$360,000
c.	$64,000	$358,000
d.	$65,000	$362,000

2. A company with a June 30 fiscal year end entered into a $3,000,000 construction project on April 1 to be completed on September 30. The cumulative construction-in-progress balances at April 30, May 31, and June 30 were $500,000, $800,000, and $1,500,000, respectively. The interest rate on company debt used to finance the construction project was 5% from April 1 through June 30 and 6% from July 1 through September 30. Assuming that the asset is placed into service on October 1, what amount of interest should be capitalized to the project on June 30?

   a. $11,666
   b. $18,750
   c. $75,000
   d. $90,000

Lecture 8.08

3. On January 2, 20X5, Lem Corp. bought machinery under a contract that required a down payment of $10,000, plus twenty-four monthly payments of $5,000 each, for total cash payments of $130,000. The cash equivalent price of the machinery was $110,000. The machinery has an estimated useful life of ten years and estimated salvage value of $5,000. Lem uses straight-line depreciation. In its 20X5 income statement, what amount should Lem report as depreciation for this machinery?

    a. $10,500
    b. $11,000
    c. $12,500
    d. $13,000

4. In January 20X4, Vorst Co. purchased a mineral mine for $2,640,000 with removable ore estimated at 1,200,000 tons. After it has extracted all the ore, Vorst will be required by law to restore the land to its original condition at an estimated cost of $180,000. Vorst believes it will be able to sell the property afterwards for $300,000. During 20X4, Vorst incurred $360,000 of development costs preparing the mine for production and removed and sold 60,000 tons of ore. In its 20X4 income statement, what amount should Vorst report as depletion?

    a. $135,000
    b. $144,000
    c. $150,000
    d. $159,000

Lecture 8.10

5. When should a long-lived asset be tested for recoverability?

    a. When external financial statements are being prepared.
    b. When events or changes in circumstances indicate that its carrying amount may not be recoverable.
    c. When the asset's carrying amount is less than its fair value
    d. When the asset's fair value has decreased, and the decrease is judged to be permanent.

6. During the year, there had been significant decreases in the fair market value of Roger Co's manufacturing equipment. The following information regarding the costs associated with the equipment was gathered:

Original cost of the equipment	$700,000
Accumulated depreciation	400,000
Expected net future cash inflows (undiscounted) related to the continued use and eventual disposal of the equipment	275,000
Fair value of the equipment	225,000

    How much impairment loss should be reported on Roger Co's income statement for the year?

    a. $ 25,000
    b. $ 50,000
    c. $ 75,000
    d. $475,000

Property, Plant and Equipment (PP&E) — Section 8

Lecture 8.12

7. Yola Co. and Zaro Co. are fuel oil distributors. To facilitate the delivery of oil to their customers, Yola and Zaro exchanged ownership of 1,200 barrels of oil without physically moving the oil. Yola paid Zaro $30,000 to compensate for a difference in the grade of oil. On the date of the exchange, cost and market values of the oil were as follows:

	Yola Co	Zaro Co.
Cost	$100,000	$126,000
Market values	120,000	150,000

In Zaro's income statement, what amount of gain should be reported from the exchange of the oil assuming the transaction lacked commercial substance?

   a. $0
   b. $ 4,800
   c. $24,000
   d. $30,000

8. May Co. and Sty Co. exchanged nonmonetary assets. The exchange is not expected to significantly affect the future cash flows for either May or Sty. May paid cash to Sty in connection with the exchange. To the extent that the amount of cash exceeds a proportionate share of the carrying amount of the asset surrendered, a realized gain on the exchange should be recognized by

	May	Sty
a.	Yes	Yes
b.	Yes	No
c.	No	Yes
d.	No	No

9. Amble, Inc. exchanged a truck with a carrying amount of $12,000 and a fair value of $20,000 for a truck and $4,000 cash in a transaction that lacked commercial substance. The fair value of the truck received was $16,000. At what amount should Amble record the truck received in the exchange?

   a. $ 7,000
   b. $ 9,600
   c. $12,000
   d. $15,000

Lecture 8.14

10. Under IFRS, when an entity chooses the revaluation model as its accounting policy for measuring PP&E, which of the following is correct?

   a. When an asset is revalued, the entire class of PP&E to which the asset belongs must be revalued.
   b. When an asset is revalued, individual assets within a class of PP&E to which that asset belongs can be revalued.
   c. Revaluations of PP&E must be made at least every 3 years.
   d. Increases in an asset's carrying value as a result of the first revaluation must be recognized as a component of profit or loss.

11. A company that presents its financial statements under IFRS is using the revaluation model to account for its fixed assets. In 20X1, it recognized a $50,000 impairment loss. During 20X2, those assets increased in value by $75,000. How will the increase be reported?

    a. In profit or loss in the amount of $75,000.
    b. In other comprehensive income in the amount of $75,000.
    c. With $50,000 reported in profit or loss and the remaining $25,000 in other comprehensive income.
    d. Impairment recoveries are not recognized.

CLASS SOLUTIONS

1. (c) The costs to be allocated to land will include the purchase price of $60,000, the legal costs incurred to purchase it of $2,000, and the net cost of demolishing the old building of $2,000 for a total of $64,000. The $8,000 in architects' fees relate to preparing plans for the building and will be capitalized along with the construction costs of $350,000 to give a building cost of $358,000.

2. (a) Capitalized interest is the lesser of actual or avoidable interest. The answer is calculated by first figuring out the avoidable interest, then comparing it to actual interest paid during the year, with the lesser number being the amount the entity can capitalize.

To find avoidable interest, multiply the weighted average accumulated expenditures for the applicable period by the applicable interest rate.

The interest rate change on July 1 is extraneous, potentially distracting information. It is unnecessary for solving the problem because the company has a June 30 fiscal year end and the question asks for capitalized interest as of June 30. The 5% annual interest rate in effect prior to July 1 will be used, prorated for the 3-month period in question.

Here are the weighted average accumulated expenditures for the three-month period:

- $500K spent in April – applies to all 3 months, so 3/3 (April, May, June)
- $300K spent in May ($800 - 500) - 2 months, so 2/3 (May, June)
- $700K spent in June ($1500 - 800) - 1 month, so 1/3 (June only)

Thus, 500(3/3) + 300(2/3) + 700(1/3) = $933,333 in weighted average accumulated expenditures.

Avoidable interest equals $933,333 x 5% (3/12), or $11,666.

Because the problem states nothing of actual interest incurred, we must assume the avoidable interest was lower than actual total interest incurred, and that the full amount of avoidable interest, or $11,666, may thus be capitalized.

3. (a) The machine will be recorded at its cash equivalent price of $110,000. Under straight-line, the depreciable basis will be the cost of $110,000 minus the salvage value of $5,000 or $105,000. This will be allocated over the 10-year life of the property at $10,500 per year.

Machinery	110,000	
Discount on N.P.	20,000	($130,000 – $110,000)
Notes payable		120,000 (24 x $5,000)
Cash		10,000

4. (b) Since Vorst must restore the property to its original condition at an estimated cost of $180,000 and incurred $360,000 in preparing the mine for production, the total cost associated with the mine is $2,640,000 + $180,000 + $360,000 or $3,180,000. When the ore has been extracted, Vorst expects to receive $300,000 from the sale of the property, indicating a depletion base of $2,880,000. With expected production of 1,200,000 tons, depletion will be $2.40 per ton. In 20X4, depletion will be $2.40 x 60,000 tons or $144,000.

5. (b) When certain circumstances occur, a review for an impairment loss should be made. For example, a significant decrease in the market value of an asset, a significant adverse change in legal factors, etc. If the review indicates impairment, then the recoverability test is performed. If the sum off the expected future net cash flows from the asset is less than the carrying value of that asset, then an impairment has occurred. When it is tested for impairment, it is done using a 2-step method under which the first step involves testing the asset for recoverability. The second step involves comparing the carrying value to the fair value. The amount of the impairment adjustment would be the difference between the carrying amount of the asset and the fair value of the asset. Answer (a) is incorrect because goodwill and intangibles with indefinite useful lives other than goodwill are required to be tested for impairment at least annually, but long-lived assets are only required to be tested when there is reason to believe they have been impaired, not whenever financial statements are being prepared. Answer (c) is incorrect because depreciable assets are not required to be tested for impairment unless the entity has reason to believe that the asset has been impaired. Answer (d) is incorrect because the entity does not evaluate whether or not the decline is permanent.

6. (c) When a long-lived asset is impaired, which is when the carrying value exceeds its fair value, the asset is written down to its fair value and an impairment loss is recognized for the difference. In this case, the carrying value is ($700,000 - $400,000) $300,000 and the fair value is $225,000, resulting in an impairment loss of $75,000.

7. (b) Since this transaction lacks commercial substance, it is generally recorded at book value. When such an exchange involves both monetary and nonmonetary assets, it is accounted for as if it were the equivalent of 2 sales. Zora is receiving cash of $30,000 and oil worth $120,000, for a total of $150,000, indicating the cash is 20% of the total. It is in exchange for oil with a carrying value of $126,000 resulting in a total gain of $24,000. Since the cash portion represents 20% of the transaction, 20% of the gain, or $4,800, will be recognized.

8. (c) When a company is involved in a nonmonetary exchange that is not expected to significantly affect cash flows, it is a transaction that lacks commercial substance and will generally recognized at book value. When the transaction involves both monetary and nonmonetary assets, the entity receiving monetary consideration will treat it as two separate transactions, one monetary and one nonmonetary and will recognize gain on the monetary portion. Since Sty is receiving cash, only stay may recognize a gain.

9. (b) Since this transaction lacks commercial substance, it is generally recorded at book value. When such an exchange involves both monetary and nonmonetary assets, it is accounted for as if it were the equivalent of 2 sales. Amble is receiving cash of $4,000 and a truck worth $16,000, for a total of $20,000, indicating the cash is 20% of the total. Since the carrying value is $12,000, that leaves a gain of $8,000. We will recognize the portion of the gain that is received in cash which is 20% x $8,000 ($20,000 − $12,000) = $1,600. So Amble would credit the old truck for $12,000, and also credit the gain of $1,600 they would debit cash for the $4,000 received leaving a balance for the new truck of $9,600.

New	9,600		
Cash	4,000		
Old		12,000	
Gain		1,600	(8,000 x 20% = 1,600)

Property, Plant and Equipment (PP&E)　　　　　　　　　　　　　　　　　　　　　Section 8

10. (a) If an item of PP&E under IFRS is revalued, the entire class of which the asset belongs must also be revalued. Answer (b) is incorrect because the entire class of which the asset belongs must be revalued rather than the individual asset. Answer (c) is incorrect because under the revaluation method, revaluation must be done periodically and reasonably frequently. There is no specific requirement that revaluation be every 3 years. Answer (d) is incorrect because under the revaluation method, increases in an asset's carrying value are recognized in other comprehensive income. They are only recognized in profit or loss to the extent that they represent recoveries of previously recognized losses.

11. (c) Under the revaluation method, increases in the value of an asset are recognized in profit or loss only to the extent of previously recognized losses. Any excess gains are recognized in other comprehensive income (OCI). In this case, $50,000 of the $75,000 increase in value represents a recovery of a previously recognized loss and will be reported in profit or loss. The remaining $25,000 will be recognized in OCI.

Section 8   Property, Plant and Equipment (PP&E)

Lecture 8.05

TASK-BASED SIMULATIONS

Task-Based Simulation 1

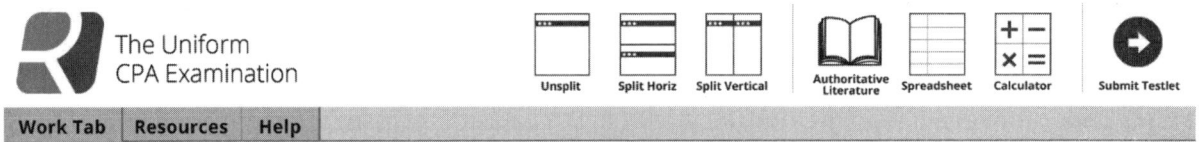

For **items 1 through 6,** determine for each item whether the expenditure should be capitalized or expensed as a period cost.

		Capitalize	Expense
1.	Freight charges paid for goods held for resale.	○	○
2.	In-transit insurance on goods held for resale purchased FOB shipping point.	○	○
3.	Interest on note payable for goods held for resale.	○	○
4.	Installation of equipment.	○	○
5.	Testing of newly purchased equipment.	○	○
6.	Cost of current year service contract on equipment.	○	○

Task-Based Simulation 2

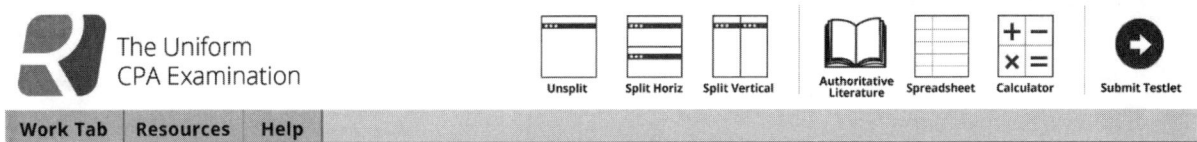

Question Number 2 consists of 8 items. Select the best answer for each item.

During 20X2, Sloan, Inc. began a project to construct a new corporate headquarters. Sloan purchased land with an existing building for $750,000. The land was valued at $700,000 and the building at $50,000. Sloan planned to demolish the building and construct a new office building on the site. Items 1 through 8 represent various expenditures by Sloan for this project.

Required:

For each expenditure in items 1 through 8, select from the list below the appropriate accounting treatment.

- **L.** Classify as land and do not depreciate.
- **B.** Classify as building and depreciate.
- **E.** Expense.

Items to be answered:

		(L)	(B)	(E)
1.	Purchase of land for $700,000.	○	○	○
2.	Interest of $147,000 on construction financing incurred after completion of construction.	○	○	○
3.	Interest of $186,000 on construction financing paid during construction.	○	○	○
4.	Purchase of building for $50,000.	○	○	○
5.	$18,500 payment of delinquent real estate taxes assumed by Sloan on purchase.	○	○	○
6.	$12,000 liability insurance premium during the construction period.	○	○	○
7.	$65,000 cost of razing existing building.	○	○	○
8.	Moving costs of $136,000.	○	○	○

Section 8   Property, Plant and Equipment (PP&E)

Lecture 8.08

Task-Based Simulation 3

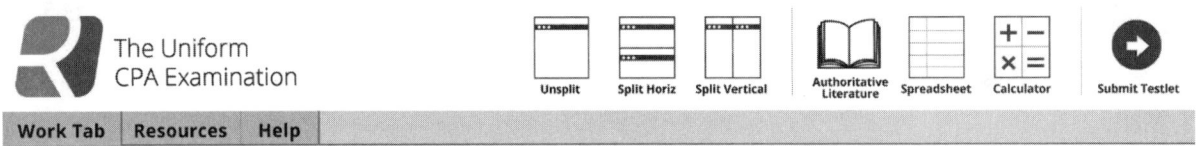

On January 2, 20X2, Gray purchased a manufacturing machine for $864,000. The machine has an eight-year estimated life and a $144,000 estimated salvage value. Gray expects to manufacture 1,800,000 units over the life of the machine. During 20x3, Gray manufactured 300,000 units.

Required:

Calculate depreciation expense on the manufacturing machine for 20x3 for each method listed.

		Amount
1.	Straight-line.	
2.	Double-declining balance.	
3.	Sum-of-years' digits.	
4.	Units of production.	

Property, Plant and Equipment (PP&E) — Section 8

Lecture 8.12

Task-Based Simulation 4

Situation

- Link Co. purchased an office building and the land on which it is located by paying $800,000 cash and assuming an existing mortgage of $200,000. The property is assessed at $960,000 for realty tax purposes, of which 60% is allocated to the building.
- Link leased construction equipment under a seven-year capital lease requiring annual year-end payments of $100,000. Link's incremental borrowing rate is 9%, while the lessor's implicit rate, which is not known to Link, is 8%. Present value factors for an ordinary annuity for seven periods are 5.21 at 8% and 5.03 at 9%. Fair value of the equipment is $515,000.
- Link paid $50,000 and gave a plot of undeveloped land with a carrying amount of $320,000 and a fair value of $450,000 to Club Co. in exchange for a plot of undeveloped land with a fair value of $500,000. The land was carried on Club's books at $350,000. This transaction is considered to lack commercial substance; the configuration of cash flows from the land acquired is not expected to be significantly different from the configuration of cash flows of the land exchanged.

Calculate the following amounts to be recorded by Link.

Items to be answered:

		Amount
1.	Building.	
2.	Leased equipment.	
3.	Land received from Club on Link's books.	
4.	Land received from Link on Club's books.	

Task-Based Simulation 5

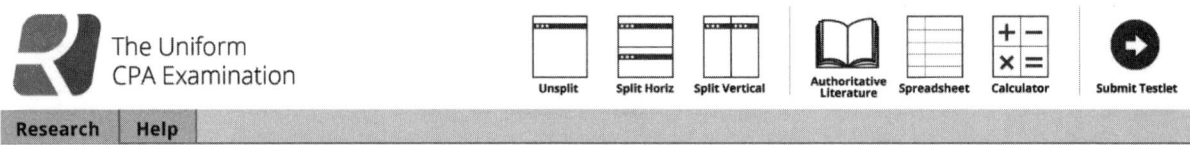

A client has discontinued manufacturing a specific product and, as a result, has retired certain machinery and equipment that was used in the manufacturing process. The client intends to attempt to sell the assets to another manufacturer. Identify the location in professional standards that indicates how a long-lived asset classified as held for sale should be measured.

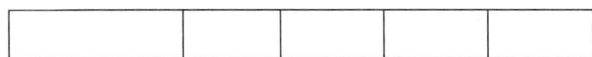

Task-Based Simulation 6

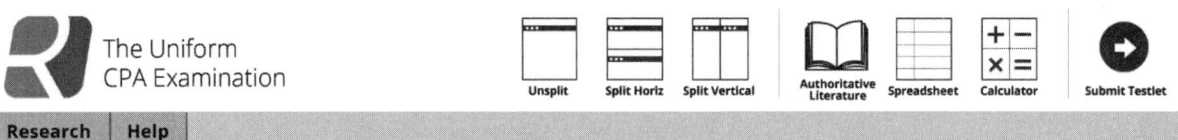

A company that sells office furniture is exchanging inventory with another company to accommodate a customer that is seeking furniture of a specific color. The inventory received is virtually interchangeable, other than color, with the inventory being traded. Identify the location in professional standards that indicates when a nonmonetary transaction should be measured at the recorded amount.

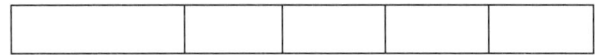

Property, Plant and Equipment (PP&E) — Section 8

TASK-BASED SIMULATION SOLUTIONS

Task-Based Simulation Solution 1

		Capitalize	Expense
1.	Freight charges paid for goods held for resale.	●	○
2.	In-transit insurance on goods held for resale purchased FOB shipping point.	●	○
3.	Interest on note payable for goods held for resale.	○	●
4.	Installation of equipment.	●	○
5.	Testing of newly purchased equipment.	●	○
6.	Cost of current year service contract on equipment.	○	●

Explanation of solutions

1. **C** — Costs incurred in getting an asset ready for its intended use are capitalized. This would include freight charges paid for goods held for resale as the goods must be transported to the company in order for the company to be able to sell them.

2. **C** — Costs incurred in getting an asset ready for its intended use are capitalized. This would include in-transit insurance on goods held for resale purchased F.O.B. shipping point since the goods become the responsibility of the purchaser as soon as they are picked up by the common carrier. The purchaser will insure the goods to make certain that they arrive intact which is necessary in order for the purchaser to be able to resell the goods.

3. **E** — Interest on notes payable for goods held for resale is not considered a cost incurred in getting the goods necessary for their intended use and would not be capitalized. Goods held for resale are generally purchased with the expectation that they will be paid for on a short-term basis and the obligation, accounts payable, does not generally bear interest.

4. **C** — Equipment cannot be used until it is installed. As a result, costs of installation represent costs incurred in getting the asset ready for its intended use and would be capitalized.

5. **C** — Testing of newly purchased equipment is necessary in preparing the equipment for use in that it allows the company to make certain that the equipment is not in need of adjustment. As a result, the cost of testing will be capitalized.

6. **E** — The cost of a service contract on equipment is related to the use of the equipment and is not incurred in getting the equipment ready for use. As a result, it will be recognized as expense and would not be capitalized.

TASK-BASED SIMULATION SOLUTION 2

1. L — The purchase price of land is recognized as land and is not subject to depreciation.

2. E — Interest may only be capitalized up to the point in time that an asset being constructed is ready for its intended use. Once the construction of the building is completed, it is ready for its intended use and interest will be recognized as expense in the period incurred.

3. B — Interest incurred during the construction of an asset for the company's use is capitalized and added to the cost of the asset. Since the interest relates to the construction loan on the building, it will be added to the cost of the building and depreciated over the life of the building.

4. L — When land and building are purchased in a single transaction, a portion of the purchase price is allocated to the building if the company intends to use it. Since the building purchased by Sloan will be demolished, the entire purchase price of the land and building will be included in the cost of the land.

5. L — Delinquent property taxes paid by a buyer of property are considered part of the purchase price of the property. Since Sloan purchased the land and building with the intention of demolishing the building, the entire purchase price, including the delinquent taxes, will be included in the cost of the land.

6. B — Premiums for liability insurance during the course of construction of a building are considered one cost in getting the building ready for its intended use. As a result, it will be capitalized as part of the cost of the building and will be depreciated over the life of the building.

7. L — The cost of razing an existing building on land is part of the cost of preparing the land for its intended use, the construction of the building. As a result, the cost of razing the existing building will be capitalized as part of the cost of the land.

8. E — Moving costs are considered a cost of doing business and will be recognized as expense in the period incurred.

Task-Based Simulation Solution 3

1. Under straight-line, depreciation will be equal to the depreciable basis divided by the useful life.

Cost	$864,000
Salvage value	144,000
Depreciable basis	$720,000
Useful life	÷ 8 years
Annual depreciation	**$90,000**

2. Under double-declining balance, salvage value is ignored. In each year, the carrying value will be multiplied by double the straight-line depreciation rate to calculate the year's depreciation. With a useful life of 8 years, the straight-line rate is 1/8 or 12.5% giving a double-declining balance rate of 2 x 12.5% or 25%. Since 20X3 is the 2nd year of the asset's useful life, depreciation will be calculated for 20X2 to determine the carrying value for 20X3.

   Depreciation in 20X2 will be $864,000 x 25% or $216,000. As a result, the carrying value will be reduced to $864,000 - $216,000 or $648,000. Depreciation in 20X3 will be $648,000 x 25% or **$162,000**.

3. Under sum-of-the-years'-digits, depreciation will be equal to the depreciable basis multiplied by a fraction. The numerator of the fraction will be 8 in the 1st year (20X2), 7 in the 2nd year (20X3) and so on. The denominator will be 8 x (8 + 1) ÷ 2 or 36.

Cost	$864,000
Salvage value	144,000
Depreciable basis	$720,000
Fraction	7/36
20X3 depreciation	**$140,000**

4. Under units of production, the depreciable basis multiplied by a fraction. The numerator of the fraction will be the production for the current year, 300,000 units in 20X3. The denominator will be the total estimated production of 1,800,000 units.

Cost	$864,000
Salvage value	144,000
Depreciable basis	$720,000
Fraction	300,000/1,800,000
20X3 depreciation	**$120,000**

Section 8 — Property, Plant and Equipment (PP&E)

Task-Based Simulation Solution 4

1. **($600,000)** The total cost of the land and building is equal to the cash paid of $800,000 plus the mortgage assumed of $200,000 for a total of $1,000,000. The cost will be allocated to the land and building using the ratios in the realty tax assessment. Since the assessment allocated 60% to the building, 60% of the cost, or **$600,000** would be recorded as building.

2. **($503,000)** Equipment acquired under a capital lease is recorded at the present value of the minimum lease payments using the lessee's incremental borrowing rate unless the rate implicit in the lease is known to the lessee and is lower than the lessee's rate and also provided that the amount does not exceed the fair value of the equipment. Even though the rate implicit in the lease is lower than Link's incremental borrowing rate, it is not known by Link and cannot be used. Link will record the leased equipment at $100,000 x 5.03 or **$503,000**, which does not exceed the fair value of the equipment.

3. **($370,000)** When a nonmonetary transaction lacks commercial substance, it is generally recognized at book value and neither party recognizes a gain on the transaction. When the transaction also involves cash, the party receiving the cash will recognize a portion of the gain proportionate to the cash portion of the total fair value of consideration exchanged. Link is giving cash, rather than receiving it, and will recognize the transaction at the carrying values of the assets given, including the land of $320,000 and cash of $50,000 for a total of **$370,000**

4. **($315,000)** Club is giving land with a carrying value of $350,000 for cash of $50,000 and land with a fair market value of $450,000 or a total of $500,000 indicating a gain of $150,000. Since Club is receiving cash, a portion of the gain will be recognized equal to the ratio of the cash received to the total proceeds multiplied by the total gain.

    $50,000/$500,000 x $150,000 = $15,000

    As a result, the transaction will be recorded with a credit to the old land of $350,000, a credit to a gain on disposal of $15,000, and a debit to cash of $50,000. The amount required to balance the entry will be a debit to the new land for **$315,000**.

Task-Based Simulation Solution 5

| FASB ASC | 360 | 10 | 35 | 43 |

Task-Based Simulation Solution 6

| FASB ASC | 845 | 10 | 30 | 3 |

Section 8 — Property, Plant and Equipment (PP&E)

Lecture 8.15

DOCUMENT REVIEW SIMULATION

Document Review Simulation 1

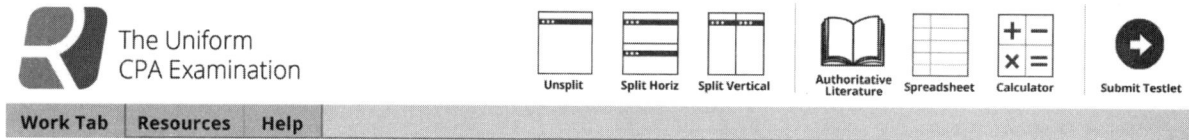

Prepare a roll forward of the property, plant and equipment account balance using various sources of information.

Newberry Enterprises, Inc. is a retailer of fishing rods and reels. During the year, the company had five property, plant, and equipment transactions. In preparation of the year-end closing, James Fitzpatrick, Property, Plant, and Equipment Account Manager, has reviewed documents and the Schedule of Property, Plant, and Equipment and prepared a memo regarding recommendations for adjustments regarding the property, plant, and equipment transactions.

Review the memo from Mr. Fitzpatrick and make any changes necessary to ensure it is accurate and consistent with the information and documents provided.

Note: if required, round your final computations to the nearest dollar.

Newberry Enterprises

To: Sandra Norman, Controller
From: James Fitzpatrick
Date: December 31, 20X6
Re: Recommendations for adjustments regarding Property, Plant, and Equipment Transactions

I have reviewed the records and documents regarding the property, plant and equipment acquisitions and disposals for the current year. Below are my findings and recommendations for adjustments.

On 1/2/20X6, the company sold equipment, with an original cost of $100,000, for $85,000 cash. A $30,000 gain on the sale was reported. **1) In reviewing the transaction, $15,000 of related accumulated depreciation was correctly removed from the books.**

On 2/23/20X6, the company purchased land and building located at 129 East Freemont Ave. from Reynolds Realtors. The building was demolished to ready the land for future use. Later in the year, the land was converted to a parking lot for employees. The total cost allocated to the land is the acquisition costs adjusted for costs to prepare the land for its intended use. **2) Therefore, the total cost allocated to the land is $229,200 and $22,620 to land improvements.**

Newberry Enterprises purchased a new computerized point of sale system from Logan Equipment Company on 6/15/20X6. The equipment was delivered in July. Test runs were completed prior to

Property, Plant and Equipment (PP&E) — Section 8

the equipment being placed into service on August 1, 20X6. In addition, a 2-year extended warranty was purchased. **3) Accordingly, the equipment is recorded at $83,800.**

On 7/1/20X6, the company purchased, at auction, warehouse equipment and an undeveloped parcel of land for $50,000. The fair market value of the equipment is $16,000 and the fair market value of the land is $64,000. **4) Since this is a lump sum purchase, the purchase price is allocated as follows: $16,000 to equipment and $34,000 to land.**

Newberry Enterprises purchased a repossessed office building for $610,000. At closing, the company paid $7,000 in delinquent real estate taxes in addition to $1,200 for its pro rata share of current year real estate taxes. Because it was a repossession, the other closing costs and related fees of $12,800 were paid by the bank. Based on tax records, 10% of the purchase price is allocated to the land. **5) The purchase price is allocated as follows: $61,000 to the land and $549,000 to the office building.**

Newberry uses the following depreciable life for new acquisitions: land improvements- 15 years; buildings- 30 years; equipment -10 years. In addition, the company uses the straight-line depreciation method, no residual value, and takes ½ year deprecation for all assets in year of acquisition. According to my computations, the depreciation expense rerated to the new additions during the year is as follows: **6) Land improvements - $754; Buildings - $9,150; Equipment - $4,815.**

As result of the transactions incurred during the year, the year-end balances for the assets are as follows: **7) Land - $727,900, Land improvements- $42,300, Buildings - $2,345,300, Equipment- $2,443,800.**

Regards,

James Fitzpatrick
Property, Plant, and Equipment Account Manager

Resources

Schedule of Property, Plant, and Equipment

Schedule of Property, Plant, and Equipment
For the Year Ended December 31, 20X6

	1/01/20X6 Balance	Additions	Disposals	12/31/20X6 Balance
Cost				
Land	$400,000			
Land Improvements	24,000			
Buildings	1,790,000			
Equipment	2,450,000			
Total Cost	$4,664,000			
Accumulated Depreciation				
Land	$0			
Land Improvements	(3,600)			
Buildings	(674,250)			
Equipment	(934,700)			
Total Accumulated Depreciation	($1,612,550)			

Adjusting entry for depreciation expense.

The following adjusting entry was made on December 20, 20X6 regarding the depreciation expense for the year. It does **not** reflect any depreciation for the assets acquired during the year.

Account	Debit	Credit
Depreciation Expense	282,650	
Accumulated Depreciation - Land Improvements		1,850
Accumulated Depreciation - Buildings		62,300
Accumulated Depreciation - Equipment		218,500

Property, Plant and Equipment (PP&E) — Section 8

E-mail regarding the operating costs for the parking lot.

The controller received an e-mail from one of the accounting clerks on 12/29/X6:

From: kfitie@newberryenterprises.com
Sent: December 29,20X6
To: snorman@newberryenterprise.com
Subject: Operating costs- new parking lot

Sasha:

In response to your question regarding the amount for operating costs associated with the new employee parking lot, I report a total of $4,320 was incurred during the year. Please let me know if you have any questions.

Katie

Katie Fite, Staff Accountant
Newberry Enterprises, Inc.

Items related to property acquired at 129 East Freemont Ave.

Invoice
Peter Moyer and Associates
Attorneys at Law

Date: March 18, 20X6

To: Newberry Enterprises, Inc.

For legal services rendered in the acquisition of the land and building located at 129 East Freemont Ave.

Total due: $850

Newberry Enterprises, Inc. Cash Receipts	
Date:	April 4, 20X6
Received from:	James Granger
Amount:	$3,000
For:	Salvage material from razed building at 129 East Freemont Ave.

Section 8 Property, Plant and Equipment (PP&E)

Select check register items

Below are excerpts from the check register for other transactions regarding the property, plant, and equipment.

Date	Check number	Payee	Amount	Memo
2/23/20X6	12447	Reynolds Realtors, Inc.	$190,200	Purchased land and building - 129 Freemont Ave.
3/25/20X6	12599	Columbia Demolitions, Inc.	$38,150	Demolition of building - 129 Freemont Ave.
5/31/20X6	13911	Mc Daniel Grading and Paving Co.	$18,300	Paving of parking lot - 129 Freemont Ave.
6/25/20X6	16100	Logan Equipment Company	$650	Test runs on the newly installed digital point of sale computerized equipment systems
8/1/20X6	16543	Logan Equipment Company	$3,200	Prepaid for 2-year extended warranty for the digital point of sale computerized systems

Invoice for equipment purchase

Logan Equipment Company
893 Industrial Drive
Gainesville, Fla.

Sales Invoice # 890
Date: June 14, 20X6
Sold to: Newberry Enterprises, Inc.

20 - Model #2015 Digital point of sale computerized equipment systems

Price per unit $3,800	$76,000
Shipping charges	$550
Installation charges	$2,000
Sales tax	$4,600
Total due	**$83,150**

Property, Plant and Equipment (PP&E)   Section 8

Items for Analysis

In reviewing the transaction, $15,000 of related accumulated depreciation was correctly removed from the books.

1. Choose an option below:

   - [Original text] In reviewing the transaction, $15,000 of related accumulated depreciation was correctly removed from the books.

   - In reviewing the transaction, $45,000 of related accumulated depreciation should have been removed from the books.

   - In reviewing the transaction, a $15,000 loss should have been recorded.

   - In reviewing the transaction, no gain or loss should have been recorded.

Therefore, the total cost allocated to the land is $229,200 and $22,620 to land improvements.

2. Choose an option below:

   - [Original text] Therefore, the total cost allocated to the land is $229,200 and $22,620 to land improvements.

   - Therefore, the total cost allocated to the land is $188,050 and $22,620 to land improvements.

   - Therefore, the total cost allocated to the land is $226,200 and $18,300 to land improvements.

   - Therefore, the total cost allocated to the land is $229,200 and $18,300 to land improvements.

Accordingly, the equipment is recorded at $83,800.

3. Choose an option below:

   - [Original text] Accordingly, the equipment is recorded at $83,800.

   - Accordingly, the equipment is recorded at $86,350.

   - Accordingly, the equipment is recorded at $87,000.

   - Accordingly, the equipment is recorded at $83,150.

Since this is a lump sum purchase, the purchase price is allocated as follows: $16,000 to equipment and $34,000 to land.

4. Choose an option below:

   - [Original text] Since this is a lump sum purchase, the purchase price is allocated as follows: $16,000 to equipment and $34,000 to land.

   - Since this is a lump sum purchase, the purchase price is allocated as follows: $25,000 to equipment and $25,000 to land.

   - Since this is a lump sum purchase, the purchase price is allocated as follows: $12,500 to equipment and $37,500 to land.

   - Since this is a lump sum purchase, the purchase price is allocated as follows: $10,000 to equipment and $40,000 to land.

©Roger CPA Review

Section 8 — Property, Plant and Equipment (PP&E)

The purchase price is allocated as follows: $61,000 to the land and $549,000 to the office building.

5. Choose an option below:
   - [Original text] The purchase price is allocated as follows: $61,000 to the land and $549,000 to the office building.
   - The purchase price is allocated as follows: $61,120 to the land and $550,080 to the office building.
   - The purchase price is allocated as follows: $61,700 to the land and $555,300 to the office building.
   - The purchase price is allocated as follows: $61,820 to the land and $556,380 to the office building.

Land improvements - $754; Buildings - $9,150; Equipment - $4,815.

6. Choose an option below:
   - [Original text] Land improvements - $754; Buildings - $9,150; Equipment - $4,815.
   - Land improvements - $554; Buildings - $9,273; Equipment - $5,600.
   - Land improvements - $466; Buildings - $10,167; Equipment - $4,850.
   - Land improvements - $610; Buildings - $9,255; Equipment - $4,690.
   - Land improvements - $1,210; Buildings - $18,510; Equipment - $8,380.
   - Land improvements - $1,210; Buildings - $9,255; Equipment - $9,380.

Land - $727,900, Land improvements- $42,300, Buildings - $2,345,300, Equipment- $2,443,800.

7. Choose an option below:
   - [Original text] Land - $727,900, Land improvements- $42,300, Buildings - $2,345,300, Equipment- $2,443,800.
   - Land - $700,400, Land improvements- $46,620, Buildings - $2,400,000, Equipment- $2,483,800.
   - Land - $746,200, Land improvements- $28,320, Buildings - $2,338,300, Equipment- $2,443,800.
   - Land - $727,900, Land improvements- $46,620, Buildings - $2,338,300, Equipment- $2,483,800.

DOCUMENT REVIEW SIMULATION SOLUTION

Document Review Simulation Solution 1

1. In reviewing the transaction, $45,000 of related accumulated depreciation should have been removed from the books.

    The amount of accumulated depreciation to be removed from the books is determined by reconstructing the journal entry and solving for the accumulated depreciation.

Cash	85,000	
Accumulated Depreciation	?	
Equipment		100,000
Gain on Sale of Equipment		30,000

    Since equipment sold for $85,000 resulted in a gain of $30,000, the carrying value of the equipment must be $30,000 lower than the proceeds or $55,000. With an original cost of $100,000, the carrying value of the equipment would be $55,000 if accumulated depreciation was $45,000.

2. Therefore, the total cost allocated to the land is $226,200 and $18,300 to land improvements.

    The total cost to be allocated to the land must be determined. It is the acquisition costs, plus legal fees plus costs to prepare the land for its intended use, reduced by any salvage proceeds. The purchase price and demolition costs can be found in the check register. The cash proceeds can be found within the documents.

Purchase price	$190,200
Legal Fees	$850
Demolition costs	$ 38,150
Salvage proceeds	($3,000)
Cost of land	**$226,200**

    The paving cost ($18,300) is assigned to land improvements and is depreciable. The $4,320 in operating costs associated with maintaining the parking lot are treated a period costs.

    Therefore, the total cost allocated to the land is $226,200 and $18,300 to land improvements.

3. Keep original text: Accordingly, the equipment is recorded at $83,800.

    The total cost of the equipment is the invoice amount plus the cost of the test runs. ($83,150 per + $650 from check register = $83,800) The $3,200 paid (per check register) for the extended warranty is not part of the purchase price but is treated a prepaid operating expense.

4. Since this is a lump sum purchase, the purchase price is allocated as follows: $10,000 to equipment and $40,000 to land.

   The purchase is allocated between the equipment and land, based on the fair market values.

   - Fair market value of equipment and land:
     $16,000 + $64,000 = $80,000

   - Purchase price allocated to equipment:
     ($16,000/$80,000) x $50,000 = $10,000

   - Purchase price allocated to land:
     ($64,000/$80,000) x $50,000 = $40,000

5. The purchase price is allocated as follows: $61,700 to the land and $555,300 to the office building.

   The purchase price includes the delinquent real estate taxes, but the current year real estate taxes are a period cost.

   - Total purchase price is $610,000 + $7,000 delinquent taxes, or $617,000.
   - 10% is allocated to land – $61,700 – and the remainder is assigned to the building – $555,300.

6. Land improvements - $610; Buildings - $ 9,255; Equipment - $4,690.

   Use the correct totals for the additions to each category. Use straight-line method and assume there is no residual value for the assets. Apply the given depreciable life and take statutory ½ year depreciation.

   - Land improvements depreciation = $18,300 / 15 years x 1/2 = $610.
   - Building depreciation = $555,300 / 30 years x 1/2 = $9,255
   - Equipment = $93,800* / 10 years x 1/2 = $4,690

   *The $93,800 figure is from the $83,800 for the computerized point of sale equipment and the $10,000 allocated to the warehouse equipment in the lump sum transaction.

Property, Plant and Equipment (PP&E) — Section 8

7. Keep original text: <u>Land - $727,900, Land improvements- $42,300, Buildings - $2,345,300, Equipment- $2,443,800.</u>

   Correct. Roll forward the schedule of property, plant, and equipment by starting with the beginning balances given, increase by the cost of additions and decrease by the cost of disposals

	1/01/20X6 Balance	Additions	Disposals	12/31/20X6 Balance
Cost				
Land	$400,000	$327,900[a]	0	$727,900
Land Improvements	24,000	18,300[b]	0	$42,300
Buildings	1,790,000	555,300[c]	0	$2,345,300
Equipment	2,450,000	93,800[d]	(100,000)[e]	2,443,800
Total Cost	$4,664,000	$995,300	($100,000)	$5,559,300

   (a) $327,900 = $226,200 + $40,000 + $61,700.
   (b) $18,300 = cost of the paving the parking lot.
   (c) $555,300 = the allocate portion to the building
   (d) $93,800 = $83,800 + $10,000
   (e) $100,000 = cost of disposed equipment

Section 9 – Intangibles

Section 9 – Intangibles
Corresponding Lectures

Watch the following course lectures with this section:

Lecture 9.01 – Intangible Assets
Lecture 9.02 – Goodwill
Lecture 9.03 – Computer Software costs and Other Assets
Lecture 9.04 – Intangibles – Class Questions
Lecture 9.05 – Intangibles under IFRS
Lecture 9.06 – Intangibles under IFRS – Class Questions

EXAM NOTE: Please refer to the AICPA FAR Blueprint in the Introduction to find a listing of the representative tasks (and their associated skill levels—i.e., Remembering and Understanding, Application, and Analysis) that the candidate should be able to perform based on the knowledge obtained in this section.

Intangibles

Lecture 9.01

INTANGIBLE ASSETS

Intangible assets refer to assets of a company which lack physical substance and provide economic benefits through the rights and privileges associated with their possession. They may be identifiable or unidentifiable. They may also be externally acquired (purchased at fair value) or internally developed **(ASC 350)**. They come in **3 basic forms**:
- **Knowledge**
- **Legal rights & Identifiable intangibles**
- **Goodwill (unidentifiable intangible)**

Knowledge

Knowledge is developed by a process of **research and development (R&D)**. *Research* is aimed at the discovery of new knowledge that will result in a new product or process or a significant improvement to an existing product or process. *Development* is the conversion of that new knowledge into a plan or design for a new product or process. Market research, R&D performed under contract for others and market testing activities are not considered research and development costs and are accounted for separately. Matching the costs of research and development to benefits is virtually impossible, since much of the work will result in failure, or benefits of indefinite value and duration. As a result of this tremendous uncertainty, research and development costs are **expensed** as incurred, in accordance with the conservatism principle. The only exception is for the acquisition of fixed assets to be used in research. When such assets have possible future benefits, they should be capitalized initially, and the costs amortized into research and development over their useful life. Equipment purchased for current research and development projects only, should be immediately expensed as R&D.

Costs should **not** be treated as **research and development** when they are directly related to current revenue, such as:
- Research performed for others for a fee.
- Periodic design changes to existing products.
- Costs for setting up production of a commercially viable product.

These costs are considered part of cost of sales, and will be capitalized and recognized as appropriate.

Legal Rights and Identifiable Intangibles

These types of intangible assets include patents, copyrights, trademarks, franchises, leasehold improvements and licenses.

The costs incurred to legally protect product and process ideas resulting from research and development are not part of it, but are instead a form of legal right known as a ***patent.***
- Capitalize cost of obtaining legal protection.
- Include cost of successful defense in court.
- Unsuccessful defense – expense the legal costs and possibly the entire patent.
- Do not include research & development of product or process.
- Maximum 20 year life, but use shorter of useful or legal life.

The cost of a patent includes the legal costs of obtaining it and, if necessary, defending it in court against infringement by other companies. If a legal defense of the patent is unsuccessful, all costs should be expensed, since no legal benefit exists in that case. A patent that has been purchased from another party is capitalized at the purchase price

Other legal rights include:
- **Copyright** – protection of artistic works, including books, recordings, and computer software. The copyright period is for the life of the creator plus 70 years (or 95 years total for works made for hire), but the costs should be amortized over it useful life.
- **Trademark** – exclusive use of an identifying name for a product or process. External acquisition costs are amortized over their useful life. Indefinite number of renewals for periods of 10 years each.
- **Franchise** – operation of a business unit under contractual arrangements with another party.

In general, the cost of these other assets is determined similarly to patents: purchase prices to the extent the benefits were obtained from other parties and legal expenditures associated with protecting them.

When a tenant has a long-term lease on real estate, and has incurred costs to improve the property, the resulting **leasehold improvements** should be capitalized and amortized over the benefit period. This will be the shorter of the:
- **Useful life** of the improvements.
- **Legal life** of the lease, including extensions that are reasonably assured of occurring.

After Acquisition

Finite Useful life Intangibles (subject to amortization) – Intangible assets with definite lives (Finite useful life) are amortized over their estimated useful lives in accordance with the matching principle. When a range of lives is possible, the shortest alternative should be used, in accordance with the conservatism principle. The amount to be amortized is its cost minus residual value. Test these assets annually for *impairment* using the undiscounted present value approach, which is similar to the approach used for fixed assets held for use.

Similar to property, plant, and equipment, these assets are evaluated to determine if events or conditions indicate a likelihood of **impairment**. If there is no indication, no further testing is required. If, however, events or conditions indicate it is likely that the asset is impaired, it will be tested using the undiscounted present value approach, which is similar to the approach used for fixed assets held for use.

In determining the useful life, consideration should be given to any legal limits on the existence of the right. *Patents and copyrights* have legal limits on their lives set by law. *Franchises* have legal limits based on the related contracts. To determine the ***useful lives*** must consider:
- The expected use of the asset by the entity,
- Legal, regulatory, or contractual provisions that may limit the useful life,
- The effects of obsolescence, competition, and other economic factors,
- The expected maintenance expenditures required.

Indefinite Useful Life Intangibles (not subject to amortization) - intangible assets and Goodwill with indefinite useful lives are NOT amortized, but rather **tested at least annually for**

impairment. If no legal, regulatory, contractual, competitive, economic, or other factors limit the useful life, it is considered to be indefinite.

Before testing an identifiable intangible with an indefinite useful life for impairment, an entity has the option, but not the requirement, to perform a qualitative analysis. If the qualitative analysis does not indicate impairment, no further testing is generally required until the next assessment anniversary date.

There are several indications of impairment:
- Cost factors – An increase in costs associated with the use of the intangible, such as raw materials or labor, could adversely affect the fair value of the asset.
- Financial performance – A decrease in cash flows, revenues, or earnings associated with the use of the intangible could adversely affect the fair value of the asset.
- Environment – A change in the legal, regulatory, contractual, political, or business environment may adversely affect the fair value of an intangible asset.
- Entity-specific events – Changes in management or key personnel, strategy, or customers, and events like potential litigation or bankruptcy may adversely affect the fair value of an intangible asset.
- Industry and market considerations – An increase in competition, the effects of obsolescence, a change in demand, or a change in other economic factors may adversely affect the fair value of an intangible asset.
- Macroeconomic conditions – Changes in general economic conditions, limitations on the access to capital, fluctuations in foreign currency exchange rates, and other changes to the equity and credit markets may adversely affect the value of an intangible.

If the entity believes that one or more of these factors indicates that it is *more likely than not* that the intangible has been impaired, the intangible will be tested for impairment. Intangibles with an indefinite useful life, other than goodwill, are tested for impairment by comparing the carrying value of the asset to its fair value.

The **fair value** will be determined on the basis of one of the following approaches:
- The **market approach** uses prices and other relevant information generated by market transactions involving identical or comparable assets, liabilities, or groups of assets and liabilities.
- The **income approach** converts expected future amounts, such as revenues or cash flows, to a single current amount applying present value concepts.
- The **cost approach** measures the amount that would be currently required to replace the service capacity of an asset.

If *impaired*, a loss is recognized in an amount equal to the excess of **the asset's *carrying value* over its *fair value*. Subsequent reversal** of a previously recognized impairment loss **is *prohibited*.**

Intangibles with indefinite lives (such as trademarks) are not amortized but are tested for impairment on an annual basis. Intangible assets with definite useful lives, including those with lives in excess of 40 years (such as a long-term franchise agreement), are amortized over such useful lives.

There are three different **methods of amortization** that can be used:
- **Straight-line** – Costs are recognized equally over the useful life.
- **Units of sales** – Costs are allocated based on the sales to date as a percentage of estimated total sales.
- **Net realizable value** – Sufficient amortization is recorded to reduce the carrying value of the intangible to the estimated remaining future benefits.

The method of amortization chosen should be the most conservative, meaning the one that reduces the carrying value of the intangible to the lowest amount.

Lecture 9.02

Goodwill

Goodwill is known as the unidentifiable intangible since its value cannot be directly determined. It is instead represented by the excess of what a buyer is willing to pay for a business over the value of the net identifiable assets, including other intangible assets, but not goodwill on the books of the acquired company.

In a business combination, goodwill is assigned to one or more reporting units. A reporting unit can be an operating segment or one level below. The amount assigned to an individual reporting unit is the excess of the fair value of that reporting unit over the fair value of the net underlying assets in the reporting unit.

If one entity acquires 100% of another entity, it is assumed that the fair value of the consideration given is the fair value of the entity reported. That amount will be compared to the net of:

+ The fair value of all identifiable tangible and intangible assets acquired, which may include assets that are not on the financial statements of the acquired entity, minus

− The fair value of all liabilities assumed

In most cases, the fair value of the consideration given will exceed the fair value of the underlying net assets, in which case the difference would be goodwill. In rare circumstances the fair value of the underlying net assets exceeds the fair value of consideration given, in which case the difference is recognized as a gain on bargain purchase by the acquiring entity.

For example, assume one entity acquires all of the stock of another entity for $1,000,000. The acquired entity has the following assets and liabilities:

	Book value	Fair value
Current assets	$ 350,000	$ 350,000
Plant and equipment, net	600,000	850,000
Intangibles, excluding goodwill	0	100,000
Total identifiable assets	$ 950,000	$ 1,300,000
Liabilities assumed	500,000	500,000
Value of underlying net assets	$ 450,000	$ 800,000
Total consideration		1,000,000
Implied goodwill		$ 200,000

The total amount of goodwill will then be assigned to one or more reporting units.
- The acquired entity may be *integrated into the acquiring entity* without maintaining separate books and records for the acquired entity.

- - The assets and liabilities of the acquired entity, including goodwill, are recorded on the books and records of the acquiring entity.
  - The entity, as a whole, is considered the reporting unit with the goodwill.
- The acquiring entity may *maintain separate books and records* for the acquired entity.
  - The acquiring entity will recognize an investment in subsidiary on its books.
  - Consolidated financial statements will be prepared each period.
  - The acquired entity will be considered the reporting unit with the goodwill.
- The acquiring entity may not only maintain separate books and records for the acquired entity but may actually maintain more than one set of books and records if the acquired entity consists of more than one department, operation, or other natural business unit.
  - The acquiring entity, for example, may maintain separate units for a research division, a manufacturing division, and a sales and distribution division.
  - Each division would be considered a separate reporting unit.
  - Goodwill would be allocated among the reporting units based on the differences between the value of each reporting unit and the fair value of its underlying net assets.

Since it is impossible to verify the value of goodwill in the absence of an actual transaction, it may only be recorded on the balance sheet when it results from the purchase of another business. A company may not record as goodwill the internal costs of developing it or restoring it.

Goodwill has an indefinite useful life and, similar to other intangibles with indefinite useful lives it is tested for impairment **at least annually**. Goodwill is considered impaired when the carrying value of the reporting unit with which it is associated exceeds that reporting unit's fair value.

The goodwill associated with each reporting unit is required to be evaluated separately. In addition to the annual impairment tests, the entity may have reason to believe that goodwill has been impaired between impairment dates. If the entity does determine that it is more likely than not that goodwill has been impaired between the most recent evaluation date and the date of the financial statements, an additional impairment test will be performed for financial statement purposes.

Various factors will be qualitatively evaluated in determining if it is more likely than not that the carrying value of the reporting unit exceeds its fair value. These include:
- Macroeconomic conditions, such as general limitations on the availability of capital
- Industry and market considerations, such as an increase in the competitive environment
- Cost factors, such as increases in the costs of raw material or labor
- Overall financial performance, such as declining profits or cash flows
- Events specific to the entity, such as changes in management
- Events affecting the reporting unit, such as a change in the composition of its assets
- In some cases, a sustained decrease in the price of shares of stock

If any of these, or other factors, indicate reasonable likelihood that the carrying value of the reporting unit exceeds its fair value, the entity will evaluate goodwill for impairment using a 2 step approach, which is the method used for testing goodwill for impairment when performing the annual evaluation.
- The 2-step approach for evaluating goodwill for impairment can be cumbersome and expensive.
- Entities have the option, although it is not a requirement, to evaluate the above factors, along with other relevant information, to determine if it is more likely than not that goodwill has been impaired.

- o If there is no reason for the entity to believe that it is more likely than not that goodwill has been impaired based on such an evaluation, the 2 step approach is not required.
- o The entity may decide to proceed directly to the 2 step approach without performing the qualitative analysis.

The 2-Step Approach for Goodwill Impairment Testing

Step 1 in the 2 step process involves comparing the carrying value of the reporting unit to its fair value. The carrying value of the reporting unit will be known to the entity since it is the amount reflected in the books and records being maintained for the reporting unit. The fair value will represent the amount that the entity would be able to sell the reporting unit for in an orderly transaction between market participants.
- If the fair value of the reporting unit is equal to, or greater than, it's carrying value, it is generally assumed that goodwill is not impaired and no further testing is required.
- If the fair value of the reporting unit is lower than its carrying value, it is assumed that goodwill has been impaired and the amount of the impairment loss is measured in step 2.

In rare circumstances, the entity may have to perform step 2 of the goodwill impairment test even though the carrying value of the reporting unit is below its market value.
- When the carrying value of the reporting unit is equal to zero or a negative amount, it is presumed that the fair value is at least equal since it is not likely that it will have a fair value below zero.
- In such cases, the entity will qualitatively evaluate various factors, including those indicated above, to determine if it is more likely than not that goodwill has been impaired.
- If so, the entity will be required to perform step 2.

Step 2 in the 2 step process involves determining the fair value of goodwill. Since goodwill is valued on the basis of the reporting entity it is associated with, the process involves the following:
- The fair value of all of the reporting unit's identifiable assets and liabilities will be measured.
- Some items will be measured according to existing authoritative literature. For example,
  - o Cash and cash equivalents is valued at face value.
  - o Short-term receivables are valued at net realizable value.
  - o Inventories are valued at replacement cost subject to floor and ceiling limitations.
- Remaining items will be measured applying the generic definition of fair value.
  - o It is the price that would be received to sell an asset or paid to transfer a liability in an orderly transaction between market participants at the measurement date.
  - o For financial assets and for liabilities, fair value is generally the present value of expected cash flows.
  - o For nonfinancial assets, the entity considers the asset's highest and best use, which might be in use, such as in the case of a productive asset, or might be in exchange, such as in the case of an asset held for investment purposes.
- The fair value of the underlying net assets will be compared to the fair value of the reporting unit, as measured in step 1.
  - o The difference represents the fair value of goodwill
  - o Goodwill will be written down to that amount and an impairment loss will be recognized for the difference.

Once goodwill has been written down due to impairment, the impaired amount becomes the goodwill's new carrying value. This amount is used for comparison in future assessments. If it is determined that goodwill increases in value, **recoveries are not recognized**.

Impairment loss	X (I/S – income from continuing operations)
Goodwill	X

For example: In a business combination, Push Corporation acquired all of the outstanding stock of Shove, Inc. for $7,500,000 at a time when Shove's underlying net assets had a fair value of $6,900,000 in the transaction. As a result, **goodwill of $600,000** was recognized. Push maintains separate accounting records for Shove, which is considered a separate reporting unit.

During the current period, due to some very aggressive marketing tactics, Shove's reputation was damaged and Push has determined that it is more likely than not that the goodwill has been impaired. As a result, Push will perform an impairment test in relation to Shove's goodwill.

In the first step, Push will compare Shove's carrying value to its market value. The carrying value on the date of the test is $8,325,000, which is readily determinable from the separate accounting records being maintained. The fair value, determined using an appropriate valuation technique, most likely employing the same approach or approaches used to determine how much Push would originally purchase Shove for, turned out to be $7,900,000.

Push next determines the fair value of Shove's underlying net assets as follows:

Cash	$ 350,000
Accounts receivable	1,250,000
Inventories	3,000,000
Other current assets	200,000
Plant and equipment	5,750,000
Intangibles	2,000,000
Total	$12,550,000
Current liabilities	(950,000)
Long-term debt	(4,100,000)
Underlying net assets	$ 7,500,000
Fair value of reporting unit	7,900,000
Remaining goodwill	**$ 400,000**

Goodwill would be written down from $600,000 to $400,000 and an impairment loss of $200,000 would be recognized in income.

Alternative Accounting Approach for Nonpublic Entities (Goodwill)

The Private Company Council (PCC) of the FASB established an alternative accounting approach that is available to nonpublic entities when accounting for goodwill to reduce the burden associated with testing goodwill for impairment. This came about because of the nonpublic companies concerns about the cost and complexity of testing goodwill for impairment. Therefore the PCC decided to simplify the process.

When the alternative accounting approach is elected, the entity will begin amortizing its goodwill. It will be *amortized* on a **straight-line basis** over its *useful life* not to exceed **10 years**. Goodwill

will also be **tested for impairment** at the company-wide level, only when a **triggering event** occurs that would more likely than not, reduce the fair value below its carrying amount.

Since goodwill will be amortized, the carrying value decreases each period, making it less likely that its carrying amount will exceed its fair value and that goodwill will be impaired. As a result, impairment testing is only required in those periods in which the entity believes that it is more likely than not that goodwill has been impaired.

If the entity determines that it is NOT more likely than not, no further testing is required. If, however, it appears that it is more likely than not that goodwill has been impaired, referred to as a *triggering event*, the entity will test goodwill for impairment.

Like a publicly held entity, the nonpublic entity will consider such factors (triggering events) as economic conditions, competition, changes in costs, and changes to the regulatory environment to determine if there is reason to believe that it is more likely than not, or, in other words, that there is a greater than 50% probability that goodwill has been impaired.

A nonpublic entity performing an impairment assessment has the option of performing it on the entity level or the reporting unit level. If the entity level is elected, which would also be disclosed in the Summary of Significant Accounting Policies along with the election to apply the alternative accounting approach, the entity will combine all components of goodwill and perform a single **one-step impairment test** (no 2 step test) for the entity as a whole.
- The fair value of the entity is compared to its carrying value.
- If the fair value is lower than the carrying value, the entire difference is attributed to goodwill and recognized as an impairment loss.

Since goodwill cannot be reduced below zero, if the amount of the impairment loss exceeds the carrying value of goodwill, the entity will have to evaluate its other assets to determine what impairment additional losses should be recognized.

Lecture 9.03

Computer Software

In the case of **computer software** developed to **sell, lease or market as a product**, these costs associated with converting a technologically feasible program into final commercial form are capitalized. Costs prior to technological feasibility are expensed as research and development, and costs incurred after software sales begin are inventoried and included in cost of sales.

Amortization of capitalized software costs is calculated using a two-step process:

First, amortization is calculated using the more conservative of straight-line and the relative sales value approach:
- The straight-line amount is calculated by dividing the remaining carrying value as of the beginning of the period by the remaining useful life, also as of the beginning of the period.
- The amount under the relative sales value approach is calculated by establishing a ratio with the current period's sales in the numerator and the total estimated sales for the remaining life of the software, including the current period's sales, in the denominator.

$$\frac{\text{Current Period's Sales}}{\text{Current Period's Sales + Estimated Future Sales}}$$

Amortization is equal to the ratio multiplied by the carrying value of the software as of the beginning of the period.

The larger of these two amounts will be recognized as amortization expense.

In the second step, the new carrying value of the software, after the amortization from the first step, is compared to the net realizable value of the software. If the carrying value is greater, the excess is also written off as amortization expense. For purposes of this calculation, the net realizable value of the software is the amount expected to be generated from future sales less the costs associated with completion, disposal, maintenance, and customer support.

Example:

- 5 years
- S/L = 1/5 = 20%
- Ratio = 100 revenue / 400 expected total revenue = 25%
- **Amortization will be 25% of carrying value.**
- New carrying value is 285, NRV is 240 → additional 45 amortization expense.

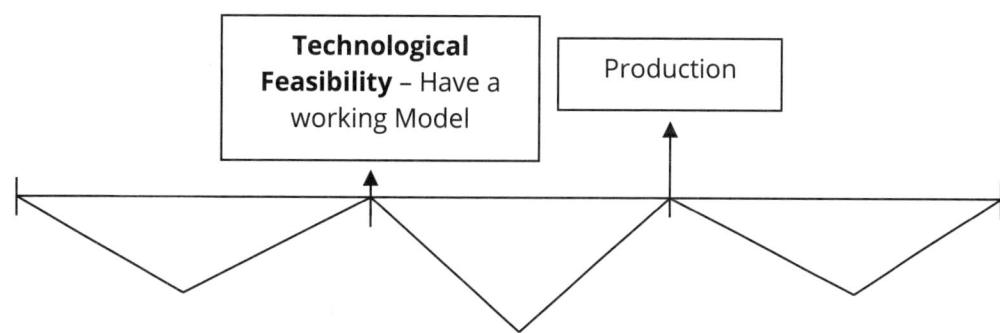

Technological Feasibility – Have a working Model		**Production**
Costs incurred during this phase = 1) Program 2) Design 3) Coding & Testing **R&D Expense**	**Costs incurred during this phase =** 1) Coding & Testing after Tech Feas. 2) Product Masters **SOFTWARE costs**	**Costs incurred during this phase =** 1) Duplication 2) Training Materials 3) Packaging **These are PRODUCTION COSTS** → **A part of Inventory**

If the **computer software** was developed for ***internal use only***, costs incurred in the preliminary project stage and costs incurred in training, data conversion and maintenance should be expensed as R&D. Costs incurred after the preliminary project stage and for upgrades and enhancements should be capitalized and amortized on a straight-line basis. Capitalization of the costs should cease when the software project is substantially complete and ready for its intended use.
- If the entity later decides to market the software to outsiders, net proceeds received should be applied first to the carrying amount of the software until the CV has reached zero, then recognized as revenue.

When an entity enters into a ***cloud computing arrangement***, an analysis is performed to determine whether some or all of the arrangement represents a software license:
- If the entire arrangement is considered a software license, the entire cost, including the present value of future payments, is treated as an intangible and accounted for similar to other licenses. It will be *capitalized* and a determination will be made as to whether or not it has a finite useful life.
- If the arrangement does not include a software license, the entire amount is treated as a service contract with the *expense recognized* in the period in which the benefit is derived.
- If the arrangement represents a combination, the total cost will be allocated between the software license and the service contract.

Other Assets

In order to account for differences between the time of payment and the time of recognition for revenues and expenses, it is often necessary to accrue or defer items.
- **Accrued revenue** – An amount that is being recognized on the income statement prior to collection. An accrued revenue is a receivable, reported as an asset.
- **Deferred expense** – An amount that is being paid prior to recognition on the income statement. A deferred expense is generally referred to as a prepaid expense, reported as a current asset.

Similarly, an entity may have an **accrued expense**, an expense that has been incurred but not paid, which is reported as a current liability. It may also have **deferred revenue,** also referred to as unearned revenue, which is revenue received prior to being earned and is reported as a liability.

Prepaid Insurance

One common example of a deferred expense is insurance. Premiums are paid in advance to cover a period of one or more years, but costs must be allocated over the period covered by the policy.

For example, assume a client paid an annual insurance premium of $240 on 4/1/X1 to cover the period ended 3/31/X2, then renewed the policy for another year at $360 on 4/1/X2. At the end of each year, the policy in place has 3 months of coverage left out of the original 12, so that prepaid insurance must be reported on the balance sheet. The appropriate amounts are:

12/31/X1 - $240 x 3 / 12 = $60

12/31/X2 - $360 x 3 / 12 = $90

There are two ways to determine insurance expense in 20X2. One is to account for the cash payment in 20X2 and adjust for the change in prepaid insurance:

| Intangibles | Section 9 |

Insurance expense (balance)	330	
Prepaid insurance	30	
Cash		360

The other is to determine the monthly allocation of insurance expense for both policies:

4/1/X1 to 3/31/X2 - $240 / 12 = $20 per month

4/1/X2 to 3/31/X3 - $360 / 12 = $30 per month

In calendar 20X2, the expenses are:

Old policy – 1/1/X2 to 3/31/X2 - $20 x 3 = $60

New policy – 4/1/X2 to 12/31/X2 - $30 x 9 = $270

Total insurance expense in 20X2 is $60 + $270 = $330.

Royalties

Royalties often include both accrued and deferred amounts. A publishing company may pay some royalties to authors based on book sales that have occurred (accrued expenses), and pay other authors advances on expected future book sales (deferred expenses).

For example, assume the following information applies to a client who is obligated to pay royalties to authors of various books published by the client:

Accrued royalties, 1/1/X1	100
Prepaid royalties, 1/1/X1	80
Accrued royalties, 12/31/X1	115
Prepaid royalties, 12/31/X1	85
20X1 royalty payments	500

The easiest way to determine the royalty expense for the year is with a journal entry that explains the changes in all of the above accounts:

Royalty expense (balance)	510	
Prepaid royalties	5	
Accrued royalties		15
Cash		500

Alternatively, we may be asked to calculate royalties owed from sales information. For example, let's say the client receives royalty payments of 10% on sales by another company of a product developed by the client, with payments for the sales period 1/1 to 6/30 received on 7/15, and payments for the sales period 7/1 to 12/31 received on 1/15. Sales information from the other company indicated:

7/1/X1 to 12/31/X1	600
1/1/X2 to 6/30/X2	540
7/1/X2 to 12/31/X2	670

Royalties receivable at the balance sheet dates are $60 at 12/31/X1 and $67 at 12/31/X2. Royalty revenue in 20X2 is $121, representing 10% of the total sales of $1,210 for the year.

Life Insurance

When a corporation takes out insurance on the life of an officer, it will sometimes select a policy that builds a cash value over time (**cash surrender value**). Since this value doesn't require the death of the officer, it is considered an asset. The company may borrow against this cash value, but since it doesn't actually have to repay the loan (this will simply reduce the proceeds in the event of the officer's death), outstanding loans against life insurance are simply subtracted from the asset. When life insurance premiums are paid, any increase in the cash value is capitalized, and the remainder expensed.

For example, assume a policy has a *cash surrender value* of $10,000 at the beginning of the year. During the year, a premium of $50,000 is paid, and the cash surrender value at the end of the year is $16,000. The entry for the premium payment is:

Cash surrender value	6,000	
Life insurance expense	44,000	
Cash		50,000

Franchise Agreements

Revenue on a franchise agreement should be recognized when the franchisor has substantially performed all material services and conditions, and collectability is reasonably assured. Direct franchise costs are deferred until the related revenue is recognized.

Sinking Fund

A company will sometimes be required to set aside amounts for the future repayment of bonds. The cash and earnings will be accumulated in a sinking fund account, and classified as a long-term asset (as long as the bonds repayment is related to bonds that are long-term liabilities). The earnings will be recognized as ordinary income.

Organization Costs

The expenses associated with forming an organization, including the legal costs of incorporation, should all be **expensed immediately** for financial accounting purposes.

Lecture 9.04

CLASS QUESTIONS

Please see the Class Questions and Class Solutions for this Lecture at the end of this Section.

Lecture 9.05

INTANGIBLE ASSETS UNDER IFRS

IFRS prescribes accounting for intangible assets that in many respects is significantly different from US GAAP. IFRS requires an entity to recognize intangible assets, whether acquired from others or internally generated, if certain conditions are met:
- The entity is able to reliably measure the cost of the asset.
- The asset's expected future economic benefits are likely to flow to the entity

Only **identifiable intangibles that lack physical substance** are recognized. An identifiable intangible is either:
- It is separable, which means it can be sold, transferred, licensed, exchanged, or otherwise disposed of
- It arises from contractual or legal rights

Acquired intangibles are recognized at cost, including direct costs of preparing the asset for its intended use.

Neither internally generated goodwill nor assets resulting from **research** may be capitalized. In addition, internally generated brands, mastheads, publishing titles, customer lists, and similar items cannot be capitalized. Other internally generated identifiable intangibles that result from **development are capitalized if** the entity can demonstrate that certain conditions are all met:
- It is technically feasible to complete the asset for use or sale.
- The entity has the intent to complete the asset and the availability of resources to do so.
- The ability to use or sell the asset.
- The asset will generate probable future economic benefits.
- Resources are available to complete the development.
- Costs incurred during the development of the intangible can be reliably measured.

An intangible asset may be accounted for under either the **cost model (CM)** or the **revaluation model (RM)**, applying the same methodology as is used for property, plant, and equipment.

The revaluation model may only be used, however, when there is an active market for the asset such that a fair value can be reliably determined. In addition, when an intangible asset is accounted for under the revaluation model, all assets in its class are also required to be valued using the revaluation model unless there is no active market for them.
- Under the **Cost Model (CM),** the asset is depreciated to its *residual value*
  - Each significant part of the asset is amortized separately
  - The method should reflect the pattern based on the economic benefits the entity obtains from the use of the asset
  - Amortization is recognized in income unless it is included in the cost of another asset such as manufactured inventory

- Under the **Revaluation Model (RM),** the asset is periodically adjusted to its estimated fair value
  - Revaluations to fair value must be made regularly to assure that the carrying amount is not significantly different from fair value
  - The asset is reported at its revalued amount less amortization and any impairments from the date of revaluation to the balance sheet date
  - Changes in value are generally recognized in income

- Increases in value prior to any decreases are recognized in other comprehensive income.
- Decreases in value first offset cumulative amounts of increases in other comprehensive income with the excess reported in income
- Increases in value occurring subsequent to decreases are first recognized in income to the extent they offset decreases previously recognized in income with the excess reported in other comprehensive income

The residual value of an asset is the estimated amount that would be received upon disposal on the financial statement date:
- The amount is net of costs of disposal.
- The asset is assumed to be of the age and in the condition that is expected when the asset is ready for disposal.

Under IFRS, an asset may not be reported at an amount that exceeds its recoverable amount, which is the greater of the amount it will generate through use or the amount that will be generated through disposal, net of costs of disposal. When an asset's carrying value exceeds its recoverable amount, an **impairment** loss is recognized.
- If either an asset's disposal value or its value in use exceeds its carrying value, the asset is not impaired.
- The value in use takes into account the time value of money and the effects of uncertainty.
- If impaired, the loss will be the difference between the carrying amount and the greater amount.

An impairment loss is recognized in the period incurred:
- If the asset is accounted for under the CM, the impairment loss is recognized immediately in **profit or loss**.
- If the asset is accounted for under the RM, the impairment loss is a **revaluation decrease**

An impairment test in which the entity estimates the recoverable amount of an asset is only required for most assets when there is an indication that the asset has been impaired. Certain intangibles are required to be tested for impairment regardless of whether or not there is an indication of impairment:
- Intangibles with indefinite useful lives
- Intangibles not yet ready for use by the entity

On each financial statement date, the entity determines if there is an indication that assets have been impaired. In addition, it also assesses whether a previously recognized impairment no longer exists, in which case it is **reversed.** How the reversal is accounted for will depend on how the asset is being accounted for.
- Under the CM, impairment reversals are recognized up to the amount of previously recognized impairment losses.
- Under the RM, impairment reversals are treated as revaluation adjustments.
    - Increases in the value of an impaired asset are recognized in income to the extent that they offset previously recognized losses.
    - Any remainder is recognized in other comprehensive income (OCI).

Intangibles   Section 9

Intangible Assets: Cost Model (CM) or Revaluation Model (RM)
(like PP&E to OCI)

(RM requires that FV be determined in an active market)

Intangible Asset	30,000	
Cash		30,000

Choose one of the following measurement models
- Cost model (CM)
- Revaluation model (RM)

Cost Model (CM) (record Amortization and Impairment loss, like normal)

Amortization Expense	5,000	
Accumulated Amortization		5,000

Impairment loss CM [CV – recoverable amt (≥ net selling price or value in use)]

Impairment Loss (**I/S**) or Amort exp	2,000	
Accumulated Amortization of		
Intangible Asset (Impairment)		2,000

Reversal of Impairment loss CM (NEW) (up to previously recognized Imp loss)

Accumulated Amortization/Intang asset	2,000	
Impairment recovery (**I/S**)		2,000

Revaluation Model (RM) (CV = revalued amount = Fair Value at Revaluation date)

Intangible Asset	30,000	
Revaluation Surplus (**OCI**)		30,000

Now Amortize and test for Impairment as normal at new value

If carrying amount is *decreased* due to revaluation

Revaluation Surplus (to 0)	30,000	
Revaluation Loss (I/S)	10,000	
Intangible Asset (or Accum Amort)		40,000

Reversal of Impairment loss RM (up to previously recognized Imp loss)

Intangible Asset (or Accum Amort)	12,000	
Revaluation gain (I/S)		10,000
Revaluation Surplus (**OCI**)		2,000

Intangible Assets	
GAAP	**IFRS**
- Internally generated intangible assets may NOT be capitalized. - All research and development costs are recognized as *expense* as incurred. - Intangible assets are recognized at Cost model (CM) and all except goodwill and those with indefinite useful lives are amortized over their useful lives - Qualitative analysis allowed prior to annual 2 step impairment test for goodwill and 1 step test for intangibles other than goodwill with indefinite useful lives. - Recoveries of value of impaired assets are NOT recognized.	- Internally generated identifiable intangible assets may be capitalized. - All research costs are expensed as incurred, but *development costs* may be *capitalized* if certain conditions apply. - Revaluation model (RM) allowed if fair value reasonably estimable - Most intangible assets are recognized using the cost model and all except goodwill and those with indefinite useful lives are amortized over their useful lives, but those with a readily determinable fair value based on an active market may use the revaluation model (RM), similar to fixed assets. - Goodwill and intangibles with indefinite useful lives tested for impairment at least annually. - Recoveries of value of impaired assets are recognized in income to the extent of losses previously recognized.

Lecture 9.06

CLASS QUESTIONS

Please see the Class Questions and Class Solutions for this Lecture at the end of this Section.

Intangibles   Section 9

CLASS QUESTIONS

Work through the below Class Questions while following along with the respective lectures. Once this is complete, you can begin independently practicing what you've learned by quizzing yourself on this course section in your Interactive Practice Questions (IPQ), which can be found in your online Student Dashboard. Your IPQ simulates the computer-based testing experience, and will also help you understand how concepts are applied to the exam. Each question includes answer explanations from expert CPAs that will help you determine why you answered a question correctly or incorrectly. This is key to your success on the CPA Exam.

Lecture 9.04

1. Cody Corp. incurred the following costs during 20X3:

Design of tools, jigs, molds, and dies involving new Technology	$125,000
Modification of the formulation of a process	160,000
Troubleshooting in connection with breakdowns during commercial production	100,000
Adaptation of an existing capability to a particular customer's need as part of a continuing commercial activity	110,000

   In its 20X3 income statement, Cody should report research and development expense of

   a. $125,000
   b. $160,000
   c. $235,000
   d. $285,000

2. On January 2, 20X5, Judd Co. bought a trademark from Krug Co. for $500,000. Judd retained an independent consultant, who estimated the trademark's remaining life to be fifty years. Its unamortized cost on Krug's accounting records was $380,000. In Judd's December 31, 20X5 balance sheet, what amount should be reported as accumulated amortization?

   a. $ 7,600
   b. $ 9,500
   c. $10,000
   d. $12,500

3. After an impairment loss is recognized, the adjusted carrying amount of the intangible asset shall be its new accounting basis. Which of the following statements about subsequent reversal of a previously recognized impairment loss is correct?

   a. It is prohibited
   b. it is required when the reversal is considered permanent
   c. it must be disclosed in the notes to the financial statements
   d. it is encouraged, but not required

4. On January 2, 20X3, Paye Co. purchased Shef Co. at a cost that resulted in recognition of goodwill of $200,000. During the first quarter of 20X3, Paye spent an additional $80,000 on expenditures designed to maintain goodwill. In its December 31, 20X3 balance sheet, what amount should Paye report as goodwill?

    a. $180,000
    b. $200,000
    c. $252,000
    d. $280,000

5. Under ASC 350, goodwill should be tested periodically for impairment

    a. For the entity as a whole.
    b. At the subsidiary level.
    c. At the industry segment level.
    d. At the operating segment level or one level below.

6. Mark incurred the following computer software costs for the development and sale of software programs during the current year:

Planning costs	$ 50,000
Design of the software	150,000
Substantial testing of the project's initial stages	75,000
Production and packaging costs for the first month's sales	500,000
Costs of producing product masters after technological feasibility was established	200,000

    The project was not under any contractual arrangement when these expenditures were incurred. What amount should Mark report as research and development expense for the current year?

    a. $200,000
    b. $275,000
    c. $500,000
    d. $975,000

Lecture 9.06

7. Under IFRS, what valuation methods are used for intangible assets?

    a. The cost model or the fair value model.
    b. The cost model or the revaluation model.
    c. The cost model or the fair value through profit or loss model.
    d. The revaluation model or the fair value model.

8. Under IFRS, an entity that acquires an intangible asset may use the revaluation model for subsequent measurement only if

    a. The useful life of the intangible asset can be reliably determined.
    b. An active market exists for the intangible asset.
    c. The cost of the intangible asset can be measured reliably.
    d. The intangible asset is a monetary asset.

9. Under IFRS, which of the following is a criterion that must be met in order for an item to be recognized as an intangible asset other than goodwill?
    a. The item's fair value can be measured reliably.
    b. The item is part of the entity's activities aimed at gaining new scientific or technical knowledge.
    c. The item is expected to be used in the production or supply of goods or services.
    d. The item is identifiable and lacks physical substance.

CLASS SOLUTIONS

1. (d) FASB ASC Topic 730 (Research and Development) defines research as planned search or critical investigation aimed at discovery of new knowledge with the hope that such knowledge will be useful in developing a new product or service or a new process or technique or in bringing about a significant improvement to an existing product or process. This would include the design of tools, jigs, molds, and dies involving new technology of $125,000 and the modification of the formulation of a process of $160,000 for a total of $285,000. Troubleshooting breakdowns during commercial production would be an operating expense. The cost of adapting existing capability to a particular customer's needs as part of a continuing commercial activity would be considered a product cost, ultimately charged to cost of sales. Neither would be considered research or development.

2. (c) When an intangible has a useful life that can be determined, the intangible is amortized over that period. As a result, the $500,000 cost will be amortized over 50 years at the rate of $10,000 per year. December 31, 20X5 is the end of the first year during which Judd owned the patent indicating that accumulated amortization would include only one year's amount, or $10,000. The carrying value on Krug's books is not relevant.

3. (a) Once an impairment loss is recognized, the reduced carrying value is considered the new cost basis and is used for all future impairment tests. Further reductions are recognized as additional impairments but recoveries are not recognized.

4. (b) Goodwill is initially recorded at the amount by which consideration given in a business combination exceeds the fair value of the underlying net assets acquired. Once recognized, goodwill remains at its original amount until such time as it may be impaired, at which time it is either reduced or eliminated with the recognition of an impairment loss. Costs incurred to maintain goodwill are recognized as expense as incurred.

5. (d) When goodwill is recognized in a business combination, it is allocated among all of the reporting units included in the acquisition. A reporting unit may be an operating segment or may be at a lower level if an operating segment consists of more than one reporting unit. Answer (a) is incorrect because goodwill is only tested for the entity as a whole when an acquired entity is not treated as a separate reporting unit and the assets acquired and the liabilities assumed, including goodwill, are treated as assets and liabilities of the reporting entity as a whole. Answer (b) is incorrect because goodwill is only tested at the subsidiary level when an acquired subsidiary consists of only one reporting unit. Answer (c) is incorrect because goodwill is only tested at the industry segment level when all of an entity's operations in that industry segment are conducted by a single acquired entity that consists of a single reporting unit.

6. (b) When developing computer software, costs incurred up to the point at which technological feasibility is achieved are recognized as research and development costs and reported as expenses in the period incurred. Once technological feasibility is achieved, costs incurred up until production begins are capitalized to the software. Costs incurred when the software is in production are included in inventory and cost of sales. In this case, the costs incurred before reaching technological feasibility include the planning costs of $50,000, the design costs of $150,000, and the testing during the initial stages of $75,000 for a total of $275,000. The $200,000 cost of producing masters would be capitalized to the software and the $500,000 in production and packaging costs would be recognized in inventory.

Intangibles   Section 9

7. (b) IFRS provides for two methods of accounting for intangibles, the cost method or the revaluation method. Answer (a) is incorrect because IFRS allows the use of the cost model for accounting for intangibles but does not allow the use of the fair value method. Its use is limited to certain investments, derivatives, and, under certain circumstances, property and equipment. Answer (c) is incorrect because IFRS allows the use of the cost model for accounting for intangibles but does not allow the use of the fair value through profit or loss model. It is used to account for certain investments. Answer (d) is incorrect because IFRS allows the use of the revaluation model for accounting for intangibles but does not allow the use of the fair value method. Its use is limited to certain investments, derivatives, and, under certain circumstances, property and equipment.

8. (b) The revaluation model may be applied to an intangible asset provided there is an active market for the asset allowing for a reliable measure of fair value at a given balance sheet date. Answer (a) is incorrect because being able to determine the useful life of an intangible is not a requirement for use of the revaluation model. Answer (c) is incorrect because an entity must be able to reliably measure the cost of an intangible asset in order to record it initially. This does not, however, affect the model used for subsequent valuation of the intangible, which could be either the cost model or the revaluation model. Answer (d) is incorrect because intangible assets are not monetary assets.

9. (d) Under IFRS, an intangible is defined as an identifiable nonmonetary asset without physical substance. Answer (a) is incorrect because it is necessary to be able to reliably measure the fair value of an intangible in order to apply the revaluation method after initial recognition. It is not required, however, to initially recognize the intangible. Answer (b) is incorrect because the cost of an entity's activities aimed at gaining new scientific or technical knowledge is considered research and is required to be recognized as an expense in the period incurred. Answer (c) is incorrect because the expected use of an intangible may determine the method and term over which it will be amortized and may determine whether amortization expense will be treated as part of cost of sales or an operating expense. It will not, however, affect whether or not it is recognized as an intangible.

TASK-BASED SIMULATIONS

Task-Based Simulation 1

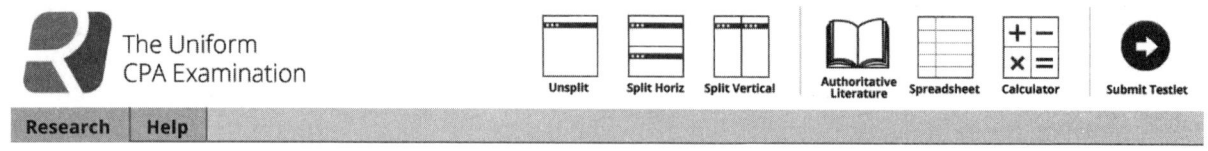

A client has recently spent a large amount of money increasing benefits to employees and establishing programs to boost morale in the belief that it will increase the loyalty of the workers and add value to the company. The client wishes to capitalize the costs. Identify the location in professional standards that indicates how to account for costs of internally developing, maintaining, or restoring intangible assets that are not specifically identifiable.

Task-Based Simulation 2

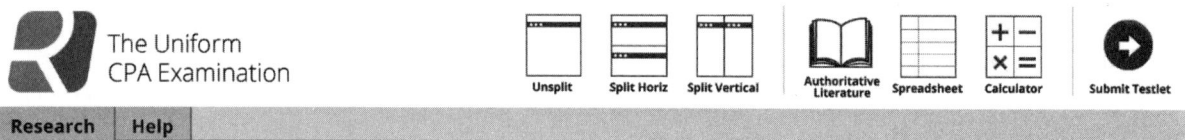

A company entered into a business combination and recognized goodwill in one of the reporting units acquired. After performing a qualitative evaluation, the company has decided that it needs to test goodwill for impairment. Identify the location in professional standards that indicates what comparison is made when performing the first step of the goodwill impairment test.

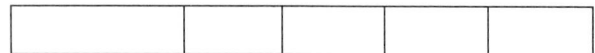

TASK-BASED SIMULATION SOLUTIONS

Task-Based Simulation Solution 1

| FASB ASC | 350 | 30 | 25 | 3 |

Task-Based Simulation Solution 2

| FASB ASC | 350 | 20 | 35 | 4 |

Section 10 - Receivables

Section 10 – Receivables
Corresponding Lectures

Watch the following course lectures with this section:

Lecture 10.01 – Receivables
Lecture 10.02 – Sale and Pledging of Receivables
Lecture 10.03 – Interest on Receivables
Lecture 10.04 – Receivables – Class Questions
Lecture 10.05 – Loans and Receivables under IFRS
Lecture 10.06 – Receivables – Document Review Simulation

EXAM NOTE: Please refer to the AICPA FAR Blueprint in the Introduction to find a listing of the representative tasks (and their associated skill levels—i.e., Remembering and Understanding, Application, and Analysis) that the candidate should be able to perform based on the knowledge obtained in this section.

Receivables

Lecture 10.01

RECEIVABLES

Accounts receivable arise from the sale of goods or the performance of services. If not related to the normal operations such as amounts due from officers, employees or stockholders, then they are reported separately from trade accounts receivable (ASC 310).

- **Valuation of Receivables**
    - A/R should be reported at their **net realizable value (NRV)**. The NRV is the gross amount of A/R less estimates of amounts that won't be collected due to:
        - **Uncollectible accounts receivable** (discussed below)
        - **Discounts** for prompt payment (ex. 2/10, N/30)
            - **Gross method** – show at gross, if discount is taken, considered a reduction of sales.
            - **Net method** – show at net, if discount not taken, considered interest income.
        - **Trade discounts** – Recorded net of any sale or trade discounts.
        - **Sales returns and allowances** – An estimate of amounts expected to be returned in the future. Considered a reduction of Sales and Receivables.

Sales returns (contra to sales)	X	
Allowance for sales returns (contra to A/R)		X

- **Uncollectible Accounts Receivable**

A/R	100	
Sales		100
Bad Debt expense	5	
Allowance for Uncollectible		
accounts (Doubtful accounts)		5

NRV = 95

There are three different ways of calculating bad debt expense. Two methods are considered GAAP using the allowance approach, the other method, the Direct write-off method is not GAAP, but is used for tax purposes.

- **Direct Write-off method**
    - Bad debt expense is recognized when a specific account is determined to be uncollectible. No valuation account is used.
    - A/R is reduced when accounts written off & recorded as bad debt expense.
    - **Violates GAAP** in two ways (but used for tax purposes)
        - **Not Matching** – bad debt expense not recorded at time of sale.
        - **Not Conservative** – A/R carried at face amount which will overstate the A/R balance in the Balance sheet.

Bad Debt Expense   X
    A/R   X

The two acceptable methods are:
- **Income statement approach - % of Credit sales method**
    - Base expense on a percentage of Credit Sales
    - Record expense at point of sale. The emphasis is on the **matching** principle.
    - Credit Sales
      <u>x % estimate of amounts not collectible</u>
      Bad debt expense (Actual JE)

    - Allowance for bad debts reduces carrying amount of A/R to net realizable value
        - Referred to as valuation account.
        - Reported as contra-asset to A/R.
        - Increased when bad debt expense recorded.
        - Decreased when accounts written off.
        - Increased when recoveries occur.

Allowance for Uncollectible accounts

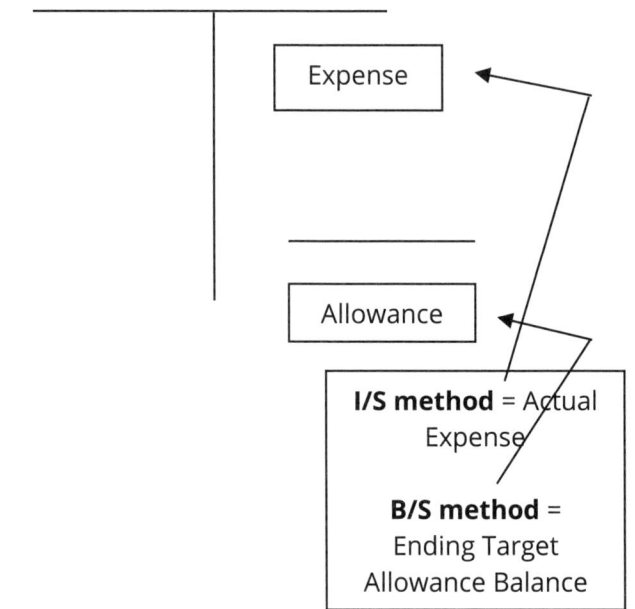

- **Balance sheet approach - % of receivables method.**
    - Aging of A/R
    - Age all the outstanding A/R's.
    - Emphasis on **Asset valuation** principle.

    - Outstanding A/R
      <u>x Uncollectible % of A/R (management estimate)</u>
      Allowance for bad debts (Target amount)
        - Separate calculation may be done for different A/R categories based on age.

Receivables Section 10

- Entry is made to adjust allowance to calculated amount – offset is adjustment to bad debt expense.

> **Aging Schedule**
> (Example) (an estimate)
> 0 – 20 days   2%
> 21 – 60 days   3%

To record bad debt expense
Bad Debt Expense	X	
Allowance (B/S)		X

Write-Off receivables
Allowance	X	
A/R		X

Note: When write-off a receivable there is No net effect on value.

Recovery of A/R (2 JE's)
A/R	X	
Allowance		X
Cash	X	
A/R		X

Accounts Receivable			Allowance for Uncollectible Accounts	
Beginning balance				Beginning balance
Sales	Collections			Bad debt expense
	Write offs	Write offs		
Recoveries				Recoveries
Ending balance				Ending balance

Lecture 10.02

Sale and Pledging of Receivables

On occasion, a client will want to generate cash from a receivable without waiting until it is collected from the customer. There are **4 basic techniques** available:
- **Pledging** – the client borrows the necessary cash, and "pledges" (offers) the receivable to the lender as collateral to secure the loan. When this occurs it must be *adequately disclosed* in a footnote in the financial statements.

- **Assigning** – the client borrows the necessary cash, and agrees to use the proceeds from the receivable to repay the lender. Sometimes, the customer is notified to make payment directly to the lender instead of the client.
- **Factoring** – a company converts it A/R into cash by assigning or selling it either with or without recourse to a factor
    - **Sale without recourse** – the client sells the receivable to another party (a factor), with the buyer assuming the risk that the receivable may not be collectible.
    - **Sale with recourse** – the client sells the receivable to another party, with the buyer retaining the right to demand the client make good on the receivable if the customer does not pay as promised.

Transfers and Servicing of Financial Assets (ASC 860)

Entities in general, and financial institutions in particular, transfer financial assets to other entities. The transfer may involve a single entire financial asset, such as a mortgage loan receivable; a group of financial assets, such as an entity's accounts receivable; or a participating interest in a financial asset, such as a percentage of the entire financial instrument.
- When a component of a financial asset that is not considered a participating interest is transferred, it will be accounted for as a secured borrowing with pledge of collateral.
- A component of a financial instrument is **a participating interest** if it has certain characteristics:
    - It represents a proportionate interest in the entire instrument.
    - All cash flows from the instrument, other than those allocated as compensation for services, are divided proportionately among participating interest holders.
    - The rights of all participating interests have the same priority and are not subordinated to one another.
    - All participating interests must agree in order for a party to pledge or exchange the entire financial instrument.

The accounting for a transfer of a financial instrument, group of financial instruments, or a participating interest in a financial interest is determined on the basis of whether or not the transferor has surrendered control of the instrument.
- If control has been surrendered, the transfer will be recognized as a sale, along with a related gain or loss.
- If control has NOT been surrendered, the transfer will be recognized as a secured borrowing with the financial instrument pledged as collateral.

Control of a financial instrument has been surrendered (considered a **sale**) only when all of the following three conditions are met:
1. The transferred financial instruments have been *isolated* from the transferor and *beyond the reach of the transferor* or its creditors, including creditors in bankruptcy.
2. Transferees have the *right to pledge or exchange* the asset it received without restrictions and without providing more than a trivial benefit to the transferor.
3. The transferor does *not maintain effective control* over the financial instrument, considering all of the transferor's continuing involvements with the instrument. The transferor does maintain effective control when:
    a. An agreement, entered into contemporaneously with the transfer, both entitles and obligates the transferor to repurchase or redeem the transferred financial assets at a fixed or determinable price.
    b. An agreement allowing the transferor the unilateral ability to require the transferee to return specific financial assets.

Receivables   Section 10

c. An agreement allowing the transferee to require the transferor to repurchase the transferred financial assets at a price significantly favorable to the transferee.

Unless all 3 of these conditions are satisfied, the financial asset is considered to have been merely **pledged or assigned** as collateral for a loan (**borrowing** transaction).

In the cases of **pledging or assigning**, the company remains the legal owner of the financial asset, and simply records a liability for the amount borrowed:

Cash	X	
Note Payable		X

Notes to the financial statements will indicate the dollar amount of the financial assets that have been pledged or assigned. Alternatively, the company can identify these amounts on the face of the balance sheet:

A/R Assigned	X	
A/R		X

The remaining entries include normal entries to record interest and principal payments on the note, and collection of the receivables.

If control is surrendered and the transfer is **accounted for as a sale**, two other issues should be considered.
- A **factor's holdback** (also referred to as *"Due from factor"*) is an amount which provides a margin of protection against sales discounts, sales returns and allowances, and disputed accounts.
- A **recourse obligation** (*probable uncollectible accounts*) is an amount included as protection for the transferee against uncollectible accounts; such obligations result in a continuing interest in the asset.

To illustrate, assume an entity with accounts receivable that are expected to have a net realizable value of $35,000 transfers them to another entity for $30,000.

If control is not surrendered, the transaction will be recognized as a secured borrowing:

Cash	30,000	
Interest expense	5,000	
Note payable		35,000

If control is surrendered, and the transferee withholds $5,000 from the proceeds for protection against future reductions resulting from returns, allowances, or disputed amounts, the transaction will be reported as a sale:

Cash	25,000	
Due from factor (withheld amount)	5,000	
Loss on sale of receivables	5,000	
Accounts receivable		35,000

- **Factoring** - The sale of short-term accounts receivable. A factoring fee is applied by the buyer, and is a straight percentage of the factored receivables.
- **Discounting** - The sale of long-term notes receivable. A discount rate is applied by the buyer, and is an annualized rate that will vary depending on the length of time until collection is due.

In the case of sales, the buyer of the receivable becomes the legal owner of it, and the client reduces the carrying value of the receivables to zero, reporting a gain or loss for the difference between the proceeds from sale and the carrying value of the receivable. There is, however, a major difference between the treatment of sales without recourse (as most, though not all, factoring involves) and sales with recourse (as most, though not all, discounting involves).

In the case of a **sale without recourse**, the seller is relieved of any obligation on the receivable. Thus, if the buyer of the receivable is unable to collect from the customer, they cannot require the seller of the receivable to compensate them.
- The transferee (buyer) bears the risk of uncollectible accounts
- The transferee does not, however, bear the risk of goods being returned, allowances made for nonconforming goods, or disputed balances.

For example, assume the client has gross accounts receivable of $100,000, and an allowance for bad debts of $8,000. On that date, the client *factors all of the receivables without recourse*, and the buyer charges a factoring fee of 9% of the face amount ($100,000 x 9% = $9,000). The entry is as follows:

Cash and Amount due from Factor (holdback)	91,000	
Loss on factoring	1,000	
Allowance for bad debts	8,000	
Accounts receivable		100,000

Notice that the client removes the entire allowance for bad debts, since the risk of collectability has been transferred to the buyer of the receivables (w/o recourse).

When receivables are **factored with recourse**, the client is liable for uncollectible accounts, and must report an estimated liability for the additional amounts that are expected to be paid to the buyer.

For example, if $100,000 accounts receivable with an allowance for bad debts of $8,000 has been **factored with recourse**, the buyer charging a 3% factoring fee on the face value ($100,000 x 3% = $3,000), the entry is:

Cash and Amount due from Factor (holdback)	97,000	
Loss on factoring	3,000	
Allowance for bad debts	8,000	
Liability on Transferred receivable		100,000
Estimated recourse liability		8,000

Receivables — Section 10

If the buyer is subsequently able to collect only $91,000, and the client is required to pay $9,000 on the uncollectible accounts, an additional loss is recorded as follows:

If the company sells the accounts receivable to a factor in a transaction considered a *borrowing transaction*, this would be considered factoring with recourse.

Estimated recourse liability	8,000	
Loss on factoring	1,000	
Cash		9,000

Cash	X	
Factor's holdback	X	
Interest expense (discount)	X	
Liability on transferred		X

When an interest bearing note receivable is sold to a bank, the usual process is known as **discounting**. The bank first determines the maturity value of the note, meaning the total payment of principal and accrued interest that is due at maturity. This amount is then reduced by a discount rate, and the bank pays the net result. Notes receivable that have been discounted *with recourse* are reported on the balance sheet with a corresponding contra account (notes receivable discounted). Notes receivable discounted *without recourse* have essentially been sold and should be removed from the balance sheet.

For example, assume the client sells inventory on 6/30/X1 for $100,000, and receives a one-year note for $100,000 bearing interest at 10% (the market rate of interest). The entry for the sale (we'll ignore cost of sales for this illustration) is:

6/30/X1	Note receivable	100,000	
	Sales		100,000

That same day, the client discounts the note at a bank at a 10% discount rate. The amount to be received is calculated as follows:

Face value	100,000
Interest at maturity (10%)	<u>10,000</u>
Maturity value	110,000
Discount (10%)	<u>11,000</u>
Net paid by bank	<u>99,000</u>

Notice the client is not collecting the face value, even though the bank rate is the same as the effective rate on the note, because bank interest is computed on the maturity value. The entry for the discounting activity is:

6/30/X1	Cash	99,000	
	Loss on discounting	1,000	
	Note receivable		100,000

If the note has been **discounted with recourse**, the client should disclose a contingent liability for the amount that might have to be paid if the customer defaults to the bank.

Both the interest rate on a note and the discount rate charged by a bank are annual rates, so the calculations are affected by the holding period.

      Face amount
+   **Interest** (Interest = Face x Interest rate x Term)
=   **Maturity value**
-    **Discount** (Discount = Maturity value x Discount rate x Time Remaining)
=   **Proceeds**

Accounting for Transfers of Participating Interests

An entity may have only a **participating interest** in a financial instrument. In order to be considered a participating interest, certain characteristics must apply:
- The interest represents a proportionate interest in the entire instrument.
- All cash flows from the instrument are divided proportionately among all participating interests.
- Each participating interest is given the same priority.
- No entity has the ability to pledge or exchange the entire instrument without the consent of all participating interest holders.

When a transfer of a participating interest qualifies as a sale, the transaction is accounted for as follows:
1. Consideration received is recognized at its fair value.
2. The carrying value of the entire instrument is allocated between the participating interest transferred and the interests retained on the basis of their relative fair values.
    a. The portion allocated to the participating interest sold is eliminated.
    b. The difference between that and the fair value of consideration received is recognized as a gain or loss in earnings
3. The remaining carrying value becomes the carrying value of the retained interests.

For example, assume a company has a note receivable with a face and carrying value of $580,000. The entity decides to transfer 40% of the note for $260,000 to another entity at a time when the fair value of the receivable is $650,000. As a result, the fair value of the 40% participating interest being transferred is $260,000 and the fair value of the retained interests is $390,000. The carrying value will be allocated as follows:
- Participating interest transferred - $260,000/$650,000 x $580,000 = $232,000
- Retained interests - $390,000/$650,000 x $580,000 = $348,000

There would be a gain on sale:

        Sales price $260,000
        Basis $232,000
        Gain $ 28,000

The resulting entry would be:

	Debit	Credit
Cash	260,000	
Gain on sale		28,000
Note receivable		232,000

Servicing of Financial Assets

Financial assets, notes receivable in particular, require what is referred to as **servicing**. Servicing of a note receivable includes such administrative functions as sending debtors monthly statements, collecting payments, allocating payments between principal and interest, and sending tax information forms to the debtor. It is fairly common for the seller of a financial asset or a participating interest in a financial asset to retain the obligation to service the receivable, referred to as servicing rights.

- The entity with the servicing rights may not receive any compensation or may receive compensation that is below the fair compensation for performing the servicing obligations, in which case the entity has a *servicing liability*.
- The entity may receive compensation that exceeds the fair compensation for performing the servicing obligations, in which case the entity has a *servicing asset*.

In addition to recognizing a service asset or liability when servicing rights are retained upon the sale of a financial instrument or a participating interest in one, an entity will also recognize a servicing asset or liability when it acquires or assumes a servicing obligation for a financial instrument in which it has no direct interest.

A **servicing asset or servicing liability** is initially recognized at its **fair value**, regardless of whether or not consideration was received. Once recognized, servicing assets or liabilities may be accounted for under either of two methods:

- **Amortization method**
    - The asset, when revenues will exceed costs, or liability, when costs will exceed revenues, is amortized over the period during which servicing income (asset) or loss (liability) will be recognized.
    - The amortization will be in proportion to the amount of income or loss.
    - The asset or liability is assessed for impairment (asset) or increased obligation (liability) at each reporting date.

- **Fair value method**
    - The servicing asset or liability is adjusted to fair value on each reporting date.
    - Increases or decreases are reported in earnings.
    - Selecting the fair value method involves an irrevocable election.

In addition to servicing assets and liabilities, there are other ways in which financial instruments are divided with some of the various components being transferred and others retained. One component is referred to as an **interest-only strip (i-o strip).** Sometimes they are retained as part of the consideration for the portion of the instrument transferred. In other cases, they are considered compensation for the service obligations.

- I-o strips are considered financial instruments, not servicing assets.
- The entity receives a proportionate amount of each interest payment received.
- They are reported at fair value when received.
- They are subsequently accounted for as available for sale securities or trading securities, as appropriate.

Securitization

Financial assets may be securitized in order to make them easier to transfer. Securitization is the process of converting financial assets into securities. It is accomplished when a group of homogeneous securities are combined into a pool and transferred into an entity referred to as a securitization mechanism. A group of mortgage notes receivable, for example, may be transferred to a real estate investment trust (REIT). Shares in the trust can then be sold to investors as securities.

Payments received by the securitization mechanism may be classified as either:
- Payments used to pay off debt securities, referred to as *pay-through*; or
- Payments attributed to investors, referred to as *pass-through*.

In certain circumstances, referred to as *revolving period securitizations*, receivables are transferred at the inception and also periodically thereafter. During the term, referred to as the revolving period, cash collections are used to purchase additional receivables from the transferor.

EXAMPLE: *Assume an entity sells a loan for $44,000, retaining servicing rights and a 1% interest only strip. The loan has a book value of $45,000 and, on the date of transfer, the fees that will be received for the servicing is expected to exceed the cost of performing the servicing, resulting in a servicing asset with a fair value of $4,100. The i-o strip has an estimated fair value of $2,200 at the date of transfer.*

Proceeds consist of:

Cash	$44,000
Servicing rights (at fair value)	4,100
I-O strip (at fair value)	2,200
Total	$50,300

Since the carrying value of the receivable was $45,000, there would be a gain on sale of $5,300. The journal entry would appear as follows:

Cash	44,000	
Servicing rights	4,100	
I-O strip	2,200	
Note receivable		45,000
Gain on sale		5,300

Accounting for Collateral

When a debtor provides a creditor with collateral for a loan, the accounting for it will depend on who retains control of the collateral. In most circumstances, the transferor (debtor) retains control of the collateral.
- It remains as an asset on the debtor's financial statements.
- The fact that it is collateral for a debt is disclosed.
- The transferee (creditor) does not recognize the asset in its financial statements.

Upon default, the creditor will take control of the collateral.
- The debtor will eliminate the carrying value of the asset, the carrying value of the debt and related accounts, such as accrued interest, and recognize a gain or loss for the difference.
- The creditor will recognize the asset at fair value, derecognize the receivable, and recognize a gain or loss (generally a loss), as appropriate.

Receivables
Section 10

When the transferee has control of the collateral, it recognizes an asset and a corresponding liability, recognizing the obligation to return the collateral upon settlement of the debt instrument. Since the transferor will no longer have possession of the collateral, it will be reported as a receivable.

If the debtor defaults:
- The creditor will eliminate the receivable and the liability to return the collateral with the difference representing a gain or loss.
- The debtor will eliminate the liability and the receivable with the difference representing a gain or loss.

Impairments (Income statement) (ASC 360)

A receivable is evaluated for impairment any time it appears that any or all payments will not be received when they are scheduled to be.
- Appears won't collect the amount loaned
- Write loan down to **either**
    1. Present value of future principal and interest inflows
    2. Loan's market price
    3. Fair value of the collateral

Bad debt expense	X	
Allowance for impaired loan		X

US GAAP requires entities to assess whether financial assets are **impaired** and recognize the impairment. If a note receivable is impaired, the loss is measured by the creditor as the difference between the investment in the loan (usually the principle plus accrued interest) and the expected future cash flows discounted at the loan's historical effective interest rate. US GAAP recognizes the uncollectible amount through an *allowance account*. Unlike IFRS, US GAAP **prohibits the reversal of impairment losses**.

Lecture 10.03

Interest on Receivables (ASC 310)

- A/R occurs in the ordinary course of business, so record at **Face value**.
- L/T receivables are not in the ordinary course of business, so record at **Present Value (P.V.)**
- The **future value factor** is equal to 1 divided by the present value factor. For example, an investment of $10,000 in two years at 10% would accumulate to the principal multiplied by the future value factor. In this case the $10,000 × 1/0.826 = $12,107.

  o **Notes received solely for cash** (assume rate is fair)

N/R	10,000	
Cash		10,000

  o **Notes received for goods or services**
    1. Note receivable at a **reasonable rate**. The PV of the note is the same as the Face amount. Assume the asset book value is 6000.

Notes receivable	10,000	
Discount on N/R		0 → cv = 10,000
Asset		6000
Gain on sale		4000

Non-interest bearing notes (Zero-Interest-Bearing Notes)

2. If the interest rate is not stated or is unreasonable, use the **FMV of the goods or the FMV of the note,** whichever is more easily determinable. Assume the FMV of the asset is 9000.

Notes receivable	10,000	
Discount on N/R		1000 → cv = 9,000
Equipment		6000
Gain on sale		3000

3. If the interest rate is not stated, the FMV of the goods or the FMV of the note is not determinable, **IMPUTE** an interest rate. Use a reasonable rate for a note of this type. PV of a note in 2 years at 10% is .8265 x 10,000 = 8,265.

Notes receivable	10,000	
Discount on N/R		1735 → cv = 8265
Equipment		6000
Gain on sale		2265

- When interest rate isn't fair, the fair rate must be imputed
  - Receivable is carried at the present value of payments discounted at fair interest rate.
  - Periodic interest income accrues based on fair rate.

As a general rule, businesses don't bother charging interest on accounts receivable expected to be collected within 30 days, and the AICPA permits a company to **ignore the interest component** or choose an unusual rate so long as **two conditions** are satisfied:
- The entire receivable will be collected within a year
- The terms of the sale are customary in the trade

For long-term receivables and short-term sales **not** consummated under **customary trade terms,** however, the entity is normally required to compute interest income using a fair rate of interest.

If the client is not assessing a fair interest rate on a receivable resulting from a sale, we must impute interest, which means determining the implicit rate of interest being charged. In such a case, it is assumed that some or all of the interest may have been included in the quoted sales price.

It may also be necessary to impute interest on a receivable obtained in connection with a loan, if the repayment includes provisions requiring the borrower to provide goods or services or other consideration in addition to cash payments. It is assumed that some or all of the interest may be represented by the value of the consideration provided.

Imputing interest is not appropriate when a loan involves a straight repayment of the cash with no other conditions, since there is no account to which the interest can be attributed.

Let's look at an example of imputing interest on a sale. Assume that the client sells a product on 1/1/X1 for $1,000, with payment not due for 3 years and no interest to be assessed. Since the period of collection exceeds one year, we must assume that a portion of the quoted selling price actually represents interest, rather than being part of the true sales price of the product. There are two reasonable approaches to determining the true sales price:
- **Cash selling price** - The price being charged by the client for sales to customers who pay in full on the date of sale.
- **Present value** - The cash flow of the receivable discounted at a fair interest rate.

Normally, the first approach is preferred, since cash selling price is more verifiable and, therefore, a more reliable measurement. The latter approach requires the determination of a fair rate of interest, and there can be reasonable disagreement as to the appropriate rate to utilize.

Assume, however, that the cash selling price is not determinable, and that a fair interest rate of 10% is determined. The present value of $1 for 3 years at 10% is .751, so that the present value of $1,000 payment due in 3 years is $751. The sale is recorded as follows:

1/1/X1	Note receivable	1,000	
	Discount on note		249
	Sales		751

The discount on note, which is simply the difference between the gross receivable and the present value of the receivable, is a form of unearned interest income.

Once a receivable is recorded, it will bear interest using the appropriate rate. In the previous example, after recording a note receivable of $1,000 with a discount of $249 at 1/1/X1, the company will report interest over the 3 years until the note comes due. The interest is based on the carrying value of the note, which is the gross note less the unamortized discount. Since the imputed interest rate is 10%, the original note of $1,000 - $249 = $751 will result in interest income of $75, recorded as follows:

12/31/X1	Discount on note	75	
	Interest income		75

This will increase the carrying value of the note by $75 for the subsequent period, so that interest income will also increase. A schedule showing the interest income in each period follows:

	20X1	20X2	20X3
Gross receivable	1000	1000	1000
Unamortized	249	174	91
Carrying value	751	826	909
Interest rate	10%	10%	10%
Interest Income	75	83	91

Interest Amortization

CV	x	Effective Interest Rate	=	Interest Income	(face x stated x time) cash payment =		Amortization of Discount/ Premium
8,265	x	10%	=	826	- 0	=	826
+826							
9,091	x	10%	=	909	- 0	=	909
+909							
10,000							

Lecture 10.04

CLASS QUESTIONS

Please see the Class Questions and Class Solutions for this Lecture at the end of this Section.

Lecture 10.05

LOANS AND RECEIVABLES UNDER IFRS

Under IFRS, loans and receivables are not given special recognition but, instead, follow the accounting treatment that is prescribed for financial assets. A loan, note, account, or other receivable is considered a financial asset, which is defined similarly under IFRS as it is under GAAP. A receivable is a **financial asset** because it represents a contractual right to receive cash.

IFRS 9 describes three categories of financial assets. The first category applies to all financial assets meeting two requirements:
- The objective of the business model under which they were received is to hold them in order to collect the cash flows.
- The contractually scheduled cash flows solely represent payments of principal and interest.

Financial assets falling into the first category are accounted for at **amortized cost**. Under the amortized cost method, the receivable is initially recognized at its fair value plus or minus transaction costs directly attributable to the acquisition or issue of the financial asset. In the case of receivables:
- Accounts receivable result from providing goods or services to a debtor and are measured at fair value, which is presumably the sales price of the goods or services.
- Notes and loans receivable generally result from providing money and are measured at the amount paid plus transaction costs, which might include, for example, a payment to an attorney for drawing up the note.

The receivable is subsequently measured by applying payments received to interest, applying the effective interest method, and then to principal. In addition, the entity is required to assess whether there is reason to believe that the receivable has been impaired as of the *end of each reporting period*. When there is objective evidence that an **impairment loss** has occurred:
- The receivable is written down to the present value of expected future cash flows using the original effective rate.
- The loss is recognized in profit or loss.
- The asset may be reduced or an allowance account may be used.

Receivables   Section 10

- Decreases in impairment losses may be recognized in profit or loss by reversing previously recognized impairment losses provided reversals do not exceed losses recognized.

As an alternative, an entity can recognize a financial asset that falls into this first category at **fair value**.
- It is accomplished by designating the financial asset as measured at fair value through profit or loss (FVTPL) when the asset is initially recognized.
- The designation is irrevocable.

In addition, all financial assets that do not meet both of the two conditions for accounting at amortized cost are also reported at fair value.
- If the business model involves holding the instrument to collect cash flows and selling the instrument when conditions are favorable, it will be accounted for at fair value with unrealized gains and losses reported in other comprehensive income.
- All remaining financial assets are reported at fair value with unrealized gains and losses reported in profit or loss

In either of the latter two cases, the asset is adjusted to its fair value as of the end of each reporting period and any increase or decrease occurring since the last accounting period would be recognized in either comprehensive income, if the objective of the entity is to collect cash flows and sell the instrument, or profit or loss in all other circumstances.

IAS 1 establishes guidelines for the presentation of financial statements. It requires financial statements to include a statement of financial position that presents, among other things, trade and other receivables; and financial assets, excluding those that are reported separately such as receivables or cash and cash equivalents. In addition, an entity is required to present current and non-current assets and liabilities separately in the statement of financial position unless it is more appropriate to present the financial statements on the liquidity basis. Assets are classified as **current** if any of the following conditions apply:
- The asset will be realized, sold, or consumed within one operating cycle;
- The asset is being held for trading purposes;
- The asset is expected to be realized within 12 months of the date of the financial statements; or
- The asset is cash or a cash equivalent that is not restricted.

Receivables are required to be reported separately into accounts receivable from trade customers, receivables from related parties, and other amounts including prepayments.

Transaction costs attributable to the acquisition of the receivable are included in the carrying value, reducing the effective rate.

IFRS still uses the **allowance method**, however instead of using the word "allowance", IFRS uses the word "**provision**". The provision for credit losses recognized on financial assets that are either measured at amortized cost or are measured at fair value through other comprehensive income will be determined based on an understanding of credit losses:
- If credit losses have not increased significantly since initial recognition, the provision will be equal to 12 months of expected credit losses.
- If credit losses have increased significantly since initial recognition, the provision will be equal to credit losses expected over the lifetime of the financial asset.

Loans and Receivables	
US GAAP	**IFRS**
• Transaction costs attributable to acquisition of receivable not included in carrying value. • Loans receivable tested for impairment when entity has reason to believe receivable is impaired. Impairment loss is NOT recovered. • "Allowance for"	• Transaction costs attributable to acquisition of receivable included in carrying value reducing effective rate. • Required to be tested for impairment each period end. Impairment loss may be recovered. • "Provision for"

Lecture 10.06

CLASS QUESTIONS

Please see the Class Questions and Class Solutions for this Lecture at the end of this Section.

CLASS QUESTIONS

Work through the below Class Questions while following along with the respective lectures. Once this is complete, you can begin independently practicing what you've learned by quizzing yourself on this course section in your Interactive Practice Questions (IPQ), which can be found in your online Student Dashboard. Your IPQ simulates the computer-based testing experience, and will also help you understand how concepts are applied to the exam. Each question includes answer explanations from expert CPAs that will help you determine why you answered a question correctly or incorrectly. This is key to your success on the CPA Exam.

Lecture 10.04

1. There are a variety of ways to calculate the allowance for bad debt expense. Which of the following methods emphasizes asset valuation, the balance sheet approach?

    a. Aging the receivables.
    b. Direct write-off.
    c. Gross sales.
    d. Credit sales less returns and allowances.

2. Which method of recording uncollectible accounts expense is consistent with accrual accounting?

	Allowance	Direct write-off
a.	Yes	Yes
b.	Yes	No
c.	No	Yes
d.	No	No

3. Inge Co. determined that the net value of its accounts receivable at December 31, 20X3, based on an aging of the receivables, was $325,000. Additional information is as follows:

Allowance for uncollectible accounts—1/1/X3	$ 30,000
Uncollectible accounts written off during 20X3	18,000
Uncollectible accounts recovered during 20X3	2,000
Accounts receivable at 12/31/X3	350,000

    For 20X3, what would be Inge's uncollectible accounts expense?

    a. $ 5,000
    b. $11,000
    c. $15,000
    d. $21,000

4. Gibbs Co. uses the allowance method for recognizing uncollectible accounts. Ignoring deferred taxes, the entry to record the write-off of a specific uncollectible account

    a. Affects neither net income nor working capital.
    b. Affects neither net income nor accounts receivable.
    c. Decreases both net income and account receivable.
    d. Decreases both net income and working capital.

Section 10 Receivables

5. When the allowance method of recognizing uncollectible accounts is used, the entries at the time of collection of a small account previously written off would

   a. Increase the allowance for uncollectible accounts.
   b. Increase net income.
   c. Decrease the allowance for uncollectible accounts.
   d. Have no effect on the allowance for uncollectible accounts.

6. When the allowance method of recognizing bad debt expense is used, the allowance would decrease when a (an)

   a. Account previously written off is collected.
   b. Account previously written off becomes collectible.
   c. Specific uncollectible account is written off.
   d. Provision for uncollectible accounts is recorded.

7. At January 1, 20X4, Jamin Co. had a credit balance of $260,000 in its allowance for uncollectible accounts. Based on past experience, 2% of Jamin's credit sales have been uncollectible. During 20X4, Jamin wrote off $325,000 of uncollectible accounts. Credit sales for 20X4 were $9,000,000. In its December 31, 20X4, balance sheet, what amount should Jamin report as allowance for uncollectible accounts?

   a. $115,000
   b. $180,000
   c. $245,000
   d. $440,000

8. Roth, Inc. received from a customer a one year, $500,000 note bearing annual interest of 8%. After holding the note for six months, Roth discounted the note at Regional Bank at an effective interest rate of 10%. What amount of cash did Roth receive from the bank?

   a. $540,000
   b. $523,810
   c. $513,000
   d. $495,238

CLASS SOLUTIONS

1. (a) An asset valuation approach is used to determine what adjustment must be made to the asset to reflect its value resulting in the recognition of bad debt expense as the amount needed to accommodate that adjustment. An income measurement approach is used to determine bad debts expense by using a percentage of gross or net sales resulting in an adjustment to the carrying value based on the amount of bad debt expense measured. The direct write-off method, which is not allowed under GAAP, applies neither the asset valuation nor the income measurement approach.

2. (b) The allowance method of recognizing bad debt expense is consistent with accrual accounting since bad debt expense is recognized in the period in which sales are recognized. The direct write-off method is not consistent with accrual accounting since bad debt expense is not recognized until it is determined that a specific account will be uncollectible, not necessarily the same period in which the sales revenue was recognized.

3. (b) With accounts receivable of $350,000 and a net value of $325,000, there should be an allowance for uncollectible accounts of $25,000. The allowance for doubtful accounts is increased by bad debt expense and decreased by write-offs, net of recoveries. If the beginning allowance was $30,000 and net write-offs were $16,000 ($18,000 - $2,000), the balance in the allowance would be $14,000 ($30,000 - $16,000) before recognizing bad debts expense. It would require bad debt expense of $11,000 to increase the unadjusted balance of $14,000 to the proper balance of $25,000 ($25,000 - $14,000 = $11,000).

4. (a) The entry to write-off an uncollectible account requires a debit to the allowance for doubtful accounts, reducing it, and a credit to accounts receivable, also reducing it. As a result, net accounts receivable remains unchanged as do net income and working capital.

5. (a) When an account that had been written off is subsequently collected, the account will first be reinstated with increases to both accounts receivable and the allowance for uncollectible accounts. The collection is then recorded with an increase in cash and a decrease in accounts receivable. The net effect is that cash is increased as is the allowance for uncollectible accounts. There is no effect on net income.

6. (c) Adjustments are made to the allowance account to recognize bad debt expense, which increases it; write-off a specific account, which decreases it; and reinstate an account that has previously been written off, which increases it. Only writing off a specific account decreases the allowance.

7. (a) The allowance for doubtful accounts is increased when bad debt expense is recognized and decreased when an account is written off. Bad debt expense is 2% of credit sales of $9,000,000 or $180,000. If $325,000 in accounts receivable were written off, the balance would be $260,000 + $180,000 - $325,000 = $115,000.

8. (c) Roth will first calculate the maturity value of the note, which will be the face of $500,000 plus one year's interest at 8% or $40,000. Since the note is being discounted after 6 months, the bank will receive $540,000 after six months. The discount will be $540,000 x 10% x 6/12 or $27,000. As a result, Roth will receive $540,000 - $27,000 or $513,000 from the discounting.

TASK-BASED SIMULATIONS

Task-Based Simulation 1

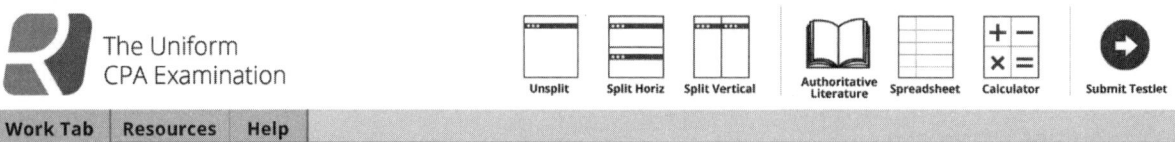

Required:

Sigma Co. began operations on January 1, year 1. On December 31, year 1, Sigma provided for uncollectible accounts based on 1% of annual credit sales. On January 1, year 2, Sigma changed its method of determining its allowance for uncollectible accounts by applying certain percentages to the accounts receivable aging schedule as follows:

Days past invoice date	Percent deemed to be uncollectible
0–30	1%
31–90	5%
91–180	20%
Over 180	80%

In addition, Sigma wrote off all accounts receivable that were over one year old. The following additional information relates to the years ended December 31, year 2, and year 1:

	Year 2	Year 1
Credit sales	$3,000,000	$2,800,000
Collections	2,915,000	2,400,000
Accounts written off	27,000	None
Recovery of accounts previously written off	7,000	None
Days past invoice date at 12/31		
0–30	300,000	250,000
31–90	80,000	90,000
91–180	60,000	45,000
Over 180	25,000	15,000

Receivables

Items to be answered:

Complete the following schedules showing the calculation of the allowance for uncollectible accounts at December 31, year 2 and the calculation for uncollectible accounts expense for year 2.

Sigma Company
SCHEDULE OF CALCULATION OF ALLOWANCE FOR UNCOLLECTIBLE ACCOUNTS
December 31, Year 2

	Amounts of accounts receivable	Percentage of uncollectible accounts	Allowance for bad debts
0 to 30 days			
31 to 90 days			
91 to 180 days			
Over 180 days			
Total accounts receivable			
Total allowance for uncollectible accounts			

Schedule of Uncollectible Accounts Expense

Balance December 31, year 1	
Write-offs during year 2	
Recoveries during year 2	
Balance before year 2 provision	
Required allowance at December 31, year 2	
Year 2 Provision	

Task-Based Simulation 2

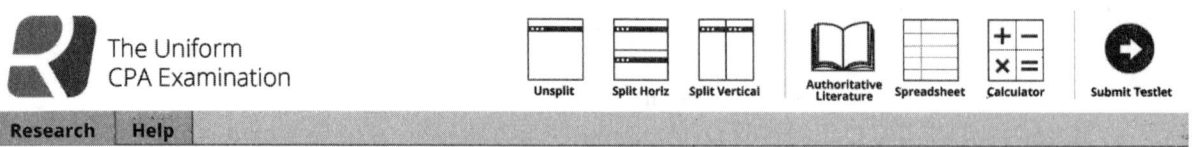

A client has notes receivable from officers and is trying to determine if they may be combined with other notes receivable on the balance sheet. Identify the location in professional standards that indicates whether receivables from officers may be combined with other receivables on the balance sheet.

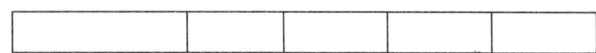

Task-Based Simulation 3

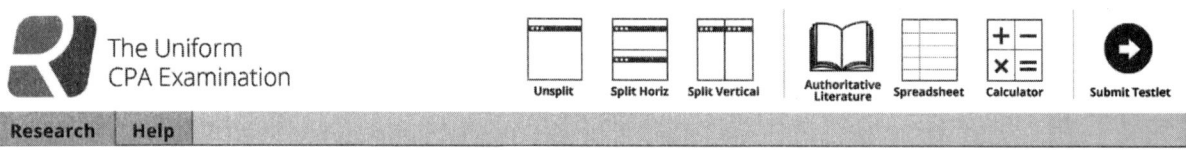

A company has transferred a note receivable to another entity in a transaction that it believes should be recognized as a sale. The auditor is not certain if the company actually surrendered control of the receivable and should record it as a borrowing transaction. Identify the location in professional standards that indicates the conditions that must be met in order for the transfer to be recognized as a sale.

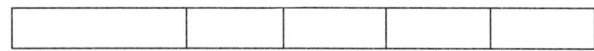

TASK-BASED SIMULATION SOLUTIONS

Task-Based Simulation Solution 1

SCHEDULE OF CALCULATION OF ALLOWANCE FOR UNCOLLECTIBLE ACCOUNTS
December 31, Year 2

	Amounts of accounts receivable	Percentage of uncollectible accounts	Allowance for bad debts
0 to 30 days	$300,000	X 1%	$3,000
31 to 90 days	80,000	X 5%	4,000
91 to 180 days	60,000	X 20%	12,000
Over 180 days	25,000	X 80%	20,000
Total accounts receivable	$465,000		
Total allowance for uncollectible accounts			$39,000

Schedule of Uncollectible Accounts Expense

Balance December 31, year 1	$28,000 ($2,800,000 X 1%)
Write-offs during year 2	($27,000) (given)
Recoveries during year 2	7,000 (given)
Balance before year 2 provision	8,000
Required allowance at December 31, year 2	39,000 (from above – target)
Year 2 Provision	$31,000

SCHEDULE OF CALCULATION OF ALLOWANCE FOR UNCOLLECTIBLE ACCOUNTS

To complete the schedule of calculation of allowance for uncollectible accounts, the information provided will first be inserted for year 2. The first column will be the amounts of invoices falling into each column, $300,000, 0 to 30 days, $80,000 31 to 90, and so on. The total will simply be the sum of $300,000 + $80,000 + $60,000 + $25,000 = $465,000.

The next column will be completed by inserting the provided percentages such as 1% for 0 to 30 days, 5% for 31 to 90 days, and so on. An allowance amount is next calculated for each line by multiplying the amount in the first column by the percentage in the next column. The results are:

$300,000 x 1% = $3,000

$80,000 x 5% = $4,000

$60,000 x 20% = $12,000

$25,000 x 80% = $20,000

As a result, the total is $39,000, which represents the required ending balance in the allowance for doubtful accounts.

Schedule of Uncollectible Accounts Expense

The schedule of uncollectible accounts expense will be completed as follows:
- In year 1, bad debts expense was 1% of credit sales of $2,800,000 for an expense of $28,000. Since no accounts were written off or recovered during the period, $28,000 would also be the balance in the allowance at December 31, year 1.
- Write-offs during year 2 are given as $27,000, which would reduce the allowance.
- Recoveries during year 2 are given as $7,000, which would increase the allowance.

As a result, the unadjusted balance in the allowance account is $28,000 - $27,000 + $7,000 = $8,000.

As determined above, the required ending balance is $39,000.

The amount of expense needed to attain the required ending balance is $39,000 - $8,000 = $31,000.

Task-Based Simulation Solution 2

| FASB ASC | 310 | 10 | 45 | 13 |

Task-Based Simulation Solution 3

| FASB ASC | 860 | 10 | 40 | 5 |

Receivables   Section 10

Lecture 10.06

DOCUMENT REVIEW SIMULATION

Document Review Simulation 1

 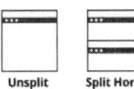 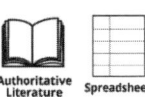

You are a new Supervisory Accountant at Sportsman Company, reporting to the controller. On your second day with Sportsman, a staff member named Junior Accountant quit his job with no notice.

One day later, it is time to prepare closing entries for March. The controller has asked you to review and correct, if necessary, the general ledger account for Accounts Receivable (A/R) prepared by Junior Accountant. You have been provided with access to the same materials and information pertaining to the A/R subsidiary ledger (subledger) that Junior Accountant had in preparing the general ledger balance. You were also informed that the March A/R beginning balance of $489,300 balanced with the A/R subledger as of March 1, 2016.

Review the general ledger account for Accounts Receivable prepared by Junior Accountant to ensure it is accurate and consistent with the information and documents provided. Report your findings, including any changes you deem necessary, to the Sportsman Company controller.

Sportsman Company

To: Roula Khan, Controller
From: CPA Candidate, Supervisory Accountant
Date: April 2, 20X6
Re: A/R General Ledger Balance

Per your request, I have reviewed the A/R general ledger balance prepared by Junior Accountant.

1. The 22 March sales return credit entry of $1,200 is correct.

2. The 25 March officer loan write-off credit entry of $12,500 is correct.

3. The 29 March assignment credit entry of $17,000 is correct.

4. The 29 March customer account write-off debit entry of $25,600 is correct.

5. The 29 March customer account recovery credit entry of $14,000 is correct.

6. The 31 March credit sales debit entry of $636,250 is correct.

7. The 31 March collections credit entry of $314,800 is correct.

8. The March ending balance of $791,650 is correct.

Regards,

CPA Candidate
Supervisory Accountant

Resources

Junior Accountant's General Ledger A/R Account

Account: Accounts Receivable				Account Number : 120	
Date	Description	Post Ref.	Debit	Credit	Balance
3/1/2016	Beginning balance				489,300
3/22/2016	Sales return			1,200	488,100
3/25/2016	Write-off officer loan			12,500	475,600
3/29/2015	Assignment			17,000	458,600
3/29/2016	Write-off customer accounts		25,600		484,200
3/29/2016	Recovery			14,000	470,200
3/31/2016	March sales		636,250		1,106,450
3/31/2016	March collections			314,800	791,650

Assignment Memo

> To: Junior Accountant
> From: Zach Barnes, Accounts Receivable Clerk
> Re: Assignment of Accounts Receivable
> Date: March 29, 2016
>
> Per instructions of the controller, we have finalized the assignment of the following accounts receivables and made the required adjustments to the subsidiary accounts receivable ledger:
> 3/29/16: Transferred accounts receivable with a net realization value of $20,000 for $17,000 to Fastcash Finance Company. Fastcash withheld $2,000 from the proceeds for projected future reductions. We have surrendered control of these receivables.
>
> -Zach

Sales Report

Sportsman Company	
Monthly Sales Report- March, 2016	
Cash sales	$360,850
Credit sales	$275,400
Total gross sales	$636,250
Less: sales returns	($12,000)
Net sales	$648,250

I was told that the sales returns were all on credit sales - JA.

Cash Receipts Report

Sportsman Company	
Cash Receipts Report - March, 2016	
Cash sales	$360,850
Collections on credit sales	$314,800
Total cash receipts	$675,650

Email from Credit Manager

From:	mvisalia@sportsman.com
Sent:	March 29, 20X6
To:	'jr.accountant@highsteppers.com'
Subject:	Inventory questions

Hello Junior Accountant:

Per your question regarding customer write-offs, our policy is to write off bad debt when the account is placed in collection. We would rather do that than carry an inflated A/R balance and see our Days Sales Outstanding numbers suffer. In other words, it keeps the A/R balance clean and meaningful. We can always recover accounts that do end up getting collected.

For your reference, that's just one approach. Other companies might wait until they actually receive written notice from the collection agency that an account proves uncollectible, or until the customer files for bankruptcy, or the company's lawyers advise of a possible write-off situation, or what have you. There is the argument that, if you're too quick to write off an account, it goes 'out of sight out of mind' and the company has less pressure to either collect on that account or ensure new customers are creditworthy.

Anyway, since the weekend is upon us, I can tell you that for March accounts placed into collection totaled $25,600 and recoveries totaled $14,000. The latter is just for one account where the customer called and promised they're going to pay and assured us they will pay very soon. We believe them, so we consider it a recovery, but we haven't actually collected on the account yet. We're not going to tell you to write off or recover any accounts on Saturday or Sunday, haha. Enjoy your weekend!
McKenzie

McKenzie Visalia, Credit Manager
Sportsman Company
mvisalia@sportsman.com

Excerpt from Board Meeting Minutes

Sportsman Company
Minutes of Special Meeting of March 22, 20X6

Members Present: All seven members present.

Agenda items:
1. Approval of agreement to a settlement in product liability suit against the Company by A.C. Sident.
2. Motion to deem $12,500 loan to Teresa Sconder, former officer of the Company, uncollectible.
3. Approval of new business casual dress code for Company headquarters.

Actions taken:
1. Agenda item #1 not approved.
2. Agenda item #2 approved.
3. Agenda item #3 approved by majority.

Receivables
Section 10

Items for Analysis

The 22 March sales return credit entry of $1,200 is correct.

1. Choose an option below:
   - [Original text] The 22 March sales return credit entry of $1,200 is correct.
   - [Delete text]
   - The 22 March sales return entry should be a debit entry of $1,200.
   - The 22 March sales return entry should be a debit entry of $14,000.
   - The 22 March sales return entry should be a credit entry of $14,000.
   - The 22 March sales return entry should be a debit entry of $12,000.
   - The 22 March sales return entry should be a credit entry of $12,000.
   - The 22 March sales return entry should be removed.

The 25 March officer loan write-off credit entry of $12,500 is correct.

2. Choose an option below:
   - [Original text] The 25 March officer loan write-off credit entry of $12,500 is correct.
   - [Delete text]
   - The 25 March officer loan write-off should be a debit entry of $12,500.
   - The 25 March officer loan write-off should be dated 22 March.
   - The 25 March officer loan write-off should be removed because the loan should be turned over to a collection agency before being deemed uncollectible.
   - The 25 March officer loan write-off should be removed.

The 29 March assignment credit entry of $17,000 is correct.

3. Choose an option below:
   - [Original text] The 29 March assignment credit entry of $17,000 is correct.
   - [Delete text]
   - The 29 March assignment entry should be a debit entry of $17,000.
   - The 29 March assignment entry should be a credit entry of $18,000.
   - The 29 March assignment entry should be a debit entry of $18,000.
   - The 29 March assignment entry should be a credit entry of $20,000.
   - The 29 March assignment entry should be a debit entry of $20,000.
   - The 29 March assignment entry should be removed.

The 29 March customer account write-off debit entry of $25,600 is correct.

4. Choose an option below:
   - [Original text] The 29 March customer account write-off debit entry of $25,600 is correct.
   - [Delete text]
   - The 29 March customer account write-off entry should be a credit entry of $25,600.
   - The 29 March customer account write-off entry should be a debit entry of $14,000.
   - The 29 March customer account write-off entry should be a credit entry of $14,000.
   - The 29 March customer account write-off entry should be removed.

The 29 March customer account recovery credit entry of $14,000 is correct.

5. Choose an option below:
   - [Original text] The 29 March customer account recovery credit entry of $14,000 is correct.
   - [Delete text]
   - The 29 March customer account recovery entry should be a debit entry of $14,000.
   - The 29 March customer account recovery entry should be a credit entry of $25,600.
   - The 29 March customer account recovery entry should be a debit entry of $25,600.
   - The 29 March customer account recovery entry should be a credit entry of $25,600.
   - The 29 March customer account recovery entry should be removed until the customer begins paying on the account.
   - The 29 March customer account recovery entry should be removed.

The 31 March credit sales debit entry of $636,250 is correct.

6. Choose an option below:
   - [Original text] The 31 March credit sales debit entry of $636,250 is correct.
   - [Delete text]
   - The 31 March credit sales entry should be a credit entry of $636,250.
   - The 31 March credit sales entry should be a debit entry of $275,400.
   - The 31 March credit sales entry should be a debit entry of $263,400.
   - The 31 March credit sales entry should be a debit entry of $314,800.

Receivables   Section 10

The 31 March collections credit entry of $314,800 is correct.

7. Choose an option below:
   - [Original text] The 31 March credit sales debit entry of $314,800 is correct.
   - [Delete text]
   - The 31 March credit sales entry should be a debit entry of $314,800.
   - The 31 March credit sales entry should be a credit entry of $275,400.
   - The 31 March credit sales entry should be a credit entry of $263,400.
   - The 31 March credit sales entry should be a credit entry of $360,850.

The March ending balance of $791,650 is correct.

8. Choose an option below:
   - [Original text] The March ending balance of $791,650 is correct.
   - [Delete text]
   - The March ending balance should be $406,300.
   - The March ending balance should be $409,300.
   - The March ending balance should be $383,800.
   - The March ending balance should be $392,300.

DOCUMENT REVIEW SIMULATION SOLUTION

Document Review Simulation Solution 1

1. <u>The 22 March sales return entry should be a credit entry of $12,000.</u>

   The Sales Report document shows credit sales returns of $12,000. When credit sales are returned, there will be a **credit** to A/R, decreasing the A/R balance, and a debit to Sales returns and allowances, a contra-sales account. There will also be entry increasing Inventory and decreasing cost of sales. Junior Accountant had mistakenly entered the sales return amount as a debit of $1,200.

2. <u>The 25 March officer loan write-off should be removed.</u>

   A loan receivable from an officer is not part of trade accounts receivable. The credit of $12,500 should be charged against the loan receivable account and a loss recorded. The write-off of the loan will have no impact on the A/R balance.

3. <u>The 29 March assignment entry should be a credit entry of $20,000.</u>

   The assignment is treated as a sale of the accounts receivables, since control is given up. The journal entry is as follows:

Cash	15,000	
Due from factor	2,000	
Loss on sale of receivable	3,000	
Accounts receivable		20,000

4. <u>The 29 March customer account write-off entry should be a credit entry of $25,600.</u>

   The email from the credit manager states that customer write-offs for March amounted to $25,600. When an account is written off, there is a debit to either Bad debt expense or Allowance for Uncollectible Accounts, with a corresponding **credit** entry to Accounts Receivable. Junior Accountant had incorrectly entered a debit to Accounts Receivable.

5. <u>The 29 March customer account recovery entry should be a debit entry of $14,000.</u>

   The email from the credit manager states that one account, in the amount of $14,000, needed to be recovered, but no actual collections had yet been made on the account. That means there should simply be a debit entry in the amount of $14,000 to record the account being reinstated as a receivable and a credit to the allowance account. Junior Accountant had incorrectly entered a credit to A/R.

6. The 31 March credit sales entry should be a debit entry of $275,400.

    The Sales Report shows that credit sales for March were $275,400. Credit sales returns are handled in a separate entry.

Cash	360,850	
Accounts receivable	275,400	
Sales		636,250

7. Keep original text: 31 March collections credit entry of $314,800 is correct.

    The Cash Receipts Report shows that March cash collections were indeed $314,800.

8. The March ending balance should be $406,300.

    After accounting for March's transactions, the ending balance should be $406,300:

Account: Accounts Receivable				Account Number : 120	
Date	Description	Post Ref.	Debit	Credit	Balance
3/1/2016	Beginning balance				489,300
3/22/2016	Sales return			12,000	477,300
3/25/2016	Write-off officer loan		N/A	N/A	477,300
3/29/2015	Assignment			20,000	457,300
3/29/2016	Write-off customer			25,600	431,700
3/29/2016	Recovery		14,000		445,700
3/31/2016	March sales		275,400		721,100
3/31/2016	March collections			314,800	$ 406,300

Section 11 – Bonds & Present Value Tables

Corresponding Lectures

Watch the following course lectures with this section:

Lecture 11.01 – Bond Terminology
Lecture 11.02 – Present Value Tables – Time Value of Money
Lecture 11.03 – Issuance of Bonds – Journal Entry
Lecture 11.04 – Bond Retirement
Lecture 11.05 – Bonds – Class Questions
Lecture 11.06 – Bonds with Detachable Warrants
Lecture 11.07 – Bonds with Warrants – Class Questions
Lecture 11.08 – Bonds under IFRS
Lecture 11.09 – Bonds under IFRS – Class Questions
Lecture 11.10 – Bond TBS – Class Questions

EXAM NOTE: Please refer to the AICPA FAR Blueprint in the Introduction to find a listing of the representative tasks (and their associated skill levels—i.e., Remembering and Understanding, Application, and Analysis) that the candidate should be able to perform based on the knowledge obtained in this section.

Bonds & Present Value Tables

Lecture 11.01
BOND TERMINOLOGY

A bond is a borrowing agreement in which the issuer promises to repay a certain amount of money (Face/Par value) to the purchaser, after a certain period of time (term), at a certain interest rate (Effective, Yield, Market rate). This is covered by ASC 470/835.

- **Term bond** – a bond that will pay the entire principal upon maturity at the end of the term
- **Serial bond** – a bond in which the principal matures in installments.
- **Debenture bonds** – unsecured bonds that are not supported by any collateral.
- **Stated, face, coupon, nominal rate** – the rate printed on the bond. Represents the amount of cash the investor will receive every payment.
- **Carrying amount** – this is the net amount at which the bond is being reported on the issuer's balance sheet, and equals the face value of the bond plus the **premium** (when the bond was issued above face value) or minus the **discount** (when the bond was issued below face value) and minus any **bond issue costs**. It is also called the book value or reported amount. It will initially be the same as issue price, net of issue costs, but gradually approaches the face value as time passes, since the premium or discount and the bond issue costs are amortized as an adjustment to interest expense over the life of the bond.
- **Effective rate**, Yield, Market Interest rate – this is the actual rate of interest the issuer is paying on the bond based on the issue price. The effective rate is often called the market rate of interest or yield.
- When the bond is issued at a **premium**, the effective rate of interest will be lower than the stated rate, since the cash interest and principal repayment are based on face value, but the company actually received more money than that.
- When the bond is issued at a **discount**, the effective rate of interest will be higher than the stated rate, since the issuer must pay cash interest and principal based on a higher amount than the funds actually received upon issuance.
- **Convertible bond** – a bond that is convertible into common stock of the debtor at the bondholder's option.
- **Callable bond** – a bond which the issuer has the right to redeem prior to its maturity date.
- **Covenants** – restrictions that borrowers must often agree to.

When an entity issues bonds, or incurs any debt, it may incur costs in the form of fees paid to a financial institution, sometimes referred to as "points" or other fees, to an attorney for drawing up documents, or to regulators or others in order to be able to print up and issue its bonds. These costs, referred to as issue costs, are treated as a contra-liability, reducing the carrying value of the debt. Issue costs are amortized with the amortization treated as an adjustment to interest expense.

FASB ASC Topic 825 (Financial Instruments) provides that a company may elect the fair value option for reporting financial assets and financial liabilities. If the fair value option is elected for a financial liability (bonds), the requirements of FASB ASC 470 no longer apply. Instead, the financial liability is reported at fair value at the end of each reporting period, and the resulting gain or loss is reported in earnings of the period.

Section 11 — Bonds & Present Value Tables

If an entity does not elect the fair value option, the bond is recorded at its issue price, and the effective interest method is used to amortize any premium or discount on the bond and any bond issuance costs. The remainder of this section will focus on the pricing of the bond using the effective interest method of amortizing a bond as required by FASB ASC 470.

Issuance of Bonds (example)

Face value of bonds	$1,000,000
Term	5 years
Stated interest rate	8%
Effective rate/Market rate/Yield	a) 8%, b) 10%, c) 6% (3 examples)

a. Bond issued at **Par value** where market rate of interest (8%) equals the stated rate (8%).

```
Cash                        1,000,000
    Bonds Payable                       1,000,000
```

Each year interest will be paid for $1,000,000 (face) x 8% (stated rate) = $80,000 per year

```
Interest expense               80,000
    Cash                                   80,000
```

b. Bond issued at a discount, since the stated rate of 8% is lower than the market rate of 10%, the only reason an investor would purchase this bond is if it would effectively yield 10%. In order to do so, the issuer must sell the bond at a **DISCOUNT** (the actual cash proceeds must be precisely computed using present value factors and are only estimated in this journal entry).

```
Cash                          900,000
Discount                      100,000
    Bonds Payable                      1,000,000
```

The **discount must be amortized** over the life of the bond. Let's assume we are using straight-line amortization of $20,000 year (100/5yrs=20).

```
Interest expense              100,000
    Discount                               20,000
    Cash                                   80,000
```

c. Bond issued for a premium, since the stated rate of 8% is higher than the Market rate of 6%. Investors are paying a **PREMIUM** to acquire this bond (the actual cash proceeds must be precisely computed using present value factors and are only estimated in this journal entry).

```
Cash                        1,100,000
    Premium                               100,000
    Bonds Payable                       1,000,000
```

Bonds & Present Value Tables   Section 11

The premium must be amortized over the life of the bond. (100/5=20)

Interest expense	60,000	
Premium	20,000	
Cash		80,000

The next consideration is how to calculate the proceeds from the issuance of the bonds. The above examples assumed the proceeds were given at 900,000 to 1,100,000. To calculate the **Present Value of the proceeds** two amounts need to be P.V.
- **PV of the Face** of the bonds (Face x P.V. of a lump sum using the effective interest rate)
- **PV of the interest** as an annuity (Face x stated rate x time = interest x PV of an Ordinary annuity at the effective interest rate)
    - The sum of these two amounts represents the PV of the bonds.
    - If *semi-annual* interest is being paid, take the years x 2 and the interest rate/2
        - Ex. 5 yr bonds at 10% semi-annual. Use the PV table for 10 periods @ 5%.

In some circumstances, a problem will not require the use of present value to calculate the proceeds from issuance. It may instead express the sales price of the bond in terms of a **percentage of face value**.
- When bonds are issued at *101*, for example, the proceeds would be 101% of face value.
- If they are issued at *98*, the proceeds would be 98% of face value.

Lecture 11.02

Present Value Tables - Time Value of Money (ASC 835)

To determine the exact selling price of a bond requires the use of present value concepts. Money that is received at a future date is less valuable than money received immediately, and present value concepts relate future cash flows to the equivalent present dollars. Present value is defined as the current measure of an estimated future cash inflow or outflow, discounted at an interest rate for the number of periods between today and the date of the estimated cash flow. Many decisions require adjustments related to the time value of money:
- **Present Value of Amount (lump sum)** – this is used to examine a single cash flow that will occur at a future date and determine its equivalent value today. The amount you need to invest today, for how many years, at what interest rate, to get $1 back in the future.
- **Present Value of Ordinary Annuity** – this refers to repeated cash flows on a systematic basis, with amounts being paid at the *end* of each period (it may also be known as an *annuity in arrears*). Bond interest payments are commonly made at the end of each period and use these factors.
- **Present Value of Annuity Due (Now)** – this refers to repeated cash flows on a systematic basis, with amounts being paid at the *beginning* of each period (it may also be known as an *annuity in advance* or special annuity). Rent payments are commonly made at the beginning of each period and use these factors.
- **Future Values (compound interest)** – these look at cash flows and project them to some future date, and include all three variations applicable to present values. This is the amount that would accumulate at a future point in time if $1 were invested now. The future value factor is equal to 1 divided by the present value factor. For example, an investment of $10,000 in two years at 10% would accumulate to the principal multiplied by the future value factor. In this case the $10,000 × 1/0.8265 = $12,100.

Present and Future Value Tables*

Future Value (Amount) of $1

(n) Periods	6%	8%	10%	12%	15%
1	1.060	1.080	1.100	1.120	1.150
2	1.124	1.166	1.210	1.254	1.323
3	1.191	1.260	1.331	1.405	1.521
4	1.262	1.360	1.464	1.574	1.749
5	1.338	1.469	1.611	1.762	2.011
10	1.791	2.159	2.594	3.106	4.046
15	2.397	3.172	4.177	5.474	8.137
20	3.207	4.661	6.728	9.646	16.367
30	5.743	10.063	17.449	29.960	66.212
40	10.286	21.725	45.259	93.051	267.864

Present Value of $1

(n) Periods	6%	8%	10%	12%	15%
1	0.943	0.926	0.909	0.893	0.870
2	0.890	0.857	0.826	0.797	0.756
3	0.840	0.794	0.751	0.712	0.658
4	0.792	0.735	0.683	0.636	0.572
5	0.747	0.681	0.621	0.567	0.497
10	0.558	0.463	0.386	0.322	0.247
15	0.417	0.315	0.239	0.183	0.123
20	0.312	0.215	0.149	0.104	0.061
30	0.174	0.099	0.057	0.334	0.015
40	0.097	0.046	0.022	0.011	0.004

Future Value (Amount) of an Ordinary Annuity of $1

(n) Periods	6%	8%	10%	12%	15%
1	1.000	1.000	1.000	1.000	1.000
2	2.060	2.080	2.100	2.120	2.150
3	3.184	3.246	3.310	3.374	3.473
4	4.375	4.506	4.641	4.779	4.993
5	5.637	5.867	6.105	6.353	6.742
10	13.180	14.486	15.937	17.549	20.304
15	23.276	27.152	31.772	37.280	47.580
20	36.786	45.762	57.275	72.052	102.444
30	79.058	113.283	164.494	241.333	434.745
40	154.762	259.056	442.592	767.091	1779.090

Present Value of an Ordinary Annuity of $1

(n) Periods	6%	8%	10%	12%	15%
1	0.943	0.926	0.909	0.893	0.870
2	1.833	1.783	1.736	1.690	1.626
3	2.673	2.577	2.487	2.402	2.283
4	3.465	3.312	3.170	3.037	2.855
5	4.212	3.993	3.791	3.605	3.352
10	7.360	6.710	6.144	5.650	5.019
15	9.712	8.559	7.606	6.811	5.847
20	11.470	9.818	8.514	7.469	6.259
30	13.765	11.258	9.427	8.055	6.566
40	15.046	11.924	9.779	8.243	6.642

Present Value of an Annuity Due of $1

(n) Periods	6%	8%	10%	12%	15%
1	1.000	1.000	1.000	1.000	1.000
2	1.943	1.926	1.909	1.893	1.870
3	2.833	2.783	2.736	2.690	2.626
4	3.673	3.577	3.487	3.402	3.855
5	4.465	4.312	4.170	4.037	3.855
10	7.802	7.247	6.759	6.328	5.772
15	10.295	9.244	8.367	7.628	6.724
20	12.158	10.604	9.365	8.366	7.198
30	14.591	12.158	10.370	9.022	7.550
40	15.949	12.879	10.757	9.233	7.638

* All values rounded to the nearest thousandth of a percent

Converting From One Annuity to Another:

In some cases, when attempting to determine the present value of a stream of interest payments, an ordinary annuity, the only table available may be for an annuity due. To determine the present value of the ordinary annuity, either:
- Use the factor for 1 more period and subtract 1.0 from it, or
- Use the factor for the appropriate number of periods and divide it by 1 + the interest rate
    - The factor for an ordinary annuity for 4 years at 8% is 3.312.
    - This can be derived by using the factor for 5 years for an annuity due, 4.312, and subtracting 1.0 to get 3.312
    - This can also be derived by dividing the factor for an annuity due of 4 years, 3.577, by 1 + the interest rate, or 1.08, to get 3.312

In other cases, when attempting to determine the present value of a stream of rent payments, an annuity due, the only table available may be for an ordinary annuity. To determine the present value of the annuity due, either:
- Use the factor for 1 less period and add 1.0 to it, or
- Use the factor for the appropriate number of periods and multiply it by 1 + the interest rate
    - The factor for an ordinary annuity for 4 years at 8% is 3.577.
    - This can be derived by using the factor for 3 years for an ordinary annuity, 2.577, and adding 1.0 to get 3.577
    - This can also be derived by multiplying the factor for an ordinary annuity of 4 years, 3.312, by 1 + the interest rate, or 1.08, to get 3.577

Actual factors for $1 are typically provided in tables to be multiplied by the cash flows in exam problems.

Example, assume that a company can earn 10% on its money. If it had to wait one year to receive a dollar, that would be the equivalent to them of 91 cents today (rounding all information to the nearest penny). The reason is that 91 cents invested at 10% would earn approximately 9 cents over the next year, and become a dollar. The way this relationship is expressed is by saying that the present value of 1 at 10% for 1 period = 0.91.

For multiple years at 10%, the factors (rounded) are:

Years	Factor
1	0.91
2	0.83
3	0.75
4	0.68
5	0.62
Ordinary Annuity	**3.79**

An ordinary annuity refers to payments being made at the end of each period, and is simply the sum of the value of each of the payments. In the above, the present value of an ordinary annuity of 1 at 10% for 5 periods = 3.79, meaning that getting one dollar each year for the next 5 years is the equivalent of getting $3.79 immediately. Another way to express it is to say that a person who paid $3.79 today to obtain an annuity of $1 per year for the next 5 years is earning a 10% rate of return on their investment.

Bonds & Present Value Tables

Section 11

Assume the following facts on the issuance of a single bond:

Face Value	$1,000
Stated Rate	8%
Effective Rate	10%
Issue Date	1/1/X1
Pay Dates for Interest	12/31
Due Date for Principal	12/31/X5
PV of 1 at 10% for 5 periods	0.62
PV of ordinary annuity at 10% for 5 periods	3.79

To determine the selling price of this term bond on 1/1/X1, the interest payments of $1,000 x 8% = $80 per year and the principal payment of $1,000 due in 5 years will be discounted at the effective rate of return of 10%, as follows:

Item	Amount	PV Factor	Present Value
Principal	$1,000	0.62	$620
Interest (Annuity)	$80	3.79	$304
Total			$924

Notice that, as expected, the selling price of the bond is less than face value, because the effective rate of interest of 10% exceeds the stated rate of 8%.

The entry to record the issuance is as follows:

1/1/X1	Cash	924	
	Unamortized discount	76	
	Bond payable		1,000

Occasionally, a company will issue a zero-coupon bond, which refers to a bond that pays no periodic interest (0% coupon rate of interest). The bondholder only receives the face value of the bond at maturity.

Lecture 11.03

Journal Entry at Issuance (with BIC and Accrued Interest)

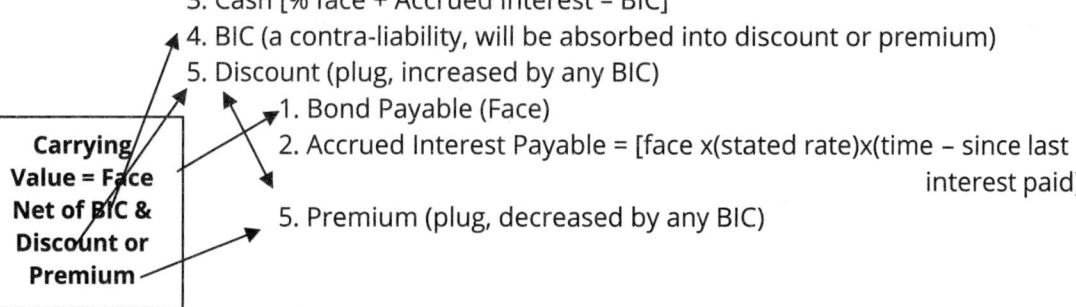

3. Cash [% face + Accrued Interest – BIC]
4. BIC (a contra-liability, will be absorbed into discount or premium)
5. Discount (plug, increased by any BIC)
   1. Bond Payable (Face)
   2. Accrued Interest Payable = [face x(stated rate)x(time – since last interest paid)
5. Premium (plug, decreased by any BIC)

Carrying Value = Face Net of BIC & Discount or Premium

Note: The carrying value **(CV)** of the bonds is Bonds Payable (1), net of the discount or premium (5), and net of BIC (4).

The bond payable is reported in **noncurrent liabilities**, net of bond issue costs and either net of unamortized discount or including unamortized premium.

The FASB has not yet provided practical guidance for recording BIC given the requirements of ASU 2015-03. It is unlikely that BIC will be tested closely on the exam before such guidance is provided. Just in case, here are examples of how BIC would most likely be recorded at issuance:

Example: BIC and Discount

Roger Co. issues $1,000,000 in 3% 10-year bonds when the market rate of interest is 5%. Bond issue costs are $20,000. Interest is paid annually, and there is no accrued interest.

Present value of lump sum at 5% after 10 periods: 0.6139

Present value of ordinary annuity at 5% over 10 periods: 7.7217

The cash proceeds will be (($1,000,000 x 0.6139) + ($30,000 x 7.7217)), or $845,551.

The discount is $1,000,000 - $845,551, or $154,449. Instead of the $20,000 in BIC being entered as a separate debit, it will be added to the discount amount, causing the discount to be reported as $154,449 + $20,000, or $174,449. This will balance because the $20,000 cash paid in BIC reduces the cash proceeds by $20,000, to $845,551 - $20,000, or $825,551.

Journal entry at issuance:

Cash, net of BIC paid	825,551	
Discount including BIC	174,449	
Bonds payable		1,000,000

Example: BIC and Premium

Roger Co. issues $1,000,000 in 5% 10-year bonds when the market rate of interest is 3%. Bond issue costs are $20,000. Interest is paid annually, and there is no accrued interest.

Present value of lump sum at 3% after 10 periods: 0.74409

Present value of ordinary annuity at 3% over 10 periods: 8.5302

The cash proceeds will be (($1,000,000 x 0.7441) + ($50,000 x 8.5302)), or $1,170,610.

The premium is $1,170,610 - $1,000,000, or $170,610. Instead of the $20,000 in BIC being entered as a debit, it will be netted against the premium amount, causing the premium to be reported as $170,610 - $20,000, or $150,610. This will balance because the $20,000 cash paid in BIC reduces the cash proceeds by $20,000, to $1,170,610 - 20,000, or $1,150,610.

Journal entry at issuance:

Cash, net of BIC paid	1,150,610	
Premium, net of BIC		150,610
Bonds payable		1,000,000

Accrued Interest Payable

A bond isn't always sold when it is dated. The 8% bond dated 1/1/X1 in our earlier example might, for example, not be issued to the public until 4/1/X1. Even so, interest accrues from the date on the bond, so the buyer is immediately credited for 3 months of interest ($1,000 x 8% x 3/12 of a year = $20), and will receive a full year of interest ($1,000 x 8% = $80) on 12/31/X1. To be equitable, the buyer will be required to pay an additional $20 on 4/1/X1 when purchasing the bond, and the issuer will report the amount as accrued interest payable, reported as a current liability. Assume, for this example that the bond itself sells for 93. The entry to record the issuance on 4/1/X1 is:

4/1/X1	Cash	950	
	Unamortized discount	70	
	Bonds payable		1000
	Accrued interest payable		20

The bond payable will be reported at $1,000 - $70 = $930. Notice that the reported amount refers to the carrying value of the bond, and is equal to the face value of the bond payable plus the unamortized premium or minus the unamortized discount. Accrued interest, like deferred bond issue costs, is not included in the carrying value of the bond.

Bond Issue Costs (BIC)

Bond Issue costs (BIC) – costs directly associated with the issuance of the bonds are a deduction from the carrying amount *(Contra Liability) of the bonds* and are amortized over the period of time the bonds are outstanding using the effective interest method. As a general rule, BIC are amortized, along with discount or premium, as an adjustment to interest expense. BIC may include:
- Printing and engraving of the bond certificates
- Legal and accounting fees
- Underwriter commissions
- Promotion costs (printing the prospectus)

Due to the simplification initiative, BIC had been recognized as a deferred charge thus creating different balance sheet presentation requirements for debt discounts, premiums and issue costs. As shown in the examples above, BIC will most likely be added to a discount or netted against premium, then amortized along with the discount or premium using the effective interest method. By simplifying it, it eliminated the conflicts with FASB concept statement No. 6, Elements of F/S and also more aligns BIC with the IFRS requirements.

As mentioned earlier, the discount or premium may be amortized over the time period that the bonds are *outstanding* using the straight-line method (not GAAP), or the effective interest method (interest method). The Interest method is preferred and is GAAP. The Straight line method may be used only if it is not materially different from the effective interest method.

Discount Amortization

Face	-	Discount	=	CV	x	Effective interest rate	-	Interest expense	(face x stated x time) cash payment		Amortization of Discount
$1,000,000	-	100,000	=	900,000	x	10%	=	90,000	-	80,000 =	10,000
	-	10,000		+10,000							
1,000,000	-	90,000	=	910,000	x	10%	=	91,000	-	80,000 =	11,000
	-	11,000	=	+11,000							
1,000,000	-	79,000	=	921,000	x	10%					

JE 1)   Interest expense   90,000
            Discount   10,000
            Cash   80,000

JE 2)   Interest expense   91,000
            Discount   11,000
            Cash   80,000

Note: When amortizing a discount, the interest expense increases each year, and the amortization of the discount increases each year.

Premium Amortization

Face	+	Premium	=	CV	x	Effective interest rate	-	Interest expense	(face x stated x time) cash payment		Amortization of Premium
$1,000,000	+	100,000	=	1,100,000	x	6%	=	66,000	-	80,000 =	14,000
	-	14,000		-14,000							
1,000,000	+	86,000	=	1,086,000	x	6%	=	65,000	-	80,000 =	15,000
	-	15,000	=	-15,000							
1,000,000	+	71,000	=	1,071,000	x	6%					

JE 1)   Interest expense   66,000
            Premium   14,000
            Cash   80,000

JE 2)   Interest expense   65,000
            Premium   15,000
            Cash   80,000

Note: when amortizing a premium, the interest expense decreases each year, but the amortization of the premium increases each year.

Bonds & Present Value Tables — Section 11

Lecture 11.04

Bond Retirement

Bonds may be called or retired prior to maturity. When this happens, it is reported as a gain/loss on the issuer's income statement. Pursuant to FASB ASC 470, it will be classified as part of continuing operations. The journal entry is basically the opposite of the original issuance. The plug to balance the entry is **gain/loss**.

Bonds Payable (face)	X	
Premium (unamortized)	X	
Loss (plug)	X	
BIC (unamortized)		X
Discount (unamortized)		X
Cash (amount to retire)		X
Gain (plug)		X

Bond Sinking Funds

A fund set up for the retirement of bonds. The balance is treated as a noncurrent asset until the bonds mature. Any interest or dividends earned are added to the sinking fund balance and reported as income.

Lecture 11.05

CLASS QUESTIONS

Please see the Class Questions and Class Solutions for this Lecture at the end of this Section.

Lecture 11.06

Bonds with Detachable Stock Purchase Warrants (2 Securities)

A warrant is a security that can be sold or exercised by the bondholder, while still keeping the bond. Since it is separable, it is as if two securities were issued, therefore a value must be given to both securities. The value for the warrant is included in APIC.
- If the FMV of both securities is known, the **relative FMV approach** is used.
- If the FMV of only one security is known, the other is a Plug.
- The amount for warrants is recorded in **APIC-Warrants**.
- If *Non-detachable* stock purchase warrants, no separate value is given
- If the warrants expire, close them out into APIC.

Ex: $800 par value of bonds with warrants is issued for $900. The relative FMV of bonds to warrants is 80% bonds, 20% warrants.

Bonds with Warrants
-FMV of Bond WITHOUT warrant
-FMV of Warrants
Total FMV

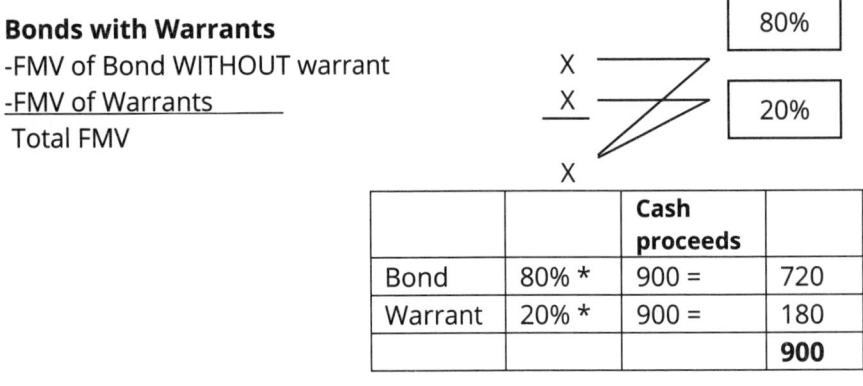

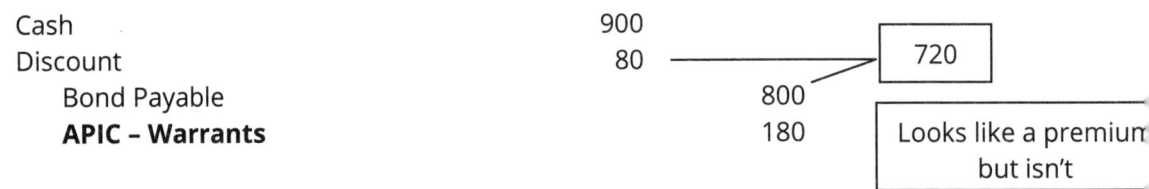

		Cash proceeds	
Bond	80% *	900 =	720
Warrant	20% *	900 =	180
			900

Cash	900	
Discount	80	720
Bond Payable		800
APIC – Warrants		180 → Looks like a premium but isn't

Disclosures should be made regarding the combined aggregate amount of maturities and sinking fund requirements for all long-term-borrowings for each of the **next 5 years** and in the aggregate.

Lecture 11.07

CLASS QUESTIONS

Please see the Class Questions and Class Solutions for this Lecture at the end of this Section.

Lecture 11.08

BONDS UNDER IFRS

IFRS does not differentiate bonds from other financial liabilities. Like other financial liabilities, and similar to bonds accounted for under US GAAP, bonds are accounted for at **amortized cost** using the **effective interest method**. The straight-line method of amortization may NOT be used.

The entity may, in certain circumstances, irrevocably elect to recognize the financial liability at fair value through profit or loss (FVTPL). If that election is not made, however:
- The bond is initially recognized at its fair value minus transaction costs that are directly attributable to the issuance.
- In most cases, the transaction price is assumed to be fair value.
  - If fair value is determined using a quoted market price in an active market for an identical liability, differences from transaction price are recognized as gain or loss.
  - In all other cases, any differences are deferred by reducing the carrying amount of the liability and including them in the calculation of the effective interest rate in applying the effective interest method.

A bond may be recognized at **fair value through profit or loss (FVTPL)** when it will result in more relevant information. This would be the case if it eliminates a measurement or recognition inconsistency (an accounting mismatch) or if the bond is part of a group of financial instruments that are managed and evaluated based on fair values. When the entity elects to report a bond payable at fair value through profit or loss:
- The liability is adjusted to its **fair value** on each reporting date.
- Any increase or decrease in fair value is recognized in **profit or loss**.

A bond is derecognized, or removed from the statement of financial position only when the obligation is discharged or cancelled. Any difference between the carrying amount of the liability and the consideration paid upon settlement is recognized in profit or loss.

Bonds	
GAAP	**IFRS**
• Straight-line method of amortization may be used, if results do not materially differ from effective interest method.	• Straight-line method of amortization is not allowed.

Lecture 11.09

CLASS QUESTIONS

Please see the Class Questions and Class Solutions for this Lecture at the end of this Section.

Lecture 11.10

CLASS QUESTIONS

Please see the Class Questions and Class Solutions for this Lecture at the end of this Section.

CLASS QUESTIONS

Work through the below Class Questions while following along with the respective lectures. Once this is complete, you can begin independently practicing what you've learned by quizzing yourself on this course section in your Interactive Practice Questions (IPQ), which can be found in your online Student Dashboard. Your IPQ simulates the computer-based testing experience, and will also help you understand how concepts are applied to the exam. Each question includes answer explanations from expert CPAs that will help you determine why you answered a question correctly or incorrectly. This is key to your success on the CPA Exam.

Lecture 11.05

1. Hancock Co.'s December 31, 20X3 balance sheet contained the following items in the long-term liabilities section:

    Unsecured
    9.375% registered bonds ($25,000 maturing annually beginning in 20X7) $275,000
    11.5% convertible bonds, callable beginning in 20X11, due 20X23 $125,000

    Secured
    9.875% guaranty security bonds, due 20X23 $275,000
    10.0% commodity backed bonds ($50,000 maturing annually beginning in 20X8) $200,000

    What are the total amounts of serial bonds and debenture bonds?

	Serial bonds	Debenture bonds
a.	$ 475,000	$400,000
b.	$ 475,000	$125,000
c.	$ 450,000	$400,000
d.	$ 200,000	$650,000

2. On June 30, 20X3, King Co. had outstanding 9%, $5,000,000 face value bonds maturing on June 30, 20X8. Interest was payable semiannually every June 30 and December 31. King did not elect the fair value option for reporting its financial liabilities. On June 30, 20X3, after amortization was recorded for the period, the unamortized bond premium and bond issue costs were $30,000 and $50,000 respectively. On that date, King acquired all its outstanding bonds on the open market at 98 and retired them. At June 30, 20X3, what amount should King recognize as gain before income taxes on redemption of bonds?

    a. $ 20,000
    b. $ 80,000
    c. $120,000
    d. $180,000

Bonds & Present Value Tables   Section 11

3. The following information pertains to Camp Corp.'s issuance of bonds on July 1, 20X3:

Face amount	$800,000
Term	Ten years
Stated interest rate	6%
Interest payment dates	Annually on July 1
Yield	9%

	At 6%	At 9%
Present value of one for ten periods	0.558	0.422
Future value of one for ten periods	1.791	2.367
Present value of ordinary annuity of one for ten periods	7.360	6.418

What should be the issue price for each $1,000 bond?

a. $1,000
b. $ 864
c. $ 807
d. $ 700

Lecture 11.07

4. On January 1, year 1, Boston Group issued $100,000 par value, 5% five-year bonds when the market rate of interest was 8%. Interest is payable annually on December 31. The following present value information is available:

	5%	8%
Present value of $1 (n = 5)	0.78353	0.68058
Present value of an ordinary annuity (n = 5)	4.32948	3.99271

What amount is the value of net bonds payable at the end of year 1?

a. $88,022
b. $90,064
c. $100,000
d. $110,638

5. On December 30, 20X3, Fort, Inc. issued 1,000 of its 8%, ten-year, $1,000 face value bonds with detachable stock warrants at par. Each bond carried a detachable warrant for one share of Fort's common stock at a specified option price of $25 per share. Immediately after issuance, the market value of the bonds without the warrants was $1,080,000 and the market value of the warrants was $120,000. In its December 31, 20X3 balance sheet, what amount should Fort report as bonds payable?

a. $1,000,000
b. $ 975,000
c. $ 900,000
d. $ 880,000

Lecture 11.09

6. Roger Corp issued corporate bonds on January 25th for $1,000,000. Roger reports their financial statements in accordance with IFRS. What valuation method should Roger use to report their bonds on their statement of financial position at year end?
   a. Amortized cost only
   b. Fair value method only
   c. Fair value through profit or loss only
   d. Either Amortized cost or Fair value through profit or loss

7. On January 3, 20X2, Europa, Ltd. Invested $198,000 in 6% bonds with a face value of $300,00 that mature on December 31, 20X20 and pay interest annually on December 31 each year. Europa intends to hold the bond for the purpose of collecting the scheduled cash flows and expects to earn a 10% rate of return. At December 31, 20X2, the bonds had a fair value of $205,000. Europa prepares its financial statements in accordance with IFRS and did not elect to carry the investment at fair value through profit and loss. What amount or amounts will Europa report in its income statement for the year ended December 31, 20X2 and what will be the carrying value of the investment at December 31, 20X2?

   a. Interest income of $18,000 and a gain of $7,000 with carrying value of $205,000.
   b. Interest income of $19,800 with a carrying value of $199,800.
   c. Interest income of $19,800 and a gain of $5,200 with a carrying value of $205,000.
   d. A gain of $7,000 with a carrying value of $205,000.

CLASS SOLUTIONS

1. (a) Serial bonds include those that require periodic principal payments, including the 9.375% unsecured registered bonds of $275,000, and the 10.0% secured commodity backed bonds of $200,000 for a total of $475,000. Debenture bonds are unsecured bonds, which includes the 9.375% registered bonds of $275,000 and the 11.5% convertible bonds of $125,000, for a total of $400,000.

2. (b) The cost of redeeming the bonds at 98 is 98% of the face value of $5,000,000 or $4,900,000. On the date of redemption, the bonds had a carrying value equal to its face of $5,000,000, plus an unamortized premium of $30,000, or $5,030,000. This is reduced by unamortized bond issue costs of $50,000 to give a net amount of $4,980,000, which is the amount used to recognized gain or loss on redemption. Compared to the amount paid of $4,800,000, there is a gain on retirement, before tax, of $80,000.

The journal entry to record the redemption would be:

Bonds Payable	5,000,000	
Premium	30,000	
Bond Issue costs		50,000
Cash		4,900,000 (5,000,000 x .98)
Gain		80,000

3. (c) Each bond consists of a lump sum of $1,000 to be paid at the end of 10 years and an ordinary annuity of $60 per year for 10 years, which consists of annual interest payments equal to 6% of $1,000, payable at the end of each period. The proceeds from the issuance of each $1,000 bond will be the sum of the present value of those two components:

Amount		PV factor		PV
$1,000	x	422	-	$422
60	x	6.418	-	385
				$807

4. (b) Bond proceeds at issuance will equal the present value of the lump sum principal payment and the cash coupon interest payments, discounted at the **effective** interest rate of 8%:

	8%	
Present value of $1 (n = 5)	0.68058	x $100,000 = $68,058
Present value of an ordinary annuity (n = 5)	3.99271	x $5,000 = $19,964

Bond proceeds are $68,058 + $19,964, or $88,022, resulting in a discount of $100,000 - $88,022, or $11,978, at issuance.

A discount amortization table allows the calculation of carrying value at the end of year 1:

Face	-	Discount	=	CV	x	Effective interest rate	-	Interest expense	(face x stated x time) cash payment	Amortization of Discount
$100,000	-	11,978	=	88,022	x	8%	=	7,042 -	5,000 =	2,042
		- 2,042		+2.042						
$100,000	-	9,936	=	**90,064**						

The carrying value of the bond after the interest payment at the end of year 1 is $88,022 + $2,042, or $90,064, which is the answer.

5. (c) The proceeds of bonds issued with **detachable** warrants are allocated between the bonds and the warrants based upon their relative FMV at the time of issuance. Since the bonds had a fair value of $1,080,000 and the warrants a fair value of $120,000, the total of the fair values is $1,200,000.
- The bonds account for $1,080,000/$1,200,000 or 90% of the proceeds of $1,000,000 or $900,000.
- The warrants account for $120,000/$1,200,000 or 10% of the proceeds of $1,000,000 or $100,000.

The bonds will be recorded at face of $1,000,000 minus a discount of $100,000 for a net amount of $900,000.

6. (d) In general, IFRS requires a financial liability to be reported at amortized cost. Only certain financial liabilities, such as derivatives, are recognized at fair value. IFRS does, however, allow an entity to make an irrevocable election to report financial liabilities at fair value through profit or loss. As a result, a bond may be reported at either amortized cost or fair value through profit and loss.

7. (b) Since Europa intends to hold the bond for the purpose of collecting the scheduled cash flows, it will account for the bond at amortized cost. Under the amortized cost approach, Europa will recognize interest income equal to the yield rate of 10% applied to the $198,000 carrying value of the bond, resulting in interest income of $19,800. Since the amount received will be the stated rate of 6% applied to the face value of $300,000, interest received will be $18,000, resulting in the amortization of discount in the amount of $1,800. The resulting carrying value of the bond will be ($198,000 + $1,800) $199,800. Under the amortized cost method, the investment is not adjusted to fair value.

Bonds & Present Value Tables   Section 11

Lecture 11.10

TASK-BASED SIMULATIONS

Task-Based Simulation 1

  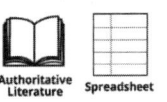

Hamnoff, Inc.'s. $50 par value common stock has always traded above par. During 20X1 Hamnoff had several transactions that affected the following balance sheet accounts:

I. Bond discount
II. Bond premium
III. Bonds payable
IV. Common stock
V. Additional paid-in capital
VI. Retained earnings

Required:

For each of the following items, determine whether the transaction Increased, Decreased, or had No effect for each of the items in the chart.

	Bond discounts	Bond premium	Bond payable	Common stock	Additional paid-in capital	Retained earnings
1. Hamnoff issued bonds payable with a nominal interest rate that was less than the market rate of interest.						
2. Hamnoff issued convertible bonds, for an amount in excess of the bonds' face amount.						
3. Hamnoff issued common stock when the convertible bonds described in item 2. were submitted for conversion. Each $1,000 bond was converted into twenty common shares. The book value method was used for the early conversion.						
4. Hamnoff issued bonds, with detachable stock warrants, for an amount equal to the face amount of the bonds. The stock warrants have a determinable value.						
5. Hamnoff declared and issued a 2% stock dividend.						

Section 11   Bonds & Present Value Tables

Task-Based Simulation 2

 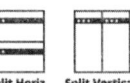

Work Tab | Resources | Help

Situation

On January 2, 20X4, North Co. issued bonds payable with a face value of $480,000 at a discount. The bonds are due in 10 years and interest is payable semiannually every June 30 and December 31. On June 30, 20X4, and on December 31, 20X4, North made the semiannual interest payments due, and recorded interest expense and amortization of bond interest.

Required:

Items 1 through 7, contained in the partially-completed amortization table below, represent information needed to complete the table. For each item, select from the following lists the correct numerical response.

	Cash	Interest expense	Amortization	Discount	Carrying amount
1/2/X4					(3)
6/30/X4	(2)	18,000	3,600	(1)	363,600
12/31/X4	$14,400	(6)	(7)		

Annual Interest Rates: Stated (4)
                       Effective (5)

Rates			Amounts			
A	3.0%		G	$ 3,420	P	$ 21,600
B	4.5%		H	$ 3.600	Q	$116,400
C	5.0%		I	$ 3,780	R	$120,000
D	6.0%		J	$ 3,960	S	$123,600
E	9.0%		K	$ 14,400	T	$360,000
F	10.0%		L	$ 17,820	R	$363,600
			M	$ 18,000	V	$367,200
			N	$ 18,180	W	$467,400
			O	$ 18,360	X	$480,000

Task-Based Simulation 3

   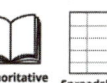 

Situation

On July 1, 20X7, Ring Co. issued $250,000, 14% bonds payable at a premium. The bonds are due in ten years. Interest is payable semiannually every June 30 and December 31. On December 31, 20X7, and June 30, 20X8, Ring made the semiannual interest payments due and recorded interest expense and amortization of bond premium.

With the proceeds of the bond issuance, Ring retired other debt. Ring recorded a gain on the early extinguishment of the other debt.

Required:

Items 1 through 7, contain in the partially completed amortization table below, represent formulas used to calculate information needed to complete the table. Select your answers from the following list of formulas. Each formula may be selected once, more than once, or not at all. "Stated interest rate" and "effective interest rate" are stated on an annual basis.

	Cash paid	Interest expense	Amortization	Carrying amount	Unamortized premium
7/1/X7				**(1)**	
12/31/X7	**(2)**	$14,100	**(3)**	$349,100	**(4)**
6/30/X8	$17,500	**(5)**	$3,536	**(6)**	

Effective Annual Interest Rate: (7)

Formulas	
A. Face amount X stated interest rate.	J. (Face amount x stated interest rate) x ½.
B. Face amount x effective interest rate.	K. (Face amount x effective interest rate) x ½.
C. Carrying amount x stated interest rate.	L. (Carrying amount at the beginning of the period x stated interest rate) x ½.
D. Carrying amount x effective interest rate	
E. Present value of face amount + present value of all future interest payments at date of issuance	M. (Carrying amount at the beginning of the period x effective interest rate) x ½
F. Carrying amount of bonds in the previous period -amortization for the current period.	N. Carrying amount - face amount.
G. Carrying amount of bonds in the previous period + amortization for the current period.	O. (Interest expense/carrying amount at the beginning of the period) x 2.
	P. (Cash paid/carrying amount) x 2.
H. Cash paid - interest expense.	Q. Face amount - unamortized premium.
I. Cash paid + interest expense.	

Task-Based Simulation 4

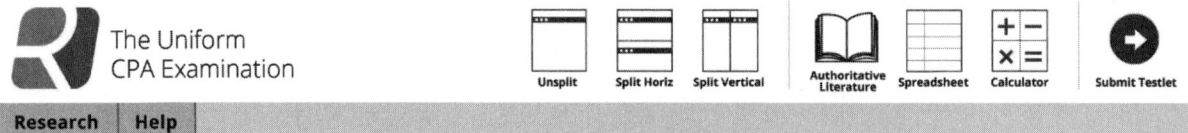

A client is issuing bonds with detachable stock purchase warrants. Identify the location in professional standards that indicates how the proceeds from the sale of debt with detachable stock purchase warrants are accounted for.

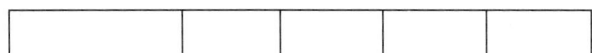

Task-Based Simulation 5

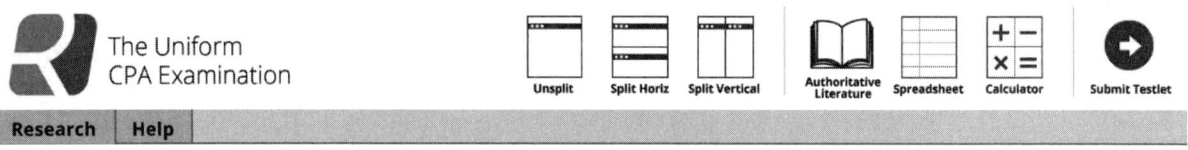

An entity retired a bond for less than the carrying value and is trying to decide if it should recognize a gain or amortize the difference over the remaining term of the bond. Identify the location in professional standards that indicates how the difference is accounted for.

Bonds & Present Value Tables — Section 11

TASK-BASED SIMULATION SOLUTIONS
Task-Based Simulation Solution 1

1. When bonds are issued with a nominal or stated rate that is below the market rate of interest, the bonds will be issued at a discount resulting in the following journal entry:

   Cash (proceeds equal to present value of
     principal and interest payments at
     market interest rate)
   Bond discount (difference)
       Bonds payable (face)

   As a result, bond discount and bonds payable (I & III) increase (I) while all other items (II, IV, V, & VI) remain unchanged (N).

2. The issuance of convertible bonds is recorded in the same manner as bonds that are not convertible. Since the bonds were issued for an amount in excess of face, the difference is a bond premium and will be recorded with the following entry:

   Cash
       Bonds payable (face)
       Bond premium (difference)

   As a result, bond premium and bonds payable (II & III) increase (I) while all other items (I, IV, V, & VI) remain unchanged (N).

3. Each $1,000 bond is convertible into 20 shares of $50 par common stock indicating that the par value of the stock will equal the face amount of the bonds. Since the bonds were issued at a premium, the carrying value of the bonds exceeds the par value of the stock indicating that the excess will be recognized as additional paid-in capital. The entry would be:

   Bonds payable (face)
   Bond premium (unamortized balance)
       Common stock (par)
       Additional paid-in capital (difference)

   As a result, bond premium and bonds payable (II & III) decrease (D), common stock and additional paid-in capital (IV & V) increase (I), and the remaining items (I & VI) remain unchanged (N).

4. When bonds are issued with detachable stock purchase warrants, a portion of the proceeds is allocated to the warrants, which will be recorded in additional paid-in capital.. Since the entire proceeds are equal to the face value of the bonds and a portion is being allocated to the warrants, the portion allocated to the bonds is less than the face amount indicating a discount. The entry would be:

   Cash (proceeds)
   Bond discount (difference)
       Bonds payable (face)
       Additional paid-in capital (amount
         allocated to warrants)

   As a result, bond discount, bonds payable, and additional paid-in capital (I, III, & V) increase (I) while the other items (II, IV, & VI) remain unchanged (N).

5. A stock dividend decreases retained earnings for the fair market value of the stock. Since the stock is trading at an amount that is greater than the par value, the excess is recognized as additional paid-in capital. The entry would be:

> Retained earnings (fair value of stock)
> > Common stock (par)
> > Additional paid-in capital (difference)

As a result, common stock and additional paid-in capital (IV & V) increase (I), retained earnings (VI) decreases (D), and the other items (I, II, & III) remain unchanged (N).

Bonds & Present Value Tables   Section 11

Task-Based Simulation Solution 2

	Cash	Interest expense	Amortization	Discount	Carrying amount
1/2/X4					**360,000 (3)**
6/30/X4	**14,400 (2)**	18,000	3,600	**116,400 (1)**	363,600
12/31/X4	$14,400	**18,180 (6)**	**3,780 (7)**		

Annual Interest Rates: Stated **(6%) (4)**
                        Effective **(10%) (5)**

1) Q   Since the bonds have a face value of $480,000 and a carrying value of $363,600 at 6/30/X4, the difference represents a discount of $116,400.

2) K   Interest payments on term bonds are the same amount every period. Since interest of $14,400 was paid on 12/31/X4, the same amount would have been paid on 6/30/X4.

3) T   The carrying value of the bonds at 6/30/X4 is $363,600 after recognizing amortization of the discount in the amount of $3,600. Since amortization of discount increases the carrying value of the bonds, the carrying value must have been $363,600 - $3,600 or $360,000 at 1/2/X4.

4) D   Interest payments equal the face value of bonds multiplied by the stated rate of interest. Interest payments amount to $14,400 every six months or $28,800 each year. Since interest payments = face x stated rate, the stated rate = interest payments divided by the face amount of the bonds or $28,800 ÷ $480,000 or 6%.

5) F   Interest expense is equal to the carrying amount of the bonds multiplied by the effective rate of interest. Since the carrying amount of the bonds was $360,000 at 1/2/X4 and interest expense for 6 months is $18,000, interest = carrying amount x effective rate x time or $18,000 = $360,000 x effective rate x 6/12 or $18,000 ÷ ($360,000 x 6/12) or 10%.

6) N   Interest expense is equal to the carrying amount of the bonds multiplied by the effective rate of interest. Interest for the period from 7/1 to 12/31/X4 would be $363,600 x 10% x 6/12 or $18,180.

7) I   Amortization of bond discount is the difference between interest expense for the period and the amount of interest paid. For the period ended 12/31/X4, interest expense is $18,180 compared to $14,400 paid. As a result, amortization of discount is the difference of $3,780.

Task-Based Simulation Solution 3

	Cash paid	Interest expense	Amortization	Carrying amount	Unamortized premium
7/1/X7				(1)	
12/31/X7	(2)	$14,100	(3)	$349,100	(4)
6/30/X8	$17,500	(5)	$3,536	(6)	

Effective Annual Interest Rate: (7)

1)   E   The initial carrying amount of a bond is equal to the proceeds from the issuance of the bond. Proceeds will be equal to the present value of the payments to be made including the present value of the principal to be paid in a lump sum at the end of the bond term and the periodic interest payments in the form of a semiannual annuity. The present value is calculated using the effective interest rate.

2)   J   The cash paid on December 31, 20X7 represents the semiannual interest amount. This will be equal to the $250,000 face of the bonds multiplied by the 14% stated interest rate. Since interest is paid semiannually, the result is multiplied by ½ year. The amount of interest paid will be the same in each semiannual period.

3)   H   Amortization of bond premium is equal to the difference between the amount of interest paid and the amount of interest expense for the same period.

4)   N   The balance of the unamortized bond premium is equal to the difference between the $349,100 carrying amount of the bond and the $250,000 face value.

5)   M   Interest expense is calculated using the effective interest method. It is equal to the carrying value of the bond multiplied by the effective rate of interest. Since interest is paid semiannually, the result is multiplied by ½ year.

6)   F   Amortization of bond premium reduces the carrying amount of the bond. The carrying amount on any given interest date will be the previous carrying amount less the amortization of bond premium in the current semiannual period.

7)   O   Interest expense for a semiannual period is calculated by multiplying the carrying value of the bond at the beginning of the period by the effective interest rate and multiplying the result by ½. If the amount of interest expense is known, the formula can be modified to calculate the effective interest rate by dividing interest expense by the carrying value of the bond at the beginning of the period and multiplying the result by 2.

Task-Based Simulation Solution 4

FASB ASC	470	20	25	2

Task-Based Simulation Solution 5

FASB ASC	470	50	40	2

Section 12 – Accounting for Leases
Corresponding Lectures

Watch the following course lectures with this section:

Lecture 12.01 – Accounting for Leases – Operating Lease
Lecture 12.02 – Accounting for Leases – Capital Lease
Lecture 12.03 – Lease Payment Example
Lecture 12.04 – Non-Operating Leases
Lecture 12.05 – Leases involving Real Estate
Lecture 12.06 – Sale-Leaseback
Lecture 12.07 – Leases – Class Questions and TBS
Lecture 12.08 – Leases under IFRS
Lecture 12.09 – Leases under IFRS – Class Questions

EXAM NOTE: Please refer to the AICPA FAR Blueprint in the Introduction to find a listing of the representative tasks (and their associated skill levels—i.e., Remembering and Understanding, Application, and Analysis) that the candidate should be able to perform based on the knowledge obtained in this section.

Accounting for Leases

Lecture 12.01

ACCOUNTING FOR LEASES – OPERATING LEASE

Note: The FASB's Accounting Standards Update 2016-2 makes major changes to lease accounting, but the changes will not become effective on the CPA Exam until the Q1 2019 testing window. Because these changes are not testable until 2019, they are not covered in this edition of the course.

A lease is a contract, which conveys the right to possess and use the lessor's property for a specified period of time in return for periodic cash payments by the lessee to the lessor. Our goal is to recognize the true substance over the form of the lease. It may be a true rental (Operating lease) or it could be a purchase and sale, which transfers substantially all the rights and risks of ownership (Capital lease/Non operating) (ASC 840).

Lessor	**Lessee**
Operating	Operating
Non-operating	Capital
• Sales type	
• Direct financing	

Operating Leases

A lease where the rights and risks of ownership don't transfer, considered a "true rental."
- **Lessor**
    - Depreciates the asset
    - Direct lease costs (commissions, legal fees) are amortized S/L over the lease term.
    - Executory costs (taxes, insurance and maintenance) are recognized as incurred.
    - Lease bonus is deferred (unearned revenue) and amortized over the life of the lease.
    - Rent received in advance is considered unearned (deferred revenue).
    - Security deposits
        - Nonrefundable – unearned revenue until earned
        - Refundable – liability until returned.
    - Uneven rental payments are recognized *uniformly* (evenly) over the lease term (free rent for example)
    - Termination costs should be measured and recognized at fair value at the date the agreement is terminated.

- **Lessee**
    - Lease rent expense is recognized uniformly (evenly) (free rent)
    - Lease bonus is considered an asset and amortized S/L over the lease term.
    - Leasehold improvements are reported with PP&E and amortized over the shorter of:
        - Lease term
        - Useful life
    - Refundable security deposits are assets (receivable)

- o Early termination costs must be recognized immediately at fair value by Lessee.

- **Disclosure**
    - o A general description of the leasing arrangements.
    - o Minimum lease payments for each of the **next 5 years** and in the aggregate.

For example, assume the client has signed a 5-year rental contract at $10,000 per year on 1/1/X1, but as an inducement to enter the agreement, the client has been offered the first six months free. This means that the first year rent payment will only be for the last six months of the year, and the payments will be:

20X1	5,000
20X2	10,000
20X3	10,000
20X4	10,000
20X5	10,000
Total	45,000

Since the total payments are $45,000, rent expense each year is $45,000 / 5 years = $9,000. In 20X1, the entry is:

Rent expense	9,000	
Accrued rent payable (balance)		4,000
Cash		5,000

In each of the years 20X2 to 20X5, the entry is:

Rent expense	9,000	
Accrued rent payable (balance)	1,000	
Cash		10,000

The accounting for a lease by the lessor is similar: rental income is recognized on a straight-line basis over the rental period. Keep in mind, however, that the owner will probably have various expenses associated with the asset being rented, including depreciation expense to be recognized over the useful life of the asset.

For example, assume that the property being rented in the previous example had just been purchased by the owner on 1/1/X1 for $70,000, and had a 10-year life and no expected salvage value. The entry by the lessor for the 20X1 rent is:

Cash	5,000	
Accrued rent receivable	4,000	
Rent income		9,000

Assuming straight-line depreciation is used on the asset, it is recorded as:

| Depreciation expense | 7,000 | |
| Accumulated depreciation | | 7,000 |

Lecture 12.02

ACCOUNTING FOR LEASES – CAPITAL LEASE

A lease where the rights and risks of ownership have transferred from the lessor to the lessee. In substance it's a purchase, although in form it's a lease. The lessee therefore recognizes both an asset and a liability at the present value of the minimum lease payments (MLP) not to exceed fair market value (FMV), while the lessor will account for such a lease as either an operating, sales-type or a direct financing lease.

If the lease meets one of the following four criteria, the lessee accounts for the lease as a capital lease, as if he OWNS it. If not, it is considered an operating lease.
1. The lease transfers **ownership** of the property to the lessee by the end of the lease term. (**Transfers title – TT**).
2. The **Written** lease contains a bargain purchase option. (**BPO**)
3. The noncancellable lease term is equal to **75%** (**Seventy-five**) or more of the estimated economic life of the property at inception.
4. The Present Value of the minimum lease payments is equal to **90%** (**Ninety**) or more of the FMV of the property at Inception.

If the beginning of the lease term falls within the *last 25%* of the total estimated economic life of the leased property, criterion #3 and #4 shall not be used for purposes of classifying the lease.

A lease that satisfies at least one of these criteria is classified as a capital lease. A lease that does not satisfy any of these criteria is reported as an **operating lease**.

Noncancellable Lease Term

The noncancellable lease term is the minimum period of time during which the lease is expected to be in force. It includes:
- *Initial lease term*. This is the original term of the lease that does not include any renewal periods.
- **Bargain renewal periods** – These are periods for which the lessee has the option to renew the lease at a rate that is expected, as of the date of the inception of the lease, to be lower than the market rate making it likely that the lease will be renewed.
- **Penalty for nonrenewal** – When a lease contains a provision that requires the lessee to pay a significant penalty to the lessor for not renewing the lease, it is assumed that the lease will be renewed to avoid the penalty and the renewal period is included in the noncancellable lease term.
- **Leases containing a BPO** – When a lease contains a BPO, it is assumed that the lessee will exercise it. As a result, it is assumed that the noncancellable lease term will include the initial lease term and any renewal periods up to the point that the BPO can be exercised. Since it is assumed that the lessee will exercise a BPO, the noncancellable lease term would not extend beyond the point at which it could be exercised.

Minimum Lease Payments

Minimum lease payments represent the minimum amount that the lessee will pay, or that the lessor will receive, under the terms of the lease during the noncancellable lease term. The minimum lease payments include:
- **Base rent** – This is the amount of rent the lessee is required to pay to the lessor over the noncancellable term of the lease. It may be in the form of a periodic payment for the

entire duration of the lease, or may be an amount that increases over time. These payments are included if the amount is fixed or can be readily determined based on information that is available at the inception of the lease.
- o This includes the minimum lease payments during the initial lease term.
- o It also includes the minimum lease payments during any renewal periods that are included in the noncancellable lease term.

- **BPO** – As indicated, when a lease contains a BPO, it is assumed that the lessee will exercise it. As a result, the amount of the BPO will be included in the minimum lease payments. For purposes of calculating present value, it will be treated as a lump sum paid at the end of the noncancellable lease term.

- **Penalties** – When a lease contains penalties for nonrenewal that are not so severe as to make it likely that the lessee will renew the lease to avoid the penalty, it is assumed that the lease will not be renewed and the penalty will be paid, making it part of the minimum lease payments.

- **Residual value** – When a lease does not contain a BPO and when title does not transfer to the lessee at the end of the lease term, the property subject to the lease will be returned to the lessor at the termination of the lease. In some cases, the lessee guarantees that the property will be worth at least a certain amount, referred to as a residual value guarantee. In other cases, the residual value is guaranteed by a third party, separate from the lessee, such as the asset's manufacturer. When the neither the lessee nor a third party provide such a guarantee, the lessor has an unguaranteed residual value.
    - o *Guaranteed residual value (guaranteed by lessee)* – Lessee and lessor both include the amount in the minimum lease payments.
    - o *Guaranteed residual value (guaranteed by third party)* – Only the lessor includes the amount in minimum lease payments.
    - o *Unguaranteed residual value* – Only the lessor includes the amount in minimum lease payments.

Minimum lease payments exclude certain payments from the lessee to the lessor. These are recognized as income by the lessor and as expense by the lessee in the periods in which they become due.
- **Contingent rents** – These are rents that are subject to the occurrence of some event in the future. They may include:
    - o Additional rents due based on usage of the asset or some other criteria, such as sales in excess of a base amount.
    - o Rent increases based on the change in an index or comparable factor, such as increases in the consumer price index.

- **Executory costs** – These are costs for taxes, insurance, or maintenance of the leased property.

The lessee records the lease at the lower of:
- **FMV** (A new implicit interest rate must be calculated)
- **PV of the minimum lease payments**
    - o Periodic payments (annual payment)
    - o BPO as a lump sum
    - o Guaranteed residual value as a lump sum

Accounting for Leases — Section 12

- *Guaranteed residual value* is considered part of the "minimum lease payment" and is reflected in the lessor's lease receivable account, whether guaranteed by the lessee or a third party, and the lessee's lease payable account if guaranteed by the lessee.
- The present value of the *unguaranteed residual value* should be included in the lessor's net investment in the lease at PV of a lump sum, unless the lease transfers title to the leased asset or there is a bargain purchase option.

  o Penalty for failure to renew (if any)
  o Don't include executory costs (taxes, insurance, maintenance) since they are expensed as incurred.

To determine the PV of the payments use:
- Incremental borrowing rate – discount rate the lessee would pay in the lending market to purchase the leased asset.
- Unless both:
  o Lessee **knows** the lessor's **implicit rate** AND
  o Implicit rate is **lower** than the incremental borrowing rate.

Note: The lessor always uses the rate implicit in the lease.

Lecture 12.03

Lease Payments

If the first payment is made on day 1, it is all principal, if the payment is made at year end the amount of principal and interest needs to be calculated. The Effective interest method is used (same as Bonds) in amortizing the lease payments.

EXAMPLE: 8 year lease of $75,000 per year. P.V. of the MLP = $428,415, 1st payment of $75,000 on day 1, Implicit rate = 11% (known by Lessee), Incremental borrowing rate = 12%. 10-year useful life. Includes Title Transfer at end of lease term.

Lease Liability	X	Incremental or Implicit Interest Rate	=	Interest Expense/ Income	-	Lease Payment	=	Amortization of Lease Liability
428,415		11%						
(75,000)								
353,415		11%	=	38,876	-	75,000	=	36,124
(36,124)								
317,291		11%	=	34,902	-	75,000	=	40,098
(40,098)								
277,193								

Day one

    Leased Asset   428,415
        Lease Liability   428,415

First Payment (day 1)

Lease Liability	75,000	
Cash		75,000

Second Payment (one year later)

Lease Liability	36,124	
Interest Expense	38,876	
Cash		75,000

Depreciation (lessee depreciates the asset)
- Criteria 1 or 2 (TT/BPO)
    - Ownership of the asset has transferred.
        - Depreciate over useful life
        - Take out salvage value

- Criteria 3 or 4 (75/90)
    - Rights and risks of ownership have transferred without ownership
        - Depreciate over **shorter** of useful life and lease term.
        - Ignore salvage value
            Example:
            - Assume the asset will live 10 years using the Straight-Line (S/L) depreciation method.

Depreciation expense	42,841 (428,415/10yrs)
Accumulated Depreciation	42,841

Note: Of the Liability of $353,415, the amount of $36,124 represents a *current liability* and the balance of $317,291 is a *non-current liability*.

Disclosures
The following is required to be disclosed:
- A description of the entity's leasing activities
- Gross amount of assets recorded under capital leases
- Minimum lease payments for each of the **next 5 years** and in the aggregate.

Lecture 12.04

NON-OPERATING LEASES – LESSOR
If the lease meets one of the four criteria, and BOTH of the following criteria, the lease is accounted for by the lessor as either a sales-type lease or direct financing lease. If both criteria are not met, the lease is an operating lease by the lessor, but is still a capital lease by the lessee. The two criteria are:

1. **Collectability** of the lease payments is reasonably assured.

2. There are **no significant uncertainties** regarding unreimbursable costs to be incurred by the lessor (**Measurability**).

Sales Type Lease

A lease where the seller is usually a manufacturer or dealer of the asset, and uses the lease as a way of selling the asset on an installment basis. The Fair value of the leased property differs from the cost, which creates a dealer's profit or loss. Includes both:
- **Profit/loss** in the period of sale, and
- **Interest revenue** to be earned over the lease term using the effective interest method.

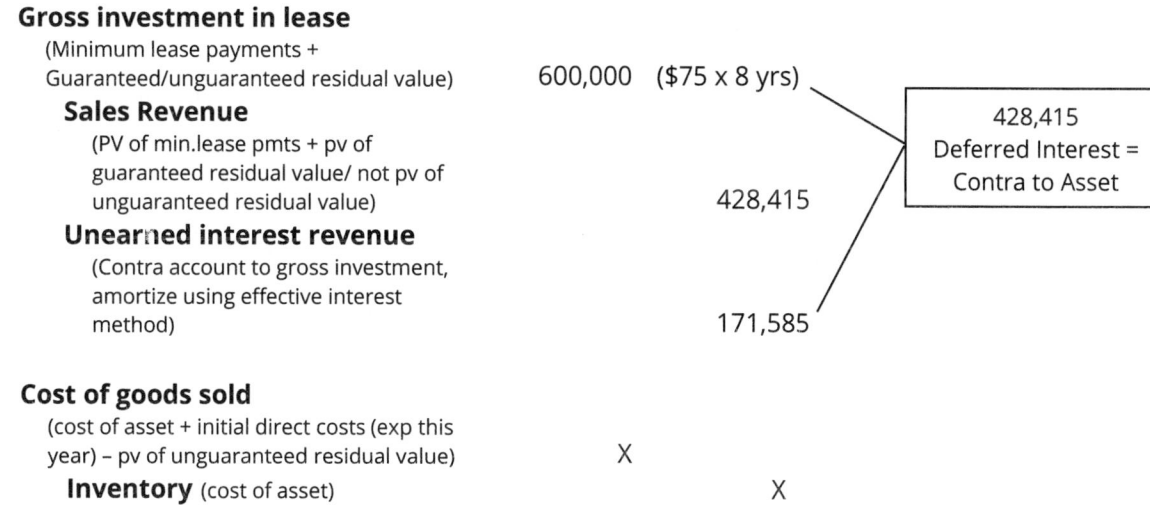

Gross investment in lease (Minimum lease payments + Guaranteed/unguaranteed residual value)	600,000	($75 x 8 yrs)
Sales Revenue (PV of min.lease pmts + pv of guaranteed residual value/ not pv of unguaranteed residual value)		428,415
Unearned interest revenue (Contra account to gross investment, amortize using effective interest method)		171,585
Cost of goods sold (cost of asset + initial direct costs (exp this year) – pv of unguaranteed residual value)	X	
Inventory (cost of asset)		X

428,415 Deferred Interest = Contra to Asset

Note: The above journal entries can be summarized as the following, resulting in the same gain:

Gross investment in lease (Minimum lease payments + Guaranteed/unguaranteed residual value)	600,000	($75 x 8 yrs)
Inventory		300,000
Unearned interest revenue (Contra account to gross investment, amortize using effective interest method)		171,585
Gain		128,415

Note: The lessor always uses the Implicit rate, the gain or loss is recognized in the period of sale and the interest is recognized over the life of the lease using the effective interest method.

Cash	75,000	
Gross Investment in Lease (Receivable)		75,000

At the end of the first year of the lease term (first anniversary of the inception of the lease), interest income is recognized:

Unearned interest rev (Def'd Rev)	38,876	
Interest Income		38,876

Direct Financing Lease

A lease where the lessor is financing the acquisition of an asset by the lessee but is not earning a manufacturer's or dealer's profit. The present value of the minimum lease payments will be equal to the fair value of the property and the lessor will earn only interest income.

Lease payment receivables	X	(min lease payments + residual value)
Equipment		X
Unearned interest revenue		X

Disclosures
- Future minimum lease payments
- Unguaranteed residual value
- Earned income
- Future payments to be received over the **next 5 years.**

Lecture 12.05

LEASES INVOLVING REAL ESTATE

Leases involving real estate create special problems due to the fact that land has an indefinite useful life. As a result, when analyzing a lease involving real estate, special rules are applied in determining if the lease is an operating lease or a capital lease for the lessee or a nonoperating lease (sales-type or direct financing) for the lessor.

When leases involve **land only**:
- The lessee will consider only the first two criteria in classifying the lease. If it does not transfer title or contain a BPO, it is an operating lease
- If the transfer of title criterion is met, assuming the lessor's two separate criteria are also met, the lessor:
    - Will report the lease as a sales-type lease if there is a manufacturer's or dealer's profit or loss
    - Will report the lease as a direct financing lease if there is no profit or loss
- If the BPO criterion is met, the lessor will account for the lease as a sales-type lease or a direct financing lease, as appropriate.

When leases involve **land and building** and either of the first two criteria are met (transfer of title or BPO), the **lessee** will capitalize the land and building separately. If neither of the first two criteria are met, the lessee will determine if the land is significant.
- If the fair value of the land is *less than 25%* of the total fair value, it is ignored and the lease is treated as a building lease only. It is capitalized if either of the latter two criteria are met.
- If the fair value of the *land ≥ 25%,* the land and building are considered separately.
    - If the portion attributed to the building meets either of the latter two criteria, the building will be capitalized and the land portion will be an operating lease.
    - If neither of the latter two criteria are met, the entire lease will be accounted for as a single operating lease

When leases involve land and building and the first criterion is met (transfer of title), the **lessor** will evaluate if there is a manufacturer's or dealer's profit or loss.
- If so, the lease will be accounted for as a sales-type lease with the land and building accounted for as a single unit.

Accounting for Leases
Section 12

- If not:
    - If the lease meets both of the seller's criteria, it will be accounted for as a direct financing lease.
    - If it does not meet both of the seller's criteria, it will be accounted for as an operating lease.

When leases involve land and building and the second criterion is met (BPO), the lessor will evaluate if there is a manufacturer's or dealer's profit or loss.
- If so, the lease will be accounted for as an operating lease.
- If not:
    - If the lease meets both of the seller's criteria, it will be accounted for as a direct financing lease.
    - If it does not meet both of the seller's criteria, it will be accounted for as an operating lease.

When leases involve land and building and neither the first nor the second criteria are met, the lessor will determine if the land is significant.
- If the fair value of the land < 25% of the fair value of the leased property, the land and building will be treated as a single lease.
    - If either of the latter criteria are met and both of the lessor's criteria are met, the lease will be classified as a direct financing or sales-type lease, as appropriate.
    - If neither of the latter criteria are met or either of the lessor's criteria are not met, the lease will be accounted for as an operating lease.
- If the fair value of the land ≥ 25% of the total fair value of the leased property, the land and building will be treated as separate leases.

Lecture 12.06

SALE-LEASEBACK

The property owner sells the property, then immediately leases all or part of it back from the new owner. It is considered two separate and distinct economic transactions. The leaseback may either be an operating lease or a capital lease (If 1 of the 4 criteria are met.), but we also need to see what *portion of the rights* to the leaseback property are retained.

- If PV of rental payments is ≥ 90% of fair value of the property at inception, this implies that the seller-lessee retains **substantially all** the rights to the use of the property and the leaseback is accounted for as a *Capital lease*.
    - Defer all gain and offset against depreciation expense.

Cash	200		
Equipment		120	
Deferred gain		80	(amortize over 4yrs = $20)
Leased asset	200	(Depreciate over 4 yrs = $50)	
Obligation under Capital lease		200	

- If PV of rental payments is >10% but < 90% of FV, leaseback could be either *Operating or Capital lease* based on 1 of 4 criteria (TT, BPO, 75, 90)
    - Defer gain up to P.V. of leaseback payments, recognize rest immediately
    - If capital lease, offset against depreciation expense

- o If operating lease, offset against rent expense

- If PV of rental payments is ≤10% of FV, this implies that the seller only retains a minor portion of the rights to use the property, the sale and leaseback are considered separate transactions. The sale is recognized and the leaseback is considered an *Operating Lease*.
  - o Recognize all gain immediately

Cash	200	
Equipment		120
Deferred gain		80 (amortize over 4yrs = $20)

Prepaid rent (payment at beginning of period)	50	
Cash		50

Capital Leaseback

Gain or loss is deferred and amortized over the period used for depreciating the asset as a reduction of depreciation expense.
- The deferred gain is reported as an asset valuation allowance to the leased asset account.
- A loss is deferred and amortized as prepaid rent if the carrying amount (BV) of the asset sold is greater than the sales price, but the fair value exceeds the carrying amount (BV).
- A loss is recognized immediately if the carrying amount is greater than the fair value.

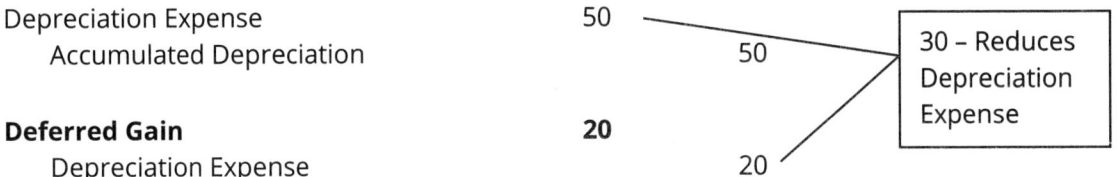

Depreciation Expense	50	
Accumulated Depreciation		50
Deferred Gain	20	
Depreciation Expense		20

30 – Reduces Depreciation Expense

Operating Leaseback

Gain or loss is also generally deferred when the leaseback is an operating lease.
- Gain or loss is deferred and amortized over the term of the lease as a reduction of rent expense. The deferred gain is considered a deferred credit.
- If Sale-leaseback occurs in the last 25% of an asset's economic life, classify as an operating lease.

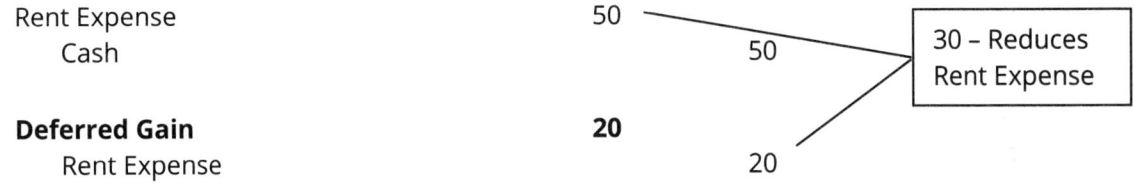

Rent Expense	50	
Cash		50
Deferred Gain	20	
Rent Expense		20

30 – Reduces Rent Expense

An artificial loss on sale occurs when the sales price is lower than the fair value of the property on the date of the sale. In all cases, the lessee (seller) should immediately recognize a Real loss when the FV ($90) of the property at the time of the leaseback is less than the Book value ($100). An artificial loss, which is the difference between the sales price ($85) and the FV ($90) should be

Accounting for Leases
Section 12

deferred. Since we are recognizing the $10 Real loss, the remaining $5 will be deferred and amortized as an addition to depreciation expense.

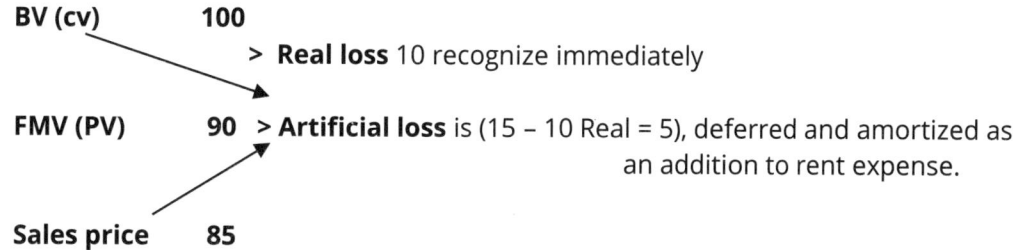

Note: A modification of a capital lease that converts it to an operating lease is treated as a sale-leaseback.

Impairment Loss (ASC 360)

If the *future cash flows* are less than the *carrying amount* of the asset, impairment loss is recognized. Impairment loss recognized is the amount by which the **carrying amount** of the asset **exceeds** the **fair value** of the asset. Similar to Goodwill and PP&E impairment (Held for Use), the loss is **not recovered**.

An entity evaluates depreciable assets and amortizable intangibles for impairment when there is an indication that the asset has been impaired. One factor that would indicate that an asset has been impaired is a decline in its fair value. This affects the accounting for leases as follows:
- A lessor with an asset subject to an operating lease, and a lessee with an asset that results from a capital lease may be required to recognize an impairment loss.
- A seller-lessee in a sale-leaseback transaction may be required to recognize an impairment loss on the asset being sold.

Lecture 12.07
CLASS QUESTIONS

Please see the Class Questions and Class Solutions for this Lecture at the end of this Section.

Lecture 12.08
LEASES UNDER IFRS

All leases are either finance leases or operating leases. Finance leases are those that transfer substantially all of the *rights and risks* of ownership to the lessee, regardless of whether title is actually transferred. All other leases are operating leases.

Rights of ownership include:
- The benefit of profitable operation over the asset's economic life
- *The benefit of appreciation in value or realization of a residual value*

Risks of ownership include:
- The possibility of losses due to idle capacity or obsolescence
- Reductions in returns due to changing economic conditions

Whether or not substantially all of the rights and risks of ownership are transferred is a matter of professional judgment.

Certain factors, individually or in combination, will ordinarily be indicative of a **finance lease:**
- Title transfers by the end of the lease term (TT).
- The lease contains a purchase option that is sufficiently lower than expected market value to make it reasonably certain that it will be exercised (BPO).
- The lease term is for the *major part* of the asset's useful life.
- The present value of the minimum lease payments, at the inception of the lease, is *substantially equal* to the fair value of the asset.
- The asset can only be used by the lessee without major modification.

In addition, certain situations, individually or in combination, may be indicative of a finance lease:
- Lessor losses associated with the lessee's cancellation of the lease are borne by the lessee.
- Lessee incurs gains or losses resulting from fluctuations in the fair value of the residual asset.
- The lessee can renew the lease at rents that are substantially below market.

Note: Leases recognized as capital leases under US GAAP would qualify as finance leases under IFRS.

Leases involving land and buildings are treated as separate leases due to the fact that land has an indefinite useful life.

Once a lease is classified under IFRS, the classification is only modified if the lessor and lessee modify the terms of the lease. This will be considered the termination of the original lease and entering into a new lease.

The **lessee** records a **finance lease** by recognizing a liability in an amount equal to the lower of the fair value of the leased asset or the present value of the minimum lease payments. An asset is recognized in the amount of the liability plus any initial direct costs incurred by the lessee.
- The present value is calculated using the rate implicit in the lease
  - May not be readily determinable
  - Lessee's incremental borrowing rate used instead
- Fair value is the amount for which the asset would be exchanged between knowledgeable and willing parties in an arm's length transaction.

In subsequent periods, minimum lease payments are allocated to interest, calculated under the interest method, with the remainder reducing the lease obligation. Contingent rents are charged to expense as incurred.

The asset is depreciated using the same approach that would be used for a comparable owned asset. If ownership is not anticipated, the asset will be depreciated over the shorter of its useful life or the lease term.

A lessee's **disclosures** for a **finance lease** will include:
- A reconciliation of future minimum lease payments to their present value

- Total future minimum lease payments, and their present values, for
  - The next year
  - The period including the second through the fifth year
  - Periods beyond five years
- Contingent rentals expensed for the period

Lease payments in an **operating lease**, similar to US GAAP, are recognized on a straight-line basis over the term of the lease unless another systematic pattern is more representative.

The lessee will also **disclose**, for an **operating lease**, total future minimum lease payments for:
- The next year
- The period including the second through the fifth year
- Periods beyond five years

A **lessor** recognizes a **finance lease** by reporting an asset as a receivable in an amount equal to the net investment in the lease. The net investment includes the present value of the minimum lease payments.
- For lessors that are not manufacturers or dealers, **initial direct costs** are added to the receivable and the effective interest rate is adjusted accordingly.
- For lessors that are manufacturers or dealers, initial direct costs are recognized as an expense in the period in which the sale is recognized.

Subsequent collections of minimum lease payments are allocated to finance income using the interest method applying a constant rate. Contingent rentals are recognized as income when earned.

For **finance leases**, the lessor will **disclose**:
- A reconciliation of future minimum lease payments to their present value
- Total future minimum lease payments, and their present values, for
  - The next year
  - The period including the second through the fifth year
  - Periods beyond **five years**
- Unearned finance income
- Unguaranteed residual values
- Contingent rentals recognized as revenue for the period

A lessor recognizes income from an **operating lease** on a straight-line basis.

The lessor will also **disclose**, for an **operating lease:**
- Total future minimum lease payments for:
  - The next year
  - The period including the second through the fifth year
  - Periods beyond **five years**
- Contingent rents recognized in income for the period

Accounting for a **sale-leaseback** by a seller-lessee depends on the classification of the leaseback.
- If the lease is a finance lease, any profit is deferred and amortized over the lease term.
- If the lease is an operating lease, profit or loss is recognized immediately if it is clear that the sale occurred at fair value.
  - If the sales price exceeds market, the excess profit is deferred and amortized over the period that the asset will be used

o If the sales price is below market, profit or loss is recognized immediately unless a loss will be compensated by future lease payments below market, in which case it will be deferred and amortized and allocated in proportion to future lease payments.

Impairment of Assets

Assets recognized as a result of capitalizing a lease are tested for impairment in the same manner as fixed assets. Impairment is tested using a single step approach under which the carrying value of the asset is compared to its fair value. Fair value is determined using an appropriate valuation, considering the asset's highest and best use, which may be in exchange or may be in use.

Since the asset may be accounted for using either the cost model or the revaluation model:
- Under the **cost model**, impairment losses are recognized in income as are recoveries to the extent of losses previously recognized.
- Under **the revaluation method**, decreases in the value of the asset are recognized in profit or loss, as are increases in value to the extent of losses previously recognized in profit or loss. Increases in value that are exceed losses previously recognized in profit or loss are reported in other comprehensive income.

Impairment losses may be recognized as depreciation expense or may be recognized separately as impairment losses.

IFRS allows **reversals** of previously recognized impairment losses.

Leases	
US GAAP	**IFRS**
• Lessee reports as capital lease if one of certain criteria are met (TT, BPO, 75, 90) and otherwise as operating lease • Lessee recognizes initial direct costs as expense when incurred • Lessor reports as sales-type, direct financing, or leveraged if certain criteria met & otherwise as operating • If the fair value of the land at inception represents 25% or more of the total fair value, the lessee must consider the components separately when evaluating the lease.	• Lessee reports as *finance lease* if risks & rewards of ownership transferred & otherwise as operating • Lessee capitalizes initial direct costs for a finance lease • Lessor reports as finance lease if risks & rewards of ownership transferred & otherwise operating • When land and buildings are leased, elements of the lease are considered separately when evaluating the lease unless the amount for the land element is immaterial.

Lecture 12.09

CLASS QUESTIONS

Please see the Class Questions and Class Solutions for this Lecture at the end of this Section.

CLASS QUESTIONS

Work through the below Class Questions while following along with the respective lectures. Once this is complete, you can begin independently practicing what you've learned by quizzing yourself on this course section in your Interactive Practice Questions (IPQ), which can be found in your online Student Dashboard. Your IPQ simulates the computer-based testing experience, and will also help you understand how concepts are applied to the exam. Each question includes answer explanations from expert CPAs that will help you determine why you answered a question correctly or incorrectly. This is key to your success on the CPA Exam.

Lecture 12.07

1. Lease M does not contain a bargain purchase option, but the lease term is equal to 90% of the estimated economic life of the leased property. Lease P does not transfer ownership of the property to the lessee at the end of the lease term, but the lease term is equal to 75% of the estimated economic life of the leased property. How should the lessee classify these leases?

	Lease M	**Lease P**
a.	Capital lease	Operating lease
b.	Capital lease	Capital lease
c.	Operating lease	Capital lease
d.	Operating lease	Operating lease

2. For a capital lease, the amount recorded initially by the lessee as a liability should normally

   a. Exceed the total of the minimum lease payments.
   b. Exceed the present value of the minimum lease payments at the beginning of the lease.
   c. Equal the total of the minimum lease payments.
   d. Equal the present value of the minimum lease payments at the beginning of the lease.

3. On December 31, 20X3, Day Co. leased a new machine from Parr with the following pertinent information:

Lease term	6 years
Annual rental payable at beginning of each year	$50,000
Useful life of machine	8 years
Day's incremental borrowing rate	15%
Implicit interest rate in lease (known by Day)	12%
Present value of annuity of 1 in advance for 6 periods at	
12%	4.61
15	4.35

The lease is not renewable, and the machine reverts to Parr at the termination of the lease. The cost of the machine on Parr's accounting records is $375,500. At the beginning of the lease term, Day should record a lease liability of

a. $375,500
b. $230,500
c. $217,500
d. $0

4. On December 31, 20X3, Roe Co. leased a machine from Colt for a five-year period. Equal annual payments under the lease are $105,000 (including $5,000 annual Executory costs) and are due on December 31 of each year. The first payment was made on December 31, 20X3, and the second payment was made on December 31, 20X4. The five lease payments are discounted at 10% over the lease term. The present value of minimum lease payments at the inception of the lease and before the first annual payment was $417,000. The lease is appropriately accounted for as a capital lease by Roe. In its December 31, 20X4 balance sheet, Roe should report a lease liability of

a. $317,000
b. $315,000
c. $285,300
d. $248,700

5. Oak Co. leased equipment for its entire nine-year useful life, agreeing to pay $50,000 at the start of the lease term on December 31, 20X1, and $50,000 annually on each December 31 for the next eight years. The present value on December 31, 20X1, of the nine lease payments over the lease term, using the rate implicit in the lease, which Oak knows to be 10%, was $316,500. The December 31, 20X1, present value of the lease payments using Oak's incremental borrowing rate of 12% was $298,500. Oak made a timely second lease payment. What amount should Oak report as capital lease liability in its December 31, 20X2, balance sheet?

a. $350,000
b. $243,150
c. $228,320
d. $0

6. A six-year capital lease that specifies equal minimum annual lease payments expires on December 31st. The payments being made represent both interest and a reduction in the net lease liability. The portion of the minimum lease payment in the fifth year applicable to the reduction of the net lease liability should be:

a. Less than in the fourth year.
b. More than in the fourth year.
c. The same as in the sixth year.
d. More than in the sixth year.

Lecture 12.09

7. Sara Corp. prepares its financial statements in accordance with IFRS. Sara Corp. signed a lease to rent fixed assets for a period of ten years. The lease payments of $15,000 per year are due on January 1st of each year. At the end of the lease term, Sara may purchase the equipment for a BPO of $175. The equipment has an estimated useful life of 12 years. Sara prepares its financial statements in accordance with IFRS. How should the lease be classified in Sara's financial statements?

    a. Operating lease.
    b. Capital lease.
    c. Finance lease.
    d. Sales-type lease.

8. Cecilia Corp., who prepares their financial statements in accordance with IFRS, entered into a lease for both a building and the Land upon which the building resides. The lease is a 20 year lease. At the end of the lease term, the building will revert back to the lessor. The life of the building is estimated to be 20 years. How should Cecilia account for the lease in their financial statements?

    a. The lease is recorded as a finance lease.
    b. The lease is recorded as an operating lease.
    c. The land is recorded as an operating lease and the building is recorded as a finance lease.
    d. The land is recorded as a finance lease, and the building is recorded as an operating lease.

CLASS SOLUTIONS

1. (b) When a lease meets any of four criteria, it is accounted for as a capital lease by the lessee. Only if none of the four criteria are met does the lessee recognize the lease as an operating lease. One of the four criteria is that the noncancellable lease term is equal to or greater than 75% of the useful life of the leased property. This is true of both Lease M, which is for 90% of the asset's economic life, and Lease P, which is for 75% of the asset's economic life. Both would be capital leases.

2. (d) When a lease qualifies as a capital lease, the lessee recognizes an asset and a lease obligation equal to the present value of the minimum lease payments as of the inception of the lease. The present value is lower than the total of the minimum lease payments, not either higher or equal.

3. (b) Since the lease is for 6 years and the asset's useful life is 8 years, the lease is for 75% of the useful life of the property and will be accounted for as a capital lease. A lease obligation will be recognized in an amount equal to the present value of the minimum lease payments using the rate implicit in the lease since it is known to the lessee and lower than the lessee's incremental borrowing rate. As a result, the lease obligation will be $50,000 x 4.61 or $230,500. Answer (a) is incorrect because $375,500 is the lessor's carrying value of the property, which is not relevant to the lessee. Answer (c) is incorrect because $217,500 would be the present value using the lessee's incremental borrowing rate, which would only be used if either the rate implicit in the lease was not known or if it was higher than the lessee's incremental borrowing rate. Neither is the case. Answer (d) is incorrect because $0 would be correct if the lease did not qualify as a capital lease but, since the lease term = 75% of the asset's useful life, it is a capital lease.

4. (d) The equal annual payments of $105,000 include executory costs of $5,000 per year, which are recognized as expense in the period incurred, and minimum lease payments of $100,000 per year, which are applied to interest expense and the lease obligation using the interest method.
- The initial lease obligation is $417,000.
- The first payment of $100,000 is made at the inception, before any interest has accrued, and is applied entirely to the obligation, reducing it to $317,000.
- The second payment will first be applied to interest with the remainder reducing the obligation.
    - Interest is $317,000 x 10% or $31,700.
    - The principal reduction is the difference of $68,300, reducing the obligation to ($317,000 - $68,300) $248,700.

5. (b) Since the lease is for the entire 9 year life of the property, it is a capital lease. The lease obligation will initially be determined using the rate implicit in the lease since it is known to the lessee and lower than the lessee's incremental borrowing rate. At 10%, the initial obligation would have been recognized in the amount of $316,500.
- The first payment is made at the inception of the lease and does not include interest, resulting in a reduction of $50,000 to $266,500.
- The second payment will be applied to interest first, with the remainder applied to reducing the lease obligation.
    - Interest will be $266,500 x 10% or $26,650.
    - The remainder of the $50,000 payment, $23,350, reduces the principal balance to $243,150.

Answer (a) is incorrect because that is the gross amount of the remaining payments, but the obligation would be equal to the present value, not the gross amount. Answer (c) is incorrect because this would be the balance in the lease obligation after the second payment if the lessee capitalized the lease using its incremental borrowing rate of 12%. Answer (d) is incorrect because since the lease is a capital lease, there will be a lease obligation.

6. (b) Payments made on a capital lease are first applied to interest with the remainder reducing the lease obligation. As the lease obligation declines each year, the amount recognized as interest expense also decreases. When lease payments are equal, as the interest portion declines, the principal reduction increases. As a result, the principal reduction in the fifth year would be greater than the fourth year and smaller than the reduction in the sixth year.

7. (c) Under IFRS, a lease can only be an operating lease or a finance lease. It is a finance lease if it transfers substantially all of the rights and risks of ownership as indicated by both the fact that the lease term is for substantially all of the asset's useful life (10 years of 12 years) and the lease contains what appears to be a bargain purchase option. Answer (a) is incorrect because under IFRS, a lease can only be an operating lease or a finance lease. It is a finance lease if it transfers substantially all of the rights and risks of ownership as indicated by both the fact that the lease term is for substantially all of the asset's useful life (10 years of 12 years) and the lease contains what appears to be a bargain purchase option. Answers (b) and (d) are incorrect because under IFRS, leases are either operating leases or finance leases. There are no capital leases or sales-type leases.

8. (c) Under IFRS, when a lease involves land and building, it is separated into two leases and the land portion is accounted for separately from the building portion. Since the building lease is for 100% of the building's 20 year useful life, it clearly transfers substantially all of the rights and risks of ownership and will be accounted for as a finance lease. There is nothing to indicate that substantially all of the rights and risks associated with the land are transferred and the land lease will be accounted for as an operating lease.

TASK-BASED SIMULATIONS

Task-Based Simulation 1

Required:

Situation

On January 2, 20X1, Elsee Co. leased equipment from Grant, Inc. Lease payments are $100,000, payable annually every December 31 for twenty years. Title to the equipment passes to Elsee at the end of the lease term. The lease is noncancellable.

- The equipment has a $750,000 carrying amount on Grant's books. Its estimated economic life was twenty-five years on January 2, 20X1.
- The rate implicit in the lease, which is known to Elsee, is 10%. Elsee's incremental borrowing rate is 12%.
- Elsee uses the straight-line method of depreciation.

The rounded present value factors of an ordinary annuity for twenty years are as follows:

12%	7.5
10%	8.5

Items to be answered:

Prepare the necessary journal entries, without explanations, to be recorded by Elsee for

1. Entering into the lease on January 2, 20X1.

2. Making the lease payment on December 31, 20X1.

3. Expenses related to the lease for the year ended December 31, 20X1.

4. Making the lease payment on December 31, 20X2.

Task-Based Simulation 2

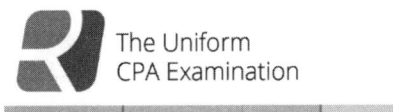

Required:

Situation

On January 2, 20X1, Starbucks leased equipment from Folgers. Lease payments are $150,000, payable annually every January 2 for 25 years. Title to the equipment passes to Starbucks at the end of the lease term. The lease is noncancellable.

Additional facts:

The equipment has a $1,250,000 carrying amount on Folgers' books. Its estimated economic life was 30 years at the inception of the lease.

The rate implicit in the lease, known to Starbucks, is 8%. Starbucks' incremental borrowing rate is 10%.

Starbucks uses the straight-line method of depreciation.

The rounded present value factors of an annuity due for 25 years are as follows:

```
      10%    9.98
       8%   11.53
```

Items to be answered:

Prepare the necessary journal entries, without explanations, to be recorded by Starbucks for:

- Entering into the lease on January 2 of the current year.
- Making the lease payments on January 2, 20X1 and 20X2.
- Expenses related to the lease for the current year, ended December 31, 20X1 and 20X2.
- Determine the amounts that will appear on Starbucks' balance sheet in relation to the lease as of December 31, 20X2.

Section 12   Accounting for Leases

Task-Based Simulation 3

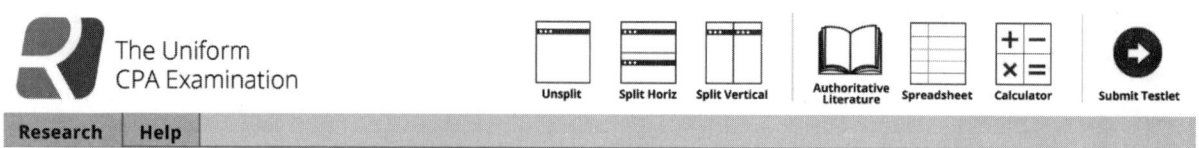

Your client has incurred a variety of costs to find a lessee to enter into an operating lease for its property, to determine whether or not prospective lessees were appropriate, and to draw up the lease. Your client is trying to determine if these costs are to be recognized as expense or deferred. Identify the location in professional standards that indicates how a lessor determines what is included in initial direct costs that can be deferred.

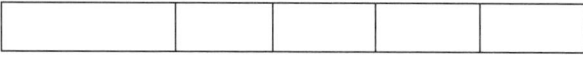

Task-Based Simulation 4

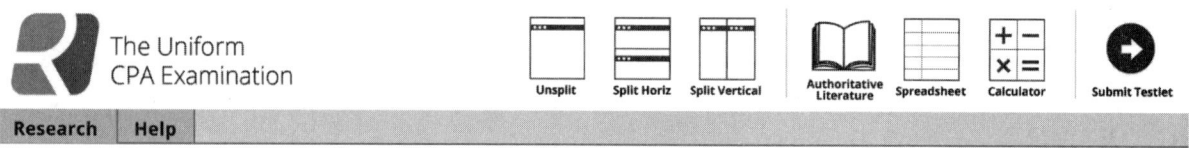

An entity has entered into a lease that transfers title of the property to the entity at the end of the lease term. The entity has determined it is a capital lease and is trying to determine the amount to be recognized as an asset and liability. Identify the location in professional standards that indicates how a capital lease asset and a capital lease obligation are initially measured.

TASK-BASED SIMULATION SOLUTIONS

Task-Based Simulation Solution 1

At 1/2/X1, the inception of the lease, Elsee will record the lease as a capital lease since title transfers (TT), but they could also qualify since lease term of 20 years and the useful life of 25 years equals 20/25 = 80%, which is ≥ 75% of useful life. Elsee then records both an asset and a liability equal to the present value of the minimum lease payments. The present value will be based on the 10% rate implicit in the lease since it is lower than Elsee's incremental borrowing rate of 12% and the rate implicit in the lease is known to Elsee. The present value will be $100,000 x 8.5 or $850,000.

	Leased equipment	850,000	
	Lease liability		850,000

Lease Liability	X	Incremental or Implicit Interest Rate	=	Interest Expense/ Income	-	Lease Payment	=	Amortization of Lease Liability
850,000		10%		85,000		100,000		15,000
(15,000)								
835,000		10%	=	83,500	-	100,000	=	16,500
(16,500)								
818,500		10%						

The payment was then made on 12/31/X1 at the end of the year. As a result, it will be allocated to both principal and interest.

	Lease liability	15,000	
	Interest expense	85,000	
	Cash		100,000

At December 31, 20X1, depreciation will be recognized. Even though the lease is only for a 20 year period, title transfers to Elsee at the end of the lease term. As a result, Elsee will depreciate the asset over its economic life of 25 years. Annual depreciation will be $850,000 / 25 years or $34,000.

	Depreciation expense	34,000	
	Accumulated depreciation		34,000

The payment on 12/31/X2 will be recorded as follows, using the amounts from the table:

	Lease liability	16,500	
	Interest expense	83,500	
	Cash		100,000

Task-Based Simulation Solution 2

At 1/2/X1, the inception of the lease, Starbucks will record an asset and a liability equal to the present value of the minimum lease payments. The present value will be based on the 8% rate implicit in the lease since it is lower than Starbucks' incremental borrowing rate and the rate implicit in the lease is known to Starbucks. The present value will be $150,000 x 11.53 or $1,729,500.

Leased equipment	1,729,500	
Lease liability		1,729,500

Lease Liability	X	Incremental or Implicit Interest Rate	=	Interest Expense/ Income	-	Lease Payment	=	Amortization of Lease Liability
1,729,500								
(150,000)								
1,579,500		8%	=	126,360	-	150,000	=	23,640
(23,640)								
1,555,860		8%	=	124,469	-	150,000	=	25,531
(25,531)								
1,530,329								

The payment on 1/2/X1 is at the inception of the lease. As a result, it will all be allocated to principal.

Lease liability	150,000	
Cash		150,000

At December 31, 20X1, depreciation will be recognized. Even though the lease is only for a 25-year period, title transfers to Starbucks at the end of the lease term. As a result, Starbucks will depreciate the asset over its economic life of 30 years. Annual depreciation will be $1,729,500 / 30 years or $57,650.

Depreciation expense	57,650	
Accumulated depreciation		57,650

Interest will be accrued on the lease liability. The liability had a balance of $1,729,500 – $150,000 or $1,579,500 for the entire year. At 8%, interest will be $126,360.

Interest expense	126,360	
Interest payable		126,360

The payment on 1/2/X2 will be recorded as follows, using the amounts from the table:

Interest payable	126,360	
Lease liability	23,640	
Cash		150,000

At December 31, 20X2, depreciation and interest expense will be recorded.

Depreciation expense	57,650	
Accumulated depreciation		57,650
Interest expense	124,469	
Interest payable		124,469

The following items will appear on Starbucks' balance sheet dated December 31, 20X2:

The leased equipment will be reported in the noncurrent asset section of the balance sheet along with other property, plant, and equipment. The amount will be:

Original cost	$1,729,500
Accumulated depreciation	115,300
Carrying value	$1,614,200

The current portion of the lease obligation will be reported as a current liability. It will equal the principal reduction that will be made in the following year

Payment due on Jan 2	$150,000
Interest	124,469
Current portion of lease liability	$25,531

The remainder of the lease obligation will be reported as a noncurrent liability. The amount will be:

Balance of lease obligation at 12/31	$1,555,860
Current portion	25,531
Long-term liability	$1,530,329

Task-Based Simulation Solution 3

| FASB ASC | 840 | 20 | 25 | 17 |

Task-Based Simulation Solution 4

| FASB ASC | 840 | 30 | 30 | 1 |

Section 13 - Liabilities

Section 13 – Liabilities
Corresponding Lectures

Watch the following course lectures with this section:

Lecture 13.01 – Current Liabilities
Lecture 13.02 – Contingencies
Lecture 13.03 – Interest on Notes Payable
Lecture 13.04 – Troubled Debt Restructuring
Lecture 13.05 – Liabilities – Class Questions & TBS
Lecture 13.06 – Liabilities under IFRS
Lecture 13.07 – Liabilities under IFRS – Class Questions
Lecture 13.08 – Contingencies – Document Review Simulation

EXAM NOTE: Please refer to the AICPA FAR Blueprint in the Introduction to find a listing of the representative tasks (and their associated skill levels—i.e., Remembering and Understanding, Application, and Analysis) that the candidate should be able to perform based on the knowledge obtained in this section.

Liabilities

Lecture 13.01

CURRENT LIABILITIES

Current Liabilities are liabilities that will be settled within one year or the Operating cycle whichever is longer. Current Liabilities are valued at their NRV or settlement value. They include accounts payable, accrued expenses, dividends payable, income taxes payable, current portion of L/T debt (ASC 210/405).

Accounts Payable

Accounts payable generally represents amounts due to vendors resulting from the purchase of merchandise.
- Liabilities incurred in obtaining goods and services from vendors in the ordinary course of business.
- **Discounts** for prompt payment (ex. 2/10, N/30)
    - **Gross method** – Purchases are shown at gross, if the discount is taken, it is considered a reduction of Cost of Sales.

Purchases	100	
A/P		100
A/P	100	
Cash		90
Discount		10 (COGS ↓)

-
    - **Net method** – Purchases are shown at net, if the discount is not taken, considered interest expense.

Purchases	90	
A/P		90
A/P	90	
Expense	10	
Cash		100

Goods in Transit
- **FOB shipping point**
    - Title passes when *shipped* by seller (placed with carrier).
    - Included in buyer's books at year-end as both Inventory and an A/P.

- **FOB destination**
    - Title passes when *received* by buyer (tendered to buyer).
    - Included in seller's books until received by buyer. Not included in buyer's books as an A/P until the goods are received.

Section 13																																Liabilities

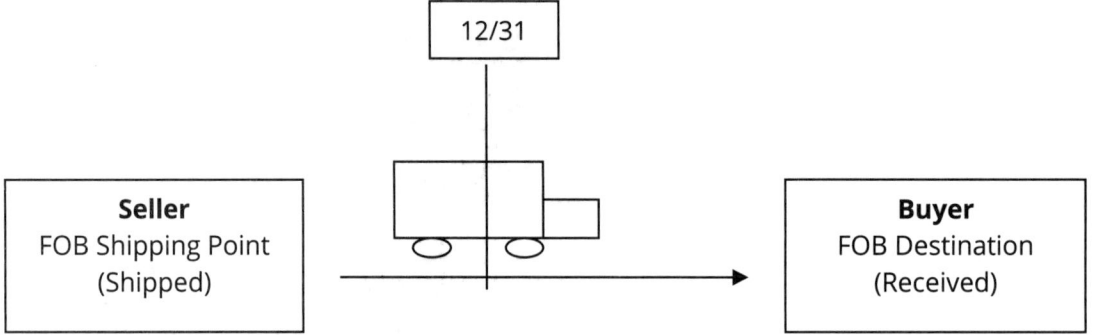

Estimated and Accrued Amounts

- **Accrued Liabilities/Expenses (Current Liability)**
    - An expense that is **incurred but not yet paid** in cash.
        - Ex: unpaid salaries or taxes at year end.
            - **Employees share** of taxes that the employer withholds are not an expense of the employer, even though they are a liability.

Expense (I/S)	X	
Accrued Liability		
(Salaries payable / B/S)		X
Accrued Liability	X	
Cash		X

- **Prepaid Expenses (Current Asset)**
    - Expenses paid in cash, but not yet incurred.
        - Ex. Prepaid rent

Prepaid Expense	X	
Cash		X
Expense (I/S)	X	
Prepaid Expense		X

- **Deferred Revenues (Current Liability)**
    - Revenue collected but not yet earned.
        - Ex. Rent collected or subscriptions collected in advance or gift certificates issued, but not yet redeemed.

Cash	X	
Unearned Revenue (B/S)		X
Unearned Revenue	X	
Revenue (I/S)		X

Liabilities   Section 13

- **Revenue Receivable (Current Asset)**
  - Revenue earned but not yet collected
    - Ex: revenue earned but still due from customer.

Receivable	X	
Revenue (I/S)		X
Cash	X	
Receivable		X

For Example: Assume a company paid $65,000 in expenses. Its beginning balance in accrued expenses was $7,500 and the ending balance was $9,000. The beginning balance in prepaid expenses was $3,800 and the ending balance was $4,100.

Using a journal entry approach, we know that there was a cash payment, recognized with a credit to cash, of $65,000. Accrued expenses increased by $1,500. An increase in a liability is a credit. Prepaid expenses increased by $300. Prepaid expenses are assets and an increase is a debit. The amount required to balance the entry is $66,200, representing the amount of expenses incurred.

Expenses (plug)	66,200	
Prepaid expenses ($4,100 - $3,800)	300	
Cash (given)		65,000
Accrued expenses		
($9,000-$7,500)		1,500

Warranty Costs

Products sold by the client often include **warranties** promising repairs or replacement for a limited time period. In most cases, it is impossible to determine how much of the sales price is for the product, and how much for the warranty commitment. As a result, revenue is recognized in its entirety on the date of sale, and the estimated warranty cost accrued at the same time.

The method of estimation to be used is the percentage of sales approach. It is similar to the equivalent approach for bad debts.

For example, assume a client has cash sales of $1,000 in 20X1, its first year of operations. The products are covered by a 2-year warranty, and the client estimates that costs equal to 1% of sales will have to be spent in the first year of the warranty, and 3% of sales in the second and final year of the warranty (repairs are expected to increase as the products get older). Let's also assume the client has spent $6 on warranty repairs in 20X1.

The entry to record sales is:

Cash	1000	
Sales		1000

At the same time, warranty costs estimated to total 4% of sales over the warranty periods are reported:

Warranty expense	40	
Estimated warranty liability		40

The amount spent on actual repairs is applied to the liability:

Estimated warranty liability	6	
Cash		6

Service Contracts

Many retail stores offer **service contracts** in connection with goods sold. Unlike warranties, service contracts are priced and sold separately, so it is possible to identify the revenue associated with them. As a result, proceeds from the sale of a service contract are systematically allocated over the period of the contract. In this case, actual repair costs are simply recorded as they occur in expenses.

One problem with the allocation of revenue, however, is that a straight-line approach isn't justified, since the amount of repairs and replacements will normally increase as products get older, so more of the revenue is earned later in the contract period.

For example, assume a 4-year service contract is being sold to customers. Rather than expect that 25% of servicing will take place in each year, it might be more reasonable to expect a steady increase over time, so that 10% of total service is rendered in the first year of the contract, 20% in the second year, 30% in the third year, and 40% in the final year of the contract. Although there will even be a difference between the first 6 months and the last 6 months of each year, let's assume that the pace of repairs within each year is even. If $100 of contracts are sold in 20X1 throughout the year, the entry for the collection of contract money is:

Cash	100	
Deferred service revenue		100

At the end of the year, revenue for the time that has elapsed on the average contract is:

12/31/X1	Deferred service revenue	5	
	Service revenue		5

Notice that only 5%, not 10%, has been earned by the end of 20X1. This is because the service contracts were sold throughout the year, not all on 1/1/X1, so the average contract is only one-half of a year, not a full year, old at 12/31/X1.

Coupons or Premiums

Many companies issue coupons for discounts on their products, distributing them through newspapers, mailings, and other means. The costs associated with these coupons are uncertain, since many of the coupons will never actually be used. For those that are used, the actual cost to the issuer will usually be greater than the face value of the coupon, since merchants redeeming coupons are usually reimbursed for handling costs associated with processing them.

To determine the estimated liability for unredeemed coupons at the balance sheet date, take the following steps:
1. Determine the total face value of the coupons issued.
2. Add the handling fee percentage promised to merchants.
3. Multiply by the percentage of coupons expected to be redeemed.
4. Subtract payments already made to merchants for redeemed coupons.

Liabilities   Section 13

In determining the estimated liability for unredeemed coupons, ignore any coupons that expired long enough before the balance sheet date so that redemption is no longer considered to have any reasonable chance of occurring.

For example assume the client has issued the following coupons, and is attempting to determine the liability for unredeemed coupons at 12/31/X1:

Face value	$500
Expiration date	12/31/X1
Handling fee paid to merchants	20%
Normal time merchants take to process coupons	One month
Payments to merchants in 20X1	$300
Total coupons expected to be redeemed	60%

In applying the steps indicated the results are:

1. There are $500 in coupons.
2. The handling fee of 20% adds $100 to the possible cost, making it $600.
3. 60% of coupons are expected to be redeemed, costing $360.
4. $300 has already been paid out, so that a remaining liability for unredeemed coupons of $60 exists.

Compensated Absences (ASC 710)

In addition to regular pay, many employees are entitled to vacation and sick pay. Recognition of the cost of these compensated absences must take into consideration two accounting issues:
- **Matching** – costs should be recognized at the time employees render the services that entitle them to compensated absences.
- **Faithful Representation (Neutrality)** – costs should only be recognized if they have been paid or are likely to be paid in the future.

As a general rule, a company will report a liability for future compensated absences if **all four** of the following conditions are met:
- The obligation for compensation for future absences results from services already provided by the employees.
- The right to compensation for future absences either vests or accumulates.
- Payment is probable.
- The amount of the payment can be reasonably estimated.

When employees have performed the services, they are typically credited for a specific number of days of compensation, which should be computed at the wage rate expected to be in effect when these days are utilized. If wage rates are adjusted, the liability should also be adjusted.

For vacation days, the recognition of costs is required if the days **accumulate** or **vest**. Accumulation means that days not taken in the current period may be used in a future period. Vesting means that days not used will be paid in cash at the time of the employee's termination of service with the company. Accumulated vacation days are almost certain to be used by an employee at some time if they are in danger of losing them.

For sick days, the recognition of costs is only required if the pay vests, and is permitted but not required if the pay only accumulates but doesn't vest. The reason for this distinction is that sick days often are never used by an employee, especially if company policy is to require actual proof of sickness (such as a note from a doctor). A company which allows the use of sick days without evidence of sickness, and essentially treats such days as additional vacation days, must accrue such costs when experience suggests they will probably be used.

For example, assume that a company pays its employees an average of $100 per day, and that there are 50 unused vacation days and 10 unused sick days at 12/31/X1 which accumulate but do not vest. Also assume that the company is giving a 10% raise to all employees, effective 1/1/X2. The company **must** accrue the vacation pay:

12/31/X1 Vacation pay expense   5500
                     Liability for unused vacation days   5500

The company **may** accrue the sick pay:

          Sick pay expense   1100
                     Liability for unused sick days   1100

Finally, a client may receive **refundable deposits** on containers for products sold by the company. The deposit must be reported as a liability when collected, but may later become revenue if there is an expiration date on the right of the customer to claim the refund.

For example, assume the company collects deposits of $1 on containers used to transport the company's product to customers, and that customers must return the containers by the end of the calendar year following the year of the sale to receive a refund on the deposit. The following information applies to the first two years in which this policy applies:

Number of sales in 20X1	50
20X1 containers returned in 20X1	30
20X1 containers returned in 20X2	15
Number of sales in 20X2	60
20X2 containers returned in 20X2	40

In 20X1, entries are made for containers delivered and returned:

          Cash   50
                     Liability for refundable deposits   50

          Liability for refundable deposits   30
                     Cash   30

In 20X2, similar entries are made:

          Cash   60
                     Liability for refundable deposits   60
          Liability for refundable deposits   55
                     Cash   55

Liabilities   Section 13

Additionally, an entry is made at 12/31/X2 for the expiration of the time allotted for the return of the remaining 20X1 containers (50 − 30 − 15 = 5):

Liability for refundable deposits	5	
Container revenue		5

Accrued & Deferred Amounts

Some companies pay **bonuses** to top-level executives based on the overall results of the organization. The calculation of these bonuses can get complicated, because they often are based on income in excess of certain amounts, and sometimes the bonus percentage is based on what income will be after the bonus is paid rather than before.

For example, a company may pay the president a bonus equal to 10% of income in excess of $400 after the bonus is deducted. Expressed using basic algebra, the bonus (B) on income (I) before deducting the bonus is:

B = 10% (I − B − 400)

If income before deduction of the bonus is $510, the bonus formula will be solved as follows (10% will be expressed as .1):

B = .1 (510 − B − 400)

The dollar amounts inside the parentheses can be combined:
B = .1 (110 − B)
The items inside the parentheses can be individually multiplied by .1:
B = 11 − .1B
Then .1B is added to both sides:
1.1B = 11
Then both sides are divided by 1.1:
B = 10

Some companies collect **subscriptions on publications** to be delivered in the future. On the exam, these commonly involve directories or other annual or semi-annual publications. As deferred revenues, these must be reported as earned only when the publications are delivered to customers.

For example, let's say the client publishes a directory twice a year, sending the May 15 edition to subscribers that have paid by April 30, and the November 15 edition to those who have paid by October 31. At 12/31/X1, unearned revenue of $190 exists. During 20X2, the client collects $1,200 evenly through the year, and publishes as promised.

To determine the subscription revenue in 20X2, consider that the 5/15/X2 publication earns the money collected up to 4/30/X2. Based on the information, cash collections in 20X2 are at the rate of $1,200 / 12 = $100 per month. Thus, $400 came in during the first 4 months, and this was earned along with the $190 from the start of the year (which presumably represented collections in 20X1 after 10/31/X1), for a total of $590 revenue recognized on 5/15/X2. The 11/15/X2 publication earns money collected between 5/1/X2 and 10/31/X2, which at the rate of $100 per month comes to $600 for those six months. The total revenue in 20X2 is $590 + $600 = $1,190. A single entry reflecting all of the year's activity in 20X2 is:

Cash	1200	
Unearned subscription revenue (balance)		10
Subscription revenue		1190

Payroll taxes need to be accrued at the time related payroll expenses are recognized. It is important, however, to distinguish employer taxes from the employee taxes on payroll. The latter are not costs of the company, but instead represent withholdings from the gross pay of the employees. As a result, only employer taxes meet the definition of accrued expenses (costs recognized on the income statement before payment).

For example, let's assume social security taxes under FICA are assessed at an 8% rate for employers with an equal amount withheld from the paycheck of employees, that the employer pays unemployment taxes under FUTA at a 3% rate, and that federal income taxes are withheld from employee paychecks.

If an employee earns $100 gross pay for a period, and is required to have $15 withheld for federal income taxes, the entry to account for the paycheck and related taxes is as follows:

Payroll expense	100	
Payroll tax expense	11	
Cash		77
Accrued payroll taxes liability		11
Withholdings due to IRS		23

Dividends Payable

Dividends are considered a **Current Liability** when they are **declared** whether related to Common stock or Preferred Stock. Dividend in Arrears on cumulative Preferred stock are not a liability, but must be disclosed in the notes to the financial statements.

Lecture 13.02

Contingencies (ASC 450)

A gain or loss that may occur in the future as a result of an existing condition.
- **Contingent Liabilities** – the event occurs before the balance sheet date, but the resolution is contingent upon a future event. We are concerned with the existence of the liability.
    - Examples include:
        - Obligations related to product warranties.
        - Pending or threatened litigation.
        - Guarantees of indebtedness of others (Suretyship).
        - Obligations related to product defects.
        - Threat of expropriation of assets.
        - Collectibility of receivables.

Liabilities
Section 13

- **Loss Contingencies**
    - **Remote** – slight chance of occurring
        - Don't Disclose
        - Don't Accrue.

    - **Reasonably Possible** – more than Remote, less than Probable.
        - Do Disclose – Disclose nature and range of loss
        - Don't Accrue – Fair presentation.

    - **Probable** – "Likely" to occur
        - If **not Estimable**
            - Do Disclose – Nature and range of loss
            - Don't Accrue
        - If **Estimable**
            - Do Disclose – Nature and range of loss
            - Do Accrue
                - Conservatism / Matching

A **remote** contingency is a loss that is reasonably certain **not** to occur. There are virtually unlimited numbers of different things that can go wrong in a business, and to attempt to identify all of them in the financial report would actually defeat the attempt to fairly present the company. It would distract the user from more significant risks with greater chances of occurring. **Although disclosure of remote contingencies isn't forbidden, it is only required in one circumstance: when the client has guaranteed the debt of another party.**

If a loss is **reasonably possible**, it must be disclosed in the notes to the financial statements, including the nature of the contingency and the range of possible losses. Accrual of the loss on the financial statements is forbidden, since the loss is still not probable. Accrual would bias the presentation of the financial numbers to the downside, violating the **neutrality** ingredient of **Faithful Representation**, one of the primary qualitative characteristics of accounting information. The client may, however, appropriate a portion of retained earnings for reasonably possible losses so as to indicate that these amounts are not available to pay dividends to shareholders.

When a loss is **probable** it will, of course, be disclosed. In addition, though, we should accrue the expected amount of loss. The problem is that it is difficult to establish a verifiable number for the loss. If it is possible to estimate an amount, this will be reported on the income statement and reduce net assets on the balance sheet.

For example, if the client is being charged with breach of contract in a case which the client's attorney believes is probably going to be lost, and the contract in question specified the monetary damages for breach at $300,000, or the client has insurance coverage that will limit their loss to $300,000 in any event, the entry might be:

Estimated losses from legal claims	300,000	
Estimated liability from legal claims		300,000

- o **If a Range of Loss**
  - Accrue amount "most Likely" to occur.
  - If any amount is as likely as the rest, accrue the minimum amount in the range and disclose the range.

- o **Unasserted Claims** (ex. potential lawsuit – not yet initiated)
  - If not probable that claim will be asserted
    - No Disclosure/ No Accrual
  - If Probable that the claim will be asserted
    - Look at likelihood of Loss
    - Remote, Reasonably Possible, Probable.

- o **Uninsured Losses** – potential loss for which company has no insurance.
  - If don't expect condition to occur, do nothing
  - If expect to occur, Disclose.
  - If occurred, Accrue and Disclose.

- **Gain Contingencies**
  - o Disclose if Reasonably possible or Probable, the nature and amount.
  - o Never accrue until realized
    - Conservatism.

Loss Contingency

	Disclose	Accrue
Remote – Slight	No	No
Reasonably Possible	Yes	No
Probable & Estimable	Yes	**Yes**
Probable & Not Estimable	Yes	No

Estimated Loss (I/S)
Estimated Liability (B/S)

Gain Contingency

	Disclose	Accrue
Remote = Slight	No	No
Reasonably Possible	Yes	No
Probable & Estimable	Yes	**No**

Subsequent Events

Events occurring during the time interval between the balance sheet date but before the date that the financial statements are issued or are available to be issued, may have an impact in one of **two ways:**

- **Type 1** – Some events provide evidence of **conditions existing** at the balance sheet date that require **adjustment (recognized)**. For example, the bankruptcy filing of a customer on January 4, 20X1 may indicate that a receivable from that customer at December 31, 20X0 ought to be written off. Another example might be the settlement of a litigation for an amount different than the amount that had been accrued.

- **Type 2** – Some events do not affect the balance sheet, as the **condition did NOT exist** at the balance sheet date, but still represent important information that should be **disclosed (non-recognized)** to assist users of the financial statements in interpreting them. For example, a fire that destroyed the company's main warehouse on January 4, 20X1 does not change the inventory balance at December 31, 20X0, but would affect the significance of that inventory and suggest possible future difficulties. Other examples include: sale of bonds or issuance of stock, purchase of a business, fire or flood loss, receivable loss.

Subsequent to B/S date but before issue financial statements.
- Two types:
  - **Type I**
    - Condition **Existed at B/S date**. Ex. Lawsuit is settled or IRS assessment.
    - Accrue and Disclose (recognized). Use Original Report date 3/1.
  - **Type II**
    - Condition **did not Exist** at B/S date. Ex. Issue bonds after year end.
    - **Disclosure (non-recognized)**, but do not Accrue. Either Dual date report or date report as of event date (if after field work date).

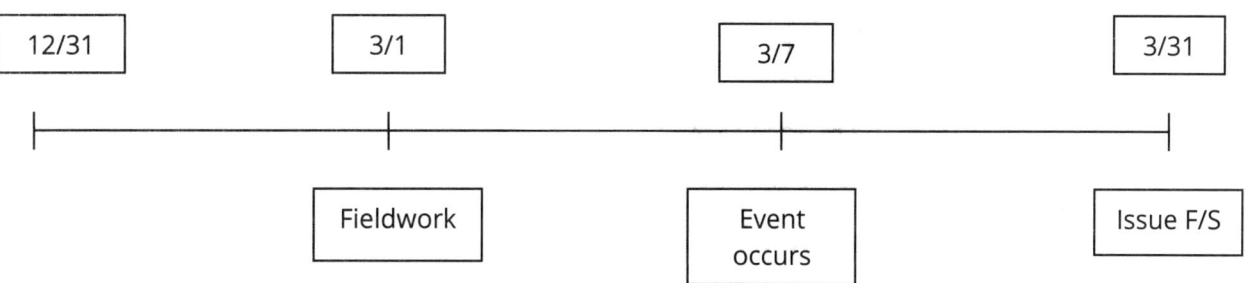

Lecture 13.03

Interest on Notes Payable

Interest on notes payable is calculated similarly to interest on notes receivable.
- If N/P occurs in the ordinary course of business, record at **Face value**. (Don't present value)
- L/T payables are recorded at **Present Value (P.V.)**
- If Long-term notes are payable in installments, the principal amounts that are due within the next 12 months or the operating cycle whichever is longer, must be reported as current liabilities, called **current portion of long-term debt**.

Note: When violation of a debt covenant gives the lender the right to call the debt, and the lender does not waive this right, this violation should typically result in the classification of the entire debt as **current** by the borrower.

- Notes Payable may be non-interest-bearing, interest bearing, or bear a rate of interest that is not considered a fair rate. When this is the case, the same rules that apply to Notes Receivable also apply to Notes Payable.

  - **Notes received/paid solely for cash** (assume rate is fair)

N/R	X	Cash	X	
Cash		X	**Notes Payable**	X

- **Notes received/paid for goods or services**
  - Note receivable at a **reasonable rate**. The PV of the note is the same as the Face amount. (face)

Notes receivable	10,000		Asset	X	
Asset		X	N/P		X
Gain		X			

Non-interest bearing notes
- If the interest rate is not stated or is unreasonable, use the **FMV of the goods or the FMV of the note,** whichever is more easily determinable. Assume the FMV of the asset is 9000.

Notes receivable	10,000	
Discount on N/R		1000 → cv = 9000
Equipment		6000
Gain on sale		3000

Asset	9000	
Discount on N/P	1000	→ cv = 9000
N/P		10,000

- If the interest rate is not stated, the FMV of the goods or the FMV of the note is not determinable, **IMPUTE** an interest rate. Use a reasonable rate for a note of this type. PV of a note in 2 years at 10% is .8265 x 10,000 = 8265.

Notes receivable	10,000	
Discount on N/R		1735 > cv = 8265
Equipment		6000
Gain on sale		2265

Asset	8265
Discount on N/P	1735
Notes Payable	**10,000**

When interest rate isn't fair, the fair rate must be **imputed**
- Receivable/Payable is carried at the present value of payments discounted at fair interest rate.
- Periodic interest income/expense accrues based on fair rate.

In some cases, an entity may generate cash by issuing a note payable and discounting it with another entity or a financial institution. An entity, for example, may issue a noninterest-bearing note that matures in one year, discounted at a bank at a rate of 8%.

- The maturity value will be equal to the face value since it is a noninterest-bearing note.

- A discount will be computed by multiplying the maturity value (face value in the case of noninterest-bearing notes) by the discount rate.

Liabilities Section 13

- The rsult, adjusted for the length of time from the date of discounting to maturity, will be recorded as a discount.

The entry will be:

Cash (for net proceeds)	X	
Discount on note payable (maturity amt x discount rate x time)	X	
Note payable (face amount)		X

The discount is then amortized according to the entity's policies. The effective interest method is generally preferred but straight-line is also used.

Refinancing of Short-Term Obligations on a L/T basis

Obligations maturing within one year or the operating cycle, whichever is longer are considered Short-Term. If the company **intends** to refinance the obligation on a L/T basis, it is classified as L/T.

- **Intent & Ability:**
    - Actually **issuing L/T debt** or Equity securities after the balance sheet date, but prior to the issuance of the financial statements.

    - Signing a **firm agreement** to refinance the obligation with a lender or investor that has the financial ability to provide the financing.

Special Loss Contingencies

- **Guarantees of Indebtedness (Suretyship)**
    - Guaranteeing the debt of another → Must be **disclosed**

- **Unconditional Purchase Obligation (Purchase Committments)**
    - If obligated to purchase goods for a period of time at a fixed price, the liability is disclosed for each of the 5 years following the Balance Sheet date.
        - Accrue loss if the market value of the item falls below the purchase price. The loss will be for the Minimum quantity required to be purchased.

- For example, assume the client signed a 3 year contract at 1/1/X1 agreeing to purchase 1,000 units per year of particular goods at 10 cents per unit. At 12/31/X1, the notes must disclose the fixed obligations for the remaining contract:
    20X2 100
    20X3 100

    Assume, however, that the goods in question become obsolete during 20X1, and at the time the financial statements for 20X1 are being issued, the client estimates that the best alternative available will be to sell the goods for scrap for 2 cents per unit. In addition to writing down any inventory on hand at 12/31/X1 to market, the client must accrue a liability for the 8 cent loss expected on the unconditional obligation to purchase 2,000 additional units over the next two years:

Estimated loss on purchase commitment	160	
Estimated liability on purchase commitment		160

Lecture 13.04

Troubled Debt Restructuring (ASC 470)

When a Debtor cannot pay a debt as it comes due, the debt is considered a Troubled Debt. In evaluating whether a restructuring constitutes a troubled debt restructuring, a creditor must separately conclude that **both** of the following exist:
1. The restructuring constitutes a *concession.*
2. The debtor is experiencing *financial difficulties.*

There are three ways to restructure the debt:
- **Transfer of Property:**
    - Debtor
        - **Gain/Loss on troubled debt restructuing** - Difference between the C.V. of the debt and the FMV of the asset giving up.
        - **Gain/Loss on disposal of asset** – Difference between FMV of asset giving up and B.V. of asset giving up.
    - Creditor
        - Records new asset at FMV and recognizes a **Loss on restructuring**. This is the loss on the difference between what was owed to them and the FMV received.

- **Equity interest in the debtor is issued:**
    - Equity is recorded as if issued for FMV.
    - **Gain** on restrcturing on difference between the C.V. of the debt and the FMV of the equity.

- **Modification of Terms**
    - Reduction of the interest rate.
    - Extension of the maturity date.
    - Reduction of the face amount of the debt and accrued interest.
        - **If Future payments < Obligation**
            - Gain to Debtor
            - Loss to Creditor
        - **If Future payments > Obligation**
            - No gain or loss
            - Considered an adjustment to the interest rate.

Troubled Debt Restructuring Example:

A. I have debt of 600, will give up an asset with a FMV of 500 and a BV of 300.
B. Give stock with a par value of 200 and a FMV of 300.
C. Modify the terms.

	Debtor	**Creditor**
CV Debt = 600	100 Gain on restructuring	(100) Loss on restructuring
FMV of asset giving = 500		
BV of asset giving up = 300	200 Gain/Loss on disposal of asset	

A. Transfer Asset

N/P	600		**Loss** - restructuring	100	
Asset		300	Asset	500	
Gain on restructuring		100	N/R		600
Gain on Disposal		200			

B. Transfer Equity

N/P	600		Investment in stock	300	
Common Stock		200	**Loss** - restructuring	300	
APIC		100	N/R		600
Gain on restructuring		300			

C. Modify Terms

For example, assume the client has a $500 note payable outstanding, with interest payments of 10%, or $50, due at the end of each calendar year until the note matures. At 12/31/X1, the client is unable to make the required annual interest payment, and the creditor agrees to restructure the debt by forgiving the missed payment, reducing the principal on the note to $400, and requiring 10%, or $40, interest payments on 12/31/X2 and 12/31/X3, with the note principal due 12/31/X3.

On 12/31/X1, prior to restructuring, the client had a $500 note payable and $50 accrued interest payable, for a total liability of $550. The restructured loan will require two interest payments of $40 each and principal of $400, for a total of $480 in future payments. The difference of $550 - $480 = $70 is the gain on restructuring, recorded as follows:

12/31/X1	Note payable	500	
	Accrued interest payable	50	
	Note payable		480
	Gain on restructuring		70

Notice that the new note doesn't distinguish principal and interest. This is because the client isn't even going to repay $550 owed before restructuring, so there really isn't any additional interest being paid. All future payments are applied to the note payable.

The accounting by the creditor is different. To be conservative, the payments under the new arrangement are discounted at a fair interest rate before comparing them with the liability. Assuming the 10% rate in this example is fair, the new note has a present value of $400, and is recorded as such:

12/31/X1	Note receivable	400	
	Loss on restructuring	150	
	Note receivable		500
	Accrued interest receivable		50

Normal interest income of $40 per year will be recognized over the next two years.

Fair Value Option ASC 825

According to FASB ASC Topic 825 (Financial Instruments), an entity has the option, but not the requirement, to report some or all of its financial instruments at fair value. Among those financial instruments that may be reported at fair value are recognized financial assets and financial liabilities.

- **Financial assets** include cash, evidence of ownership in another entity, or a contract that conveys to one entity a right to either:
    o Receive cash or another financial instrument from another entity, or
    o Exchange other financial instruments on potentially favorable terms with the other entity.

- **Financial liabilities** include contracts that impose on the entity an obligation to either:
    o Deliver cash or another financial instrument to another entity, or
    o Exchange other financial instruments on potentially unfavorable terms with the other entity.

A debtor may elect the fair value option for some of its liabilities without making the election for others, even if they are similar. When a debtor elects the fair value option for a liability, that liability will be reported at its fair value on any given balance sheet date. Any decrease or increase required to adjust the liability to its fair value is recognized as a gain or loss in the income statement in the period of change.

The election of the fair value option by a debtor does not affect the accounting by the creditor. The creditor has a similar option to recognize the receivables at fair value.

If the fair value option is not elected for liabilities, a debtor will account for them using traditional approaches covered in this section.

Bankruptcy ($15,775)
- Concerned with the distribution of assets in a liquidation.
    o **Secured Creditors** – perfected security interest
        ▪ Fully secured – the value of the collateral covers the debt owed.

- Partially secured – the value of the collateral is less than the debt owed. The remaining balance becomes an unsecured claim.

  o **Priority Claims** (paid one level at a time / **STOP-IT Drunk Driver**)
  - **S**upport and Alimony payments
  - **T**rustee, Attorney and accountant fees
  - **O**wed to involuntary gap creditors
  - **P**ayroll within 180 days up to $12,850
  - **I**ndividual consumer deposits up to $2,850
  - **T**ax claims w/i 3 years of the filing
  - **Drunk Driver** injury claims

  o **General (unsecured) creditors**

Lecture 13.05

CLASS QUESTIONS

Please see the Class Questions and Class Solutions for this Lecture at the end of this Section.

Lecture 13.06

CURRENT LIABILITIES UNDER IFRS

IFRS defines a financial liability as any liability that is a contractual obligation to deliver cash or another financial asset, a contractual obligation to exchange financial instruments under potentially unfavorable conditions, or a contract that may be settled in the entity's own equity instruments. Financial assets and liabilities are reported at **cost**, with an option to report them at **fair value.**

Two important differences between IFRS and GAAP:
1. Under GAAP, **short-term obligations expected to be refinanced** may be reported in the noncurrent liability section of the balance sheet if the company has the intent and ability to refinance. IFRS allows such a liability to be reported as noncurrent only if the entity expects, and has the discretion, to refinance or roll over the obligation for at least twelve months after the reporting period under a loan facility that is in place as of the balance sheet date. If refinancing or rolling over the obligation is not at the discretion of the entity, such as when there is no arrangement for refinancing in place, the entity will classify the obligation as a current liability.

2. IFRS distinguishes between **contingencies** and **provisions**. Provisions are considered liabilities that are uncertain in timing or amount. A provision is recognized as a liability when three conditions are met:
   a. The entity has a present obligation as a result of a past event
   b. It is probable that an outflow of resources will be required
   c. The amount of the obligation can be reliably estimated.

Provisions are distinguished from other liabilities and accruals.
- Other liabilities, such as trade payables, are obligations to pay for goods or services that have been received or supplied and have either been invoiced or have been agreed upon with the supplier.

- Accruals, such as for payroll or accrued vacation pay, or for goods or services that have been received or supplied but have not been invoiced or agreed upon with the supplier.

Accruals are often reported with trade payables. Provisions, on the other hand, which may include, for example, provisions for warranty costs, are reported separately.

Under IFRS, a contingent liability is either:
- A possible obligation arising from past events that will be confirmed only upon the occurrence or nonoccurrence of some future event that is not entirely within the control of the entity, or
- A present obligation arising from a past event that is not recognized because either:
  - It is not probable that a future outflow of resources will be required, or
  - The amount of the outflow cannot be reliably estimated.

All provisions are actually contingencies because they are uncertain as to timing or amount. IFRS, however, uses the term **contingency** to describe a potential liability that is **not recognized on the balance sheet**. A contingency that is recognized is referred to as a **provision**.

Similar to GAAP, contingent assets are not recognized. Unlike GAAP, however, they are required to be disclosed when an inflow of economic benefits is probable. When realization of income is virtually certain, the inflow is not considered a contingency and is recognized.

IFRS describes **subsequent events**, which are events occurring after the financial statement date but prior to the issuance of financial statements, as **events after the reporting period**. Although they do not use the same terminology, IFRS describes two types of subsequent events, similar to Type 1 and Type 2 events that are described by US GAAP.
- Certain events provide evidence of conditions that **existed** at the balance sheet date.
  - These require adjustments to the financial statements.
  - They are equivalent to Type 1 events.

- Certain events indicate conditions that arose after the balance sheet date (didn't exist)
  - These do not require adjustments to the financial statements.
  - They are disclosed if material.
  - They are equivalent to Type 2 events.

Monetary Current Liabilities

US GAAP	IFRS
• Short-term obligations classified as long-term if entity can demonstrate *intent & ability* to refinance on long-term basis	• Short-term obligations classified as long-term if entity has entered into *agreement* to refinance on long-term basis
• Does not distinguish between contingencies and provisions, considering both as contingencies.	• Considers *provisions* to be liabilities that are uncertain as to timing or amount and *contingencies* as: - Possible obligations arising from past events that may or may not be confirmed **or** - Present obligations for which the outflow of resources is either not probable or not reasonably estimable
• Contingent losses recognized if *probable* and reasonably *estimable*	• Provisions recognized as liabilities but contingencies are not recognized on balance sheet.
• Contingent gains may be disclosed but never required	• Contingent gains *required* to be disclosed if probable

Lecture 13.07

CLASS QUESTIONS

Please see the Class Questions and Class Solutions for this Lecture at the end of this Section.

Lecture 13.08

CLASS QUESTIONS

Please see the Class Questions and Class Solutions for this Lecture at the end of this Section.

CLASS QUESTIONS

Work through the below Class Questions while following along with the respective lectures. Once this is complete, you can begin independently practicing what you've learned by quizzing yourself on this course section in your Interactive Practice Questions (IPQ), which can be found in your online Student Dashboard. Your IPQ simulates the computer-based testing experience, and will also help you understand how concepts are applied to the exam. Each question includes answer explanations from expert CPAs that will help you determine why you answered a question correctly or incorrectly. This is key to your success on the CPA Exam.

Lecture 13.05

1. Ames, Inc. has $500,000 of notes payable due June 15, 20X6. Ames signed an agreement on December 1, 20X5, to borrow up to $500,000 to refinance the notes payable on a long-term basis with no payments due until 20X7. The financing agreement stipulated that borrowings may not exceed 80% of the value of the collateral Ames was providing. At the date of issuance of the December 31, 20X5 financial statements, the value of the collateral was $600,000 and is not expected to fall below this amount during 20X6. In Ames' December 31, 20X5 balance sheet, the obligation for these notes payable should be classified as

	Short-term	Long-term
a.	$500,000	$ 0
b.	$100,000	$400,000
c.	$ 20,000	$480,000
d.	$ 0	$500,000

2. Lime Co.'s payroll for the month ended January 31, 20X5, is summarized as follows:

Total wages	$10,000
Federal income tax withheld	1,200

   All wages paid were subject to FICA. FICA tax rates were 7% each for employee and employer. Lime remits payroll taxes on the 15th of the following month. In its financial statements for the month ended January 31, 20X5, what amounts should Lime report as total payroll tax liability and as payroll tax expense?

	Liability	Expense
a.	$1,200	$1,400
b.	$1,900	$1,400
c.	$1,900	$ 700
d.	$2,600	$ 700

Liabilities Section 13

3. During 20X5, Haft Co. became involved in a tax dispute with the IRS. At December 31, 20X5, Haft's tax advisor believed that an unfavorable outcome was probable. A reasonable estimate of additional taxes was $200,000 but could be as much as $300,000. After the 20X5 financial statements were issued, Haft received and accepted an IRS settlement offer of $275,000. What amount of accrued liability should Haft have reported in its December 31, 20X5 balance sheet?

    a. $200,000
    b. $250,000
    c. $275,000
    d. $300,000

4. Management can estimate the amount of loss that will occur if a foreign government expropriates some company assets. If expropriation is reasonably possible, a loss contingency should be

    a. Disclosed but not accrued as a liability.
    b. Disclosed and accrued as a liability.
    c. Accrued as a liability but not disclosed.
    d. Neither accrued as a liability nor disclosed.

5. North Corp. has an employee benefit plan for compensated absences that gives employees 10 paid vacation days and 10 paid sick days. Both vacation and sick days can be carried over indefinitely. Employees can elect to receive payment in lieu of vacation days; however, no payment is given for sick days not taken. At December 31, 20X2, North's unadjusted balance of liability for compensated absences was $21,000. North estimated that there were 150 vacation days and 75 sick days available at December 31, 20X2. North's employees earn an average of $100 per day. In its December 31, 20X2, balance sheet, what amount of liability for compensated absences is North required to report?

    a. $36,000
    b. $22,500
    c. $21,000
    d. $15,000

Lecture 13.07

6. Arden, Inc., a company that prepares its financial statements in accordance with IFRS, has a $5,000,000 note payable that comes due on October 1, 20X2. The company has both the ability and the intent to refinance the obligation on a long-term basis. As of December 31, 20X1, it has entered into an agreement with a financial institution that allows it to refinance $2,000,000 for a 24-month period. In addition, it intends to issue a new 20 year $3,500,000 bond in May, 20X2 and knows that it will be able to because it has excellent credit and the bond market is very strong. How will Arden report this on their balance sheet at December 31, 20X1?

    a. The entire $5,000,000 will be reported as a noncurrent liability.
    b. $3,500,000 will be reported as a noncurrent liability and the remaining $1,500,000 will be reported as a current liability.
    c. The entire $5,000,000 will be reported as a current liability
    d. $2,000,000 will be reported as a noncurrent liability and the remaining $3,000,000 will be reported as a current liability.

7. Fergusen, Ltd., a company that prepares its financial statements in accordance with IFRS has the following pending items at December 31, 20X3.
   - The company is the defendant in a lawsuit as a result of an inadvertent violation of another entity's patent. Legal counsel has indicated that an unfavorable verdict in the amount of $250,000 is probable.
   - The company is involved in another lawsuit and their legal counsel believes that it is reasonably possible that it will result in a loss of $75,000.
   - The entity sells a product that is subject to a warranty. The estimated warranty liability as is $180,000.

   In its financial statements for the period ended December 31, 20X3, how much will be reported either on the balance sheet or in the footnotes for contingencies and how much for provisions?

   a. Contingencies of $75,000 will be disclosed and provisions of $430,000 will be accrued as a liability.
   b. A contingency of $250,000 will be accrued, a contingency of $75,000 will be disclosed, and a provision of $$180,000 will be accrued.
   c. Contingencies of $430,000 will be accrued and provisions of $75,000 will be disclosed.
   d. Contingencies of $355,000 will be accrued and provisions of $180,000 will be accrued.

Liabilities   Section 13

CLASS SOLUTIONS

1. (c) An entity may report a short-term liability that is expected to be refinanced on a long-term basis as a noncurrent asset provided the entity can demonstrate both the ability and intent to do so. Signing an agreement to refinance notes payable on a long-term basis is sufficient to support the intent and ability. The amount that may be reported as noncurrent, however, is limited to the amount the entity is able to refinance on a long-term basis as of the balance sheet date. Since Ames is limited to 80% of the value of the collateral, which is $480,000 (80% x $600,000), that is the amount that would be reported as noncurrent. The remainder would be current.

2. (d) Lime's expense will consist of its share of FICA taxes, which is 7% of wages or $700 ($10,000 x 7%). In addition to its share of FICA taxes, Lime is liable to the taxing authority for taxes withheld from employees, which will include their share of FICA taxes, also $700, and the federal income taxes withheld of $1,200, or $1,900 in total. Lime's total liability will consist of its share of FICA taxes, $700 and the $1,900 withheld for a total of $2,600.

3. (a) When a contingent liability is probable, as is the case with Haft, it will be accrued to the extent that it is reasonably estimable. Haft reasonably estimates the liability at $200,000, which is the amount to be accrued. Answer (b) is incorrect because when a contingent liability is expected to occur within a range, such as the $200,000 to $300,000 possible range to Haft, the best estimate within that range is accrued. Not the average, which would be $250,000. Answer (c) is incorrect because Haft was not aware of the amount for which the liability would be settled, $275,000, until after the financial statements were issued. As a result, they would not have been able to accrue this amount. Answer (d) is incorrect because when a contingent liability is expected to occur within a range, such as the $200,000 to $300,000 possible range to Haft, the best estimate within that range is accrued, which in this case is $200,000. If there is no amount that is a better estimate than any other within the range, the minimum amount, also $200,000 would be accrued. The $300,000 would only be accrued if that were the best estimate, which it is not in this case.

4. (a) A contingent liability that is probable and reasonably estimable is accrued and disclosed, but one that is only reasonably possible is disclosed without being accrued. Answer (b) is incorrect because the contingent liability would be disclosed and accrued as a liability if it was both reasonably estimable and probable of occurrence. It is not accrued if it is only reasonably possible. Answer (c) is incorrect because a contingent liability is only accrued if it is both probable and reasonably estimable, not if it is only reasonably possible. Regardless, if a contingent liability is accrued, it would also be disclosed. Answer (d) is incorrect because a contingent liability that is only remote is neither accrued nor disclosed. Disclosure is, however, required when a contingent liability is reasonably possible.

5. (d) A company accrues a liability for compensated absences when it is relatively certain that it will be paid. Vacation pay is required to be accrued if it either vests or accumulates. If it vests, the employee will be entitled to payment whether vacation is taken or not. If it accumulates, an employee would likely use the vacation prior to giving notice, rather than forfeit it. Sick pay, on the other hand, is only required to be accrued if it vests, because they will be entitled to payment whether used or not. If sick pay accumulates, but does not vest, there is no guarantee that the employee will get sick and qualify to use it in anticipation of giving notice and it may not be paid. As a result, North will accrue vacation pay of 150 days at $100 per day, or $15,000, but will not accrue sick pay.

6. (d) Under IFRS, a short-term obligation may be reported as noncurrent only if, as of the balance sheet date, it has entered into an agreement as of the balance sheet date to refinance the obligation for a period of at least 12 months. The intent and ability to issue a bond does not qualify. As a result, Arden would report $2,000,000 as noncurrent based on the agreement with the financial institution and the remainder would be reported as current.

7. (a) Under IFRS, a provision is a liability that is uncertain as to timing or amount. Provisions would include the $250,000 loss associated with the patent lawsuit since it results from a past event, the outflow of resources is probable, and the amount is reasonably estimable, as well as the warranty obligation of $180,000. Both of these would be recognized as liabilities for a total of $430,000. Contingencies are potential obligations that are not recognized as liabilities either because the outflow of resources is not probable or the amount is not reasonably estimable. Contingencies, which are disclosed but not accrued, would include the $75,000 potential loss associated with the other lawsuit.

Liabilities

Section 13

TASK-BASED SIMULATIONS

Task-Based Simulation 1

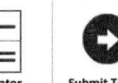

Required:

Items 1 through 6 are based on the following:

Town Company is preparing its financial statements for the year ended December 31, 20X1.

Items 1 through 6 represent various commitments and contingencies of Town at December 31, 20X1, and events subsequent to December 31, 20X1, but prior to the issuance of the 20X1 financial statements. For each item, select from the following list the reporting requirement. A reporting requirement may be selected once, more than once, or not at all.

Reporting requirement

D.	Disclosure only	B.	Both accrual and disclosure
A.	Accrual only	N.	Neither accrual nor disclosure

Section 13   Liabilities

	(D)	(A)	(B)	(N)
1. On December 1, 20X1, Town was awarded damages of $75,000 in a patent infringement suit it brought against a competitor. The defendant did not appeal the verdict, and payment was received in January 20X2.	○	○	○	○
2. A former employee of Town has brought a wrongful-dismissal suit against Town. Town's lawyers believe the suit to be without merit.	○	○	○	○
3. At December 31, 20X1, Town had outstanding purchase orders in the ordinary course of business for purchase of a raw material to be used in its manufacturing process. The market price is currently higher than the purchase price and is not anticipated to change within the next year.	○	○	○	○
4. A government contract completed during 20X1 is subject to renegotiation. Although Town estimates that it is reasonably possible that a refund of approximately $200,000 – $300,000 may be required by the government, it does not wish to publicize this possibility.	○	○	○	○
5. Town has been notified by a governmental agency that it will be held responsible for the cleanup of toxic materials at a site where Town formerly conducted operations. Town estimates that it is probable that its share of remedial action will be approximately $500,000.	○	○	○	○
6. On January 5, 20X2, Town redeemed its outstanding bonds and issued new bonds with a lower rate of interest. The reacquisition price was in excess of the carrying amount of the bonds.	○	○	○	○

Liabilities   Section 13

Task-Based Simulation 2

Required:

This question consists of 12 items. Select the **best** answer for each item.

Edge Co., a toy manufacturer, is in the process of preparing its financial statements for the year ended December 31, 20X3. Edge expects to issue its 20X3 financial statements on March 1, 20X4.

Required:

Items 1 through 12 represent various information that has not been reflected in the financial statements. For each item, the following two responses are required:

a. Determine if an adjustment is required and select the appropriate **amount**, if any, from the list below.

b. Determine (**Yes/No**) if additional disclosure is **required,** either on the face of the financial statements or in the notes to the financial statements.

Adjustment amounts
- **A.** No adjustment is required
- **B.** $100,000
- **C.** $150,000
- **D.** $250,000
- **E.** $400,000
- **F.** $500,000

Section 13 | Liabilities

Items to be answered:

1. Edge owns a small warehouse located on the banks of a river in which it stores inventory worth approximately $500,000. Edge is not insured against flood losses. The river last overflowed its banks twenty years ago.

2. During 20X3, Edge began offering certain health care benefits to its eligible retired employees. Edge's actuaries have determined that the discounted expected cost of these benefits for current employees is $150,000.

3. Edge offers an unconditional warranty on its toys. Based on past experience, Edge estimates its warranty expense to be 1% of sales. Sales during 20X3 were $10,000,000.

4. On October 30, 20X3, a safety hazard related to one of Edge's toy products was discovered. It is considered probable that Edge will be liable for an amount in the range of $100,000 to $500,000.

5. On November 22, 20X3, Edge initiated a lawsuit seeking $250,000 in damages from patent infringement.

6. On December 17, 20X3, a former employee filed a lawsuit seeking $100,000 for unlawful dismissal. Edge's attorneys believe the suit is without merit. No court date has been set.

7. On December 15, 20X3, Edge guaranteed a bank loan of $100,000 for its president's personal use.

8. On December 31, 20X3, Edge's board of directors voted to discontinue the operations of its computer games division and sell all the assets of the division. The division was sold on February 15, 20X4. On December 31, 20X3, Edge estimated that losses from operations, net of tax, for the period January 1, 20X4, through February 15, 20X4, would be $400,000 and that the gain from the sale of the division's assets, net of tax, would be $250,000. These estimates were materially correct.

9. On January 5, 20X4, a warehouse containing a substantial portion of Edge's inventory was destroyed by fire. Edge expects to recover the entire loss, except for a $250,000 deductible, from insurance.

10. On January 24, 20X4, inventory purchased FOB shipping point from a foreign country was detained at that country's border because of political unrest. The shipment is valued at $150,000. Edge's attorneys have stated that it is probable that Edge will be able to obtain the shipment.

11. On January 30, 20X4, Edge issued $10,000,000 bonds at a premium of $500,000.

12. On February 4, 20X4, the IRS assessed Edge an additional $400,000 for the 20X2 tax year. Edge's tax attorneys and tax accountants have stated that it is likely that the IRS will agree to a $100,000 settlement.

Task-Based Simulation 3

 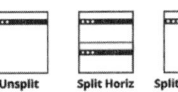 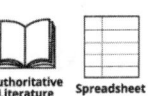
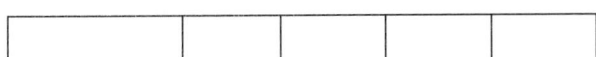

A company provides its employees a certain number of paid sick days per year, which can be accumulated and used in a future period but they do not vest. The company is trying to determine what amount they are required to accrue for sick pay. Identify the location in professional standards that indicates whether or not an employer is required to accrue a liability for nonvesting accumulating rights to receive sick pay benefits.

Task-Based Simulation 4

 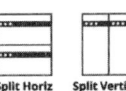 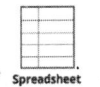 
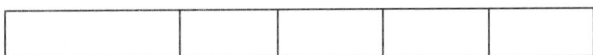

Your client is being sued and their attorney believes that an unfavorable outcome is probable. The client can estimate a potential range of losses that are likely to be incurred but cannot identify a single amount that is a better estimate than any other. Identify the location in professional standards that indicates what amount, if any, should be accrued.

Section 13 Liabilities

TASK-BASED SIMULATION SOLUTIONS

Task-Based Simulation Solution 1

	(D)	(A)	(B)	(N)
1. On December 1, 20X1, Town was awarded damages of $75,000 in a patent infringement suit it brought against a competitor. The defendant did not appeal the verdict, and payment was received in January 20X2.	○	○	●	○
2. A former employee of Town has brought a wrongful-dismissal suit against Town. Town's lawyers believe the suit to be without merit.	○	○	○	●
3. At December 31, 20X1, Town had outstanding purchase orders in the ordinary course of business for purchase of a raw material to be used in its manufacturing process. The market price is currently higher than the purchase price and is not anticipated to change within the next year.	○	○	○	●
4. A government contract completed during 20X1 is subject to renegotiation. Although Town estimates that it is reasonably possible that a refund of approximately $200,000 – $300,000 may be required by the government, it does not wish to publicize this possibility.	●	○	○	○
5. Town has been notified by a governmental agency that it will be held responsible for the cleanup of toxic materials at a site where Town formerly conducted operations. Town estimates that it is probable that its share of remedial action will be approximately $500,000.	○	○	●	○
6. On January 5, 20X2, Town redeemed its outstanding bonds and issued new bonds with a lower rate of interest. The reacquisition price was in excess of the carrying amount of the bonds.	●	○	○	○

Liabilities Section 13

Explanation of solutions:

1. (B) Since the award of damages occurred prior to the financial statement date and it is not being appealed, the $75,000 is not a contingency. It will be accrued and disclosed.

2. (N) When Town's lawyers indicate that they believe a claim is without merit, that is an indication that the probability of occurrence is only remote. A contingent liability that is probable and estimable is accrued and disclosed. One that is reasonably possible is disclosed, but not accrued. One that is only remote, however, is neither accrued nor disclosed.

3. (N) Fluctuations in the market prices of resources used or required by an entity represent the normal risks of being in business. It would be neither possible nor useful to recognize all such risks in the financial statements and neither disclosure nor accrual would be required.

4. (D) The prospect of being required to pay a refund as a result of an anticipated renegotiation of a government contract represents a contingent loss. Since it is only reasonably possible that it will occur, it will be disclosed and not accrued. If it were probable, it would be disclosed and accrued. The amount to be accrued would be the minimum amount of the range, $200,000, since there is no indication that an amount within the range of $200,000 to $300,000 is the best estimate of the loss.

5. (B) A governmental requirement to clean up toxic waste is an asset retirement obligation that is treated similarly to a contingent liability. Since a liability of $500,000 is both probable and reasonably estimable, that amount will be accrued and disclosed.

6. (D) The redemption of bonds after the balance sheet date is a subsequent event. Since it is not indicative of a condition that existed as of the balance sheet date, as the bonds were not redeemed until the following period, it is a Type 2 subsequent event that will be disclosed but will not involve an adjustment to the financial statements.

Task-Based Simulation Solution 2

1. AN — The fact that a company does not maintain an insurance policy for certain types of losses does not constitute a contingency that would be subject to accrual unless the condition that is not covered by insurance exists at the balance sheet date, it is probable that a loss will occur, and the amount of the loss can be reasonably estimated. Although the company may disclose the lack of insurance, it is not required to do so.

2. CY — When a company has an obligation for postretirement benefits, such as providing health care benefits to retired employees, an amount equal to the present value of an estimate of the expected benefits must be accrued and reported as a liability. The amount, in this case, is given as $150,000. An obligation for postretirement benefits must also be disclosed.

3. BN — Warranty expense represents a contingency that is probable, since it is likely that some products will require work that is covered by the warranty, and generally can be reasonably estimated. As a result, it requires accrual. The amount will be 1% of sales of $10,000,000 or $100,000. Since warranty expense is an ordinary cost of doing business, no special disclosure is required.

4. BY — The discovery of a safety hazard related to one of Edge's products represents a contingent liability. Since it is probable that Edge will be liable, accrual of a loss would be appropriate provided the amount can be reasonably estimated. When the amount can only be estimated in terms of a range of loss with no single amount more probable than any other, the minimum amount of the range will be accrued. Edge will accrue a loss of $100,000. In addition, since this is not an ordinary cost of doing business, disclosure is required.

5. AN — A lawsuit initiated by Edge constitutes a gain contingency. It is never appropriate to accrue a gain contingency. In addition, although Edge may disclose the gain contingency, disclosure is not required.

6. AN — Since Edge's attorneys believe the suit filed by the former employee is without merit, it represents a contingent loss that is only remote. As a result, neither accrual nor disclosure would be appropriate.

7. AY — The guarantee of a bank loan for Edge's president represents a loss contingency that would only be accrued if it were probable that the president would default requiring Edge to repay the loan. Whenever a company guarantees the indebtedness of another, however, disclosure is required.

8. AY — When a company decides to discontinue the operations of a division, it is accounted for as a disposal of a segment of a business. That means that the results of operations of the segment, as well as gains and losses on the sale of assets or settlement of liabilities associated with the segment will be reported in the discontinued operations section of the income statement. Amounts, however, are recognized in the period in which they occur. As a result, no gain or loss would be recognized in 20X3 since operations and the sale will occur in 20X4. Disclosure would be required.

9. AY — Since the warehouse fire did not occur until January 5, 20X4, after the balance sheet date, accrual would not be appropriate. The loss, however, represents a subsequent event that affects the amount reported on the balance sheet, requiring that it be disclosed.

10.	AN	The detaining of the inventory shipment on January 24, 20X4 is a subsequent event relating to a condition that did not exist at the balance sheet date. As a result, accrual would not be appropriate. In addition, since it is likely that Edge will obtain the shipment, it is not likely that a loss will be incurred and disclosure would not be required.
11.	AY	Issuance of debt after the balance sheet date is a subsequent event relating to a condition that did not exist at the balance sheet date. As a result, accrual would not be appropriate. The issuance of debt after the balance sheet date, but prior to the issuance of the financial statements, would require disclosure.
12.	BY	Although the IRS assessment occurred after the balance sheet date, it is a subsequent event that relates to a condition that did exist as of the balance sheet date since it relates to a previous tax period. It is a contingency loss that is probable and can be reasonably estimated at $100,000. As a result, it will be accrued and disclosed.

Task-Based Simulation Solution 3

FASB ASC	710	10	25	7

Task-Based Simulation Solution 4

FASB ASC	450	20	30	1

Section 13   Liabilities

Lecture 13.08
DOCUMENT REVIEW SIMULATION
Document Review Simulation 1

 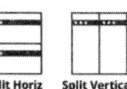 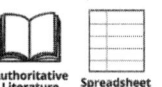

Work Tab | Resources | Help

Gallant Corporation manufactures forklifts and has a calendar year end. In conjunction with the year-end audit, the accountant for Gallant Corporation prepared a schedule of year-end contingencies to determine what amount should be recorded on the books and which items require disclosure in the financial statements for year ending December 31, 20X6. The 20X6 financial statements will be issued on March 1, 20X7. A preliminary review of subsequent events occurred through January 30, 20X7.

The schedule was reviewed by the senior auditor who made some modifications to the treatment of the contingencies. Review the memo from the senior auditor to the accountant for Gallant Corporation and make any changes necessary to ensure it is accurate and consistent with the information and documents provided.

To revise the memo, click on each segment of underlined text below and select the needed correction, if any, from the list provided.

Goings and Goings, CPAs

To:	Chad Reading, Accountant
From:	Roger Philipp, Controller
Date	February 1, 20X7
Re:	Recommendations regarding December 31, 20X6 year-end contingencies

I have reviewed your schedule of year-end contingences along with the related records and documents for the year ending December 31, 20X6. Below are my findings and recommendations for adjustments. If you have any questions, please do not hesitate to call me.

Warranty Liability and Expense
According to the controller, all of the forklifts manufactured by the company have a two-year warranty. Based on historical experience regarding warranties, Gallant estimates a warranty cost equal to 2% of sales will be incurred in the year of the sale and 4% in the second year. After reviewing the Warranty Liability and Warranty Expense accounts, I do not agree with the current 12/31/20X6 balances. In accordance with the matching principle, revenues and any related expenses must be recognized together in the same period. **1) Thus, the Warranty Expense account should have a debit balance of $28,000 and the Warranty Liability account a credit balance of $140,000.**

Line of Credit
Gallant Corporation has secured a $500,000 line of credit with the National Bank. In reviewing the terms of the agreement, the company is required to maintain $150,000 compensating cash balance at the bank. **2) Since only the compensating cash balance is required to be reflected**

on the books, I agree with the current general ledger balance of $150,000 for the Line of Credit Liability account.

Pending EPA Violations

During 20X6, the Federal government cited Gallant for several environmental (EPA) violations. After negotiating with the government, Gallant's attorney believes it is probable that government will prevail and that the company will be fined within the range of 300,000- $500,000. **3) I agree with your decision, based on the attorney's advice, not to record a contingent liability at year-end but rather wait until the fine is assessed.**

Purchase Commitment

In reviewing the accounting records, Gallant entered into a two-year contract to purchase manufacturing components with a supplier. At December 31, 20X6, there are 7,500 units remaining under the purchase agreement which the company anticipates satisfying in next 18 months. **4) Accordingly, Gallant is not required to accrue any liability but should disclose this information in the notes to financial statements.**

Pending Litigation

Gallant is involved in two ongoing lawsuits. After meeting with the attorney and reviewing the email to the controller, **5) I concur with the accrual of a $160,000 liability for the anticipated loss contingencies.**

Subsequent Events

Our preliminary review of the subsequent events revealed two items. Depending on the nature of the subsequent event, generally accepted accounting principles may require disclosure in an organization's financial statements. **6) Therefore, we will be making an adjustment for $360,000 to the year-end financial statements for both the fire loss and the final outcome of the sexual harassment lawsuit.**

Section 13 | Liabilities

Resources

Auditor's notes regarding warranty liability

Subject:	20X6 Warranty Liability
Auditor:	Larry Goings, CPA, Senior Auditor
Date:	January 6, 20X6

In order to record the estimated warranty liability at December 31, 20X6 I verified the following information:

- Warranty Policy
  On December 12, 20X6, I interviewed the controller (Roger Philipp). Per our conversation, Mr. Philipp confirmed that all of the forklifts manufactured by the company have a two year warranty. Based on historical experience regarding warranties, Gallant estimates that for sales made in 20X6, a warranty cost equal to 2% of sales will be incurred in the year of the sale and 4% in the second year.

- Forklift Sales
  Per review of the sales journal and supporting documentation, the forklift sales during 20X6 totaled $1,500,000.

- Cost of Repairs
  Per review of the actual repair tickets for the current year, the average cost of repairs is $200 per forklift. The actual cost paid for repairs under warranty during 20X6 was $28,000.

- General Ledger Balance
  The balance in the Warranty Liability account on 1/1/20X6 was $78,000 and at 12/31/20X6 the balance is a $50,000. At year-end, the Warranty Expense account has a $0 balance.

Memo from the auditor to the controller

Goings and Goings, CPAs

To:	Roger Philipp
From:	Larry Goings, CPA, Senior Auditor
Date	January 28, 20X7
Re:	Subsequent events

As part of our audit procedures we conduct a review of subsequent events that occurred after the year end reporting period, but before the financial statements will be issued. Our preliminary findings revealed the following:

- On January 15, 20X7, Gallant's manufacturing plant was damaged by a fire. The amount of the uninsured loss is $280,000.
- On January 25, 20X7, the sexual harassment lawsuit was settled. Gallant was required to pay $80,000.

Liabilities
Section 13

Journal entries made during the year regarding warranty liability

Account	Debit	Credit
Warranty Liability	78,000	
Warranty Expense		78,000
(To reverse prior year liability)		

Account	Debit	Credit
Warranty Expense	28,000	
Cash		28,000
(To record current year warranty costs)		

Account	Debit	Credit
Warranty Expense	50,000	
Warranty Liability		50,000
(To remove the credit balance in the warranty expense account)		

Memo regarding purchase commitment

Gallant Corporation

To:	Chad Reading, Accountant
From:	Roger Philipp, Controller
Date	January 1, 20X7
Re:	Purchase commitment with Gaston Supply Company

On July 1, 20X6, Gallant entered into a non-cancelable, two-year contract to purchase certain manufacturing components with a supplier. The contract calls for the purchase of 5,000 units per year at $6.50 per unit. During 20X6, we have purchased 2,500 units of our committed 10,000 units. At December 31, 20X6, I have been informed that the market price of the component part is $5.00 per unit. If you have any questions, please call me at extension #1559.

Email from attorney regarding pending EPA violations

From:	asterling@sterlingandsterling.com
Sent:	December 29, 20X6
To:	rphillip@gallantcorp.com
Subject:	Pending EPA violations

Roger:

This email is in response to your question during our meeting yesterday regarding the pending EPA violations against Gallant Corporation. According to my review of the documents, on June 15, 20X6, the Federal government cited Gallant for several environmental (EPA) violations. After meeting several times with the government on the company's behalf, I believe it is probable that Federal government will prevail. Based on the violations, I estimate that the company will be fined within the range of $300,000 - $500,000. However, I advise that you do not record a contingent liability since that will appear to be an admission of guilt.

Please let me know if you have any questions.

Arnold
Arnold Sterling, Attorney at Law
Sterling and Sterling

Line of Credit Information

Gallant Corporation has a $500,000 line of credit with the National Bank. There were no borrowings during the year-ended December 31, 20X6. Under terms of the line of credit, Gallant is required to maintain $150,000 compensating balance on deposit. Accordingly, the company made the following general journal entry:

Account	Debit	Credit
Cash-Compensating Balance	150,000	
Line of Credit Liability - National Bank		150,000
(To record compensating cash balance related to line of credit)		

Liabilities   Section 13

Email from attorney regarding pending litigation

From: asterling@sterlingandsterling.com
Sent: December 29, 20X6
To: rphilipp@gallantcorp.com
Subject: Pending litigation

Roger:
I wanted to update you on the status of the two litigation cases involving Gallant Corporation. As you know, Gallant is a plaintiff in a dispute regarding manufacturing defects. Based on merits of the case I believe it is "reasonably possible" that the company will lose. However, the damages will not exceed $100,000. Also, Gallant is being sued for sexual harassment by a former employee. After meeting with the plaintiff, I believe it is probable that the company will have to pay damages totaling $60,000. Please let me know if you have any questions.

Arnold
Arnold Sterling, Attorney at Law
Sterling and Sterling

Section 13 | Liabilities

Items for Analysis

Thus, the Warranty Expense account should have a debit balance of $28,000 and the Warranty Liability account a credit balance of $140,000.

1. Choose an option below:

    - [Original text] Thus, the Warranty Expense account should have a debit balance of $28,000 and the Warranty Liability account a credit balance of $140,000.

    - [Delete text]

    - Thus, the Warranty Expense account should have a debit balance of $28,000 and the Warranty Liability account a credit balance of $108,000.

    - Thus, the Warranty Expense account should have a debit balance of $30,000 and the Warranty Liability account a credit balance of $108,000.

    - Thus, the Warranty Expense account should have a debit balance of $28,000 and the Warranty Liability account a credit balance of $90,000.

    - [None of the choices are correct.]

Since only the compensating cash balance is required to be reflected on the books, I agree with the current general ledger balance of $150,000 for the Line of Credit Liability account.

2. Choose an option below:

    - [Original text] Since only the compensating cash balance is required to be reflected on the books, I agree with the current general ledger balance of $150,000 for the Line of Credit Liability account.

    - [Delete text]

    - For a line of credit where no borrowings have taken place, the line of credit is not recorded as a liability on the books, but rather disclosed in the notes to the financial statements.

    - When there is a line of the credit, the total amount of the credit is reflected on the books. Therefore, the balance in the Line of Credit Liability account should be $500,000.

    - When there is a compensating balance associated with a line of credit, only the difference between the total line of credit and the cash balance is reflected on the books. Therefore, the balance in the Line of Credit Liability account should be $350,000.

    - [None of the choices are correct.]

I agree with your decision, based on the attorney's advice, not to record a contingent liability at year-end but rather wait until the fine is assessed.

3. Choose an option below:

    - [Original text] I agree with your decision, based on the attorney's advice, not to record a contingent liability at year-end but rather wait until the fine is assessed.

    - [Delete text]

    - Because the outcome is deemed probable and estimable, an adjustment must be made to the books. The amount accrued should be the maximum of $500,000.

    - Because the outcome is deemed probable and estimable, an adjustment must be made to the books. The amount accrued should be limited to the minimum of $300,000.

Liabilities   Section 13

- Because the outcome is deemed probable and estimable, an adjustment must be made to the books. The amount accrued will be $400,000.

- Because the outcome is deemed probable but cannot be reasonably estimated, only disclosure in the notes to the financial statements is required.

- [None of the choices are correct.]

Accordingly, Gallant is not required to accrue any liability but should disclose this information in the notes to financial statements.

4. Choose an option below:

    - [Original text] Accordingly, Gallant is not required to accrue any liability but should disclose this information in the notes to financial statements.

    - [Delete text]

    - Accordingly, Gallant should accrue $11,250 as an estimated liability related to the purchase commitment.

    - Accordingly, Gallant should accrue $48,750 as an estimated liability related to the purchase commitment.

    - Accordingly, Gallant should accrue $37,500 as an estimated liability related to the purchase commitment.

    - [None of the choices are correct.]

I concur with the accrual of a $160,000 liability for the anticipated loss contingencies.

5. Choose an option below:

    - [Original text] I concur with the accrual of a $160,000 liability for the anticipated loss contingencies.

    - [Delete text]

    - Under the circumstances, neither of the amounts required recognition at year-end. Instead, both items should be disclosed in the notes to the financial statements.

    - Based on the attorney's opinion regarding the future outcome of the two cases, the company should accrue $60,000 for the sexual harassment lawsuit. The other lawsuit only requires disclosure in the notes to the financial statements.

    - Based on the attorney's opinion regarding the future outcome of the two cases, the company should accrue $100,000 for the manufacturing defect lawsuit. The other lawsuit only requires disclosure in the notes to the financial statements.

    - [None of the choices are correct.]

Therefore, we will be making an adjustment for $360,000 to the year-end financial statements for both the fire loss and the final outcome of the sexual harassment lawsuit.

6. Choose an option below:

    - [Original text] Therefore, we will be making an adjustment for $360,000 to the year-end financial statements for both the fire loss and the final outcome of the sexual harassment lawsuit.

    - [Delete text]

- Since neither event occurred at year-end, no adjustment is required. However, we will disclose both events in the notes to the financial statements.
- Therefore, we will be making an adjustment for $280,000 to the year-end financial statements for the fire loss. No adjustment is required for the $80,000 loss from the lawsuit since a liability was already recorded based on the estimated loss at year-end.
- Therefore, we will be making an additional adjustment for $20,000 to the year-end financial statements for the final outcome of the sexual harassment lawsuit. The fire loss will be disclosed in the notes to the financial statements since it is a condition that did not exist as of the balance sheet date.
- [None of the choices are correct.]

DOCUMENT REVIEW SIMULATION SOLUTION

Document Review Simulation Solution 1

1. [None of the choices are correct.]

   The Warranty Expense account should have a debit balance of $90,000 and the Warranty Liability account a credit balance of $140,000.

   The total estimated warranty cost of 6% (2% + 4%) is recorded in the year of the sale in accordance with the matching principle.

   Warranty expense: $1,500,000 x 6% = $90,000.

   The actual expenses incurred during are debited to the liability account. Therefore, at year-end the warranty liability account should have a $140,000 balance:

   Warranty Liability

Repairs	$28,000	1/1 bal.	$78,000
		Adj entry 12/31	$90,000
		End bal.	$140,000

2. <u>For a line of credit where no borrowings have taken place, the line of credit is not recorded as a liability on the books but rather disclosed in the notes to the financial statements.</u>

   The line of credit is not recorded on the books but disclosed in the notes to the financial statements. Note that the compensating balance requirement of $150,000 is treated as restricted cash and not as a liability.

3. <u>Because the outcome is deemed probable and estimable, an adjustment must be made to the books. The amount accrued should be limited to the minimum of $300,000.</u>

   A journal entry to record a liability on the balance sheet and a loss or expense on the income statement is required if the loss contingency is both probable and estimable. Both these conditions are met. The email from the attorney regarding the pending EPA violations clearly states the loss is probable and gives an estimated range.

   When a contingent liability can only be estimated to occur with a range where no amount within that range is more likely to be the actual loss than any other, the amount accrued is limited to the minimum amount in the estimated range. In this case, a contingent liability is recorded for $300,000.

4. <u>Accordingly, Gallant should accrue $11,250 as an estimated liability related to the purchase commitment.</u>

   When an entity enters into a noncancellable purchase commitment, at a minimum, the entity's obligation is required to be disclosed. In addition, a liability will be recognized to the extent that payments under the commitment will exceed the value that will be obtained.
   To date, the entity has purchased 2,500 units of a total of 10,000 it is obligated to purchase under the noncancellable commitment. As a result, the entity is still obligated to purchase 7,500 units. Due to a decline in price, the entity will be required to pay $6.50 per units for

items that could be purchased in the open market for $5.00. As a result, the entity is required to pay $1.50 per unit in excess of the value to be received.

As a result, a loss and estimated liability of $1.50 per unit on 7,500 units, or $11,250, will be recorded.

5. <u>Based on the attorney's opinion regarding the future outcome of the two cases, the company should accrue $60,000 for the sexual harassment lawsuit. The other lawsuit only requires disclosure in the notes to the financial statements.</u>

    A contingent liability is required to be accrued and disclosed if it is probable that a loss will be incurred and the amount of the loss can be estimated. If the amount of a probable loss cannot be reasonably estimated or if the loss is only reasonably possible, the loss will be disclosed but not accrued.

    The loss involving the product defect is only reasonably possible and disclosure is sufficient. The loss relating to the sexual harassment suit, however, is probable and estimable. As of when the entity was preparing its journal entries, information from the auditor's review of subsequent events was not known. As a result, the amount to be accrued will be the $60,000 suggested by the attorney, which was the best estimate at the time.

6. <u>Therefore, we will be making an additional adjustment for $20,000 to the year-end financial statements for the final outcome of the sexual harassment lawsuit. The fire loss will be disclosed in the notes to the financial statements since it is a condition that did not exist as of the balance sheet date.</u>

    Under GAAP, financial statements should include the effects of all subsequent events that provide additional information about conditions in existence as of the balance sheet date. Such subsequent events are termed Type 1. However, if the subsequent event provides information about conditions that did **not** exist as of the balance sheet date, it is a Type 2 subsequent event, requiring disclosure but with no adjustment required.

    Regarding the sexual harassment lawsuit, Gallant initially would have recorded the $60,000 at year end because the contingency is both probable and estimable. Because the actual settlement in January 20X7 is a Type 1 subsequent event, an adjustment to the liability on the year-end balance sheet is required. Therefore, an additional adjustment of $20,000 ($80,000 - $60,000) should be made.

    The fire is a Type 2 subsequent event because it relates to a condition that did not exist at balance sheet date. Therefore, no recognition is required on the balance sheet. Instead the event is disclosed in the footnotes to the financial statements.

Section 14 – Pensions & Postemployment Benefits

Corresponding Lectures

Watch the following course lectures with this section:

Lecture 14.01 – Types of Pension Plans
Lecture 14.02 – Pension Expense
Lecture 14.03 – Pension Presentation
Lecture 14.04 – Post-retirement Benefits other than Pensions
Lecture 14.05 – Pensions – Class Questions – M/C
Lecture 14.06 – Pensions – Class Question – TBS
Lecture 14.07 – Pensions under IFRS
Lecture 14.08 – Pensions under IFRS – Class Question

EXAM NOTE: Please refer to the AICPA FAR Blueprint in the Introduction to find a listing of the representative tasks (and their associated skill levels—i.e., Remembering and Understanding, Application, and Analysis) that the candidate should be able to perform based on the knowledge obtained in this section.

Pensions & Postemployment Benefits

Lecture 14.01

TYPES OF PENSION PLANS

An agreement between an employer and employee to give the employee benefits once they retire (**ASC 715**).
- Two types of plans under GAAP:
  - **Defined Contribution** – defined contribution plan (ex. 401K) or when the employer sets aside specific amounts during the time of service, and the retired employee receives whatever sum these contributions and earnings produce.

Pension Expense	5000	
Cash		5000

  - **Defined Benefit** - The employer guarantees certain benefits to be paid to retired employees, and is responsible for setting aside sufficient amounts to fulfill these promises
    - Two non-GAAP cash basis methods are "pay-as-you-go" (payments are expensed after someone retires) and Terminal funding (funding an annuity upon retirement).

Accounting for a **defined contribution plan** is straightforward. The company accrues the required contributions at the time services are rendered by employees, and reports pension expense. Contributions are normally required by law to be paid before the due date of the tax return in order for the contribution to be deductible on the return, so companies fund liabilities quickly.

For example, assume the client is offering a 15% defined contribution pension plan to its employees, and salaries and wages for 20X1 total $1,000. The entry to recognize pension expense is:

12/31/X1	Pension expense	150	
	Accrued pension cost		150

The liability must be paid by no more than 2 1/2 months following the close of the fiscal year. This 2 ½ month window is not affected by the recent change in C corporation tax return due dates. Assuming it is paid at that time, the entry is:

3/15/X2	Accrued pension cost	150	
	Cash		150

These two types of entries are the only ones needed for a defined contribution plan. The company is not involved in the administration of pension assets after they are contributed to the plan.

Accounting for a **defined benefit pension plan** is much more complicated, because of two special problems:
- **Matching** – pension expense must be recognized at the time of employee service, not when benefits are paid to retired employees.
- **Estimation** – costs are difficult to determine, since they depend on the lifespan of the employees, changes in wage rates, and the rates of return earned on pension investments.

To compute pension expense, the services of an **actuary** will be required. The actuary will, among other responsibilities, compute the pension obligation three different ways. Each computation is of the amount the company would need to have set aside in a plan today to be able to pay benefits to employees for service to date. This may also be described as the actuarial present value of future benefits to be paid. It is described as actuarial because it takes into account such factors as life expectancy, and it is described as being a present value because it takes into account the time value of money and the delay between the time that an expense is accrued and when it is paid.

- **Vested benefit obligation** (**VBO**) – what is owed if an employee is terminated immediately. The VBO is the actuarial present value of vested benefits, which are those benefits that the employee is entitled to that are not contingent on remaining in the employment of the entity (if **quit**).

- **Accumulated benefit obligation** (**ABO**) – what is owed for service to date if the employee continues in employment until normal retirement age at *current wage rates*. The actuarial present value of benefits attributed by the pension benefit formula to employee services rendered before a specified date and based on employee services and compensation *prior to that date* (salaries **received to date**) **(Faithful Representation)**.

- **Projected benefit obligation** (**PBO**) – What is owed for service to date if the employee continues in employment until normal retirement age and receives periodic adjustments to pay for increased experience and general inflation based on *future wage rates*. The present value of the obligation is determined under the **benefits-years-of-service method.** So the PBO is the actuarial present value as of a date of all benefits attributed by the pension benefit formula to employee service rendered prior to that date. The PBO is measured using assumptions as to future compensation levels if the pension benefit formula is based on those future compensation levels (salaries **to be received**) **(Relevance)**.

In some pension plans, benefits earned are not affected by changes in future compensation. When an employee's compensation increases over time, benefits earned after the change in compensation are calculated using the new compensate rate, but benefits already earned are not adjusted for the change in rate. These plans are referred to as **flat-benefit or non-pay-related plans**.

In other plans, benefits earned are affected by changes in future compensation. When an employee's compensation increases over time, not only are those benefits earned after the change calculated using the new compensation rates, but benefits already earned are also adjusted for the change in rate. These plans are referred to as **pay-related, final-pay, final-average-pay, or career-average-pay plans.**

In a flat-benefit or non-pay-related plan, the ABO will be equal to the PBO. In all other cases, the PBO, which does take anticipated future pay increases into account, will be greater than the ABO.

Pensions & Postemployment Benefits   Section 14

The VBO and the ABO are calculated for disclosure purposes and provide information about the entity's obligations if the plan was to be discontinued.

The most useful of the three computations to the accountant determining pension expense is PBO, since this represents the most realistic estimate of pension costs of a going concern. As a result, it is used in the calculations applied in determining pension expense and in determining the amount of a pension-related asset or liability that will appear on the balance sheet.

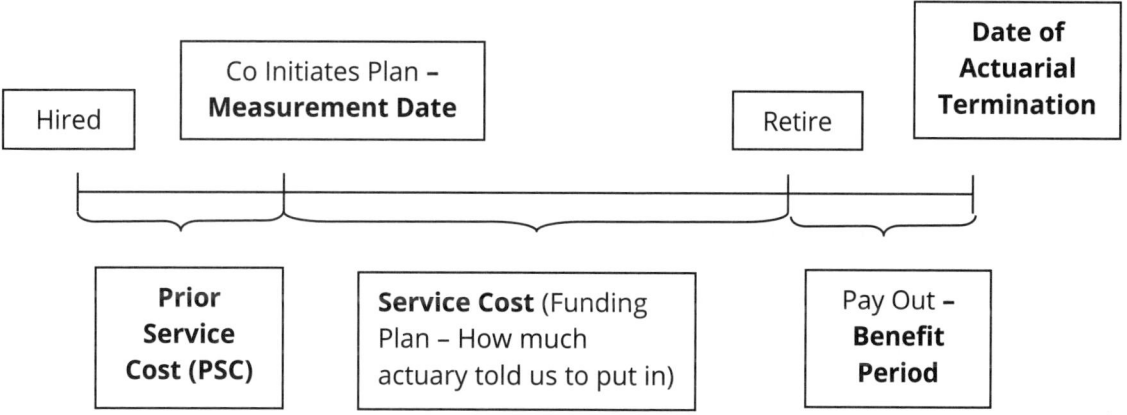

- Based on **Assumptions made by an Actuary**
    o Salary
    o Life expectancies
    o Interest rates
    o Years employed
    o Costs of administering the plan
    o Turnover rates

Section 14   Pensions & Postemployment Benefits

Lecture 14.02

Pension Expense

To compute, **pension expense (Pension Cost)**, up to seven different amounts may need to be determined:

Pension Expense (Pension Cost) (A-SPIDER)

+ **S**ervice Cost
- Actuarial present value of benefits attributed to services performed during the period
- Increase in PBO for 1 year

+/- **P**rior Service Cost (PSC) Amortization
- Cost associated with service years before plan was implemented or amended.
- Calculation = Beginning PSC / Average Service Life *or* expected future years-of-service amortization method.

+ **I**nterest Cost
- Change in PBO resulting from passage of time.
- Calculation = Beginning PBO x Discount Rate (Settlement Rate).

-(Actual **R**eturn on PLAN Assets)
- Actual earnings of pension plan during the period.
  - Calculation = Ending PA – Beginning PA – Contribution Made + Benefits Paid (or)
  - Beg FV of Plan Assets x Actual Return

+ **D**eferred Gain (unrecognized pension gain/ - loss)
- When Actual Investment results differ from long-run Expected returns.
- Calculation = Return on PA – Beginning PA x Expected Rate of Return

- (**E**xcess amortization of deferred gain/ +loss)
- Unrecognized gains or losses included in accumulated other comprehensive income
- Amortization if deferrals get too large (**corridor approach**)
  - Minimum amortization calculation:
    - Deferred gain or loss at beginning of year.
    - Minus 10% of Plan Assets or beg PBO, whichever is higher.
    - Excess / Average Service Life

+/-**A**mortization of Existing Net Obligation or Net Asset at implementation

=   **Pension Expense/Cost**

The first items are based on the PBO, and the last items are based on the pension plan assets that have been set aside by the company.

+ *Service cost* is the increase in PBO that results from employee service in the current period. The complex actuarial computations used to determine service cost are beyond the scope of the CPA exam, but service cost is the primary component of pension expense each year, since it matches the pension cost to each period of service by the employee. It represents the amount that would need to be set aside by the company each year over the service life of an employee to fund promised benefits after retirement (**increase in PBO for 1 year**).

+/- Prior service cost is the PBO that results from establishing (or amending) a plan that gives employees credit for work performed **before** the date the plan was adopted. Since most defined benefit plans give employees credit for all years of service since the original date of hire, the prior service cost on the date a plan is established is often enormous. This cost should be amortized systematically over the **average service time** of the employees in order to conform to the matching principle.
- When a plan is initiated, PSC will consist of the actuarial present value of benefits that employees are retroactively entitled to as a result of being employed by the entity prior to initiation of the plan.
    - This is initially recognized with a credit to the PBO and a debit to other comprehensive income (OCI).
    - The amount is amortized as an increase in pension expense.

- When a plan is amended, the PBO may increase or decrease as a result.
    - If benefits are reduced or the retirement age is postponed, the PBO will decrease.
    - If benefits are increased or the retirement age is accelerated, the PBO will increase.
    - The decrease or increase will result in a debit or credit, respectively, to the PBO with the offset to OCI

There are two different approaches for calculating amortization of PSC to determine the amount that will be added to, or deducted from, pension expense. On the exam, the **straight-line method** is normally used.
- Divide beginning PSC by the average expected remaining service lives of employees expected to receive benefits **(Beg PSC / Avg Svc Life)**.
- If, for example, an entity had 100 employers expected to begin retiring at the rate of 10 per year over the next 10 years:
    - 10 employees would have an expected remaining service life of 1 year each for a total of 10 years.
    - 10 employees would have an expected remaining service life of 2 years each, for a total of 20 years.
    - The total expected remaining service life of the 100 employees would be: 10+20+30+40+50+60+70+80+90+100 = 550.
    - With 100 employees, the average expected remaining service period would be 5.5 years (550/100)

The theoretically preferred approach is to assign an equal amount to each future service period for each covered employee. Using the same information from the previous example:
- In the first year, all 100 employees would be covered resulting in amortization of 100/550 x PSC.
- In the second year, 10 employees would have retired and the 90 remaining employees would be covered, resulting in amortization of 90/550 x PSC

+ Interest cost is the increase in PBO that results from the passage of time. Since PBO is a present value computation, it includes an interest rate assumption (discount rate) for promised future benefits. As time passes, the company gets closer to the date benefits must be paid, so the present value grows. On the exam, interest cost is equal to the PBO at the beginning of the year multiplied

by the discount rate (**Settlement rate** – rate at which the plan's obligations could be settled) **(Beg PBO x Disc Rate)**.

- (Actual Return on plan assets) refers to the earnings of the investments in the pension plan. This represents the change in the value of the pension assets over the course of the year after adjusting for contributions and withdrawals. It includes:
- Interest and dividends accrued on investments
- Unrealized gains or losses on investments acquired during the period or held for the entire period
- Realized gains or losses on sales of investments net of unrealized gains or losses previously recognized

The value used is the market-related value of plan assets (securities/real estate), not the historical cost of the securities. Keep in mind that the actual return is subtracted from pension expense, not added to it, since it represents earnings of the plan that reduce the amount the company will have to fund. The fair value of plan assets will be increased by contributions to the plan and decreased by distributions from the plan. The remainder of the change in the fair value of plan assets during the period represents the actual return on plan assets.

The actual return equals the market-related value of plan assets at the end of the year minus the value at the beginning of the year minus contributions made to the plan plus withdrawals made from the plan (End PA – Beg PA – Contributions + Withdrawals).

- **2** ways to calculate **Actual Return on Plan Assets**

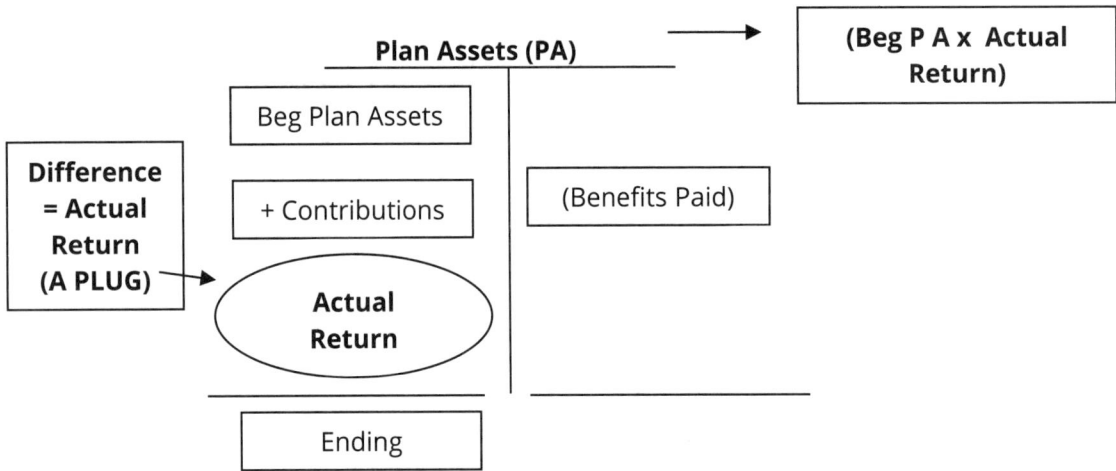

+ Deferred gain (- loss) Unrecognized pension gain is the portion of pension investment income that is believed to be the result of short-term variations from the long-run expected return on investments. The expected return on plan assets, which is used to calculate service cost, is the long-term expected return. It is likely that the actual return in any given year will be lower or higher than the expected return but that, over the long-term, the differences will substantially offset. To avoid large variances in pension expense from period to period that may result from changes in the actual return, pension expense is calculated using the expected return with any difference accumulated in OCI.
- The actual gain on plan assets reduces pension expense since, the greater the return on plan assets, the less the company will need to contribute to the plan.

Pensions & Postemployment Benefits — Section 14

- Pension expense is then adjusted for the difference between the actual return and the expected return on plan assets.
    - Expected return is equal to beginning plan assets x the expected rate of return.
    - If the actual return is greater, the difference is added back to pension expense.
    - If the actual return is lower, the difference is deducted from pension expense.
    - The net effect is that pension expense will include the expected, rather than the actual return on plan assets.

- Excess Amortization of Deferred prior pension gain (loss amortization) is needed when the deferred gains or losses get too large. Although it is anticipated that returns in excess of expected returns will be offset by returns that are lower than expected returns over the long term, this may not be the case.
- The expected rate may not have been a good estimate.
- Economic or market conditions may differ from expectations.

When it does not appear that deferred gains and losses will offset one another, the difference will be amortized to make certain it is properly recognized in pension expense. To determine the amount of amortization, a **corridor approach** is used.
- As of the beginning of the period, the accumulated net deferred gain or loss is compared to 10% of the *greater of* the beginning balance in the PBO or the fair value of plan assets.
    - **([Beg Deferred Amt – 10% (Higher of Beg PBO or Beg PA)] / Avg Svc Life).**
- If the accumulated net deferred gain or loss is larger than the greater of those two, the excess is amortized.
- Amortization will be at least the excess divided by the average expected remaining service life of active employees covered by the plan.
    - Amortization of a net gain reduces pension expense.
    - Amortization of a net loss increases pension expense.

+/-Amortization of Existing Net Obligation or Net Asset at implementation
When the company first adopted FASB 87 after 1986, there may have been a transition adjustment for the difference between the PBO and the Fair Value of Plan assets.
- If the **PBO > F.V.** of plan assets, then the amortization of the <u>net obligation</u> will *increase* pension expense/cost.
- If **F.V > PBO**, then the <u>Net Asset</u> amortization will *decrease* pension expense/cost.
    - This amount should be amortized over the larger of **15 years** or the **average remaining service life.**

= Pension Expense (Pension Cost) (A-SPIDER)

Lecture 14.03
PENSION PRESENTATION

To Fund the Plan

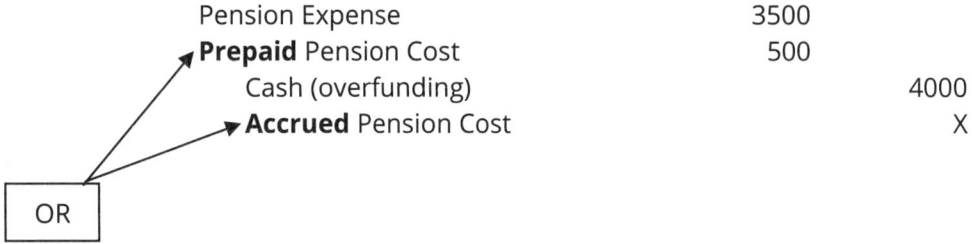

Pension Expense	3500	
Prepaid Pension Cost	500	
Cash (overfunding)		4000
Accrued Pension Cost		X

OR

Funding of pension plans does not necessarily occur at the same time as pension expense is recorded. If expensing exceeds funding, an accrued pension cost liability account is created. If funding exceeds expensing, a prepaid pension cost asset account is created. Plans where the fund is under the control of the employer are considered unfunded.

    For example, if pension expense of $90 is computed in the first year of a plan, and the client contributes only $50 to the pension plan, the following entry is made:

Pension expense/cost	90	
Accrued pension cost (balance)		40
Cash		50

If the client instead contributes $100, the entry is:

Pension expense/cost	90	
Prepaid pension cost (balance)	10	
Cash		100

ASC 715 requires reporting the funded status of a pension plan on the balance sheet. Both overfunded and underfunded plans must be reported on the balance sheet as either assets or liabilities.

The funded status is the difference between the **ending *projected benefit obligation*** and the **ending *fair value of the plan assets*** at the measurement date (fiscal year end). If the plan is overfunded, a *noncurrent asset* is recorded on the balance sheet. If the plan is underfunded, either a *current liability, a noncurrent liability*, or both are reported on the balance sheet. In other words, the funding status of plans may NOT be netted (overfunded plans may not be netted with underfunded plans). The measurement date for a defined benefit plan is as of the date of the employer's fiscal year-end statement of financial position.

A defined benefit plan that has a fiscal year-end that does not coincide with a month-end may have difficulty in determining fair values of certain plan assets and obligations as of the measurement date. A company with a 52/53 week year, for example, may have a fiscal year-end that is the last Friday in March. As a practical expedient, a defined benefit plan with a fiscal year-end that does not coincide with a month-end may elect to use the month-end closest to the fiscal year-end as its measurement date.

- An entity with more than one defined benefit plan would be required to make a similar election for all plans.

- The practical expedient must be applied consistently from year to year.

Plan assets and obligations are required to be adjusted for significant changes occurring between the fiscal year-end and the month-end being used as the measurement date. This will include the effects of contributions, plan amendments, settlements, or curtailments. Adjustments are not made, however, for the effects of events that are not the result of the entity's activities such as changes in market prices or interest rates.

Any gains and losses not already recognized as pension expense are recognized in **Accumulated other comprehensive income** (net of tax). ASC 715 also requires that if a plan is amended and either increases or decreases the projected benefit obligation, this amount should be recognized as either a prior service cost or credit. Prior service costs or credits should be amortized over the future periods of service of the employees expected to receive benefits.

Example: Ending PBO 800, ending FV plan assets 600, accrued pension cost 50 (target 200-50=150), tax rate 30%,

Excess adjustment of PBO and FV of Plan assets at year end (Other Comprehensive Income - OCI)	105 (150 x 70%)
Deferred Tax asset	45 (150 x 30%)
Accrued Pension Cost (Liability for Pension Benefits)	150

To account for the change in the Projected Benefit Obligation (PBO):

Beginning of year PBO
+ Service cost
+ Interest cost
± Prior service cost or credit (from changes to plan in current year in full)
± Actuarial gain or loss (from changes in actuarial assumptions)
– Benefits paid
End of year PBO

- o Notice that amortization of PSC, gains/losses and transition amounts don't affect the PBO in the current year, however they do affect pension expense/cost for the year.

- **Disclosures:**
   - o A reconciliation of the Pension benefit obligation (*PBO*) showing the components separately (**A SPIDER**).
   - o A reconciliation of the *fair value of plan assets* with the components shown separately.
   - o The *funded status* of the plan and the amounts recognized and not recognized in the balance sheet.
   - o For defined benefit plans, the accumulated benefit obligation.
   - o The benefits expected to be paid in each of the next five years and in the aggregate for the five years thereafter.
   - o The net periodic benefit cost recognized with the components.

- On a weighted-average basis, *rates and assumptions used* for the assumed discount rate, rate of compensation increase and expected long-term rate of return on plan assets.
- An explanation of any significant changes in the plan assets or the benefit obligation.
- A detailed description of the plan including employee groups covered.
- The net gain or loss and net prior service cost or credit recognized in other comprehensive income (OCI) for the period, and any reclassification adjustments of OCI (amortization of items) that are recognized in pension cost.
- The amounts in accumulated OCI that have not yet been recognized as pension costs, showing separately the net gain or loss, the net prior service cost or credit, and net transition asset or obligation
- The amounts in accumulated OCI expected to be recognized as components of pension cost over the fiscal year-end that follows the most recent balance sheet presented, showing separately net gain or loss, net prior service cost or credit, and net transition asset or obligation
- The amount and timing of any plan assets expected to be returned to the employer during the next 12-month period (or operating cycle, if longer) after the most recent balance sheet.

Financial Reporting by Pension Plans

A **defined benefit pension plan** will provide annual financial statements consisting of:
- A statement reporting **net assets available for benefits** as of the end of the fiscal year.
- A statement reporting **changes in net assets available for benefits** for the fiscal year.
- Information about the actuarial present value of **accumulated plan benefits**, which may be as of either:
  - The beginning of the current fiscal year; or
  - The end of the current fiscal year.
- Information about significant effects of other factors affecting the actuarial resent value of accumulated plan benefits.

A **defined contribution pension plan** will provide annual financial statements consisting of:
- A statement reporting **net assets available for benefits** as of the end of the fiscal year.
- A statement reporting **changes in net assets available for benefits** for the fiscal year.

The statement of net assets available for benefits is required to present total assets, total liabilities, and net assets available for benefits, reflecting all investments at fair value.
- Investments of a defined contribution pension plan that are considered fully benefit-responsive are measured at contract value, rather than at fair value.
- As a practical expedient, when the plan's year-end does not fall on a month-end, fair values may be determined based on the closest month-end.
  - Contributions, distributions, or other significant events occurring between the month-end and fiscal year-end are to be disclosed.
  - The entity will also disclose the election to use the practical expedient in its summary of significant accounting policies and the date as of which investments are valued.

Lecture 14.04

POST-RETIREMENT BENEFITS OTHER THAN PENSIONS

Some companies provide employees with other postretirement benefits that are not in the form of cash payments. Common examples are:
- Health care benefits
- Life insurance coverage
- Legal services
- Day care
- Tuition assistance and housing subsidies

Post Retirement Benefit Expense
+Current service cost
+Interest cost on APBO
-(Actual Return on Plan Assets)
+Amortization of PSC
-(Gain amortization for changes in APBO)
±Amortize transition amount (net obligation) (longer of 20 years or average service life)
Net postretirement benefit expense/cost

Transition costs represent the increase or decrease in the amount reported as an asset or liability for postretirement benefits that resulted from adopting GAAP reporting. It may be amortized as an increase or decrease in the expense over the longer of 20 years or the average remaining service life of active participants. As an alternative, the entire amount may be taken into income in the period of transition.

Similar formula as for pensions, but DON'T use PBO → Use APBO (Accumulated Postretirement Benefit Obligation)
- Accrue if –
    a) Probable & Estimable
    b) Accumulates or Vests
    c) Services have already been performed.

ASC 715 also requires that companies disclose the status of *overfunded and underfunded postretirement plans* on their balance sheets and any adjustment is also made to Other Comprehensive Income (OCI). Overfunded plans are aggregated with the total reported as an asset while underfunded plans are also aggregated with the total reported as a liability.

Most of these benefits are based on the length of service of the employees and do not vary based on wage levels, so there is no need to compute a projected benefit obligation and costs are based on the accumulated postretirement benefit obligation (**APBO**). The computations are similar to those involving the costs of pension plans, with **two major differences**:

1. Costs are not generally funded during the service period, so there are no assets to account for and costs generally include only service cost and interest cost (and amortization of prior service cost if the plan credits employees for service prior to the adoption of the plan).

2. Employees usually qualify for full benefits after a certain number of years, and costs should be **matched to the period of service** required to qualify, not the entire service

time of the employee up to retirement. The obligation must be fully accrued by the date the employee is fully eligible for the benefits.

For example, assume the client is providing the most common postretirement benefit, health care coverage for retirees, and requires the employee to have completed 10 years of service to qualify for full coverage after retirement. If an employee is hired at the age of 48, and works until age 65, the service cost of the benefits is recognized over the period from age **48 to 58**, since the employee does not need to continue working beyond that point for the employer to be obligated.

Disclosures

- The accumulated Postretirement benefit obligation (APBO)
- A brief plan description
- A summary of significant accounting policies
- The assumed trend in the rate of health care costs that was used to measure the expected cost of benefits covered by the plan.
- The effects on APBO, service cost and interest cost of a 1% increase or decrease of the trend rates for health care costs.
- Information about contributions and legally required reserves.
- The status of overfunded and underfunded post-retirement plans

ASC 712 deals with **nonretirement postemployment benefits**, which are all types of benefits provided to a former or inactive employee, beneficiary, or dependent, that is not provided through a pension or postretirement plan. These might include salary continuation, supplemental unemployment benefits, severance benefits, disability benefit, job training and counseling, or continuation of such benefits as health care or life insurance coverage.

Sometimes these benefit are in the form of *special termination benefits* that are offered to an employee as compensation for termination. These are recognized as a loss and liability when the offer is accepted by the employee and the amount of the benefits is subject to reasonable estimation.

Termination benefits that an employer is contractually obligated to provide are treated similarly to contingent liabilities. They are accrued when it becomes probable that employees will be entitled to the benefits and the amounts can be reasonably estimated. The amount will include any lump sum payments and the present values of future payments.

Financial Reporting by Health and Welfare Plans

A **defined benefit health and welfare plan** will provide annual financial statements consisting of:
- A statement reporting **net assets available for benefits** as of the end of the fiscal year.
- A statement reporting **changes in net assets available for benefits** for the fiscal year.
- Information about the **plan's benefit obligations** as of the end of the current fiscal year.
- Information about significant effects of other factors affecting the plan's benefit obligations.

A **defined contribution health and welfare plan** will provide annual financial statements consisting of:
- A statement reporting **net assets available for benefits** as of the end of the fiscal year.
- A statement reporting **changes in net assets available for benefits** for the fiscal year.

The statement of net assets available for benefits is required to present total assets, total liabilities, and net assets available for benefits, reflecting all investments at fair value.
- Investments of a defined contribution health and welfare plan that are considered fully benefit-responsive are measured at contract value, rather than at fair value.
- As a practical expedient, when the plan's year-end does not fall on a month-end, fair values may be determined based on the closest month-end.
  - Contributions, distributions, or other significant events occurring between the month-end and fiscal year-end are to be disclosed.
  - The entity will also disclose the election to use the practical expedient in its summary of significant accounting policies and the date as of which investments are valued.

Lecture 14.05

CLASS QUESTIONS

Please see the Class Questions and Class Solutions for this Lecture at the end of this Section.

Lecture 14.06

CLASS QUESTIONS

Please see the Class Questions and Class Solutions for this Lecture at the end of this Section.

Lecture 14.07

PENSIONS AND OTHER EMPLOYEE BENEFITS UNDER IFRS

IFRS deals with all employee benefits in a single standard, IAS 19, **Employee Benefits**. It defines employee benefits as all forms of consideration given to an employee by an entity in exchange for services rendered by that employee. Categories of employee benefits include:
- **Short-term benefits** that are provided to current employees and are expected to be settled within one year of the end of the period.
- **Post-employment benefits**, other than termination benefits.
- **Termination benefits**, which are provided to employees that result from termination of an employee before the normal retirement date or acceptance by an employee of benefits in exchange for terminating employment with the entity.
- **Other employee benefits**.

Short-Term Employee Benefits include salaries and wages; vacation and sick pay; profit-sharing or bonuses; and nonmonetary benefits such as medical coverage, cars, or free or discounted goods or services. They are recognized in their undiscounted amounts in the period in which the employee renders the services that earn the benefits.

Paid absences, including vacation, sick pay, and compensation for jury duty fall into two categories:
- Those that accumulate are recognized in the period during which the employee's entitlement to payment increases.
- Those that do not accumulate are recognized in the period of the absence.

Costs associated with profit-sharing and bonus plans are recognized when the entity has a present obligation to make the payments and the amount can be reasonably estimated. A present obligation to make the payments only exists if the entity has no realistic alternative other than to make the payments.

Postemployment Benefits include pensions, lump sum retirement payments, and other postemployment benefits such as life insurance and continued medical care. Plans involving establishing a separate entity to which contributions are made, such as pension plans, are not distinguished from plans for which no such separate entity is established. They are identified, however, as defined contribution plans and defined benefit plans.

For **defined contribution plans**, the entity recognizes an expense in the amount of the defined contribution in the period in which the employee performs the services. When the amount is not expected to be fully paid within 12 months of the end of the reporting period, the amount will be recognized at its present value, discounted by reference to the market yields on high quality corporate bonds as of the end of the reporting period.

Accounting for **defined benefit plans**, requires a 4 step process.
1. Determine the surplus or deficit
    a. The cumulative cost, including those earned for services earned in the current period and prior periods, is determined using the ***projected unit credit method***, an actuarial technique.
    b. The amount is discounted to its present value, resulting in the ***defined benefit obligation (DBO)***
    c. The amount is reduced by the fair value of plan assets (PA), if any.
    d. The difference is the surplus, if PA exceed the DBO, or a deficit if the opposite is true.
2. The net amount is adjusted for any effect of limiting a defined benefit asset to the *asset ceiling*, which is the present value of economic benefits that will be realized in the form of either refunds from the plan or reductions in future contributions to the plan.
3. The expense to be recognized in profit or loss is determined, incorporating three components.
    a. Current service cost is the increase in the DBO as a result of services performed by employees in the current period.
    b. Past service cost and any gain or loss on settlement.
        i. Past service cost is the adjustment to the present value of the DBO that results from an amendment or curtailment of the plan, generally recognized when the amendment or curtailment occurs.
        ii. Gains or losses on settlements are the difference between the present value of the DBO being settled and the settlement amount, recognized when the settlement occurs.
    c. Net interest on the net defined benefit liability or asset, calculated using the same discount rate applied for defined contribution plans.
4. Components of the remeasurement of the defined benefit liability or asset that are recognized in OCI are identified. These include:
    a. Actuarial gains and losses.
    b. The return on plan assets, other than amounts included in net interest.
    c. Any change in the effect of the asset ceiling, other than amounts included in net interest.

Pensions & Postemployment Benefits — Section 14

The net defined benefit liability or asset is recognized in the statement of financial position. An asset is limited to the lower of the surplus in the defined benefit plan and the asset ceiling.

Termination Benefits are reported as a liability at the earlier of either:
- The date on which the entity can no longer withdraw the offer of those benefits; or
- The date on which the entity recognizes the costs of restructuring.

Termination benefits are measured similarly to *short-term employee benefits* when they are expected to be settled within 12 months of the end of the reporting period in which they are recognized. Otherwise, they are recognized in the same manner as *other long-term employee benefits*.

Other Long-Term Employee Benefits include long-term paid absences, such as sabbatical leave; long-term disability benefits; and deferred remuneration. For other long-term employee benefits, the entity recognizes the net total of the following items in profit or loss:
- Service cost
- Net interest
- Remeasurements of the net defined benefit liability or asset

Another specific rule of IFRS is that the **netting of pension plan assets and liability balances** is only permissible when there is a legally enforceable right to use the assets of one plan to settle the obligations of another plan.

Pensions and Other Employee Benefits	
US GAAP	**IFRS**
• Vacation pay that accumulates or vests and sick pay that vests are required to be accrued. • The benefits-years-of-service method is applied in calculations for defined benefit pension plans. • Corridor approach used for recognizing actuarial gains or losses in pension expense.	• Vacation pay and sick pay that accumulate are required to be accrued. • The projected unit credit method is applied in calculations for defined benefit pension plans. • Actuarial gains and losses recognized immediately in other comprehensive income.

Lecture 14.08

CLASS QUESTIONS

Please see the Class Questions and Class Solutions for this Lecture at the end of this Section.

Section 14   Pensions & Postemployment Benefits

CLASS QUESTIONS

Work through the below Class Questions while following along with the respective lectures. Once this is complete, you can begin independently practicing what you've learned by quizzing yourself on this course section in your Interactive Practice Questions (IPQ), which can be found in your online Student Dashboard. Your IPQ simulates the computer-based testing experience, and will also help you understand how concepts are applied to the exam. Each question includes answer explanations from expert CPAs that will help you determine why you answered a question correctly or incorrectly. This is key to your success on the CPA Exam.

Lecture 14.05

1. The following information pertains to Kane Co's defined benefit pension plan:

Accrued pension cost, January 1, 20X4	$ 2,000
Service cost	19,000
Interest cost	38,000
Expected and actual return on plan assets	22,000
Amortization of unrecognized prior service cost	52,000
Employer contributions	40,000

    The ending fair value of plan assets is $750,000 and the ending projected benefit obligation is $850,000. Ignoring income taxes, in its December 31, 20X4 balance sheet, what is the required adjustment to accrued pension cost (Liability)?

    a. $45,000
    b. $49,000
    c. $51,000
    d. $87,000

2. Payne, Inc. implemented a defined-benefit pension plan for its employees on January 2, 20X3. The following data are provided for 20X3, as of December 31, 20X3:

Projected benefit obligation	$103,000
Plan assets at fair value	78,000
Net periodic pension cost	90,000
Employer's contribution	70,000
Unfunded prior service cost	4,000

    What debit entry should Payne make, based only on the preceding date, in other comprehensive income for the year ended December 31, 20X3?

    a. $0
    b. $1,000
    c. $5,000
    d. $25,000

Pensions & Postemployment Benefits	Section 14

3. Visor Co. maintains a defined benefit pension plan for its employees. The service cost component of Visor's net periodic pension cost is measured using the

   a. Unfunded Accumulated benefit obligation.
   b. Unfunded Vested benefit obligation.
   c. Projected benefit obligation.
   d. Expected return on plan assets.

4. Interest cost included in the net pension cost recognized by an employer sponsoring a defined benefit pension plan represents the

   a. Amortization of the discount on unrecognized prior service costs.
   b. Increase in the fair value of plan assets due to the passage of time.
   c. Increase in the projected benefit obligation due to the passage of time.
   d. Shortage between the expected and actual returns on plan assets.

5. The following information pertains to Seda Co.'s pension plan:

Actuarial estimate of projected benefit obligation at 1/1/X5	$72,000
Assumed discount rate (settlement rate)	10%
Service costs for 20X5	18,000
Pension benefits paid during 20X5	15,000

   If **no** change in actuarial estimates occurred during 20X5, Seda's projected benefit obligation at December 31, 20X5 was

   a. $64,200
   b. $75,000
   c. $79,200
   d. $82,200

6. Which of the following disclosures is not required of companies with a defined benefit pension plan?

   a. A description of the plan.
   b. The amount of pension expense by component.
   c. The weighted-average discount rate.
   d. The estimates of future contributions for the next five years.

7. According to ASC 715, an employer sponsoring a defined benefit pension plan must report a liability on the balance sheet equal to

   a. The current year pension cost that was not funded.
   b. The difference between the fair value of plan assets less the accumulated benefit obligation.
   c. The difference between the accumulated benefit obligation and the projected benefit obligation.
   d. The difference between the fair value of plan assets less the projected benefit obligation.

8. Arroz Corporation implemented a defined benefit pension plan for its employees on January 2, 20X4. The following data are provided for 20X6 and as of December 31, 20X6:

Projected benefit obligation	$600,000
Accumulated benefit obligation	550,000
Plan assets at fair value	420,000
Pension cost for 20X6	180,000
Pension contribution for 20X6	150,000

Assume that as of January 1, 20X6, Arroz's pension plan was fully funded, and there were no recorded pension assets or liabilities on the balance sheet. Assuming a tax rate of 40%, what is the net effect of the required adjustment on accumulated other comprehensive income on December 31, 20X6?

a. $90,000 decrease.
b. $108,000 decrease.
c. $36,000 decrease.
d. $0

Lecture 14.08

9. Which of the following is an actuarial technique that is used in IFRS to account for defined benefit pension plans?

a. Projected-unit-credit method.
b. Benefit-years-of-service method.
c. Accumulated benefits method.
d. Vested years of service method.

Pensions & Postemployment Benefits Section 14

CLASS SOLUTIONS

1. (c) Pension expense for 20X4 will be equal to service cost + interest – expected and actual return on plan assets + amortization of prior service cost for a total of ($19,000 + $38,000 - $22,000 + $52,000) $87,000. Since the employer contribution was $40,000, the accrued pension cost will increase by $47,000 to $49,000. If the ending PBO is $850,000 and the ending fair value of plan assets is $750,000, the plan is underfunded by $100,000. With an accrued pension liability of $49,000, an additional liability of $51,000 is needed.

2. (c) With a projected benefit obligation of $103,000 and plan assets of $78,000, Payne must report a minimum pension liability of $25,000. Payne contributed only $70,000 to the plan based on pension cost of $90,000 indicating that there is already an accrued pension liability of $20,000. In order to achieve an accrued pension liability of $25,000, Payne will need to accrue an additional liability of $5,000, indicating a debit entry to OCI of $5,000 for the period.

3. (c) Service cost is the increase in the projected benefit obligation that represents the benefits earned as a result of services performed for the company during the current year. Service cost is not affected by whether the plan is funded or unfunded. Answer (a) is incorrect because the unfunded accumulated benefit obligation is the unpaid portion of the actuarial present value of benefits earned to date without taking into account future increases in compensation. It represents the amount that would be owed if the pension plan were to be terminated but all employees were to receive their benefits upon retirement. It is not used to calculate service cost. Answer (b) is incorrect because the unfunded vested obligation is the unpaid portion of the actuarial present value of benefits earned to date that are not contingent on future employment. It represents the amount that the company would be required to pay in benefits if all employees were terminated on the balance sheet date. It is not used to calculate service cost. Answer (d) is incorrect because the expected return on plan assets is a component that reduces pension expense while service cost increases it. It is not used to calculate service cost.

4. (c) Interest cost is a component of pension expense that is calculated by multiplying the beginning balance of the PBO by the discount rate. It represents the increase in the PBO due to the passage of time. Answer (a) is incorrect because unrecognized prior service cost is included in the PBO, on which the interest is calculated. As a result, amortization of the discount on unrecognized prior service cost is included in interest cost, but it is not what interest cost constitutes in its entirety. Answer (b) is incorrect because unlike the PBO, which is recognized at its present value, the fair value of plan assets does not automatically increase due to the passage of time. It increases or decreases based on the earnings on investments in the plan, which may include interest, dividends, and realized and unrealized gains and losses. Answer (d) is incorrect because the difference between the expected and actual return on plan assets is a gain or loss that is deferred and amortized as a component of pension expense only when the accumulated amount exceeds 10% of the greater of the PBO or plan assets.

5. (d) With a discount rate of 10% and a beginning balance in the PBO of $72,000, interest cost would be ($72,000 x 10%) $7,200. Combined with service cost of $18,000, pension expense is $25,200, increasing the PBO. Payments of pension benefits of $15,000 reduce the PBO resulting in an ending balance of ($72,000 + $25,200 - $15,000) $82,200.

6. (d) An entity with a defined benefit pension plan is required to disclose a description of the plan, the amount of pension expense by component, the weighted-average discount rate, and the estimate of future contributions for the next fiscal period, not the next five years.

7. (d) An entity with a defined benefit pension plan is required to report a liability to the extent to which the fund is underfunded or an asset to the extent to which it is overfunded. Funding is determined by comparing the PBO to the fair value of plan assets and a liability is recognized when the PBO exceeds plan assets. Answer (a) is incorrect because when some or all of the current period's pension cost is not funded, the unfunded portion is recognized as an accrued liability, which is considered in determining if an additional liability is required to comply with the requirement. Answers (b) and (c) are incorrect because funding is determined by comparing the PBO, not the ABO, to the fair value of plan assets and a liability is recognized when the PBO exceeds plan assets.

8. (a) The plan is underfunded by $180,000, the amount by which the PBO of $600,000 exceeds the plan assets of $420,000, requiring that the entity recognize a liability in that amount. With pension cost of $180,000 in the current year and a contribution of $150,000, the entity would recognize an accrued liability for the difference of $30,000. As a result, an additional liability of $150,000 is required. The tax effect of ($150,000 x 40%) $60,000 will be recognized as a deferred tax asset and the remaining $90,000 would be a decrease to OCI.

9. (a) While GAAP allows the use of various methods, IFRS requires that the PBO and service cost be determined using the projected-unit-credit method.

Lecture 14.06

TASK-BASED SIMULATIONS

Task-Based Simulation 1

Situation

The following information pertains to Sparta Co.'s defined benefit pension plan.

Discount rate	8%
Expected rate of return	10%
Average service life	12 years
At January 1, 20X5:	
Projected benefit obligation	$600,000
Fair value of pension plan assets	720,000
Unrecognized prior service cost	240,000
Unamortized prior pension gain	96,000
At December 31, 20X5:	
Fair value of pension plan assets	825,000

Service cost for 20X5 was $90,000. There were no contributions made or benefits paid during the year. Sparta's unfunded accrued pension liability was $8,000 at January 1, 20X5. Sparta uses the straight-line method of amortization over the maximum period permitted.

Items to be answered:

Calculate the following **amounts** for Sparta's pension cost for 20X5.

1. _____ Interest cost
2. _____ Expected return on plan assets
3. _____ Actual return on plan assets
4. _____ Amortization of prior service costs
5. _____ Minimum amortization of unrecognized gain

Section 14 — Pensions & Postemployment Benefits

For the following items determine whether the component **Increases, Decreases, or has No effect** on Sparta's unfunded accrued pension liability.

		Increase	Decrease	No effect
6.	Service cost	○	○	○
7.	Interest cost	○	○	○
8.	Actual return on plan assets	○	○	○
9.	Amortization of prior service costs	○	○	○
10.	Amortization of unrecognized pension gain	○	○	○

Pensions & Postemployment Benefits — Section 14

Task-Based Simulation 2

   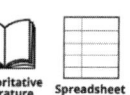

Your client has established a defined contribution pension plan for its employees. The plan requires the company to make contributions for period during which the employee is performing services and reduced contributions for a period after the employee retires. Identify the location in professional standards that indicates how those costs should be accounted for.

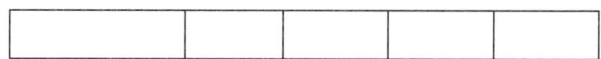

Task-Based Simulation 3

An entity has a defined benefit pension plan for which the projected benefit obligation (PBO) exceeds the fair value of plan assets. As a result, the entity will be recognizing an unfunded accrued pension liability and is trying to determine what the offset will be when it records the journal entry. Identify the location in professional standards that indicates how to record the accrual of a liability to recognize the unfunded status of the pension plan.

TASK-BASED SIMULATION SOLUTIONS

Task-Based Simulation Solution 1

1. $ 48,000   Interest cost

2. $ 72,000   Expected return on plan assets

3. $105,000   Actual return on plan assets

4. $ 20,000   Amortization of prior service costs

5. $ 2,000   Minimum amortization of unrecognized gain

Explanations:

1. Interest cost is equal to the beginning PBO of $600,000 multiplied by the discount rate of 8%, which is $48,000.

2. The expected return on plan assets is equal to the beginning balance in plan assets of $720,000 multiplied by the expected rate of return of 10% to provide an expected return of $72,000.

3. The actual return on plan assets is the increase of $105,000 during the period ($825,000 - $720,000) after adjusting for contributions made to the plan and benefits paid from the plan, neither of which occurred. As a result, the actual return would be the entire increase of $105,000.

4. Since Sparta uses straight-line amortization over the maximum period, unamortized prior service costs of $240,000 will be amortized over the expected average service life of covered employees of 12 years resulting in amortization of ($240,000/12) $20,000.

5. An unrecognized gain is amortized when the amount as of the beginning of the period exceeds 10% of the greater of the beginning PBO or the beginning fair value of plan assets. In this case, the fair value of plan assets was greater at $720,000 vs $600,000. Unrecognized gains of $96,000 exceed 10% of PA of $72,000 by $24,000. This will be amortized over the expected average service life of employees, which is 12 years, resulting in amortization of $2,000 ($24,000/12).

For the following items determine whether the component **Increases, Decreases, or has No effect** on Sparta's unfunded accrued pension liability.

Pensions & Postemployment Benefits — Section 14

The unfunded accrued pension liability is the excess of the PBO over the fair value of plan assets. It is increased by pension cost. It is decreased by contributions to the plan and earnings on plan assets. It is not affected by the payment of benefits since that decreases both the PBO and plan assets for the same amount.

		Increase	Decrease	No effect
6.	Service cost	●	○	○
7.	Interest cost	●	○	○
8.	Actual return on plan assets	○	●	○
9.	Amortization of prior service costs	●	○	○
10.	Amortization of unrecognized pension gain	○	●	○

Explanations:

6. (I) – Service cost increases pension cost, so that would also increase unfunded accrued pension liability.

7. (I) – Interest cost increases pension cost, so that would also increase unfunded accrued pension liability.

8. (D) – Actual return on plan assets decreases pension cost, but this is netted with the deferred gain to get the expected return on plan assets.

9. (I) – Amortization of PSC increases pension cost since we are increasing employee benefits, this increases our cost or pension expense for the period.

10 (D) – The amortization of the unrecognized pension gain would decrease pension cost for the period since we are now using up our gain and amortizing it into the pension cost. If we had to amortize a loss, that however would increase our pension cost.

Task-Based Simulation Solution 2

| FASB ASC | 715 | 70 | 35 | 1 |

Task-Based Simulation Solution 3

| FASB ASC | 715 | 30 | 25 | 4 |

Section 15 – Stockholders' Equity
Corresponding Lectures

Watch the following course lectures with this section:

Lecture 15.01 – Stockholders' Equity
Lecture 15.02 – Treasury Stock
Lecture 15.03 – Preferred Stock, APIC and Stock Option
Lecture 15.04 – Retained Earnings and Dividends
Lecture 15.05 – Presentation
Lecture 15.06 – Stockholder's Equity – Class Questions M/C
Lecture 15.07 – Stockholder's Equity – Class Question TBS
Lecture 15.08 – Stockholder's Equity under IFRS
Lecture 15.09 – Stockholder's Equity under IFRS – Class Question

EXAM NOTE: Please refer to the AICPA FAR Blueprint in the Introduction to find a listing of the representative tasks (and their associated skill levels—i.e., Remembering and Understanding, Application, and Analysis) that the candidate should be able to perform based on the knowledge obtained in this section.

Stockholders' Equity

Lecture 15.01

STOCKHOLDERS' EQUITY

Presentation of Stockholders' Equity section (ASC 505):

- **Preferred stock**
    - Disclose shares authorized, issued, outstanding
    - Disclose dividend and liquidation preference
    - Disclose cumulative and participation rights

- **Common stock**
    - Disclose shares authorized, issued, outstanding
    - Net treasury shares under **par value method** from total
      (*contra C/S*)

- **Additional paid-in capital**
    - Preferred stock
    - Common Stock
    - Treasury Stock
    - Warrants
    - Employee stock options

- **Noncontrolling Interest in "S"**

- **Retained earnings** (Appropriated/Unappropriated)

- **Accumulated other comprehensive income (DENT)**
  (Prominently displayed)
    - **D**erivative cash flow hedges
    - **E**xcess adjustment of Pension PBO and FV of Plan assets at yr end
    - **N**et unrealized gain or loss on available-for-sale securities
    - **T**ranslation adjustments for Foreign Currency

- **Treasury stock**
    - Report only if under **cost** method (*contra-equity*)

Common Stock

A corporation begins operations by issuing stock in order to raise funds. It will obtain the authority to issue shares from the state of incorporation. All corporations will issue some form of common stock, which normally has a **par value (Certificate of Incorporation) or stated value (Board of directors)** assigned to it. The issue price of the stock, however, is virtually always greater than the par, and this excess goes to additional paid-in capital (APIC), and is identified specifically as being from common stock.

For example, if a corporation is authorized to issue $10 par value common stock, and issues a single share for $13, the entry is:

Cash	13	
Common stock		10
APIC-CS		3

If the stock is issued in exchange for **property** other than cash, the property is recorded at **fair market value.**

If **multiple securities** are issued (stocks and bonds or common and preferred stock), the *relative Fair market value method* should be used.

If stock is **repurchased and retired**, the accounts credited at the time of issuance are debited. If the repurchase price is lower than the original issuance price, the difference is credited to APIC from stock retirements. If the repurchase price is higher, the remainder is normally debited to retained earnings (after debiting any APIC that exists from previous stock retirements that exists).

For example, if the above share is **repurchased at $12** and retired, the entry is:

Common stock	10	
APIC-CS	3	
APIC-Retired stock		1
Cash		12

If, instead, it is **repurchased at $15**, the retirement entry is:

Common stock	10	
APIC-CS	3	
Retained earnings	2	
Cash		15

If the client had APIC-Retired stock from previous transactions, the debit to retained earnings would have been made to that account instead. If the difference, however, was greater than the balance in APIC-Retired stock, it would be reduced to zero and the remainder would reduce retained earnings.

A company will sometimes obtain **stock subscriptions** from potential shareholders for new offers of the stock. A down payment is received at the time of the subscription, and the remainder when the stock is issued.

Stockholder's Equity   Section 15

Assume the client is planning to issue shares of its $10 par value stock at $30 per share, and obtains subscriptions from potential buyers, who are required to make a $3 down payment with the subscription and pay the balance when the stock is issued to them. The entry when the subscription is **taken out** is:

Cash	3	
Subscriptions receivable	27	
Common stock subscribed		10
APIC-CS		20

When the balance is paid and **stock issued**, the entry is:

Cash	27	
Common stock subscribed	10	
Subscriptions receivable		27
Common stock		10

If a company does not issue stock within a certain time period after subscription, the potential investor is entitled to a **refund** of the down payment and **cancellation of the contract.** If the company failed to issue stock in the example, the refund entry is:

Common stock subscribed	10	
APIC-CS	20	
Cash		3
Subscriptions receivable		27

If, on the other hand, the potential buyer breaches the subscription contract and refuses to purchase it when available, the company is normally entitled to **keep the down payment** as an estimate of damages from breach, and records the cancellation as follows:

Common stock subscribed	10	
APIC-CS	20	
APIC-Forfeited subscriptions		3
Subscriptions receivable		27

If shareholder **donates** stock back to corporation, the entry would be:

Treasury Stock	X (@ FMV)	
APIC-T/stk		X

Lecture 15.02

Treasury Stock

Often, shares are repurchased but not retired. These **treasury shares** are *not paid dividends and are not voted*, so they reduce the number of shares outstanding. They are considered **authorized, issued, but not outstanding**. When the company intends to hold the shares indefinitely, it will account for treasury shares under the **par value method**. The entry is similar to retirement, except that the debit to common stock is instead, recorded to treasury stock, and any APIC-Retired stock is instead recorded as APIC-TS. Treasury shares held under the par value method are not reported directly on the financial statements, but reduce the amount shown as common stock.

- **Treasury stock (two methods)**
  - Cost Method
  - Par Value Method (Legal / stated value method)

Ex. Issue 20,000 shares of $5 Par value C/S @ $25 per share.

1. **Cost Method** (Cost In, Cost Out → Until Retire)			**Par Value Method** (Legal method) (Par In, Par Out)		
Cash	500,000		Cash	500,000	
C/S (20($5))		100,000	C/S (20($5))		100,000
APIC – C/S (20($20))		400,000	APIC – C/S (20($20))		400,000
2. **Repurchase 2,000 @ $19**					
Treasury Stock – Cost	38,000		APIC – C/S (2000(20))	40,000	
Cash		38,000	T/S (2000(5))	10,000	
			Cash		38,000
			APIC – T/S		12,000
3. **Resell 700 @ $22**					
Cash	15,400		Cash	15,400	
APIC – TS/RE	**X**		T/S (700(5))		3,500
T/S (19(700))		13,300	APIC – C/S		11,900
APIC – TS		**2,100**	Like a new issuance		
4. **Resell 500 @ $15**					
APIC – T/S	2,000		Cash	7,500	
Cash	7,500		T/S (500(5))		2,500
T/S (500(19))		9,500	APIC – CS		5,000
5. **RETIRE 300** – No longer ISSUED or OUTSTANDING					
C/S (300($5))	1,500		C/S	1,500	
APIC c/s (300($20))	6,000		T/S		1,500
T/S (300($19))		5,700			
APIC – T/S		1,800			

(OR applies to step 3)

NOTE: Under the Par value method, T/S is considered a *contra C/S* account.
    Under the Cost method, T/S is considered a *contra Equity* account.

If one share of $10 par value stock that was originally issued for $13 was reacquired under the **par value method** at $12, the entry would have been:

Treasury stock	10	
APIC-CS	3	
APIC-TS		1
Cash		12

Stockholder's Equity

If reacquired at $15, the entry would have been:

Treasury stock	10	
APIC-CS	3	
Retained earnings	2	
Cash		15

APIC-TS and/or APIC-Retired stock would have been debited instead of retained earnings to the extent that such amounts existed from previous transactions.

A subsequent resale of these shares is reported in a similar manner to a new issuance, except that treasury stock is credited for the par value of the shares instead of common stock. If the share reacquired in either of the transactions on this page is subsequently resold at $18, the entry is:

Cash	18	
Treasury stock		10
APIC-CS		8

Notice that the credit to APIC is on common stock, not treasury stock.

When shares are reacquired with the intention of reselling them soon thereafter, the treasury shares are accounted for under the **cost method**. Using this approach, the shares are recorded at cost and reported separately on the financial statements as the last account in stockholders' equity. There is no difference between shares repurchased below the original issue price or above it. If the shares mentioned earlier are acquired for $12, the entry under the cost method is:

Treasury stock	12	
Cash		12

A subsequent resale at $18 is recorded as follows:

Cash	18	
Treasury stock		12
APIC-TS		6

Notice that the APIC is from treasury stock. The APIC-CS from the original issuance is not disturbed. If someone donates Stock back to the company than they would record this as follows:

Treasury Stock	10	
APIC Treasury Stock		10

In some jurisdictions, retained earnings is restricted as to the payment of dividends when an entity has treasury stock. Such a restriction is required to be disclosed and will generally be in an amount equal to the cost of the treasury shares that the entity has on hand. As a result, if the shares were retired or sold without consideration, the cost represents the maximum amount by which retained earnings would be reduced.

Donated stock is the companies own stock that was donated back to them by a shareholder. It is recorded at its FMV. The journal entry is below:

Donated Treasury Stock	10	
APIC Treasury Stock		10

Lecture 15.03

Preferred Stock

Preferred Stock refers to stock similar to a debt instrument with two advantages over common stock:

- **Dividends** – preferred shares must be paid a dividend before the company is allowed to pay the common shareholders a dividend.
- **Liquidation** – if the corporation liquidates, preferred shareholders must be paid before the common shareholders.

The **dividend preference** for preferred shares is based on a stated dividend rate that is computed on the par (or stated) value of the shares. Keep in mind that dividends are optional, however, and a company may decide not to pay any dividends at all in a particular year to any shareholders. The preferred shareholders have a dividend preference, not a dividend guarantee.

To see how the allocation of dividends is computed, assume a client has two types of stock outstanding at 12/31/X6, at which time $300 of dividends are declared:

Type of shares	Par value	Shares	Total
10% Preferred stock	$100	4	$400
Common stock	$1	100	$100

Of the $300 in dividends, the first $400 x 10% = $40 must be paid to the preferred shareholders, based on the dividend preference. The remaining $260 is paid to the common shareholders.

Along with the stated annual preference, preferred shareholders may be paid additional amounts if the shares are:

- **Cumulative** – dividends missed in earlier years must also be paid before the common shareholders receive anything.
- **Participating** – if the common shareholders get a dividend that is a higher rate on its par value than the stated rate on the preferred shares, the preferred shareholders must get the same higher rate.
- **Convertible** – the preferred shareholder has the option of converting their stock for common stock at a specified ratio.
- **Callable** – the corporation has the option of repurchasing the preferred stock at a specified price.
- **Preferred with Warrants** – the warrants are convertible into shares of common stock.

Assume, for example, that the company in the preceding example paid the same $300 in 20X6, but paid no dividends in the 5 years 20X1 to 20X5. Notwithstanding their preference, the preferred shareholders received nothing in those years. If the stock is not cumulative, the preferred shareholders will still only receive $400 x 10% = $40. If, however, the stock is cumulative, then the $40 preferences missed for 5 years result in $200 of **dividends in arrears** at 12/31/X5. In 20X6, when $300 is paid, the preferred shareholders will collect $240 and the common shareholders $60, determined as follows:

Amount	Shareholders	Reason
$200	Preferred	Dividends in arrears
$40	Preferred	Annual preference
$60	Common	Remainder

If the preferred shares are not cumulative, but are participating, they will still receive more than their annual preference when $300 is paid in 20X6. First, they receive $400 x 10% = $40 as their annual preference. Next, the common shareholders are paid, but only until they are also receiving 10% on their par value, or $100 x 10% = $10. The remaining $250 is allocated to the preferred and common shares based on their relative par values:

Type of shares	Total par value	Percentage of combined
Preferred	$400	80%
Common	$100	20%
Total	$500	100%

Thus, the preferred shares get an additional $250 x 80% = $200 and the common shares an additional $250 x 20% = $50. The preferred shareholders end up receiving $40 + $200 = $240 and the common shareholders $10 + $50 = $60. In each case, the shareholders are getting dividends equal to 60% of par value, so the preferred shares are fully participating in the large dividend.

When a company liquidates, preferred shareholders are paid first, based on the amount of their **liquidation preference**. Unless specifically stated, this is usually the same as the par value of the preferred shares. Remember, however, that a liquidating distribution is still a form of dividend, so preferred shareholders must also be paid dividends in arrears on top of their liquidation preference. The remainder is paid to common shareholders. The amount that each outstanding common share is entitled to receive is known as **book value per common share**. The calculation of BV per C/S share is Common Shareholders equity / Common shares outstanding.

To demonstrate the calculation of liquidation payments and book value, assume the stockholders' equity section of the client is as follows on 12/31/X1, and that no dividends have been paid in 20X1:

Account	Amount
8% Cumulative Pfd stock - 5 shares authorized and issued @ $100 par, $110 liquidation value	$500
C/S – 5,000 shares authorized, 103 shares issued @ $1 par	$103
APIC	$200
Retained earnings	$223
Treasury stock, at cost – 3 shares @ $12	($36)
Stockholders' equity	$990

The preferred shareholders are entitled to receive the liquidation preference of $110 x 5 shares = $550 and the dividends in arrears of $500 x 8% = $40, for a total of $590. The common shareholders receive the remaining equity of $990 - $590 = $400. The book value per share of preferred stock is $590 / 5 = $118, and the book value per share of common stock is $400 / 100 = $4. Notice that the book value is based on the shares outstanding.

Additional Paid-In-Capital (APIC)

There are many forms of additional paid-in capital (APIC) (contributed capital) that may be included in the stockholders' equity section of the balance sheet, including:
- **Common stock** – the portion of the issue price of common stock that exceeded the par (or stated) value of the shares.
- **Preferred stock** – The portion of the issue price of preferred stock that exceeded the par (or stated) value of the shares.
- **Retired stock** – Repurchase and retirement of shares below the original issue price.
- **Treasury stock** – Repurchase of shares below the original issue price under the par value method and resale of shares above the repurchase price under the cost method.
- **Warrants** – The amount allocated to the value of detachable warrants that are issued with bonds or preferred stock.

Companies may issue securities that give the holders the right to buy shares of stock at an established price for a specific period of time. Examples of these securities are **stock rights** which are often issued to existing shareholders, **stock options** which are often issued to officers or employees, and **stock warrants** which are often issued to bondholders.

Stock rights (sometimes called *preemptive or subscription rights*) are contractual rights held by existing shareholders to purchase a proportional share of new shares in the same class, to preserve their preexisting ownership percentage (prevent dilution of ownership).

There are, however, many other types of transactions that may affect APIC. One common category of transactions is referred to as **share based compensation**, which may include transactions with **employees or** with **nonemployees**. Regardless of whether the share based compensation is in a transaction with employees or with nonemployees, the entity will recognize the goods or services received when goods are obtained or services are received. In addition, the entity will recognize an increase in either *equity* or *liabilities*.
- When the transaction is for goods that provide a future value, such as inventory, an asset is recognized that is reported in earnings when the asset is sold or consumed.
- When the transaction is for services, they are recognized in income as they are consumed.

When applying the rules, it is important to distinguish if the share-based payments are being made to **employees or nonemployees**, and if they are considered **Equity or a Liability.**

A share-based transaction with **nonemployees**, which is addressed in **ASC 505**, will be measured on the basis of the most reliable information available. The amount will be whichever is more reliable between:
- The fair value of the goods or services received; or
- The fair value of the equity instruments exchanged.

Most employee stock options are considered compensatory and result in the recognition of compensation expense. Those that do not involve recognition of compensation expense are considered **noncompensatory**. To be considered noncompensatory, certain criteria must be met:
- The stock option plan must satisfy one of two conditions. **Either:**
  - The terms are comparable, and no more favorable, to terms offered to shareholders holding the same class of stock that is the subject to the plan; or
  - Any purchase discount below fair value at issuance is no greater than the costs that would have been incurred in a public offering of the securities, which is assumed to be the case if the discount is 5% or less.

Stockholder's Equity Section 15

- The plan is available to substantially all employees meeting limited employment requirements.
- The plan provides no special option features other than:
    - Permitting employees a period not to exceed 31 days to enroll in the plan once the purchase price has been determined.
    - The purchase price is determined on the basis of the market price on the date of purchase.
        - Employees may be permitted to cancel participation before the purchase date.
        - Upon cancellation, employees would be refunded amounts previously paid.

No entry is reported for the granting of noncompensatory options nor upon their expiration, and the exercise of such options is recorded as a simple issuance of shares at the exercise price paid by the employee.

For example, if a company issues **noncompensatory options** granting all employees the right to buy shares in the company's $10 par value stock for $40 per share, the exercise of an option is reported as follows:

Cash	40	
Common stock		10
APIC-CS		30

According to **ASC 718**, all share-based compensation plans that do not meet all of the criteria are compensatory, indicating that they will result in the recognition of compensation expense. A share-based transaction with *employees* will always be measured at the **fair value** of the equity instruments issued. The cost of services received from employees in a share-based transaction will be equal to either:
- The fair value of equity instruments issued as of the grant date; or
- The fair value of liabilities incurred.

(Share-based payments classified as **Equity**)
The date on which the amount of compensation is determined is considered the measurement date, which is the date on which the options are granted to employees, referred to as the grant date. In stock options are traded in active markets, making the fair value readily determinable. In other cases, particularly when dealing with nonpublic entities, the fair value of the stock options is not readily determinable (**Measurement date = Grant date**).

When that value of stock options is not readily determinable, an option pricing model will be used to determine the fair value of the options. A reliable model will take into account such factors as the exercise price, the expected life of the option, the current value of the underlying stock and the volatility of the underlying stock's price, dividends, and the risk-free interest rate.
- Originally, the FASB suggested a preference for the *Black-Scholes model* to estimate fair value. The formula used by this method is far too complicated to be learned, and no exam questions have ever asked for it to be applied.
- Recent FASB comments indicate a preference for the *binomial distribution model*, which is based on the *expected cash flow* method. Estimates are made as to the possibility of different price changes in the stock and decisions by employees to exercise, and a weighted average expectation is generated and discounted using interest rate assumptions.

A simplified example of the calculation of fair value based on the binomial distribution method follows. Assume that a company has stock selling at $30 at the time they issue stock options to key employees giving them the right to purchase company stock at $30, exercisable for a period starting in two years and ending in five years. The risk-free interest rate is 5%, the present value of $1 for 2 periods at 5% is 0.91, and the present value of $1 for 5 periods at 5% is 0.78.

The company estimates that 30% of the options will expire without ever being exercised, that 50% will be exercised in 2 years, at their earliest possible date, with the stock selling at an average $40 price, and that 20% of the options will be held as long as possible and exercised in 5 years, just before expiration, at an average $50 price. The gain to the employees who exercise the options will be the amount by which the value of the stock received exceeds the exercise price on the date of exercise. The fair value of the option under the binomial distribution method is $7.67:

Result	Stock Price	Exercise Price	Gain	Factor	PV	Pct	Weighted Value
Expire	--	--	--	--	--	30%	--
Exer 2 Yrs	$40	$30	$10	0.91	$9.10	50%	$4.55
Exer 5 Yrs	$50	$30	$20	0.78	$15.60	20%	$3.12
Fair Value							$7.67

When fair value cannot be determined with any degree of reliability, the entity will value stock options using the **intrinsic method**. Nonpublic entities may also make a one-time election to use the intrinsic method, which is an irrevocable election. Under the intrinsic method, the options are measured on the basis of the difference between the exercise price and the fair value of the share on the measurement date.
- If the fair value of the stock is greater than the exercise price, compensation will be equal to the difference multiplied by the number of options.
- If the fair value of the stock is equal to or lower than the exercise price, there will be no compensation.

No entry is required at the time stock options are granted, although many entities will recognize deferred compensation for the total amount, the number of options multiplied by the fair value of an option, with a credit to APIC from stock options outstanding.

The entity must make an accounting policy election as to how to measure the total amount of compensation, which is based on the number of options that are expected to vest and become exercisable. The **two methods** that the entity will choose between will be:

- To estimate the number of options expected to be forfeited before becoming exercisable; or

- To account for forfeitures when they occur.

Under the first approach, if a company issued 100,000 options to employees that vest over 3 years with an expected turnover rate of 2% per year, the number of options expected to be exercisable will be calculated as follows:

- Year 1 – 2% will terminate employment, resulting in forfeitures of 2% x 100,000 or 2,000, leaving 98,000 options.

- Year 2 – An additional 2% will terminate employment, resulting in forfeitures of 2% of 98,000 or 1,960, leaving 96,040 options

Stockholder's Equity

- Year 3 – An additional 2% will terminate employment, resulting in forfeitures of 2% of 96,040 or 1,921, leaving 94,119 options that are estimated to become exercisable.

Total compensation expense will be 94,119 multiplied by the fair value per option and will be recognized over the 3 year vesting period.

Assume the 100,000 options, issued on 1/1/X1, each give the employee the right to buy one share of the company's $10 par value common stock for $34, its current selling price. The option can be exercised after 1/1/X4 if the employee remains in service to the company, and expires on 12/31/X6. The company is using the fair value method, and the value at 1/1/X1 using the binomial distribution model is estimated at $6 per option.

On the **date of grant**, the entry is based on 94,119 options at $6:

1/1/X1   Deferred compensation   564,714
                         APIC-Stock options outstanding   564,714

Compensation expense is recognized over the period during which the employee is performing services for the entity in exchange for the compensation. This can be determined on the basis of the terms of the option.
- If the option is immediately exercisable, it indicates that the compensation is for services already rendered.
    - On the date of grant, the total amount of compensation will be recognized as compensation expense.
    - No deferred compensation is recognized.

- If the options are not immediately exercisable, the compensation will be recognized over the period from the grant date through the date on which the options become exercisable.
    - The date on which the options become exercisable are said to be vested
    - The period is referred to as the vesting period.

As for vesting, under a **cliff vesting** schedule, options vest all at once or 100 percent after five years of service. Under a **graded vesting schedule**, employees are 20 percent vested after three years of service and become 20 percent vested each year after that until they are 100 percent vested after seven years.

Since the employee must remain for 3 years before the option can be exercised, the **compensation expense** is allocated over that time:

12/31/X1, 12/31/X2, & 12/31/X3
              Compensation expense   188,238
                         Deferred compensation   188,238

Assuming that the entity's actual turnover is the same as estimated turnover, the same entry will be made every year. If actual turnover differs, the amounts will be adjusted prospectively.

At the time the options are exercised the journal entry would be:

Cash (94,119 x $34)	3,200,046	
APIC Stock options O/S (94,119 x $6)	564,714	
Common Stock (94,119 x $10)		941,190
APIC Common Stock (94,119 x $30)		2,823,570

Under the second approach, assuming the same facts and circumstances. In addition, actual forfeitures were 2,100 in year 1, 2,250 in year 2, and 1,950 in year 3.

On the **date of grant**, the entry is based on the total 100,000 options at $6:

1/1/X1

Deferred compensation	600,000	
APIC-Stock options outstanding		600,000

To recognize compensation expense at the end of the 1st year, first, 1/3 of the total compensation, $600,000/3 or $200,000, is recognized as compensation expense:

12/31/X1

Compensation expense	200,000	
Deferred compensation		200,000

The forfeitures are then recognized. With 2,100 options forfeited, at $6 each, total forfeitures will be $12,600, 1/3 of which relates to year 1 with the remaining 2/3 relating to years 2 and 3:

APIC-Stock options outstanding	12,600	
Compensation expense		4,200
Deferred compensation		8,400

This reduces deferred compensation to $600,000 - $200,000 - $8,400 or $391,600.

To recognize compensation expense at the end of the 2nd year, first, 1/2 of the remaining deferred compensation, $391,600/2 or $195,800, is recognized as compensation expense:

12/31/X2

Compensation expense	195,800	
Deferred compensation		195,800

The forfeitures for year 2 are then recognized. With 2,250 options forfeited, at $6 each, total forfeitures will be $13,500, 2/3 of which relates to years 1 and 2, with the remaining 1/3 relating to year 3:

APIC-Stock options outstanding	13,500	
Compensation expense		9,000
Deferred compensation		4,500

Stockholder's Equity   Section 15

This reduces deferred compensation to $391,600 - $195,800 - $4,500 or $191,300.

To recognize compensation expense at the end of the 3rd year, first, the remaining deferred compensation, $191,300, is recognized as compensation expense:

12/31/X3

Compensation expense	191,300	
Deferred compensation		191,300

The forfeitures for year 3 are then recognized. With 1,950 options forfeited, at $6 each, total forfeitures will be $11,700, all of which will be recognized:

APIC-Stock options outstanding	11,700	
Compensation expense		11,700

Disclosures

- Vesting requirements, maximum term of options granted and number of shares authorized for grants of options
- The number and weighted-average exercise of prices of each group of options
- Weighted average grant-date fair value of options granted
- Description of methods used and assumptions made in determining fair values of options
- Total compensation cost recognized for the year
- For O/S options, range of exercise prices
- For options that are being reported under the intrinsic method (only applicable to options granted before the effective date of SFAS 123 revised), pro forma disclosures of the impact on earnings if the fair value method had been used.

Share-Based Payments Classified as Liabilities

Although stock options often provide a nice benefit to employees, there are limiting factors that may make it difficult for employees to exercise them.
- They must have the cash to pay the exercise price.
- They will be taxed in the period of exercise based on the difference between the stock's market value and the option price.

To make certain that employees have the opportunity to take advantage of a share-based compensation plan, entities will often use an alternative, such as **stock appreciation rights** (SAR). A SAR works similarly to a stock option in that:
- It is granted to employees, specifying an option price.
- It is generally not immediately exercisable and vests over a period from the grant date to the exercise date at a future time.
- It is generally exercisable for a certain length of time.

A SAR may be exercised at any time from the vesting date to the expiration date. When it is exercised, rather than purchase a share of stock for the exercise price, the employee will be compensated for the difference between the market value of the share on the exercise date and the exercise price (**measurement date = settlement/exercise date**).

For publicly-held companies, compensation related to share-based plans classified as liabilities is the same as for those classified as equity in that both are recognized on the basis of fair value. The measurement date, however, is the date of settlement.

Nonpublic entities may recognize share-based payment arrangements as liabilities either at fair value or at intrinsic value and will make a policy decision as to which.

Since the share-based payment will be made in cash, rather than through the issuance of shares, the transaction results in the recognition of a liability instead of equity. Unlike stock option rights, where the total amount of compensation for the plan is determined on the grant date, compensation in a SAR plan is measured in each reporting period.

For example, assume an entity has given its president 100 stock appreciation rights on 1/1/X1, exercisable on 12/31/X3 and expiring on 12/31/X5. The stock price on various dates was as follows:

1/1/X1	$20
12/31/X1	$23
12/31/X2	$26
12/31/X3	$25
12/31/X4	$27
12/31/X5	$30

In the first year, the **stock increased $3**, indicating total compensation of $300 ($3 x 100 rights). Since only 1/3 of the vesting period has elapsed, only 1/3 of the compensation expense will be recognized:

Compensation expense	100	
Liability for appreciation rights		100

In the second year, the stock increase to $26, indicating that total compensation of $600 ($6 x 100 rights). Since 2/3 of the vesting period has elapsed, 2/3 of the compensation expense, $400, has been incurred. Compensation expense of $100 was previously recognized, requiring recognition of an additional $300 in the current period:

Compensation expense	300	
Liability for appreciation rights		300

At the end of the third year, the stock price has declined to $25 per share, indicating total compensation expense of $500 ($5 x 100). Since $400 has been incurred in the preceding two periods, and additional $100 in compensation expense will be recognized in the current period.

Compensation expense	100	
Liability for appreciation rights		100

As of the end of 20X4, the SARs have not been exercised. As a result, the liability is remeasured with any adjustment recognized in the current period as an increase or decrease to compensation expense. Since the price is now $27, total compensation is $700. This is compared to the $500 recognized to date requiring additional compensation expense of $200.

Compensation expense	200	
Liability for appreciation rights		200

Finally, on 12/31/X5, when the SARs are getting ready to expire, the president exercises them. At that point, the value of the stock is $30 per share, indicating compensation of $10 per share or $1,000. The liability has a balance of $700, requiring the following entry:

Compensation expense	300	
Liability for appreciation rights	700	
Cash		1,000

Lecture 15.04

Retained Earnings (RE)

Retained Earnings represents the accumulated earnings since inception of the company that have not been paid out to shareholders in the form of a dividend. At the end of each accounting year, net income is closed into retained earnings. In addition, retained earnings is periodically reduced for dividends. There are three dates relevant to each dividend:

- **Declaration date** - the board of directors commits to the dividend.

RE	X	
Dividends Payable		X

- **Record date** - The shareholders at this date are identified as the ones entitled to the dividend (no Journal entry)

- **Payment date** - distribution is made to the shareholders of record.

Dividends Payable	X	
Cash		X

- **Types of Dividends**
    - Cash
    - Property (FMV @ date of declaration)
    - Scrip (Interest bearing Note Payable)
    - Liquidating (return of capital)
    - Stock - Small (FMV) / Large (Par)
    - Stock split

	Cash Dividend	Scrip – Give dividend but no money	Stock Dividend

	RE 25
	   Cash 25
		RE 25
		   Note Payable 25
			Small < 20 – 25% - FMV
			RE 25
			   CS 20
			   APIC 5

		Partial Liquidating Dividend
		RE 15
		APIC 10
		   Cash 25
			Large > 20 – 25% - Par
			RE 20
			   CS 20

Net effect on Stkhldrs equity = 20	**Property (FMV)**
	RE 25
	   Asset 20
	   Gain 5
		Person receiving Liq Div
		Cash 25
		   Div income 15
		   Investment 10
			Stock Splits – Double shares, Half par
			CS (10(10)) 100
			   CS (20(5)) 100

- **Note**: All dividends reduce Stockholders Equity except for Stock dividends and Stock splits.

The corporation charges retained earnings on the **declaration date**, since the liability is created at that time. For example, if the board declares dividends totaling $500 on 4/1/X1, payable on 4/28/X1 to shareholders of record on 4/21/X1, the entries are:

4/1/X1   Retained earnings   500
           Dividends payable   500

This records the obligation. Identifying the actual payees doesn't change any account balances, so the next entry is on the **payment date**:

4/28/X1   Dividends payable   500
           Cash   500

When a dividend exceeds the balance of retained earnings prior to declaration, the amount of the dividend in excess of retained earnings represents a return of contributed capital, and is known as a **liquidating dividend**. For example, if the board declares the $500 dividend on 4/1/X1 as above, but the balance in retained earnings is only $400 before recording the dividend, the entry is:

4/1/X1   Retained earnings   400
           Additional paid-in capital   100
              Dividends payable   500

When a company pays a dividend in the form of **property** other than cash, this is known as a **dividend-in-kind**. Such dividends are treated as simultaneous sales of property and distributions of cash, and results in gains or losses.

For example, assume the client declares a dividend-in-kind of land on 7/1/X1, payable on 7/15/X1. The land originally cost $300, is worth $800 on 7/1/X1, and $820 on 7/15/X1. The entry on the declaration date is:

7/1/X1   Retained earnings   800
           Dividends payable   800
           Land   500
              Gain on land   500

Stockholder's Equity   Section 15

On the payment date, the entry is:

7/15/X1	Dividends payable	800	
	Land		800

The price appreciation after the declaration date is ignored, since the commitment to distribute the land effectively sells it.

Stock dividends are not actual distributions of assets from a company, but represent transfers of capital from retained earnings to contributed capital accounts. Total stockholders' equity is unchanged. There are two types of stock dividends:
- **Ordinary stock dividends** – These are small stock dividends (typically less than 20%), and are recorded at the fair market value of the stock at the time of the dividend.
- **Stock splits effected in the form of stock dividends** – These are large stock dividends (typically more than 25%), and are recorded at the par value of the stock.

For example, assume a client has outstanding 100 shares of $10 par value stock with a fair market value of $30 per share. If a **5%** (5 shares) **stock dividend** is declared and paid, it is reported at $30 per share:

Retained earnings	150	
Common stock		50
APIC-CS		100

If a **100%** (100 shares) **stock dividend** is declared, it is reported at $10 per share:

Retained earnings	1000	
Common stock		1000

The reason for the difference is that the fair market value of the stock is not deemed to be a realistic estimate after a large stock dividend takes place, since it will substantially reduce the selling price of the shares. Dividends between 20% and 25% do not take place on the exam, since it is difficult to determine which classification they should have.

Stock splits in which old stock is exchanged for new stock are accounted for by adjusting the par value of the new shares for the split. If a 2-1 stock split occurred in the above situation, the 100 shares of $10 par stock would have been replaced by 200 shares of $5 par stock. Since total par value is unchanged, no entry is made. A reverse stock split does the opposite by reducing the number of shares outstanding and proportionally increases the par value.

Retained earnings are assumed to be available for the payment of dividends, so when a company faces contingent liabilities that may require large payments in the future, it will often **appropriate** a portion of the retained earnings to indicate to its shareholders its unavailability for dividend payments.

If a company wishes to appropriate $100,000 of retained earnings for possible losses related to pending lawsuits, the entry is:

Retained earnings-Unappropriated	100,000	
Retained earnings-Reserve for lawsuits		100,000

Notice that the above entry has no impact on net assets or net income, and doesn't actually change retained earnings, either. It is considered a disclosure on the face of the financial statements, and is appropriate for reasonably possible costs or costs that are probable but not estimable. The above entry is not used for probable and estimable losses, which should be accrued on the income statement and reduce net assets.

When the reserve is no longer needed, the above entry is reversed. This is appropriate whether or not the costs actually occur, since the effects of the contingency will be reflected directly if and when they do result in losses.

In general, retained earnings may not be increased except when net income is closed into it. An exception is when a company has a **quasi-reorganization (fresh start) (ASC 852)**. Since new companies always begin with retained earnings of $0, a company with a deficit in retained earnings has the ability to eliminate that deficit by reorganizing as a new company. Accounting principles, therefore, allow a company to restate its accounts as if they had reorganized. This requires shareholder approval.

Usually, a company involved in a quasi-reorganization will take the opportunity to adjust the carrying amount of assets to market values, and may adjust the par value of the stock as well. If the entry doesn't balance, the difference adjusts APIC.

For example, assume a client has the following balance sheet:

Assets	900
Liabilities	200
$10 par common stock	800
APIC	500
RE	(600)
Liabilities and stockholders' equity	900

They elect a quasi-reorganization. Assets are reduced to market value of $800, and the par value of the shares reduced to $5. The entry is:

Common stock	400	
APIC (balance)	300	
Assets		100
Retained earnings		600

The reason the par value of the stock is often reduced (as in this example) is that APIC cannot be debited for an amount that exceeds its balance before the quasi-reorganization.

Lecture 15.05

Presentation (ASC 205)

The presentation of stockholders' equity in a balance sheet may include as many as **7 categories**, presented in the following order:
- Preferred stock
- Common stock
- Additional paid-in capital
- Noncontrolling interest (minority interest)
- Retained earnings
- Accumulated other comprehensive income
- Treasury stock, at cost

Stock accounts are known as the **legal capital** of the corporation, and are listed from the most senior security (the one entitled to dividends first) to the most junior. If a company has one class of preferred stock and one class of common stock, the preferred stock is listed first.

Preferred stock is shown at the total par (or stated) value of shares issued less shares held in treasury under the par value method. On the face of the balance sheet as part of the account name, the company must disclose:
- Par value per share
- Liquidation value per share (if different from par value)
- Dividend preference rate or amount per share
- Cumulative (if applicable)
- Participating (if applicable)
- Shares authorized
- Shares issued
- Shares outstanding

Common stock is also shown at the total par value of shares issued less shares held in treasury under the par value method. On the face of the balance sheet as part of the account name, the company must disclose:
- Par value per share
- Shares authorized
- Shares issued
- Shares outstanding

Additional paid-in capital is listed immediately after the stock accounts, and includes all contributed capital in excess of the legal capital of the company. Some of the types of APIC are from:
- Preferred stock
- Common stock
- Retired stock
- Treasury stock
- Warrants
- Employee stock options (less deferred compensation)
- Expired stock options

Noncontrolling interest, sometimes referred to as the minority interest, arises when a reporting entity prepares consolidated financial statements that include a subsidiary in which the parent owns less than 100%. This may include an entity:

- With which the reporting entity has entered into a business combination in which it acquired a majority of the equity shares, in which case the noncontrolling interest represents the minority portion not owned.
- That is a variable interest entity (VIE) in which it has a controlling financial interest but does not own a majority of the equity. In this case, the noncontrolling interest represents the equity of the consolidated VIE that is not owned by the reporting entity, generally a majority.

The noncontrolling interest of a consolidated subsidiary is initially recognized at its fair value on the date of the combination. In many cases, this will be measured at the market price of a single share multiplied by the number of shares held by stockholders other than the reporting entity. It will be adjusted for the noncontrolling interest's share in income, comprehensive income, and distributions.

The noncontrolling interest of a VIE will be determined in the same manner when the VIE is not a related entity. When the VIE is a related entity, however, the consolidation is reported using the VIE's book values, rather than fair values, and the noncontrolling interest is the portion of the VIE's reported equity that is not owned by the reporting entity.

Net income includes all components of income for both the reporting entity and all consolidated entities and is allocated between the portion attributable to the reporting entity and the portion attributable to the noncontrolling interest. Other comprehensive income, including components of the reporting entity and consolidated entities, is also allocated.

The noncontrolling interest is a component of stockholders' equity and is required to be presented in the equity section of the balance sheet.

Stockholder's Equity

Retained earnings is reported next. The details of the changes in the account are reported in a separate **statement of retained earnings**, which might appear as follows:

	XYZ Corporation Statement of Retained Earnings For the Year Ended December 31, 20X3
Retained earnings, 12/31/X2 – as previously reported	$600
Prior period adjustment to correct inventory, net of $80 taxes	120
Retained earnings, 1/1/X3 – adjusted	720
Net income for the year ended 12/31/X3	260
Less dividends	(100)
Retained earnings, 12/31/X3	880

The next section is for **accumulated other comprehensive income (OCI) - (DENT)**, which reflects cumulative changes in net assets resulting from certain transactions not included in net income and not affecting retained earnings including:
- **D**erivative Cash flow hedges.
- **E**xcess adjustment of Pension PBO and FV of Plan assets at year end
- **N**et unrealized changes in the value of marketable securities
- **T**ranslation gains and losses from foreign currency

Tax effects may be reported on each of the accounts or in the aggregate for the section. In certain cases, the items included in this section may be debit balances, resulting in contra-equity accounts being reported.

Treasury stock is presented last on the balance sheet, but only for stock that is being held under the cost method (treasury shares held under the par value method are netted directly against the stock accounts presented earlier). It is always a contra-equity account. Included in the account name must be disclosures of:
- Number of shares held
- An indication that the shares are reported at cost

An example of the stockholders' equity section of the balance sheet follows:

XYZ Corporation
Stockholders' Equity
December 31, 20X3

Preferred stock, $100 par value, $105 liquidation value, 8% cumulative, 100 shares authorized, issued, and outstanding		$10,000
Common stock, $1 par value, 4,000 shares authorized, 1,000 shares issued, 900 shares outstanding		1,000
Additional paid-in capital		5,000
Noncontrolling Interest		400
Retained earnings		12,400
Accumulated other comprehensive income:		
Foreign currency translation gains	$1,800	
Net unrealized losses on available-for-sale securities	(300)	
	1,500	
Less taxes	(600)	900
		29,700
Less common stock in treasury, 100 shares at cost		(1,200)
Total stockholders' equity		$28,500

Assuming there are no dividends in arrears on preferred stock, the **book value** of the common stock is computed as follows:

Stockholders' equity	$28,500
Preferred stock liquidation value	(10,500)
Common stock equity	18,000/
Divided by common shares outstanding	900 =
Book value per common share	$20

Stockholder's Equity

Statement of Changes in Stockholders' Equity

When significant changes occur in stockholder's equity, companies are required to disclose them. Here is an example of such a statement taken from the financial statements of Marriott, International:

MARRIOTT INTERNATIONAL, INC. (DEC)
CONSOLIDATED STATEMENTS OF SHAREHOLDERS' EQUITY
Fiscal Years 20X1
(In millions)

Common Shares Outstanding		Total	Equity Attributable to Marriott Shareholders					Equity Attributable to Noncontrolling Interests
			Class A Common Stock	Additional Paid-In Capital	Retained Earnings	Treasury Stock, at Cost	Accumulated Other Comprehensive Income (Loss)	
366.9	Balance at year-end 20X0	$1,585	$5	$3,644	$3,286	-$5,348	-$2	—
—	Net income	198	—	—	198	—	—	—
—	Other comprehensive loss	-24	—	—	—	—	-24	—
—	Dividends	-135	—	—	-135	—	—	—
9.5	Employee stock plan issuance	182	—	9	-137	310	—	—
-43.4	Purchase of Treasury stock	-1,425	—	—	—	-1,425	—	—
—	Spin-off of Marriott Vacations Worldwide Corporation	-1,162	—	-1,140	—	—	-22	—
333	Balance at year-end 20X1	($781)	$5	$2,513	$3,212	($6,463)	($48)	$—

Equity Securities Classified as Debt

Some financial instruments issued by an entity have characteristics of both debt and equity. ASC 480, Distinguishing Liabilities from Equity, requires financial instruments that embody an **obligation** of the issuing entity be reported as a liability. An obligation in this context is a duty or responsibility to transfer assets or issue equity shares. The obligation may be conditional or unconditional.

An example of an equity instrument that includes an obligation would be a put option issued by the entity. A put option entitles the holder to require to repurchase its equity securities. Settlement may be through:
- Physical settlement in which the full cash amount is transferred in exchange for all of the shares.
- Net cash settlement in which cash is paid or received based on the difference between the option price and the fair value at exercise.
- Net share settlement in which shares are issued or reacquired with a total value equal to the difference between the option price and the fair value at exercise.

In some cases, these instruments will require the entity to issue shares for an amount greater than their fair value on the date of issuance or will be the recipient of a net settlement. In such cases, the instruments would be reported as assets.

Instruments that may be reported as liabilities or assets include:
- Mandatorily redeemable financial instruments;
- Obligations to repurchase equity shares by issuing assets; and
- Certain obligations to issue a variable number of shares.

Mandatorily redeemable instruments are always reported as liabilities unless redemption is only required upon liquidation or termination of the entity. An instrument that is redeemable only upon the occurrence of an event that is not certain to occur is not considered mandatorily redeemable. The instrument will be recognized as a liability when:
- The event has occurred;
- The condition is resolved; or
- The event has become certain to occur.

An **obligation to repurchase equity shares by transferring assets**, such as a forward purchase contract or a put option, is classified as a liability, unless it is an outstanding share, if two characteristics apply:
1. There is an obligation to repurchase the entity's equity securities or has an obligation that is calculated on the basis of the fair value of the shares; and
2. The obligation does, or may, ultimately require settlement by the transfer of assets.

An instrument that gives the holder the right to require the entity to transfer assets is always reported as a liability.

In some cases, an entity may have an **obligation to issue a variable number of shares**. These are reported as liabilities when the monetary value of the shares the entity will be required to issue is based on:
- A fixed monetary amount such that the number of shares will be determined essentially by dividing that amount by the fair value per share at settlement; or
- An index other than the fair value of the entity's equity shares, such as a financial instrument that is indexed to the Dow Jones Industrial Average; or

Stockholder's Equity

- A relationship that varies inversely to the fair value of the entity's equity securities, such as a written put option that can be satisfied by net share settlement.

Equity securities of an entity that are reported as liabilities are not considered in the calculation of earnings per share. This includes mandatorily redeemable securities as well as forward contracts, such as put options, to repurchase equity shares.

When all of the shares of an entity are mandatorily redeemable, all will be reported in the liability section, identified as shares subject to mandatory redemption. As a result, there will be no stockholders' equity section and amounts for common stock, APIC, and retained earnings are disclosed.

For example, a closely-held corporation is formed by 5 friends, and a single class of common stock is issued. There is a provision requiring the corporation to repurchase the shares of any shareholder who dies by the payment of cash equal to the net book value of the shares on the latest financial statement date prior to the death. In such a circumstance, the common stock is treated as a liability. The balance sheet might appear as follows:

Five Buddies Corporation

Total Assets	$10,000,000
Liabilities other than shares	$ 3,000,000
Shares subject to mandatory redemption	7,000,000
Total Liabilities	$10,000,000

Lecture 15.06
CLASS QUESTIONS
Please see the Class Questions and Class Solutions for this Lecture at the end of this Section.

Lecture 15.07
CLASS QUESTIONS
Please see the Class Questions and Class Solutions for this Lecture at the end of this Section.

Lecture 15.08
STOCKHOLDERS' EQUITY UNDER IFRS

IFRS deals with stockholders' equity in a variety of pronouncements. IAS 1, Presentation of Financial Statements, requires the presentation of a **statement of changes in equity** for each period presented as a component of a complete set of financial statements.

Certain items may either be presented in the statement of changes in equity or the footnotes to the financial statements. These include:
- An analysis of each item of comprehensive income for each component of equity.
- Dividends recognized as distributions to owners, including dividends per share.

IAS 1 also requires that the **Statement of Financial Position** include:
- Noncontrolling interests; and
- Issued capital and reserves attributable to owners of the reporting entity.

Certain information related to equity may be presented either in the **statement of financial position** or in the footnotes to the financial statements. This includes the following for each class of share capital:
- Shares authorized, issued and fully paid, and issued but not fully paid.
- Par value per share or an indication that it is no par stock.
- A reconciliation of the beginning and ending number of shares.
- Rights, preferences, and restrictions related to that class of shares.
- Shares held by the entity or related parties.
- Shares reserved for issuance to satisfy obligations under option plans and contracts.

The entity will also provide a description of each reserve including its nature and purpose.

Additional **disclosures** are required of an entity that has **puttable** financial instruments that are classified as equity, including:
- Summarized information about amounts classified as equity.
- Objectives, policies, and processes for complying with obligations to repurchase or redeem instruments when the put option is exercised by the holder.
- Changes from previous periods.
- Expected cash outflows on repurchase or redemption.
- Information regarding the means of determining the expected cash outflows.

\When appropriate, additional disclosures are required. These include information about dividends including amounts proposed or declared before issuance of the financial statements that are not recognized during the period. The entity is also required to disclose any cumulative preferred dividends not recognized.

IAS 32, Financial Instruments: Presentation, includes various requirements that relate to the accounting and reporting of certain financial instruments that would be classified as capital. It indicates that a financial instrument would be classified as **equity if two conditions are met:**
- The instrument does not contain a contractual obligation to deliver cash or another financial asset or exchange financial assets or liabilities on potentially unfavorable terms.
- For instruments that will, or may, be settled by issuance of equity instruments, it must be either:
  - A non-derivative instrument that does not include an obligation to deliver a variable number of its equity instruments; or
  - A derivative that will be settled by exchanging a fixed amount of financial assets for a fixed number of its equity instruments.

A **puttable financial instrument** is generally reported as a liability but is classified as equity if it has certain features.

Instruments that contain an **obligation to deliver a pro rata share of net assets** to another party on liquidation is reported as equity if has the following characteristics.
- The holder is entitled to a proportionate share of net assets upon liquidation.
- The instrument is part of a class of instruments, all with identical features, that is subordinate to all other classes of instruments.

With the exception of puttable instruments, the primary factor that indicates an instrument is an **equity instrument** instead of a liability is that the instrument does not require the entity to
- Deliver cash or another financial asset; or
- Exchange financial assets or liabilities on potentially unfavorable terms.

IAS 32 requires that **compound financial instruments** be bifurcated, accounting for components representing financial assets, financial liabilities, and equity instruments separately. IFRS 9, *Financial Instruments*, addresses the measurement of financial instruments. It describes equity instruments as a residual interest in the entity's assets after settlement of its liabilities. As a result, the proceeds from issuance of a compound instrument are allocated:
- First to the nonequity components in amounts equal to their fair values.
- The residual amount, the difference between the fair value of the compound instrument and the fair value of the nonequity components, is allocated to the equity component.

Unlike convertible bonds, convertible preferred stock is not considered a compound instrument. It is instead recognized as preferred stock.
- The conversion feature, including terms for conversion, would be disclosed.
- Conversion is accounted for using the book value method.

IAS 32 also indicates that dividend distributions are reported directly in equity and that costs associated with equity transactions are accounted for as reductions to equity and are disclosed separately.

Treasury shares are deducted from equity. There are **3 methods** of accounting for treasury shares, Cost method, Par value method and the **Constructive retirement method**. The constructive retirement method is similar to the par value method, however, when shares are repurchased, the entry is to common stock as opposed to treasury stock since the company generally does not intend to reissue the shares.
- No gain or loss is recognized in income as a result of transactions in an entity's own equity instruments.
- The amount paid or received is reported as an adjustment directly to equity.

The entity will disclose the amount of treasury shares held.

Statement of Comprehensive Income under IFRS

The statement of comprehensive income may be presented in either one statement or in two statements. The two-statement approach presents a statement of profit and loss displaying components of profit or loss, and then presents a second statement, which begins with profit or loss and displays the components of comprehensive income. Items that are included (**DENT-R**)
- **D**erivative Cash Flow hedges effective portion of gains and losses on hedging instruments in a cash flow hedge.
- **E**xcess Amortization of actuarial gains and losses on defined benefit pension plans,
- **N**et unrealized gains and losses on remeasuring available-for-sale financial assets
- **T**ranslation gains and losses from foreign currency translations,
- Changes in **R**evaluation surplus for plant, property, and equipment, intangibles, etc.

Each component of comprehensive income should be stated separately on the statement of comprehensive income.

Share-Based Payments under IFRS

IFRS 2, Share Based Payment, provides measurement principles and requirements for three types of share-based payments.

Equity-settled share-based payment transactions
- The entity issues equity instruments in exchange for goods or services.
- The transaction is measured at the fair value of the goods or services received.

Cash-settled share-based payment transactions
- The entity incurs liabilities in exchange for goods or services.
- The amount of the liability is based on the price or value of the entity's shares or other equity instruments.
- The transaction is measured at the fair value of the liability.

Share-based payment transactions that may be settled with cash or equity instruments
- The entity or the supplier of the goods or services has a choice as to the form of settlement.
- If the entity has incurred a liability, the cash-settled share-based approach is applied to the transaction or to the portion of it to which a liability applies.
- The equity-settled share-based approach is used if no liability is incurred or to the portion of the transaction that did not involve a liability.

Disclosures will include:
- The nature and extent of share-based payment arrangements;
- The means by which fair values were determined; and
- The effect on profit or loss and financial position.

Shareholders' equity must include:
- Common stock (Share Capital) – number authorized, issued, and outstanding
- *Preference shares* (e.g., preferred stock) -must be reported separately including number of shares authorized, issued, and outstanding.
    - Preference shares that are redeemable at the option of the holder must be classified as liabilities.
- *Share Premium* – APIC account
- *Reserves* – a Revaluation account
- *Treasury shares* repurchased are stated at **cost** and shown as a reduction to shareholders' equity.
- *Accumulated other comprehensive income (DENT-R)* is reported in the shareholders' equity section of the balance sheet
- *Noncontrolling interests* are disclosed as a separate item in the equity section of the balance sheet.

Stockholders' Equity

US GAAP	IFRS
• Provides comprehensive guidelines for recognizing equity transactions, reporting equity, and providing equity disclosures. • Recognizes compound instruments, such as convertible preferred stock, as preferred stock, disclosing conversion feature. • OCI includes DENT • Treasury stock accounting is either Cost method or Par value method	• Guidance predominantly limited to disclosure as nature of transactions and reporting affected by jurisdiction. • Requires bifurcation of compound instruments into liability and equity components. • OCI includes DENT-**R** • Treasury stock accounting has 3 methods, Cost, Par value and the Constructive retirement method.

Earnings Per Share will be discussed in another Section.

Lecture 15.09

CLASS QUESTIONS

Please see the Class Questions and Class Solutions for this Lecture at the end of this Section.

CLASS QUESTIONS

Work through the below Class Questions while following along with the respective lectures. Once this is complete, you can begin independently practicing what you've learned by quizzing yourself on this course section in your Interactive Practice Questions (IPQ), which can be found in your online Student Dashboard. Your IPQ simulates the computer-based testing experience, and will also help you understand how concepts are applied to the exam. Each question includes answer explanations from expert CPAs that will help you determine why you answered a question correctly or incorrectly. This is key to your success on the CPA Exam.

Lecture 15.06

1. On April 1, 20X3, Hyde Corp., a newly formed company, had the following stock issued and outstanding:
   - **Common stock, no par, $1 stated value, 20,000 shares originally issued for $30per share.**
   - Preferred stock, $10 par value, 6,000 shares originally issued for $50 per share.

   Hyde's April 1, 20X3 statement of stockholders' equity should report

	Common stock	Preferred stock	Additional paid-in capital
a.	$ 20,000	$ 60,000	$820,000
b.	$ 20,000	$300,000	$580,000
c.	$600,000	$300,000	$ 0
d.	$600,000	$ 60,000	$240,000

2. ASP Corporation was organized on January 2, 20X3, with 100,000 authorized shares of $10 par value common stock. During 20X3 ASP had the following capital transactions:

   January 5—issued 75,000 shares at $14 per share.
   December 27—purchased 5,000 shares at $11 per share.

   ASP used the par value method to record the purchase of the treasury shares. What would be the balance in the paid in capital from treasury stock account at December 31, 20X3?

   a. $0
   b. $ 5,000
   c. $15,000
   d. $20,000

3. A company declared a cash dividend on its common stock on December 15, 20X3, payable on January 12, 20X4. How would this dividend affect stockholders' equity on the following dates?

	December 15, 20X3	December 31, 20X3	January 12, 20X4
a.	Decrease	No effect	Decrease
b.	Decrease	No effect	No effect
c.	No effect	Decrease	No effect
d.	No effect	No effect	Decrease

Stockholder's Equity   Section 15

4. Ole Corp. declared and paid a liquidating dividend of $100,000. This distribution resulted in a decrease in Ole's

	Paid-in capital	Retained earnings
a.	No	No
b.	Yes	Yes
c.	No	Yes
d.	Yes	No

5. Instead of the usual cash dividend, Evie Corp. declared and distributed a property dividend from its overstocked merchandise. The excess of the merchandise's carrying amount over its market value should be

   a. Ignored.
   b. Reported as a separately disclosed reduction of retained earnings.
   c. Reported in other comprehensive income, net of income taxes.
   d. Reported as a reduction in income from continuing operations.

6. The stockholders' equity section of Brown Co.'s December 31, 20X3 balance sheet consisted of the following:

Common stock, $30 par, 10,000 shares authorized and outstanding	$300,000
Additional paid-in capital	150,000
Retained earnings (deficit)	(210,000)

   On January 2, 20X4, Brown put into effect a stockholder approved quasi reorganization by reducing the par value of the stock to $5 and eliminating the deficit against additional paid-in capital. Immediately after the quasi reorganization, what amount should Brown report as additional paid-in capital?

   a. $ (60,000)
   b. $150,000
   c. $190,000
   d. $400,000

Items 7 and 8 are based on the following:
On January 2, 20X8, Kine Co. granted Kristin, its president, compensatory stock options to buy 1,000 shares of Kine's $10 par common stock. The options call for a price of $20 per share and are exercisable for three years following the grant date. Kristin exercised the options on December 31, 20X8. The market price of the stock was $50 on January 2, 20X8, and $70 on December 31, 20X8. The fair value of a similar stock option with the same terms was $28 on the grant date.

7. What is compensation expense for 20X8 for the share-based payments?

   a. $ 9,333
   b. $10,000
   c. $20,000
   d. $28,000

8. By what net amount should stockholders' equity increase as a result of the grant and exercise of the options?

    a. $20,000
    b. $30,000
    c. $50,000
    d. $70,000

Lecture 15.09

9. There are a variety of ways to account for treasury stock under IFRS. Which of the following is NOT a method that may be used to account for treasury stock under IFRS?

    a. Cost method.
    b. Par value method.
    c. Retained earnings method.
    d. Constructive retirement method.

Stockholder's Equity — Section 15

CLASS SOLUTIONS

1. (a) The amount reported for stock, both common and preferred, is the par value, if there is one, and the stated value if there is not. If there is neither a stated nor a par value, the amount reported will be the proceeds. Common stock consisted of 20,000 shares with a $1 stated for a total of $20,000. Preferred stock consists of 6,000 shares with a $10 par value for a total of $60,000. The remainder of the proceeds would be recognized as additional paid-in capital, consisting of $580,000 from the issuance of the common shares ($600,000 - $20,000) and $240,000 from the issuance of the preferred shares ($300,000 - $60,000) for a total of $820,000.

2. (c) Under the par value method, the purchase of 5,000 treasury shares would be recorded with a debit to treasury stock for the par value of (5,000 x $10) $50,000 and a debit to APIC for the original amount of (5,000 x $4) $20,000. The total reduction to equity is $70,000 resulting from a payment of cash of (5,000 x $11) $55,000. The difference of $15,000 would be recognized as APIC from treasury stock.

3. (b) On December 15, when the dividends are declared, an entry is prepared recognizing a liability for the amount of the dividend and a reduction to stockholders' equity in the form of an account entitled dividends declared. At December 31, dividends declared will be closed into retained earnings, but there is no net effect on stockholders' equity. When the dividend is paid the following January 12, the entry will eliminate the liability and reduce cash without affecting stockholders' equity.

4. (d) Dividends paid out of earnings are recognized as reductions of retained earnings. Distributions that are not paid out of earnings are considered liquidating dividends. They reduce additional paid-in capital, not retained earnings.

5. (d) A property dividend is recognized, for all practical purposes, in a two-step process. First, the property is adjusted to fair value as if it were sold for that amount, resulting in the recognition of a gain or loss. A dividend is then recognized with a reduction to retained earnings in an amount equal to the fair value of the property. If the merchandise had a carrying value that exceeded its market value, a loss would be recognized for the difference. The loss will be recognized as a component of income from continuing operations.

6. (c) In recording a quasi-reorganization, the retained earnings deficit of $210,000 is eliminated and the amount reported as common stock is reduced to recognize the reduction in par from $30 to $5. This amounts to a reduction of (10,000 x $25) $250,000. Since this is greater than the increase in retained earnings, the entry will be balanced with an increase of $40,000 to APIC resulting in a balance of $190,000.

7. (d) The fair value of the stock option at date of grant was $28 indicating total compensation of ($28 × 1,000 shares) $28,000. The entire amount is recognized because the options are exercisable immediately, which indicates that the compensation is for services already provided.

8. (a) The grant of the options will involve the recognition of compensation expense and APIC in the amount of $28,000, the fair value of the options. Since compensation expense reduces net income and, therefore, retained earnings, there is no effect on stockholders' equity. When the option is exercised, there will be a debit to cash for the proceeds of $20,000 and a net credit to stockholders' equity accounts for the same amount.

9. (c) Under IFRS, treasury stock may be accounted for under the cost method, the par value method, or the constructive retirement method. There is no retained earnings method for accounting for treasury stock under IFRS.

Lecture 15.07

TASK-BASED SIMULATIONS

Task-Based Simulation 1

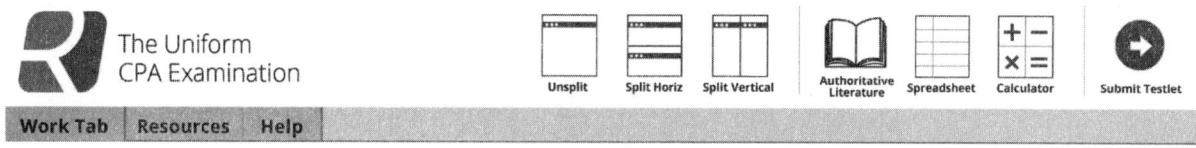

Min Co. is a publicly held company whose shares are traded in the over-the-counter market. The stockholders' equity accounts at December 31, 20X1, had the following balances:

Preferred stock, $100 par value, 6% cumulative; 5,000 shares authorized; 2,000 issued and outstanding	$200,000
Common stock, $1 par value, 150,000 shares authorized; 100,000 issued and outstanding	100,000
Additional paid-in capital	800,000
Retained earnings	1,586,000
Total stockholders' equity	$2,686,000

Transactions during 20X2 and other information relating to the stockholders' equity accounts were as follows
- February 1, 20X2 — Issued 13,000 shares of common stock to Ram Co. in exchange for land. On the date issued, the stock had a market price of $11 per share. The land had a carrying value on Ram's books of $135,000, and an assessed value for property taxes of $90,000.
- March 1, 20X2 — Purchased 5,000 shares of its own common stock to be held as treasury stock for $14 per share. Min uses the cost method to account for treasury stock. Transactions in treasury stock are legal in Min's state of incorporation.
- May 10, 20X2 —Declared a property dividend of marketable securities held by Min to common shareholders. The securities had a carrying value of $600,000; fair value on relevant dates were

Date of declaration (May 10, 20X2)	$720,000
Date of record (May 25, 20X2)	758,000
Date of distribution (June 1, 20X2)	736,000

- October 1, 20X2 — Reissued 2,000 shares of treasury stock for $16 per share.
- November 4, 20X2 — Declared a cash dividend of $1.50 per share to all common shareholders of record November 15, 20X2. The dividend was paid on November 25, 20X2.

- December 20, 20X2 — Declared the required annual cash dividend on preferred stock for 20X2. The dividend was paid on January 5, 20X3.
    - January 16, 20X3 — Before closing the accounting records for 20X2, Min became aware that no amortization had been recorded for 20X1 for a patent purchased on July 1, 20X1. Amortization expense was properly recorded in 20X2. The patent was properly capitalized at $320,000 and had an estimated useful life of eight years when purchased. Min's income tax rate is 30%. The appropriate correcting entry was recorded on the same day.
    - Adjusted net income for 20X2 was $838,000.

Calculate the following amounts to be reported on Min's financial statements at December 31, 20X2.

		Amount
1.	Prior period adjustment, 20X2	
2.	Preferred dividends, 20X2	
3.	Common dividends—cash, 20X2	
4.	Common dividends—property, 20X2	
5.	Number of common shares issued at December 31, 20X2	
6.	Amount of common stock issued	
7.	Additional paid-in capital, including treasury stock transactions	
8.	Treasury stock	

Items 9 and 10 represent other financial information for 20X1 and 20X2.

		Amount
9.	Book value per share at December 31, 20X1, before prior period adjustment	
10.	Numerator used in calculation of 20X2 earnings per share for the year	

Task-Based Simulation 2

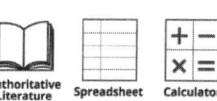

An entity wishes to communicate to users of its financial statements that it is not likely to pay dividends because it is accumulating funds for a future acquisition. It is considering using an appropriation of retained earnings. Identify the location in professional standards that indicates whether or not an entity may recognize an appropriation of retained earnings.

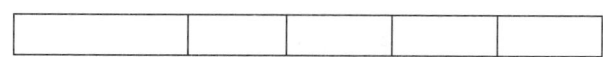

Task-Based Simulation 3

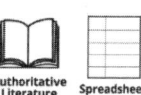

A client has established a stock option plan for its employees. It is trying to determine the amount at which the award should be recognized. Identify the location in professional standards that indicates the basis used to measure a share based payment transaction with employees.

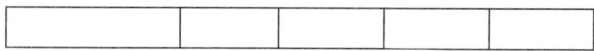

TASK-BASED SIMULATION SOLUTIONS

Task-Based Simulation Solution 1

Because of the format of this question, the most effective approach is to first scan the information provided to familiarize yourself with what is available. Next evaluate each requirement and find the information that is relevant to it.

1. ($14,000) A prior period adjustment would be appropriate for recording a correction of an error. In this case, an error was discovered in that an intangible with a limited useful life was not amortized in the previous year. Annual amortization will be the cost of the asset divided by its useful life ($320,000/8) or $40,000 per year. Since the intangible was acquired on July 1, only ½ year's amortization, $20,000, will be recognized. The adjustment will be a credit to the intangible, or accumulated amortization, for $20,000. The tax effect of ($20,000 x 30%) $6,000 will be recognized as a debit to taxes receivable, if the correction is also being made for tax purposes, or a deferred tax asset or liability if not. The remainder of $14,000 is the prior period adjustment, recorded as a reduction to beginning retained earnings.

2. ($12,000) The facts indicate that the required annual preferred dividend was declared on December 20 and paid the following January 5. The dividend will be calculated as a percentage of par value. Since the 6% preferred stock has a total par value of $200,000, the preferred dividend is ($200,000 x 6%) $12,000.

3. ($165,000) A cash dividend of $1.50 per common share was declared on November 4, to shareholders of record on November 15. Dividends are not paid on treasury shares and the dividend will be calculated on the basis of the number of shares issued and outstanding on November 15. There were 100,000 shares outstanding at the beginning of the year. On February 1, 13,000 shares were issued, on March 1, 5,000 treasury shares were acquired, and on October 1, 2,000 of the treasury shares were reissued. As a result, there were (100,000 + 13,000 – 5,000 + 2,000) 110,000 shares outstanding on November 15, resulting in a cash dividend to common stockholders of (110,000 x $1.50) $165,000.

4. ($720,000) Property dividends are recognized at an amount equal to the fair value of the property on the declaration date. If the fair value differs from the carrying value, a gain or loss on disposal is recognized for the difference. The property dividend was declared on May 10, at which time the fair value of the property, and the amount of the dividend, was $720,000.

5. (113,000) The number of shares issued does not take into account treasury stock. As a result, the 100,000 shares issued at the beginning of the year would be increase by the 13,000 issued on February 1, for a total of 113,000. The 5,000 treasury shares purchased and the 2,000 resold affect shares outstanding but not shares issued.

6. ($113,000) The amount reported for common stock issued would be the number of shares issued multiplied by the par or stated value per share. There were a total of 113,000 shares issued, including the 100,000 issued at the beginning of the year and the 13,000 issued on February 1. At a par value of $1 per share, the amount of common stock is (113,000 x $1) $113,000.

Stockholder's Equity

7. ($934,000) To determine the total APIC, each transaction will have to be analyzed. The beginning balance of APIC is $800,000. The 13,000 shares issued for land on February 1 would be recognized at their fair value of $11 per share, including $10 per share, or $130,000 APIC. Under the cost method, the purchase of treasury shares does not affect APIC, but the subsequent resale of 2,000 shares does. The shares cost $14 per share, or $28,000, and they were resold for $16 per share or $32,000. The difference of $4,000 would be recognized in APIC. The resulting total is ($800,000 + $130,000 + $4,000) $934,000.

8. ($42,000) As a result of the purchase of 5,000 shares of treasury stock on March 1, and the resale of 2,000 shares on October 1, there are 3,000 shares in the treasury at December 31. Under the cost method, they are recognized at their cost of $14 per share or $42,000.

9. ($24.86) The total book value of common stock is equal to total stockholders' equity minus amounts attributable to preferred shareholders. The book value per share is that amount divided by the number of common shares outstanding at the end of the period. Since there is no liquidation preference for preferred stock and cumulative dividends were apparently not in arrears, the only portion of stockholders' equity that is attributable to preferred stockholders is the par value of preferred stock. All remaining accounts are attributable to the common stockholders. Common stock at the end of year 1 was $100,000, APIC was $800,000, and retained earnings was $1,586,000, for a total of $2,486,000, excluding preferred stock. There were 100,000 shares issued and outstanding, resulting in book value per share of ($2,486,000/100,000) $24.86 per share.

10. ($826,000) The numerator in the calculation of earnings per share consists of net income attributable to common stockholders. This will be equal to net income minus preferred dividends. In the case on noncumulative preferred stock, preferred dividends include those declared during the period. When it is cumulative, preferred dividends consist of the current dividend, whether declared or not. Adjusted income is given as $838,000. The preferred dividend is $12,000, leaving the difference of $826,000 as net income attributable to common stockholders.

Task-Based Simulation Solution 2

FASB ASC	505	10	45	3

Task-Based Simulation Solution 3

FASB ASC	718	10	30	2

Section 16 - Earnings Per Share (EPS)

Section 16 – Earnings Per Share
Corresponding Lectures

Watch the following course lectures with this section:

Lecture 16.01 – Reporting Earnings Per Share
Lecture 16.02 – Earnings Per Share – Diluted
Lecture 16.03 – Earnings Per Share – Treasury Stock Method
Lecture 16.04 – Earnings Per Share – Class Questions
Lecture 16.05 – Earnings Per Share Under IFRS

EXAM NOTE: Please refer to the AICPA FAR Blueprint in the Introduction to find a listing of the representative tasks (and their associated skill levels—i.e., Remembering and Understanding, Application, and Analysis) that the candidate should be able to perform based on the knowledge obtained in this section.

Earnings Per Share (EPS)

Lecture 16.01

REPORTING EARNINGS PER SHARE

A publicly-held company is required to present earnings per share (EPS) for Basic and Dilutive EPS on the **face** of the income statement for **(ASC 260):**
- **Income from continuing operations (ONT – I)**
- **Net income**

The company must also present EPS for **discontinued operations**, which may be presented **either** on the *face* of the statement or in the *notes* to the financial statements.

A company does not present other Comprehensive income or total comprehensive income on a per share basis. Cash flows per share are also not disclosed.

If a company has only common stock, preferred stock, and other instruments that cannot be converted into common stock (no options or convertible securities outstanding) it has a **simple capital structure** and reports a single EPS number for each of the above categories. If a company has outstanding options or convertible securities, it has a **complex capital structure** and must present two EPS numbers for each of the above categories:
- **Basic**
- **Diluted**

Basic Earnings Per Share

The calculation of EPS in a simple capital structure (and basic EPS in a complex capital structure) follows. We'll use the calculation of net income for all of these examples.
Earnings per share is, of course, earnings divided by shares:
- **Earnings** = Net income minus preferred stock dividends.
- **Shares** = Weighted average common shares outstanding during the year.

Since EPS is being computed for the **common stock**, earnings must be reduced by dividends payable to preferred shareholders. If the preferred stock is **not cumulative**, only dividends actually declared during the year are subtracted. If the preferred shares are **cumulative**, the annual dividend preference is subtracted each year, regardless of whether or not it is declared or paid, since the amounts not paid accumulate and will never be payable to common shareholders. The effect of participating preferred shares is more complicated and appears to be beyond the scope of CPA exam testing.

Simple (Basic) Capital Structure

Net Income
- Preferred Div's (All Cumulative and Non-cumulative only if declared)
$ Available to C/S
_____
(1) Wtd avg. # c/s outstanding (div's and splits – Retroactive)

As an example of the computation of earnings for EPS purposes, assume a company has the following capital structure:

8% Preferred stock	$400
Common stock	100

The company reports net income of $932 for the year and declares no dividends. If the preferred stock is not cumulative, common stock earnings are $932. If the preferred stock is cumulative, then the missed dividend of $400 x 8% = $32 accumulates and will be paid to the preferred shareholders eventually, reducing the earnings applicable to common stock to $932 - $32 = $900. It doesn't matter if there are dividends in arrears from earlier years, since those amounts would have been subtracted in determining EPS of those earlier years, and wouldn't be subtracted again this year.

1 - Weighted Average number of shares of common stock outstanding

The determination of the **number of shares** to include in the denominator of the calculation can be very tricky. The amount to be used is the weighted average of the number of common shares outstanding during the year. As a result, shares sold to the public during the year must be prorated for the portion of the year they were outstanding.

For example, assume the following facts applied to the client for the first two years of its existence:

Issued, 1/1/X1	500
Issued, 7/1/X1	100
Issued, 10/1/X1	300
Outstanding, 12/31/X1	900

Although the number of shares outstanding at 12/31/X1 is 900, only 500 of these shares (those issued at the start of 20x0) were outstanding throughout 20X1. The 100 shares issued on 7/1/X1 were only outstanding for half of the year, and the shares issued 10/1/X1 for the final quarter of the year. The calculation of weighted average shares for 20X1 is:

```
500 x 12/12 = 500
100 x  6/12 =  50
300 x  3/12 =  75
Total         625
```

The reason for prorating shares issued during the year is that the funds received from issuance are only available for productive use by the corporation from that point on, not the entire year. This would **not** be the case, however, if shares are issued as a result of (**Retroactive**):
- **Stock dividends**
- **Stock splits**
- **Delayed issuance for earlier consideration (Stock Subscriptions)**

In these cases, the shares are treated as if they had always been outstanding and are included at full amount for the current year. They are also included for earlier years that are shown in *comparative financial statements*. In the case of a reverse stock split, these would retroactively *reduce* shares outstanding for all periods presented.

For example, assume that the 100 shares issued on 7/1/X1 were the result of a 20% stock dividend on the 500 shares outstanding previously. Since all shares are going to previous shareholders, they are treated as if they always had these additional shares. The calculation for 20X1 is:

```
500 x 1 = 500
100 x 1 = 100
300 x ¼ =  75
Total     675
```

Example: On 1/1 100,000 shares of C/S are outstanding. On April 1st, 80,000 shares are issued. On July 1st, a 10% stock dividend is issued. On September 1st, 18,000 shares of Treasury Stock are repurchased. On December 31st a 2 for 1 stock split occurs. Calculate the weighted average number of shares of C/S outstanding at 12/31.

1/1 100,000 shares o/s x 100% =	100,000
4/1 80,000 shares issued x 9/12 =	60,000
7/1 10% dividend issued 160,000 x 10% =	16,000
9/1 18,000 shares of Treasury Stock repurchased x 4/12 =	(6,000)
	170,000
12/31 a 2 for 1 stock split occurs	x 2
Weighted average number of c/s outstanding at 12/31 =	**340,000**

Lecture 16.02

Diluted EPS

2 - The If-Converted Method

The calculation of **diluted EPS** (assume anyone who "*could convert*" does so) for a company with **convertible Preferred stock or Convertible Bonds** starts with the computation just discussed, which is called **basic EPS.** For convertible securities, the following adjustments are made in the calculation:
- **Numerator** – earnings are increased by the dividends or after-tax interest expense that would not have been due if the securities had been converted to common stock at the beginning of the year.
- **Denominator** – shares are increased by the additional number of common shares that would have been outstanding if the securities had been converted. The convertible preferred stock or convertible debt is assumed to have been converted at the beginning of the period, or at the time of issuance, whichever is later. No weighting is "required".

If the calculation results in an EPS number which is higher than the basic EPS number, then the security is **anti-dilutive** and not included in the reported diluted EPS. To determine whether or not an item is anti-dilutive, each item is considered separately in sequence from most to least dilutive. One would normally consider options and warrants first.

> ## Complex (Diluted) Capital Structure (Could convert)
>
> **Net Income Available to C/S**
> + (2) Preferred Div's (not net of tax)
> + (2) Interest expense saved from convertible Bonds (net of tax)
> + (3) $0 (from Treasury stock)
> ___
>   (1) Wtd avg. # c/s outstanding (div's and splits – Retroactive)
> + (2) # of shares convertible security is converted into for both Pfd stock and convertible bonds (not weighted)
> + (3) Incremental # of C/S outstanding from Treasury stock method at average market price. (Not weighted)

For example, assume that a company reporting $932 net income for the year has the following capital structure, which did not change during the year:

Preferred stock, $100 par, 8% cumulative, 4 shares, each convertible into 10 shares of common stock	$400
Common stock, $1 par, 100 shares	100

To calculate **basic EPS:**

Earnings = Net income – PS dividends = $932 - $32 = $900
Shares = 100
Basic EPS = $900 / 100 = $9.00

If the preferred shares had been converted at the beginning of the year, the $32 in preferred dividends would not have been owed and there would have been 4 x 10 = 40 additional common shares. To calculate diluted EPS:

Earnings = $900 + $32 = $932
Shares = 100 + 40 = 140
Diluted EPS = $932 / 140 = $6.66

The **conversion of a bond ("if converted method")** requires considering the tax effect, since the reduction of interest expense is accompanied by an increase in taxable income. It is assumed that the conversion occurred at the *beginning of the earliest period reported* (or at the time of *issuance*, if later).

For example, assume a client with $800 of net income and an effective tax rate of 30% had the following capital structure throughout the year:

6% Convertible bond, $1,000 face value, convertible into 20 shares of common stock	$1,000
Common stock, $1 par, 200 shares	200

Earnings Per Share (EPS) — Section 16

Basic EPS is computed as follows:
Earnings = $800
Shares = 200

Basic EPS = $800 / 200 = $4.00

The conversion of the bonds would have eliminated the $1,000 x 6% = $60 in interest expense, but would have increased taxes by $60 x 30% = $18, so the net savings is only $60 - $18 = $42.

Diluted EPS is computed as follows:
Earnings = $800 + $42 = $842
Shares = 200 + 20 = 220

Diluted EPS = $3.83

Lecture 16.03

3 - The Treasury Stock Method

The effect of **options** on diluted EPS is to first increase the shares by the number that would have been issued if the options had been exercised, then decrease the shares by the number that could have been repurchased by the corporation (at the **average CS market price** during the year) with the proceeds from exercise. This is known as the **treasury stock method.** The exercise of options has no effect on earnings, since options pay no dividends or interest. If market prices change in the future, previously reported EPS should not be adjusted retroactively, leave it as it was reported.

For example: If 40,000 options are issued at an option price of $15 per share when the average market price is $20 per share, what is the dilutive effect?

```
40,000 options which are convertible into 40,000 shares of c/s
x $15 option price
$600,000
                                              40,000
600,000/$20 avg. mkt price   =              - 30,000 shares of treasury stock
                                              10,000 shares dilutive effect.
```

Another method of calculating the *incremental number of shares outstanding* is:

Number of shares − (number of shares x exercise price) = additional shares outstanding
               Average market price

$$40,000 - \frac{(40,000 \times \$15)}{\$20} = 10,000$$

Section 16   Earnings Per Share (EPS)

Lecture 16.04

CLASS QUESTIONS

Please see the Class Questions and Class Solutions for this Lecture at the end of this Section.

Lecture 16.05

EPS UNDER IFRS

IAS 33, like US GAAP, requires an entity whose shares are traded in a public market to provide EPS and indicates that other entities presenting EPS information should do so in accordance with the same provisions. *Basic EPS* is provided in all circumstances where EPS is either required or presented. In addition, entities with potentially dilutive securities outstanding will provide *diluted EPS* information as well.

EPS is calculated on the basis of profit or loss. When the statement presenting the results of operations reports profit or loss from continuing operations, EPS information is presented for it as well.

Basic EPS is profit or loss attributable to ordinary equity holders divided by the weighted average ordinary shares outstanding. The amount attributable to ordinary equity holders would be adjusted for after-tax amounts of:
- Preference dividends; and
- Difference on settlement of preference shares (liquidation preference).

For purposes of the calculation, preference dividends are the same as under US GAAP and include:
- After-tax dividends declared during the current period on noncumulative preference shares; and
- Current period's after-tax dividends on cumulative preference shares, whether declared or not.

Also like US GAAP, IAS indicates that weighted average shares are adjusted for all periods presented for events or transactions that change the number of shares outstanding without a corresponding change in resources, such as a stock split or stock dividend that increases the number of shares without bringing additional resources to the entity.

Diluted EPS takes into account the effect of those outstanding securities that are dilutive. The weighted average number of shares outstanding is increased for the number of ordinary shares the dilutive securities would cause to be issued and profit or loss attributable to ordinary shareholders is adjusted for the effects of those conversions. This might include, for example, adding back after-tax interest on a convertible bond that is assumed to be converted into ordinary shares.

While the effect of dilutive options, rights, and warrants affects diluted EPS in the same manner for IFRS and US GAAP, it is described differently under IFRS. Basically, the effect is:
- The proceeds from issuance at the exercise price is determined.
- Those proceeds are divided by the average market price of shares for that period.
- The difference is added to the weighted average shares outstanding in the computation of diluted EPS (this is similar to the treasury stock method).

Earnings Per Share (EPS) — Section 16

CLASS QUESTIONS
Work through the below Class Questions while following along with the respective lectures. Once this is complete, you can begin independently practicing what you've learned by quizzing yourself on this course section in your Interactive Practice Questions (IPQ), which can be found in your online Student Dashboard. Your IPQ simulates the computer-based testing experience, and will also help you understand how concepts are applied to the exam. Each question includes answer explanations from expert CPAs that will help you determine why you answered a question correctly or incorrectly. This is key to your success on the CPA Exam.

Lecture 16.04

1. Strauch Co. has one class of common stock outstanding and no other securities that are potentially convertible into common stock. During 20X2, 100,000 shares of common stock were outstanding. In 20X3, two distributions of additional common shares occurred: On April 1, 20,000 shares of treasury stock were sold, and on July 1, a 2-for-1 stock split was issued. Net income was $410,000 in 20X3 and $350,000 in 20X2. What amounts should Strauch report as basic earnings per share in its 20X3 and 20X2 comparative income statements?

	20X3	20X2
a.	$1.78	$3.50
b.	$1.78	$1.75
c.	$2.34	$1.75
d.	$2.34	$3.50

2. West Co. had earnings per share of $15.00 for 20X3 before considering the effects of any convertible securities. No conversion or exercise of convertible securities occurred during 20X3. However, possible conversion of convertible bonds, not considered common stock equivalents, would have reduced earnings per share by $0.75. The effect of possible exercise of common stock options would have increased earnings per share by $0.10. What amount should West report as diluted earnings per share for 20X3?

    a. $14.25
    b. $14.35
    c. $15.00
    d. $15.10

3. Ute Co. had the following capital structure during 20X2 and 20X3:

Preferred stock, $10 par, 4% cumulative, 25,000 shares issued and outstanding	$ 250,000
Common stock, $5 par, 200,000 shares issued and outstanding	1,000,000

    Ute reported net income of $500,000 for the year ended December 31, 20X3. Ute paid no preferred dividends during 20X2 and paid $16,000 in preferred dividends during 20X3. In its December 31, 20X3 income statement, what amount should Ute report as basic earnings per share?

    a. $2.42
    b. $2.45
    c. $2.48
    d. $2.50

4. The if-converted method of computing earnings per share data assumes conversion of convertible securities as of the

   a. Beginning of the earliest period reported (or at time of issuance, if later).
   b. Beginning of the earliest period reported (regardless of time of issuance).
   c. Middle of the earliest period reported (regardless of time of issuance).
   d. Ending of the earliest period reported (regardless of time of issuance).

5. In determining earnings per share, interest expense, net of applicable income taxes, on convertible debt that is dilutive should be

   a. Added back to weighted-average common shares outstanding for diluted earnings per share.
   b. Added back to net income for diluted earnings per share.
   c. Deducted from net income for diluted earnings per share.
   d. Deducted from weighted-average common shares outstanding for diluted earnings per share.

6. Timp, Inc. had the following common stock balances and transactions during 20X6:

1/1/X6 Common stock outstanding	30,000
2/1/X6 Issued a 10% common stock dividend	3,000
7/1/X6 Issued common stock for cash	8,000
12/31/X6 Common stock outstanding	41,000

   What were Timp's 20X6 weighted-average shares outstanding?

   a. 30,000
   b. 34,000
   c. 36,750
   d. 37,000

7. The following information is relevant to the computation of Chan Co.'s earnings per share to be disclosed on Chan's income statement for the year ending December 31:

   - Net income for 20X2 is $600,000.
   - $5,000,000 face value 10-year convertible bonds outstanding on January 1. The bonds were issued four years ago at a discount which is being amortized in the amount of $20,000 per year. The stated rate of interest on the bonds is 9%, and the bonds were issued to yield 10%. Each $1,000 bond is convertible into 20 shares of Chan's common stock.
   - Chan's corporate income tax rate is 25%.

   Chan has no preferred stock outstanding, and no other convertible securities. What amount should be used as the numerator in the fraction used to compute Chan's diluted earnings per share assuming that the bonds are dilutive securities?

   a. $ 130,000
   b. $ 247,500
   c. $ 952,500
   d. $1,070,000

Earnings Per Share (EPS)

8. On June 30, 20X8, Lomond, Inc. issued twenty $10,000, 7% bonds at par. Each bond was convertible into 200 shares of common stock. On January 1, 20X9, 10,000 shares of common stock were outstanding. The bondholders converted all the bonds on July 1, 20X9. The following amounts were reported in Lomond's income statement for the year ended December 31, 20X9:

Revenues	$977,000
Operating expenses	920,000
Interest on bonds	7,000
Income before income tax	50,000
Income tax at 30%	15,000
Net income	$ 35,000

What is Lomond's 20X9 diluted earnings per share?

a. $2.50
b. $2.85
c. $2.92
d. $3.50

9. Coffee Co. had the following information related to common and preferred shares during the year:

Common shares outstanding,	1/1	700,000
Common shares repurchased,	3/31	20,000
Conversion of preferred shares,	6/30	40,000
Common shares repurchased,	12/1	36,000

Coffee reported net income of $2,000,000 at December 31. What amount of shares should Coffee use as the denominator in the computation of basic earnings per share?

a. 684,000
b. 700,000
c. 702,000
d. 740,000

CLASS SOLUTIONS

1. (b) The 2-for-1 stock split is accounted for retroactively as if it occurred on 1/1/X2. As a result, shares outstanding would have been 200,000 in 20X2 for the entire year, which would be the weighted average for that year. Divide that into earnings of $350,000 and EPS for 20X2 is $1.75. In 20X3, after adjusting for the stock split, there would have been 200,000 shares outstanding from 1/1 through 4/1, when the treasury shares were sold. Since the 20,000 treasury shares were sold before the stock split, they would be affected as well and would be the equivalent of 40,000 shares. As a result, there would have been the equivalent of 240,000 shares outstanding from 4/1 through 12/31. Weighted average shares outstanding would consist of (200,000 x 3/12 + 240,000 x 9/12) 230,000 shares. Divide that into earnings of $410,000 and EPS for 20X3 is $1.78.

2. (a) Diluted EPS takes into account the effects of all potentially dilutive securities that are dilutive and would decrease EPS, such as the convertible bonds, and ignores those that are antidilutive and would increase EPS, such as the stock options. As a result, diluted EPS would be ($15.00 - $.75) $14.25.

3. (b) Since the preferred stock is cumulative, the current dividend, which is 4% of the par value or ($250,000 x 4%) $10,000 reduces net income attributable to common stockholders. Net income attributable to common stockholders is ($500,000 - $10,000) $490,000, which is divided by the 200,000 shares of common stock outstanding all year. The result is basic EPS of $2.45.

4. (a) The if-converted method of computing earnings per share assumes that convertible securities are converted at the beginning of the earliest period reported or, if later, at the time of issuance.

5. (b) In computing dilutive EPS, dilutive convertible securities are accounted for under the if-converted method. The number of common shares that the securities are convertible into are added to the weighted average common shares outstanding. In addition, the net of tax interest on convertible bonds, and dividends on convertible preferred stock are added back to income to measure income attributable to common stockholders.

6. (d) In computing weighted average shares outstanding, stock dividends and stock splits are assumed to have occurred retroactively, as of the beginning of the earliest period presented. If the 3,000 shares issued in the stock dividend had been issued on 1/1, there would have been 33,000 shares outstanding for ½ year (33,000 x ½ = 16,500) and 41,000 outstanding for the latter ½ year (41,000 x ½ = 20,500). Weighted average shares outstanding would be (16,500 + 20,500) 37,000 shares.

7. (c) Since it is assumed that the convertible bonds are dilutive, the interest on the bonds, net of tax, will be added back to net income to compute diluted EPS. The $5,000,000 bonds have a stated rate of 9%, indicating that interest is paid at the rate of $450,000 per year. There is discount amortization of $20,000, increasing interest expense on the bonds to $470,000. The tax effect will be 25% or $117,500 and the net amount to be added to net income will be ($470,000- $117,500) $352,500. This will be added to net income of $600,000 to give income attributable to common stockholders of $952,500 for diluted EPS.

8. (b) When convertible securities are converted into common stock during the period, it is assumed that they were converted as of the beginning of the earliest period presented for the purpose of computing diluted EPS. If the bonds had been converted at 1/1, the $7,000 in bond interest would not have been incurred. At a 30% tax rate, however, the increase to income would result in an increase to income tax of ($7,000 x 30%) $2,100. As a result, net income attributable to common stockholders would increase by the net of $4,900 to $39,900.

Each of the 20 bonds is convertible into 200 shares of stock. As a result, if they had been converted as of 1/1, there would have been an additional 4,000 shares outstanding for the year, increasing the number outstanding all year to 14,000. Diluted EPS would be ($39,900/14,000) $2.85 per share.

9. (c) There were 700,000 shares outstanding for 3 months from 1/1 to 3/31 at which time 20,000 shares were repurchased, reducing the total outstanding to 680,000. There were 680,000 shares outstanding for 3 months from 4/1 to 6/30 at which time 40,000 shares were issued, increasing the total to 720,000 shares. There were 720,000 shares outstanding for 5 months from 7/1 to 12/1 at which time 36,000 shares were repurchased, reducing the total to 684,000. There were 684,000 shares outstanding for 1 month from 12/1 to 12/31. As a result, weighted average shares outstanding were (700,000 x 3/12 + 680,000 x 3/12 + 720,000 x 5/12 + 684,000 x ½) 702,000.

TASK-BASED SIMULATIONS

Task-Based Simulation 1

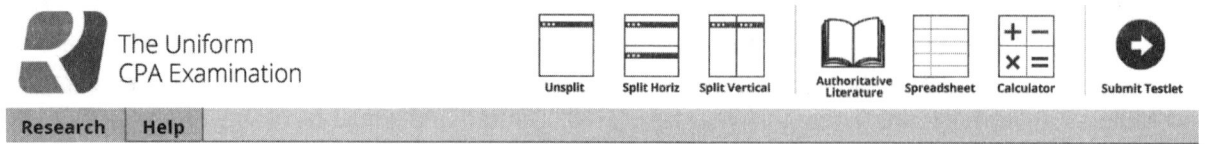

Your client is in the process of filing with the SEC in anticipation of a public offering. The client is uncertain as to whether or not it is required to provide earnings per share information. Identify the location in professional standards that indicates what entities are required to present earnings per share.

Task-Based Simulation 2

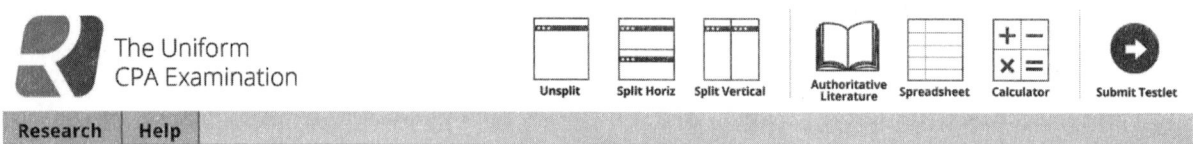

An entity with both cumulative and noncumulative preferred stock is calculating basic earnings per share data and is trying to determine how to account for preferred dividends. Identify the location in professional standards that indicates how to account for preferred dividends in the calculation of basic earnings per share.

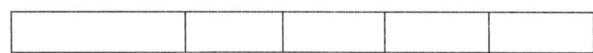

TASK-BASED SIMULATION SOLUTIONS

Task-Based Simulation Solution 1

| FASB ASC | 260 | 10 | 15 | 2 |

Task-Based Simulation Solution 2

| FASB ASC | 260 | 10 | 45 | 11 |

Section 18 – Accounting Changes and Error Corrections

Corresponding Lectures

Watch the following course lectures with this section:

Lecture 18.01 – Accounting Changes, Principle and Estimate
Lecture 18.02 – Accounting Changes, Entity and Error
Lecture 18.03 – Financial Statement Disclosures
Lecture 18.04 – Accounting Changes – Class Questions – M/C
Lecture 18.05 – Accounting Changes – Class Questions – TBS
Lecture 18.06 – Accounting Changes under IFRS
Lecture 18.07 – Accounting Changes under IFRS – Class Question

EXAM NOTE: Please refer to the AICPA FAR Blueprint in the Introduction to find a listing of the representative tasks (and their associated skill levels—i.e., Remembering and Understanding, Application, and Analysis) that the candidate should be able to perform based on the knowledge obtained in this section.

Accounting Changes and Error Corrections

Lecture 18.01

ACCOUNTING CHANGES

FASB ASC 250 defines an accounting change as a change in accounting principle, a change in estimate, or a change in the reporting entity. The correction of an error in previous financial statements is not an accounting change.

The **three types** of accounting changes are:
1. Change in accounting principle
2. Change in accounting estimate
3. Change in reporting entity

ASC 250 is the result of a broader effort to improve the comparability of cross-border financial reporting by working with the *International Accounting Standard Board (IASB)* toward developing a single set of high-quality accounting standards.

1 - Change in Accounting Principle (*Retrospective* approach)

A **change in accounting principle** is:
- A change from one generally accepted principle to another one that is also generally accepted when there are two or more acceptable alternative accounting treatments.
- A change to a generally accepted principle when the one previous in use is no longer acceptable.
- A change in the method of applying an accounting principle.

An entity may only change an accounting principle if either the change is required as a result of an authoritative pronouncement or the entity can justify the change in that it is preferable. In many cases, authoritative pronouncements that require a change in accounting principles provide transition guidance indicating how the change is to be implemented. When provided, those guidelines are required to be followed.

A change in accounting principles, assuming no transition guidance is provided, is accounted for by applying the new principle **retrospectively**. This is accomplished as follows:
- The cumulative effect of the change on periods prior to the earliest period presented is reflected in the carrying values of assets and liabilities as of the beginning of the earliest period presented.
- An offsetting adjustment, if necessary, is generally made to the opening balance of retained earnings but may be to another component of equity or net assets, as appropriate.
- Financial statements for each period presented will reflect application of the new accounting principle.

To account for the change in accounting principle under ASC 250:
The financial statements for all years impacted should be *retrospectively restated.* A retrospective application is the application of a different accounting principle to previously issued financial statements, as if that principle had always been used. This is done as of the **beginning of the first period presented**.
1. Financial statements for each individual prior period presented are adjusted to reflect the **period-specific effects** of applying the new accounting principle.
2. An offsetting adjustment is made to the opening balance of retained earnings for that period (the beginning of the first period presented).

Note that this change in treatment removes the accounting change from the Income Statement and moves it to the Statement of Retained Earnings.

Change from GAAP to GAAP
- Change in the valuation method for inventory (FIFO, etc.)
- Change to or from the full-cost method in the extractive industry
- Changes in construction accounting (ex: completed contract to percentage of completion).
    - A change in depreciation method is considered not distinguishable from a change in estimate and is treated as a change in estimate and accounted for on a *prospective basis*. It is called ***a change in accounting principle inseparable from a change in accounting estimate***.

Only the **direct effects** of the change are recognized. An example of a direct effect is an adjustment to an inventory balance due to a change in inventory valuation method. Related changes, such as the effect on deferred taxes or impairment adjustment are also considered direct effects and must be recognized.

Indirect effects are any changes to current or future cash flows that result from making a change in accounting principle. An example of an indirect effect is a change in a profit sharing or royalty payment based on revenue or net income. Any indirect effects of the change are reported in the period in which the accounting change is made.

If it is impracticable to determine the cumulative effect to any of the prior periods, the new accounting principle is applied as if the change was made **prospectively** at the earliest date practicable.

Footnote disclosures to the financial statements are required for a change in accounting principle. They include:
- The nature and reason for the change, and explanation as to why the new method is preferable
- The method of applying the change
- A description of the prior period information that is retrospectively adjusted
- The effect of the change on income from continuing operations, net income, and any other affected financial statement line item, and any affected per share amounts for the current period and all periods adjusted retrospectively
- The cumulative effect of the change on retained earnings or other components of equity or net assets as of the earliest period presented
- If retrospective application is impracticable, the reason, and a description of how the change was reported
- A description of the indirect effects of the change, including amounts recognized in the current period, and related per share amounts

Accounting Changes and Error Corrections Section 18

- Unless impracticable, the amounts of indirect effect of the change and the per share amounts for each prior period presented

For example, showing both methods, assume a client operating on a calendar year used the weighted average method for inventory costing through the end of 20X1, and that ending inventory at 12/31/X1 was $700. In 20X2, the client changed to the FIFO method. Had FIFO always been in use, inventory at 12/31/X1 would have been $900. Assume the change is also being made for tax purposes (if not, use Deferred tax liability instead of Current tax liability), and that the client's effective tax rate in 20X1 and 20X2 is 40%.

Since the change must be made as of the *beginning* of the fiscal year, an entry is required on 1/1/X2 to adjust inventory to the method and record the related tax effect:

Inventory	**From Weighted Average**	**To FIFO**
12/31/X1	700	
1/1/X2		900

1. To record the change to the FIFO method of inventory costing using **ASC 250**, the following journal entry would be prepared in 20X2:

Inventory	200	
Current income tax liability		80 (200 x 40%)
Retained Earnings		120 (200 x 60%)

2. To record the change to the FIFO method of inventory costing using **APBO 20 (OLD METHOD)**, the following journal entry would be prepared in 20X2 (no longer GAAP):

Inventory	200	
Current income tax liability		80 (200 x 40%)
Cumulative effect on prior years of accounting change (I/S)		120 (200 x 60%)

Note that this change in treatment removes the accounting change from the *Income Statement* and moves it to the Statement of *Retained Earnings*.

The tax effect of a change in principle occurs even if the change is not made for tax purposes. The only difference is that the tax effect will be reported as a deferred income tax liability instead of current.

If it is *impracticable* to determine the cumulative effect to any of the prior periods, the new accounting principle is applied as if the change was made **prospectively** at the earliest date practicable. If for example a company changed inventory valuation from FIFO ***to LIFO*** and it is impracticable to determine the cumulative effect of applying this change retrospectively because records of inventory purchases and sales are no longer available for all prior years, then prior periods are presented as if it had carried forward the 20X0 ending balance in inventory (measured on a FIFO basis) and begun applying the LIFO method to its inventory beginning January 1, 20X1.

2 - Change in Accounting Estimate – (*Prospective* Method)

A **change in estimate** has the effect of adjusting the carrying value of an existing asset or liability or affecting the subsequent accounting for existing or future assets or liabilities.
- Changes in accounting estimates result from the availability of new information.
- **Examples** may include bad debts; inventory obsolescence; sales discounts and sales returns and allowances, service lives and salvage values of depreciable or amortizable assets, and warranty obligations.

A change in accounting estimate is not applied to prior periods but is instead applied *prospectively*. It may affect the current period only, such as the writing off of a receivable that had not previously been reserved against; or may affect the current and future periods, such as a determination that a higher percentage of credit sales than expected are proving uncollectible.

It may be difficult to distinguish between a change in accounting principle and a change in accounting estimate, such as a change in the **method for depreciating or amortizing an asset**. Such a change is a change in the method of applying a generally accepted accounting principle, indicating it is a change in accounting principle. It is also recognition of the fact that the estimate of the pattern of benefits to be derived from the asset has changed. When *a change in accounting principle is inseparable from a change in accounting estimate*, it is accounted for as a **change in accounting estimate** (**Prospectively**).

When making the change:
1. Prior periods are NOT adjusted.
2. Current year, use the New Basis (new number of years, new percentages, etc.) and future periods if the change affects both. (called Prospective)
   Note: If the accounting change is *inseparable* from a change in principle, treat as a change in estimate.
   Disclose – the impact of the change on the current accounting period.

Since estimates, by their nature, are not exact figures, it can be expected that changes in estimate will occur on a continuous basis. As a result, no special reporting is needed: the new estimate is simply used from the **date of revision** onward. In the case of allowance accounts, the amount is simply adjusted with the other side of the entry being reported in continuing operations. For example, if the allowance for bad debts is revised, an entry to adjust the allowance will be offset by a change to the bad debt expense account. There are no special disclosures required.

Lecture 18.02

3 - Change in Reporting Entity – (*Retrospective* Adjustment)

A **change in reporting entity** results in financial statements that are essentially those of a different reporting entity, consisting primarily of:
- Presenting consolidated financial statements in place of individual financial statements for each entity.
- Changing the specific subsidiaries making up groups for which consolidated financial statements are prepared.
- Changing the entities included in combined financial statements.
- Changes between the use of the equity method of accounting and consolidation of a subsidiary without a change in the ownership percentage of stock.

A change due to a change in ownership, such as a business combination reported under the acquisition method, is not a change in reporting entity. It is a change in the actual entity and subject to different accounting and reporting guidelines.

A change in reporting entity is applied retrospectively and all prior periods' financial statements that are presented are modified to reflect the new reporting entity as if that had been the reporting entity as of the beginning of the earliest period presented.

When making this change:
1. Prior periods presented are corrected.
2. Any remaining balance affects beginning Retained Earnings (net of tax), as a prior period adjustment.

The accounting for these changes requires the use of the **retrospective approach**, meaning that the presentation of all items in current and comparative previous years' financial statements will be as if the combination of companies in the current financial statements were always the same. Since these changes affect virtually every account on the balance sheet and income statement, computational problems on this type of change are generally beyond the scope of the exam.

1 - Correction of an Error / Prior Period Adjustment – (*Retroactive* Adjustment)

Although a **correction of an error** is not considered an accounting change, it is accounted for in a manner similar to a change in accounting principle. When an error that had been made in a prior period's financial statements is discovered, it is reported as an error correction and the prior financial statements are restated. Although restatement is accomplished in the same manner as the recognition of a change in accounting principles, there is a distinction in the presentation and disclosure.

To report a correction of an error:
- The cumulative effect of the error on periods prior to the earliest period presented is reflected in the carrying values of assets and liabilities as of the beginning of the earliest period presented.
- An offsetting adjustment, if necessary, is generally made to the opening balance of retained earnings as a ***prior period adjustment*** but may be to another component of equity or net assets, as appropriate.
- Financial statements for each period presented will reflect the correction of the effects of the error on that period's financial statements.

    Examples include:
    - Change from NON-GAAP to GAAP (cash to accrual, direct write-off method for bad debts to an allowance approach)
    - A mathematical error
    - Mistakes in applying GAAP (failure to record depreciation expense)
    - Inventory Errors

Statement of Retained Earnings	
Beginning RE	$xxx
+/-**Prior period adjustment** (net of tax)	**xx**
Adjusted beginning RE	xxx
+ Net income	xx
- Dividends	(xx)
Ending Retained earnings	$xxx

If it is discovered in the current year that an error has been made in accounting in a prior one, the affected accounts are adjusted as of the beginning of the current year, and reported as a prior period adjustment to beginning retained earnings. It will be reported on the Statement of Retained Earnings of the current year, unless comparative financial statements are being issued, in which case the accounting of the prior years will be corrected directly. If only some of the prior years affected are being presented, the presented ones are corrected and the remaining effects are shown on the Statement of Retained Earnings of the earliest year being presented. The approach to correction of an error is an example of the retroactive approach. Retroactive application is the restatement of previously issued financial statements to correct an error.

Inventory errors correct themselves after 2 years. If, however, an inventory error is found in the first and or second year, an adjustment may be required to both the balance sheet and the income statement. For example, if ending inventory of X1 is overstated, that means COGS for X1 is understated, so NI for X1 is overstated. In X2, the beginning inventory will now be overstated (since X1 ending inventory is now X2 beginning), so X2 COGS is overstated and NI for X2 is now Understated. Therefore RE at the end of X2 is now correct (X1 income Over and X2 is Under, so it is a wash).

Required **Disclosures** for a Correction of an Error include:
- The effect of the correction on each financial statement line item and any per-share amounts for all prior periods presented.
- The cumulative effect of the restatement on retained earnings or other components of equity as of the beginning of the earliest period presented.
- A statement that previously issued financial statements have been restated.

Lecture 18.03

FINANCIAL STATEMENT DISCLOSURES (ASC 235)

Financial statements must be accompanied by informative disclosures which will assist in understanding and interpreting the financial statements

Summary of Significant Accounting Policies

One note that is always included is the **summary of significant accounting policies** (**1st footnote**). This note identifies the choices made by the client for those items that have more than one acceptable approach under GAAP. This discusses the accounting principles selected where GAAP allows alternatives (such as the choice of inventory costing method), the methods of applying those principles as well as other information about unusual or innovative principles that the client is applying.

Accounting Changes and Error Corrections

Examples include:
- Revenue recognition policies
- Inventory costing system (e.g., FIFO, LIFO)
- Depreciation method (e.g., straight-line, sum-of-the-years' digits)
- Long-term construction accounting method (e.g., percentage-of-completion, completed-contract)
- Criteria for classification of investments (e.g., cash equivalents, trading securities)

There is no disclosure of methods required when only one method is acceptable, such as the use of expensing for research and development costs or the inclusion of cash in bank at the reconciled account balance. The user of the financial statements only needs to be informed when there was a different approach that might have been used, so as not to be confused by differences resulting from accounting methods that vary from company to company.

Long-Term Obligations

Another disclosure that is necessary in the notes to the financial statements for almost every company is for **long-term obligations**. To assist the user in identifying potential cash flow problems in future years, this disclosure must report legal commitments to cash payments in connection with:
- Notes and bonds payable (including obligations to make payments to a sinking fund)
- Leases (both operating and capital)
- Unconditional purchase obligations extending more than 1 year

All **fixed and determinable** payment obligations of the client as of the balance sheet must be disclosed, but a distinction is made between those payments due within 5 years of the balance sheet date and those not due until after that time:
- Payments due within the **next 5 years** will be identified year by year.
- All payments due after that are **aggregated** into a single amount.

For example, if a client signs an 8-year lease agreement on 7/1/X1 requiring payments of $10,000 per year beginning with the date of signing, a disclosure of the long-term obligations in the notes to the 12/31/X1 financial statements would appear as follows:

20X2	$10,000
20x3	$10,000
20x4	$10,000
20x5	$10,000
20x6	$10,000
After 12/31/X6	$25,000
Total	**$75,000**

Related parties – this discusses major transactions with related parties (owners, management, employees, affiliates) and identifies all parties who control or are controlled by the entity, even if no transactions have occurred with them. Special disclosure is not required when a transaction is obviously with a related party, such as dividends (that are obviously being paid to owners), and wages (that are obviously being paid to employees in the ordinary course of business).

There is **no requirement to disclose** related-party transactions if they are either:
- Compensation arrangements with employees (including management) arising in the ordinary course of business, or

- Eliminated in the preparation of combined or consolidated financial statements.

The AICPA has stated that coverage of related party transactions will be exclusive to the AUD exam as of 1 April 2017.

Other Comprehensive Basis of Accounting (OCBOA) – Special Purpose Frameworks

Financial statements may be prepared in conformity with a comprehensive basis to accounting other than GAAP, referred to as a special purpose framework. Some different methods include:
- Cash receipts and disbursements basis
- Income tax basis
- A method prescribed by a regulatory agency

In addition to normal disclosures, a description of the basis being used and its major differences from U.S. generally accepted accounting principles should be provided in the notes to the financial statements.

Prospective Financial Statements

Prospective financial information is any information about the future, and is considered an Attestation engagement, discussed in the Audit exam. There are 2 types of statements:
- **Forecast** – what management **expects** to occur in the future (General or Limited use).
- **Projection** – what management believes will occur given certain **hypothetical** assumptions (Limited use only).
    - Must perform work using due professional care and in accordance with GAAP.
    - A summary of significant accounting policies and assumptions must be disclosed.
    - The services that may be performed include an Examination, Compilation or Agreed-upon-procedures report.

Lecture 18.04

CLASS QUESTIONS

Please see the Class Questions and Class Solutions for this Lecture at the end of this Section.

Lecture 18.05

CLASS QUESTIONS

Please see the Class Questions and Class Solutions for this Lecture at the end of this Section.

Lecture 18.06

ACCOUNTING POLICIES, CHANGES IN ACCOUNTING ESTIMATES AND ERRORS UNDER IFRS

IAS 8 addresses the selection and disclosure of accounting policies as well as changes in accounting policies, changes in accounting estimates, and corrections of errors. It requires an entity to follow IFRS when applicable and to apply judgment in selecting policies when specific IFRS do not apply.

In applying judgment, the requirements of IFRS dealing with similar matters should be considered and, when there are no analogous requirements, the conceptual framework should be considered. The change in accounting policies are permitted as long as they result in information that is both:
- *Relevant* to the decision-making needs of users; and
- *Reliable*, including being representationally faithful, reflective of the economic substance rather than the form of the issue, free of bias, prudent, and complete.

In general, accounting policies should be applied consistently for similar transactions, events, and conditions. The only circumstances under which IFRS allows a **change in accounting policy** is when either it is required by an IFRS or it results in financial statements that provide information that is more **Relevant and more Reliable**. The accounting for a change in accounting policy is **similar to US GAAP** requirements for a **change in accounting principle**.
- If a new requirement specified by an IFRS includes transition guidance, it should be followed.
- If there is no transition guidance, or if the change is voluntary, the change will be applied **retrospectively**.

Disclosures differ slightly if the change is required by IFRS or voluntary but essentially include the title of the IFRS, if applicable, or the reasons the change is preferable; the nature of the change; the amounts of adjustments to financial statement items; and the effects on basic and diluted EPS, if applicable.

IAS 8 recognizes **changes in accounting estimates** in a manner similar to US GAAP. Like US GAAP, they include changes to estimates related to:
- Bad debts
- Inventory obsolescence
- Fair value
- Useful lives or patterns of consumption of assets
- Warranty obligations

In general, the effect of a change in accounting estimate is recognized **prospectively**. To the extent, however, that the change affects the carrying value of assets and liabilities, it is recognized in the period of change.

IAS 8 requires that **errors in prior period financial statements** are to be corrected **retrospectively** in the first set of financial statements issued after the error is discovered.
- Amounts presented for prior periods on a comparative basis will be restated.
- Opening balances will be restated for portions of errors occurring before the beginning of the earliest period presented.

Under IFRS, when an entity makes a retrospective restatement, the entity must present **3 balance sheets and 2 of each of the other financial statements**.

Change in Reporting Entity: Doesn't exist under IFRS

Accounting Changes

US GAAP	IFRS
• Change in reporting entity recognized with retrospective restatement • Uses term *principle*	• No provision for *change in reporting entity* • Uses term *policy*

Lecture 18.07

CLASS QUESTIONS

Please see the Class Questions and Class Solutions for this Lecture at the end of this Section.

Accounting Changes and Error Corrections   Section 18

CLASS QUESTIONS

Work through the below Class Questions while following along with the respective lectures. Once this is complete, you can begin independently practicing what you've learned by quizzing yourself on this course section in your Interactive Practice Questions (IPQ), which can be found in your online Student Dashboard. Your IPQ simulates the computer-based testing experience, and will also help you understand how concepts are applied to the exam. Each question includes answer explanations from expert CPAs that will help you determine why you answered a question correctly or incorrectly. This is key to your success on the CPA Exam.

Lecture 18.04

1. ASC 250 specifies that the effects of a change in accounting principle should be recorded on a prospective basis when the change is from the

    a. Cash basis of accounting for vacation pay to the accrual basis.
    b. Straight-line method of depreciation for previously recorded assets to the double-declining balance method.
    c. Presentation of statements of individual companies to their inclusion in consolidated statements.
    d. Completed-contract method of accounting for long-term construction-type contracts to the percentage-of-completion method.

2. On January 1, 20X6, Jones Construction, Inc. changed to the percentage-of-completion method of income recognition for financial statement reporting but not for income tax reporting. Jones can justify this change in accounting principle. As of December 31, 20X5, Jones compiled data showing that income under the completed-contract method aggregated $700,000. If the percentage-of-completion method had been used, the accumulated income through December 31, 20X5, would have been $880,000. Assuming an income tax rate of 40% for all years, ASC 250 requires that the cumulative effect of this accounting change to be reported by Jones as

    a. An increase in construction-in-progress for $180,000 in the 20X5 balance sheet.
    b. A decrease in the beginning balance of retained earnings for $108,000 in 20X6.
    c. A cumulative effect adjustment of $108,000 on the 20X6 income statement.
    d. An increase in ending retained earnings of $180,000 in 20X5.

3. In 20X6, Brighton Co. changed from the individual item approach to the aggregate approach in applying the lower of FIFO cost or market to inventories. ASC 250 requires that the change should be reported in Brighton's financial statements as a

    a. Change in estimate on a prospective basis.
    b. Cumulative effect of change in accounting principle on the current year income statement.
    c. Retrospective application to the earliest period presented if practicable.
    d. Prior period adjustment with a separate disclosure.

4. On January 1, 20X2, Union Co. purchased a machine for $528,000 and depreciated it by the straight-line method using an estimated useful life of eight years with no salvage value. On January 1, 20X5, Union determined that the machine had a useful life of six years from the date of acquisition and will have a salvage value of $48,000. An accounting change was made in 20X5 to reflect these additional data. The accumulated depreciation for this machine should have a balance at December 31, 20X5, of

   a. $292,000
   b. $308,000
   c. $320,000
   d. $352,000

5. During 20X9, Steve Company discovered that the ending inventories reported on its financial statements were incorrect by the following amounts:

20X7	$60,000 understated
20X8	75,000 overstated

   Steve uses the periodic inventory system to ascertain year-end quantities that are converted to dollar amounts using the FIFO cost method. Prior to any adjustments for these errors and ignoring income taxes, Steve's retained earnings at January 1, 20X9, would be

   a. Correct.
   b. $ 15,000 overstated.
   c. $ 75,000 overstated.
   d. $135,000 overstated.

Lecture 18.07

6. How would IFRS account for a change in accounting policy/principle?

   a. On a prospective basis.
   b. On a retrospective basis.
   c. By restating the financial statements.
   d. By a cumulative adjustment on the income statement.

7. Under IFRS, changes in accounting policies are

   a. Permitted if the change will result in a more reliable and more relevant presentation of the financial statements.
   b. Permitted if the entity encounters new transactions, events, or conditions that are substantively different from existing or previous transactions.
   c. Required on material transactions, if the entity previously accounted for similar, though immaterial, transactions under an unacceptable accounting method.
   d. Required if an alternate accounting policy gives rise to a material change in assets, liabilities, or the current-year net income.

CLASS SOLUTIONS

1. (b) A change from the straight-line method of depreciation for previously recorded assets to the double-declining balance method is a change in accounting principle that cannot be distinguished from a change in accounting estimate. As a result, it is accounted for prospectively as a change in accounting estimate. Answer (a) is incorrect because a change from the cash basis to the accrual basis of accounting for vacation pay is a change from an unacceptable principle to an acceptable one, which is considered a correction of an error. A correction of an error is accounted for retrospectively. Answer (c) is incorrect because a change in the companies included in consolidated financial statements is a change in reporting entity that is accounted for retrospectively. Answer (d) is incorrect because a change from the completed-contract method to the percentage-of-completion method for long-term construction-type contracts is a change in accounting principle and is accounted for retrospectively.

2. (a) A change from completed-contract to percentage-of-completion is a change in accounting principle that is given retrospective application. The carrying value of assets and liabilities are adjusted as of the beginning of the earliest period presented with an offset to retained earnings. In this case, there would be an increase (debit) to construction in progress of $180,000. Since the change is made for the financial statement, but not for tax, it creates a temporary difference and a deferred tax liability of ($180,000 x 40%) $72,000. The difference would be an increase (credit) to beginning retained earnings. Answer (b) is incorrect because the difference would be an increase (credit) to beginning retained earnings, not a decrease. Answer (c) is incorrect because the difference, which is the cumulative effect of the change, would be an increase (credit) to beginning retained earnings, not an income statement item. Answer (d) is incorrect because the adjustment would not be to ending retained earnings.

3. (c) A change in the method of applying an accounting principle, such as a change from the individual item approach to the group approach for evaluating the lower of cost or market price of inventory, is accounted for through retrospective application to the extent it is practicable. Answer (a) is incorrect because a change from the individual item approach to the group approach in evaluating the lower of cost or market price of inventory is a change in the method of applying an accounting principle, which is accounted for retrospectively as a change in accounting policy. It is not considered a change in accounting estimate. Answer (b) is incorrect because the cumulative effect of the change is recognized as an adjustment to the beginning retained earnings of the earliest period presented. It is not reported on the income statement. Answer (d) is incorrect because a prior period adjustment would be the accounting for a correction of an error, not a change in accounting principle.

4. (a) Changes in the useful life and salvage value of a depreciable asset are changes in accounting estimates that are accounted for prospectively. As of 1/1/X5, 3 years of the original 8 year life had elapsed and accumulated depreciation would have been ($528,000 x 3/8) $198,000 resulting in a book value of $330,000 at that date. With a salvage value of $48,000, the remaining depreciable basis is $282,000, and depreciation will be $94,000 per year ($282,000/3) for each of the next 3 years, its remaining useful life. At the end of 20X5, accumulated depreciation would be ($198,000 + $94,000) $292,000.

5. (c) Since one year's ending inventory is the next year's beginning inventory, a misstatement in one period "corrects itself" in the next period. The understatement in 20X7 resulted in an overstatement to 20X7 cost of sales and an understatement to 20X8 cost of sales resulting in no net effect. The overstatement of inventory at 12/31/X8 resulted in an understatement of cost of sales and an overstatement of pre-tax income by $75,000. If taxes are ignored, this is the amount by which 1/1/X9 retained earnings is overstated.

6. (b) Like US GAAP, IFRS requires that changes in accounting principles to be reported on a retrospective basis, which involves adjusting prior period financial statements to reflect the change.

7. (a) IFRS allows a change in an accounting in one of two circumstances. It is permitted if the change is required by an IFRS or if the change will result in financial statements that are reliable more relevant. Answer (b) is incorrect because adopting an accounting policy for new transactions, events or conditions that are substantively different from existing or previous transactions is not considered a change in accounting policy as the entity previously had no policy to change from. Answer (c) is incorrect because a change from an unacceptable accounting method to an acceptable one is not considered a change in accounting policy but a correction of an error. Answer (d) is incorrect because the fact that the change will materially affect assets, liabilities, or net income is not sufficient to require the change be made.

Accounting Changes and Error Corrections — Section 18

Lecture 18.05

TASK-BASED SIMULATIONS

Task-Based Simulation 1

   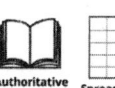 

Situation
On January 2, 20X2, Quo, Inc. hired Reed to be its controller. During the year, Reed, working closely with Quo's president and outside accountants, made changes in accounting policies, corrected several errors dating from 20X1 and before, and instituted new accounting policies.

Quo's 20X2 financial statements will be presented in comparative form with its 20X1 financial statements.

Required:

Items 1 through 10 represent Quo's transactions.
List A represents possible classifications of these transactions as: a change in accounting principle, a change in accounting estimate, a correction of an error in previously presented financial statements, or neither an accounting change nor an accounting error.

List B represents the general accounting treatment for these transactions. These treatments are
- **Retrospective application approach**—Apply the new accounting principle to all prior periods presented showing the cumulative effect of the change in the carrying value of assets and liabilities at the beginning of the first period presented, and adjust financial statements presented to reflect period-specific effects of the change.
- **Retroactive restatement approach**—Restate the 20X1 financial statements and adjust 20X1 beginning retained earnings if the error or change affects a period prior to 20X1 financial statements.
- **Prospective approach**—Report 20X2 and future financial statements on the new basis, but do **not** restate 20X1 financial statements.

Items to be answered:

For each item, select one from List A and one from List B.

List A *(Select one treatment)*
A. Change in accounting principle.

B. Change in accounting estimate.
C. Correction of an error in previously presented financial statements.
D. Neither an accounting change nor an accounting error.

List B *(Select one approach)*
X. Retrospective application approach.
Y. Retroactive restatement approach.
Z. Prospective approach.

Items to be answered:

		List A **Treatment** (A) (B) (C) (D)	List B **Approach** (X) (Y) (Z)
1.	Quo manufactures heavy equipment to customer specifications on a contract basis. On the basis that it is preferable, accounting for these long-term contracts was switched from the completed-contract method to the percentage-of-completion method.	○ ○ ○ ○	○ ○ ○
2.	As a result of a production breakthrough, Quo determined that manufacturing equipment previously depreciated over fifteen years should be depreciated over twenty years.	○ ○ ○ ○	○ ○ ○
3.	The equipment that Quo manufactures is sold with a five-year warranty. Because of a production breakthrough, Quo reduced its computation of warranty costs from 3% of sales to 1% of sales.	○ ○ ○ ○	○ ○ ○
4.	Quo changed from LIFO to FIFO to account for its finished goods inventory.	○ ○ ○ ○	○ ○ ○
5.	Quo changed from FIFO to average cost to account for its raw materials and work in process inventories.	○ ○ ○ ○	○ ○ ○
6.	Quo sells extended service contracts on its products. Because related services are performed over several years, in 20X2, Quo changed from the cash method to the accrual method of recognizing income from these service contracts.	○ ○ ○ ○	○ ○ ○
7.	During 20X2, Quo determined that an insurance premium paid and entirely expensed in 20X1 was for the period January 1, 20X1, through January 1, 20x3.	○ ○ ○ ○	○ ○ ○
8.	Quo changed its method of depreciating office equipment from an accelerated method to the straight-line method to more closely reflect costs in later years.	○ ○ ○ ○	○ ○ ○
9.	Quo instituted a pension plan for all employees in 20X2 and adopted the accounting standards related to pensions. Quo had not previously had a pension plan.	○ ○ ○ ○	○ ○ ○
10.	During 20X2, Quo increased its investment in Worth, Inc. from a 10% interest, purchased in 20X1, to 30%, and acquired a seat on Worth's board of directors. As a result of its increased investment, Quo changed its method of accounting for investment in subsidiary from the cost adjusted for fair value method to the equity method. Quo did not elect to use the fair value method to report its 30% investment in Worth.	○ ○ ○ ○	○ ○ ○

Accounting Changes and Error Corrections   Section 18

Task-Based Simulation 2

Situation

Falk Co. began operations in January, 20X1. On January 2, 20X2, Falk Co. hired a new controller. During the year, the controller, working closely with Falk's president and outside accountants, made changes in existing accounting policies, instituted new accounting policies, and corrected several errors dating from prior to 20X2.

Falk's financial statements for the year ended December 31, 20X2, will not be presented in comparative form with its 20X1 financial statements.

Required:

List A represents possible classifications of these transactions as a change in accounting principle, a change in accounting estimate, correction of an error in previously presented financial statements, or neither an accounting change nor an error correction.

List B represents the general accounting treatment required for these transactions. These treatments are

- Retrospective application approach—Apply the new accounting principle to all prior periods presented showing the cumulative effect of the change in the carrying value of assets and liabilities at the beginning of the first period presented, and adjust financial statements presented to reflect period-specific effects of the change.
- Retroactive restatement approach—Adjust 20X2 beginning retained earnings if the error or change affects a period prior to 20X2.
- Prospective approach—Report 20X2 and future financial statements on the new basis, but do not adjust beginning retained earnings or include the cumulative effect of the change in the 20X2 income statements.

List A—Type of change
(Select one)
A. Change in accounting principle.
B. Change in accounting estimate.
C. Correction of an error in previously presented financial statements.
D. Neither an accounting change nor an error correction.

List B—General accounting treatment
(Select one)
X. Retrospective application approach.
Y. Retroactive restatement approach.
Z. Prospective approach.

Items to be answered:

For Items 1 and 2, select a classification for each transaction from List A and the general accounting treatment required to report the change from List B.

	List A Type of Change				List B Accounting Treatment		
	(A)	(B)	(C)	(D)	(X)	(Y)	(Z)
1. Falk manufactures customized equipment to customer specifications on a contract basis. Falk changed its method of accounting for these long-term contracts from the completed-contract method to the percentage-of-completion method because Falk is now able to make reasonable estimates of future construction costs.	○	○	○	○	○	○	○
2. Based on improved collection procedures, Falk changed the percentage of credit sales used to determine the allowance for uncollectible accounts from 2% to 1%.	○	○	○	○	○	○	○

Task-Based Simulation 3

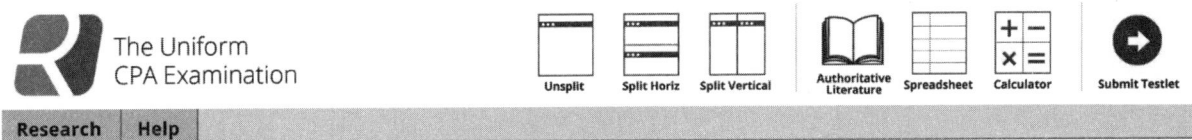

A client wishes to change the method by which it values inventory from FIFO to average because it believes average will provide more relevant information and, as a result, is preferable. Identify the location in professional standards that indicates when a reporting entity should change an accounting principle.

Task-Based Simulation 4

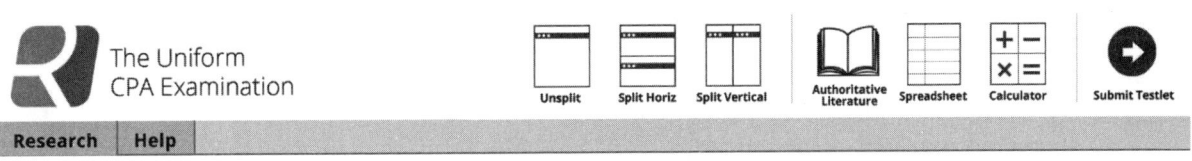

In the current period, a reporting entity has appropriately decided to consolidate an entity that was previously accounted for under the equity method, despite the fact that there was no change in its investment in the entity. Identify the location in professional standards that indicates how this change in reporting entity should be reported.

TASK-BASED SIMULATION SOLUTIONS

Task-Based Simulation Solution 1

		List A Treatment				List B Approach		
		(A)	(B)	(C)	(D)	(X)	(Y)	(Z)
1.	Quo manufactures heavy equipment to customer specifications on a contract basis. On the basis that it is preferable, accounting for these long-term contracts was switched from the completed-contract method to the percentage-of-completion method.	●	○	○	○	●	○	○
2.	As a result of a production breakthrough, Quo determined that manufacturing equipment previously depreciated over fifteen years should be depreciated over twenty years.	○	●	○	○	○	○	●
3.	The equipment that Quo manufactures is sold with a five-year warranty. Because of a production breakthrough, Quo reduced its computation of warranty costs from 3% of sales to 1% of sales.	○	●	○	○	○	○	●
4.	Quo changed from LIFO to FIFO to account for its finished goods inventory.	●	○	○	○	●	○	○
5.	Quo changed from FIFO to average cost to account for its raw materials and work in process inventories.	●	○	○	○	●	○	○
6.	Quo sells extended service contracts on its products. Because related services are performed over several years, in 20X2, Quo changed from the cash method to the accrual method of recognizing income from these service contracts.	○	○	●	○	○	●	○
7.	During 20X2, Quo determined that an insurance premium paid and entirely expensed in 20X1 was for the period January 1, 20X1, through January 1, 20X3.	○	○	●	○	○	●	○

Accounting Changes and Error Corrections — Section 18

#	Description	C1	C2	C3	C4	C5	C6	C7
8.	Quo changed its method of depreciating office equipment from an accelerated method to the straight-line method to more closely reflect costs in later years.	○	●	○	○	○	○	●
9.	Quo instituted a pension plan for all employees in 20X2 and adopted the accounting standards related to pensions. Quo had not previously had a pension plan.	○	○	○	●	○	○	●
10.	During 20X2, Quo increased its investment in Worth, Inc. from a 10% interest, purchased in 20X2, to 30%, and acquired a seat on Worth's board of directors. As a result of its increased investment, Quo changed its method of accounting for investment in subsidiary from the cost adjusted for fair value method to the equity method.	○	○	○	●	○	○	●

Section 18 — Accounting Changes and Error Corrections

Explanation of solutions

1. (A, X) A change in the method of accounting for a long-term construction contract is a change in accounting principle and is given retrospective treatment.

2. (B, Z) A change in the useful life of a depreciable asset is a change in accounting estimate that is accounted for prospectively.

3. (B, Z) A change in the estimated cost of fulfilling a warranty obligation is a change in accounting estimated that is accounted for prospectively.

4. (A, X) A change from LIFO to FIFO is a change in accounting principle that is given retrospective treatment.

5. (A, X) A change from FIFO to average cost is a change in accounting principle that is given retrospective treatment.

6. (C, Y) A change from the cash method to the accrual method for recognizing income is a change from an unacceptable accounting principle to an acceptable one. It is considered a correction of an error and requires restatement of prior period financial statements.

7. (C, Y) Recognizing the entire 2 year premium as an expense in the first year is an error. A correction of an error is accounted for by retroactively restating prior period financial statements.

8. (B, Z) A change in the method of calculating deprecation is a change in accounting principle that cannot be distinguished from a change in accounting estimate. As a result, it is accounted for as a change in accounting estimate and is applied prospectively.

9. (D, Z) When a company adopts a new accounting principle for a transaction that is new or unlike previous transactions, it is not considered an accounting change but rather the establishment of an accounting policy. It is neither an accounting change nor an error but it is accounted for by applying the approach prospectively to the current and future periods.

10. (D, Z) An increase in ownership from 10% to 30%, coupled with acquiring a seat on the board of directors gives the company the ability to exercise significant influence over the investee and would require a change from the cost method to the equity method. This would not be considered an accounting change or a correction of an error. Requirements under ASC 323 indicate that when an investment qualifies for the equity method, it is to be applied on a *prospective basis* only, with no need to restate period financial statements.

Accounting Changes and Error Corrections — Section 18

Task-Based Simulation Solution 2

	List A Type of Change				List B Accounting Treatment		
	(A)	(B)	(C)	(D)	(X)	(Y)	(Z)
1. Falk manufactures customized equipment to customer specifications on a contract basis. Falk changed its method of accounting for these long-term contracts from the completed-contract method to the percentage-of-completion method because Falk is now able to make reasonable estimates of future construction costs.	●	○	○	○	●	○	○
2. Based on improved collection procedures, Falk changed the percentage of credit sales used to determine the allowance for uncollectible accounts from 2% to 1%.	○	●	○	○	○	○	●

Explanation of solutions

1. (A, X) A change in the method of accounting for long-term construction contracts is a change in accounting principle. It is applied retrospectively to prior period financial statements.

2. (B, Z) A change in the percentage of credit sales expected to be uncollectible is a change in accounting estimate. It is accounted for prospectively by applying the change to the current period and to future periods.

Task-Based Simulation Solution 3

| FASB ASC | 250 | 10 | 45 | 2 |

Task-Based Simulation Solution 4

| FASB ASC | 250 | 10 | 45 | 21 |

Section 19 – Accounting for Income Taxes
(Deferred Taxes)

Corresponding Lectures

Watch the following course lectures with this section:

Lecture 19.01 – Accounting for Income Taxes – Permanent Diff.
Lecture 19.02 – Accounting for Income Taxes – Temporary Diff.
Lecture 19.03 – Deferred Tax Liability Example
Lecture 19.04 – Deferred Tax Asset Example
Lecture 19.05 – Deferred Taxes – Class Questions
Lecture 19.06 – Equity Method, NOL, Classification
Lecture 19.07 – Deferred Taxes – Class Questions
Lecture 19.08 – Deferred Taxes – Class Questions - TBS
Lecture 19.09 – Deferred Taxes under IFRS
Lecture 19.10 – Deferred Taxes under IFRS – Class Question

EXAM NOTE: Please refer to the AICPA FAR Blueprint in the Introduction to find a listing of the representative tasks (and their associated skill levels—i.e., Remembering and Understanding, Application, and Analysis) that the candidate should be able to perform based on the knowledge obtained in this section.

Accounting for Income Taxes (Deferred Taxes)	Section 19

Accounting for Income Taxes (Deferred Taxes)

Lecture 19.01

ACCOUNTING FOR INCOME TAXES

Financial statements are governed by GAAP, and income taxes are governed by the Internal Revenue Code. Because of the differences between the recognition and measurement of book and taxable income, the amount of income tax expense and the amount of income taxes payable allocable to continuing operations are often different. These differences may result in future taxable amounts, deferred tax liabilities, or could result in future deductible amounts, deferred tax assets.

Deferred Income Taxes (ASC 740)

Deferred income taxes (ASC 740) result from differences between the carrying values for book purposes and the tax bases of assets and liabilities of the client. Some of these differences will result in future taxable amounts, requiring the recognition of deferred tax liabilities, and others will result in future deductible amounts, requiring the reporting of deferred tax assets.

The **Liability method** is used to report deferred income tax expense. Calculate the current and deferred income tax asset/liability (Balance Sheet Approach), and the plug is income tax expense.

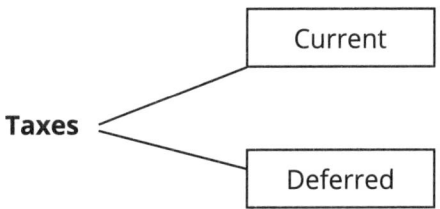

For example: assume the client is reporting income before taxes on the 20X1 financial statement of $200 and has an effective tax rate of 20% in the current year and 30% in future years. They received municipal bond interest of $60, and MACRS deductions exceeded depreciation on the financial statements by $40. The calculation of current income tax expense is as follows:

Income Tax **Expense**	**32 (Current 20, Deferred 12)**	
Current Tax Liability	20 (100 x 20%)	
Deferred Tax Liability	12 (40 x 30%)	

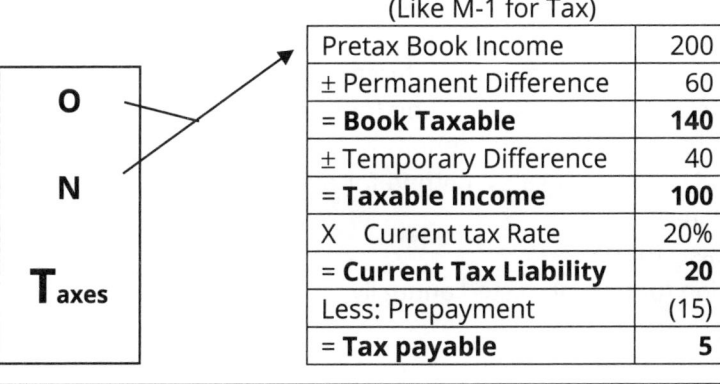

Notice the current tax liability/payable is based on the current tax return income of $100 x the current tax rate of 20%. The deferred tax liability/payable is based on the change in the deferred income tax asset or liability from the beginning to the end of the reporting period of $40 x 30%, which is the future enacted tax rate.

There are **two types of differences** between pretax GAAP income and taxable income, Permanent differences and Temporary differences.

Since books are generally maintained by a corporation on a GAAP basis, certain adjustments will have to be made from book income in order to determine taxable income. Some of these differences are the result of **Permanent differences** in reporting, which refers to items on the income statement that are not taxable or deductible under present law.

There are also differences between GAAP and taxable income that result from items being taxable or deductible in a different period than the item is reported on the income statement. These are called **Temporary Differences.**

Permanent Difference

A **Permanent** difference is a difference that will appear on either the financial statements or the tax return, but not both. They do not result in deferred tax differences since they will never reverse. Some examples:
- Municipal bond interest (not taxable)
- Dividends received deduction (DRD) (not a book deduction)
- Life insurance expense, when the company is the beneficiary (not tax deductible)
- Life insurance proceeds
- Fines or penalties (not tax deductible)
- 50% meals and entertainment for tax (100% for book)
- Federal income tax payments

Lecture 19.02

Temporary Differences

Temporary differences represent differences between the tax bases of assets or liabilities and their reported amounts in the financial statements (books) that will result in taxable or deductible amounts in the future. These differences will reverse over time. Goodwill is considered a temporary difference. The differences are reported as an asset or liability, resulting either in taxable or deductible amounts.

Deferred tax Liabilities (*taxable temporary difference – **TTD***) are expected future tax liabilities that arise because future Taxable income is expected to be **greater** than future Book income due to these temporary differences. Examples include:
- Depreciation methods for tax and book may be different (accelerated depreciation for tax)
- Investments accounted for under the equity method for book, and cost method for tax. (More income for book today, so owe government money later)
- Accrual Sales for book, and installment sales method for tax (more book income today, owe government money later)
- Prepaid expenses (cash basis for tax).
- Goodwill (15 yr amortization for tax and tested annually for GAAP)

Accounting for Income Taxes (Deferred Taxes) — Section 19

Deferred tax *Assets* (*deductible temporary difference – DTD*) are expected future tax deductible differences that arise because future Taxable income will be *less* than future Book income due to temporary differences. Examples include:
- Warranty expense for book today, but deductible for tax when you pay it (Tax expense is less today, so income is higher)
- Rent, Royalty & Interest received in advance is taxed when received, but for book, when earned.
- Bad debt expense – for tax, use direct write-off, for books an allowance approach.
- Contingent Liabilities

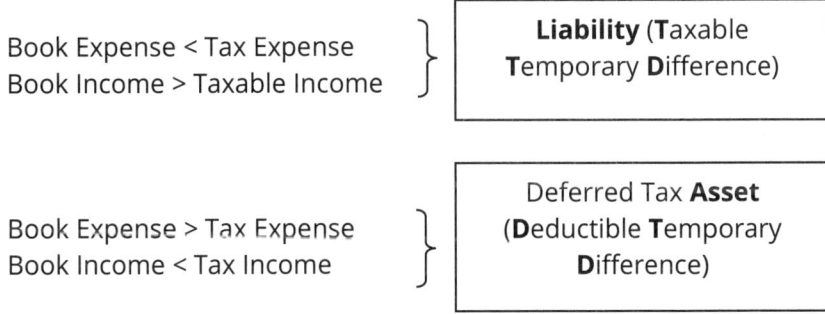

Book Expense < Tax Expense
Book Income > Taxable Income
} **Liability** (**T**axable **T**emporary **D**ifference)

Book Expense > Tax Expense
Book Income < Tax Income
} Deferred Tax **Asset** (**D**eductible **T**emporary **D**ifference)

Lecture 19.03

Deferred Tax Liability Example

EXAMPLE: Rog Co. prepays a $50 expense at the start of the year that is for the next 5 years. For book purposes our expense is $50/5 = $10/yr as we are using accrual accounting. For tax purposes, we deduct all $50 today as we are using the cash basis. Assume the current tax rate is 20%, and the future rate is 30%.

	Book			**Tax**		
X1	Expense	10		Expense	50	
	Prepaid expense	40		Cash		50
	Cash		50			
X2	Expense	10		Expense	0	
	Prepaid		10	Cash		0

If income in X1 was $150 before this $50 expense and $200 in X2,

X1			**X2**	
$150			$200	
book	tax		book	tax
150	150		200	200
-10	-50		-10	-0
140	100 x 20% = $20		190	200 x 30%=$60
	Current tax liability			

Difference is $40 which will reverse at $10 per year, if future tax rate is 30%, $40x30% = **$12 deferred tax liability**

Difference is $10, so the difference starts to reverse out. We then measure the remaining Liability of $30 (40-10) at the future tax rate of 30%, and that gives us a new **Target Liability of $9.**

Note: The cumulative difference is analyzed over time to determine the amount needed in the deferred tax liability account at year end.

The Journal entries would be:

X1	Income tax expense	32	(20 current/12 defd)
	Deferred tax Liability		12
	Current tax Liability		20
X2	Income tax expense	57	(60 current/3 defd)
	Deferred tax liability	3	(to get to target of $9)
	Current tax Liability		60

The calculations of current and deferred taxes for 20X1 are:

Year	20X1	20X2	20X3	20X4	20X5
Taxable	100	0	0	0	0
Accounting	140	(10)	(10)	(10)	(10)
Difference	(40)	10	10	10	10
Rate	20%	30%	30%	30%	30%
Current tax	20				
Deferred tax		3	3	3	3 = 12

The current income tax expense on the $100 of taxable income at the effective 20% rate is $20, and is recorded as follows (assuming no prepayments):

Presentation on the Income Statement:	**X1**		**X2**
Provision for income taxes			
Current	($20)	Current	($60)
Deferred	($12)	Deferred	$ 3
Total provision for income taxes	($32)		($57)

Note: The tax rate used is the **Enacted tax rate**. That is the rate expected to be in effect when the temporary difference is paid or realized.

The *Effective Tax Rate* is the Average rate at which pretax profits are being taxed. It is calculated by taking the income tax expense divided by its net income before taxes.

Accounting for Income Taxes (Deferred Taxes) — Section 19

Lecture 19.04

Deferred Tax Asset Example

EXAMPLE: Rog Co. receives Rental Revenue in advance of $50 at the start of the year that is for the next 5 years. For book purposes our Revenue is $50/5 = $10/yr, as we are required to use the Accrual method. For tax purposes all $50 would be recognized today as we are a cash basis taxpayer, so we have prepaid the tax due, creating a deferred tax asset. Assume the current tax rate is 20%, and the future rate is 30%.

	Book			**Tax**		
X1	Cash	50		Cash	50	
	Rent Rev		10	Rent Rev		50
	Unearned Rev		40			
X2	Unearned Rev	10		Unearned	0	
	Rent Rev		10	Rent Rev		0

If income in X1 was $150 before this $50 Revenue and $200 in X2,

```
     X1                              X2
   $150                            $200
Book      tax                   book      tax
150       150                   200       200
+10       +50                   +10       +0
160       200 x 20% = $40       210       200 x 30% = $60
current tax liability
```

Difference is $40 which will reverse at $10 per year, if future tax rate is 30%, $40x30% = **$12 deferred tax asset**

Difference is $10, so the difference starts to reverse out. We then measure the remaining asset of $30 (40-10) at the future tax rate of 30%, and that gives us a new **Target Asset of $9.** That means we need to reduce the deferred tax asset from 12 down to 9.

Note: The cumulative difference is analyzed over time to determine the amount needed in the deferred tax asset account at year end.

The Journal entries would be:

X1	Income tax expense	28	(current 40/defd 12)
	Deferred tax Asset	12	
	Current tax liability		40
X2	Income tax expense	63	(current 60/defd 3)
	Deferred tax Asset		3 (to get to target of $9)
	Current tax liability		60

When a company has a **Deferred tax asset**, it must determine if it is "more likely than not" (50% or more likelihood) that some or all of the asset will not be realized. If this is the case, a **deferred tax asset valuation allowance** is established for the portion that is not expected to be realized. This is a contra-asset to the deferred tax asset, thus reducing it.

If for example we had a deferred tax asset of $12, but we only expect to use $8, that means it is more likely than not that $4 will not be realized. Therefore a deferred tax asset valuation allowance must be established for $4. By recording this allowance, we are increasing our Income tax expense by $4 from $28 to $32.

Valuation Allowance → **Deferred Tax Asset Valuation Allowance**

Income Tax Expense	32	
Deferred Tax Asset	12	
Current Tax Liability		40
Deferred Tax Asset Valuation Allowance		4

Lecture 19.05

CLASS QUESTIONS

Please see the Class Questions and Class Solutions for this Lecture at the end of this Section.

Lecture 19.06

Equity Method Effects on Deferred Taxes

If an investment is accounted for under the **Equity method**, two differences need to be accounted for. There would be a Dividend Received Deduction (DRD) difference and also a deferred tax difference.

The calculation of taxes on significant investments in the common stock of other companies is unusually complex. This results from the use of the equity method of accounting for book purposes and the dividends-received deduction on dividends taxed when received.

For example, assume the client has made a 30% investment giving them significant influence over the activities of the investee, and that the following information applies to 20X1, the first year the investment is held:

Investee net income	500
Investee dividends paid	100
Dividends-received deduction	80%
Investor taxable income	700
Investor pretax accounting income	844
20X1 effective tax rate	35%
Expected tax rate in 20X2 and beyond	25%

All undistributed earnings are expected to be distributed and reported as dividend income in future years.

Accounting for Income Taxes (Deferred Taxes)   Section 19

The difference of $144 between the taxable and accounting income results from the difference in treatment of the income from the investment. For GAAP purposes, the equity method of accounting caused the investor to pick up their share of the earnings of the investee which is $500 x 30% = $150. The dividend on the tax return is $100 x 30% = $30, but due to the 80% dividends-received deduction, only 20% of that $30 dividend, or $6, is taxed.

In future periods, the $400 of undistributed earnings of the investee will be distributed, with 30%, or $120, going to the investor. Due to the dividends-received deduction, only $24 of those dividends will be in future taxable income. The schedule to compute current and deferred taxes follows:

Year	20X1	Future
Taxable income	700	24
Accounting income	844	0
Difference	(144)	24
Rate	35%	25%
Current tax	245	
Deferred tax		6

Notice that the $144 difference in the current year is not the same as the future taxable amounts of $24, since most of the dividends will not be taxed in future periods.

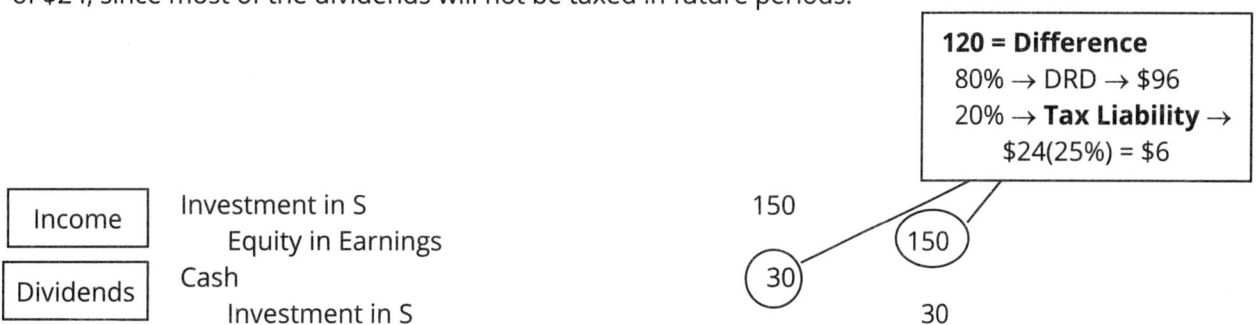

Note: The difference of $120 will be distributed in the future therefore resulting in future cash receipts. A TTD of $120 results, but is subject to an 80% DRD, so only $24 will be taxable at the future rate of 25% = $6 deferred tax Liability.

Net Operating Losses (NOL)

Net Operating Losses (NOL) may be carried **back 2 years and forward 20 years**. When carried back it may be applied as a reduction of taxable income in those periods which results in an income tax refund receivable. If an operating loss is carried forward, the tax effects are recognized to the extent that the tax benefit is more likely than not to be realized. Tax carryforwards should be recognized as deferred tax assets in the period they occur. For example:

	Income	**Enacted rates**		**taxes paid**
20X1	$250	20%		
20X2	$100	20%	=	$20
20X3	$300	30%	=	$90
20X4	**($500)**	35%		
20X5	$600	40%		

In 20X4 we have a loss of $500, so we carry it back two years and offset prior year's income. $500-$100-$300= $100 (NOL carryforward benefit). We will get a refund of the taxes we paid in X2 of $20 (100 x 20%) + $90 (300 x 30%) from X3. That would give us an income tax refund receivable of $110. We would also have a deferred tax asset of $100 (carryforward) x 40% for the benefit we get to use next year.

Income tax refund receivable	$110 (90 + 20)	
Deferred tax asset	40 (100 x 40%)	
Income tax benefit		150 (Income statement)

Note: If do not expect to realize the entire deferred tax asset, a valuation allowance may be needed.

Classification on the Balance Sheet

Deferred tax assets and liabilities have traditionally been classified as either current or noncurrent and were classified on the balance sheet accordingly. In an attempt to simplify the accounting for income taxes, all deferred tax assets and liabilities are now classified as **noncurrent** amounts on the balance sheet. This simplification became effective on the CPA Exam 1 January 2017.

The **net** amount of all deferred tax assets and liabilities, along with any related valuation allowance, is presented on the balance sheet as a **single noncurrent amount**.

Example:

Noncurrent Deferred Tax Asset	10	
Noncurrent Deferred Tax Liability		30
Noncurrent Tax Asset Valuation Allowance		5

Net balance sheet presentation: **Noncurrent** deferred tax Liability of 25

Disclosure

Certain disclosures are required in relation to the items reported on the balance sheet. In general, they may be provided on the face of the financial statements, in supplementary schedules, or in the notes to the financial statements. These include:
- The components of the net deferred tax asset or liability reported on the balance sheet, including:
    - The total of all deferred tax liabilities;
    - The total of all deferred tax assets; and
    - The total deferred tax asset valuation allowance recognized, along with the net change in the allowance for the period.
- The amounts of operating loss carryforwards and tax credit carryforwards along with their expiration dates.

An entity will also provide disclosures about ***temporary differences***. The specific disclosures are different for public and nonpublic entities.
- Public entities will disclose the approximate tax effect of each type of temporary difference and carryforward that affects deferred tax assets or liabilities.

- Nonpublic entities will disclose the types but are not required to disclose the approximate tax effects.

For each year presented, the significant components of income tax expense arising from continuing operations are disclosed.
- Current tax expense or benefit
- Deferred tax expense or benefit
- Investment tax credits
- Government grants
- Benefits of operating loss carryforwards
- Adjustments to deferred tax assets or liabilities resulting from changes in tax laws, tax rates, or the entity's tax status
- Adjustment to the beginning valuation allowance due to changes in judgment about the realizability of deferred tax assets

In this example, the numbers would be netted on the Balance Sheet to show a $25 noncurrent tax Liability, as a result of netting the deferred tax Asset of $10, offset by a $5 valuation allowance, with the deferred tax Liability of $30. Let's look at a **detailed example**. A client with taxable income of $500 at an effective tax rate of 30% in 20X1 and an expected tax rate of 40% in 20X2 and beyond has the following differences between book and tax reporting as of the end of 20X1, its first year of operations:

Rent collected in advance on one-year lease agreement	150
Excess of MACRS deduction on tax return over GAAP depreciation	250
Municipal bond interest	120
Prepaid insurance on policy with 3-year remaining life	300

Current income taxes are $500 x 30% = $150.

Rent collected in advance is included in this year's taxable income, but is a current liability that will only be reported in revenue on the financial statement next year. Since this will cause next year's taxable income to be lower than financial statement income, it is a future deductible amount resulting in a deferred tax asset of $150 x 40% = $60.

The depreciation difference, reflected in fixed assets in the noncurrent asset section, will cause future tax deductions to be smaller, and taxable income higher, so it is a future taxable amount resulting in a deferred tax liability of $250 x 40% = $100.

As stated above, as a result of ASU 2015-17 all deferred tax assets and deferred tax liabilities are classified as **noncurrent**.

Municipal bond interest does not result in any difference in carrying values, and is not a part of future financial statement or taxable income.

Prepaid insurance was deducted on the tax return when paid, but will result in reductions of book income equally over the next 3 years under the matching principle with no tax deductions in those years. As a result, the $300 is a future taxable amount resulting in $300 x 40% = $120 of deferred tax liabilities.

Summarizing the tax accounts from this example:

Current income taxes on taxable income	150
Deferred tax asset on rent	60
Deferred tax liability on depreciation	100
Deferred tax liability on insurance	120

After the netting of deferred tax assets and deferred tax liabilities, the **balance sheet** will report the following:

Current Liabilities
Current income taxes payable   150

Noncurrent Liabilities
Deferred tax liability   160

On the **income statement**, the following will be reported in continuing operations:
- Current income tax expense   150
- Deferred income tax expense   160

Lecture 19.07

CLASS QUESTIONS

Please see the Class Questions and Class Solutions for this Lecture at the end of this Section.

Lecture 19.08

CLASS QUESTIONS

Please see the Class Questions and Class Solutions for this Lecture at the end of this Section.

Lecture 19.09

DEFERRED TAXES UNDER IFRS

IAS 12, Income Taxes, requires an entity to recognize **current tax** for current and prior periods as a liability to the extent that the taxes are unpaid ("liability method").
- When tax payments exceed amounts owed, the difference is recognized as an asset.
- The tax benefit of tax loss carrybacks are also recognized as an asset.

Current tax assets and liabilities are measured at the amount expected to be paid, or recovered from, taxing authorities upon filing of the entity's tax returns for all tax jurisdictions to which the entity is subject.

Current tax assets and liabilities may be *offset* against one another if the entity has the legal right of offset and it intends to either settle or recover the amount on a net basis or to realize the asset and settle the liability at the same time.

Accounting for Income Taxes (Deferred Taxes) — Section 19

Under IFRS, all deferred tax assets and liabilities are classified as **Non-Current only** on the statement of financial position. GAAP now aligns with IFRS in this treatment of deferred tax assets and liabilities, as a result of ASU 2015-17.

IFRS also requires an entity to recognize a *deferred tax liability for all taxable temporary differences*, with few exceptions. These include the initial recognition of goodwill or the initial recognition of an asset or liability in a transaction that has no effect on either financial statement or taxable income and that was not part of a business combination.
- A temporary difference (TD) is defined as a difference between the financial statement carrying value of an asset or liability and its tax basis.
- A taxable temporary difference (TTD) will result in taxable income when the asset is recovered or the liability is settled.
- A deductible temporary difference (DTD) will result in reductions to taxable income when the asset is recovered or the liability is settled.

Deferred tax assets are also recognized for all deductible temporary difference but the amount is *limited* to amounts for which it is probable (more likely than not) that taxable profits will be available against which the DTD can be applied. This will be the case when there are TTD's that are expected to reverse either:
- In the same period as the reversal of the DTD; or
- In periods into which a tax loss can be carried back or forward.

Deferred tax assets are also recognized for carryforwards of unused tax losses and tax credits. They too, however, are limited to amounts for which it is expected that future profit will be available against which to apply them.

Deferred tax assets that are not recognized because it is not probable that there will be taxable profits against which to apply them when they reverse, are reevaluated at the end of each reporting period to determine if a change in circumstances has made it probable that there will be taxable profits.

Under IFRS and now GAAP, all deferred tax assets and liabilities **are considered noncurrent**. They are measured by multiplying the amount of a TTD or a DTD by the tax rate that is expected to apply when the temporary difference reverses. The rate to be used is one that has been **enacted or substantially enacted** by the end of the reporting period.
- US GAAP requires the entity to use a future enacted tax rate and disallows the use of a substantially enacted rate.
- A substantially enacted future tax rate is one that has been announced by the taxing authority, if it has the substantive effect of actual enactment, but may require several months before it is actually enacted.

In general, both current and deferred taxes are recognized in the determination of profit or loss for the period. That is not the case, however, when the taxes arise:
- From a transaction that is not recognized in profit or loss, such as one affecting other comprehensive income or is recorded directly in some other equity account.
- From a business combination.

Deferred tax assets and liabilities may be *offset* against one another only if the entity has the legal right of offset and the tax amounts relate to the same taxing authority (Ex: same country).

IAS 12 requires **disclosure of**:
- The major components of tax expense, disclosed separately.

- Aggregate amounts relating to items applied directly to equity.
- Income tax related to each component of OCI.
- An explanation of the relationship between financial statement income and income tax expense.
- Tax rate changes
- Amounts and date of expiration of DTDs and unused tax losses and credits that did not result in the recognition of a deferred tax asset.
- For each type of temporary difference, unused tax loss, and unused tax credit:
    - The amount of deferred tax assets and liabilities recognized in the statement of financial position.
    - Deferred tax income or expense recognized in profit or loss that is not apparent from amounts recognized on the statement of financial position.

Deferred Income Taxes	
US GAAP	**IFRS**
• Deferred tax assets are recognized in full but valuation allowances reduce them to the amount that is *more likely than not* to be realized. • Measure deferred tax assets and liabilities using the future enacted tax rate.	• Deferred tax assets are recognized only when reasonably assured of realization and only to the extent it is probable that they will be realized. • Measure deferred tax assets and liabilities using **either** the future enacted or *substantially enacted* tax rate

Lecture 19.10

CLASS QUESTIONS

Please see the Class Questions and Class Solutions for this Lecture at the end of this Section.

Accounting for Income Taxes (Deferred Taxes) — Section 19

CLASS QUESTIONS

Work through the below Class Questions while following along with the respective lectures. Once this is complete, you can begin independently practicing what you've learned by quizzing yourself on this course section in your Interactive Practice Questions (IPQ), which can be found in your online Student Dashboard. Your IPQ simulates the computer-based testing experience, and will also help you understand how concepts are applied to the exam. Each question includes answer explanations from expert CPAs that will help you determine why you answered a question correctly or incorrectly. This is key to your success on the CPA Exam.

Lecture 19.05

1. For the year ended December 31, 20X3, Tyre Co. reported pretax financial statement income of $750,000. Its taxable income was $650,000. The difference is due to accelerated depreciation for income tax purposes. Tyre's effective income tax rate is 30% and Tyre made estimated tax payments during 20X3 of $90,000. What amount should Tyre report as current income tax expense for 20X3?

    a. $105,000
    b. $135,000
    c. $195,000
    d. $225,000

2. Dunn Co.'s 20X3 income statement reported $90,000 income before provision for income taxes. To compute the provision for federal income taxes, the following 20X3 data are provided:

Rent received in advance	$16,000
Income from exempt municipal bonds	20,000
Depreciation deducted for income tax purposes in excess of depreciation reported for financial statements purposes	10,000
Enacted corporate income tax rate	30%

    If the alternative minimum tax provisions are ignored, what amount of current federal income tax liability should be reported in Dunn's December 31, 20X3 balance sheet?

    a. $18,000
    b. $22,800
    c. $24,600
    d. $21,000

Lecture 19.07

3. Black Co., organized on January 2, 20X3, had pretax accounting income of $500,000 and taxable income of $800,000 for the year ended December 31, 20X3. The only temporary difference is accrued product warranty costs that are expected to be paid as follows:

20X4	$100,000
20X5	50,000
20X6	50,000
20X7	100,000

Black has never had any net operating losses (book or tax) and does not expect any in the future. There were no temporary differences in prior years. The enacted income tax rates are 35% for 20X3, 30% for 20X4 through 20X6, and 25% for 20X7. In Black's December 31, 20X3 balance sheet, the deferred income tax asset should be

   a. $ 60,000
   b. $ 70,000
   c. $ 85,000
   d. $105,000

4. Because Jab Co. uses different methods to depreciate equipment for financial statement and income tax purposes, Jab has temporary differences that will reverse during the next year and add to taxable income. Deferred income taxes that are based on these temporary differences should be classified in Jab's balance sheet as a

   a. Contra account to current assets.
   b. Contra account to noncurrent assets.
   c. Current liability.
   d. Noncurrent liability.

5. When dealing with deferred taxes, which of the following should be disclosed in a company's financial statements?

   I. The types and amounts of existing temporary differences
   II. The types and amounts of existing permanent differences
   III. The nature and amount of each type of operating loss and tax credit carryforward

   a. I and II only
   b. I and III only
   c. II and III only
   d. I, II, and III

Lecture 19.10

6. Which of the following is true regarding reporting deferred taxes in financial statements prepared in accordance with IFRS?

   a. Deferred tax assets and liabilities are classified as current and noncurrent based on their expiration dates.
   b. Deferred tax assets and liabilities may only be classified as noncurrent.
   c. Deferred tax assets are always netted with deferred tax liabilities to arrive at one amount presented on the balance sheet.
   d. Deferred taxes of one jurisdiction are offset against another jurisdiction in the netting process.

CLASS SOLUTIONS

1. (c) Current tax expense is calculated by multiplying taxable income, which is given as $650,000, by the tax rate of 30%. As a result, current tax expense is $195,000.

2. (b) Financial statement income be increased by the $16,000 of rent received in advance because it is taxable in the year received. It will be reduced by the $20,000 municipal bond interest because it is not table. It will also be reduced by the additional $10,000 in depreciation that will be deducted for tax purposes. As a result, taxable income will be ($90,000 + $16,000 - $20,000 - $10,000) $76,000. At a tax rate of 30%, current income tax expense and the current federal tax liability will be ($76,000 x 30%) $22,800.

3. (c) Black will calculate a deferred tax asset by multiplying the amount of the warranty liability that will be incurred in each future period by the enacted future tax rate for that period and combining the amounts. A total of $200,000 will be paid during the period from 20X4 through 20X6, when the tax rate will be 30%. As a result, those amounts will generate a deferred tax asset of $60,000. The remaining $100,000 will be incurred in 20X7 when the tax rate will be 25%, resulting in an additional deferred tax asset of $25,000 and a total deferred tax asset of $85,000.

4. (d) A difference in methods for computing depreciation for financial statement and tax purposes is a temporary difference. Since the reversal will add to future taxable income, it is apparently a taxable temporary difference, which will result in a deferred tax liability. Answers (a) and (b) are incorrect because deferred taxes are not presented as a contra account. Answer (c) is incorrect because all deferred tax assets and liabilities are now reported as noncurrent.

5. (b) An entity is required to disclose information about the nature and amount of temporary differences and the nature and amount of each operating loss and tax credit carryforward, including when they expire. There is no requirement to disclose information about the types and amounts of permanent differences.

6. (b) Under IFRS, deferred tax assets and liabilities are always reported as noncurrent, which is now also true under GAAP. Under IFRS, deferred tax assets may only be offset against deferred tax liabilities if they relate to the same tax jurisdiction, which is also true under GAAP.

TASK-BASED SIMULATIONS

Task-Based Simulation 1

Required:

The following partially completed worksheet contain Lane Co.'s reconciliation between financial statement income and taxable income for the three years ended April 30, 20X3, and additional information.

Lane Co.
INCOME TAX WORKSHEET
For the Three Years Ended April 30, 20X3

	April 30, 20X1	April 30, 20X2	April 30, 20X3
Pretax financial income	$900,000	$1,000,000	$1,200,000
Permanent differences	100,000	100,000	100,000
Temporary differences	200,000	100,000	150,000
Taxable income	$600,000	$ 800,000	$ 950,000
Cumulative temporary differences (future taxable amounts)	$200,000	$(2)	$ 450,000
Tax rate	20%	25%	30%
Deferred tax liability	$ 40,000	$ 75,000	$ (4)
Deferred tax expense	--	$ (3)	--
Current tax expense	$ (1)	--	--

The tax rate changes were enacted at the beginning of each tax year and were not known to Lane at the end of the prior year.

Items to be answered:

Items 1 through 4 represent amounts omitted from the worksheet. For each item, determine the amount omitted from the worksheet. Select the amount from the following list. An answer may be used once, more than once, or not at all.

Amount

A.	$ 25,000	H.	$135,000
B.	$ 35,000	I.	$140,000
C.	$ 45,000	J.	$160,000
D.	$ 75,000	K.	$180,000
E.	$100,000	L.	$200,000
F.	$112,500	M.	$300,000
G.	$120,000	N.	$400,000

Specific audit objective

1. Current tax expense for the year ended April 30, 20X1.
2. Cumulative temporary differences at April 30, 20X2.
3. Deferred tax expense for the year ended April 30, 20X2.
4. Deferred tax liability at April 30, 20X3.

Section 19 Accounting for Income Taxes (Deferred Taxes)

Task-Based Simulation 2

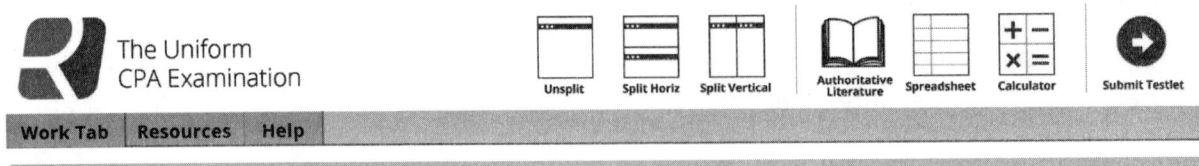

Required:

Items 1 through 4 describe circumstances resulting in differences between financial statement income and taxable income. For each numbered item, determine whether the difference is

List
A. A temporary difference resulting in a deferred tax asset.
B. A temporary difference resulting in a deferred tax liability.
C. A permanent difference.

Items to be answered:

Indicate the classification of each item. An answer may be selected once, more than once, or not at all.

	A Temporary difference DTA	B Temporary difference DTL	C Permanent difference
1. For plant assets, the depreciation expense deducted for tax purposes is in excess of the depreciation expense used for financial reporting purposes.	○	○	○
2. A landlord collects some rents in advance. Rents received are taxable in the period in which they are received.	○	○	○
3. Interest is received on an investment in tax-exempt municipal obligations.	○	○	○
4. Costs of guarantees and warranties are estimated and accrued for financial reporting purposes.	○	○	○

Task-Based Simulation 3

A client is preparing its deferred tax provision and is trying to determine what rate to use. A tax bill that will change its tax rate was passed and enacted shortly after the client's year-end. Identify the location in professional standards that indicates what tax rate should be used to measure deferred taxes.

Section 19   Accounting for Income Taxes (Deferred Taxes)

TASK-BASED SIMULATION SOLUTIONS

Task-Based Simulation Solution 1

Specific audit objective	(A)	(B)	(C)	(D)	(E)	(F)	(G)	(H)	(I)	(J)	(K)	(L)	(M)	(N)
1. Current tax expense for the year ended April 30, 20X1.	○	○	○	○	○	○	●	○	○	○	○	○	○	○
2. Cumulative temporary differences at April 30, 20X2.	○	○	○	○	○	○	○	○	○	○	○	○	●	○
3. Deferred tax expense for the year ended April 30, 20X2.	○	●	○	○	○	○	○	○	○	○	○	○	○	○
4. Deferred tax liability at April 30, 20X3.	○	○	○	○	○	○	○	●	○	○	○	○	○	○

Explanation of solutions

1. (G) Current income tax expense is always equal to taxable income, given as $600,000, multiplied by the tax rate, also given as 20%, resulting in current taxes of $120,000.

2. (M) The cumulative temporary differences at 4/30/X2 can be determined in one of two ways. The deferred tax liability is calculated by multiplying the cumulative differences by the tax rate. If there is a deferred tax liability of $75,000 when the rate is 25%, there must be cumulative temporary differences of $300,000 ($300,000 x 25% = $75,000). This can also be determined by adding the $200,000 in temporary differences in the first year to the $100,000 identified in the second year.

3. (B) Deferred tax expense in any year is measured as the change in the net amount of all deferred tax assets and liabilities. There was a deferred tax liability of $40,000 at 4/30/X1, and $75,000 at 4/30/X2 indicating an increase of $35,000, which will be deferred tax expense.

4. (H) The deferred tax liability will be equal to the cumulative temporary differences of $450,000 multiplied by the 30% tax rate, resulting in a deferred tax liability of $135,000.

Task-Based Simulation Solution 2

	A Temporary difference DTA	B Temporary difference DTL	C Permanent difference
1. For plant assets, the depreciation expense deducted for tax purposes is in excess of the depreciation expense used for financial reporting purposes.	○	●	○
2. A landlord collects some rents in advance. Rents received are taxable in the period in which they are received.	●	○	○
3. Interest is received on an investment in tax-exempt municipal obligations.	○	○	●
4. Costs of guarantees and warranties are estimated and accrued for financial reporting purposes.	●	○	○

Explanation of solutions

1. (B) When an entity deducts more depreciation for tax purposes than for financial statement purposes, there will be a reduced depreciation deduction in future periods and the entity will be required to pay additional taxes. This is a taxable temporary difference that will result in a deferred tax liability.

2. (A) Rents are taxed in the earlier of the year in which they accrue or the year in which they are received. When rents are received in advance, they are taxed when received but they are recognized in income subsequently when earned. As a result, they will not be taxed in future periods and represent a deductible temporary difference that will result in a deferred tax asset.

3. (C) Interest received on tax exempt municipal obligations is not taxable and is a difference with no future tax effect, also referred to as a permanent difference.

4. (A) Estimated guarantees and warranties reduce financial statement income in the period accrued but are not deductible until the costs are actually incurred in a subsequent period. When they are incurred, they will reduce future taxable income and represent a deductible temporary difference that will result in a deferred tax asset.

Task-Based Simulation Solution 3

| FASB ASC | 740 | 10 | 30 | 8 |

Section 20 - Interim Financial Reporting

Section 20 – Interim Financial Reporting

Corresponding Lectures

Watch the following course lectures with this section:

Lecture 20.01 – Interim Financial Reporting
Lecture 20.02 – Interim Financial Reporting – Class Question
Lecture 20.03 – Interim Financial Reporting under IFRS
Lecture 20.04 – Interim Reporting under IFRS – Class Question

EXAM NOTE: Please refer to the AICPA FAR Blueprint in the Introduction to find a listing of the representative tasks (and their associated skill levels—i.e., Remembering and Understanding, Application, and Analysis) that the candidate should be able to perform based on the knowledge obtained in this section.

Interim Financial Reporting   Section 20

Interim Financial Reporting

Lecture 20.01

INTERIM FINANCIAL REPORTING

Companies that issue annual financial statements typically issue interim reports on a **quarterly** basis as well. In general, the application of **generally accepted accounting principles** to a report covering three months will be no different than for a report covering one year, since an interim period is an integral part of the overall year. Timeliness is emphasized over reliability. These statements should be marked "unaudited". As a result **(ASC 270)**:

- **Revenues** are recognized in each quarter as earned and realized (for example, estimates must be made each quarter when applying the percentage-of-completion method of construction accounting to determine the profit in each period).
- **Expenses** are matched to each quarter (for example, a property tax bill covering an entire year must be allocated equally to the four quarters).
- **Accounting Changes** made in an interim period are to be reported by retrospective application.

For example, assume a client received an annual rental payment of $300 from a client on 1/2/X1 and paid a $100 property tax bill covering all of calendar year 20X1 on 3/15/X1. The effects of these items on the interim reports in the 20X1 are:

Quarter	1st	2nd	3rd	4th
Rent income	75	75	75	75
Property tax	(25)	(25)	(25)	(25)

One item that may need special consideration is the provision for income taxes. When preparing an annual report, the company already knows its taxable income for the year and can compute its income tax provision with full knowledge of the applicable tax rates and available tax credits.

When computing income taxes at an interim date, however, the company must make an estimate of the **effective annual tax rate** that it believes will be applicable for that entire year. This should take into account estimates of total taxable income for the year and any tax planning strategies the company plans to adopt during the year.

The estimate of the effective annual tax rate should be updated at each interim date, and the provision for income taxes in later quarters will be based on the current estimated rate applied to cumulative income reduced by provisions reported in early periods.

For example, if a client has income of $100 in the first quarter of 20X1 and expects the effective annual tax rate for all of 20X1 to be 25%, then the provision for income taxes in the first quarter will be $100 x 25% = $25. If the client has an additional $150 of income in the second quarter, and revises their estimate of the effective annual tax rate for all of 20X1 to 30%, then the provision for income taxes in the second quarter will be calculated as follows:

Income in 2nd quarter of 20X1	150
Income in 1st quarter of 20X1	100
Income for 6 months ended 6/30/X1	250
Expected effective annual tax rate	30%
Income taxes for 6 month period	75
Less: Amount reported in 1st quarter	(25)
Income tax provision in 2nd quarter	50

Another item requiring special handling on interim reports is **inventory**. The use of inventory estimation techniques is permissible for interim reports. A special problem, however, involves fluctuations in inventory values at interim dates.

Since interim periods are integral parts of the entire year, they must be computed in a manner that will result in consistent presentations with the full year. A company sometimes experiences declines in inventory values at interim dates that are **expected to be recovered** by year-end. In these cases, inventory should **not** be written down to market at the interim date. On the other hand, if a decline in value is not expected to be recovered before year-end, then the inventory should be written down.

For example, assume a client has suffered a substantial drop in the replacement cost of their inventory at the end of the first quarter, but believes these values will recover before the end of the year. The decline in market will not be reported in the first quarter. If the client is incorrect, and values do not recover by the end of the year, the decline will be reported in the fourth quarter.

On the other hand, assume a decline occurs in the first quarter, and the client **does not believe prices will recover** by year-end. They will write down the inventory to market in the first quarter. If the client is incorrect, and values recover in the third quarter of the year, the increase in market will have to be reported in the third quarter to offset the decline reported in the first quarter. Any increase in value in the third quarter that exceeds the decline reported in the first quarter is ignored, since inventory is not valued at market when it is higher than cost.

> **To Summarize:**
>
> - Property taxes, bonuses, depreciation – allocate to all quarters
> - Inventory losses – in that quarter
> - Major expenses - in that quarter, unless benefit future quarters then allocate.
> - **D**iscontinued operations – in that quarter
> - **Income tax expense** is estimated each quarter using the rate expected for the entire year.

SEC Reporting Requirements under Regulation S-K

Quarterly report (Form 10-Q) provides quarterly information similar to that in the 10-K but in less detail. Quarterly financial statements are **reviewed** by public accountants. The company files three Form 10-Qs every year and the Form 10-K contains the quarterly results for the fourth quarter. The Form 10-Q must include the following financial statements.
    a. An interim balance sheet as of the end of the most recent fiscal quarter, and a balance sheet as of the end of the preceding fiscal year. It will include only major captions and

items representing less than 10% of total assets that have not changed by more than 25% may be combined with other items.

b. Interim statements of income for (1) the most recent fiscal quarter, (2) for the period between the end of the preceding fiscal year and the end of the most recent fiscal quarter, and (3) for the corresponding periods of the preceding fiscal year. It will also include only major captions. Items representing less than 15% of average net income for the 3 most recent fiscal years that have not changed by more than 20% when compared to the corresponding preceding fiscal period's statement of income may be combined with other items.

c. Interim statements of cash flows for (1) the period between the end of the preceding fiscal year and the end of the most recent fiscal quarter, and for (2) the corresponding period of the preceding fiscal year. The statement is abbreviated and reports a single figure for net cash flows from operating activities and only reports individual changes from investing and financing activities if they exceed 10% of average net cash flows from operating activities for the preceding 3 years.

d. The statement of changes in equity may also be presented.

Disclosures are limited to those needed to avoid the financial information being presented from being misleading. Information that was included with the most recent annual financial statements that have not changed significantly may be omitted.

Form 10-Qs are due **40 days** after the end of the fiscal quarter for accelerated and large accelerated filers (**45 days** for all other registrants including non-accelerated filers and small reporting companies).

Lecture 20.02

CLASS QUESTIONS

Please see the Class Questions and Class Solutions for this Lecture at the end of this Section.

Lecture 20.03

INTERIM REPORTING UNDER IFRS

IFRS does not mandate interim reporting. If interim statements are issued, the entity must use the same accounting policies as used in year-end financial statements. Its interim financial statements must include, as a minimum the following:
- A condensed statement of financial position;
- A condensed statement or condensed statements of profit or loss and other comprehensive income;
- A condensed statement of changes in equity;
- A condensed statement of cash flows; and
- Selected notes.

Lecture 20.04

CLASS QUESTIONS

Please see the Class Questions and Class Solutions for this Lecture at the end of this Section.

Section 20   Interim Financial Reporting

CLASS QUESTIONS

Work through the below Class Questions while following along with the respective lectures. Once this is complete, you can begin independently practicing what you've learned by quizzing yourself on this course section in your Interactive Practice Questions (IPQ), which can be found in your online Student Dashboard. Your IPQ simulates the computer-based testing experience, and will also help you understand how concepts are applied to the exam. Each question includes answer explanations from expert CPAs that will help you determine why you answered a question correctly or incorrectly. This is key to your success on the CPA Exam.

1. Conceptually, interim financial statements can be described as emphasizing

    a. Timeliness over reliability.
    b. Reliability over relevance.
    c. Relevance over comparability.
    d. Comparability over neutrality.

2. For interim financial reporting, a company's income tax provision for the second quarter of 20X3 should be determined using the

    a. Effective tax rate expected to be applicable for the full year of 20X3 as estimated at the end of the first quarter of 20X3.
    b. Effective tax rate expected to be applicable for the full year of 20X3 as estimated at the end of the second quarter of 20X3.
    c. Effective tax rate expected to be applicable for second quarter of 20X3.
    d. Statutory tax rate for 20X3.

3. Wilson Corp. experienced a $50,000 decline in the market value of its inventory in the first quarter of its fiscal year. Wilson had expected this decline to reverse in the third quarter, and in fact, the third quarter recovery exceeded the previous decline by $10,000. Wilson's inventory did not experience any other declines in market value during the fiscal year. What amounts of loss and/or gain should Wilson report in its interim financial statements for the first and third quarters?

	First quarter	Third quarter
a.	$0	$0
b.	$0	$10,000 gain
c.	$50,000 loss	$50,000 gain
d.	$50,000 loss	$60,000 gain

4. Which of the following is true regarding the disclosure requirements regarding interim financial statements under IFRS?

    a. Interim financial statements are required.
    b. If interim financial statements are presented, four basic financial statements and selected notes are required.
    c. If interim financial statements are presented, at least a balance sheet and profit and loss are required.
    d. Interim financial statements must be presented with the most recent annual financial statements.

CLASS SOLUTIONS

1. (a) Two primary characteristics of accounting information is that it is relevant, in that it is timely and will be provide information that is helpful for the decision-making activities of the user; and that it is reliable, in that it is verifiable, representationally faithful, and free of bias. Interim financial reports are designed to provide users with timely information, useful in the making of decisions, at the sacrifice of reliability. Answer (b) is incorrect because interim financial reports are prepared during the annual period to provide users with information that is relevant in that it is timely and useful in their decision-making activities. Due to the speed with which they are required to be developed, interim reports sacrifice reliability for timeliness, a component of relevance, not the other way around. Answer (c) is incorrect because while a primary characteristic of financial information is its relevance, comparability is a secondary characteristic. Interim financial statements are prepared applying the same principles and procedures that are used in preparing annual financial statements and comparability need not be sacrificed. Answer (d) is incorrect because although neutrality may be sacrificed in the haste of preparing interim financial statements, but it is not in order to achieve comparability, which should be achieved by applying the same accounting principles and policies to the preparation of the interim financial information that are applied in the preparation of annual information.

2. (b) Each interim period is considered to be an integral part of the annual period and expectations for the annual period are reflected in the interim report. The income tax expense should be calculated using the estimated annual effective tax rate. The estimated tax rate should be updated as of the end of each interim period, such as the second quarter in this case. Answer (a) is incorrect because the estimated tax rate should be updated as of the end of the second quarter, not the first. Answer (c) is incorrect because the income tax expense should be calculated using the estimated annual effective tax rate, not the rate that is applicable to that quarter. Answer (d) is incorrect because the income tax expense for an interim period should be calculated using the estimated annual effective tax rate. This will be a function of the statutory rate but may also include a variety of other items, depending on the various components of the entity's income and whether it is subject to special rates, limited deductibility, or other matters.

3. (a) In general, declines in the value of inventory are recognized in the interim period in which they occur. This is not the case, however, if they are expected to be recovered in a subsequent interim period that is part of the same annual period. When they are expected to be recovered in a subsequent interim period, the loss is only recognized to the extent that it is not expected to be recovered. If the inventory achieves a value that is higher than its original carrying value, the additional gain is not recognized.

4. (b) IFRS does not require an entity to prepare interim financial statements. It does, however, specify that, if an entity does provide interim financial statements, it will include a minimum of four condensed financial statements and selected notes. Those include statements of financial position; profit or loss and other comprehensive income, or separate statements; changes in equity; and cash flows. There is no requirement that they be accompanied by the most recent annual financial statements.

TASK-BASED SIMULATIONS

Task-Based Simulation 1

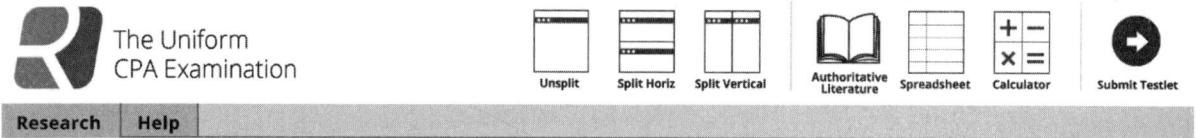

A company determines its inventory using the periodic FIFO approach based on a physical count for its annual financial statements. It is trying to determine what alternative approaches might be available for interim reporting purposes. Identify the location in professional standards that indicates how an entity may measure its inventory for interim reporting.

Task-Based Simulation 2

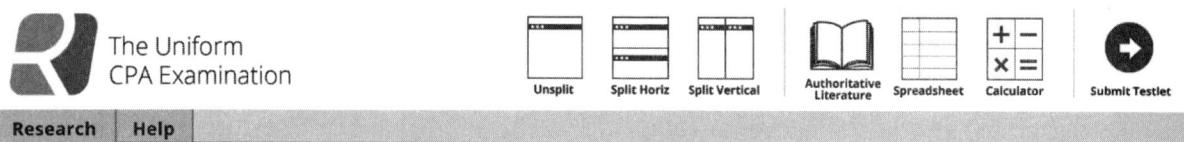

In preparing its interim financial statements, an entity recognizes that its tax rate, based on its 1st quarter income, would be substantially lower than its estimated tax rate for the entire fiscal period. Identify the location in professional standards that indicates what tax rate should be used in the preparation of interim financial statements.

TASK-BASED SIMULATION SOLUTIONS

Task-Based Simulation Solution 1

| FASB ASC | 270 | 10 | 45 | 6 |

Task-Based Simulation Solution 2

| FASB ASC | 740 | 2700 | 30 | 5 |

Section 21 – Segment Reporting

Corresponding Lectures

Watch the following course lectures with this section:

Lecture 21.01 – Segment Reporting
Lecture 21.02 – Segment Reporting – Class Questions
Lecture 21.03 – Segment Reporting under IFRS
Lecture 21.04 – Segment Reporting under IFRS – Class Question

EXAM NOTE: Please refer to the AICPA FAR Blueprint in the Introduction to find a listing of the representative tasks (and their associated skill levels—i.e., Remembering and Understanding, Application, and Analysis) that the candidate should be able to perform based on the knowledge obtained in this section.

Segment Reporting (≥10%)

Lecture 21.01

SEGMENT REPORTING

Publicly-held companies (not non-public or not-for-profit) are required to report certain key information about significant segments of their business, referred to as **reportable segments**. The definition of "segment" is based on a concept known as the **management approach**, in which a segment represents any group of activities with revenues and expenses that is regularly evaluated by management as a single unit.

According to FASB ASC 280, a segment is a component of a public entity that has 3 characteristics:
- It is involved in business activities that may result in earning revenues and incurring expenses, whether external or internal.
    - External activities involve transactions with other entities.
    - Internal activities involve transactions with other components of the same public entity.
- Its performance is evaluated by management for the purposes of resource allocation.
- Financial information identifiable to the component is available.

Different segments can be in the same line of operations, as long as management evaluates them separately for internal purposes. Segments may be identified, for example, by:
- *Activity*, such as manufacturing components making up one segment and distribution centers, another.
- *Product*, such as those components distributing heavy equipment making up one segment and those distributing software making up another.
- *Customers*, such as those components making sales domestically making up one segment and those selling internationally making up another.

There are three different ways to identify a reportable segment. A segment is reportable if it contributes at least **10% of the total for all segments** of one or more of the following:
- **Revenues**
- **Assets**
- **Profits**

The **revenue** test is based on combined revenues of all segments, including those resulting from intersegment sales. This is the case even though consolidated revenues on the income statement will eliminate intersegment activity.

For example, assume the client has 4 industry segments with the following revenue information:

Segment	Sales to Unaffiliated Companies (Outside)	Intersegment Sales	Total Sales
A	20	25	45
B	150	45	195
C	35	0	35
D	95	30	125
Total	300	100	**400**

- Although consolidated revenue on the income statement is reported at $300, the 10% test is applied to total sales of $400, so segments with total sales of at least $40 are reportable. Segments A, B, and D are reportable, and C is not. There is also a 75% test, discussed below, that requires that the total external revenue reported by segments is less than 75% of total external revenues, additional reportable segments are required to be included. That criterion is met in this case - 75% of 300 (the unaffiliated revenue = 225. Reportable Segments A. B and D = 265 which is at least 75%.

The 10% test applying to **profits** is the most complex. First, the calculated amount for each segment represents **operating income** only (sales reduced by cost of sales and selling, general, and administrative expenses). Furthermore, expenses incurred at the overall corporate level (such as the salaries of the company's top officers) are excluded from the computations. Common costs, however, must be included and allocated among the various segments; using an appropriate technique (the technique to use is always identified in exam questions).

For example, assume that the company had total sales of $1,000, of which $300 occurred in segment C. Segment C had operating expenses of $90. The company as a whole had $200 of common expenses, and allocates common costs based on sales. The operating profit of Segment C is computed as follows:

Sales	300
Operating expenses	90
Income before common costs	210
Common costs – 200 x (300 / 1000)	60
Operating profit	150

All segments having **operating profits** are combined, and all segments having operating losses are combined. The **10% test** is applied to the **higher** of the combined profits or combined losses. In performing this test, absolute values are considered. This means it does not matter if the larger total is the total of the segments with profits or losses. Ten percent of the number represented by the larger total is the threshold. In addition, it does not matter if the segment earned a profit or incurred a loss. If the amount of component's profit or loss is at least equal to the threshold amount, it is a reportable segment.

Let's assume the four industry segments of a business have the following operating income figures:

Segment	Operating Profit (Loss)
A	1850
B	(190)
C	150
D	(310)

The combined operating profits are $1,850 + $150 = $2,000, and the combined operating losses are $190 + $310 = $500. Since $2,000 is higher, the 10% test requires a segment to have $200 or higher net profit or loss, so that segments A and D are the reportable segments.

The 10% test applied to **assets** includes identifiable assets only, not goodwill. There are no special complications and this is rarely tested.

In addition to reporting significant segments based on the management approach, a public company should also report data for **foreign operations** (geographic areas) if such operations contributed at least 10% of total revenues or total identifiable assets. Reporting of revenues should separately identify sales to unaffiliated customers and intersegment sales.

Finally, a company should report revenues from **major customers**, referring to those that individually provided at least 10% of consolidated revenues.

There must be enough segments separately reported so that at least *75% of unaffiliated revenues (to outsiders)* is shown by reportable segments. If the 75% test is not satisfied, additional segments must be designated as reportable (even if don't meet the 3 tests) until the test is satisfied.
- Don't exceed 10 reported segments – combine smaller
- Report aggregate information for all non-key segments
- Not required to disclose allocated costs and expenses of reportable segments.
- An enterprise may consider *aggregating two or more* operating segments if they have similar economic characteristics and if the segments are similar in each of the following areas:
  - Nature of products and services
  - Production process
  - Type of customers
  - Methods used to distribute their products or services
  - Nature of regulatory environment

Disclosure - An enterprise must disclose the following general information:
- General information, including how reportable segments are identified and the types of products and services from which each reportable segment derives its revenues.
- Certain info about the basis of measurement for reported segment profit or loss and segment assets.
  - Internal and external revenues
  - Interest income and expense
  - Depreciation, depletion, and amortization expense and other significant noncash items
  - Unusual items

- o   Equity in net income of equity method investees
- Income tax reconciliations of the segment amounts to the enterprise amount, including revenues, profit or loss, and assets
- Interim period information
- Enterprise-wide disclosures
  - o   External product and service revenue
  - o   Geographic area revenue including both domestic and foreign revenue.
  - o   Geographic area Long-lived assets.
  - o   Information about major customers (> 10% revenue).

Reportable Segment ≥ 10%

a. **Operations in Different Industries** (test #1,2,3) → Meet any of 3 tests, disclose ALL 3

b. **Foreign Operations** (Geographic areas) (test #1 & 3) → Meet any 1, disclose ALL 3

c. **Major Customer or Export Sales** (test #1) → Meet, disclose ONLY 1

Three Tests

1) **Revenue** = If segment's revenues ≥ 10% of Company's total revenue (includes intercompany/intersegment sales & transfers)

2) **Profit/Loss** = If segment's P/L ≥ 10% of Combined operating Profit/Loss of all segments that had a Profit/Loss.
   - Includes allocated common costs
   - Excludes Corporate level expenses
     - o   Interest
     - o   Income taxes
     - o   Gain/loss from discotinued ops

3) **Segments asset test** = If segments assets ≥ 10% of Company's identifiable assets

75% Test
- There must be enough segments separately reported so that at least *75% of unaffiliated revenues (To outsiders)* is shown by reportable segments. If the 75% test is not satisfied, additional segments must be designated as reportable (even if don't meet the 3 tests) until the test is satisfied. NOTE: On the page 1 example, 75% of 300 (the unaffiliated revenue = 225. Reportable Segments A. B and D = 265 which is at least 225, so the 75% rule is met.

Segment Reporting

Lecture 21.02

CLASS QUESTIONS

Please see the Class Questions and Class Solutions for this Lecture at the end of this Section.

Lecture 21.03

SEGMENT REPORTING UNDER IFRS

IFRS 8 is very similar to US GAAP in that a company still uses the management approach and still applies the same 3 thresholds mentioned earlier, the Revenue test, Profit/Loss test and Asset test. The 75% rule also still applies.

Lecture 21.04

CLASS QUESTIONS

Please see the Class Questions and Class Solutions for this Lecture at the end of this Section.

Section 21 Segment Reporting

CLASS QUESTIONS

Work through the below Class Questions while following along with the respective lectures. Once this is complete, you can begin independently practicing what you've learned by quizzing yourself on this course section in your Interactive Practice Questions (IPQ), which can be found in your online Student Dashboard. Your IPQ simulates the computer-based testing experience, and will also help you understand how concepts are applied to the exam. Each question includes answer explanations from expert CPAs that will help you determine why you answered a question correctly or incorrectly. This is key to your success on the CPA Exam.

Lecture 21.02

1. Correy Corp. and its divisions (each is an operating segment) are engaged solely in manufacturing operations. The following data (consistent with prior years' data) pertain to the operations conducted for the year ended December 31, 20X3:

(Industry operating segment)	Total revenue	Operating profit	Identifiable assets at 12/31/03
A	$10,000,000	$1,750,000	$20,000,000
B	8,000,000	1,400,000	17,500,000
C	6,000,000	1,200,000	12,500,000
D	3,000,000	550,000	7,500,000
E	4,250,000	675,000	7,000,000
F	1,500,000	225,000	3,000,000
	$32,750,000	$5,800,000	67,500,000

In its segment information for 20X3, how many reportable segments does Correy have?

   a. Three.
   b. Four.
   c. Five.
   d. Six.

2. ABC Co. had the following revenues and expenses that occurred relating to their operating segments during the year:

Sales to unaffiliated customers	$1,000,000
Intersegment sales of products	400,000
Interest earned on loans to other segments	30,000
General corporate expenses	25,000

In order to qualify as a reportable segment, the segments revenue must exceed

   a. $143,000
   b. $140,000
   c. $140,500
   d. $100,000

Page 21-6 ©Roger CPA Review

Segment Reporting
Section 21

3. There is a method in segment reporting to help define what constitutes a "segment". The method that is used under ASC 280 is called

    a. Segment approach.
    b. Revenue approach.
    c. Profit or Loss approach.
    d. Management approach.

Lecture 21.04

4. Rocket Corporation prepares its financial statements in accordance with IFRS. For segment reporting purposes, which tests must Rocket apply to determine if a unit or component is an operating segment?

    a. Revenue test and asset test.
    b. Revenue test, asset test, and profit or loss test.
    c. Revenue test, asset test, and expense test.
    d. Revenue test, asset test, and cash flow test.

CLASS SOLUTIONS

1. (c) A segment is reportable if it represents at least 10% of the activities of the overall entity. The 10% test is applied to revenues, assets, and profits and if the segment's amount is at least 10% of the total for any one of those factors, it is a reportable segment. Segments A, B, C, and E are reportable segments under all 3 tests. Segment D is a reportable segment because its identifiable assets are 11.1% of the total, exceeding the 10% minimum. As a result, all 5 are reportable segments.

2. (b) When applying the revenue test to determine if a segment is a reportable segment, the segment's revenues are compared to the total for the entity. Total revenues include revenues from intersegment sales. Revenues do not, however, include interest earned, which is reported as other income, not revenue. It also doesn't include general corporate expenses, as those stay at the corporate level. As a result, total revenue is ($1,000,000 + $400,000) $1,400,000 and any segment with 10% revenues of $140,000 or above will be a reportable segment.

3. (d) The method for determining what segments are part of an entity is referred to as the management approach. This is because segments are identified as those activities involving revenues and expenses that are evaluated by management. As a result, management may decide to identify segments by type of activity, such as manufacturing and sales; product, such as clothing and accessories; geographical location; or some other criteria.

4. (b) Similarly to US GAAP, entities use three tests under IFRS for segment reporting purposes, a revenue test, a total asset test and a profit or loss test to identify reportable segments.

TASK-BASED SIMULATIONS

Task-Based Simulation 1

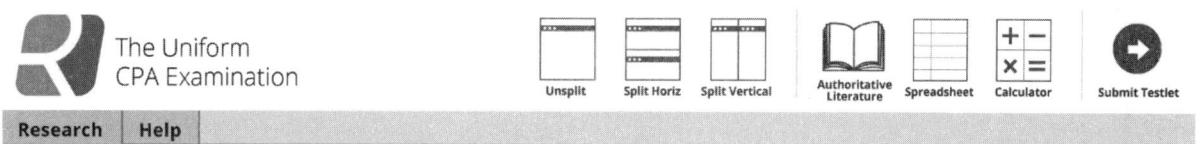

After several business combinations, a company is organized into numerous operating segments segregated on the basis of the natures of their operations and the geographical markets they serve. As a result, the company is trying to determine which of its numerous operating segments are large enough to be reported separately. Identify the location in professional standards that indicates quantitative thresholds that are used to determine if an operating segment should be reported separately.

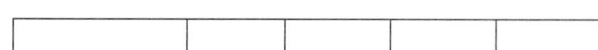

Task-Based Simulation 2

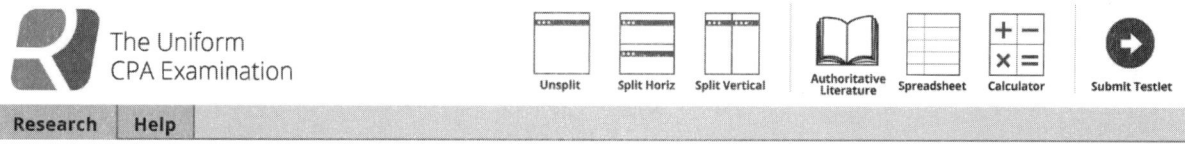

A client has identified several reportable segments and is trying to determine what information it should report in regard to its profit or loss and assets. Identify the location in professional standards that indicates what information should be reported in regard to profit or loss and assets for reportable segments.

TASK-BASED SIMULATION SOLUTIONS

Task-Based Simulation Solution 1

| FASB ASC | 280 | 10 | 50 | 12 |

Task-Based Simulation Solution 2

| FASB ASC | 280 | 10 | 50 | 22 |

Section 22 – Installment Sales and Cost Recovery Method

Corresponding Lectures

Watch the following course lectures with this section:

Lecture 22.01 - Installment Sales and Cost Recovery Method
Lecture 22.02 - Installment Sales – Class Questions
Lecture 22.03 – Revenue Recognition under IFRS
Lecture 22.04 – Revenue Recognition under IFRS – Class Question

EXAM NOTE: Please refer to the AICPA FAR Blueprint in the Introduction to find a listing of the representative tasks (and their associated skill levels—i.e., Remembering and Understanding, Application, and Analysis) that the candidate should be able to perform based on the knowledge obtained in this section.

Installment Sales and Cost Recovery Method

Lecture 22.01

RECOGNIZING REVENUE

When a client makes a sale in which payments will be spread out over more than one accounting period, this is referred to as an installment sale. Under GAAP, this sale should normally be reported in conformity with the earnings principle, meaning that 100% of income is reported on the date of sale **(ASC 605)**.

The use of the installment method, in which income is reported as the cash is collected, normally violates GAAP. It is, however, permitted in those circumstances when there is a substantial doubt as to the collectability of the receivable, based on the conservatism principle. The installment method is also commonly used for tax purposes.

When installment sales are reported normally, in accordance with the earnings principle, the sales and cost of sales are recognized immediately. Current and long-term portions of the installment receivable will be reported separately, and interest income will accrue normally on the unpaid balance, based on the principles discussed in the section on receivables.

When collection of installments is not reasonably assured, and the installment method is determined to be appropriate, income will be recognized each period based on the portion of the sales price that has been collected in that period. The amount recognized will equal the cash collected in the period multiplied by the gross profit percentage on the sale. Deferred gross profit will be reported on the balance sheet as a contra-asset to the installment receivable, and will equal the face value of the remaining receivable multiplied by the gross profit percentage on the sale.

Methods of Recognizing Revenue

An entity generally recognizes revenue when it is earned, but when realization is uncertain, alternative approaches may be required.
- **Accrual method**
    - Use when collection is reasonably assured and
    - Degree of collectability is estimable
    - Profit is recognized when earned and realizable.
        - Normal GAAP

- **Installment sales approach**
    - **Collection is not reasonably assured**
    - **Profit is recognized as cash is collected.**
        - More conservative

- **Cost recovery method**
    - **Collection not reasonably assured**
    - **No basis for determining whether or not collectible**
    - **No profit recognized until the entire cost is recovered.**
        - Most conservative

Section 22 — Installment Sales and Cost Recovery Method

Installment Sales Method (For TAX)

When it is uncertain as to whether the total amount of a receivable will be collected and the amount that will be collected is not readily determinable, the installment method will be applied.
- Only used when there is no way to reasonably estimate the degree of collectability.
- Allows revenue to be deferred and recognized each year in proportion to the cash collected during that year – Conservatism.

Two calculations:

- **Gross Profit recognized**
    - Cash collected x Gross Profit % = Profit recognized (I/S)

- **Deferred Gross Profit**
    - Receivable balance x Gross Profit % = Deferred Profit (B/S)

(**Gross Profit** = Sales – COGS)
(**Gross Profit %** = Gross Profit/ Sales Price)

Normal Accrual Method – profit is recognized at point of sale.

Cash	150	
AR	750	
Sales		900
COGS	540	
Inventory		540

Gross Profit = 360 (900 – 540)
Gross Profit % = 40% (360/900)

Installment Sales method – profit is recognized as cash is collected

Cash	150	
AR	750	
Sales		900
COGS	540	
Inventory		540

Installment Sales and Cost Recovery Method — Section 22

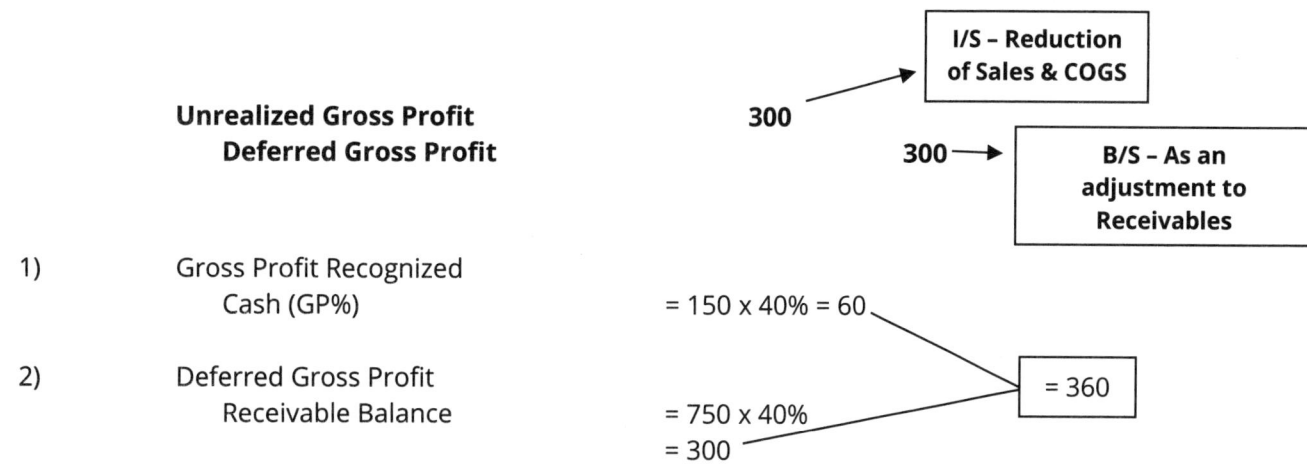

| | | Unrealized Gross Profit | 300 | |
| | | Deferred Gross Profit | | 300 |

1) Gross Profit Recognized
   Cash (GP%) = 150 x 40% = 60

2) Deferred Gross Profit
   Receivable Balance = 750 x 40%
   = 300

= 360

For example, assume a client has made a sale on 12/31/X1 of $100 of an item that cost $70, and is collecting $20 of the sales price on the date of sale, with the remaining $80 (plus interest) to be collected in future years. The calculation of realized gross profit in 20X1 and deferred gross profit at 12/31/X1 follows:

Sales	100	Collected	20	Receivable	80
COGS	70	GP%	30%	GP%	30%
GP	30	Realized GP	6	Deferred GP	24

Note that the realized and deferred gross profit figures can be used to determine the cash collected and receivable balances, respectively, by using the gross profit percentage as a divisor instead of a multiplier. For example, the cash collected of $20 equals the $6 realized profit divided by the 30% profit percentage.

In the year the sale takes place, the client reports the entire sales price and cost of sales on the income statement, then defers the profit not recognized by the end of the year. In subsequent years, the additional profit is recognized as cash is collected, and interest income is reported as well.

For example, assume that in the previous example with the sale of $100, cost of sale of $70, and down payment on 12/31/X1 of $20, the remaining $80 is to be collected in four installments of $20 each on December 31, 20X2, 20X3, 20X4, and 20X5, plus interest at the market rate of 10% on the unpaid balance. Looking only at the income statement entries related to this single sale and collections, the following would appear:

Year	20X1	20X2	20X3	20X4	20X5
Sales	100	---			---
Less: COGS	70	---			---
Gross profit	30	---			---
Less: Unrealized-current sales	24	---			---
Realized-current sales	6	---			---
Realized-prior sales	---	6	6	6	6
Realized-total	6	6	6	6	6
Interest income	---	8	6	4	2
Net income	6	14	12	10	8

Study the numbers until you're comfortable with how they were determined. The realized profit each year represents the cash collected multiplied by the profit percentage, and the interest income is 10% of the receivable outstanding throughout the year.

Since the installment method is used in cases of uncertain collectability, receivables will occasionally be written off. In such cases, both the receivables and deferred gross profit accounts will be reduced.

For example, assume that $100,000 of sales with 40% gross profit rates took place in 20X1, that $30,000 was collected, and that $10,000 of accounts were written off during the year. At 12/31/X1, the remaining installment receivables are $100,000 - $30,000 - $10,000 = $60,000, and deferred gross profit is $60,000 x 40% = $24,000.

Also keep in mind that profit must be computed separately on each sale, to determine the gross profit percentage to be applied to all collections in both the current and subsequent years.

Cost Recovery Method

In extremely rare cases, such as when sales are made to customers with a very high probability of defaulting, the seller may be permitted to use the cost recovery method. Under this approach, all collections, including those identified as principal and interest, are applied to the cost of sales, with no gross profit realized until collections exceed costs. Further amounts are reported as realized gross profit until gross collections exceed the sales price, and remaining amounts are reported as interest income.

- Used when collection is very doubtful (most conservative approach)
- No income or profit is recognized until the entire cost is recovered.
- All profit is recorded as deferred gross profit.
- Defer all 360 until cost is recovered (540) – Next dollar becomes profit (interest income) after the whole 540 is recovered.

Unrealized Gross Profit	360
Deferred Gross Profit	360

For example, in the earlier example of a $100 sale and $70 cost of sale, with principal payments of $20 per year, and interest payments from 20X2 to 20X5 of $8, $6, $4, and $2, respectively, the cost recovery method would report the first $70 collected as cost recovery, the next $30 as realized gross profit, and the remaining amounts above $100 as interest income. Assuming all payments are made, the schedule of income is as follows:

Year	20X1	20X2	20X3	20X4	20X5
Principal payment	20	20	20	20	20
Interest payment	---	8	6	4	2
Total payment	20	28	26	24	22
Cumulative payments	20	48	74	98	120
Realized profit	0	0	4	24	2
Interest income	0	0	0	0	20

Notice there is no profit until 20X3, when cumulative payments of $74 exceed the cost of sales of $70. In 20X5, once cumulative payments reached the sales price of $100, the remaining $20 was reported at interest income.

Other Revenue Recognition Topics

Sometimes an entity may arrange to sell **multiple** goods and/or services as part of one sale. Special consideration must be given to the amount and timing of revenue recognition under such a **multiple-element arrangement**.

For instance, Roger Co. may sell a customer a Rogetron 3000, plus a 3-year service contract for the device, for a total of $5,000. Roger Co. also sells Rogetron 3-year service contracts separately. Because the service contract has its own standalone value, it is considered a separate element. The $5,000 sale of the device plus service contract is considered a **multiple-element arrangement** as per ASC 605-25.

The transaction price will be allocated between the two separate elements, with revenue recognized when it is both **earned** and **realizable**. Assuming no issues with collectability or return policy, revenue for the Rogetron 3000 will be recognized immediately. Revenue on the 3-year service contract will be allocated over the 3-year term of the contract.

The **relative fair value method** is commonly used to allocate the transaction price among the separate elements of a multiple-element arrangement. If the Rogetron 3000 normally sells separately for $4,750, and the 3-year service contract normally sells separately for $528, the $5,000 transaction price for both will be allocated 4,750 / 5,278, or 90%, to the Rogetron, and 528 / 5,278, or 10%, to the service contract:

Cash	5,000	
Revenue – Rogetron 3000		4,500
Deferred Revenue –		500
Service Contract		

Another difficulty arises with revenue recognition for arrangements involving **continuous delivery**. The most common such arrangements are long-term construction contracts, which will be covered in the next section.

Lecture 22.02

CLASS QUESTIONS

Please see the Class Questions and Class Solutions for this Lecture at the end of this Section.

Lecture 22.03

REVENUE RECOGNITION UNDER IFRS

IAS 18 - Revenue, defines revenue as "the gross inflow of economic benefits during the period arising in the course of the ordinary activities of an entity when those inflows result in increases in equity, other than increases relating to contributions from equity participants." Revenue is measured on the basis of the fair value of the consideration received or receivable by the entity.

Revenue is recognized from the *sale of goods* if **all five** of the following criteria are met:
1. The significant risks and rewards of ownership of the goods are transferred to the buyer,
2. The entity does not retain either a continuing managerial involvement or control over the goods,
3. The amount of revenue can be measured reliably,
4. It is probable that economic benefits from the transaction will flow to the entity, and
5. The costs associated with the transaction can be measured reliably.

Revenue can be recognized from *rendering services* when the outcome of rendering services can be estimated reliably. The amount of revenue to be recognized is determined in a manner that is very similar to as the *percentage-of-completion method*. Revenue is recognized on the basis of the stage of completion of the project as of the end of the reporting period. Progress payments or advances from customers are not used to determine the stage of completion. To qualify for recognition **4 conditions** must be satisfied:
1. The amount of revenue can be measured reliably,
2. It is probable that economic benefits will flow to the entity,
3. The stage of completion at the end of the reporting period can be measured reliably,
4. The costs incurred and to complete the transaction can be measured reliably.

If the outcomes cannot be estimated reliably, then revenue should be recognized using the **cost recovery method**. The cost recovery method recognizes revenue only to the extent that the expenses recognized are recoverable. Note that IFRS **does not** permit use of the *completed contract method*, which is allowed for US GAAP.

In May, 2014, the International Accounting Standards Board (IASB) issued IFRS 15, Revenue from Contracts with Customers, discussed in a previous section, which replaces the standards indicated above. The effective date of IFRS 15 has been deferred to 2018. As a result, the standards discussed above will be relevant until that time.

Installment Sales and Cost Recovery Method

In addition, revenues from **interest, royalties, and dividends** are recognized when it is *probable* that an economic benefit will flow to the entity and the amount can be *reasonably measured*.
- Interest revenues are recognized using the effective interest method.
- Royalties are recognized on the accrual basis.
- Dividends are recognized when the shareholder obtains the right to receive payment.

An entity will *disclose its revenue recognition policies* and amounts from each significant category of revenues, including those from:
- The sale of goods;
- Rendering services;
- Interest;
- Royalties; and
- Dividends

Lecture 22.04

CLASS QUESTIONS

Please see the Class Questions and Class Solutions for this Lecture at the end of this Section.

CLASS QUESTIONS

Work through the below Class Questions while following along with the respective lectures. Once this is complete, you can begin independently practicing what you've learned by quizzing yourself on this course section in your Interactive Practice Questions (IPQ), which can be found in your online Student Dashboard. Your IPQ simulates the computer-based testing experience, and will also help you understand how concepts are applied to the exam. Each question includes answer explanations from expert CPAs that will help you determine why you answered a question correctly or incorrectly. This is key to your success on the CPA Exam.

Lecture 22.02

1. Luge Co., which began operations on January 2, 20X3, appropriately uses the installment sales method of accounting. The following information is available for 20X3:

Installment accounts receivable, December 31, 20X3	$800,000
Deferred gross profit, December 31, 20X3 (before recognition of realized gross profit for 20X3)	$560,000
Gross profit on sales	40%

    For the year ended December 31, 20X3, cash collections and realized gross profit on sales should be

	Cash collections	Realized gross profit
a.	$400,000	$320,000
b.	$400,000	$240,000
c.	$600,000	$320,000
d.	$600,000	$240,000

2. According to the installment method of accounting, gross profit on an installment sale is recognized in income

    a. On the date of sale.
    b. On the date the final cash collection is received.
    c. In proportion to the cash collection.
    d. After cash collections equal to the cost of sales have been received.

3. Income recognized using the installment method of accounting generally equals cash collected multiplied by the

    a. Net operating profit percentage.
    b. Net operating profit percentage adjusted for expected uncollectible accounts.
    c. Gross profit percentage.
    d. Gross profit percentage adjusted for expected uncollectible accounts.

Installment Sales and Cost Recovery Method   Section 22

Lecture 22.04

4. For an entity that has not yet adopted the recent revenue recognition standards, which revenue recognition method should be used under IFRS, if the outcome of rendering services cannot reliably be estimated?
    a. Installment method
    b. Completed contract method
    c. Cost recovery method
    d. Percentage-of-completion method

CLASS SOLUTIONS

1. (d) With a 40% gross profit on sales and an installment receivable of $800,000 at 12/31/X3, deferred gross profit at 12/31/X3 would be ($800,000 x 40%) $320,000. Since the unadjusted balance is $560,000, deferred gross profit will be reduced and realized gross profit would be recognized for the difference of $240,000. The realized gross profit represents 40% of collections. As a result, collections can be determined by dividing the realized gross profit of $240,000 by 40% to give collections of $600,000.

2. (c) Under the installment method of accounting, the gross profit percentage on a sale is calculated and revenue is recognized by multiplying that percentage by amounts collected. Revenue, as a result, is recognized in proportion to collections. Answer (a) is incorrect because revenue is recognized on the date of sale under the accrual basis, not the installment method. Answer (b) is incorrect because there is no method of recognizing revenue that postpones recognition until the final payment is received unless collections prior to that point did not at least equal cost of sales or, under the completed contract method, the last payment is received upon completion of the contract. Answer (d) is incorrect because profit is recognized after collections equal cost of sales under the cost recovery method, not the installment method.

3. (c) Under the installment method of accounting, the gross profit percentage on a sale is calculated and revenue is recognized by multiplying that percentage by amounts collected. Answer (a) is incorrect because the net operating profit percentage, which would be income from operations divided by total revenues, is not used. Answer (b) is incorrect because the net operating profit percentage adjusted for expected uncollectible accounts is not used. Answer (d) is incorrect because the gross profit percentage is not adjusted for expected uncollectible accounts.

4. (c) IFRS, like US GAAP, requires the use of the cost recovery method when the outcome of rendering services cannot be measured reliably. Answer (a) is incorrect because the percentage-of-completion method is used when costs and revenues can be measured reliably and the stage of completion is determinable. Answer (b) is incorrect because the completed contract method is not allowable under IFRS. Answer (d) is incorrect because the installment method is used when the outcome can be reliably estimated but the degree of uncollectibility of the receivable is not readily determinable. Once IFRS 15, Revenue from Contracts with Customers, is applied, the correct answer would be (b). When a contract does not qualify for revenue recognition while the performance obligation is being met, the new standard requires that revenue be recognized only when the performance obligation has been satisfied, comparable to the completed contract approach.

Installment Sales and Cost Recovery Method — Section 22

TASK-BASED SIMULATIONS

Task-Based Simulation 1

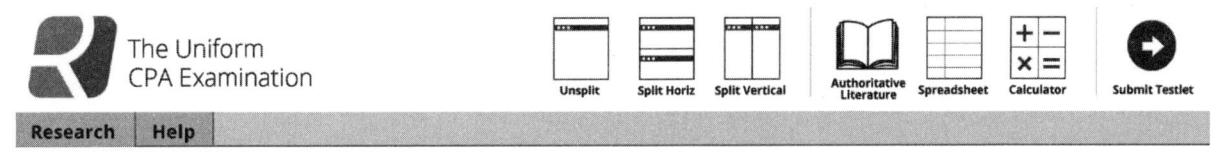

A client has entered into certain revenue related transactions in which the collection of the sales price is not reasonably assured. The client wishes to determine if it should account for the sale using the installment sales method. Identify the location in professional standards that indicates when it is appropriate to use the installment sales method.

Task-Based Simulation 2

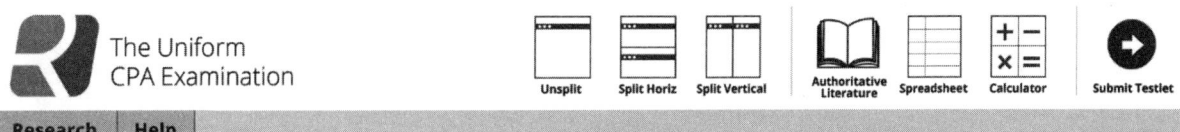

Your client has appropriately decided to use the cost recovery method to recognize revenue on a specific material transaction. The client is asking how much revenue and expense to recognize, if any. Identify the location in professional standards that indicates how to determine the amounts of revenue and expense to recognize under the cost recovery method.

TASK-BASED SIMULATION SOLUTIONS

Task-Based Simulation Solution 1

| FASB ASC | 605 | 10 | 25 | 3 |

Task-Based Simulation Solution 2

| FASB ASC | 605 | 10 | 25 | 4 |

Section 23 – Long-Term Construction Contracts

Corresponding Lectures

Watch the following course lectures with this section:

Lecture 23.01 – Long-Term Construction Contracts
Lecture 23.02 – Long-Term Construction Contracts – Class Questions
Lecture 23.03 – Long-Term Construction Contracts under IFRS

EXAM NOTE: Please refer to the AICPA FAR Blueprint in the Introduction to find a listing of the representative tasks (and their associated skill levels—i.e., Remembering and Understanding, Application, and Analysis) that the candidate should be able to perform based on the knowledge obtained in this section.

Long-Term Construction Contracts

Lecture 23.01

LONG-TERM CONTRACTS FOR CONSTRUCTION

Long Term contracts often provide that the seller (builder) may bill the purchaser at intervals, as it reaches various points in the project. There are two methods of accounting for Long-Term construction contracts, the Completed Contract Method and the Percentage-of-Completion Method. The Percentage-of-Completion method is recommended when **Collection is assured** and when **costs to complete** the contract and **estimates of progress toward the completion** of the contract are reasonably dependable **(ASC 605).**

Under either method, costs incurred on the contract are inventoried as they occur in a construction in progress account, while billings are accumulated in a current liability account called billings on uncompleted contracts. Notice that both accounts are current, not long-term. This is because the income from such contracts is realized in only one operating cycle of the company, and when that cycle is longer than a year, items that normally would seem to be long-term are classified as current.

When using the completed contract method, spending, billing, and collections each year are recorded in entries affecting various balance sheet accounts, but no income statement entries are made until the year the contract is completed (except when there is an anticipated loss on the overall contract). When using the percentage-of-completion method, an entry is made at the end of each period to report an appropriate portion of the total income expected from the contract.

The percentage-of-completion method is more consistent with the principles of revenue recognition, since revenue is recognized as it is earned by the performance of work and as it is realized through billings and collections. It should be preferred when reasonable estimates can be made at the end of each period as to both:
- Expected profit at completion
- Progress toward completion

The completed contract method is preferred when these conditions cannot be satisfied or when there is significant uncertainty as to whether the contract will actually be performed by both sides, based on the modifying convention of **conservatism.** If change from one method to the other, it is considered a change in accounting principle and accounted for retrospectively.

Percentage-of-Completion Method

The percentage-of-completion method is used when costs can be measured, when the progress toward completion can be reliably determined, and when the amount of revenue to be earned is known.
- Profit is recognized in each period of the contract. The amount of profit recognized is determined on the accrual basis taking into account the estimated profit on the contract, the portion of the contract that is completed (% complete), and any profit that has been previously recognized.
- More consistent with the revenue recognition principle.
- Better **Matching.**

Long-Term Construction Contracts

Accounting during year
- o **Billings** are added to billings on uncompleted contracts.

    A/R   850
        Billings   850

- o As **cash is collected**, the Receivable is reduced.

    Cash   800
        A/R   800

- o As **Costs are incurred**, they are added to Construction in Progress **(CIP)**.

    Construction in Progress (CIP)   700
        Cash   700

- o **Profits** are added to Construction in Progress **(CIP)** based on the formula below.

    CIP   100
        Cash Income   700

    Profit is calculated in steps:
    1. Total contract – estimated total cost = estimated total profit.
    2. Costs to date / estimated total cost = % of completion.
    3. Estimated total profit x % of completion = GP to date.
    4. GP to date – GP to date at end of last period = GP in current period.
        - GP added to construction in Progress (CIP) account.

- o At year end, Billings and CIP are netted on the **balance sheet** to report either:
    - **Current Asset** (Costs + profit in excess of billings)
    - **Current liability** (Billings in excess of costs + profits)

- o **Anticipated Losses** are always recognized **Immediately**.

Percentage of Completion
(Cost-to-Cost Method)

Costs **INCURRED to date** (700)
─────────────────────────── = **Percentage** of Completion (%) 700/3500 = 20%
TOTAL construction Costs   X Total Profit **   4,000 - 3,500 =   500
(Actual + estimated **to** complete)   Profit Recognized to Date   100
(700 + 2,800 = 3,500)

                        - (Profit Previously Recognized/in previous years) 0

                        = Profit to recognize This Year   **100**

- **Total Profit will always change, so use new profit amount.
- Anticipated Losses are Recognized immediately under both methods.

Long-Term Construction Contracts — Section 23

Class Example: Roger Builders has agreed to construct a building for CPA Inc at a total contract price of $4,000,000. The estimated construction costs at inception are $3,000,000 and the actual costs for both years 1 and 2 are below. The construction was completed after year 2.

Total contract price = $4,000,000
Estimated costs = $3,000,000
Estimated Profit = $1,000,000

	Cumulative Year 1	Year 2
Costs incurred to date	$700,000	$1,650,000
Estimated costs to complete	2,800,000	1,650,000
Billings	850,000	1,800,000
Cash collections	800,000	1,500,000

	Completed Contract Method – ENTRIES	Percentage of Completion – ENTRIES

Billings	Construction Receivable X
	   Billings X
		Construction Receivable 850
		   Billings 850

Collections	Cash X
	   Construction Receivable X
		Cash 800
		   Construction Receivable 800

Costs	Construction In Progress (CIP) X
	   Cash X
		CIP 700
		   Cash 700

Recognize Profit	**NONE – No income until done	CIP 100
		   Gross profit on CIP (I/S) 100
		
		(CIP 100
		(Construction Expense 700 (3,500,000 x 20%)
		   Construction Revenue 800 (4,000,000 X20%)

Yr 2
CIP   250
(Construction Expense   950   (3,300,000 x 50% - 700)
   Construction Revenue 1200 (4,000,000 x 50% = 2000)
               (2000-800=1200)

Net the Billings and CIP accounts on the B/S at the end of each year
850
(800)
(50) Liability

- If a net Debit, considered an asset.
- If a net Credit, considered a liability.

Completed-Contracted Method (Conservatism)

- Report no profit until the job is finished. Violates the matching concept.
- Still accumulate costs in the CIP account
- Billings still accumulated in the Billings account.
    - At year end net CIP and Billings, similar to the Percentage-of-completion method.
- Considered inappropriate unless:
    - Percentage-of-completion cannot be determined.
    - Total costs cannot be estimated.
- Recognize all anticipated losses immediately.

To show how revenues and profits under the percentage-of-completion method are computed each year, let's use the following example. A contractor has signed a fixed price contract for $1,000 on 1/1/X1 to build a house. The following events occur in the first 2 years of the job:

Year	20X1	20X2
Spending	150	200
Cumulative	150	350
Estimated costs to complete	600	350
Estimated total costs	750	700
Cost-to-cost percentage	20%	50%
Billings	210	220
Cumulative	210	430
Collections	180	210
Cumulative	180	390

The cost-to-cost percentage represents the cumulative costs incurred divided by the estimated total costs of the job as of the end of each year. This is the normal method used on the exam to determine the percentage of completion, and is used in this example.

To calculate income each year, use the following steps:
1. Compare the total contract price with the estimated total costs of the job at the end of that year to determine estimated total profits.
2. Multiply the total profit by the percentage of completion to determine the profit to date.
3. Subtract profits recognized in earlier years to determine the profit to be reported in the current year.
4. If the exam question asks for revenue rather than profit, add the current period expenses to the profit that needs to be reported, and the result is revenue.

The calculations for the first 2 years of this contract are:

Year	20X1	20X2
Contract price	1000	1000
Estimated total costs	750	700
Estimated total profit	250	300
Percentage complete	20%	50%
Profit to date	50	150
Earlier years' profits	---	50
Current period profit	50	100
Current costs	150	200
Current revenue	200	300

Notice that an alternative method of deriving revenue is to multiply the contract price by the percentage of completion. In 20X1, $1,000 x 20% = $200 revenue. In 20X2, $1,000 x 50% = $500 cumulative revenue, reduced by the $200 reported in the prior year to $300 for the current year.

Long-Term Construction Contracts Section 23

The entries in 20X1 for spending, billings, and collections are as follows:

Construction in progress	150	
Cash		150
Accounts receivable	210	
Billings on uncompleted contracts		210
Cash	180	
Accounts receivable		180

Actually, the credit to cash in the first entry may be made to other balance sheet accounts reflecting construction costs, such as various accrued expenses and payables, and accumulated depreciation on assets used for construction.

Assuming the completed contract method has been used, these are the only entries made each year. On the balance sheet at 12/31/X1, the construction in progress and billings on uncompleted contracts accounts are not reported separately, but are netted together for each contract. For those contracts where construction in progress exceeds billings, the net amount is reported as a current asset. For those contracts where billings exceed construction in progress, the net amount is reported as a current liability. In the above case, the amounts reported are:

Current assets
Accounts receivable 30

Current liabilities
Billings in excess of related costs 60

In order to see the additional entry required under the percentage-of-completion method, let's repeat the earlier calculation of 20X1 income for convenience:

Year	20X1
Contract price	1000
Estimated total costs	750
Estimated total profit	250
Percentage complete	20%
Profit to date	50
Earlier years' profits	---
Current period profit	50
Current costs	150
Current revenue	200

In 20X1, an entry is made to report revenues and profits as follows:

Construction in progress	50	
Construction expense	150	
Construction revenue		200

Notice that the profit is added to the inventory account. This will also affect the reporting of excess billings on the balance sheet. At 12/31/X1, the accounts presented will be:

Current assets
Accounts receivable 30

Current liabilities
Billings in excess of related costs and profits 10

The accounts receivable represent the billings of $210 minus collections of $180. The billings of $210 also exceed the $150 costs plus $50 profits by $10.

All of the calculations under the percentage-of-completion method have been based on the assumption that the contract would eventually result in a profit. Occasionally, though, a contract will incur sufficient cost overruns so as to result in a loss to the contractor. When estimated total costs exceed the contract price, the excess should be immediately reported on the income statement in its entirety as an estimated loss, regardless of which method was chosen for the recognition of contract profits. If profits were reported in earlier years under the percentage-of-completion method, these will have to be reversed as well.

Lecture 23.02

CLASS QUESTIONS
Please see the Class Questions and Class Solutions for this Lecture at the end of this Section.

Lecture 23.03

LONG-TERM CONSTRUCTION CONTRACTS UNDER IFRS

IAS 11, Construction Contracts, allows recognition of revenue on construction contracts during the contract period under a method that is comparable to the **percentage-of-completion method** (stage of completion) allowed under US GAAP. The method may be applied when the outcome of the contract can be reasonably estimated.

In a *fixed cost* contract, the outcome can be reasonably estimated if:
- Contract revenue is reliably *measurable*
- It is *probable* that the economic benefits of the contract will flow to the entity;
- *Costs to complete* the contract and the stage of completion can be reliably measured; and
- *Costs attributable to the contract* can be clearly identified and reliably measured.

In a *cost plus* contract, the outcome can be reasonably estimated if:
- It is *probable* that the economic benefits of the contract will flow to the entity; and
- *Costs* attributable to the contract can be clearly *identified* and reliably *measured,* regardless of whether or not they are reimbursable.

Similar to US GAAP, the stage of completion may be determined on the basis of inputs, such as costs incurred to date as a ratio to total estimated costs; or on the basis of outputs, such as having an engineer estimate the stage of completion of a project.

If the outcomes cannot be estimated reliably, then revenue should be recognized using the **cost recovery method** *(zero profit method).* The cost recovery method recognizes revenue only to the extent that the expenses recognized are recoverable. Note that IFRS does **Not** permit use of the **completed contract method**, which is allowed for US GAAP.

Long-Term Construction Contracts

When the total cost of a contract is expected to exceed the contract price, that contract will result in a loss. Regardless of the method of accounting being applied, when a loss on a contract is anticipated, it is recognized in income immediately.

When IFRS 15, Revenue from Contracts with Customers, becomes effective, the standards related to long-term construction contracts will be superseded. Long-term construction contracts will then be accounted for applying the same principles that apply to other contracts.
- If the contract qualifies for recognition of revenue as the performance obligation is being satisfied, a method similar to the percentage-of-completion approach will be applied.
- If the contract does not meet the requirements for recognition as the performance obligation is being satisfied, it is not recognized until the performance obligation has been satisfied, comparable to the completed contract approach.

IFRS 15 becomes effective on the CPA Exam in January 2018.

Revenue Recognition of Construction Contracts	
US GAAP	**IFRS**
• If certain criteria are met, construction contracts are accounted for using the percentage-of-completion (stage of completion). Otherwise the completed contract method is used.	• The completed contract method is never allowed for construction contracts. If certain criteria are met, the percentage-of-completion method is used. Otherwise, revenue recognition is limited to the costs incurred, using the cost recovery (zero profit) method.
	• As a result of IFRS 15, long-term construction contracts will be accounted for applying the same principles as applied in other revenue-related transactions. In most cases, the revenues will be recognized as performance obligations are being met as opposed to when they have been met.

CLASS QUESTIONS

Work through the below Class Questions while following along with the respective lectures. Once this is complete, you can begin independently practicing what you've learned by quizzing yourself on this course section in your Interactive Practice Questions (IPQ), which can be found in your online Student Dashboard. Your IPQ simulates the computer-based testing experience, and will also help you understand how concepts are applied to the exam. Each question includes answer explanations from expert CPAs that will help you determine why you answered a question correctly or incorrectly. This is key to your success on the CPA Exam.

Lecture 23.01

1. A company used the percentage-of-completion method of accounting for a five-year construction contract. Which of the following items will the company use to calculate the income recognized in the third year?

	Progress billings to date	Income previously recognized
a.	Yes	No
b.	No	Yes
c.	No	No
d.	Yes	Yes

2. When should an anticipated loss on a long-term contract be recognized under the percentage-of-completion method and the completed-contract method, respectively?

	Percentage-of-completion	Completed-contract
a.	Over life of project	Contract complete
b.	Immediately	Contract complete
c.	Over life of project	Immediately
d.	Immediately	Immediately

3. ABC Co, is working on a construction type contract. They have been using the percentage-of-completion method to account for costs and revenues. The contract was started in 20X5 and was completed in 20X7 for a fixed price of $9,000,000. The following cost information was given to you, their accountant:

	December 31 20X5	20X6
Cumulative contract costs incurred	$3,900,000	$6,300,000
Estimated total cost at completion	7,800,000	8,100,000

   ABC Co. wants to know how much income they should recognize for the year ended 20X6?

   a. $100,000
   b. $300,000
   c. $600,000
   d. $700,000

Long-Term Construction Contracts — Section 23

CLASS SOLUTIONS

1. (b) Under the percentage-of completion method, the cumulative profit earned as of the end of the period is calculated by multiplying the percentage-of-completion of the project by the total estimated profit. This is reduced by profits previously recognized. Process billings are not a factor.

2. (d) When a long-term contract is expected to result in a loss, the total amount of the loss is estimated and recognized immediately under both the completed contract and the percentage-of-completion methods. Under the percentage-of-completion method, the amount of loss recognized includes reversing any profits previously recognized.

3. (a) At 12/31/X6, costs of $6,300,000 were incurred out of a total estimated cost of $8,100,000, indicating that the project is 7/9 complete. With a contract price of $9,000,000, total profit is estimated at $900,000 and 7/9 or $700,000 is the profit to date. Applying the same approach to the preceding period, costs of $3,900,000 out of a total of $7,800,000 indicated that the project was estimated to be 50% complete. Estimated profit at that time was ($9,000,000 - $7,800,000) $1,200,000, 50% of which, or $600,000 would have been recognized. As a result, the profit recognized in 20X6 will be ($700,000 - $600,000) $100,000.

TASK-BASED SIMULATIONS

Task-Based Simulation 1

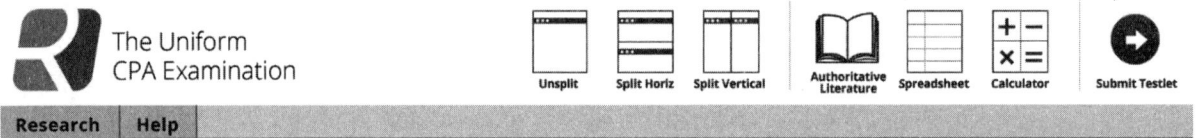

A company is applying the percentage-of-completion method to a long-term construction contract for the first time. It wants to know what approaches should be followed in estimating the cost to complete the contract. Identify the location in professional standards that indicates how the cost to complete a contract is estimated.

Task-Based Simulation 2

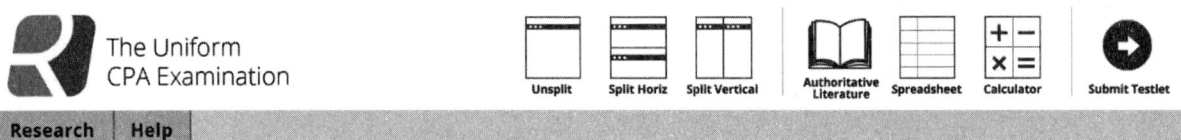

An entity is applying the percentage-of-completion method to a long-term construction contract and has some contracts for which costs and estimated profits exceed billings and others for which billings exceed costs and estimated profits. The entity is trying to determine how these amounts should be reported on its balance sheet. Identify the location in professional standards that indicates what amounts will be included in current assets and current liabilities under the percentage-of-completion method.

TASK-BASED SIMULATION SOLUTIONS

Task-Based Simulation Solution 1

| FASB ASC | 605 | 35 | 25 | 44 |

Task-Based Simulation Solution 2

| FASB ASC | 605 | 35 | 45 | 3 |

Section 24 – Going Concern Issues
Corresponding Lecture

Watch the following course lecture with this section:

Lecture 24.01 – The Going Concern Assumption
Lecture 24.02 – The Going Concern Assumption – Class Questions

EXAM NOTE: Please refer to the AICPA FAR Blueprint in the Introduction to find a listing of the representative tasks (and their associated skill levels—i.e., Remembering and Understanding, Application, and Analysis) that the candidate should be able to perform based on the knowledge obtained in this section.

Going Concern Issues

Lecture 24.01

THE GOING CONCERN ASSUMPTION (ASC 205)

When an entity prepares its financial statements in accordance with GAAP, its management is required to evaluate whether or not there is *substantial doubt* as to whether or not the entity will be able to continue as a *going concern* within one year after the date that the financial statements are issued. The evaluation is required every time the entity prepares financial statements. When making the evaluation, management will consider:
- The entity's financial position
- Sources of liquidity
- Recognized and unrecognized conditional and unconditional obligations that are either due or anticipated to be due within one year
- Funds needed to maintain the entity for one year
- Other factors, including negative trends; internal matters, such as labor difficulties; external matters, such as the loss of a significant customer or supplier; or other indications of financial difficulty

There is substantial doubt about an entity's ability to continue as a going concern when events and conditions indicate that it is probably that the entity will not be able to meet its obligations when they come due sometime within a one year period. The period begins on the date on which the financial statements are issued, or on the date on which they are available to be issued, whichever is earlier.

If management determines that there is substantial doubt as to the entity's ability to continue as a going concern, it will evaluate any plans that it perceives will mitigate that doubt. Plans will only be considered that both:
- Are *probable* of being implemented effectively; and
- Will *mitigate* the conditions or events raising the substantial doubt.

Even when there is substantial doubt as to an entity's ability to continue as a going concern, it will apply GAAP in preparing its financial statements but will be required to provide certain disclosures. The entity will **disclose**:
- The principal events or conditions responsible for the conclusion that substantial doubt exists;
- Management's evaluations of the significance of those events;
And:
- A description of management's plans that are expected to alleviate the doubt, or
- If management's plans are not expected to alleviate the substantial doubt, a description of management's plans that are intended to mitigate the events or conditions.

Lecture 24.02

CLASS QUESTIONS

Please see the Class Questions and Class Solutions for this Lecture at the end of this Section.

CLASS QUESTIONS

Work through the below Class Questions while following along with the respective lectures. Once this is complete, you can begin independently practicing what you've learned by quizzing yourself on this course section in your Interactive Practice Questions (IPQ), which can be found in your online Student Dashboard. Your IPQ simulates the computer-based testing experience, and will also help you understand how concepts are applied to the exam. Each question includes answer explanations from expert CPAs that will help you determine why you answered a question correctly or incorrectly. This is key to your success on the CPA Exam.

Lecture 24.02

1. Which of the following conditions or events most likely would cause Shield Company's management to consider whether the entity's ability to continue as a going concern is impaired?

    a. Accounts receivable are pledged as collateral.
    b. Arrearages in preferred stock dividends are paid.
    c. Restrictions on the disposal of principal assets are present.
    d. Usual trade credit from suppliers is denied.

2. After considering negative trends and financial difficulties, Surefoot's management seeks a plan to strengthen the entity's ability to continue as a going concern. Which of the following is the most viable plan?

    a. Increase current dividend distributions.
    b. Increase ownership equity.
    c. Purchase assets formerly leased.
    d. Reduce existing lines of credit.

3. Valley Company is trying to convince its auditor of its ability to continue as a going concern for a reasonable period of time. Which of Valley's plans would its controller most likely suggest as a mitigating factor?

    a. Accelerate research and development projects related to future products.
    b. Accumulate treasury stock at prices favorable to Valley's historic price range.
    c. Negotiate reductions in required dividends being paid on preferred stock.
    d. Purchase equipment and production facilities currently being leased.

CLASS SOLUTIONS

1. (d) An inability to obtain trade credit from suppliers is an indication of financial problems that might indicate an entity's ability to continue as a going concern is impaired. Accounts receivable often are pledged as collateral, not only when there is a going concern problem. Restrictions on the disposal of principal assets, while uncommon, do not indicate a going concern problem. Payment of preferred dividends in arrears indicates a cash surplus; a cash deficit would cause doubts about an entity's ability to continue as a going concern.

2. (b) By increasing ownership equity, the entity may be able to bring additional funds into the entity—mitigating the risk of being unable to continue as a going concern. Increasing dividends, reducing lines of credit, and purchase assets under lease, would all require the entity to use cash and would lessen the entity's ability to continue as a going concern.

3. (c) An entity's ability to generate cash flow is the most essential factor to the auditor in assessing the ability to continue as a going concern. Paying lower amounts of future dividends would be an example. Accelerating research and development expenditures, accumulating treasury stock, and purchasing equipment, may all be good strategies for the long-term health of the entity, but all are examples of spending money in the immediate future, which would not mitigate an immediate going concern problem.

TASK-BASED SIMULATIONS

Task-Based Simulation 1

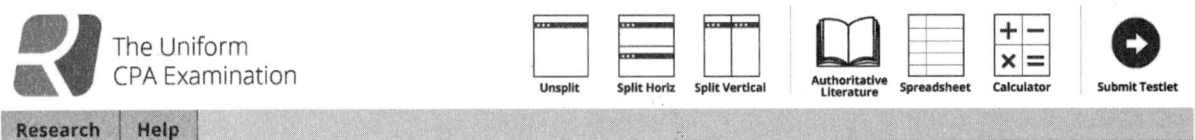

You are the new controller for Dammerung Co., a firm for which there is substantial doubt as to its ability to continue as a going concern, even after considering management's plans. You must prepare information to be disclosed in the notes to Dammerung's financial statements, but are unsure as to what, exactly, you must disclose beyond a statement indicating there is substantial doubt about the entity's ability to continue as a going concern. Identify the location in professional standards that indicates what information should be disclosed to users when there is substantial doubt regarding an entity's ability to continue as a going concern, even after considering management's plans.

TASK-BASED SIMULATION SOLUTION

Task-Based Simulation Solution 1

| FASB ASC | 274 | 40 | 50 | 13 |

Section 25 – Statement of Cash Flows

Corresponding Lectures

Watch the following course lectures with this section:

Lecture 25.01 – Statement of Cash Flows
Lecture 25.02 – Statement of Cash Flows – Class Questions
Lecture 25.03 – Statement of Cash Flows – Direct Method
Lecture 25.04 – Statement of Cash Flows – Indirect Method
Lecture 25.05 – Statement of Cash Flows – Class Questions
Lecture 25.06 – Preparing a Statement of Cash Flows
Lecture 25.07 – Statement of Cash Flows – Class Question - TBS
Lecture 25.08 – Statement of Cash Flows under IFRS
Lecture 25.09 – Statement of Cash Flows under IFRS – Class Question

EXAM NOTE: Please refer to the AICPA FAR Blueprint in the Introduction to find a listing of the representative tasks (and their associated skill levels—i.e., Remembering and Understanding, Application, and Analysis) that the candidate should be able to perform based on the knowledge obtained in this section.

Statement of Cash Flows

Lecture 25.01

STATEMENT OF CASH FLOWS

The statement of cash flows is consistently tested on the CPA exam, usually as either several multiple choice questions or as part of a simulation **(ASC 230).**

The statement of cash flows is a **required** financial statement whenever a company is presenting the results of operations for a year **(ASC 305)**. The primary **purpose** is to provide detailed information about an entity's cash inflows and outflows (Sources and Uses). We are also interested in their Investing and Financing activities.

In the statement of cash flows, we measure the change in Cash and **Cash Equivalents**. A Cash equivalent is a financial instrument that is **both**:
- Easily convertible into a known amount of cash (**highly liquid**), and
- **Original maturity of 3 months or less** from the date of purchase. Since it is so close to maturity, this presents very little risk of change in value, due to changes in interest rates. (Ex. Treasury bills, commercial paper & money market funds)

There are 3 categories of activities in the statement of cash flows:
- **Operating Activities** – Inflows and outflows of cash related to the production of income from continuing operations. All transactions that are NOT investing and financing activities are considered operating.
    - Collections on sales from customers
    - Cash payments for COGS and SGA
    - Interest received and paid
    - Dividends received
    - Acquisition and disposal of trading securities
    - Payments for income taxes
    - All other receipts/disbursements that do not stem from transactions defined as Investing or Financing activities.

- **Investing Activities** – Investing in yourself or others.
    - Principal collections or **L**oans made by the entity (interest and dividends received are Operating)
    - Acquisition or disposal of available-for-sale or held-to-maturity **I**nvestments (Not Trading)
    - Acquisition or disposal of **P**roperty, plant & equipment and intangibles

Acquisition			**Disposal**		
PP&E	47		Cash	15	
Cash		47	Accumulated		
			Depreciation	37	
			Equipment		47
			Gain on sale		5

- **Financing Activities** – Issuing Debt or Equity
    o Proceeds from issuing or payments for retiring Bonds (interest is Operating)
    o Issuance or Reacquisition of stock or Treasury stock
    o Borrowing or repaying a loan
    o Dividends paid to shareholders (dividends received is Operating)

Examples of **Financing activities**

	Dr.	Cr.
Cash	X	
Common stock		X
Preferred stock		X
APIC		X
N/P		X
Bonds Payable		X

Roger Company
Statement of Cash Flows
FYE December 31, 20X3

	Dr.	Cr.	Change
Cash flows from **Operating** activities			
Net cash *provided (used)* by operating activities			**$135**
Cash flows from **Investing** activities			65
Net cash provided (used) by investing activities			
Cash flows from **Financing** activities			
Net cash provided (used) by financing activities			(50)
Net Increase or Decrease in cash			$150
+ Beginning cash balance			+100
Ending cash balance			$250

Lecture 25.02

CLASS QUESTIONS

Please see the Class Questions and Class Solutions for this Lecture at the end of this Section.

Lecture 25.03

Operating Activities

There are two acceptable approaches to preparing the Operating activities section of the statement of cash flows:

- **Direct method** – (direct cash approach – preferred method) Cash sources and uses related to each account in income from continuing operations are listed individually.
    - Sales are adjusted for changes in A/R
    - COGS are adjusted for changes in both Inventory and A/P.
    - Selling expenses may be adjusted for changes in Allowance for uncollectible A/R and Accumulated depreciation if they are included in selling expense.
    - Interest expense is adjusted for amortization of bond discount or premium.
    - Income tax expense is adjusted for changes in current and deferred taxes.

    Note 1: Gains and losses from sale of Investments (other than trading), and expenses not requiring the use of cash (depreciation, amortization) are not reported.

    Note 2: If selling expense includes depreciation or bad debt expense, they should be deducted since they do not involve the payment of cash.

- **Indirect method** – (reconciliation approach) Income from continuing operations is reconciled to net cash flow from operating activities by adjusting for differences related to changes in balance sheet operating accounts (such as accounts receivable, inventory, and accounts payable) and noncash income items (such as depreciation, amortization, and deferred income taxes).
    - Both are acceptable methods, but if the statement is prepared using the direct method, the indirect method MUST be presented as a supplementary schedule.

Roger Company
Income Statement
FYE December 31, 20X3

Sales	$600
COGS	(200)
Selling expense (Includes bad debt expense of $20)	(100)
General & administrative expenses	(40)
Depreciation expense	(50)
Interest expense	(30)
Equity in earnings of Investee	10
Income tax expense	(60)
Gain on sale of Avail-for-sale security (AFS)	10
Net Income	**$140**

Statement of Cash Flows

Selected Balance Sheet account changes for the year

Increase in A/R	$80
Increase in investment under Equity method	10
Increase in Inventory	30
Increase in A/P	20
Increase in Allowance for uncollectible receivables	20
Increase in Accumulated Depreciation	50
Decrease in Bond Discount	5
Decrease in deferred tax liability	10
Increase in Taxes Payable	40

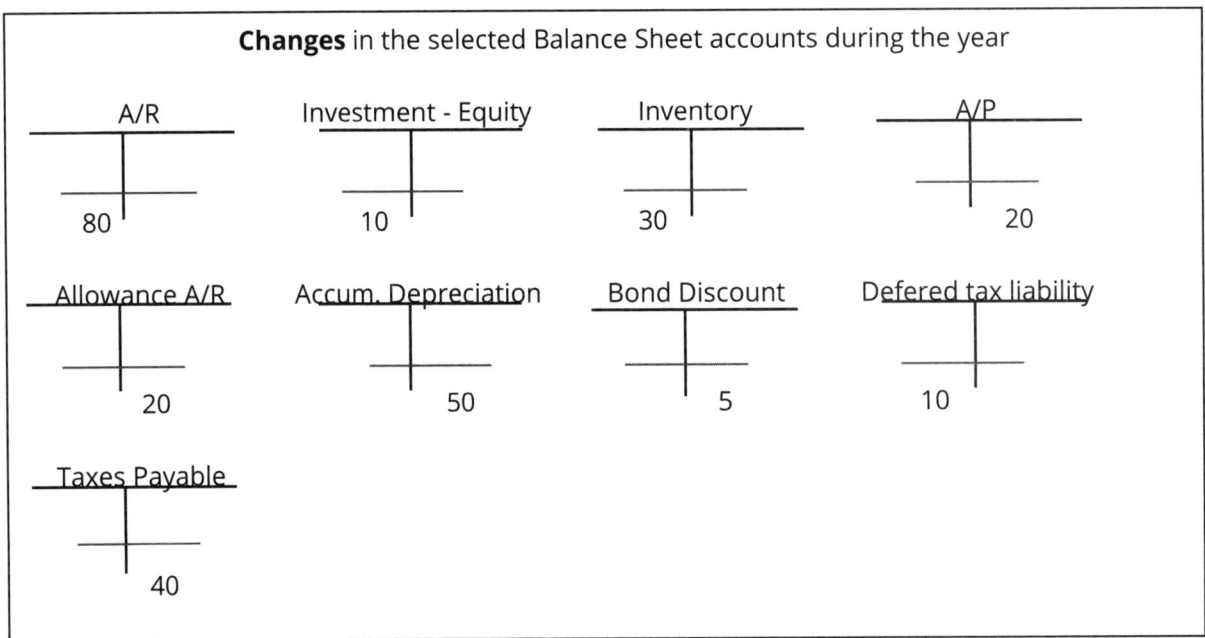

Direct Method (direct cash approach)

Take every income statement item and convert from the Accrual method of accounting back to Cash.

1. **Cash collected from Customers** (A/R increased by 80)

CASH (Plug)	520	
A/R (Change in A/R)	80	
Sales		600

2. **Payments for Purchases** (Inventory increased by 30 and A/P increased by 20)

COGS	200	
Inventory (change)	30	
A/P (change)		20
CASH (plug)		210

3. **Payments for Selling expenses** (Allowance for bad debts increased by 20, bad debts is considered a selling expense).

Selling expenses	100	
Allowance for Uncollectible receivables		20
CASH		80

4. **Payments for G & A expense**

G & A expense	40	
CASH		40

5. **Depreciation expense** – Ignore under the direct method, since there was no effect on cash.

Depreciation expense	50	
Accumulated depreciation		50

6. **Interest expense** (amortization of Discounts or Premiums changed by 5. Is covered in more detail in the Bond section).

Interest expense	30	
Amortization of discount		5
CASH		25

7. **Equity in earnings** – when an investment is accounted for under the Equity method, as the Investee earns income, the investor recognizes their share of the income on their Income Statement, even though they have not yet received cash.

Investment under the equity method	10	
Equity in earnings of Investee		10

8. **Income tax expense** (Deferred tax liability decreased by 10, taxes payable increased by 40)

Income tax expense	60	
Deferred tax liability	10	
Income taxes payable		40
CASH		30

9. **Gain on sale of investment** – Assume an Available-for-sale (AFS) investment that had an original cost of $50, was sold for $60. The cash proceeds would be considered an Investing activity, so the gain is a non-operating gain and should not be part of Operating activities.

CASH	60	
Investment		50 (cost)
Gain on sale of AFS		10

Operating activities (direct method)	**Dr.**	**Cr.**	**Change**
Cash collected from customers	$520		
Payments for purchases		$210	
Payments for selling expenses		80	
Payments for G & A expenses		40	
Payments for Interest		25	
Payments for Taxes		30	
Net cash **provided** by Operating activities	$520	$385	**$135**

Note: Under the direct method, non-operating Gains and losses are ignored. Non-cash items such as depreciation, bad debt expense, amortization expense and Equity in Earnings are also ignored unless already included in Selling expense (bad debt expense in this example), then adjust.

Lecture 25.04
Indirect Method (Reconciliation Approach)

When applying the indirect method, begin with **Net Income** and make 3 types of adjustments.
1. **Non-cash items are adjusted** (Depreciation and Amortization expense is added back, equity in earnings is deducted)

2. **Non-operating items** are adjusted (deduct the gain from sale of an Available-for-sale security, since this is an Investing activity)

3. Changes in the balances of **accrual related accounts are adjusted** (A/R, Inventory, A/P, Allowance for uncollectible accounts receivable, Amortization of Discount, and taxes)

Operating activities (indirect method)	Dr.	Cr.	Change
Net income	$140		
Depreciation expense	50		
Equity in earnings		$10	
Gain on sale of AFS investment		10	
Increase in A/R		80	
Increase in Inventory		30	
Increase in A/P	20		
Increase in Bad debts (allowance)	20		
Amortization of Discount	5		
Decrease in Deferred tax liability		10	
Increase in tax payable	40		
Net cash *provided* by operating activities	$275	$140	**$135**

Indirect method:
Begin with **Net Income of $140.** The following adjustments are then made:

1. **Non-cash items are adjusted.** Since Depreciation and Amortization expense did not result in the use of any cash but was deducted from Net Income, the depreciation expense is added back to Net income ($50). Income from the investment held under the Equity method was also received, but it did not result in the inflow of any cash. Since the income recorded as "equity in earnings" was included as income, but did not result in the inflow of any cash, the income is deducted from Net income ($10).(Note: under the direct method, these were ignored)

2. **Non-operating items are adjusted.** The sale of the AFS investment resulted in a $10 gain. The cash proceeds from the sale of an investment is an Investing activity, however, the gain would have been included in the Income Statement. Since the gain was NOT from Operating activities, it must be deducted from Net Income ($10). (Note: under the direct method, this was ignored)

Cash	60	
Investment		50 (cost)
Gain on sale		10

3. **Changes in the balances of accrual related accounts are adjusted.** As we did for the direct method, all the changes in the balances must be accounted for. For example, A/R increased by $80. Therefore, the amount included for sales was $600, but the actual cash inflow was only $520, so we must take out the $80. Basically, if an **asset Increased, it is a deduction** on the indirect method, if a **Liability increased, such as A/P of $20, it is an addition** to the indirect method.

Note: Net cash provided/used by operating activities should be the **same** under either the Direct or the Indirect method. The Direct method is preferred by the FASB.

Supplementary Disclosures
- If **direct method** is used:
    - Schedule to **reconcile net income** to cash flow from operations
        - Identical to indirect method of preparing operating activities section.
    - Schedule of **non-cash** investing and financing activities
        - Transactions having no effect on cash
            - Conversion of bonds to stock.
            - Purchase financed entirely by loan.

- If **indirect method** is used:
    - Cash payments for Interest and Income Taxes must be **Disclosed.**
    - Schedule of **non-cash** investing and financing activities.

- **Cash flows per share** are *NOT Disclosed*

Cash to Accrual

Another topic regularly tested on the exam is the conversion of cash basis financial statements to the accrual basis. Many questions will provide the amount of cash paid for an expense, or received for a revenue item. The increases and decreases in related accrual accounts such as accounts receivable, accounts payable, prepaid expenses, or accrued expenses, are also provided. The question will require the calculation of the appropriate accrual basis amount.

A similar approach should be used to solve these questions as is used for solving questions calling for items to be reported on a statement of cash flows under the direct method, referred to as the journal entry approach. In applying this approach:
- Debit or credit cash for the amount given
- Debit or credit the related accrual accounts for the increase or decrease
- The amount required to balance the entry will be the accrual basis amount for the revenue or expense item.

Assume, for example, that a company reported cash receipts from customers of $345,000. Accounts receivable had a beginning balance of $29,000 and an ending balance of $31,000. Sales can be calculated by adding the $31,000 ending accounts receivable to cash receipts of $345,000 and deducting $29,000, resulting in sales of $347,000.
- Revenues = Cash received + increase (or - decrease) in accounts receivable
- Revenues = $345,000 + $2,000 = $347,000

Cash Receipts (given)	345,000	
Increase in A/R	2,000	
Sales (plug)		347,000

The same methodology is applied when converting cash paid for merchandise into cost of goods sold. Cash paid for merchandise is increased by the ending accounts payable balance, representing goods purchased in the current period but not yet paid for, and reduced by the beginning balance to exclude payments made in the current period for goods purchased in previous periods. The result will be goods purchased during the period, but not cost of goods sold.

Purchases will be increased by beginning inventory, representing goods purchased in previous periods that may have been sold in the current period, and decreased by ending inventory, representing goods purchased in the current period or prior periods but that is not yet sold. The result will be cost of sales.
- Cash payments for merchandise + increase (or - decrease) in accounts payable = purchases
- Purchases - increase (or + decrease) in inventory = cost of goods sold

Cost of Goods Sold (plug)	X	
Inventory (Increase in Inventory)	X	
Cash paid (given)		X
A/P (Increase in A/P)		X

Lecture 25.05

CLASS QUESTIONS

Please see the Class Questions and Class Solutions for this Lecture at the end of this Section.

Lecture 25.06

PREPARING A STATEMENT OF CASH FLOWS

The CPA exam will periodically require candidates to prepare a statement of cash flows. The problem will generally provide:
- A comparative balance sheet with beginning and ending balances and a column showing the increase or decrease in the individual accounts
- A summarized income statement
- Additional information about specific transactions

These problems can best be solved when a systematic approach is applied. The following approach can be used to solve any such CPA exam problem and will enable you to complete the problem easily within the time allotted and provide the maximum points.

The procedures to be followed are:
1. Set up the statement of cash flows in a 3-column format.
   o The 1st column will be for increases, the 2nd for decreases, and the 3rd for the net change to an item.
   o Leave ample space for each category of cash flows, with operating activities generally having the most transactions.
   o If the problem calls for the use of the direct method and a supplementary schedule reconciling net income to cash flows, set up the supplementary schedule using a similar 3-column format.
   o At the bottom of the statement, fill in the amounts for the net increase or decrease in cash and the beginning and ending balances of cash.

2. Set up T-accounts for each balance sheet account, other than cash.
   o The increase or decrease can be placed on the appropriate debit or credit side of the T-account.
   o Leave room above the increase or decrease to enter transactions

3. Analyze the additional information provided, preparing journal entries for the transactions. Post the debits and credits in the appropriate schedules.

   Begin with net income. Put the amount in the increase column of the operating activities section of the statement of cash flows. If the direct method is used, enter it in the increase column of the supplementary schedule. In either case indicate that it is "Net income". In addition, enter the same amount on the credit side of the retained earnings T-account.

   For all additional entries:
   - Entries to balance sheet accounts other than cash will go into the T-accounts
   - Debits or credits to cash will go into the appropriate section of the statement with debits in the increase column and credits in the decrease column.
   - Debits or credits to income statement accounts will go into the operating activities section of the statement. If the problem calls for the direct method, these entries will go into the supplementary schedule instead.

4. Any unreconciled differences in the balance sheet T-accounts should be eliminated with the offsetting debit or credit going into the appropriate section of the statement of cash flows.

5. If the problem calls for the direct method, complete the operating activities section of the statement by using the income statement and the related balance sheet accounts. In all cases, complete the statement with subtotals for each section.

CLASS EXAMPLE

The comparative balance sheet for Ruiz Corporation at December 31, 20X1 and 20X0 is as follows:

Ruiz Corporation
Comparative Balance Sheet
December 31, 20X1 and 20X0 (000's omitted)

	20X1	20X0	Increase (Decrease)
Assets			
Cash	$ 550	$ 430	$ 120
Short-term investments	400	100	300
A/R, net	100	100	---
Inventory	540	460	80
Long-term investments	1,500	1,600	(100)
Plant assets	4,100	3,400	700
Accum Dep	(1,200)	(1,200)	---
Total Assets	$5,990	$4,890	$1,100
Liabilities & S/E			
A/P	$ 170	$ 175	$ (5)
Dividends payable	400	240	160
Short-term bank debt	325	---	325
Long-term debt	510	400	110
C/S, $10 par	700	600	100
APIC	820	700	120
R/E	3,065	2,775	290
Total Liab & S/E	$5,990	$4,890	$1,100

The following additional information is available:
- Net income was $790.
- A long-term investment was sold for $135. There were no other transactions affecting long-term investments. All investments are classified as available-for-sale securities.
- Cash dividends of $500 were declared.
- Building costing $600 and having a carrying amount of $350 was sold for $350.
- Equipment costing $110 was acquired through issuance of long-term debt.
- 10,000 shares of common stock were issued for $22 a share.

Required:

Prepare a statement of cash flows using the indirect method. Do not prepare schedules for supplementary disclosures.

CLASS SOLUTION

The quickest way to solve the problem is to prepare the journal entries that must have taken place during the year to explain the changes in all the accounts, then post to the statement of cash flows those debits and credits that involve income statement accounts to the operating activities section (O), entries to cash associated with asset acquisitions and disposals in the investing activities section (I), and entries to cash associated with creditor and shareholder transactions in the financing activities section (F). In the journal entries below, each item that would be posted to the statement of cash flows is identified by section in parentheses.

The entries that are most obvious are those based on the additional information.

1. To report net income of $790, the entry is:

Net income (O)	790	
Retained earnings		790

2. The long-term investment sold for $135 must have had a cost of $100 based on the decrease in the investment account, so the entry is:

Cash (I)	135	
Gain on sale of investment (O)		35
Long-term investments		100

3. The declaration of $500 in dividends is recorded as follows:

Retained earnings	500	
Dividends payable		500

4. The sale for $350 of the building that cost $600 and has a carrying value of $350 is reported as follows:

Cash (I)	350	
A/D	250	
Plant assets		600

5. The acquisition of $110 of equipment by issuing long-term debt is as follows:

Plant assets	110	
Long-term debt		110

6. The issuance of 10,000 shares of stock at $22 per share is recorded as follows:

Cash (F)	220	
CS, par $10		100
APIC		120

    At this point, it is clear that more entries are needed, since the changes in several of the accounts have not yet been explained. Look at each account on the balance sheet that hasn't yet been explained by the previous six entries, and prepare the most logical entry to explain the change.

7. The short-term investments increased by $300, presumably by purchase. The likely entry is:

Short-term investments	300	
Cash (I)		300

   Accounts receivable didn't change, so no entry is needed.

8. Inventory increased by $80 during the year. This is probably the result of a large number of entries for purchases and sales, and isn't easy to determine. Using the indirect method, however, it is only necessary to identify the net change in inventory as an adjustment to cost of sales in the operating section, so the entry is as follows:

Inventory	80	
Increase in inventory (O)		80

   The decrease in long-term investments of $100 was already explained with entry (5) above.

9. Plant assets already were reduced in entry (3) by $600 and increase in entry (4) by $110, for a net decrease of $490. Since, however, plant assets ended the year $700 higher than they began, there must have been purchases totaling $1,190 that weren't identified previously, (1,190 – 600 + 110 = 700). The likely entry is:

Plant assets	1,190	
Cash (I)		1,190

10. Accumulated depreciation didn't change during the year, but entry (3) required a decrease of $250 when the building was sold, so there must have been an increase of $250 not yet identified. Clearly, this is from the normal depreciation entry:

Depreciation expense (O)	250	
A/D		250

11. The decrease in accounts payable is the result of multiple transactions and under the indirect method can simply be assumed to be an adjustment to cost of goods sold in the operating section:

Accounts payable	5	
Decrease in accounts payable (O)		5

12. Dividends payable increased $500 when dividends were declared in entry (2), but the net change for the year was an increase of only $160, so there must have been a decrease of $340 resulting from dividends payments (500 – 340 = 160):

Dividends payable	340	
Cash (F)		340

13. The only reason for short-term debt to increase by $325 is borrowing:

    Cash (F)   325
        Short-term bank debt   325

The increase of $110 in long-term debt was explained by entry (4) already. The increases in common stock and APIC were explained by entry (6). The increase of $290 in retained earnings was explained by entries (1) and (2) (790 – 500 = 290).

Now that all of the accounts have been explained, all necessary entries must have been prepared. The resulting statement of cash flows is:

Ruiz Corporation
Statement of Cash Flows
December 31, 20X1

DESCRIPTION	DEBITS	CREDITS	NET CHANGE
OPERATING ACTIVITIES			
Net income	790 (1)		
Gain on sale of investment		35 (2)	
Increase in inventory		80 (8)	
Depreciation expense	250 (10)		
Decrease in accounts payable		5 (11)	
Net from operating activities	**1040**	**120**	**920**
INVESTING ACTIVITIES			
Proceeds from building sale	350 (4)		
Proceeds from sale of investment	135 (2)		
Cost of short-term investments		300 (7)	
Payments for plant asset purchase		1,190 (9)	
Net from investing activities	**485**	**1,490**	**(1,005)**
FINANCING ACTIVITIES			
Proceeds from stock issuance	220 (6)		
Dividends paid		340 (12)	
Proceeds of short-term bank loan	325 (13)		
Net from financing activities	**545**	**340**	**205**
Increase in cash			**120**
Cash at beginning of year			430
Cash at end of year			550

Statement of Cash Flows — Section 25

Lecture 25.07

CLASS QUESTIONS

Please see the Class Questions and Class Solutions for this Lecture at the end of this Section.

Lecture 25.08

STATEMENT OF CASH FLOWS UNDER IFRS

The requirements under IFRS for preparing and presenting a statement of cash flows are very similar to the requirements under US GAAP. Similarly, IAS 7, Statement of Cash Flows, requires an entity to present a statement of cash flows for every period for which the entity is presenting financial statements. The statement will present inflows and outflows of cash and cash equivalents, which are defined in the same way in IAS 7 as in US GAAP, classified as operating, investing, or financing.

Operating, investing, and financing activities are defined essentially the same under IFRS as under US GAAP.

One significant difference is the reporting of interest and dividends.
Interest paid:
- Is considered an operating activity by a financial institution.
- May be reported as either an outflow for operating activities or for financing activities by other entities.

Interest and dividends received:
- Are considered operating activities by a financial institution.
- May be reported as either an inflow from operating activities or from investing activities by other entities.

Both US GAAP and IFRS allow an entity to report cash flows from operating activities under either the **direct method or the indirect method**. Both consider the direct method the preferred method. IAS 7, however, also allows the use of a ***modified indirect method***. Under this approach:
- The statement shows revenues and expenses as reported in the statement of comprehensive income.
- Adjustments are made for changes in inventories and operating receivables and payables.

In general, cash flows are required to be reported on a gross basis. Cash received from an activity cannot be offset against cash payments for a related activity. In some circumstances, however, net reporting is allowed.
- Both US GAAP and IFRS allow net reporting for items that are large in amount, have short-term maturities, and for which turnover is quick.
- IFRS also allows an entity to net cash receipts and disbursements on behalf of customers when they better reflect the activities of the customer than the reporting entity.
    - A property management company, for example, may be collecting rents on behalf of a customer and remitting them to the customer within a short period of time.
    - Reporting the rent receipts as operating cash inflows and the remittances as operating outflows may give the wrong impression about the operations about the property management company, allowing for net reporting.

IAS 7 prohibits an entity from including **noncash** investing and financing transactions on the statement of cash flows. They are required to be disclosed elsewhere in the financial statements and provide all relevant information.

IAS 7 also requires an entity to disclose:
- All components of cash and cash equivalents
- A reconciliation of the changes in each item to amounts reported in the statement of cash flows.

Statement of Cash Flows	
US GAAP	**IFRS**
• Allows direct method or indirect method of reporting operating activities	• Allows direct, indirect, or *modified direct method* showing rev & exp & changes in working capital accounts in operating activities
• Interest & div received reported as operating activities	• Interest & dividends received are investing activities unless lending is normal business activity (operating)
• Interest paid is operating	• Interest paid may be financing
• Negative cash balance reported as current liability	• Negative cash balance reported as negative cash equivalent

Asher Industries
IFRS Consolidated Financial Statements
December 31 20X2

Consolidated Statement of Cash Flows

For the year ended 31 December
In thousands of euro

	Note	20X2	20X1
Cash flow from operating activities			
Profit for the period		6,224	3,956
Adjustments for:			
Depreciation		5,010	5,102
Amortization of intangible assets	17	785	795
(Reversal of) impairment losses on PP&E	16	(393)	1,123
Impairment losses on intangible assets	17	116	285
Reversal of impairment losses on intangible assets	17	(100)	-
Impairment losses on assets classified as held for sale	8	25	-
Change in fair value of biological assets	18	(650)	(50)
Net change in biological assets due to (births) deaths	18	(11)	(15)
Change in fair value of investment property	19	(120)	(100)
Net finance costs	14	849	1,196
Share of profit of equity accounted investees	20	(467)	(587)
Gain on sale of PP&E	11	(26)	(100)
Gain on sale of discontinued operation, net of income tax	7	(516)	-
Employee benefit curtailment gain	29	(100)	-
Equity-settled share-based payment transactions	30	755	250
Income tax expense	15	2,503	1,756
		13,884	13,611
Change in inventories		(686)	2,305
Change in current biological assets due to sales	18	127	63
Change in intangible assets	17	(95)	-
Change in trade and other receivables		(12,993)	(1,318)
Change in prepayments		870	(800)
Change in trade and other parables		5,153	(2,450)
Change in provisions and employee benefits		299	320
Change in deferred income, including government grant	31	(28)	-
Cash generated from operating activities		6,531	11,731
Interest paid		(1,604)	(1,529)
Income tax paid		(400)	(1,400)
Net cash from operating activities		4,527	8,802
Cash flows from investing activities			
Interest received		211	155
Dividends received		369	330
Proceeds from sale of PP&E		1,177	481
Proceeds from sale of investments		987	849
Disposal of discontinued operation, net of cash disposed of	7	10,890	-
Acquisition of subsidiary, net of cash acquired	9	(2,125)	-
Acquisition of PP&E		(15,857)	(2,408)
Acquisition of investment property	19	(200)	-
Plantations and acquisitions of non-current biological assets	18	(305)	(437)
Acquisition of other investments		(319)	(2,411)
Development expenditure	17	(1,235)	(495)
New cash used in investing activities		(6,407)	(3,936)
Cash flows from financing activities			
Proceeds from issue of share capital	26	1,550	-
Proceeds from issue of convertible notes	28	5,000	-
Proceeds from issue of redeemable preference shares	28	2,000	-
Proceeds from sale of own shares	26	30	-
Proceeds from exercise of share options	26	50	-
Proceeds from settlement of derivatives		5	11
Payment of transaction costs related to loans and borrowings	28	(311)	-
Acquisition of non-controlling interests	9	(200)	-
Repurchase or own shares	26	-	(280)
Repayments of borrowings		(5,132)	(4,492)
Payment of finance lease liabilities	28	(254)	(214)
Dividends paid	26	(1,243)	(524)
Net cash from (used in) financing activities		1,495	(5,499)
Net decrease in cash and cash equivalents		(385)	(633)
Cash and cash equivalents at 1 January		1,568	2,226
Effect of exchange rate fluctuations on cash held		(12)	(25)
Cash and cash equivalents at 31 December	25	1,171	1,568

Lecture 25.09
CLASS QUESTIONS

Please see the Class Questions and Class Solutions for this Lecture at the end of this Section.

Statement of Cash Flows	Section 25

CLASS QUESTIONS
Work through the below Class Questions while following along with the respective lectures. Once this is complete, you can begin independently practicing what you've learned by quizzing yourself on this course section in your Interactive Practice Questions (IPQ), which can be found in your online Student Dashboard. Your IPQ simulates the computer-based testing experience, and will also help you understand how concepts are applied to the exam. Each question includes answer explanations from expert CPAs that will help you determine why you answered a question correctly or incorrectly. This is key to your success on the CPA Exam.

Lecture 25.02

1. Mend Co. purchased a three-month US Treasury bill. Mend's policy is to treat as cash equivalents all highly liquid investments with an original maturity of three months or less when purchased. How should this purchase be reported in Mend's statement of cash flows?

    a. As an outflow from operating activities.
    b. As an outflow from investing activities.
    c. As an outflow from financing activities.
    d. Not reported.

2. In a statement of cash flows, if used equipment is sold at a gain, the amount shown as a cash inflow from investing activities equals the carrying amount of the equipment

    a. Plus the gain.
    b. Plus the gain and less the amount of tax attributable to the gain.
    c. Plus both the gain and the amount of tax attributable to the gain.
    d. With **no** addition or subtraction.

3. Alp, Inc. had the following activities during 20X3:

    - Acquired 2,000 shares of stock in Maybel, Inc. for $26,000. Alp intends to hold the stock as a long-term investment.
    - Sold an investment in Rate Motors for $35,000 when the carrying value was $33,000.
    - Acquired a $50,000, four-year certificate of deposit from a bank. (During the year, interest of $3,750 was paid to Alp.)
    - Collected dividends of $1,200 on stock investments.

    In Alp's 20X3 statement of cash flows, net cash used in investing activities should be

    a. $37,250
    b. $38,050
    c. $39,800
    d. $41,000

Lecture 25.05

4. Lino Co.'s worksheet for the preparation of its 20X3 statement of cash flows included the following:

	December 31	January 1
Accounts receivable	$29,000	$23,000
Allowance for uncollectible accounts	1,000	800
Prepaid rent expense	8,200	12,400
Accounts payable	22,400	19,400

Lino's 20X3 net income is $150,000. What amount should Lino include as net cash provided by operating activities in the statement of cash flows?

   a. $151,400
   b. $151,000
   c. $148,600
   d. $145,400

5. Bob, a consultant, keeps his accounting records on a cash basis. During the current year, Bob collected $200,000 in fees from clients. At December 31st of the previous year, Bob had accounts receivable of $40,000. At December 31st of the current year, Bob had accounts receivable of $60,000, and unearned fees of $5,000. On an accrual basis, what was Bob's service revenue for the current year?

   a. $175,000
   b. $180,000
   c. $215,000
   d. $225,000

Lecture 25.09

6. Apple Co. incurred some interest expense. In their statement of cash flows prepared under IFRS, where would this expense show up?

   a. Operating activities.
   b. Either in operating activities or financing activities.
   c. Financing activities.
   d. In investing activities or financing activities.

CLASS SOLUTIONS

1. (d) The purchase of a 3 month US Treasury bill is an exchange of one cash equivalent, cash, for another, a highly liquid instrument with an original maturity of 3 months or less. As a result, there is no inflow or outflow of cash or cash equivalents and the transaction would not be reported in a statement of cash flows.

2. (a) The sale of equipment for cash results in a cash inflow from investing activities equal to the amount received. If the asset is sold at a gain, the proceeds will be the carrying value plus the gain. If it is sold at a loss, they will be the carrying value minus the loss. Answers (b) and (c) are incorrect because payments for income taxes, including the tax on a gain on sale of equipment, are reported as operating outflows. Answer (d) is incorrect because there is an addition for the gain or a subtraction for the loss in this case.

3. (d) Cash flows from investing activities will include an outflow of $26,000 to purchase stock, an inflow of the $35,000 in proceeds from the sale of an investment, and an outflow of $50,000 to purchase a 4-year certificate of deposit, which is not a cash equivalent because of the long-term maturity. Dividends collected are inflows from operating activities. As a result, net cash outflows for investing activities are (-$26,000 + $35,000 - $50,000) $41,000.

4. (a) A $6,000 increase in accounts receivable indicates that collections were actually lower than sales for the period. In calculating cash flows from operating activities, the increase would decrease net income. A $200 increase in the allowance for doubtful accounts results from the recognition of bad debts expense, which reduced income without requiring the use of cash. It will be added to income. A $4,200 decrease in prepaid rent indicates that some of the rent that had been prepaid in an earlier period was used toward the current period's expense, requiring less cash for rent. It will also be added to income. A $3,000 increase in accounts payable indicates that the entity did not pay for all of the purchases included in cost of sales, requiring the use of less cash. It will also be added to income. As a result, cash flows from operating activities will be ($150,000 - $6,000 + $200 + $4,200 + $3,000) $151,400.

5. (c) The $200,000 collected from clients would be a revenue under the cash basis. However, it must get adjusted for the amounts earned, but not collected. That would be from the change in accounts receivable for the year. Since the A/R balance increased, that represents money earned, but not yet received. So A/R increased by $20,000 (change from $40,000 at beginning of year to $60,000 at year end). This will increase revenue by $20,000 to $200,000 + $20,000 = $220,000. There were also unearned fees of $5,000. This represents cash collected, but not yet earned. This will reduce revenues by $5,000, as it is already included in the original $200,000 received. So ending revenue on an accrual basis will be $200,000 + $20,000 - $5,000 = $215,000.

6. (b) Under IFRS, an entity may report payments for interest as either a cash outflow for operating activities or for financing activities. Answer (a) is incorrect because it is not required to be reported in operating activities. Answer (c) is incorrect because it is not required to be reported in financing activities. Answer (d) is incorrect because interest received may be reported as a cash inflow from investing activities, although it is not required.

Section 25 Statement of Cash Flows

Lecture 25.07

TASK-BASED SIMULATIONS

Task-Based Simulation 1

 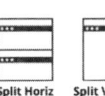 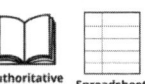

Situation

The following is a condensed trial balance of Probe Co., a publicly held company, after adjustments for income tax expense.

Probe Co.
CONDENSED TRIAL BALANCE

	12/31/X10 Balances Dr. (Cr.)	12/31/X9 Balances Dr. (Cr.)	Net change Dr. (Cr.)
Cash	$ 484,000	$ 817,000	$(333,000)
Accounts receivable, net	670,000	610,000	60,000
Property, plant, and equipment	1,070,000	995,000	75,000
Accumulated depreciation	(345,000)	(280,000)	(65,000)
Dividends payable	(25,000)	(10,000)	(15,000)
Income taxes payable	(60,000)	(150,000)	90,000
Deferred income tax liability	(63,000)	(42,000)	(21,000)
Bonds payable	(500,000)	(1,000,000)	500,000
Unamortized premium on bonds	(71,000)	(150,000)	79,000
Common stock	(350,000)	(150,000)	(200,000)
Additional paid-in capital	(430,000)	(375,000)	(55,000)
Retained earnings	(185,000)	(265,000)	80,000
Sales	(2,420,000)		
Cost of sales	1,863,000		
Selling and administrative expenses	220,000		
Interest income	(14,000)		
Interest expense	46,000		
Depreciation	88,000		
Loss on sale of equipment	7,000		
Gain on redemption of bonds	(90,000)		
Income tax expense	105,000		
	$ 0	$ 0	$195,000

Statement of Cash Flows   Section 25

Additional Information:

- During 20X10 equipment with an original cost of $50,000 was sold for cash, and equipment costing $125,000 was purchased.
- On January 1, 20X10, bonds with a par value of $500,000 and related premium of $75,000 were redeemed. The $1,000 face value, 10% par bonds had been issued on January 1, 20X1, to yield 8%. Interest is payable annually every December 31 through 20X20.
- Probe's tax payments during 20X10 were debited to Income Taxes Payable. Probe recorded a deferred income tax liability of $42,000 based on temporary differences of $120,000 and an enacted tax rate of 35% at December 31, 20X9; prior to 20X9 there were no temporary differences. Probe's 20X10 financial statement income before income taxes was greater than its 20X10 taxable income, due entirely to temporary differences, by $60,000. Probe's cumulative net taxable temporary differences at December 31, 20X10, were $180,000. Probe's enacted tax rate for the current and future years is 35%.
- 60,000 shares of common stock, $2.50 par, were outstanding on December 31, 20X9. Probe issued an additional 80,000 shares on April 1, 20X10.
- There were no changes to retained earnings other than dividends declared.

Items to be answered:

PART A

For each transaction in **items 1 through 6 two responses are required**:

- Determine the **amount** to be reported in Probe's 20X10 statement of cash flows prepared using the **direct method**.
- Select from the list the appropriate **classification** of the item on the statement of cash flows.

    O.   Operating
    I.   Investing
    F.   Financing
    S.   Supplementary information
    N.   Not reported on Probe's statement of cash flows

		Amount	Classification of Activity				
			(O)	(I)	(F)	(S)	(N)
1.	Cash paid for income taxes		O	O	O	O	O
2.	Cash paid for interest		O	O	O	O	O
3.	Redemption of bonds payable		O	O	O	O	O
4.	Issuance of common stock		O	O	O	O	O
5.	Cash dividends paid		O	O	O	O	O
6.	Proceeds from sale of equipment		O	O	O	O	O

Section 25   Statement of Cash Flows

Task-Based Simulation 2

Items to be answered:

PART B
Using all the information given in TBS #1, Prepare a statement of cash flows using the **indirect method**.

Required:

Complete the following statement of cash flows using the **indirect method** for Probe Co.

Probe Co.
STATEMENT OF CASH FLOWS
For the Year Ending 12/31/X10

	Cash Source	Cash Use
Operating Activities		
Investing Activities		
Financing Activities		
Net increase/decrease in Cash		
+ Beginning Cash balance		
Ending Cash balance		

Page 25-24   ©Roger CPA Review

Task-Based Simulation 3

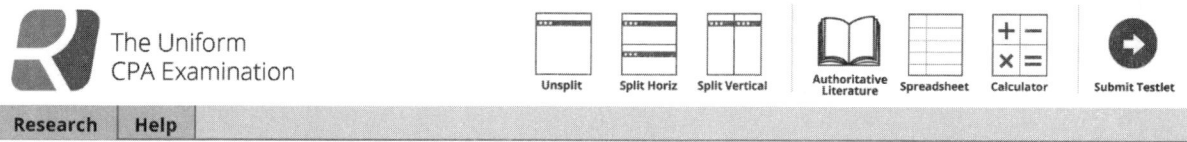

An entity has a very seasonal business and, as a result, uses its line of credit regularly. It takes out advances frequently and repays them within 30 to 60 days. The entity is trying to determine if it should report each advance as a source of cash and each repayment as a use on its statement of cash flows or if it may report the amounts on a net basis. Identify the location in professional standards that indicates whether cash receipts and cash payments related to debt may be reported on a net basis.

Task-Based Simulation 4

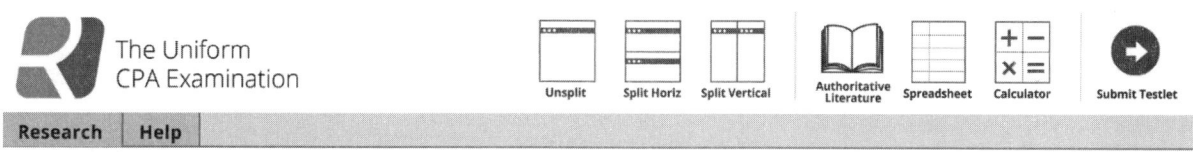

A client is using the direct method to report cash flows from operating activities on its statement of cash flows. In order to keep its financial statements as short as possible, it would prefer to use the minimum number of line items in that section of its statement. Identify the location in professional standards that indicates the minimum classes of operating cash receipts and payments that should be reported on a statement of cash flows when applying the direct method.

Section 25   Statement of Cash Flows

TASK-BASED SIMULATION SOLUTIONS

Task-Based Simulation Solution 1

		Amount	Classification of Activity
1.	Cash paid for income taxes	174,000	Operating Activity (Supplementary Info if Indirect method)
2.	Cash paid for interest	50,000	Operating Activity (Supplementary info if indirect method)
3.	Redemption of bonds payable	485,000	Financing Activity
4.	Issuance of common stock	255,000	Financing Activity
5.	Cash dividends paid	65,000	Financing Activity
6.	Proceeds from sale of equipment	20,000	Investing

Explanations:

1. Cash paid for income taxes can be calculated as follows:
   - Income tax expense is $105,000.
   - There is a $90,000 decrease in income taxes payable, indicating that the entity paid $90,000 in addition to the current expense.
   - Deferred income taxes payable increased by $21,000, indicating that this portion of income tax expense was not actually paid.
   - As a result, payments for income taxes are $105,000 + $90,000 - $21,000 = $174,000

2. Cash paid for interest can be calculated as follows:
   - Interest expense is $46,000
   - The unamortized premium on bonds decreased by $79,000, of which $75,000 was eliminated due to the redemption of bonds, indicating amortization of $4,000
   - Amortization of bond premium decreases interest expense and should be added back to determine interest payments
   - As a result, payments for interest are $46,000 + $4,000 = $50,000

3. The payment for the redemption on bonds payable can be calculated as follows:
    - On the date of redemption, the bonds had a face value of $500,000 and unamortized premium of $75,000, resulting in a carrying value of $575,000.
    - The bonds were redeemed at a gain of $90,000, indicating that it cost the company less than their carrying value to redeem them.
    - As a result, the payment to redeem the bonds would be $575,000 - $90,000 = $485,000

4. The proceeds from issuance of common stock can be calculated as follows:
    - The company issued 80,000 shares of $2.50 par value common stock, which has a total par value of $200,000, the increase to common stock.
    - There was an increase in additional paid-in capital of $55,000 and, since there is no indication of any other stock related transactions, it must have been derived from the issuance of the common stock.
    - As a result, proceeds from the sale of the stock would be $200,000 |+ $55,000 = $255,000

5. Payments for dividends can be calculated as follows:
    - The $80,000 decrease in retained earnings is indicated as being entirely due to the declaration of dividends.
    - Dividends payable increased by $15,000, indicating that the entity paid $15,000 less than the amount declared.
    - As a result, payments for dividends were $80,000 - $15,000 = $65,000

6. Proceeds from the sale of equipment can be calculated as follows:
    - The cost of the equipment sold was $50,000
    - Depreciation expense for the period was $88,000, but the increase in accumulated depreciation was only $65.000.
    - As a result, the difference of $23,000 represents the accumulated depreciation on the equipment sold.
    - The book value of the equipment sold was, therefore, $50000 - $23,000 = $27,000
    - There was a loss of $7,000 on the sale of equipment, indicating that it was sold for $7,000 less than the book value.
    - As a result, proceeds from the sale of equipment were $27,000 - $7,000 = $20,000

Task-Based Simulation Solution 2

<table>
<tr><td colspan="4" align="center">*Probe Co.*
STATEMENT OF CASH FLOWS
For the Year Ending 12/31/X10</td></tr>
<tr><td></td><td>Cash Source</td><td>Cash Use</td><td></td></tr>
<tr><td>**From Operating Activities**</td><td></td><td></td><td></td></tr>
<tr><td>Net income</td><td>195,000</td><td></td><td></td></tr>
<tr><td>Loss on sale of equipment</td><td>7,000</td><td></td><td></td></tr>
<tr><td>Gain on redemption of bonds</td><td></td><td>(90,000)</td><td></td></tr>
<tr><td>Depreciation Expense</td><td>88,000</td><td></td><td></td></tr>
<tr><td>Increase in Account Receivable</td><td></td><td>(60,000)</td><td></td></tr>
<tr><td>Decrease in Income Tax Payable</td><td></td><td>(90,000)</td><td></td></tr>
<tr><td>Increase in Deferred Tax payable</td><td>21,000</td><td></td><td></td></tr>
<tr><td>Amortization of Premium on Bond</td><td></td><td>(4,000)</td><td></td></tr>
<tr><td>**Net cash provided from operating activities**</td><td>$311,000</td><td>($244,000)</td><td>**$67,000**</td></tr>
<tr><td></td><td></td><td></td><td></td></tr>
<tr><td>**From Investing Activities**</td><td></td><td></td><td></td></tr>
<tr><td>Sale of equipment</td><td>20,000</td><td></td><td></td></tr>
<tr><td>Purchase of equipment</td><td></td><td>(125,000)</td><td></td></tr>
<tr><td>**Net cash used from investing activities**</td><td>$20,000</td><td>($125,000)</td><td>**($105,000)**</td></tr>
<tr><td></td><td></td><td></td><td></td></tr>
<tr><td>**From Financing Activities**</td><td></td><td></td><td></td></tr>
<tr><td>Redeem bonds</td><td></td><td>(485,000)</td><td></td></tr>
<tr><td>Issue common stock</td><td>255,000</td><td></td><td></td></tr>
<tr><td>Payment of dividends</td><td></td><td>(65,000)</td><td></td></tr>
<tr><td>**Net cash used from financing activities**</td><td>$255,000</td><td>($550,000)</td><td>**(295,000)**</td></tr>
<tr><td>Net decrease in cash</td><td></td><td></td><td>(333,000)</td></tr>
<tr><td>Beginning Cash Balance</td><td></td><td></td><td>817,000</td></tr>
<tr><td>Ending Cash Balance</td><td></td><td></td><td>484,000</td></tr>
</table>

The first step in solving a problem of this sort would be to determine net income. To do so either calculate the net amount for all income statement accounts in the 12/31/X10 trial balance or simply use the amount by which the net change column does not balance. Either way, net income is $195,000, which will be put into the Operating Activities with the caption "Net Income".

Statement of Cash Flows

It is usually best to use the additional information next and analyze the transactions to determine:
- What the impact will be on the statement of cash flows; and
- How much of the differences in account balances from one year to the next can be accounted for.

1. The purchase of equipment for $125,000 would be an outflow for investing activities. Indicate that amount as a negative number with the caption "Purchase of equipment".

2. There was a sale of equipment that had cost $50,000. It was apparently sold for a loss of $7,000, the amount in the trial balance. To determine the proceeds, however, it will be necessary to determine the related accumulated depreciation.
   a. Depreciation expense is $88,000. Recognize this as an addition back to net income in the operating section, using the caption "Depreciation expense" since it is an expense that reduced income but did not require the use of cash.
   b. There was a net increase in accumulated depreciation of only $65,000 indicating that the difference of $23,000 must have been the accumulated depreciation on the asset sold, indicating it had a book value of $27,000. If it was sold at a loss of $7,000, the proceeds were $20,000.
   c. In the investing activities area, show an addition of $20,000 with the caption "Sale of equipment". In addition, since the loss reduced net income without requiring a payment in that amount, it is added back to net income in the operating activities section with the caption "Loss on sale of equipment:.

   This accounts for the changes in Property, plant, and equipment and Accumulated depreciation

3. Bonds with a face amount of $500,000 and a related unamortized premium of $75,000 were sold at a gain of $90,000. This indicates that the amount required to redeem the bonds was $90,000 less than the carrying value of the bonds or $485,000.
   a. This amount will be reported as a negative amount in financing activities with the caption "Redeem bonds".
   b. The gain on redemption will be deducted from net income in the operating activities section since it was not an operating activity that provided cash, although it was included in net income. Show the gain as a negative number with the caption "Gain on redemption of bonds".

   This accounts for the change in Bonds payable, but does not account for the entire change in the Unamortized premium on bonds.

4. The unamortized premium on bonds decreased by a total of $79,000, $75,000 of which related to the bonds that were redeemed. The remaining difference represents amortization that decreased interest expense from the higher amount actually paid.
   a. Deduct the $4,000 in amortization of bonds from net income in the operating activities section.
   b. Use the caption "Decrease in unamortized premium on bonds".

   This accounts for the change in the unamortized premium account.

5. The information about the income taxes is possibly confusing and, it turns out, irrelevant. It is not needed to complete the problem.
    a. There is a $21,000 increase in the deferred tax liability. Although the information provided explains the reasoning behind it, for the statement of cash flows, the relevant information is that the increase is included in income tax expense but did not require any payment. It will be added back to income with the caption "Increase in deferred income tax payable".

6. There is a $90,000 decrease in income taxes payable, indicating that the entity paid more in taxes than was recognized as expense during the period. This will be deducted from net income as it required the use of cash, with the caption "Decrease in income tax payable". This accounts for the changes in the income tax related accounts.

7. The issuance of the 80,000 shares of stock would account for the changes to both common stock and additional paid in capital for a total of $255,000. It will be added to financing activities with the caption "Issue common stock".
This accounts for the changes to Common stock and Additional paid-in capital.

8. Since the only change to retained earnings resulted from the declaration of dividends, they must have been declared in the amount of $80,000. There is, however, a $15,000 increase in dividends payable, indicating the amount paid was only $65,000. This will be reported as a reduction of financing activities with the caption "

9. The only items that remain on the trial balance that have not been accounted for are accounts receivable and cash. The $60,000 increase in accounts receivable indicates that some of the sales included in income were not collected. It will be deducted from operating activities with the caption "Increase in accounts receivable.

Next, it is a matter of completing the statement.
- Calculate the net amount for operating activities, which is a positive $67,000. Put in that total with the caption "Net cash flows from operating activities".
- Calculate the net amount for investing activities, which is a negative $105,000. Put that as a negative total with the caption "Net cash flows from investing activities".
- Calculate the net amount for financing activities, which is a negative $295,000. Put that as a negative total with the caption "Net cash flows from financing activities".
- Combine the three amounts to provide a net negative amount of $333,000. Put that amount below the others with the caption "Net decrease in cash"
- That will be followed with the beginning balance, putting $817,000 in the column with the caption "Cash at beginning of year".
- The net of $333,000 will then be put at the bottom with the caption "Cash at end of year".

Task-Based Simulation Solution 3

FASB ASC	230	10	45	9

Task-Based Simulation Solution 4

FASB ASC	230	10	45	25

Section 26 – Financial Statement Analysis

Corresponding Lectures

Watch the following course lecture with this section:

Lecture 26.01 – Financial Statement Analysis
Lecture 26.02 – Financial Statement Analysis – Class Questions

EXAM NOTE: *Please refer to the AICPA FAR Blueprint in the Introduction to find a listing of the representative tasks (and their associated skill levels—i.e., Remembering and Understanding, Application, and Analysis) that the candidate should be able to perform based on the knowledge obtained in this section.*

Financial Statement Analysis

Lecture 26.01
ANALYSIS OF FINANCIAL STATEMENTS

When users of financial statements examine them, they often compute certain key ratios to evaluate the company's performance. There are hundreds of different ratios that can be computed from a set of financial statements, and it isn't realistic to attempt to learn more than a handful. There are six that are tested regularly, however, that we'll discuss.

A couple of extremely common ratios used to determine the **ability of the company to cover its upcoming bills** are:
- **Current ratio**
- **Quick (acid test) ratio**

The current ratio is simply *current assets divided by current liabilities* at the balance sheet date. The quick ratio is *quick assets divided by current liabilities*. Quick assets are those that can be converted into cash rapidly, and normally include:
- Cash
- Marketable securities
- Accounts receivable

Other current assets, such as inventory and prepaid expenses, are not considered quick assets because they are difficult to convert to cash without substantial effort.

For example, assume a client had the following assets and liabilities at the balance sheet date:

Cash	100
Accounts receivable	50
Inventories	500
Trading securities	150
Machinery & equipment	180
Total assets	980
Accounts payable	60
Current portion of note payable	140
Long-term portion of note payable	400
Total liabilities	600

- Current assets = 100 + 50 + 500 + 150 = 800
- Quick assets = 100 + 50 + 150 = 300
- Current liabilities = 60 + 140 = 200
- Current ratio = 800 / 200 = 4 to 1
- Quick ratio = 300 / 200 = 1.5 to 1

Two ratios are used to measure the **efficient use of inventory:**
- **Inventory turnover ratio**
- **Number of days' sales in average inventory**

Inventory turnover ratio measures the number *of times the average inventory is sold. The formula is cost of* sales divided by average inventory. **Number of days' sales in average inventory** is a different way to measure the same thing. The formula is *average inventory divided by daily cost of sales.*

To complicate the question, the exam often doesn't provide cost of sales, and it must be computed using the standard formula:

Cost of sales = Beginning inventory + Purchases – Ending inventory

Also, it may not provide average inventory, which is computed as follows:

(Beginning Inventory + Ending Inventory) / 2

For example, assume the following facts are available:

Inventory, 1/1/X1	200
Inventory, 12/31/X1	300
Sales in 20X1	900
Purchases in 20X1	600
Working days in 20X1	250

- Cost of sales = 200 + 600 – 300 = 500
- Daily cost of sales = Cost of sales / Working days per year = 500 / 250 = 2
- Average inventory = (200 + 300) / 2 = 250
- Inventory turnover ratio = 500 / 250 = 2 times
- Number of days' sales in average inventory = 250 / 2 = 125 days

The final set of regularly-tested ratios measures the **efficiency of receivables**:
- **Receivables turnover ratio**
- **Number of days' sales in average receivables**

The **receivables turnover ratio** is *credit sales divided by average receivables*, and the **number of days' sales in average receivables** is *average receivables divided by daily credit sal*es. The questions are usually straightforward.

For example, assume the following facts apply:

Accounts receivable, 1/1/X1	100
Accounts receivable, 12/31/X1	200
Cash sales in 20X1	400
Credit sales in 20X1	750
Working days in 20X1	250

Average receivables = (Beginning A/R + Ending A/R) / 2 = (100 + 200) / 2 = 150

Daily credit sales = Credit sales / Working days per year = 750 / 250 = 3

Receivables turnover ratio = 750 / 150 = 5 times

Number of days' sales in average receivables = 150 / 3 = 50 days

- **Working capital**
    - Current assets – current liabilities
- **Current ratio**
    - Current assets / current liabilities
- **Quick ratio (acid test)**
    - (Cash + marketable securities + A/R) / current liabilities.
- **Receivables turnover**
    - Sales on credit / Average of beginning and ending A/R.
- **Number of days' sales in average receivables**
    - 360 / Receivables Turnover
- **Inventory turnover**
    - Cost of sales / Average of beginning and ending inventory.
- **Number of days' supply in average inventory**
    - 360 / Inventory Turnover **or** Average (ending) inventory / Average daily cost of goods sold
- **Length of Operating Cycle**
    - Number of days' sales   Number of days' supply
      In average receivables   in average inventory
- **Debt to Total Assets**
    - Total liabilities / total assets
- **Debt to Equity**
    - Total Liabilities (total debt) / Stockholders equity
- **Book value per common share**
    - Common stockholders' equity / number of common shares outstanding
- **Dividend payout**
    - Dividends per common share / EPS
- **Return on Total Assets**
    - Net income + Interest Expense (net of tax) / Average Total Assets

It is important to understand the ratios and their Purpose or Use.

Ratio	Formula	Purpose or Use
Liquidity – Measures of the company's short-term ability to pay its maturing obligations.		
1. Working Capital	Current assets - Current liabilities	Measures the company's solvency
2. Current ratio	<u>Current assets</u> Current liabilities	Measures short-term debt-paying ability
3. Quick or acid-test ratio	Cash, marketable securities, and <u>receivables (net)</u> Current liabilities	Measures immediate short-term liquidity
4. Current cash debt coverage ratio	Net cash provided by <u>operating activities</u> Average current liabilities	Measures a company's ability to pay off its current liabilities in a given year from its operations
5. Defensive interval ratio	Cash, marketable securities, and <u>receivables (net)</u> <u>Average daily expenditures</u>	Measures the length of time a company can continue to pay its bills with its existing liquid assets.
Activity – <u>Measures how effectively the company uses its assets</u>		
6. Receivables turnover	<u>Net credit sales</u> Average trade receivables (net)	Measures liquidity of receivables
7. Inventory turnover	<u>Cost of goods sold</u> Average inventory	Measures liquidity of inventory
8. Asset turnover	<u>Net sales</u> Average total assets	Measures how efficiently assets are used to generate sales
9. Number of days' supply in average inventory	= 360 / Inventory Turnover **or** = Average (ending) inventory / Average daily cost of goods sold	Measures number of days required to sell inventory
10. Number of days' sales in average receivables	= 360 / Receivables Turnover	Measures number of days required to collect receivables

Financial Statement Analysis — Section 26

Ratio	Formula	Purpose or Use
Profitability – Measures of the degree of success or failure of a given company or division for a given period of time.		
11. Profit margin on sales (Gross margin)	$\dfrac{\text{Net income}}{\text{Net sales}}$	Measures net income generated by each dollar of sales
12. Rate of return on assets	$\dfrac{\text{Net income}}{\text{Average total assets}}$	Measures overall profitability of assets
13. Rate of return on common stock equity (Return on equity)	$\dfrac{\text{Net income minus preferred dividends}}{\text{Average common stockholders' equity}}$	Measures profitability of owners' investment
14. Earnings per share	$\dfrac{\text{Net income minus preferred dividends}}{\text{Weighted shares outstanding}}$	Measures net income earned on each share of common stock
15. Price-earnings ratio	$\dfrac{\text{Market price of stock}}{\text{Earnings per share}}$	Measures the ratio of the market price per share to earnings per share
16. Payout ratio	$\dfrac{\text{Cash dividends}}{\text{Net income}}$	Measures percentage of earnings distributed in the form of cash dividends
Coverage – Measures of the degree of protection for long-term creditors and investors.		
17. Debt to equity	$\dfrac{\text{Total debt}}{\text{Stockholders' equity}}$	Shows creditors the corporation's ability to sustain losses
18. Debt to total assets	$\dfrac{\text{Total debt}}{\text{Total assets}}$	Measures the percentage of total assets provided by creditors
19. Times interest earned	$\dfrac{\text{Income before interest expense and taxes}}{\text{Interest expense}}$	Measures ability to meet interest payments as they come due
20. Cash debt coverage ratio	$\dfrac{\text{Net cash provided by operating activities}}{\text{Average total liabilities}}$	Measures a company's ability to repay its total liabilities in a given year from its operations
21. Book value per share	$\dfrac{\text{Common stockholders' equity}}{\text{Outstanding shares}}$	Measures the amount each share would receive if the company were liquidated at the amounts reported on the balance sheet

Lecture 26.02

CLASS QUESTIONS

Please see the Class Questions and Class Solutions for this Lecture at the end of this Section.

Section 26   Financial Statement Analysis

CLASS QUESTIONS

Work through the below Class Questions while following along with the respective lectures. Once this is complete, you can begin independently practicing what you've learned by quizzing yourself on this course section in your Interactive Practice Questions (IPQ), which can be found in your online Student Dashboard. Your IPQ simulates the computer-based testing experience, and will also help you understand how concepts are applied to the exam. Each question includes answer explanations from expert CPAs that will help you determine why you answered a question correctly or incorrectly. This is key to your success on the CPA Exam.

Lecture 26.02

1. Heath Co.'s current ratio is 4:1. Which of the following transactions would normally increase its current ratio?

    a. Purchasing inventory on account.
    b. Selling inventory on account.
    c. Collecting an account receivable.
    d. Purchasing machinery for cash.

2. During 20X3, Rand Co. purchased $960,000 of inventory. The cost of goods sold for 20X3 was $900,000, and the ending inventory at December 31, 20X3, was $180,000. What was the inventory turnover for 20X3?

    a. 6.4
    b. 6.0
    c. 5.3
    d. 5.0

CLASS SOLUTIONS

1. (b) Selling inventory on account would result in a decrease to inventory and an increase to accounts receivable for an amount equal to the inventory plus the gross profit on sale. As a result, current assets will increase without changing current liabilities, increasing the current ratio. Answer (a) is incorrect because purchasing inventory on account will increase current assets (inventory) and current liabilities (accounts payable) by the same amount. The result will be a decrease in the current ratio if it is greater than 1 to 1 and an increase if it is less than 1 to 1. Answer (c) is incorrect because collecting an account receivable would increase one current asset (cash) and decrease another (accounts receivable) by the same amount. There is no change to current assets and, therefore, no change to the current ratio. Answer (d) is incorrect because purchasing a machine for cash would decrease one current asset (cash) without affecting any other current assets or current liabilities since the machine is a noncurrent asset. A decrease in current assets with no change to current liabilities results in a decrease to the current ratio.

2. (b) Inventory turnover is cost of goods sold divided by average inventory. Average inventory is beginning inventory plus ending inventory divided by 2. If ending inventory was $180,000 and cost of goods sold was $900,000, goods available for sale were $1,080,000. With purchases of $960,000, beginning inventory must have been the difference of $120,000. As a result, average inventory is ($120,000 + $180,000)/2 = $150,000 and inventory turnover is $900,000/$150,000 = 6.0 times.

Section 27 – Inflation Accounting
Corresponding Lectures

Watch the following course lecture with this section:

Lecture 27.01 – Inflation Accounting
Lecture 27.02 – Inflation Accounting – Class Questions

EXAM NOTE: Please refer to the AICPA FAR Blueprint in the Introduction to find a listing of the representative tasks (and their associated skill levels—i.e., Remembering and Understanding, Application, and Analysis) that the candidate should be able to perform based on the knowledge obtained in this section.

Inflation Accounting

Lecture 27.01

INFLATION ACCOUNTING

Accounting for the **effects of changing prices** is **optional (ASC 255).** When the client elects to present such data as supplementary information accompanying the basic financial statements, it may present two different types of information:
- **Current cost information**
- **Price-level adjusted data**

To understand the effects of changing prices, it is important to distinguish monetary assets and liabilities from non-monetary items. A **monetary** item is an asset or liability whose value is *fixed in money terms*. Examples are:
- Cash
- Accounts and notes receivable
- Bond investments that will be held to maturity
- Prepaid expenses
- Accounts, notes, and bonds payable

A **non-monetary** item is one that does not guarantee a fixed amount of money being received or paid. Examples are:
- Inventories
- Plant and equipment
- Intangibles
- Marketable securities (including bonds that may be sold prior to maturity)

Current cost accounting reports assets on the balance sheet at replacement cost. In determining the replacement cost of fixed assets, the estimated cost of a used asset must be utilized. If this isn't available, the cost of a new asset may be adjusted for estimated depreciation.

For example, assume the client acquired a machine with a 10-year life and no expected salvage value on 1/1/X1 for $100, and that it was being depreciated on a straight-line basis. At 12/31/X3, accumulated depreciation was $30 and book value $70. In determining the current cost of the machine, the client is unable to identify a price for a 3-year-old machine, but the replacement cost for an identical new machine on 12/31/X3 was $120. By applying the same depreciation approach, accumulated depreciation is estimated at $120 x 3 / 10 = $36, and the current cost of the machine is reported at $120 - $36 = $84.

On the income statement, cost of sales is reported at the average current cost of goods sold. For example, assume the following historical information is available for FIFO calculation of cost of sales in 20X1:

	Units	Dollars
Beginning inventory	10	100
Purchases	40	440
Ending inventory	(20)	(280)
Cost of sales	30	260

The current cost of the inventory was $10 per unit at 1/1/X1 and $14 per unit at 12/31/X1, so the average current cost per unit was $12. The average current cost of goods sold was 30 units x $12 per unit = $360.

Price-level adjusted numbers continue to carry assets at historical cost, but nonmonetary items are adjusted to reflect changes in the consumer price index. For example, if land was acquired in 20X1 at $500 when the price index was 1.00, and the price index at 12/31/X3 is 1.10, the land is carried on a price-level adjusted 12/31/X3 balance sheet at $500 x 1.10 / 1.00 = $550.

Monetary assets and liabilities are not adjusted for inflation, since they do not increase in value from it. The failure of these items to increase results in a purchasing power loss when monetary assets are held and a purchasing power gain when monetary liabilities are held (since the failure of assets to rise in value is unfavorable but the failure of liabilities to increase is favorable).

To measure **purchasing power gains and losses**, a calculation is made of the change in value that would have occurred on net monetary items if they had been nonmonetary, and this is compared to their actual value. Since the calculation is being made of the gain or loss over the course of the year, all amounts are adjusted to reflect the average price level for the year.

If inflation:

Monetary ASSET	Purchasing power LOSS
Monetary LIABILITY	Purchasing power GAIN

For example, assume a client began the year with net monetary assets of $400 and ended the year with net monetary assets of $600. The price index at the beginning of the year was 1.00 and at the end of the year 1.20, with an average of 1.10.

Expressed in nominal dollars, the change during the year can be summarized as:

Beginning	$400
Increase	$200
Ending	$600

If all of the figures are adjusted to a common price level of 1.10 (the average for the year), then beginning net monetary assets are $400 x 1.10 / 1.00 = $440, the increase (which occurred over the course of the year) is $200 x 1.10 / 1.10 = $200, and the ending net monetary assets are $600 x 1.10 / 1.20 = $550. The amounts do not reconcile, though, and the discrepancy is the purchasing power loss:

Beginning	$440
Increase	$200
Subtotal	$640
Ending	$550
Discrepancy	$90

The discrepancy is a purchasing power loss to the company, because it represents the difference between what the assets would have been worth if they had benefited from inflation ($640) and what they were actually worth ($550).

Lecture 27.02
CLASS QUESTIONS

Please see the Class Questions and Class Solutions for this Lecture at the end of this Section.

CLASS QUESTIONS

Work through the below Class Questions while following along with the respective lectures. Once this is complete, you can begin independently practicing what you've learned by quizzing yourself on this course section in your Interactive Practice Questions (IPQ), which can be found in your online Student Dashboard. Your IPQ simulates the computer-based testing experience, and will also help you understand how concepts are applied to the exam. Each question includes answer explanations from expert CPAs that will help you determine why you answered a question correctly or incorrectly. This is key to your success on the CPA Exam.

Lecture 27.02

1. A company that wishes to disclose information about the effect of changing prices in accordance with ASC 255 Financial Accounting and Changing Prices, should report this information in

    a. The body of the financial statements.
    b. The notes to the financial statements.
    c. Supplementary information to the financial statements.
    d. Management's report to shareholders.

2. The following are just a few of the items that appeared on Jones Co.'s books at the end of 20X3:

Merchandise inventory	$600,000
Loans to employees	20,000

    What amount should Jones classify as monetary assets for the purpose of preparing constant dollar financial statements?

    a. $0
    b. $ 20,000
    c. $600,000
    d. $620,000

3. When computing purchasing power gain or loss on net monetary items, which of the following accounts is classified as non-monetary?

    a. Advances to unconsolidated subsidiaries.
    b. Allowance for uncollectible accounts.
    c. Unamortized premium on bonds payable.
    d. Accumulated depreciation of equipment.

4. During a period of inflation in which a liability account balance remains constant, which of the following occurs?

    a. A purchasing power gain, if the item is a non-monetary liability.
    b. A purchasing power gain, if the item is a monetary liability.
    c. A purchasing power loss, if the item is a non-monetary liability.
    d. A purchasing power loss, if the item is a monetary liability.

Inflation Accounting Section 27

CLASS SOLUTIONS

1. (c) Entities are not required to present information about changing prices. If an entity decides to present it, information about changing prices is provided in supplementary information. Answer (a) is incorrect because information about changing prices is not required and is not considered part of the basic financial statements. If an entity decides to present it, information about changing prices is presented as supplementary information, it is not in the body of the financial statements. Answer (b) is incorrect because the notes to the financial statements are designed to provide information that will enable users to better understand the information in the financial statements. Information about changing prices is voluntary, not required, and is presented in supplementary information. Since it is not part of the basic financial statements, it would be inappropriate to include it in the notes. Answer (d) is incorrect because management's report to shareholders is designed to indicate how management dispatched its responsibilities. It would not be appropriate to include information about changing prices in management's report.

2. (b) Monetary assets and liabilities are financial instruments that are fixed in amount and do not vary in dollar amount as a result of inflation. As prices increase or decrease, the dollar value of inventory will fluctuate accordingly. Regardless of changes in price level, however, receivables from employees will remain at $20,000.

3. (d) Monetary assets and liabilities are financial instruments that are fixed in amount and do not vary in dollar amount as a result of inflation. As prices increase or decrease, the dollar value of equipment would change and, since it is based on the amount reported as equipment, accumulated depreciation would as well. As a result, it is nonmonetary. Answer (a) is incorrect because as prices increase or decrease, the dollar amount of advances to subsidiaries would remain unchanged. As a result, it is monetary. Answer (b) is incorrect because as prices increase or decrease, the dollar amount of accounts receivable, and the related allowance for uncollectible accounts, would remain unchanged. As a result, it is monetary. Answer (c) is incorrect because as prices increase or decrease, the dollar amount of bonds payable, and the related unamortized premium would remain unchanged. As a result, it is monetary.

4. (b) In periods of inflation, monetary liabilities result in purchasing power gains. That is because, as prices increase, the amount of the liability does not change. As a result, the liability will be repaid with "less expensive" dollars.

TASK-BASED SIMULATIONS

Task-Based Simulation 1

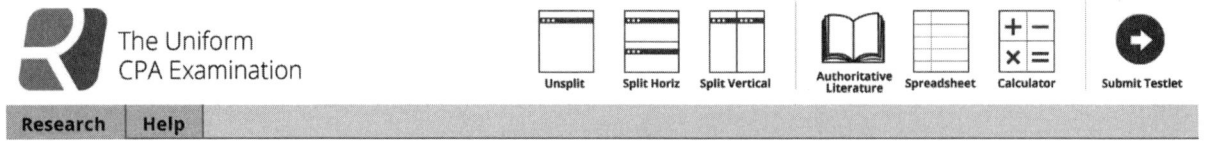

A client is trying to determine if it is required to provide supplementary information related to changing prices with its financial statements. Identify the location in professional standards that indicates whether or not an entity is required to disclose supplementary information on the effects of changing prices.

Task-Based Simulation 2

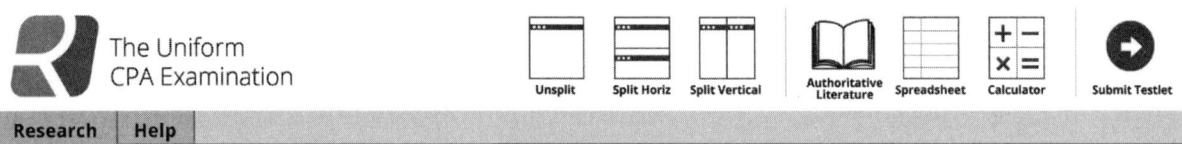

An entity has decided to provide supplementary information related to changing prices with its financial statements. It is trying to determine how to measure cost of goods sold, depreciation, depletion, and amortization in its income from continuing operations on a current cost basis. Identify the location in professional standards that indicates how cost of goods sold, depreciation, depletion, and amortization should be measured in income from continuing operations presented on a current cost basis.

TASK-BASED SIMULATION SOLUTIONS

Task-Based Simulation Solution 1

| FASB ASC | 255 | 10 | 50 | 1 |

Task-Based Simulation Solution 2

| FASB ASC | 255 | 10 | 50 | 39 |

Section 28 – Partnerships
Corresponding Lectures

Watch the following course lecture with this section:

Lecture 28.01 – Partnerships – Formation
Lecture 28.02 – Partnerships – Admission of New Partner
Lecture 28.03 – Partnerships – Class Questions

EXAM NOTE: Please refer to the AICPA FAR Blueprint in the Introduction to find a listing of the representative tasks (and their associated skill levels—i.e., Remembering and Understanding, Application, and Analysis) that the candidate should be able to perform based on the knowledge obtained in this section.

Partnerships

Lecture 28.01

ACCOUNTING FOR PARTNERSHIPS

Accounting for partnerships **differs from corporations** in two significant ways:
- A partnership isn't a taxable entity (form 1065), so no provisions are needed for current or deferred income taxes.
- The equity section does not distinguish between contributed capital and retained earnings, but instead simply identifies the capital balances of each partner.

Formation

- Assets are valued at fair value
- Liabilities assumed are recorded at their present value
- If noncash (land or equipment) contributions subject to a mortgage are made, the contributing partner's capital account is credited for the fair value of the noncash asset less the mortgage assumed by the partnership.
- Partner's capital account equals the difference between the fair value of the contributed assets less the present value of liabilities assumed.

The **allocation of equity (Operation of P/S)** represents virtually most of the testing on a typical CPA exam. Partners are credited for contributions and debited for distributions directly. Income is allocated in three steps:

1. Partners may be **allocated interest** on the average capital balances they maintained during the year.
2. One or more partners may be allocated a **fixed salary** for services rendered to the partnership.
3. The **remaining income** or loss is allocated based on the partnership agreement or, in the absence of agreement, equally (unless capital is the main income producer, as in the case of an investment partnership, in which case income is normally allocated based on capital balances).

For example, assume that Abe, Bea, and Cy are equal partners in the ABC Partnership, and maintained average capital balances during 20X1 of $50, $80, and $20, respectively. To encourage the partners to leave capital in the business, each partner is paid 10% on the capital balances they maintain. Bea runs the store, and is provided a $20 salary on top of profits. If partnership income during 20X1 totaled $71, the allocation would be as follows:

Partner	Abe	Bea	Cy	To Allocate
Average capital	50	80	20	
Income				71
10% interest	5	8	2	-15
Subtotal				56
Salary		20		-20
Subtotal				36
Profit sharing	12	12	12	-36
Allocation	17	40	14	----

Lecture 28.02

Admission of a New Partner

When partners admit a new partner into the partnership, there are *three different methods* that may be applied, depending on the terms under which the partner is being admitted. These are the bonus method, the goodwill method, and the exact method.
- Increase capital by contribution.
- Determine if capital equals agreement as to share.
    - If not, then adjust using either:
        - **Bonus method** – when the purchase price is different than the book value of the capital account purchased, bonuses are adjusted between the old and new partners' capital accounts and do not affect partnership assets.
            - Old partners share bonus based on profit and loss ratio prior to admission of new partner (**Bonus Adjust the Right – BAR**).

        - **Goodwill method** – Goodwill is recognized based upon the total value of the partnership implied by the new partner's contribution (**Goodwill Adjust the Left – GAL**).

        - **Exact method** – No goodwill or bonus is recorded. New partner capital account is equal to the assets contributed.

The **admission of a new partner** to a business often requires a reallocation of the capital balances of both the new and old partners. When this occurs, the method of reallocation that is normally used is the **bonus method (adjust the Right)**, in which the new partner transfers sufficient capital to the old partners to leave the new partner with the desired capital allocation (in rare cases, the old partners pay the bonus to the new one).

For example, assume that the DanDee partnership has two partners, Dan and Dee, who share profits on a **3:2 basis** and have capital balances of **$30 and $100**, respectively. Lyon is admitted to a **1/6 interest** in initial capital and profits in exchange for a **$50 contribution** to the partnership. The contribution may be recorded:

Cash	50	
Lyon, capital		50

At this point, however, total capital is $30 + $100 + $50 = $180, and Lyon's share of initial capital of $50 / $180 does **not** equal the 1/6 agreement. Since 1/6 of $180 is $30, not $50, Lyon will have to pay a $20 bonus to Dan and Dee, who share such bonuses as they share profits, 3 to 2. The adjustment is as follows:

Capital	Net assets	Dan	Dee	Lyon
Before admission	130	30	100	
Contribution	50			50
Subtotal	180	30	100	50
Bonus		12	8	-20
After admission	180	42	108	30

Bonus (Adjust the Right)		
Cash	50	
Capital – Lyon		30
Capital – Dan		12
Capital – Dee		8

Alternatively, the partnership may use the **goodwill method (adjust the Left)**, in which goodwill is recorded and added to the old partners' capital balances (or in rare cases, that of the new partner), so that total capital is increased to achieve the desired ratio. In this example, Lyon paid **$50 to own 1/6** of the company, so the implied value of the company is $50 x 6 = $300. Since capital equaled $180 before recording goodwill, implied goodwill is $300 - $180 = $120, and the adjustment is as follows:

Capital	Net assets	Dan	Dee	Lyon
Before admission	130	30	100	
Contribution	50			50
Subtotal	180	30	100	50
Goodwill	120	72	48	
After admission	300	102	148	50

Goodwill (Adjust the Left)		
Cash	50	
Goodwill	120	
Capital - Lyon		50
Capital – Dan		72 (120x60%)
Capital – Dee		48 (120 x 40%)

Occasionally, a partnership wishes to admit a partner and provide them with a certain fraction of initial capital **without recording either a bonus or goodwill (Exact method)**. In this case, the new partner must pay an amount to the partnership that will result in the desired initial capital allocation. For Dan and Dee to admit Lyon in this manner with a 1/6 interest in initial capital, Dan and Dee's combined accounts of $130 before admission must represent 5/6 of the new total capital. **$130 x 6 / 5 = $156**, so Lyon must contribute $156 - $130 = $26, as follows:

Capital	Net Assets	Dan	Dee	Lyon
Before admission	130	30	100	
Contribution	26			26
After admission	156	30	100	26

Notice that $26 / $156 = 1/6 already, with no need for an adjustment.

Exact method		
Cash	26	
Capital - Lyon		26

Retirement and Liquidation

When a **partner retires**, several adjustments usually need to be made:
1. Assets and liabilities are adjusted to fair market value (including goodwill) to determine the value of the retiring partner's interest.
2. The retiring partner's account is reduced by the retirement payment.
3. If the retiring partner's account is reduced below $0, a bonus is paid to adjust it properly, with the other partners paying the cost based on their relative shares of profits and losses (in rare cases, the retiring partner's account is above $0 and the bonus is paid to the surviving partners).

For example, assume that the DanDeeLyon Partnership's three partners, Dan, Dee, and Lyon, share profits and losses on a 3:2:1 basis and have capital accounts of $30, $100, and $50, respectively. Lyon retires: the partnership net assets are appraised at an amount $120 higher than book value, and Lyon is then paid $80 at retirement. The computation of the capital balances of the surviving partners, Dan and Dee, is as follows:

Capital	Net Assets	Dan	Dee	Lyon
Before retirement	180	30	100	50
Appraisal	120	60	40	20
Subtotal	300	90	140	70
Payment	(80)			(80)
Subtotal	220	90	140	(10)
Bonus		(6)	(4)	10
After retirement	220	84	136	---

When a **partnership liquidates** immediately, all of the assets and liabilities are reduced to cash, with gains and losses reported on sold assets. The resulting capital balances may represent the payments to the partners, but if one partner has been reduced to a deficit (debit) balance in capital, they often do not pay the indicated amount. In such cases, they are credited with a bonus to increase capital to $0, and the amount is taken from the other partners based on their relative sharing of losses.
- Assume all non-cash assets are sold for $0.
- Allocate the loss to all the partners based on their profit/loss percentages.
- If one partner has a deficit balance, allocate the deficit balance to the remaining partners based on their new profit/loss percentages.

For example, assume that the Dan Dee Lyon Partnership, with partners sharing profits and losses **3:2:1 and with capital balances of $30 for Dan, $100 for Dee, and $50 for Lyon, liquidates**. The sale of assets results in a **$120 loss**. The payments to the partners are computed as follows:

Capital	Net assets	Dan	Dee	Lyon
Before liquidation	180	30	100	50
Realized losses	(120)	(60)	(40)	(20)
Subtotal	60	(30)	60	30
Dan's bonus		30	(20)	(10)
Payments	60	0	40	20

In an **installment liquidation**, assets may be sold in stages. In the first stage, all assets not yet sold are written off as a total loss (because of the conservatism principle and since they aren't in cash form and cannot be used to pay partners yet). Any bonus reallocation is made as noted above. The steps involved in later stages appear to be beyond the scope of CPA exam testing.

Joint and Several Liability (ASC 405)

Partners in a partnership are said to be jointly and severally liable for the obligations of the partnership. This indicates that a third party with a legitimate claim against the partnership may be successful in an action against any of the partners or all of the partners collectively. As a result, a partner paying a disproportionate amount of the claim will have a claim against the other partners.

When a reporting entity is involved in an arrangement that creates joint and several liability, that entity, referred to as an obligor, may be required to recognize a liability. A liability will be accrued if the amount of the liability is fixed as of the reporting date and the obligation is not subject to some other authoritative method of accounting.

The amount that will be recognized as a liability will be the total of:
- The amount the obligor is required to pay under the arrangement with co-obligors.
- Additional amounts that the entity expects to pay on behalf of co-obligors.

When a liability is recognized, the offset may be to:
- Cash if the obligation is debt related.
- Expense if the obligation resulted from a loss such as an unfavorable legal settlement.
- A receivable, such as from a co-obligor, subject to evaluation for impairment or collectability.
- An equity account as a result of a transaction with an entity under common control.

Lecture 28.03

CLASS QUESTIONS

Please see the Class Questions and Class Solutions for this Lecture at the end of this Section.

CLASS QUESTIONS

Work through the below Class Questions while following along with the respective lectures. Once this is complete, you can begin independently practicing what you've learned by quizzing yourself on this course section in your Interactive Practice Questions (IPQ), which can be found in your online Student Dashboard. Your IPQ simulates the computer-based testing experience, and will also help you understand how concepts are applied to the exam. Each question includes answer explanations from expert CPAs that will help you determine why you answered a question correctly or incorrectly. This is key to your success on the CPA Exam.

Lecture 28.03

Questions 1 and 2 are based on the following:

The following condensed balance sheet is presented for the partnership of Alfa and Beda, who share profits and losses in the ratio of 60: 40, respectively:

Cash	$ 45,000
Other assets	625,000
Beda, loan	30,000
	$700,000
Accounts payable	$120,000
Alfa, capital	348,000
Beda, capita	232,000
	$700,000

1. The assets and liabilities are fairly valued on the balance sheet. Alfa and Beda decide to admit Capp as a new partner with 20% interest. No goodwill or bonus is to be recorded. What amount should Capp contribute in cash or other assets?

    a. $110,000
    b. $116,000
    c. $140,000
    d. $145,000

2. Instead of admitting a new partner, Alfa and Beda decide to liquidate the partnership. If the other assets are sold for $500,000, what amount of the available cash should be distributed to Alfa?

    a. $255,000
    b. $273,000
    c. $327,000
    d. $348,000

Partnerships

3. When property other than cash is invested in a partnership, at what amount should the noncash property be credited to the contributing partner's capital account?
   a. Fair value at the date of contribution.
   b. Contributing partner's original cost.
   c. Assessed valuation for property tax purposes.
   d. Contributing partner's tax basis.

4. When Mill retired from the partnership of Mill, Yale, and Lear, the final settlement of Mill's interest exceeded Mill's capital balance. Under the bonus method, the excess
   a. Was recorded as goodwill.
   b. Was recorded as an expense.
   c. Reduced the capital balances of Yale and Lear.
   d. Had **no** effect on the capital balances of Yale and Lear.

CLASS SOLUTIONS

1. (d) If no goodwill or bonus is to be recognized and Capp will have a 20% interest, the interests of Alfa and Beda will represent the remaining 80%. Their capital accounts total $580,000, which implies that total capital would be ($580,000/80%) $725,000. Capp will contribute 20% or $145,000.

2. (b) If other assets with a carrying value of $625,000 are sold for $500,000, there would be a loss of $125,000, 60% of which, or $75,000, would be allocated to Alfa, and 40% of which, or $50,000, would be allocated to Beda. Alfa's resulting capital account would be $273,000, which would be the maximum amount that could be distributed to Alfa.

3. (a) A contribution of property other than cash to a partnership in exchange for an equity interest in the partnership is a nonreciprocal nonmonetary transaction. It is recorded at the fair value of the noncash property contributed as of the date of the transaction.

4. (c) When the withdrawal of a partner is recorded under the bonus method, no goodwill is recognized. Instead, if the withdrawing partner is compensated with an amount lower than the partner's equity balance, that partner is said to be giving a bonus to the other partners and the difference will be added to their partnership equity balances in proportion to how they share profits and losses. If the amount paid to the withdrawing partner exceeds the partner's equity balance, as is the case here, that partner is receiving a bonus from the other partners, Yale and Lear, which will reduce their accounts proportionately.

Section 29 – Governmental Accounting Corresponding Lectures

Watch the following course lectures with this section:

Lecture 29.01 – Overview of Governmental Accounting
Lecture 29.02 – Fund Types
Lecture 29.03 – General Purpose Financial Statements
Lecture 29.04 – Fund Financial Statements and Governmental Funds
Lecture 29.05 – Proprietary Fund Financial Statements
Lecture 29.06 – Fiduciary Funds and Notes and RSI
Lecture 29.07 – Gov't Accounting, Fund Types – Class Questions
Lecture 29.08 – Component Units, Infrastructure and Major Funds
Lecture 29.09 – Fund Journal Entries – Class Example - Revenue
Lecture 29.10 – Fund Journal Entries – Class Example - Expenditures
Lecture 29.11 – Gov't Accounting, Journal Entries – Class Questions
Lecture 29.12 – Interfund Transactions
Lecture 29.13 – GASB Concept Statements
Lecture 29.14 – Gov't Accounting, Gov Wide F/S – Class Questions
Lecture 29.15 – Gov't Accounting, Journal Entries – Class Question – TBS

EXAM NOTE: Please refer to the AICPA FAR Blueprint in the Introduction to find a listing of the representative tasks (and their associated skill levels—i.e., Remembering and Understanding, Application, and Analysis) that the candidate should be able to perform based on the knowledge obtained in this section.

Governmental Accounting

Lecture 29.01

OVERVIEW OF GOVERNMENTAL ACCOUNTING

The principles of accounting by a governmental unit are different from those of a private business. A private business prepares financial statements for use by creditors and investors in making lending and investing decisions. A government's financial statements are used to make **social and political decisions**. As a result, a unique system of financial reporting has been developed, known as **modified accrual** accounting, and is used to account for most of the activities of a typical governmental entity.

Private Business	Government
Revenues – Voluntary • *Earned &* • *Realizable* • **Accrual accounting** – uses the *Economic resources measurement focus* (All resources avail.)	**Revenues** – Involuntary • *Measurable* • *Available* • **Modified accrual** – uses the *Financial resources measurement focus* (current resources) When **Received**: • income taxes, bus lic, tolls **Accrue for**: • Property taxes (60 days) • Grants –unrestricted-approved –restricted - spent
Costs • Selfish / (spend $ to make $) • Expenses, matching, dep exp.	**Costs** • Unselfish • Expenditures, no matching
Profit motivated Revenue, expenses and Retained Earnings (Net Position)	**Budget compliance** Revenue, expenditures and changes in Fund Balance

Principles

One of the principles that is central to modified accrual accounting is the **interperiod equity** concept. In general, government activity is approved and then carried out on an annual basis. The legislative body of the government approves a budget at the beginning of the year, and the employees of the government departments attempt to carry out the directives given to them over the course of that year. At the end of the period, the financial statements are utilized to evaluate the success of the departments in meeting their directives for that period.

The interperiod equity concept keeps the focus on a single period, with the revenues of the period intended to cover the spending of that period. This is, of course, consistent with the idea of trying to maintain a **balanced budget**, so that costs in the current period aren't paid by future taxpayers. At the same time, this focus on evaluating government activity one period at a time means that future periods are essentially ignored. In modified accrual accounting, a department will usually not account for long-term assets and long-term debt, since these represent those future periods.

The purchase of an asset is simply treated as a current outflow of financial resources and the proceeds from a long-term borrowing a current inflow. No depreciation is recorded on assets and interest and principal owed on long-term debt are not recorded until the periods in which they must be paid. Modified accrual accounting is easiest to understand if the interperiod equity concept focus on one period at a time is kept in mind.

In measuring the transactions under **modified accrual accounting**, the following **measurement principles** are used:

- **Revenues** – these are recognized in the period they are **available to spend**, which means collectible in the current period to pay liabilities, or within 60 days after year end. Revenues billed or collected in advance are deferred until the appropriate future period. Revenues that are not measurable are treated as available to spend once they are collected.

- **Costs** – these are recognized using the expenditure principle. Costs are recorded in the period that the obligation to pay them arises, whether this is before or after the period in which the government is actually using the assets or services. So generally costs are recorded when the related fund liability is incurred except as it relates to unmatured interest on L/T debt, as this is only recorded with it becomes legally due.

- **Reporting** – the financial statements that are prepared include a balance sheet to present the financial position and a statement of revenues, expenditures, and changes in fund balance to present the flow of financial resources during the year. There is no equivalent in modified accrual reporting to a statement of cash flows.

- **Accountability** – budgets are typically developed at the beginning of each year, and the focus of governmental financial reporting is on determination of compliance with budgets and accountability for resources. Any fund utilizing annual budgets must prepare a reconciliation of budget to actual amounts to be presented as supplementary information in the financial statements. Elected officials are accountable to their constituents.

Accounting principles for state and local governments are established by the Governmental Accounting Standards Board (GASB). They issue a variety of publications and the codification of governmental standards includes a hierarchy that identifies what constitutes GAAP for all state and local government entities and the priorities with which they should be applied.

- The highest level of governmental GAAP includes officially established accounting principles. This category includes:
    1. GASB Statements
    2. GASB Interpretations

- The second level includes:
    1. GASB Technical Bulletins
    2. AICPA Industry Auditing and Accounting Guides and AICPA Statements of Position that have been specifically been made applicable to state and local governmental entities by the AICPA and have been cleared by the GASB.

- The third level consists of:
    1. AICPA Practice Bulletins that have been specifically been made applicable to state and local governmental entities by the AICPA and have been cleared by the GASB.
    2. Consensus positions on accounting issues applicable to state and local governments established by a group of accountants organized by the GASB for that purpose (similar to the Emerging Issues Task Force)

- The final level consists of:
    1. GASB Implementation Guides
    2. Practices widely recognized and prevalent in state and local governments

When annual budgets are utilized in the accounting for a government department, *expected sources and uses* may include:
- **Estimated revenues** – revenues that are expected to be available to spend in the period.
- **Estimated other financial** sources – expected proceeds from issuance of long-term debt and operating transfers from other government departments.
- **Appropriations** – expenditures that are expected to occur in the period.
- **Estimated other financial uses** – expected operating transfers to other government departments.

Budgetary entries are made at the beginning of the year and closed out (reversed) at the end of the year. These estimated accounts are used to control expenditures, account for taxes that are being levied and estimate transfers in and out. If a balanced budget has been prepared, the sum of the estimated revenues and estimated other financial sources will equal the sum of the appropriations and estimated other financial uses. If a budgetary surplus or deficit is expected, it will be reported as an increase or decrease in the equity. The equity section of a government department using modified accrual accounting consists of **fund balances**, and the budgetary account used is **budgetary fund balance – unreserved**. It is identified as unreserved because it represents anticipated activity, but no actual legal commitments.

For example, if the legislative budget for a department using modified accrual accounting includes expected revenues of $700, bond proceeds of $200, expenditures of $500, and operating transfers to assist other departments of $250, the journal entry made at the **beginning of the fiscal year** is:

Estimated revenues	700	
Estimated other financial sources	200	
Budgetary fund balance – unreserved		150
Appropriations		500
Estimated other financial uses		250

Revenues

Revenues and inflows of resources include both exchange and non-exchange transactions:
- **Exchange transactions** – goods/services/cash of *equal value* are exchanged (GAAP).
    - Purchase electricity, water from enterprise fund.

- **Non-exchange transactions (4 types)** A transaction in which the gov gives/receives w/o directly receiving/giving equal value in exchange.

- **"Derived" tax revenues** – taxes self-assessed on exchange transactions (sales tax, income tax, motor fuel tax). A revenue when occurs.

- **"Imposed" non-exchange transactions** – taxes not derived from transactions (property taxes, fines, forfeits, special assessments). Assessed on assets or rights of non-gov. A revenue when use of money is permitted and an asset when have a legal claim.

- **"Government-mandated" non-exchange transactions** – one level of government provides funds to another level of government to be used for a specific purpose (federal grant). Revenue when the eligibility requirements are met.

- **"Voluntary" non-exchange transactions** – transactions entered into willingly by parties (unrestricted grants & voluntary donations). Revenue when the eligibility requirements are met.

When using the **modified accrual approach**, revenues are recognized when they satisfy two requirements:
- **Measurable** (quantifiable in monetary terms)
- **Available to Spend** (collectible in the current period or within 60 days of year-end)
  - Uses *the Financial Resources approach* which measures only the current financial resources available to the Government.

Several different types of taxes are *self-assessed*, meaning the taxpayer files a return on which the tax liability is calculated. Examples are:
- Income taxes
- Sales taxes

These are examples of **derived tax revenues**, and the right of the government to receive the taxes arises when the underlying events (income, sales) take place, so revenues are accrued based on the time period of the income or sales that are being taxed. Amounts collected in advance of the period to which they apply, such as overpayments of taxes in one period that are being applied to the next, are reported as deferred revenue.

Some taxes and fees are assessed on assets or rights rather than specific economic activity, and are called **imposed non-exchange transactions**. Examples are:
- Licenses and permits
- Property taxes

With respect to licenses and permits, however, the payment is optional, since the citizen may decide not to obtain the license or permit and, as a result, not pay the amount billed. Such amounts cannot be considered available to spend until the citizen decides to pay the bill, so these are not accrued in advance.

Once a property tax assessment is made, however, the government can expect to collect the amount billed to the taxpayer, since these taxes are mandatory. As a result, property taxes that have been billed usually satisfy the requirements of being measurable and available, and are **accrued** in advance of collection.

A receivable is recorded for property taxes at the time the taxes are billed. The amount to be included in revenue is not the same as the amount levied, however:

- An allowance for uncollectibles must be established.
- Amounts that are not expected to be collected soon enough to be available to spend in the current period must be deferred.

Although this may seem odd, the requirement that taxes be available to spend in the current period does not mean the taxes must be collected during the current period. When goods and services are received by the government, it will issue a voucher for payment, but is allowed up to 60 days to pay the voucher (notice this is double the normal time that businesses are given to pay an invoice). As a result, revenue that is expected to be collected in the **first 60 days of the following** fiscal year may be considered available to spend in the **current** year

For example, assume a calendar-year government levies $2,200 in *property taxes* on 11/1/X1. It expects to collect as follows:

November 20X1	400
December 20X1	900
January 20X2	300
February 20X2	250
March 20X2	225
Estimated uncollectibles	125

The entry to record the **billing** is as follows:

9/1/X1	Property Taxes receivable - current	2,200	
	Revenues		**1,850**
	Deferred revenues		225
	Allowance for uncollectibles		125

The amounts expected during 20X1 and the first two months (approximately 60 days) of 20X2 are considered available to spend in 20X1.

The deferred revenues are **reclassified** at the beginning of 20X2 when they represent the current year:

1/1/X2	Deferred revenues	225	
	Revenues		225

Collections of cash are applied to receivables or reported as revenues, depending on whether or not they were previously accrued. For example, if $2,000 of previously accrued property taxes is collected, the entry is:

	Cash	2,000	
	Property Taxes receivable - current		2,000

If licenses and permits of $500 are **received**, the entry is:

	Cash	500	
	Revenues		500

Uncollectible accounts could either be written off or reclassified from current to delinquent. If they are **written off**, the accounting is done in the same manner as private businesses, reducing the allowance and the related receivables. If $100 of uncollected property taxes is written off, the entry is:

Allowance for uncollectibles	100	
Property Taxes receivable - current		100

Once the due date for a tax bill has passed, any remaining receivables and allowance accounts may be identified as **delinquent accounts**.

Property Taxes receivable - delinquent	100	
Property Taxes receivable - current		100
Allowance for uncollectibles	100	
Allowance for uncollectibles - delinquent		100

Of course, the allowance account may be adjusted, based on an aging of the remaining receivables. Just as the original entry to the allowance account reduced the net revenues recorded, adjustments are made to the revenues account. For example, if the allowance is reduced by $25 based on an aging, the entry is:

Allowance for uncollectibles	25	
Revenues		25

So far, the only receivable we have discussed is for property taxes. Because of the restriction that revenues must be both measurable and available, the only common source other than property taxes that might be accrued is a **grant** from another government unit.

For example, if our client is a local government, and the state government authorizes a $900 **unrestricted grant** that will be paid to the local government later in the current year, the entry at the time the grant is *approved* is:

Receivable from state grant	900	
Revenues		900

The *collection* of the grant is straightforward:

Cash	900	
Receivable from state grant		900

If the state grant is **restricted**, then it is not considered available until the local government has acted in accordance with the restriction. For example, if the $900 state grant is paid to the local entity immediately, but stipulates that the money must be spent on the purchase of new equipment, the receipt of the money (assuming no prior accrual occurred) is recorded as follows:

| Cash | 900 | |
| Deferred revenues | | 900 |

When $600 of the money is *spent* on appropriate equipment, an expenditure of $600 is reported and a simultaneous entry is made to show that this portion of the grant is now available:

| Deferred revenues | 600 | |
| Revenues | | 600 |

If the remainder of the grant money is not spent, it may have to be returned to the state government:

| Deferred revenues | 300 | |
| Cash | | 300 |

The proceeds from the issuance of Long-term debt is recorded in the governmental fund as an "other financing source", not as a revenue.

| Cash | 1000 | |
| Other Financing Source | | 1000 |

Expenditures

Under modified accrual accounting, costs are reported in accordance with the expenditure principle, which means that the focus is on the outflow of financial resources to pay for the good or service rather than on the benefits resulting from the cost. Thus, there is no parallel to the matching principle, and no attempt to amortize costs that benefit multiple periods.

Because of the importance of adhering to budgets in the governmental process, the initial entry in connection with the acquisition of an asset or service is made when the **order is placed** with the vendor. An open order is known as an **encumbrance**, and can be considered a form of estimated expenditure. Unlike an appropriation, however, this represents an actual legal commitment, and requires that a portion of the fund balance be reserved.

For example, if an **order to purchase supplies is placed**, and the governmental entity estimates that the invoice for the supplies will be $900 when received, the following entry is made:

| Encumbrances | 900 | |
| Reserved for Encumbrances | | 900 |

When an **order has been filled**, two entries need to be made. The first is to cancel the encumbrance, since it is no longer an open order. This just involves reversing the entry made when the order was placed:

| Reserved for Encumbrances | 900 | |
| Encumbrances | | 900 |

The actual invoice from the vendor is also recorded. Keep in mind that it might not be for the exact same amount as was estimated in the encumbrance. If the supplies ordered earlier are billed to the government department for $890, the entry to record the approval for payment is:

Expenditures	890	
Vouchers payable		890

The actual **payment** of the voucher later on is recorded as follows:

Vouchers payable	890	
Cash		890

Notice that the purchase of the supplies is recorded as an expenditure, even though the supplies may not have been used yet. This is known as the **purchases** method. It contrasts with the approach used by private businesses to record supplies as expenses only once they are used, known as the **consumption** method.

In order to avoid exceeding budgetary limits placed on the department, the sum of the expenditures recorded to date and the open encumbrances should not exceed the appropriations. For example, if appropriations for supplies were recorded in the initial budgetary entry for $1,500, and expenditures to date are $890, open encumbrances for additional orders should not exceed $610. If it appears the budget for the year will be exceeded, the department should usually request a supplementary appropriation or other modification to the legislative budget.

Keep in mind that purchases of fixed assets are recorded as expenditures at the time of delivery of the assets to the government. Also note that the government may bypass the recording of encumbrances for repetitive expenditures, such as **salaries and wages** of employees. Note: At the end of any reporting period, the remaining balance of funds that are available for use for a city would be = Appropriations – Encumbrances – Expenditures = funds available.

Expenditures may be *categorized* in detail in several different ways:
- **Function or Program** – the category identifies the purpose or objectives of the expenditure. Examples are highways and streets, health and welfare, education, general government, **public safety**, disaster relief, and defense. Program includes drug addiction, education, and elderly. (**WHY - Purpose**)
- **Organizational Unit (department)** – this category groups expenditures based on the government's organizational structure. Examples include **police & fire departments**, city clerk, personnel department, parks and recreational departments. These can be combined to form a Function category, such as public safety.
- **Activity** – this category classifies expenditures by activity which allows the ability to measure economy and efficiency of operations. Ex: **police protection function**.
- **Character** – the category identifies the fiscal period that the benefits are expected. Examples are *debt service-past* (matured interest and principal), *current services-present* (salaries and supplies), and *capital outlay-future* (police car and construction expenditures) (**WHEN**).
- **Object** – this category identifies the types of items purchased or services obtained. Examples are personnel services, salaries, rent, utilities, depreciation, and supplies. (**WHAT - Type**)

- The statement of Revenues, Expenditures and changes in Fund balance generally reports expenditures by function within character classifications. Budgets often report expenditures by object class.
- Function must be presented in either:
  - Statement or footnotes

Closing Entries

At the end of the fiscal year, several closing entries are required under modified accrual accounting. One is to close the entry that was made at the beginning of the year to record the budget.

For example, if the legislative budget included expected revenues of $700, bond proceeds of $200, expenditures of $500, and operating transfers to assist other departments of $250, the journal entry made at the **beginning of the fiscal year** would have been:

Estimated revenues	700	
Estimated other financial sources	200	
Budgetary fund balance – unreserved		150
Appropriations		500
Estimated other financial uses		250

At the **end of the year**, the closing entry is:

Budgetary fund balance – unreserved	150	
Appropriations	500	
Estimated other financial uses	250	
Estimated revenues		700
Estimated other financial sources		200

This is simply a reversal of the opening entry, and is unaffected by the actual revenues and costs during the year.

The **second closing entry** that is needed is comparable to private businesses, and involves the *nominal accounts* created during the year for inflows and outflows related to revenues, other financing sources, expenditures, and other financing uses.

For example, if revenues recorded during the year totaled $710, other financial sources $190, expenditures $490, and other financial uses $230, the **closing entry at the end of the year** is:

Revenues	710	
Other financial sources	190	
Fund balance – unreserved		180
Expenditures		490
Encumbrances (for outstanding purchase orders)		X
Other financial uses		230

Notice that the excess of inflows over outflows of $180 is closed into fund balance – unreserved, which is the modified accrual accounting equivalent to retained earnings (or retained earnings – unappropriated) of a private business.

A third closing entry is needed for **open encumbrances**, that is, orders that were placed during the year but not fulfilled as of the end of the year. Since an encumbrance represents a legal commitment to purchase, it reduces the unreserved fund balance.

For example, assume that, during the year, orders totaling $500 were placed, and $470 of those were fulfilled, with the remaining $30 still open at year-end. As a result, there is a debit balance of $30 in Encumbrances and a credit balance of $30 in Reserved for encumbrances prior to the closing entries. The closing entry needed at year-end is:

Fund Balance – unreserved	30	
Encumbrances		30

The unreserved fund balance is reduced because of the commitment, and a separate fund balance – Reserved for Encumbrances now identifies the outstanding orders on the balance sheet. This can also be accomplished in the previous closing entry as the X above.

The fourth closing entry is needed if the government department elects to **keep track of its inventory** in the General fund. The purchase of inventory is usually recorded as an immediate expenditure (**Purchase method**). If the **Consumption method** is used, Inventory would be debited as goods are purchased. This is used in government-wide statements. It is useful, however, for the legislative body to be aware of any remaining inventories at year-end, since this may affect the budget for purchases in later years.

For example, assume that the department purchased $300 of supplies during their first year of operations, but didn't use all of them, having an inventory of $80 at the close of the fiscal year.

To account for the outstanding inventory without affecting the unreserved fund balance, the following entry is made:

Inventory of supplies	80	
Reserved for inventories		80

In subsequent years, the inventory and related reserve account are adjusted up or down to account for changes in the inventory level. For example, if the inventory of supplies at the end of the **second** year of operations is only $50, the closing entry to account for the decrease from the previous year is:

Reserved for inventories	30	
Inventory of supplies		30

It may be useful to summarize the net effect on fund balances of the various closing entries. Let's repeat all the closing entries discussed in this section (keeping in mind that the numbers used were arbitrarily selected). The starred items representing accounts whose entire balance is being eliminated as a result of the entry.

Governmental Accounting   Section 29

The closing of the **budgetary accounts**:

Budgetary fund balance – unreserved *	150	
Appropriations *	500	
Estimated other financial uses *	250	
Estimated revenues *		700
Estimated other financial sources *		200

The closing of the **nominal accounts:**

Revenues *	710	
Other financial sources *	190	
Fund balance – unreserved *		180
Expenditures *		490
Encumbrances (for outstanding po's)		X
Other financial uses *		230

The closing of the **encumbrance accounts:**

Fund Balance – unreserved	30	
Encumbrances*		30

The **adjustment to ending inventory:**

Inventory of supplies	80	
Reserved for inventories		80

If this represents the first year of operations for the specific government department, **the equity (fund balance) section** of the balance sheet will report the following amounts:

Fund balance – Unreserved	150
Fund balance – Reserved for encumbrances	30
Fund balance – Reserved for inventories	80

Lecture 29.02

Fund Types

Government activities are not all accounted for using the modified accrual method. Some activities closely resemble the activities of private businesses, and use accrual accounting. A **self-balancing set of accounts**, known as a **fund**, is established for each category of activity.

There are **3 broad categories** of funds and these contain **11 fund types**:
- **Governmental Funds** – generally have a budgetary focus and the main emphasis of reporting is the sources, uses and balances of *current financial resources*. These are for activities that are primarily funded by taxation or other mandatory payments and are virtually unique to government. **Modified accrual** accounting is used.

- **Proprietary Funds** – generally have an operations orientation and the main emphasis of reporting is determining income, financial position, changes in financial position, and cash flows using the economic resources approach. These are for activities that are primarily funded by voluntary payments for goods and services by users, and that resemble businesses. **Accrual accounting** is used, in a virtually identical fashion to private businesses.

- **Fiduciary Funds** – generally are oriented toward the accounting for assets and the main emphasis of reporting is net position and changes to net position using the economic resources approach. These are for activities that most closely resemble not-for-profit organizations, including trusts and agency activities. The trust and agency funds use **Accrual accounting**.

The **five governmental funds** as defined by GASB 54 are: **(Modified Accrual)**
- **General** – this fund accounts for and reports any activity or function by the government unit that is not being accounted for in another fund, such as ordinary operations, public safety, public works, culture and recreation. Revenue sources include income, sales, and property taxes, fees, fines, licenses, permits and grants. Unassigned fund balance.

- **Special Revenue** – these funds are used to account for and report specific revenues from *earmarked* sources that are restricted or committed to be used to finance designated activities other than Capital Projects and Debt Service. An example is a gas tax that finances repairs and maintenance of the roads. Revenue sources include fees, grants, specific taxes and other earmarked revenue sources. Restricted or committed fund balance.

- **Capital Projects** – These funds account for major acquisition or construction activities of capital assets, other than those financed by proprietary or trust funds. This fund accounts for and reports the financial resources that are restricted, committed or assigned for these types of capital outlay. An example is the construction of a city hall, convention center or a county courthouse. Revenue sources include special tax revenues, proceeds from bonds, transfers or capital grants.

- **Debt Service** – This fund is responsible for accumulating and making interest and principal payments on the tax supported debts of the governmental funds. The DSF accounts for and reports the resources that are restricted, committed or assigned for this L/T debt purpose. The expenditures may also Include premiums on issuance of bonds. Revenue sources include portions of property taxes and transfers.

- **Permanent** – These funds account for and report assets whose principal is restricted and may not be spent (nonexpendable fund), but must be invested on a permanent basis (the income is, however, spendable/expendable – endowment fund). Investments are reported at their fair values, with a few minor exceptions as per GASB 72. Revenue sources are usually from the investment earnings of the trust.

A government unit must have one general fund, but can establish as many special revenue, capital projects, and permanent funds as needed to account for the various activities that fit these categories. A debt service fund is only needed if the entity issues general obligation debts.

There are **two proprietary funds: (Accrual)**
- **Internal Service** – These funds render services or provide goods to other funds within the government entity, charging the other funds directly for those services. An example is a maintenance dept, IT dept, janitorial dept or a motor pool. Revenue sources include billings for services, grants and interest earnings.

- **Enterprise** – These funds account for activities financed by voluntary payments for goods and services rendered to the payers. Often a user fee is paid. Examples include a city-operated water utility, airports, transit systems, public hospitals, public universities, public housing, lotteries or a post office. Revenue sources include charges for services, interest and investment income, shared revenues (property or gas tax) and transfers in.

A government will establish as many enterprise and internal service funds as needed to account for activities that fit these descriptions. Although it is acceptable for these funds to receive some tax money, the majority of revenue must be earned from sales of goods or services.

There are **four fiduciary funds: (Accrual)**
- **Pension trust** (and other employee benefits) – These account for government employee pensions and other post-retirement benefits for which the government is trustee. 2 RSI schedules are required: Funding progress & employer contributions.

- **Investment trust** – these account for pooled resources that are being invested on behalf of multiple government entities for which this specific government entity is trustee.

- **Private purpose trust** – these account for resources that are being held for the benefit of private persons or organizations or other governments. Examples include a fund to hold cash for unclaimed tax refunds or escheat property as well as a scholarship fund. Could be expendable or nonexpendable.

- **Agency** – these account for collected amounts that must be transferred to other funds or outsiders. An odd characteristic of agency funds is that all of the assets held belong to others (held in a custodial capacity), so assets always equal liabilities, and the agency fund has no equity section at all. Examples include special assessments and the property tax assessor.
    - Special assessment (street lights, sidewalk)
        - Government obligated – capital projects or debt service fund.
        - Government NOT obligated – Agency fund

- Fiduciary funds account for resources held by a government in a trustee or agency capacity for other entities. The application of measurement focus and basis of accounting to fiduciary funds is similar to the one used for proprietary funds. All trust funds make use of the economic resources measurement focus and the accrual basis of accounting in the same way as proprietary funds. Agency funds, however, are a bit atypical in that they only report assets and liabilities. Accordingly, Agency funds do not report equity and do not utilize measurement focus, but do employ the **accrual basis** of accounting to recognize assets and liabilities.

To summarize, the **Modified accrual funds** are (**PD**-**C**onsents-to-**S**moking **G**rass):
- **P**ermanent
- **D**ebt service
- **C**apital projects
- **S**pecial revenue
- **G**eneral

The **Accrual funds** are (**I-PIPE-A**lot):
- **I**nternal service
- **P**ension trust

- **I**nvestment trust
- **P**rivate-purpose trust
- **E**nterprise
- **A**gency

Note: prior to the passage of GASB 34 there were two other funds and two account groups.
- **Non-expendable trust fund** – These assets are now reported in **permanent funds**.
- **Expendable trust fund** – These assets are now reported in **special revenue funds** if the government directly spends the amounts, or in **agency funds** if the government merely transfers the amounts to outsiders.
- **General long-term asset account group** – This group formerly accounted for the capital assets held by the governmental funds. The funds are now directly responsible for keeping track of these assets, and depreciation is recorded in the **government-wide financial statements** for these assets (but not in individual fund statements).
- **General long-term debt account group** – This group formerly accounted for the long-term obligations of the governmental funds for which the debt service fund was responsible, directly or indirectly, for repayment. The debt service fund is now directly responsible for keeping track of these liabilities in the **government-wide financial statements** (but not in individual fund statements).

FINANCIAL REPORTING

GASB 34, as amended by GASB 63, requires a governmental entity to provide a Comprehensive Annual Financial Report (CAFR), which consists of three sections:
- Introductory
- Financial
- Statistical

The introductory section will include a transmittal letter and the statistical section will include financial, economic, and demographic information. The focus of the accounting, however, is the financial section, which consists of five components:
1. Management discussion & analysis (MD&A)
2. Government-wide financial statements
3. Fund financial statements
4. Notes to the financial statements
5. Required supplementary information (RSI) other than MD&A

It is important to be comfortable with the content of each of the five sections. Discussion of each follows.

1 - Management Discussion & Analysis (MD&A)

The first section of the financial report is a discussion by management of the significant activities of the government as a whole during the reporting period and for the future. It also provides an overview of the government's financial activities. MDA is considered to be Required Supplementary Information (RSI). Items to be included are:
- **Comparison with prior year** – A brief discussion of the financial statements with an analysis of amounts that changed considerably from the preceding year.

- **Overall financial statements** – Condensed information from the government-wide financial statements to follow with discussion of overall results.
- **Individual fund statements** – Key account information from the individual fund statements to follow with analysis of individually significant accounts.
- **Variance analysis** – Discussion of major differences between the original and final budgets for the year, and actual results for the year.
- **Long-term activities** – Discussion of significant capital asset and long-term debt activity for the year, and the condition of infrastructure assets.
- **Expected events** – Descriptions of known facts, decisions, and conditions that may have a significant effect on future financial position and results of operations.

2 - Government-Wide Financial Statements (Accrual)

The financial statement presentation in the second section of the financial report consists of **two financial statements**: *a statement of net position and a statement of activities* for the overall government entity. The government-wide statements are prepared on **the economic resources measurement focus** and **accrual basis** of accounting. All activities of the primary government are included, with the exception of fiduciary activities, as well as discretely presented component units. These statements are designed to provide information about **Operational Accountability** which shows how effective and efficient the organization has been at using its resources, and the resources available to meet its future obligations.

2a - The Statement of Net Position

The Statement of Net Position (formally Net Assets) is a type of balance sheet, except that the form is: "Assets + Deferred *outflows* of Resources – Liabilities – Deferred *Inflows* of Resources = Net Position". This format is called the **Net Position Format**, which is encouraged, although a *balance sheet format* is also permitted (assets plus deferred outflows of resources equal liabilities plus deferred inflows of resources plus net position).
- Regardless of which format is used, however, the statement of net position will report the residual amount as the **net position**, consisting of **three components**
    - Net investment in capital assets
    - Restricted net position
    - Unrestricted net position
- Terms like net assets, fund balance, or equity should not be used.
- It is preferred to present assets and liabilities in order of liquidity

The **net investment in capital assets** is the total of capital assets reduced by accumulated depreciation and obligations, including bonds, mortgages, notes, and other borrowings, that are associated with the acquisition, construction, or improvement of capital assets.

The **restricted net position** consists of restricted assets net of liabilities and deferred inflows of resources that are related to restricted assets.

The **unrestricted net position** is the residual amount.

Deferred Outflows and Deferred Inflows of Resources

When the government consumes net assets, it is considered an outflow of resources if it is applicable to the current reporting period. **Deferred outflows** of resources represent the consumption of net assets that are applicable to a future reporting period. Deferred outflows of resources are not assets, but are similar in that they have a positive effect on net position.

- Prepaid rent, for example, would not be an example of a deferred outflow. This is because the outflow of resources, cash, is matched by the inflow of resources, prepaid rent and, as a result, net position has not decreased.
- *Grant expenditures made in advance* of the grantee meeting timing requirements on the other hand, is a deferred outflow. The outflow of resources, cash, is not matched by an inflow of resources and, as a result, net position has decreased

Similarly, inflows of resources are acquisitions of net assets that are applicable to the current reporting period. **Deferred inflows** of resources are basically the opposite of deferred outflows of resources. They are acquisitions of net assets that are applicable to a future reporting period. Deferred inflows are not liabilities, but they are similar in that they have a negative effect on net position.
- Deferred revenue, for example, would not be an example of a deferred inflow. This is because the inflow of resources, cash, is matched by incurring an obligation to perform, a liability and, as a result, net position has not increased.
- *Grant funds received in advance* of the grantee meeting timing requirements on the other hand, is a deferred inflow. The inflow of resources, cash, is not matched by an obligation as the grant funds would have been received with the passage of time and, as a result, net position has increased.

There is still a lot of confusion as to when an item is an asset or liability and when it is a deferred outflow or deferred inflow of resources, respectively. GASB 65 was issued to provide some clarification.

Many items that result from government activities may be considered **deferred outflows of resources or deferred inflows of resources**, depending on which side of the transaction the governmental entity is on. Some of the items that are addressed include:
- Current and advanced debt refunding
    - Reacquisition cost in excess of carrying value is a deferred outflow.
    - Carrying value in excess of reacquisition cost is a deferred inflow.
- Nonexchange revenue transactions
    - Imposed nonexchange revenues, such as property taxes, received or accrued in advance are deferred inflows.
    - Government-mandated and voluntary nonexchange transactions paid or received before timing requirements are met are deferred outflows or deferred inflows, respectively.
- Sales of future revenues
    - Amounts paid for the rights are deferred outflows.
    - Proceeds from sale are deferred inflows.
- Sale and leaseback transactions
    - Deferred losses are deferred outflows.
    - Deferred gains are deferred inflows.
- Grants
    - Expenditures paid before timing requirements have been met are deferred outflows.
    - Amounts received before timing requirements have been met are deferred inflows.
- Qualified hedging derivatives
    - A negative fair value is a deferred outflow.
    - A positive fair value is a deferred inflow.
- Service concession arrangements
    - Consideration paid represents deferred outflows.

- Consideration received represent deferred inflows.

If deferred outflows or deferred inflows are disclosed in the aggregate, the notes to the financial statements should describe the details of what is included in the net amounts.

GASB also describes items that are recognized as **assets or liabilities** and as current outflows (expenditures), and current inflows (revenues). Examples of items that remain as assets and liabilities include:
- Government mandated nonexchange revenue transactions
    - Amounts transmitted before eligibility requirements are met, other than timing requirements, are deferred outflows and reported as assets.
    - Amounts received before eligibility requirements are met, other than timing requirements, are deferred inflows and reported as liabilities.
- Prepaid insurance is recognized as an asset
- Commitment fees received for a commitment to originate or purchase a loan are generally recognized as liabilities

Items that will be reported as **current outflows or current inflows** include:
- Debt issue costs, other than prepaid insurance costs, are recognized as expense as incurred.
- Initial direct costs of an operating lease incurred by a lessor are recognized as expense as incurred.
- Acquisition costs related to insurance activities are recognized as expense as incurred.
- Loan origination fees other than points that are part of lending activities
    - Are recognized as revenue when received.
    - Are recognized as expense when incurred.
- Purchases of loans
    - Amounts paid to purchase loans are recognized as expense
    - Fees received related to the purchase of loans are recognized as revenues

Full accrual accounting is to be used, including the recording and depreciation of fixed assets, including infrastructure. Note that "net position" is broken down into three categories: (1) Net investment in capital assets, (2) restricted net position, and (3) unrestricted net position. The term "net investment in capital assets" is computed by taking the value of capital (fixed) assets, less accumulated depreciation, less the debt associated with the acquisition of the capital assets.

There are **four columns** on the **Statement of Net Position**:
- **Governmental activities** – Governmental activities are those that are financed primarily through taxes and other nonexchange transactions. This reports in a single column the consolidated results of all the **governmental and internal service** funds. The presentation uses **accrual** accounting, even though the government funds are all modified accrual funds. Capital assets are reported and depreciated in the asset section, and long-term debt is included in the liability section. Interfund transactions within this column are eliminated, so that the internal service fund is often effectively eliminated. Interfund transactions with the enterprise and fiduciary funds are **not** eliminated, however, so the government as a whole is not actually consolidated.

- **Business-type activities** – Business-type activities are those normally financed through user charges. This reports in a single column the consolidated results of all the enterprise funds (note it does not include internal service funds, which were accounted for in the governmental column). Accrual accounting is used here as in the individual fund accounting. Interfund transactions among the various enterprise funds are eliminated, but not transactions with other fund-types.

- **Total** – This column simply adds together the amounts from the two primary government columns for governmental and business-type activities (note that fiduciary activities were not reported in either of the two previous columns, so this total doesn't actually reflect all of the net assets held by the government).

- **Component units** – A legally separate organization for which the elected officials of a primary government are financially accountable. This reports in a single column the combined results of all the component units for which separate reporting was selected (those receiving blended treatment were already included in one of the first two columns of this statement). No eliminations are made.

So component units of the primary government could include autonomous units, such as a school district, which operate with separate budgets and management. The accounting for these **component units** may be either:

- **Separately stated (discreetly presented)** – When the management of the unit consists of separately elected officials with budgets developed separately from the primary government, and the services provided by the unit are not primarily to the government itself, separate accounting for the activities of the component unit in separate columns is usually appropriate.

- **Blended** – When the component unit serves other parts of the primary government, or is dependent on the overall government legislative body for funding or budgeting, it may be more appropriate to account for the activities of the component unit along with the remaining funds of the government. Where it serves the other departments and is paid by those departments, an internal service fund may be appropriate. Where funding is received from services to outsiders, an enterprise fund may be appropriate. Blending is also required for a component unit that was incorporated as a not-for-profit corporation with the government as the only corporate member. Shown in the *Governmental Activities column.*

- The GASB requires reporting as a component unit, an entity that raises and holds economic resources for the direct benefit of a government (ex. A library society that raises money, which will go to the government that operates the library). If meet all 3 criteria, ***discretely present*** in separate columns as a component unit.
    1. **Direct benefit** – the funds are nearly totally all for the direct benefit of the primary government, its component units, or it constituents.

    2. **Majority** – the primary government or its component unit is entitled to a majority of the economic resources received or held by the separate entity.

    3. **Significance** – the resources are significant to that primary government.

> **Component units**
> **Discrete presentation** in separate columns if:
> - A separate elected governing board
> - Legally separate
> - Fiscally independent – authority to:
>   - Determine its budget
>   - Levy taxes w/o approval
>   - Issue bonded debt w/o approval
>   - Separately stated
>
> **Blend** with other funds if activities cannot be separated, and would be misleading to exclude them.
> - The governing body of comp unit is the same as that of the primary gov
>   - A financial burden/benefit relationship exists
>   - Or mgmt of the primary gov has operational responsibility for the component unit
> - The comp unit provides services almost entirely for the benefit of the primary gov
> - The comp unit's debt is expected to be repaid by the primary gov.
>
> Place in *Governmental activities* column

Accounting for **infrastructure** assets (streets, sidewalks, highways, etc.) in the governmental activities column has several complications. The ***preferred approach*** is to account for these assets at historical cost and **recognize depreciation** (remember that the governmental activities column in the government-wide financial statements uses accrual accounting). Several governments find the recordkeeping burdensome, however, since the ongoing expenditures for repairs, maintenance, and improvements for such assets can make it difficult to gauge total costs and tend to result in lives for these assets which are, in a sense, indefinite in duration.

GASB 34, as amended by GASB 63, permits governments to omit depreciation on infrastructure assets if they can demonstrate that the regular costs incurred to maintain them give them an indefinite life. This is called the **Modified approach**. This approach may be used if (1) the government uses an asset management system to manage the infrastructure and (2) the government documents how the assets are being preserved at a minimum level established by the government.

If these conditions are met, infrastructure assets are recorded as capital expenditures and NOT depreciated; however, additions and improvements are still capitalized. Two schedules are included in the required supplementary information:

- A schedule reflecting the condition of the government's infrastructure
- A schedule comparing needed and actual expenditures of maintaining the infrastructure.

Intangible assets that are identifiable should be recognized in the statement of net position at historical cost.

2b - The Statement of Activities

The Statement of Activities reports revenues and expenses, on the full accrual basis. This is a consolidated statement except that interfund transactions are not eliminated, when those transactions are between governmental and business-type activities, and between the primary government and discretely presented component units. Expenses are reported by function. Revenues are also reported on the accrual basis and may be exchange revenues or nonexchange revenues.

Program revenues, those that are directly associated with the functional expense categories, are deducted to arrive at the net expense or revenue. Note that program revenues include (1) charges for services, (2) operating grants and contributions, and (3) capital grants and contributions, although program revenues are not limited to the three categories.

Charges for services are deducted from the function which creates the revenues. Grants and contributions are reported in the function to which their use is restricted. The net expense or

revenue is broken out between governmental activities, business-type activities, and component units, the same as in the Statement of Net Position. General revenues are deducted from the net expenses to obtain net revenues. General revenues include all taxes levied by the reporting government and other nonexchange revenues not restricted to a particular program. After that, separate additions or deductions are made for special items, extraordinary items, and transfers (between categories). If a government had contributions to term and permanent endowments and contributions to permanent fund principal, these would also be shown after general revenues. Finally, the net position at the beginning and end of the year are reconciled.

Lecture 29.04

3 - Fund Financial Statements (Governmental, Proprietary & Fiduciary)

The third section of the report includes information about individual funds and component units. In addition to government-wide statements, GASB 34, as amended by GASB 63, requires a number of fund financial statements. Most governments use fund accounting internally and prepare the government-wide statements with worksheet adjustments from this fund accounting base. Fund Financial Statements use Fiscal Accountability, which shows the organizations compliance with laws and regulations affecting its spending activities.

Fund financial statements are presented separately for the governmental, proprietary, and fiduciary fund categories. Each government has only one general fund; each other fund type may have any number of individual funds, although GASB encourages having as few funds as possible. Fixed assets and long term debt are not reported in the fund financial statements, only in the government-wide financial statements.

There will be 4 complete sets of financial statements in most cases.
- ***Governmental funds*** – (General fund, Special revenue, Capital projects, Debt service & Permanent) A **balance sheet** and **statement of revenues, expenditures, and changes in fund balance** will be prepared with columns for each major fund and a total for all minor funds. This time, the reporting will be on a **modified accrual** basis, with a reconciliation of the numbers to the government-wide financial statements that were prepared on an accrual basis (and which included the internal service funds). There is no need to identify the specific fund type (special revenue, capital projects, etc.) for the different major funds

being reported. The Balance Sheet would also include deferred outflows of resources and deferred inflows of resources, like the government wide statement of net position.

Governmental fund F/S – (modified accrual basis, Current financial resources approach, current assets and liabilities only, no fixed assets or L/T debt)

- **Balance sheet** (Current Assets + Deferred Outflows = Current Liabilities + Deferred Inflows + fund balance)
    - Fund balance (5 categories)
    - Reconcile fund balance to statement of N/A Gov. wide (Gov. Activ)
- **Statement of revenues, expenditures, and changes in fund balances**
    - Reconcile Rev. and Expenditure from Modified accrual to accrual

---

The reconciliation of the Governmental fund balance to the government-wide statement of net position includes adjustments for fixed assets, issuance of L/T Debt, debt service payments, revenue recognition, accrual of revenue and expenses (modified accrual vs accrual) and must also include the Internal Service fund. The reconciliation will appear as follows:

Alexes City
Reconciliation of Governmental Fund Balances to Net Position of Governmental Activities
December 31, 20X1

Total governmental fund balances	$10,000,000
Long-term assets used by governmental funds	61,000,000
Internal service fund balances	1,000,000
Long-term liabilities incurred by governmental funds	(30,000,000)
Net Position of governmental activities	$42,000,000

There may be constraints on how funds can be spent. As a result, there are **5 fund balance classifications** that are classified in a hierarchy that is designed to indicate the extent to which government is bound to honor those constraints. The classifications, ranging from the *most restrictive to the least restrictive*, are:

- A **nonspendable fund balance** includes funds that cannot be spent for one of two reasons:
    1. They are not in spendable form, such as assets like inventories or prepaid expenses that are not expected to be converted into cash; and long-term loans or notes receivable and property held for resale, unless they are restricted, committed, or assigned.
    2. They are legally or contractually required to be maintained, such as the principal balance of a permanent fund.

- A **restricted fund balance** includes funds that are restricted for a specific purpose. Restrictions may be:
    1. Imposed externally, such as by creditors, grantors, contributors, or the laws or regulations of others
    2. Imposed by law

- A **committed fund balance** includes funds that are required to be used for a specific purpose as a result of constraints imposed by the highest level of decision-making authority.

- An **assigned fund balance** includes funds that the government INTENDS to spend for a specific purpose but are not restricted or committed and do not require assignment by the highest level of decision-making authority.

- The **unassigned fund balance** includes all General funds that do not belong in another classification, such as not being restricted, committed or assigned to a specific purpose.

Lecture 29.05

Proprietary Funds

Proprietary funds (Internal Service & Enterprise Fund) – **A statement of net position** (Balance Sheet), **statement of revenues, expenses, and changes in fund net position, and statement of cash flows** will be prepared with columns for each major enterprise fund and a total for all minor enterprise funds. The internal service funds are reported in a separate column in these statements (note their inclusion here and **not** with the governmental funds, where they were grouped in the government-wide financial statements). The statement of **cash flows, with a few adjustments**, is similar to that of a private entity except that there are 4 sections to the statement. The sections of the statement are **(a)** Operating, (must be prepared under the direct method with a reconciliation (indirect) also presented) which does not include any interest or dividends here, **(b)** Noncapital Financing (for unsecured loans including interest expense and cash received from property taxes or grants), **(c)** Capital & related Financing (for financed purchases and sales of capital assets, normally investing and also interest expense), and **(d)** Investing, which includes both interest and dividends received (normally operating) and also includes inflows and outflows associated with loans to others. A reconciliation of operating income (not net income) to net cash flow from operating activities is required.
- Some governmental entities are involved in loan programs, such as providing low-income mortgage loans or student loans.
- The making and collecting of loans is the primary activity of such entities.
- As a result, loans made and collected by such entities, including interest, are reported as operating activities.

All accounting is on an **accrual basis**, just as it was in the government-wide financial statements.

> **Proprietary fund F/S** –(Accrual basis, Current Economic resources approach, current and non-current assets and liabilities)
>
> - **Statement of Net Position (Balance Sheet)**
> - **Statement of revenues, expenses, and changes in fund net position (fund equity)**
> - **Statement of cash flows (4 sections)**
>   - **Operating** – direct method is required (no interest/div here)
>   - **Investing**
>   - Includes interest/Div income
>   - No capital asset acq/disposal
>   - Loans made
>   - **Noncapital financing**
>   - Includes interest exp on unsecured loans
>   - Transfers, grants, subsidies and property taxes received
>   - **Capital & related financing**
>   - Includes interest exp. on secured loans for capital assets
>   - Includes financed purchases and sales of capital assets (normally investing)
>   - Reconciliation of operating income to net cash from operating activities must be provided.

Lecture 29.06

Fiduciary Funds

Fiduciary funds (Pension trust, investment trust, private purpose trust, & agency) – A **statement of fiduciary net position** and **statement of changes in fiduciary net position** will be prepared with columns for each major fiduciary fund and a total for all minor fiduciary funds. Since agency funds always have a net asset balance of zero (all assets are owed to outsiders and, therefore, have equal liabilities), they will not be included in the statement of changes in fiduciary net position only on the statement of fiduciary net position. The Trust and Agency funds use the **accrual basis** and the Economic resources approach. Remember that none of these funds were included in the government-wide financial statements.

In the above description of fund statements, it was noted that there would be a column for each major fund and then a total for all minor ones in the financial statements for each of the three fund categories (governmental, proprietary, and fiduciary). All of the following are considered major funds.

Major Funds

Major Funds - On the fund financial statements, we report by major fund category as opposed to by fund type. A major fund is:
- General fund
- Other funds representing **BOTH:**
  - **10% or more** of total category assets, liabilities, revenues or expenditures/expenses of either Governmental or Enterprise category. **&**

- - **5% or more** of total <u>entity</u> (Gov & Enterprise) assets, liabilities, revenues or expenditures/expenses.
- Any other funds that management believes are **useful** to present separately.

4 - Notes to the Financial Statements

The fourth section of the general purpose financial statements is the Notes to the financial statements. These are a required part of the basic financial statements and should provide information that is not displayed on the face of the financial statements and is essential to their fair presentation.

Notes should distinguish whether they pertain to the primary government or its discretely presented component units.

The *Basic Financial statements (BFS)* consist of 2 + 3 + 4 above. The Notes essential to fair presentation include:
- Summary of accounting policies, including:
  - A description of the government-wide financial statements
  - The basis of accounting applied, such as accrual for government-wide financial statements and proprietary and fiduciary fund statements, and modified accrual for government fund financial statements
  - Policies regarding cash and cash equivalents; capitalization and determining useful lives; and infrastructure
- Disclosures related to:
  - Cash
  - Investments
  - Significant contingent liabilities
  - Significant effects of subsequent events
  - Pensions and other postemployment benefits
  - Significant violations of legal or contractual provisions
  - Debt service requirements
  - Leases
  - Construction and other significant commitments
  - Capital assets
  - Long-term liabilities
  - Deficit in fund balance or net position
  - Interfund balances and transfers
  - Donor-restricted endowments
- Related party transactions
- A description of the reporting entity
- Segment information for enterprise funds

In addition, GASB 42 requires disclosures about *capital asset impairment* if both (a) the decline in service utility of the asset is large in magnitude, and (b) the event or change in circumstance is outside the normal life cycle of the capital asset (unexpected). If the asset is no longer to be used, it should be reported at the lower of carrying value or fair value.

5 - Required Supplementary Information (RSI) other than MD&A

The fifth and final section of the financial report includes other information required by various GASB pronouncements. The most important is **a statement of revenues, expenditures, and changes in fund balance – budget & actual**, called a ***Budgetary comparison schedule (BCS)***. This schedule is required for every governmental fund that prepared annual budgets (typically the general fund and special revenue funds, but also sometimes including others).

The **4 types of RSI**, other than MDA, that are **required** under GASB are:
- Budgetary Comparison Schedules (BCS) (sample in back)
- Information about Infrastructure Assets (for Entities Reported Using the Modified Approach)
    - A schedule reflecting the condition of the government's infrastructure,
    - A comparison of the needed and actual expenditures to maintain the government's infrastructure.
- Claims Development Information When the Government Sponsors a Public Entity Risk Pool
- 2 pension schedules:
    - Schedule of Funding Progress (for Entities Reporting Pension Trust Funds)
    - Schedule of Employer Contributions (for Entities Reporting Pension Trust Funds)

A Budgetary Comparison Schedule (BCS) may be presented as RSI or as a separate statement for the general fund and for each major special revenue fund that has a legally adopted annual budget. The BCS presents both the original and final budget as well as actual inflows, outflows, and balances (a sample is in the back).

The accounting method used for each statement is the basis that was used for the preparation of the fund's budget, even if this differs from the presentation of that fund in the financial statements in the second and third sections. Thus, a general fund which was given an annual budget prepared on the cash basis will prepare its statement of revenues, expenditures, and changes in fund balance – budget & actual on a cash basis, even though it was reported on an accrual basis in the government-wide financial statements and on a modified accrual basis in the fund financial statements.

Lecture 29.07

CLASS QUESTIONS

Please see the Class Questions and Class Solutions for this Lecture at the end of this Section.

Lecture 29.09
Class Example

The town of Shady Acres adopted the following budget for its general fund for the fiscal year:

Revenues	
Property Taxes	1800
Business Licenses	200
Total	2000

Expenditures	
Supplies	500
Stop Sign	1000
Computer	400
Total	1900

The following transactions occurred during the year:
1. The budget for the year was adopted by the town council.
2. $2,100 of property taxes were billed. $300 was expected to be uncollectible.
3. $200 was billed for renewals of business licenses.
4. Collections on property taxes turned out to be $1,900. The town wrote off $200 of the remaining delinquent balance.
5. Collections on business licenses totaled $300 as a result of new license applications.
6. Orders were placed for the supplies and computer with an expectation of the prices being equal to budgeted amounts. A contractor was found to put in the stop sign, but the town believes the cost-plus contract agreed to will result in a total bill of $1,500 when work is complete.
7. The supplies are received and a bill for $500 presented to the town by the vendor.
8. The stop sign was installed. Due to cost overruns, the final bill came to $3,000.
9. The town treasurer prepared the closing entries for the year. As of the close of the year, the computer had not yet been delivered. An inventory count revealed $100 of usable supplies still on hand.
10 The computers are received the following year at a cost of $550.

Required:

Prepare entries without explanations for the above activities of the General fund of the town.

Class Solution

Revenues

1. Set-up Budget

Estimated Revenues	2000	
Estimated other Financing Sources	0	
Budgetary Fund Balance – unreserved		100
Appropriations		1900
Estimated other financing Uses		0

2. Assess Property Taxes

Property Taxes Receivable	2100	
Allowance for Uncollectibles		300
Revenues		1800
Deferred Revenues		0

3. Bill Business Licenses

No Entry until Received

4. Collect Property Taxes

Cash	1900	
Taxes Receivable		1900

Over-collection of Property Taxes

Allowance for uncollectibles	100	
Revenues		100

Write-off Property Tax Receivables

Allowance for uncollectibles	200	
Taxes Receivable		200

5. Collect Business Licenses

Cash	300	
Revenues		300

Section 29 — Governmental Accounting

Lecture 29.10
Expenditures (Encumbrance Accounting): (not for repetitive expenditures such as salaries and rent)

6. Order Goods

Encumbrances	2400	
Reserved for Encumbrances		2400

7. Receive Supplies

Reserved for Encumbrances	500	
Encumbrances		500
Expenditures	500	
Vouchers Payable		500

8. Receive Stop Sign

Reserved for Encumbrances	1500	
Encumbrances		1500
Expenditures	3000	
Vouchers Payable		3000

9. Closing Entries
Close Budgetary entries

Appropriations	1900	
Estimated Other financing Use	0	
Budgetary Fund Balance – Unreserved	100	
Estimated Revenues		2000
Estimated Other financing Source		0

Close Actual accounts

Revenues	2200	
Fund balance – unreserved	1700	
Other Financing Sources	0	
Expenditures		3500
Encumbrances (to close out open purchase orders of 400)		400
Other financing Uses		0

To record the receipt of the computers the following year for $550 instead of $400

Encumbrance – Prior Year	400	
Fund balance – Unreserved		400
Reserved for Encumbrances	400	
Encumbrance – Prior Year		400

Governmental Accounting

This entry reverses the encumbrances which were closed at the end of the prior year to Fund Balance – Unreserved.

Receive computers the following year

Expenditures – Prior Year	400	
Expenditures	150	
Vouchers Payable		550

To Record the balance of supplies at year end

Inventories	100	
Reserved for Inventories		100

Lecture 29.11

CLASS QUESTIONS

Please see the Class Questions and Class Solutions for this Lecture at the end of this Section.

Lecture 29.12

Interfund Transactions

There are **four different** types of cash transfers that may take place between different funds:
- Operating transfers
- Quasi-external transactions
- Reimbursements
- Loans

Operating transfers, also called **interfund transfers** are the most common, and represent movements of cash from one fund to finance current period activities in another fund. It also includes establishing or closing out a fund, which used to be called *Residual equity transfers*. To distinguish them from ordinary revenues and expenditures/expenses, they are classified as **other changes**. The transferee reports the amount received as **other financial sources** if using modified accrual accounting and as **other revenues** if using accrual accounting. The transferor reports the amount paid as **other financial uses** if using modified accrual accounting and as **other expenses** if using accrual accounting. These accounts appear on the appropriate operating statements: statement of revenues, expenditures, and other changes or statement of revenues, expenses, and other changes.

For example, if $100 is sent from the general fund to the debt service fund to help finance interest payments that must be made that year, the entry in the **general fund** is:

Other financial uses	100	
Cash		100

The entry in the **debt service fund** is:

Cash	100	
Other financial sources		100

Quasi-external transactions are payments from one fund to another for services or goods that are being provided. These are reciprocal transactions, involving an earnings process, unlike the previous examples of operating and residual equity transfers, in which a transfer is made without any benefit received by the transferor. The transferee is receiving money that represents earned **revenue**, and the transferor reports the payment as an **expenditure**, if it uses modified accrual accounting and an **expense** if it uses accrual accounting.

For example, assume the town has a water utility enterprise fund whose customers include, along with the citizens of the town, the other departments of the government. If a bill of $300 is paid by the capital projects fund for water used in the current year, the entry in the **capital projects fund** is:

    Expenditures – utilities   300
        Cash   300

The entry in the **enterprise fund** is:

    Cash   300
        Revenues   300

Notice that this type of transaction could easily have taken place between unrelated entities in a normal supplier/customer relationship, and that is the reason for identifying these as quasi-external transactions.

Reimbursements are repayments from one fund to another for costs paid earlier on its behalf. The transferee will record the receipt of money as either a settlement of a **receivable** it recorded when making the payment or as a reduction of an earlier **expenditure** or **expense** it recorded. The transferor records the payment of money as the settlement of a **payable** it recorded when the other fund paid costs on its behalf or as its own **expenditure** or **expense**.

For example, assume the general fund paid $900 for 9 government employees to attend a conference, including 4 employees of the general fund itself and 5 employees of the internal service fund. The internal service fund later reimbursed the general fund $500 for its employees.

At the time of payment for the conference, the **general fund,** if it were **not** aware it was going to later be reimbursed, would have recorded:

    Expenditures – conference   900
        Cash   900

When the **internal service fund** later reimbursed the general fund, it would then have recorded:

    Expenses – conference   500
        Cash   500

This would have reduced the net expenditure of the **general fund**:

    Cash   500
        Expenditures – conference   500

On the other hand, if both funds knew at the time of the conference that the general fund would later be reimbursed, the entry in the **general fund** for its payment would have been:

Expenditures - conference	400	
Due from internal service fund	500	
Cash		900

At the same time, the **internal service fund** would have recorded:

Expenses – conference	500	
Due to general fund		500

The later reimbursement would settle the due to/due from accounts.

Loans are temporary transfers between funds that are to be repaid at a later date. They are handled through interfund **receivable** and **payable** accounts.

For example, if the enterprise fund lends $400 to the special revenue fund, the entry in the **enterprise fund** is:

Due from special revenue fund	400	
Cash		400

The entry in the **special revenue fund** is:

Cash	400	
Due to enterprise fund		400

Of course, the later repayment involves both funds making the exact opposite entries from the original loan entries.

According to GASB 34, as amended by GASB 63, transfers are reported on the government-wide statement of activities. For transfers to be reported, they must be between governmental activities and business-type activities. Two kinds of transfers that are reported on the statement of activities include (1) Permanent transfers or (2) Recurring transfers from either governmental activities to business-type activities, or vice-versa. Permanent transfers are made once, while the recurring transfers are typically made annually. A reimbursement would not be included, but a quasi-external would.

Public College and University Accounting – GASB 35

Public colleges and universities may be exclusively involved in government activities, in business-type activities, or may engage in both. If a public college or university is involved in more than one government program, or if it is involved in both government and business-type activities, it should follow the requirements for basic financial statements and RSI and present both:
- Fund financial statements
- Government-wide financial statements

If the public college or university is engaged in only one government activity, it may combine the statements using a columnar format.

Public colleges and universities that are only engaged in business-type activities are only required to present those financial statements that are required for enterprise funds. The basic financial statements and RSI will include:
- M D & A
- Enterprise fund financial statements
    - Statement of net position
    - Statement of revenues, expenses, and changes in net position
    - Statement of cash flows
- Notes to financial statements
- RSI

Lecture 29.13

Governmental Accounting (GASB) Concept Statements

The Governmental Accounting Concepts Statements form the GASB's conceptual framework which provides a foundation to guide the Board's development of accounting and financial reporting standards (much like FASB Concepts).

GASB Concept Statement #1 – Objectives of Financial Reporting

This concepts Statement **establishes the objectives** of general purpose external financial reporting by state and local governmental entities and applies to both (1). Governmental-type and (2.) Business-type activities.

The characteristics that affect financial reporting of *Governmental-type activities* are:
- **Primary** characteristics of government's structure and the services it provides:
    - The representative form of government and the separation of powers
    - The prevalence of intergovernmental revenues
    - The services provided to taxpayers

- **Control** characteristics resulting from government's structure:
    - The *budget* as an expression of public policy and financial intent and as a method of providing control
    - The use of fund accounting for control purposes

- **Other** characteristics:
    - The dissimilarities between similarly designated governments
    - The significant investment in non-revenue-producing capital assets
    - The nature of the political process.

The Board has identified three groups as the **primary users** of external state and local governmental financial reports:
- The citizenry
- Legislative and oversight bodies
- Investors and creditors.

Financial reports are used primarily to:
- Compare Actual financial results with the legally adopted budget;
- To assist in determining Compliance with finance-related laws, rules, and regulations;
- To assist in evaluating Efficiency and Effectiveness.
- To assess Financial condition and results of operations;

The Board believes that financial reporting plays a major role in fulfilling government's duty to:
- Be Publicly **Accountable** in a democratic society (taxpayer has a "right to know").
- Provide information to assist users in assessing **interperiod equity** (are current-year revenues sufficient to pay for current-year services or whether future taxpayers will be required to assume burdens for services previously provided).

State and local governmental financial reports should possess these basic characteristics: **understandability, reliability, relevance, timeliness, consistency, and comparability**.

The financial reporting **objectives set forth in GASB Concept statement #1** are:

Financial reporting should assist in fulfilling government's duty to be publicly **Accountable** and should enable users to assess that accountability by:
- Providing information to determine whether current-year revenues were sufficient to pay for current-year services
- Demonstrating whether resources were obtained and used in accordance with the entity's legally adopted budget, and demonstrating compliance with other finance-related legal or contractual requirements
- Providing information to assist users in assessing the service efforts, costs, and accomplishments of the governmental entity

Financial reporting should assist users in **evaluating the operating results** of the governmental entity for the year by:
- Providing information about sources and uses of financial resources
- Providing information about how it financed its activities and met its cash requirements
- Providing information necessary to determine whether its financial position improved or deteriorated as a result of the year's operations

Financial reporting should assist users in assessing the level of services that can be provided by the governmental entity and its **ability to meet its obligations** as they become due by:
- Providing information about its financial position and condition
- Providing information about its physical and other nonfinancial resources having useful lives that extend beyond the current year
- Disclosing legal or contractual restrictions on resources and the risk of potential loss of resources.

Governmental **Business-type activities** (run like a private business) are also subject to the objectives stated above because they are part of government so are therefore publicly **accountable**. Some business type activities are characterized by an exchange relationship involving "user charges", while others involve receiving significant operating subsidies, capital grants, or taxes from the general government.

GASB Concept Statement #2 - Service Efforts and Accomplishments (SEA) Reporting (amended by concept statement #5)

This Concepts Statement further develops the objective, elements and characteristics of service efforts and accomplishments (SEA) reporting.

The objective of **SEA** *reporting* is to provide more complete information about a governmental entity's performance than can be provided by the traditional financial statements and schedules to assist users in assessing the economy, efficiency, and effectiveness of services provided.

This would expand the amount and types of information being gathered and reported externally; The Board believes that including SEA measures as part of General Purpose External Financial Reporting (GPEFR) would represent a significant improvement in financial reporting practices for state and local governmental entities.

Ideally a governmental entity should:
- Establish and communicate clear, relevant goals and objectives
- Set measurable targets for accomplishment
- Develop and report indicators that measure its progress

The elements of SEA reporting include:
- Measures of service effort
- Measures of service accomplishments (output and outcome measures)
- Measures that relate service efforts to service accomplishments (efficiency and cost-outcome measures)
- Narrative or explanatory information

GASB Concept Statement #3 - Communication Methods in General Purpose External Financial Reports (GPEFR) That Contain Basic Financial Statements

This Concept provides a conceptual basis for selecting communication methods to present items of information within general purpose external financial reports (GPEFR) that contain basic financial statements.
- These alternative communication methods include recognition in:
  - Basic financial statements
  - Disclosure in notes to basic financial statements
  - Presentation as required supplementary information
  - Presentation as supplementary information

Each of these communication methods is defined, and criteria are developed to help the GASB or a preparer of a financial report determine the appropriate method to use to communicate an item of information.

GASB Concept Statement #4 – 7 Elements of Financial Statements

This Concepts Statement establishes definitions for the seven elements of historically based financial statements of state and local governments. Elements are the fundamental components of financial statements.

The elements of a **Statement of Financial Position** are:
- **Assets** - Resources with present service capacity that the government presently controls.
- **Liabilities** - Present obligations to sacrifice resources that the government has little or no discretion to avoid.
- A **deferred outflow of resources** - A consumption of net assets by the government that is applicable to a future reporting period.
- A **deferred inflow of resources** - An acquisition of net assets by the government that is applicable to a future reporting period.
- **Net position** - The residual of all other elements presented in a statement of financial position.

Governmental Accounting
Section 29

The elements of the **Resource Flows Statements** are:
- An ***outflow of resources*** - A *consumption* of net assets by the government that is applicable to the reporting period.
- An ***inflow of resources*** - An *acquisition* of net assets by the government that is applicable to the reporting period.

A ***Resource*** in the governmental context is an item that can be drawn on to provide services to the citizenry.

GASB Concept Statement #5 – An amendment of GASB Concepts Statement No. 2

This amendment eliminated one section and modified four sections of Concepts Statement 2, already reflected in the definition of concept #2 above.

GASB Concept Statement #6 – Measurement of Elements of Financial Statements

This statement establishes two approaches for measurement used in financial statements.

Initial amounts are more appropriate for assets that are used in the entity's business, enabling it to provide goods and services. Initial amounts are based on transaction prices or amounts assigned to an asset when it was acquired or a liability when it was assumed.

Remeasured amounts, which are more appropriate for assets that will be converted into cash, financial assets, and for liabilities when there is uncertainty regarding the amount or timing of payments, involves remeasuring an asset or liability as of the balance sheet date.

There are 4 measurement attributes that are used in financial statements. These are:
- Historical Cost – the price paid to acquire an asset or the amount received when a liability was incurred in an exchange transaction.
- Fair value – the price that would be received to sell an asset or paid to be relieved of a liability in an orderly transaction between market participants.
- Replacement cost – the amount that would be paid to obtain resources with equivalent service potential in an orderly market transaction.
- Settlement amount – the amount that would be realized from disposal of an asset or the amount at which a liability could be liquidated when there is no active market.

GASB 63

GASB No. 63 amends GASB No. 34 to incorporate deferred outflows of resources and deferred inflows of resources into the financial reporting model.

GASB 63 changes the title of the "Statement of Net Assets" to the **"Statement of Net Position"** and provides (1) that deferred outflows should be reported in a separate section following assets, and (2) deferred inflows should be reported in a separate section following liabilities. The statement then arrives at net position which includes the net effects of assets, deferred outflows of resources, liabilities, and deferred inflows of resources. Net position consists of three components:
- Net investment in capital assets
- Restricted net position
- Unrestricted net position

In addition, the title of the "Statement of Revenues, Expenses and Changes in Net Assets" changes to the **"Statement of Revenues, Expenses, and Changes in Net Position."**

Use of the **net position format** is encouraged (assets plus deferred outflows of resources minus liabilities minus deferred inflows of resources equal net position); however, use of the **balance sheet format** (assets plus deferred outflows of resources equal liabilities plus deferred inflows of resources plus net position) also is permitted under GASB Statement 63.

GASB 65

GASB 65 was established to clarify which financial statements items are still considered Assets and Liabilities and which should be reclassified as Deferred Outflows and Inflows and which are considered current period Expenditures (outflows) or current period Revenues (inflows).

GASB 66

GASB 66 amends GASB 10, *Accounting and financial reporting for Risk Financing Related Insurance Issues*, GASB 10 required state and local governments to report risk financing activities exclusively in the general fund or an internal service fund. This pronouncement removes that limitation so that the decision as to which fund the activities should be reported in will be determined based on the nature of the activity.

GASB 67 & 68 Accounting and Financial Reporting for Pensions

GASB 67 revises existing guidance for the financial reports of most pension plans, and GASB 68 *also* revises and establishes new financial reporting requirements for most governments that provide their employees with pension benefits.

The provisions of both statements apply to pension plans that are administered through trusts and have all three of the following characteristics:
- Contributions and earnings are irrevocable
- Assets are dedicated to providing pension benefits
- Plan assets are protected from creditors that are not direct creditors of the plan itself, such as creditors of the sponsoring employer, nonemployer contributors, the plan administrator, and plan members.

Reporting is different for defined benefit plans and defined contribution plans. Defined benefit plans will provide 2 financial statements along with notes to the financial statements and RSI:
- Statement of fiduciary net position
- Statement of changes in fiduciary net position

A defined benefit pension plan defines the net pension liability as the total pension liability, based on actuarial valuations performed at least every two years, minus the pension plan's fiduciary net position.

A defined contribution plan is required to provide certain information in the *notes* to the financial statements:
- Identification of the plan as a defined contribution pension plan
- Classes of plan members covered
- Authority for establishing the plan

GASB 69 Government Combinations and Disposals of Government Operations

GASB 69 identifies **three types of combinations** between or among governmental units. The three types could be accounted for as a merger, an acquisition or a transfer. In order to be considered a combination among governments, as opposed to an acquisition of assets, the services that were provided by the combining governments must continue to be provided by the government surviving the merger.

1. A **governmental merger** occurs when two or more legally separate governments combine *without an exchange of consideration*.

    - The merger may result in all combining governments ceasing to exist, replaced by a **new government**.
    - The merger may result in all but one of the combining governments being absorbed into a **continuing government**.

    A merger resulting in a new government is recognized as of the date on which the combination becomes effective. A merger involving a continuing government is recognized as of the beginning of the period in which the combination occurs. In either case, the combination is recorded by recognizing assets, deferred outflows of resources, liabilities, and deferred inflows of resources at their ***carrying values***. Any transactions that occurred between merging entities before the combination and any receivables and payables between the merging entities are eliminated.

2. A **government acquisition** occurs when a government provides *significant consideration* in exchange for another entity or its operations. The acquisition date is considered the date on which the acquiring government takes control of the other entity's assets and becomes obligated for its liabilities. In an acquisition:

    - Assets, deferred outflows of resources, liabilities, and deferred inflows of resources are ***recognized*** by applying authoritative guidance for state and local governments.
        - The acquiring government may, as a result, recognize elements that were not required to be recognized by the acquired entity.
        - Goodwill recognized by an acquired entity, or the comparable deferred outflows of resources for acquired governmental entities, are not recognized in the acquisition
    - Assets, deferred outflows of resources, liabilities, and deferred inflows of resources are measured at ***acquisition values***.
        - Acquisition value is the price that would be paid to acquire similar assets with similar service capacities, or to discharge liabilities assumed.
        - Financial statement elements related to certain items are measured using applicable guidance rather than acquisition value:
            - Employee benefit arrangements, including compensated absences, pensions and other postemployment benefits, or termination benefits.
            - Municipal solid waste landfill closure and post-closure costs and obligations for pollution remediation
            - Investments, including derivatives
    - Consideration consists of the sum of the values of assets given and liabilities incurred to the former owners.
        - Contingent liabilities, such as contingent payments to former owners, are generally recognized when probable and estimable.
        - Consideration in excess of the net position acquired is recognized as a deferred outflow of resources.
        - When consideration is less than the net position acquired, the difference generally reduces nonfinancial noncurrent assets acquired
            - If reduced to zero, the excess is recognized as a special item on the flows statement
            - The terms of the arrangement may indicate the excess is a contribution or intended to provide economic aid to the acquiring government, in which case it is recognized as a contribution.

- Acquisition costs are recognized as expenses or expenditures in the period incurred. Costs of issuing debt are recognized in conformity with the applicable guidance for debt issuance.

3. A third type of combination is a **transfer of operations** in which the operations of a government or nongovernmental entity are transferred to a new or existing governmental entity *without the transfer of consideration*. An operation is an integrated set of activities, with associated assets and liabilities, designed to provide identifiable services.

    - The transfer is recognized on the date the governmental entity obtains control of assets associated with the operation and becomes obligated for its liabilities.
    - Assets, deferred outflows of resources, liabilities, and deferred inflows of resources are measured at their ***carrying values***.

Disclosures of the combinations would include:
- A description of the combination and the reasons for the merger, acquisition or transfer.
- The date of the combination
- The amounts recognized, the consideration provided and any significant adjustments made.

GASB 69 also addresses the **disposal of government operations**. It requires a government disposing of an operation to recognize a gain or loss, if applicable, as a special item in the statement of revenues, expenditures, and changes in fund balances in the period in which the disposal occurs.
- The gain or loss takes into account the consideration received, if any, the carrying value of assets and liabilities associated with the operation disposed of, and costs directly associated with the disposal.
- Costs associated with normal activities up to the measurement date are excluded.

GASB 70 Accounting and Financial Reporting for Nonexchange Financial Guarantees

GASB 70 applies when a governmental entity provides a guarantee of another entity's obligations without receiving compensation of comparable value. It requires the recognition of a liability when facts and circumstances indicate that it is *more likely than not* that the guarantor will be required to make a payment.

GASB 71 Pension Transition for Contributions Made Subsequent to the Measurement Date – An Amendment of GASB Statement No. 68

GASB 71 amends GASB 68 by requiring the recognition of contributions made to a pension plan after the measurement date on which the liability is measured for the purposes of applying GASB 68.

GASB 72 Fair Value Measurement and Application

GASB 72 defines fair value similarly to how it is defined under GAAP. Fair value is an *exit price* that is the amount that would be received to sell an asset or the amount that would be paid to transfer a liability in an orderly transaction between market participants. It is assumed that fair value is based on transactions that occur in the governmental unit's principal market or, when there is not principal market, the most advantageous market and is not adjusted for transaction costs.

Fair value is measured on the basis of the availability of data and is determined using the market approach, using information from market transactions involving identical or comparable assets or liabilities; the cost approach, based on the amount it would cost to replace an asset's service capacity; or the income approach, based on future revenues or cash flows.

Inputs are evaluated based on their relative reliability, similarly to GAAP.
- Level 1 inputs, the most reliable, are quoted market prices for identical assets or liabilities in an active market.
- Level 2 inputs are directly or indirectly observable inputs, other than level 1 quoted prices.
- Level 3 inputs, the least reliable, are unobservable inputs, including management's assumptions.

Values assume the *highest and best use* for nonfinancial assets. It is further assumed that liabilities will be transferred as opposed to settled with the counterparty.

Investments are required to be measured at fair value, with the exception of money market investments and certain interest-earning investment contracts that mature less than one year from purchase, which may be reported at amortized cost. Investments include securities or other assets that are being held primarily for income or profit such that it's only service capacity is its ability to generate cash or to be sold to generate cash.

Certain investments are not measured at fair value:
- Money market investments
- External investment pools
- Life insurance contracts
- Synthetic guaranteed investment contracts

Disclosures will include the level of inputs used to determine fair value and the valuation techniques applied.

GASB 73 Accounting and Financial Reporting for Pensions and Related Assets That Are Not within the Scope of GASB Statement 68, and Amendments to Certain Provisions of GASB Statements 67 and 68

GASB 73 expands the scope of the accounting and reporting requirements incorporated in GASB Statement 68 to include all pensions and assets accumulated for purposes of providing those pensions.

GASB 74 Financial Reporting for Postemployment Benefit Plans Other Than Pension Plans

GASB 74 requires defined benefit other postretirement employee benefit (OPEB) plans that are administered through trusts to provide two financial statements consisting of a statement of fiduciary net position and statement of changes in fiduciary net position. It also expands the disclosure requirements for such OPEB plans.

GASB 75 Accounting and Financial Reporting for Postemployment Benefits Other Than Pensions

GASB 75 establishes standards for recognizing and measuring liabilities, deferred inflows or outflows of resources, and expenses or expenditures for defined benefit other postemployment benefit (OPEB) plans. It also provides recognition and disclosure requirements for employers with payables to defined OPEB plans that are administered through trusts and meet certain criteria.

GASB 76 The Hierarchy of Generally Accepted Accounting Principles for State and Local Governments

GASB 76 establishes a hierarchy of accounting principles generally accepted for state and local governments that consists of two categories:
- Category A – Statements of the Governmental Accounting Standards Board (GASB)
- Category B – GASB Technical Bulletins; GASB Implementation Guides; and AICPA literature that has been cleared by the GASB.

GASB 77 Tax Abatement Disclosures

GASB 77 requires state and local governments to disclose certain information about tax abatement agreements, which are agreements entered into that limit the amount of tax the entity may be able to raise. Tax abatement agreements may establish maximum tax rates that will be required to be paid or a ceiling on the tax that might be collected and are used to encourage economic development.

Disclosures about tax abatement agreements entered into by a government will include:
- Information describing the tax being abated, the authority for the abatement, criteria for eligibility, the procedures by which taxes are abated, provisions for recapture, and commitments made by recipients.
- The gross amount of taxes abated for the period.

- Other commitments made by the government as part of the tax abatement agreement.

GASB 78 Pensions Provided through Certain Multiple-Employer Defined Benefit Pension Plans

GASB78 applies to certain pension plans provided to employees of state and local governments through a cost-sharing multiple-employer defined benefit plan. It excludes these plans from the requirements of GASB 68 and establishes separate reporting and disclosure requirements for them including the recognition and measurement of pension expense, expenditures, and liabilities; note disclosures; and required supplementary information. Plans that qualify under this statement will have the following characteristics:
- The plan is not a state or local governmental pension plan;
- The plan is used to provide defined benefit pensions both to employees of state or local governments and employees of other employers; and
- The plan has no predominant state or local governmental employer.

Pension expense is measured using the economic resources measurement focus. It will be equal to the employer's required contributions to the plan for the reporting period. A liability is recognized for unpaid required contributions as of the end of the period. In addition, liabilities will be accrued and pension expense will include amounts arising during the period that result from ***separate liabilities*** of the employer to the pension plan. These may include, for example, amounts assessed to an employer as a result of joining a cost-sharing plan.

Pension expenditures will be recognized in an amount equu8al to the employer's required contributions associated with pay periods within the reporting period. Pension expenditures will also include amounts paid by the employer in relation to separate liabilities and the change in the balances of amounts normally expected to be liquidated with expendable available resources.

Disclosures will include:
- The name of the plan, the administrator of the plan and identification as a cost-sharing plan;
- Whether or not the plan issues a publicly available financial report;
- A brief description of benefit terms;
- A brief description of contribution requirements; and
- Information about employer payables, if any.

Required supplementary information will include required contributions for each of the 10 most recent fiscal years.

GASB 79 Certain External Investment Pools and Pool Participants

GASB 79 allows for investment pools to make an election to report all investments at amortized cost for financial reporting purposes. In order to qualify to make the election, the pool must meet certain criteria related to:
- How the external investment pool transacts with participants;
- Requirements for the maturity, quality, diversification, and liquidity of the portfolio; and
- The calculation and requirements of a shadow price, which is the net asset value per share calculated using total investments measured at fair value.

Investment pools not meeting the criteria, short-term debt investments with maturities within 90 days of the financial statement date are reported at amortized cost. Others are reported at the fair value on the day it became a short-term investment.

GASB 80 Blending Requirements for Certain Component Units

GASB 80 requires the blending of a component unit that was incorporated as a not-for-profit corporation with the governmental unit is the sole corporate member.

GASB 81 Irrevocable Split-Interest Agreements

GASB 81 provides accounting guidelines for accounting for irrevocable split-interest agreements in which a donor provides resources to two or more beneficiaries, including governments, which may be through trusts or other forms of agreements. In such agreements, the donor transfers resources to an intermediary who holds and administers them on behalf of the government and one or more other recipients.

Sample City
STATEMENT OF NET POSITION
December 31, 20X1

	Primary government			
	Governmental activities	Business-type activities	Total	Component units
Assets				
Cash and cash equivalents	$ 13,597,899	$ 10,279,143	$ 23,877,042	$ 303,935
Investments	27,365,221	--	27,365,221	7,428,952
Receivables (net)	12,833,132	3,609,615	16,442,747	4,042,290
Internal balances	175,000	(175,000)	--	--
Inventories	322,149	126,674	448,823	83,697
Capital assets, net of acc dep (**Infrastructure**)	170,022,760	151,388,751	321,411,511	37,744,786
Total assets	224,316,161	165,229,183	389,545,344	49,603,660
Deferred outflows				
-Grant Expenditures paid in advance of meeting timing requirements				
-Deferred *Loss* from sale/leaseback				
-Payment to acquire rights to future parking revenue				
Liabilities				
Accounts payable	6,783,310	751,430	7,534,740	1,803,332
Deferred revenue	1,435,599	--	1,435,599	38,911
Noncurrent liabilities:				
Due within one year	9,236,000	4,426,286	113,662,286	1,426,639
Due in more than one year	83,302,378	74,482,273	157,784,651	27,106,151
Total liabilities	100,757,287	79,659,989	180,417,276	30,375,033
Deferred inflows				
-Grant amounts received in Advance of meeting timing requirements				
-Deferred *Gain* from Sale/leaseback				
Net Position				
Net Investment in capital assets	103,711,386	73,088,574	176,799,960	15,906,392
Restricted for:				
Capital projects	11,705,864	--	11,705,864	492,445
Debt service	3,020,708	1,451,996	4,472,704	--
Community development projects	4,811,043	--	4,811,043	--
Other purposes	3,214,302	--	3,214,302	--
Unrestricted (deficit)	(2,904,429)	11,028,624	8,124,195	2,829,790
Total net position	**$123,558,874**	**$ 85,569,194**	**$209,128,068**	**$19,228,627**

Sample City
STATEMENT OF ACTIVITIES
For the Year Ended December 31, 20X1

		Program revenues			Net (expense) revenue and changes in net Position			
					Primary government			
Functions/Programs	Expenses	Charges for services	Operating grants and Contributions	Capital grants and contributions	Governmental activities	Business-type activities	Total	Component units
Primary government								
Governmental activities:								
General government	$ 9,571,410	$ 3,146,915	$ 843,617	$ --	$ (5,580,878)	$ --	$ (5,580,878)	$ --
Public safety	34,844,749	1,198,855	1,307,693	62,300	(32,275,901)	--	(32,275,901)	--
Public works	10,128,538	850,000	--	2,252,615	(7,025,923)	--	(7,025,923)	--
Engineering services	1,299,645	704,793	--	--	(594,852)	--	(594,852)	--
Health and sanitation	6,738,672	5,612,267	575,000	--	(551,405)	--	(551,405)	--
Cemetery	735,866	212,496	--	--	(523,370)	--	(523,370)	--
Culture and recreation	11,532,350	3,995,199	2,450,000	--	(5,087,151)	--	(5,087,151)	--
Community development	2,994,389	--	--	2,580,000	(414,389)	--	(414,389)	--
Education (payment to school district)	21,893,273	--	--	--	(21,893,273)	--	(21,893,273)	--
Interest on long-term debt	6,068,121	--	--	--	(6,068,121)	--	(6,068,121)	--
Total governmental activities	105,807,013	15,720,525	5,176,310	4,894,915	(80,015,263)	--	(80,015,263)	--
Business-type activities:								
Water	3,595,733	4,159,350	--	1,159,909	--	1,723,526	1,723,526	--
Sewer	4,912,853	7,170,533	--	486,010	--	2,743,690	2,743,690	--
Parking facilities	2,796,283	1,344,087	--	--	--	(1,452,196)	(1,452,196)	--
Total business-type activities	11,304,869	12,673,970	--	1,645,919	--	3,015,020	3,015,020	--
Total primary government	$117,111,882	$28,394,495	$5,176,310	$6,540,834	(80,015,263)	3,015,020	(77,000,243)	--
Component units								
Landfill	$ 3,382,157	$ 3,857,858	$ --	$ 11,397	--	--	--	487,098
Public school system	31,186,498	705,765	3,937,083	--	--	--	--	(26,543,650)
Total component units	$ 34,568,655	$ 4,563,623	$3,937,083	$ 11,397	--	--	--	(26,056,552)

	Governmental activities	Business-type activities	Total	Component units
General revenues:				
Taxes:				
Property taxes, levied for general purposes	51,693,573	--	51,693,573	--
Property taxes, levied for debt service	4,726,244	--	4,726,244	--
Franchise taxes	4,055,505	--	4,055,505	--
Public service taxes	8,969,887	--	8,969,887	--
Payment from Sample City	--	--	--	21,893,273
Grants and contributions not restricted to specific programs	1,457,820	--	1,457,820	6,461,708
Investment earnings	1,958,144	601,349	2,559,493	881,763
Miscellaneous	884,907	104,925	989,832	22,464
Special item—gain on sale of park land	2,653,488	--	2,653,488	--
Transfers	501,409	(501,409)	--	--
Total general revenues, special items, and transfers	76,900,977	204,865	77,105,842	29,259,208
Change in net Position	(3,114,286)	3,219,885	105,599	3,202,656
Net Position—beginning	126,673,160	82,376,829	209,033,689	16,025,971
Net Position—ending	**$123,558,874**	**$85,596,714**	**$209,139,288**	**$19,228,627**

Sample City
BALANCE SHEET (GASB 54 classifications)
GOVERNMENTAL FUNDS
December 31, 20X1

	General	HUD Programs	Community redevelopment	Route 7 construction	Other governmental funds	Total governmental funds
Assets						
Cash and cash equivalents	3,418,485	$1,236,523	$ --	$ --	$ 5,606,792	$ 10,261,800
Investments	--	--	13,262,695	10,467,037	3,485,252	27,214,984
Receivables, net	3,644,561	2,953,438	353,340	11,000	10,221	6,972,560
Due from other funds	1,370,757	--	--	--	--	1,370,757
Receivables from other governments	--	119,059	--	--	1,596,038	1,715,097
Liens receivable	791,926	3,195,745	--	--	--	3,987,671
Inventories	182,821	--	--	--	--	182,821
Total assets	9,408,550	$7,504,765	$13,616,035	$10,478,037	$10,698,303	$ 51,705,690
Deferred Outflow						
-Deferred loss on sale and leaseback of building						
Liabilities and fund balances						
Liabilities						
Accounts payable	3,408,680	$129,975	$ 190,548	$1,104,632	$ 1,074,831	$ 5,908,666
Due to other funds	--	25,369	--	--	--	25,369
Payable to other governments	94,074	--	--	--	--	94,074
Deferred revenue	4,250,430	6,273,045	250,000	11,000	--	10,784,475
Total liabilities	7,753,184	6,428,389	440,548	1,115,632	1,074,831	16,812,584
Deferred inflows						
-Deferred gain on sale and leaseback of building						
Fund balances						
Nonspendable	974,747					974,747
Restricted			100,000			100,000
Committed	40,292	41,034	19,314	5,792,587	1,814,122	7,707,349
Assigned		1,035,342	13,056,173	3,569,818	7,809,350	25,470,683
Unassigned	640,327					640,327
Total fund balances	1,655,366	$1,076,376	$13,175,487	$9,362,405	$9,623,472	**$34,893,106**

Amounts reported for governmental activities in the statement of net assets are different because:

Capital assets used in governmental activities are not financial resources and therefore are not reported in the funds. ... 161,082,708

Other long-term assets are not available to pay for current-period expenditures and therefore are deferred in the funds. ... 9,348,876

Internal service funds are used by management to charge the costs of certain activities, such as insurance and telecommunications, to individual funds. The assets and liabilities of the internal service funds are included in governmental activities in the statement of net assets. ... 2,994,691

Long-term liabilities, including bonds payable, are not due and payable in the current period and therefore are not reported in the funds. ... (84,760,507)

Net Position of governmental activities ... **$123,558,874**

NOTE: Fund balances section of balance sheet has been modified to conform with GASB 54 fund balances classifications.

Sample City
STATEMENT OF REVENUES, EXPENDITURES, AND CHANGES IN FUND BALANCES
GOVERNMENTAL FUNDS
For the Year Ended December 31, 20X1

	General	HUD programs	Community redevelopment	Route 7 construction	Other governmental funds	Total governmental funds
Revenues						
Property taxes	$51,173,436	$ --	$ --	$ --	$4,680,192	$55,853,628
Franchise taxes	4,055,505	--	--	--	--	4,055,505
Public service taxes	8,969,887	--	--	--	--	8,969,887
Fees and fines	606,946	--	--	--	--	606,946
Licenses and permits	2,287,794	--	--	--	--	2,287,794
Intergovernmental	6,119,938	2,578,191	--	--	2,830,916	11,529,045
Charges for services	11,374,460	--	--	--	30,708	11,405,168
Investment earnings	552,325	87,106	549,489	270,161	364,330	1,823,411
Miscellaneous	881,874	66,176	--	2,939	94	951,083
Total Revenues	86,022,165	2,731,473	549,489	273,100	7,906,240	97,482,467
Expenditures						
Current						
General government	8,630,835	--	417,814	16,700	121,052	9,186,401
Public safety	33,729,623	--	--	--	--	33,729,623
Public works	4,975,775	--	--	--	3,721,542	8,697,317
Engineering services	1,299,645	--	--	--	--	1,299,645
Health and sanitation	6,070,032	--	--	--	--	6,070,032
Cemetery	706,305	--	--	--	--	706,305
Culture and recreation	11,411,685	--	--	--	--	11,411,685
Community development	--	2,954,389	--	--	--	2,954,389
Education—payment to school district	21,893,273	--	--	--	--	21,893,273
Debt service						
-Principal	--	--	--	--	3,450,000	3,450,000
-Interest and other charges	--	--	--	--	5,215,151	5,215,151
Capital outlay	--	--	2,246,671	11,281,769	3,190,209	16,718,649
Total expenditures	88,717,173	2,954,389	2,664,485	11,298,469	15,697,954	121,332,470
Excess (deficiency) of revenues over expenditures	(2,695,008)	(222,916)	(2,114,996)	(11,025,369)	(7,791,714)	(23,850,003)
Other Financing Sources (Uses)						
Proceeds of refunding bonds	--	--	--	--	38,045,000	38,045,000
Proceeds of long-term capital-related debt	--	--	17,529,560	--	1,300,000	18,829,560
Payment to bond refunding escrow agent	--	--	--	--	(37,284,144)	(37,284,144)
Transfers in	129,323	--	--	--	5,551,187	5,680,510
Transfers out	(2,163,759)	(348,046)	(2,273,187)	--	(219,076)	(5,004,068)
Total other financing sources and uses	(2,034,436)	(348,046)	15,256,373	--	7,392,967	20,266,858
Special Item						
Proceeds from sale of park land	3,476,488	--	--	--	--	3,476,488
Net change in fund balances	(1,252,956)	(570,962)	13,141,377	(11,025,369)	(398,747)	(106,657)
Fund balances-beginning	2,908,322	1,647,338	34,110	20,387,774	10,022,219	34,999,763
Fund balances—ending	$1,655,366	$1,076,376	$13,175,487	$9,362,405	$9,623,472	**$34,893,106**

Sample City
STATEMENT OF NET POSITION
PROPRIETARY FUNDS
December 31, 20X1

	Business-type activities Enterprise funds			Governmental Activities internal service fund
	Water and sewer	Parking facilities	Totals	
Assets				
Current assets:				
Cash and cash equivalents	$8,416,653	$369,168	$8,785,821	$3,336,099
Investments	--	--	--	150,237
Receivables, net	3,564,586	3,535	3,568,121	157,804
Due from other governments	41,494	--	41,494	--
Inventories	126,674	--	126,674	139,328
Total current assets	12,149,407	372,703	12,522,110	3,783,468
Noncurrent assets:				
Restricted cash and cash equivalents	--	1,493,322	1,493,322	--
Capital assets:				
Land	813,513	3,021,637	3,835,150	--
Distribution and collection systems	39,504,183	--	39,504,183	--
Buildings and equipment	106,135,666	23,029,166	129,164,832	14,721,786
Less accumulated depreciation	-15,328,911	-5,786,503	-21,115,414	-5,781,734
Total noncurrent assets	131,124,451	21,757,622	152,882,073	8,940,052
Total assets	143,273,858	22,130,325	165,404,183	12,723,520
Deferred Outflows				
Payment to receive rights to future parking Revenue				
Liabilities				
Current liabilities:				
Accounts payable	447,427	304,003	751,430	780,570
Due to other funds	175,000	--	175,000	1,170,388
Compensated absences	112,850	8,827	121,677	237,690
Claims and judgments	--	--	--	1,687,975
Bonds, notes, and loans payable	3,944,609	360,000	4,304,609	249,306
Total current liabilities	4,679,886	672,830	5,352,716	4,125,929
Noncurrent liabilities:				
Compensated absences	451,399	35,306	486,705	--
Claims and judgments	--	--	--	5,602,900
Bonds, notes, and loans payable	54,451,549	19,544,019	73,995,568	--
Total noncurrent liabilities	54,902,948	19,579,325	74,482,273	5,602,900
Total liabilities	59,582,834	20,252,155	79,834,989	9,728,829
Deferred Inflows				
Net Position				
-**Net Investment in capital assets**	72,728,293	360,281	73,088,574	8,690,746
-**Restricted** for debt service	--	1,451,996	1,451,996	--
-**Unrestricted**	10,962,731	65,893	11,028,624	-5,696,055
Total Net Position	**$83,691,024**	**$1,878,170**	**$85,569,194**	**$2,994,691**

Sample City
STATEMENT OF REVENUES, EXPENSES, AND CHANGES IN FUND NET POSITION
PROPRIETARY FUNDS
For the Year Ended December 31, 20X1

	Business-type activities—Enterprise fund			Governmental activities— Internal service funds
	Water and sewer	Parking facilities	Totals	
Operating revenues:				
Charges for service	$11,329,883	$1,340,261	$12,670,144	$15,256,164
Miscellaneous	--	3,826	3,826	1,066,761
Total operating revenues	11,329,883	1,344,087	12,673,970	16,322,925
Operating expenses:				
Personal services	3,400,559	762,348	4,162,907	4,157,156
Contractual services	344,422	96,032	440,454	584,396
Utilities	754,107	100,726	854,833	214,812
Repairs and maintenance	747,315	64,617	811,932	1,960,490
Other supplies and expenses	498,213	17,119	515,332	234,445
Insurance claims and expenses	--	--	--	8,004,286
Depreciation	1,163,140	542,049	1,705,189	1,707,872
Total operating expenses	6,907,756	1,582,891	8,490,647	16,863,457
Operating income (loss)	4,422,127	(238,804)	4,183,323	(540,532)
Nonoperating revenues (expenses):				
Interest and investment revenue	454,793	146,556	601,349	134,733
Gain on disposal of capital assets	--	104,925	104,925	20,855
Interest expense	(1,600,830)	(1,166,546)	(2,767,376)	(41,616)
Miscellaneous expense	--	(46,846)	(46,846)	(176,003)
Total nonoperating revenues (expenses)	(1,146,037)	(961,911)	(2,107,948)	(62,031)
Income (loss) before contributions and transfers	3,276,090	(1,200,715)	2,075,375	(602,563)
Capital contributions	1,645,919	--	1,645,919	18,788
Transfers out	(290,000)	(211,409)	(501,409)	(175,033)
Change in net position	4,632,009	(1,412,124)	3,219,885	(758,808)
Total net position—beginning	79,059,015	3,290,294	82,349,309	3,753,499
Total Net Position—ending	**$83,691,024**	**$1,878,170**	**$85,569,194**	**$ 2,994,691**

Sample City
STATEMENT OF CASH FLOWS
PROPRIETARY FUNDS
For the Year Ended December 31, 20X1

	Business-type activities—Enterprise funds			Governmental activities—
	Water and sewer	Parking facilities	Totals	Internal service funds
Cash flows from _Operating_ activities				
Receipts from customers	$11,400,200	$ 1,345,292	$12,745,492	$15,326,343
Payments to suppliers	(2,725,349)	(365,137)	(3,090,486)	(2,812,238)
Payments to employees	(3,360,055)	(750,828)	(4,110,883)	(4,209,688)
Internal activity—payments to other funds	(1,296,768)	--	(1,296,768)	--
Claims paid	--	--	--	(8,482,451)
Other receipts (payments)	(2,325,483)	--	(2,325,483)	1,061,118
Net cash provided by operating activities	1,692,545	229,327	1,921,872	**883,084**
Cash flows from _Noncapital Financing_ activities				
Operating subsidies and transfers to other funds	(290,000)	(211,409)	(501,409)	(175,033)
Cash flows from _Capital and related Financing_ activities				
Proceeds from capital debt	4,041,322	8,660,778	12,702,100	--
Capital contributions	1,645,919	--	1,645,919	--
Purchases of capital assets	(4,194,035)	(144,716)	(4,338,751)	(400,086)
Principal paid on capital debt	(2,178,491)	(8,895,000)	(11,073,491)	(954,137)
Interest paid on capital debt	(1,479,708)	(1,166,546)	(2,646,254)	41,616
Other receipts (payments)	--	19,174	19,174	131,416
Net cash (used) by capital and related financing activities	(2,164,993)	(1,526,310)	(3,691,303)	(1,264,423)
Cash flows from _Investing_ activities				
Proceeds from sales and maturities of investments	--	--	--	15,684
Interest and dividends	454,793	143,747	598,540	129,550
Net cash provided by investing activities	454,793	143,747	598,540	145,234
Net (decrease) in cash and cash equivalents	(307,655)	(1,364,645)	(1,672,300)	(411,138)
Balances—beginning of the year	8,724,308	3,227,135	11,951,443	3,747,237
Balances—end of the year	**$ 8,416,653**	**$ 1,862,490**	**$10,279,143**	**$ 3,336,099**
Reconciliation of operating income (loss) to net cash provided (used) by operating activities				
Operating income (loss)	$ 4,422,127	$ (238,804)	$ 4,183,323	$ (540,532)
Adjustments to reconcile operating income to net cash provided (used) by operating activities:				
Depreciation expense	1,163,140	542,049	1,705,189	1,707,872
Change in assets and liabilities:				
Receivables, net	653,264	1,205	654,469	31,941
Inventories	2,829	--	2,829	39,790
Accounts and other payables	(297,446)	(86,643)	(384,089)	475,212
Accrued expenses	(4,251,369)	(11,520)	(4,239,849)	(831,199)
Net cash provided by _Operating_ activities	$ 1,692,545	$ 229,327	$ 1,921,872	$ **883,084**

Sample City
STATEMENT OF FIDUCIARY NET POSITION
FIDUCIARY FUNDS
December 31, 20X1

	Employee retirement plan	Private-purpose trusts	Agency funds
Assets			
Cash and cash equivalents	$ 1,973	$ 1,250	$ 44,889
Receivables:			
Interest and dividends	508,475	760	--
Other receivables	6,826	--	183,161
Total receivables	515,301	760	183,161
Investments, at fair value:			
US government obligations	13,056,037	80,000	--
Municipal bonds	6,528,019	--	--
Corporate bonds	16,320,047	--	--
Corporate stocks	26,112,075	--	--
Other investments	3,264,009	--	--
Total investments	65,280,187	80,000	--
Total assets	65,797,461	82,010	$228,050
Liabilities			
Accounts payable	--	1,234	--
Refunds payable and others	1,358	--	228,050
Total liabilities	1,358	1,234	$228,050
Net Position			
Held in trust for pension benefits and other purposes	$65,796,103	$80,776	

Sample City
STATEMENT OF CHANGES IN FIDUCIARY NET POSITION
FIDUCIARY FUNDS
For the Year Ended December 31, 20X1

	Employee retirement plan	Private-purpose trusts
Additions		
Contributions:		
Employer	$ 2,721,341	$ --
Plan members	1,421,233	--
Total contributions	4,142,574	--
Investment earnings:		
Net (decrease) in fair value of investments	(272,522)	--
Interest	2,460,871	4,560
Dividends	1,445,273	--
Total investment earnings	3,633,622	4,560
Less investment expense	216,428	--
Net investment earnings	3,417,194	4,560
Total additions	7,559,768	4,560
Deductions		
Benefits	2,453,047	3,800
Refunds of contributions	464,691	--
Administrative expenses	87,532	678
Total deductions	3,005,270	4,478
Change in net position	4,554,498	82
Net position—beginning of the year	61,241,605	80,694
Net Position—end of the year	$65,796,103	$80,776

Sample City
STATEMENT OF REVENUES, EXPENDITURES, AND CHANGES IN FUND BALANCES—
BUDGET AND ACTUAL (BCS)
GENERAL FUND
For the Year Ended December 31, 20X1

	Budgeted amounts		Actual amounts (budgetary basis)
	Original	**Final**	
Revenues			
Property taxes	$52,017,833	$51,853,018	$51,173,436
Other taxes—franchise and public service	12,841,209	12,836,024	13,025,392
Fees and fines	718,800	718,800	606,946
Licenses and permits	2,126,600	2,126,600	2,287,794
Intergovernmental	6,905,898	6,571,360	6,119,938
Charges for services	12,392,972	11,202,150	11,374,460
Interest	1,501,945	550,000	552,325
Miscellaneous	3,024,292	1,220,991	881,874
Total revenues	91,043,549	87,078,943	86,022,165
Expenditures			
Current			
General government (including contingencies and miscellaneous)	11,837,534	9,468,155	8,621,500
Public safety	33,050,966	33,983,706	33,799,709
Public works	5,215,630	5,025,848	4,993,187
Engineering services	1,296,275	1,296,990	1,296,990
Health and sanitation	5,756,250	6,174,653	6,174,653
Cemetery	724,500	724,500	706,305
Culture and recreation	11,059,140	11,368,070	11,289,146
Education—payment to school district	22,000,000	22,000,000	21,893,273
Total expenditures	90,940,295	90,041,922	88,774,763
Excess (deficiency) of revenues over expenditures	103,254	(2,962,979)	(2,752,598)
Other Financing Sources (Uses)			
Transfers in	939,525	130,000	129,323
Transfers out	(2,970,256)	(2,163,759)	(2,163,759)
Total other financing sources and uses	(2,030,731)	(2,033,759)	(2,034,436)
Special Item			
Proceeds from sale of park land	1,355,250	3,500,000	3,476,488
Net change in fund balance	(572,227)	(1,496,738)	(1,310,546)
Fund balances—beginning	3,528,750	2,742,799	2,742,799
Fund balances—ending	$ 2,956,523	$ 1,246,061	$ 1,432,253

Lecture 29.14
CLASS QUESTIONS
Please see the Class Questions and Class Solutions for this Lecture at the end of this Section.

Lecture 29.15
CLASS QUESTIONS
Please see the Class Questions and Class Solutions for this Lecture at the end of this Section.

CLASS QUESTIONS

Work through the below Class Questions while following along with the respective lectures. Once this is complete, you can begin independently practicing what you've learned by quizzing yourself on this course section in your Interactive Practice Questions (IPQ), which can be found in your online Student Dashboard. Your IPQ simulates the computer-based testing experience, and will also help you understand how concepts are applied to the exam. Each question includes answer explanations from expert CPAs that will help you determine why you answered a question correctly or incorrectly. This is key to your success on the CPA Exam.

Lecture 29.07

1. What is the basic criterion used to determine the reporting entity for a governmental unit?

    a. Special financing arrangement.
    b. Geographic boundaries.
    c. Scope of public services.
    d. Financial accountability.

2. Which of the following funds of a governmental unit recognizes revenues in the accounting period in which they become available and measurable?

	General fund	Enterprise fund
a.	Yes	No
b.	No	Yes
c.	Yes	Yes
d.	No	No

3. Property taxes and fines represent which of the following classes of non-exchange transactions for governmental units?

    a. Derived tax revenues.
    b. Imposed non-exchange revenues.
    c. Government-mandated non-exchange transactions.
    d. Voluntary non-exchange transactions.

4. Lake County received the following proceeds that are legally restricted to expenditure for specified purposes:

Levies on affected property owners to install sidewalks	$500,000
Gasoline taxes to finance road repairs	900,000

    What amount should be accounted for in Lake's special revenue funds?

    a. $1,400,000
    b. $ 900,000
    c. $ 500,000
    d. $0

Governmental Accounting   Section 29

5. Financing for the renovation of Fir City's municipal park, begun and completed during 20X3, came from the following sources:

Grant from state government	$400,000
Proceeds from general obligation bond issue	500,000
Transfer from Fir's general fund	100,000

   In its 20X3 capital projects fund financial statement, Fir should report these amounts as

	Revenues	Other financing sources
a.	$1,000,000	$0
b.	$ 900,000	$ 100,000
c.	$ 400,000	$ 600,000
d.	$0	$1,000,000

6. Dale City is accumulating financial resources that are legally restricted to payments of general long-term debt principal and interest maturing in future years. At December 31, 20X3, $5,000,000 has been accumulated for principal payments and $300,000 has been accumulated for interest payments. These restricted funds should be accounted for in the

	Debt service fund	General fund
a.	$0	$5,300,000
b.	$ 300,000	$5,000,000
c.	$5,000,000	$ 300,000
d.	$5,300,000	$0

7. An enterprise fund would be used when the governing body requires that

   I. Accounting for the financing of an agency's services to other government departments be on a cost-reimbursement basis.
   II. User charges cover the costs of general public services.
   III. Net income information be reported for an activity.

   a. I only.
   b. I and II.
   c. I and III.
   d. II and III.

8. For which of the following fund balance classifications is the *intent* of the governing board to use for a specific purpose a critical factor?

   a. Committed.
   b. Restricted.
   c. Assigned.
   d. Nonspendable

Lecture 29.11

Items 9 and 10 are based on the following:

Ridge Township's governing body adopted its general fund budget for the year ended July 31, 20X3, comprised of Estimated Revenues of $100,000 and Appropriations of $80,000. Ridge formally integrates its budget into the accounting records.

9. To record the appropriations of $80,000, Ridge should

   a. Credit Appropriations Control
   b. Debit Appropriations Control
   c. Credit Estimated Expenditures Control
   d. Debit Estimated Expenditures Control

10. To record the $20,000 budgeted excess of estimated revenues over appropriations, Ridge should

    a. Credit Estimated Excess Revenues Control.
    b. Debit Estimated Excess Revenues Control.
    c. Credit Budgetary Fund Balance.
    d. Debit Budgetary Fund Balance.

11. For the budgetary year ending December 31, 20X3, Maple City's general fund expects the following inflows of resources:

Property Taxes, Licenses, and Fines	$9,000,000
Proceeds of Debt Issue	5,000,000
Interfund Transfers for Debt Service	1,000,000

    In the budgetary entry, what amount should Maple record for estimated revenues?

    a. $ 9,000,000
    b. $10,000,000
    c. $14,000,000
    d. $15,000,000

12. In 20X3, New City issued purchase orders and contracts of $850,000 that were chargeable against 20X3 budgeted appropriations of $1,000,000. The actual cost of the purchase orders was $2,000,000. The journal entry to record the issuance of the purchase orders and contracts should include a

    a. Credit to Vouchers Payable of $1,000,000.
    b. Credit Reserved for Encumbrances of $850,000.
    c. Debit to Expenditures of $1,000,000.
    d. Debit to Appropriations of $850,000.

Governmental Accounting   Section 29

13. Elm City issued a purchase order for supplies with an estimated cost of $5,000. When the supplies were received, the accompanying invoice indicated an actual price of $4,950. What amount should Elm debit (credit) to Reserved for Encumbrances after the supplies and invoice were received?

    a. $ (50)
    b. $ 50
    c. $4,950
    d. $5,000

14. A balance in the Reserved for Encumbrances in excess of a balance of Encumbrances indicates

    a. An excess of vouchers payable over encumbrances.
    b. An excess of purchase orders over invoices received.
    c. An excess of appropriations over encumbrances.
    d. A recording error.

Lecture 29.14

15. A city's water enterprise fund received interest of $10,000 on long-term investments. How should this amount be reported on the Statement of Cash Flows?

    a. Operating activities.
    b. Noncapital financing activities.
    c. Capital and related financing activities.
    d. Investing activities.

16. Which event(s) should be included in a statement of cash flows for a governmental entity?

    I. Cash inflow from issuing bonds to finance city hall construction.
    II. Cash outflow from a city utility representing payments in lieu of property taxes.

    a. I only.
    b. II only.
    c. Both I and II.
    d. Neither I nor II.

17. Which of the following financial statements should be prepared for proprietary funds?

    a. Statement of revenues, expenditures, and changes in fund balances.
    b. Statement of activities.
    c. Statement of changes in proprietary net position.
    d. Statement of cash flows.

Items 18 through 20 are based on the following:

The general fund of ABC city acquired two police cars at the beginning of January 20X3, at a total cost of $40,000. The cars are expected to last for four years and have a $10,000 residual value. Straight-line depreciation is used.

18. On the balance sheet for the governmental funds at December 31, 20X3, the police cars will be reported under assets in the general fund column at which of the following amounts?

    a. $40,000
    b. $32,500
    c. $0
    d. $22,500

19. On the government-wide statement of net position at December 31, 20X3, the police cars will be reported under assets in the governmental activities column at which of the following amounts?

    a. $40,000
    b. $32,500
    c. $0
    d. $22,500

20. On the statement of revenues, expenditures, and changes in fund balances prepared for the governmental funds for the year ended December 31, 20X3, the police cars will be reported as

    a. Expenditures of $40,000.
    b. Expense of $7,500.
    c. Expenditures of $7,500.
    d. Expense of $40,000.

21. Which of the following statements is correct about the accounting for infrastructure assets using the modified approach?

    I. Depreciation expense on the infrastructure assets should be reported on the government-wide statement of activities, under the governmental activities column.

    II. Certain information about infrastructure assets reported using the modified approach is required supplementary information in the annual report.

    a. I only.
    b. II only.
    c. Both I and II.
    d. Neither I nor II.

Items 22 and 23 As of December 31, 20X5, ABC city compiled the information below for its capital assets, exclusive of infrastructure assets.

Cost of capital assets financed with general obligation debt and tax revenues	$3,500,000
Accumulated depreciation on the capital assets	750,000
Outstanding debt related to the capital assets	1,250,000

22. On the government-wide statement of net position at December 31, 20X5, under the governmental activities column, what amount should be reported for capital assets?

    a. $3,500,000
    b. $1,500,000
    c. $2,250,000
    d. $2,750,000

23. On the government-wide statement of net position at December 31, 20X5, under the governmental activities column, the information related to capital assets should be reported in the net position section at which of the following amounts?

    a. $3,500,000
    b. $1,500,000
    c. $2,250,000
    d. $2,750,000

CLASS SOLUTIONS

1. (d) A governmental unit must be fiscally accountable for its activities. They must demonstrate that the government's actions comply with decisions concerning raising and spending of public money within a budgetary period. The government must also be accountable for the operation of business-type and fiduciary activities. In defining a governmental unit, the primary criterion is identifying the activities that the governmental entity is accountable for.

2. (a) Governmental funds, which include the general fund, apply the modified accrual method of accounting under which revenues are recognized when they become available and measurable. An enterprise fund is very much like a nongovernmental business enterprise and, as a result, applies accrual basis account, recognizing revenues when earned.

3. (b) Property taxes and fines are imposed non-exchange revenues because they are assessed and not derived from transactions. Answer (a) is incorrect because derived tax revenues are those that are derived from a transaction, such as sales taxes. Answer (c) is incorrect because government mandated nonexchange transactions are funds provided by one level of government to another. Answer (d) is incorrect because voluntary nonexchange transactions are those entered into willingly by the paying party, such as grants and donations.

4. (b) Special revenue funds are used to account for revenues that are restricted or committed to be used to finance designated activities other than capital projects or debt service. This would include gasoline taxes that are designated to be used to finance road repairs. Levies against property owners may be accounted for in an agency fund if government is simply acting as a facilitator by collecting and disbursing the funds. Otherwise, they may be accounted for in a debt service fund if, for example, the levies are used to repay a bond that was issued to install the sidewalks.

5. (c) Revenues include funds that are derived from taxes, assessments, fines, and activities of the governmental unit. Funds received from the proceeds of bond issues and operating transfers to other funds are considered other financing sources and are not considered revenue.

6. (d) A debt service fund is used to make principal and interest payments on the tax supported debts of the government and collect funds for that purpose. Funds accumulated for both principal and interest are accounted for in the debt service fund. Related items that may be accounted for in the general fund include transfers made to the debt service fund for the payment of principal or interest.

7. (d) An enterprise fund is used to account for activities involving providing goods or services in exchange for voluntary payments. An enterprise fund uses accrual accounting and is accounted for similarly to a nongovernmental business enterprise and would also be appropriate when information about net income is required. Services provided by one agency to other governmental departments on a cost reimbursement basis are accounted for in internal service funds, not enterprise funds.

Governmental Accounting

8. (c) A portion of the fund balance that the governing board intends to use for a specific purpose is classified as being assigned. Answer (a) is incorrect because a committed fund balance represents encumbrances that have been made but have not yet been spent. Answer (b) is incorrect because a fund balance can only be restricted when a restriction is placed on it by an external party, not as a result of the intent of the governing board. Answer (d) is incorrect because a fund balance is considered nonspendable when the donor of the funds indicates that the principal is to remain intact.

9. (a) Ridge's budget will be recorded with a debit to estimated revenues control for $100,000, a credit to appropriations control for $80,000 and a credit to the budgetary fund balance for $20,000.

10. (c) Ridge's budget will be recorded with a debit to estimated revenues control for $100,000, a credit to appropriations control for $80,000 and a credit to the budgetary fund balance for $20,000.

11. (a) Revenues include funds that are derived from taxes, assessments, fines, and activities of the governmental unit. Funds received from the proceeds of debt issues and operating transfers for other funds are considered other financing sources and are not considered revenue.

12. (b) When purchase orders are originally issued, the entity will debit encumbrances to recognize that funds have been committed and credit Reserved for Encumbrances. When the invoice is received, the entry will be reversed. Answer (a) is incorrect because vouchers payable is credited when an invoice is received, not when a purchase order is issued. In addition, the amount would be $2,000,000, the actual cost of the purchase orders, not $1,000,000. Answer (c) is incorrect because expenditures will be debited when an invoice is received, not when a purchase order is issued. Answer (d) is incorrect because appropriations are credited when the budget is recorded and credited at the end of the period when closing entries are made. It would not be affected when purchase orders are issued.

13. (d) When a purchase order is issued, Encumbrances is debited and Reserved for Encumbrances is credited for the estimated amount, $5,000 in this case When the invoice is received, that entry is reversed and expenditures are recognized in the amount of the invoice.

14. (d) Encumbrances is debited and Reserved for Encumbrances is credited when goods or services are ordered and the entry is reversed when an invoice is received. Since both accounts are affected by the same amounts, the only reason they would not have equal balances would be a recording error.

15. (d) Unlike a business enterprise preparing a statement of cash flows under US GAAP, governmental accounting principles indicate that interest received on investments is treated as a cash inflow from investing activities.

16. (b) Governmental funds apply the modified accrual basis of accounting and would not prepare a statement of cash flows. As a result, the bond proceeds would not be reported in a statement of cash flows. Enterprise funds, including utilities, apply the accrual method of accounting and do prepare a statement of cash flows. Payments by a city utility would appear on a statement of cash flows.

17. (d) A proprietary fund is, in many ways, comparable to a for-profit business enterprise. Its financial statements consist of a statement of net position, a statement of revenues, expenses, and changes in fund net position, and a statement of cash flows. Answer (a) is incorrect because a proprietary fund has expenses, not expenditures. Answer (b) is incorrect because a proprietary fund does not provide a statement of activities. Answer (c) is incorrect because a proprietary fund does not provide a separate statement of changes in proprietary net position.

18. (c) A governmental fund reports acquisitions of capital assets, which include police cars, under the modified accrual basis of accounting as expenditures, rather than as assets. As a result, no amount will be reported under assets for the police cars on the balance sheet of a governmental fund.

19. (b) The government wide statement of net position is prepared on an accrual basis. As a result, the police cars would have initially been reported at cost of $40,000. At the end of the period, 1 year's depreciation would have been recognized. The amount would be based on the cost of $40,000 minus the salvage value of $10,000, resulting in a depreciable basis of $30,000. This is divided by the 4 year life, indicating depreciation for one year would be ($30,000/4) $7,500. As a result, the carrying value of the asset would be ($40,000- $7,500) $32,500.

20. (a) Under the modified accrual basis of accounting, amounts spent on capital assets, including police cars, are recognized as expenditures at their full cost. As a result, the statement of revenues, expenditures, and changes in fund balances will report the acquisition of the police cars as expenditures in the amount of $40,000.

21. (b) Under the modified approach, infrastructure assets are not required to be depreciated if certain requirements are met. Expenditures for assets that meet the requirements are expensed as incurred. When the modified approach is used, the government will disclose information about the condition of the assets and the cost to maintain and preserve them.

22. (d) The statement of net assets is divided into three sections: assets, liabilities, and net. In the governmental activities column, capital assets are reported in the asset section at an amount equal to cost less accumulated depreciation or ($3,500,000 - $750,000) $2,750,000.

23. (b) The statement of net assets is divided into three sections: assets, liabilities, and net. In the governmental activities column, net capital assets are reported in the net section at an amount equal to the asset cost less accumulated depreciation and outstanding debt related to the capital assets. The amount would be ($3,500,000 - $750,000 - $1,250,000) $1,500,000.

Lecture 29.15

TASK-BASED SIMULATIONS

Task-Based Simulation 1

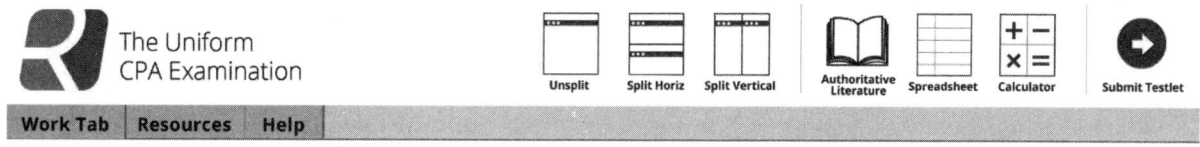

Situation:

The following information relates to Bel City, whose first fiscal year ended December 31, 20X4. Assume Bel has only the long-term debt specified in the information and only the funds necessitated by the information.

1. General fund:

- The following selected information is taken from Bel's 20X4 general fund financial records:

	Budget	Actual
Property taxes	$5,000,000	$4,700,000
Other revenues	1,000,000	1,050,000
Total revenues	$6,000,000	$5,750,000
Total expenditures	$5,600,000	$5,700,000
Property taxes receivable—delinquent		$ 420,000
Less: Allowance for estimated uncollectible taxes—delinquent		50,000
		$ 370,000

- There were no amendments to the budget as originally adopted.
- No property taxes receivable have been written off, and the allowance for uncollectibles balance is unchanged from the initial entry at the time of the original tax levy.
- There were no encumbrances outstanding at December 31, 20X4.

2. Capital project fund:

- Finances for Bel's new civic center were provided by a combination of general fund transfers, a state grant, and an issue of general obligation bonds. Any bond premium on issuance is to be used for the repayment of the bonds at their $1,200,000 par value. At December 31, 20X4, the capital project fund for the civic center had the following closing entries:

Revenues	$ 800,000	
Other financing sources —bond proceeds	1,230,000	
Other financing sources —operating transfers in	500,000	
Expenditures		$1,080,000
Other financing uses—operating transfers out		30,000
Unreserved fund balance		1,420,000

- Also, at December 31, 20X4, capital project fund entries reflected Bel's intention to honor the $1,300,000 purchase orders and commitments outstanding for the center.
- During 20X4, total capital project fund encumbrances exceeded the corresponding expenditures by $42,000. All expenditures were previously encumbered.
- During 20X5, the capital project fund received no revenues and no other financing sources. The civic center building was completed in early 20X5 and the capital project fund was closed by a transfer of $27,000 to the general fund.

3. *Water utility enterprise fund*:
- Bel issued $4,000,000 revenue bonds at par. These bonds, together with a $700,000 transfer from the general fund, were used to acquire a water utility. Water utility revenues are to be the sole source of funds to retire these bonds beginning in year 20X9.

Required:

For **Items 1 through 13,** indicate if the answer to each item is yes Y or no N.

Items 1 through 8 relate to Bel's general fund.

1. Did recording budgetary accounts at the beginning of 20X4 increase the fund balance by $50,000?
2. Should the budgetary accounts for 20X4 include an entry for the expected transfer of funds from the general fund to the capital projects fund?
3. Should the $700,000 payment from the general fund, which was used to help to establish the water utility fund, be reported as an "other financing use"?
4. Did the general fund receive the $30,000 bond premium from the capital projects fund?
5. Should a payment from the general fund for water received for normal civic center operations be reported as an "other financing use"?
6. Does the net property taxes receivable of $370,000 include amounts expected *to* be collected after March 15, 20X5?
7. Would closing budgetary accounts cause the fund balance to increase by $400,000?
8. Would the interaction between budgetary and actual amounts cause the fund balance to decrease by $350,000?

Items 9 through 13 relate to Bel's funds other than the general fund.

9. Should the capital project fund be included in Bel's government-wide statement of activities?
10. Should the water utility enterprise fund be included in Bel's government-wide statement of net position?

In which fund should Bel report capital and related financing activities in its 20X4 statement of cash flows?

11. Debt service fund.
12. Capital project fund.

Governmental Accounting — Section 29

13. Water utility enterprise fund.

For Items 14 through 19, determine the amount.

Items 14 and 15 relate to Bel's general fund.

14. What was the amount recorded in the opening entry for appropriations?
15. What was the total amount debited to property taxes receivable?

Items 16 through 19 relate to Bel's funds other than the general fund.

16. What was the completed cost of the civic center?
17. How much was the state capital grant for the civic center?
18. In the capital project fund, what was the amount of the total encumbrances recorded during 20X4?
19. In the capital project fund, what was the unreserved fund balance reported at December 31, 20X4?

TASK-BASED SIMULATION SOLUTIONS

Task-Based Simulation Solution 1

1. **N** — The budgetary accounts at the beginning of 20X4 increased the fund balance by the difference between total budgeted revenues of $6,000,000 and total budgeted expenditures of $5,600,000 or $400,000.

2. **Y** — An expected transfer of funds from the general fund to the capital projects fund will be recognized in the budgetary accounts as an estimated other financing use.

3. **Y** — The $700,000 payment from the general fund, which was used to help establish the water utility fund, would be an operating transfer out, which is reported in other financing uses.

4. **N** — A premium on the issuance of bonds is transferred to the debt service fund and is not retained by the general fund.

5. **N** — A payment from the general fund to an enterprise fund for water received for normal civic center operations will be reported as an expenditure, not as an other financing use.

6. **Y/N** — Net property taxes receivable would ordinarily include only amounts to be collected during the 20X4 calendar year or within 60 days after the end of the year. Collections expected after 3/15/X5 should not be included. As a result, either answer was accepted.

7. **N** — Closing the budgetary accounts would cause the fund balance to decrease by $400,000, not increase.

8. **N** — The budgetary accounts have no effect on the fund balance since the recording of the budgetary accounts increased the budgetary fund balance by $400,000 and the closing of the budgetary accounts decreased it by the same amount. The closing of the actual amounts increased the fund balance by $50,000.

9. **Y** — The government-wide statement of activities will include all governmental and proprietary funds, as well as component units being reported as discrete units. The capital projects fund will be included in the governmental-type activities column of the statement.

10. **Y** — The government-wide statement of net position includes all governmental and proprietary funds, as well as component units being reported as discrete units. The enterprise funds will be included in the business-type activities column of the statement.

11. **N** — A combined statement of cash flows only includes the proprietary funds. The debt service fund is a governmental fund and would not be included.

12. **N** — A combined statement of cash flows only includes the proprietary funds. The capital projects fund is a governmental fund and would not be included.

13. **Y** — A combined statement of cash flows includes all of the proprietary funds. The water utility enterprise fund is proprietary and would be included.

14. **$5,600,000** — Appropriations would be recorded upon adopting and recording the budget. The amount will be equal to the estimated expenditures of $5,600,000.

15. **$4,750,000**   Since $4,700,000 was actually collected for property taxes and there was no change in the allowance for uncollectible taxes, which was $50,000, the entry to record property taxes would have been a debit to property taxes receivable of $4,750,000, a credit to the allowance for uncollectible property taxes of $50,000, and a credit to revenues of $4,700,000.

16. **$2,473,000**   Since the capital projects fund reported expenditures of $1,080,000 in 20X4, as indicated by the closing entry, and had an unreserved fund balance of $1,420,000, the total cost of the civic center would have been $2,500,000 if the entire $1,420,000 had been spent. During 20X5, however, there was $27,000 remaining in the capital projects fund, which was transferred to the general fund when the capital projects fund was closed. As a result, the total cost was $2,500,000 - $27,000 or $2,473,000.

17. **$800,000**   The state capital grant for the civic center would have been recorded as revenues. The 20X4 closing entry for the capital projects fund indicates that revenues were $800,000. Since the other sources of financing the construction are recorded as other financing sources, $800,000 must be the amount of the state grant.

18. **$2,422,000**   During 20X4, encumbrances exceeded corresponding expenditures by $42,000. With $1,080,000 in expenditures, encumbrances that related to the expenditures must have been $1,122,000. In addition, there was $1,300,000 in encumbrances outstanding at 12/31/X4 indicating total expenditures for 20X4 of $2,422,000.

19. **$120,000**   As a result of the closing entry at 12/31/X4, there was an unreserved fund balance of $1,420,000. The intention to honor $1,300,000 in outstanding purchase orders and commitments would result in the recording of an entry involving a debit to the unreserved fund balance by $1,300,000 and a credit to the reserved for encumbrances. As a result, the remaining balance in the unreserved fund balance at 12/31/X4 would be $120,000.

Section 30 – Nonprofit Accounting
Corresponding Lectures

Watch the following course lectures with this section:

Lecture 30.01 – Nonprofit Accounting – Financial Statements
Lecture 30.02 – Contribution Revenue
Lecture 30.03 – VHWO Statement of Functional Expense
Lecture 30.04 – Contributions – Services
Lecture 30.05 – Hospitals – Private Sector
Lecture 30.06 – Nonprofit Accounting – Class Questions
Lecture 30.07 – Nonprofit Accounting – Class Question - TBS

EXAM NOTE: Please refer to the AICPA FAR Blueprint in the Introduction to find a listing of the representative tasks (and their associated skill levels—i.e., Remembering and Understanding, Application, and Analysis) that the candidate should be able to perform based on the knowledge obtained in this section.

Nonprofit Accounting

Lecture 30.01

NPO FINANCIAL STATEMENTS (FASB ASC 958)

Note: The FASB's Accounting Standards Update 2016-14 makes major changes to nonprofit accounting, but the changes will not become effective on the CPA Exam until the Q1 2018 testing window. Because these changes are not testable until 2018, they are not covered in this edition of the course.

The focus of reporting for a not-for-profit organization (NPO) is on presenting basic information for the *Entity as a whole*. NPO's focus on providing delivery of services funded with public or private resources that generally come from contributions or fees that are not taxable. NPO accounting covers **4 different groups:**
- Health care
- Colleges and universities
- Voluntary health and welfare (United Way, Red Cross, Greenpeace, Salvation Army)
- All others not above (fraternities, labor unions, museums, libraries, non profit organizations)

Accrual accounting is used and the financial statements that must be prepared for all such organizations parallel the **3 basic financial statements** (balance sheet, income statement, statement of cash flows) used by private businesses. Their reporting emphasis is on disclosing the sources of resources and how they were expended. The 3 basic statements include:
- **Statement of Financial Position**
- **Statement of Activities**
- **Statement of Cash Flows**

The Statement of Financial Position (B/S)

The Statement of Financial Position (B/S) reports assets, liabilities, and net assets (equity) of the NPO. Assets and liabilities may be classified or reported in order of liquidity and payment date. Assets restricted for long-term purposes must be reported separately from those that are not. The net asset section of the statement includes three accounts:
- **Unrestricted net assets** are those resources of the NPO that are available for the general use of the entity and can include assets set aside by the **board of trustees**, since a true restriction must come from an outside donor. Unrestricted net assets include the remainder of the net assets of an NPO after considering those that are temporarily or permanently restricted.

- **Temporarily restricted net assets** are those resources of the NPO that have been donated by a third party who has placed a restriction as to either how the resources are to be used, such as for cancer research or for the improvement of a building, or when the resources may be used, such as after a prescribed period of time or upon the occurrence of an event (**time or use/purpose**). The fact that they are temporarily restricted indicates that the resources will become unrestricted at some point (restriction will eventually **LAPSE**).

- **Permanently restricted net assets** include resources usually cash or investment securities, donated by a third party where the donor stipulates that the principal, or corpus, may never be spent, but may be invested. The earnings from that investment may be restricted or unrestricted, depending on the donor's stipulations (**endowments**).

Statement of Financial Position for a Not-for-Profit Organization

Not-for-Profit Organization
STATEMENTS OF FINANCIAL POSITION
June 30, 20X1 and 20X0
(in thousands)

	20X1	20X0
Assets		
Cash and cash equivalents	$ 75	$ 460
Accounts and interest receivable	2,130	1,670
Inventories and prepaid expenses	610	1,000
Contributions receivable	3,025	2,700
Short-term investments	1,400	1,000
Assets restricted to investment in land, buildings, and equipment	5,210	4,560
Land, buildings, and equipment	61,700	63,590
Long-term investments	218,070	203,500
Total assets	$292,220	$278,480
Liabilities and net assets		
Accounts payable	$ 2,570	$ 1,050
Refundable advance		650
Grants payable	875	1,300
Notes payable		1,140
Annuity obligations	1,685	1,700
Long-term debt	5,500	6,500
Total liabilities	10,630	12,340
	20X1	*20X0*
Net assets		
Unrestricted	**115,228**	103,670
Temporarily restricted	**24,342**	25,470
Permanently restricted	**142,020**	137,000
Total net assets	281,590	266,140
Total liabilities and net assets	$292,220	$278,480

The Statement of Activities (I/S & R/E)

The Statement of Activities (I/S & R/E) reports revenues, net assets released from restriction, and expenses. The statement separately reports the 3 categories of net assets.
- **Revenues/Gains** typically include contributions from donors and investment income. Property is included at FMV at date of gift and services are only included if professional and the NPO would have otherwise paid for them. They are reported in the appropriate column depending on whether the revenues are unrestricted, temporarily restricted, or permanently restricted. Investment income reported in the permanently restricted net asset column should only represent net capital gains or other income that will remain part of the permanent endowment.

- **Net assets released from restriction** only reports temporarily restricted net assets that became unrestricted during the year, due to the *expiration of time restrictions* or the *performance of purpose restrictions*. Identical dollar amounts are reported as positive numbers in the unrestricted net assets column and negative numbers in the temporarily restricted net assets column. There cannot be any amount reported in permanently restricted net assets since these would never be released.
- **Expenses** are reported only in the *unrestricted net assets column*. The expenditure of temporarily restricted net assets has the effect of releasing the assets from restriction, and is reported as both a release, as discussed in the preceding paragraph, and an unrestricted expense. Permanently restricted net assets cannot be spent. The expenses are categorized as either program services, support services or combined costs.

    - **Expenses** (all unrestricted)
        - Program – activities representing NPO purpose.
        - All are reported in the "unrestricted" net assets column.
        - May be classified different ways
            - **Object** – what - type of cost e.g. salaries, Dep.
            - **Function** – why – purpose e.g. health care, police, fire
            - **Character** – when – time period
                - Debt service – past
                - Current service – present
                - Capital outlay – future
                    - Functional must be presented in either:
                        - Statements
                        - Foot Notes

Statement of Activities for a Not-for-Profit Organization

Not-for-Profit Organization
STATEMENT OF ACTIVITIES
Year Ended June 30, 20X1
(in thousands)

	Unrestricted	Temporarily restricted	Permanently restricted	Total
Revenues, gains, and other support:				
Contributions	$ 8,640	$ 8,110	$ 280	$ 17,030
Fees	5,400			5,400
Income on long-term investments	5,600	2,580	120	8,300
Other investment income	850			850
Net unrealized and realized gains on long-term investments	8,228	2,952	4,620	15,800
Other	150			150
Net assets released from restrictions:				
Satisfaction of program restrictions	**11,990**	**(11,990)**		
Satisfaction of equipment acquisition restrictions	1,500	(1,500)		
Expiration of time restrictions	1,250	(1,250)		
Total revenues, gains, and other support	43,608	(1,098)	5,020	47,530
Expenses and losses:				
Program A	13,100			13,100
Program B	8,540			8,540
Program C	5,760			5,760
Management and general	2,420			2,420
Fund raising	2,150			2,150
Total expenses	31,970			31,970
Fire loss	80			80
Actuarial loss on annuity obligations		30		30
Total expenses and losses	32,050	30		32,080
Change in net assets	11,558	(1,128)	5,020	15,450
Net assets at beginning of year	103,670	25,470	137,000	266,140
Net assets at end of year	**$115,228**	**$24,342**	**$142,020**	**$281,590**

The following chart summarizes increases and decreases in net assets reported on the statement of activities:

	Unrestricted	Temp Rest	Perm Rest
Revenues	Increase	Increase	Increase
Released	Increase	Decrease	N/A
Expenses	Decrease	N/A	N/A

Lecture 30.02

Contribution Revenue (FASB ASC 958)

Many contributions received by a not-for-profit organization (NPO) are **unrestricted gifts** of cash, and are reported as revenues in the **unrestricted net assets** (UNA) section of the statement of activities:

    Cash (operating activity)   100
        Revenues (UNA)   100

It is common, however, for NPOs to *receive gifts* that are **restricted**. For example, a hospital might receive a donation of $500 with the stipulation that it be spent on the hospital's cancer research program. This causes the donation to be included in **temporarily restricted net assets** (TRNA), and is recorded as follows:

    Cash (operating activity)   500
        Revenues (TRNA)   500

Later, when the hospital actually **spends the money** on research that satisfies the restriction.

Two entries are needed. The first is to report the release of the restriction:

    Net assets released (TRNA)   500
        Net assets released (UNA)   500

The second is to report the research costs:

    Expenses (UNA)   500
        Cash   500

Note: The net of the increase in "Unrestricted net assets" (UNA) and the increase in the "Expense" (decreases -UNA) has *no net effect* on unrestricted N/A.

Finally, a donation of cash may stipulate that only the income generated from investing the cash may be spent. The donation is reported as **permanently restricted** net assets (PRNA). For example, assume $1,000,000 was donated to **endow** an ongoing cancer research program. The donation itself is reported as follows:

    Cash (financing activity)   1,000,000
        Revenues (PRNA)   1,000,000

If the money earns interest income of $40,000, that money is spendable:

    Cash   40,000
        Revenues (TRNA)   40,000

The Statement of Cash Flows

The Statement of Cash Flows is comparable to the same statement for private businesses, reporting cash flows from operating, investing, and financing activities. Either the direct or indirect method may be used.

- **Operating** activities represent most of the cash flow effects of the items reported in the **statement of activities**. Inflows include revenues collected and outflows include expenses paid. Contributions that can be spent on operations are included as well.

- **Investing** activities represent the cash flow effects of **asset** transactions. Inflows include proceeds from the sale of assets and sales of works of art, and outflows include payments for asset purchases.

- **Financing** activities represent the cash flow effects of **liability** transactions. Inflows include proceeds from loans and outflows include principal payments on loans. Contributions that are permanently restricted or may only be spent on acquisition of assets are included as well (*restricted for Long Term Purposes*). Financing activities includes 2 categories, proceeds from restricted contributions and other financing activities.

Statement of Cash flows

- **Operating activities** – flow from statement of activities
    - Direct/indirect
    - Unrestricted and temporary restricted revenues
    - Rev, exp, interest income/expense, dividend income

- **Investing activities** – flow from buying and selling assets
    - Investments acq/sold
    - PP&E acq/disposal

- **Financing activities** – flow from borrowings and repayments
    - 2 categories
        - Proceeds from restricted contribution
        - Other financing activities
    - Perm restricted revenue
    - Money restricted for L/T purpose
        - Pmt on bonds, N/P, $ restricted for Endowment,
        - Money restricted for acq of PP&E.

- Contribution revenue is usually operating
    - Contribution for long-term purpose is financing

Nonprofit Accounting   Section 30

Statement of Cash Flows for a Not-for-Profit Organization
Not-for-Profit Organization
STATEMENT OF CASH FLOWS
Year Ended June 30, 20X1
(in thousands)

Cash flows from operating activities:	
Cash received from service recipients	$ 5,220
Cash received from contributors	8,030
Cash collected on contributions receivable	2,615
Interest and dividends received	8,570
Miscellaneous receipts	150
Interest paid	(382)
Cash paid to employees and suppliers	(23,808)
Grants paid	(425)
Net cash used by operating activities	(30)
Cash flows from investing activities:	
Insurance proceeds from fire loss on building	250
Purchase of equipment	(1,500)
Proceeds from sale of investments	76,100
Purchase of investments	(74,900)
Net cash used by investing activities	(50)
Cash flows from financing activities:	
Proceeds from contributions restricted for:	
Investment in endowment	200
Investment in term endowment	70
Investment in plant	1,210
Investment subject to annuity agreements	200
	1,680
Other financing activities:	
Interest and dividends restricted for reinvestment	300
Payments of annuity obligations	(145)
Payments on notes payable	(1,140)
Payments on long-term debt	(1,000)
	(1,985)
Net cash used by financing activities	(305)
Net decrease in cash and cash equivalents	(385)
Cash and cash equivalents at beginning of year	460
Cash and cash equivalents at end of year	$ 75
Reconciliation of change in net assets to net cash used by operating activities:	
Change in net assets	$ 15,450
Adjustments to reconcile change in net assets to net cash used by operating activities:	
Depreciation	3,200
Fire loss	80
Actuarial loss on annuity obligations	30
Increase in accounts and interest receivable	(460)
Decrease in inventories and prepaid expenses	390
Increase in contributions receivable	(325)
Increase in accounts payable	1,520
Decrease in refundable advance	(650)
Decrease in grants payable	(425)
Contributions restricted for long-term investment	(2,740)
Interest and dividends restricted for long-term investment	(300)
Net unrealized and realized gains on long-term investments	(15,800)
Net cash used by operating activities	$ (30)
Supplemental data for noncash investing and financing activities:	
Gifts of equipment	$140
Gift of paid-up life insurance, cash surrender value	$80

Lecture 30.03
VHWO, Statement of Functional Expense

One specific type of NPO is a **voluntary health and welfare organization**, which provides community services financed by voluntary contributions from the general public. In addition to the 3 statements required for all NPOs, a voluntary health and welfare organization must prepare a **statement of functional expenses**. This statement is a detailed schedule of expenses broken down by function such as program expenses and support services. In such a statement, the following detail is provided:

Statement of Functional Expenses (For VHWO – Red Cross/Greenpeace)

Statement of Activities

Public support (donated) (contributions, grants, bequests, pledges, Special event revenues)
+ Revenues (earned) (membership dues, investment income, client service Revenue, fees)
- **Program expenses** (further the mission of the organization – boat dep, research, community services, public health and education)
- **Support services** (Secondary to the mission)
  - **G & A & M** –(marketing/ tax prep/print annual report)
  - **Fund raising** – (Print & mail pledge cards, maintaining donor list, merchandise sent to potential contributors, salaries of fundraisers)

Excess of revenue over expenses

- **Program services** – (Further the mission of the organization) These are expenses that are directly related to the program. For example, a relief organization might report categories for emergency relief, community education, training, research, hospice services, etc.

- **Supporting services** – (Secondary to the mission) Fund-raising expenses and General and Administrative expenses are reported.
    - **Management & General** –marketing, tax preparation, printing annual report, business management, budgeting.
    - **Fund raising** – (Print & mail pledge cards, maintaining donor list, preparing and distributing fund raising materials, and conducting other activities designed to solicit contributions)
    - **Membership development** – Soliciting for potential members and for dues, costs associated with member relations and similar activities

Management & general expenses include the ***cost of soliciting funds*** other than contributions and membership dues. This includes advertising and other costs of promoting goods or services for sale to customers; costs of responding to requests for proposals for customer-sponsored contracts, or of administering such contracts. They are not considered fund raising expenses.

For other NPOs, functional expenses may be reported in the form of a financial statement or in notes to the financial statements.

Lecture 30.04

Contributions

Donations of services are normally not recorded. However, when an organization receives donations of **professional services** that it normally would have compensated (**essential services**), the service provider is helping to defray expenses of the NPO and should be reported as a donor.

Essential if:
- Services create or enhance a non-financial asset (inventory, land, building) - OR
- The services require specialized skills (doctor, lawyer, accountant)

For example, if a hospital receives *donated time* from retired nurses that enables them to avoid hiring and paying additional workers, and the estimated amount that time would have cost the hospital is $30,000, the following entry is made:

Expenses (UNA)	30,000	
Contribution Revenue (UNA)		30,000

Notice that the donation increases the nursing expense as well as contribution revenue, and is reported in unrestricted net assets, since services that have been provided cannot be withdrawn later.

NPOs also frequently receive donations of services from volunteers providing **unskilled services** that it would **not** have contracted to obtain had they not been donated. These are excluded from the financial reporting, since they do not assist the organization in defraying its expenses.

In some cases, services may be provided by the employees of an affiliated NPO. The same basic rule applies as to whether or not to recognize those services in that essential services are recognized and nonessential ones are not. The amount at which they will be recorded will generally be the affiliated NPO's cost. If, however, the cost is significantly higher or lower than the fair value of the services, they may be reported at either the affiliated NPO's cost or the fair value.

For example, if volunteers come regularly to a hospital to visit with lonely patients and read to them, they are certainly performing a service that is valuable and appreciated. Nevertheless, if the hospital does not provide such visitations on a paid contract basis with anyone, then these donated services are not considered relevant in evaluating the NPO itself, and no entry is made.

Contributions of property are normally reported as revenues in the same manner as contributions of cash. They may be reported as unrestricted, temporarily restricted, or permanently restricted depending on the conditions of the contribution.

A special rule may be applied, however, to certain donations of **art, artifacts, or antiques.** If the NPO intends to use these items *for display* or research purposes only, the organizations cares for it themselves and if sold, the proceeds must be reinvested in other collectibles, then it is permitted to exclude the donation from its financial statements entirely. This avoids having the organization appear to possess great wealth (and, thus, not be in need of public support) when it is holding assets that cannot be used to finance the operations of the NPO. If they don't meet the above requirements, then they would recognize both and asset and a revenue.

If the NPO reserves the right to sell the asset, however, it will have to include its value on the financial statements and report a donation unless the proceeds of any sale are strictly limited to the purchase of replacement art, artifacts, or antiques. They may however show as permanently restricted N/A.

If they receive **donated materials**, they would also record both an asset and a support revenue. If however the materials are "pass through" (donated clothing), then whey would debit an expense and credit an unrestricted contribution revenue.

Gifts in kind are non-cash contributions to a nonprofit organization. They are recorded at FMV.

Marketable Securities (FASB ASC 958-320)

NPO's are required to use fair value accounting for most equity and debt investments and reports realized and unrealized gains and losses directly in the statement of activities.
- **Trading** – FMV, unrealized gains/losses on Statement of Activities.
- **Available for sale** – FMV, Unrealized gains/losses on Statement of Activities.
- **Held to Maturity** – Bonds
- Doesn't cover Equity securities

Pledges (an unconditional promise to give) that have been made to an NPO may be accrued as receivables (net of allowance) by the organization in the period in which they are made. In doing so, however, the NPO should establish an appropriate **allowance for uncollectibles**, and treat pledges that aren't due to be paid until a future period as time-restricted donations. The pledges are *recorded at P.V.* for annuities. Cash contributions however are a revenue or gain when received.

Conditional promise to give (matching funds) – Conditional promises to give are pledges that will become payable to the entity when the conditions have been met. As a result, conditional promises to give are not recognized as revenues until they become unconditional. This occurs when either:
- The conditions on which the promise depends have been substantially met.
- There is only a remote likelihood that the conditions on which the promise depends will not be met.

Funds received before conditions are substantially met are recognized as liabilities until such time as the promises become unconditional.

For example, assume that an Independence Day pledge drive by the NPO in 20X1 has netted promises totaling $20,000, with half of the pledge due by the end of the current year and the remainder due by the end of 20X2. Based on experience, the organization expects 10% of pledges not to be honored. The entry to be recorded when pledges are received is:

Pledges receivable (at P.V.)	20,000	
Allowance for uncollectible pledges		2,000
Revenues (UNA)		9,000
Revenues (TRNA)		9,000

Nonprofit Accounting

Assuming collection is as expected, the pledges collected in 20X2 effectively eliminate the time restriction:

| 12/31/X2 | Net assets released (TRNA) | 9,000 | |
| | Net assets released (UNA) | | 9,000 |

FASB ASC 958 – Agent or Trustee (like agency fund – ex. United Way)

If collect money for others such as a foundation, it can be considered either contribution revenue or a liability at FMV. It is considered a **revenue** if either:
- They have variance power over the donation to redirect the money (OR)
- The beneficiary of the donation is financially related (ongoing economic interest in the net assets of the other).

| Cash | x | |
| Contribution Revenue | | x |

- If don't meet Either of the two above, record as a **liability**

| Cash | x | |
| Refundable advance (liability) | | x |

Depreciation

FASB ASC 958 requires all nonprofit organizations to recognize depreciation in general purpose external financial statements using the *same criteria* in allocating the depreciable cost of fixed assets over their estimated useful lives as commercial enterprises.

Colleges & Universities

Private colleges and universities are subject to the same guidance as other not-for-profit organizations. Some special issues that relate to colleges and universities include:
- Tuition remissions & scholarships are revenue (if go to school, it's a revenue)
- Refunds – not revenues

Cash	12,000	
Scholarship expense	10,000	
Tuition remission	8,000	
Tuition revenue		30,000

Lecture 30.05

HOSPITALS (HEALTH CARE ORGANIZATIONS – PRIVATE SECTOR)

The two types of health care organizations are investor-owned health care entities, which provide goods and services for profit, and not-for-profit business oriented health care entities, which have no ownership interests. Not-for-profit health care organizations:
- Charge fees in order to remain self-sufficient rather than to maximize profits.
- May receive contributions from resource providers in transactions that are either nonreciprocal or are not proportionate.

Accounting and financial reporting for both types of health care organizations is consistent, although each has transactions that would not be appropriate for the other. For example:
- A not-for-profit health care organization will not have any transactions or reporting related to shareholders' equity.
- An investor-owned health care organization will not receive contributions.

Four statements are presented for a private sector not-for-profit hospital, including a balance sheet (Statement of Financial Position), a statement of Operations (Activities), a statement of Changes in Net Assets (or equity), and a statement of Cash Flows. Notes to the financial statements will also be provided. The statements may have other titles that are appropriately descriptive, such as a statement of financial position instead of the balance sheet, or a statement of activities in place of a statement of operations. The statement of cash flows, however, should be entitled as such.

- **The Balance Sheet (Statement of Financial Position)** classifies assets and liabilities as current or noncurrent on a similar basis as for profit entities, although continuing care retirement communities may report assets according to how soon they will be converted to cash and liabilities according to maturity dates.
    - Assets of a not-for-profit health care organization are identified as *unrestricted, temporarily restricted, or permanently restricted*, similarly to other not-for-profit entities. Unrestricted net assets, however, include those that are contractually limited, such as proceeds of debt that are deposited with a trustee and are limited in use by the requirements of an agreement, or assets limited to use for identified purposes as a result of an agreement with an outside party other than a grantor or donor, such as restrictions imposed by state law on many health maintenance organizations (HMOs).
    - In addition, funds that are internally designated are reported separately from those that are externally designated for some specific purpose. This may be either on the face of the financial statements or in the notes.
    - In addition:
        - Cash and claims to cash are reported separately and excluded from current assets when restricted to withdrawal or use for something other than current operations, designated for acquisition or construction of noncurrent assets, required to be segregated for the liquidation of long-term debt, or are limited to long-term use by donor restriction.
        - While receivables for health care services are generally reported at the provider's full established rates, providing *charity care* does not result in the recognition of a receivable.
        - Investments in assets that are not financial instruments are reported at amortized cost.
        - A liability will be recognized for medical malpractice claims, including an estimate of losses that will result from unreported incidents that are probable of having occurred before the end of the reporting period.
        - Potential insurance recoveries are reported as insurance receivables, not as reductions to the liability, and are evaluated for the need for an allowance for uncollectibility.

- **The statement of Changes in Net Assets** presents the other changes required by FASB ASC 954. As is true for other not-for-profit organizations, contributions restricted to long-term purposes (plant acquisition, endowment, term endowment, etc.) would not be reported in the Statement of Operations (as unrestricted revenue) but would be reported in the Statement of Changes in Net Assets as a revenue increasing temporarily restricted or permanently restricted net assets, as appropriate.

- **The statement of Cash Flows**, like other not-for-profit entities, is prepared similarly to a statement of cash flows for a private business, reporting cash flows from operating activities, from investing activities, and from financing activities.

- **The Statement of Operations (Activities)** is required to include a **performance indicator**, which may be described as *operating income, revenues over expenses, revenues and gains over expenses and losses, earned income, or performance earnings.* The performance indicator is an operating measure of a for-profit health care entity. It helps in comparing the performance across health care organizations with different organizational forms. Regardless of what description is used, the performance indicator is to be clearly labeled.
    - Not-for-profit, business-oriented health care entities are required to report the performance indicator on the same statement that presents the total changes in unrestricted net assets.

    - A description of the nature and composition of the performance indicator is to be included in the notes to the financial statements. The performance indicator ***includes*** items related to investments in debt and equity securities:
        - Dividends, interest, and similar investment income
        - Realized gains and losses
        - Unrealized gains and losses on trading securities (unrealized gains and losses on investments other than trading securities are excluded)
        - Other than temporary impairments

    - Other changes in net assets may be presented in the same statement or separately.

    - Additional classifications may be used for components within the performance indicator, such as operating and nonoperating, expendable and nonexpendable, earned and unearned, or recurring and nonrecurring.

    - Certain items are ***excluded*** from the performance indicator and are reported separately as changes in net assets.
        - Transactions with owners acting in the capacity as an owner
        - Equity transfers
        - Restricted contributions, including temporary restrictions
        - Contributions of long-lived assets or long-lived assets released from donor restrictions
        - Items reported in, or reclassified from, other comprehensive income
        - Separately reported items, such as discontinued operations
        - Unrealized gains and losses on investments other than trading securities

- o Note the separation of items above and below that line. Also note the presentation separately for depreciation, interest, and provision for bad debts. In addition, note that the net assets released from restrictions includes separate amounts for those net assets released for operations and those released for other items.
  - **Patient service revenue** – Accounted for on the **accrual basis** and includes gross billings at established rates before reductions for discounts granted to insurance groups and employees (but *excludes charity care* which isn't billed at all, but is disclosed in the financial statements). Patient service revenue includes medical services such as doctors, surgery, and most hospital stay costs.

  - **Net patient service revenue** – Patient service revenue after reductions for discounts and contractual adjustments for third-party payments (but not bad debt expense, which is claimed separately as an operating expense)
    - In some cases, the amount collectible cannot be determined at the time the services are provided, such as when a health care facility is required by law to provide emergency services, regardless of the patient's ability to pay.
    - This may result in the recognition of revenue and a relatively high provision for bad debts in the period of service.
      - When this is the case, the entity will report net patient service revenue, which will consist of patient service revenue reduced by contractual allowances and discounts and a provision for bad debts.
      - All other health care entities would still show bad debts as an operating expense, assuming they only recognize patient service revenue to the extent it expects to collect.

Donated supplies are recognized as a revenue at FMV in the period received and as either an asset or an expense.

Supplies or Expense	100	
Unrestricted contribution – other operating Revenue		100

GOVERNMENTAL HEALTH CARE ORGANIZATIONS

Governmental health care organizations are generally considered governmental entities that are engaged only in business-type activities, similar to utilities. As such, a governmental health care organization will present financial statements prepared in accordance with the same requirements applied to enterprise funds.

Statement of Operations (UNA) (Activities) – Hospital

Patient service revenue (hotel type, medical, lab)
- **(P**rovision for contractual adjustments) Medicare, employee
                                  Discounts, not charity
Net patient service revenues

+ **O**ther Operating revenues, gains & losses (**earned**)
- **Non medical** –Parking, gift shop, cafeteria, tuition (auxiliary activities)
- **Donated medicines and blankets** (supplies & equipment)
- Restricted grants
- Net assets released from restriction used for *operations*

(**O**perating Expenses) *Bad debts*, drugs, doctors, Gen & Admin, Dep, Int.
Results from operations

+ **N**on-operating Revenues (Other Income) (**unearned**)
- **Unrestricted** donations, gifts, bequests
- Unrestricted **Interest & Dividend income**
- Unrestricted grants
- Donated **services**

Excess of Rev/Gains over Exp/Losses (**Performance indicator**)
(operating income, performance earnings, earned income)

Items reported separately from performance indicator
    *Restricted donations/contributions
    *Assets released from donor restrictions for long-lived assets (PP&E)
    *Restricted Investment Income
    *Change in net unrealized gains and losses (other than trading) on unrestricted investments
    *Transfers to Parent
    *Discontinued operations
Increase in Unrestricted Net Assets (UNA)

Sample Not-for-Profit Hospital
STATEMENTS OF OPERATIONS (ACTIVITIES)
Years Ended December 31, 20X7 and 20X6

	20X7	20X6
Unrestricted revenues, gains and other support:		
Net patient service revenue	$85,156	$78,942
Premium revenue	11,150	10,950
Other revenue	2,601	5,212
Net assets released from restrictions used for operations	300	--
Total revenues, gains and other support	99,207	95,104
Expenses:		
Operating expenses	88,521	80,585
Depreciation and amortization	4,782	4,280
Interest	1,752	1,825
Provision for **bad debts**	1,000	1,300
Other	2,000	1,300
Total expenses	98,055	89,290
Operating income	1,152	5,814
Other income:		
Investment income	3,900	3,025
Excess of revenues over expenses (Performance Indicator)	5,052	8,839
Change in net unrealized gains and losses on other than trading securities	300	375
Net assets released from restrictions used for purchase of property and equipment	200	
Change in interest in net assets of Sample Hospital Foundation	283	536
Transfers to parent	(688)	(3,051)
Increase in unrestricted net assets	$ 5,147	$ 6,699

See accompanying notes to financial statements.

Sample Not-for-Profit Hospital
STATEMENTS OF CHANGES IN NET ASSETS
Years Ended December 31, 20X7 and 20X6
(in thousands)

	20X7	20X6
Unrestricted net assets:		
Excess of revenues over expenses	$ 5,052	$ 8,839
Net unrealized gains on investments, other than trading securities	300	375
Change in interest in net assets of Sample Hospital Foundation	283	536
Transfers to parent	(688)	(3,051)
Net assets released from restrictions used for purchase of property and equipment	200	--
Increase in unrestricted net assets	5,147	6,699
Temporarily restricted net assets:		
Contributions for charity care	140	996
Net realized and unrealized gains on investments	5	8
Net assets released from restrictions	(500)	--
Increase (decrease) in temporarily restricted net assets	(355)	1,004
Permanently restricted net assets:		
Contributions for endowment funds	50	411
Net realized and unrealized gains on investments	5	2
Increase in permanently restricted net assets	55	413
Increase in net assets	4,847	8,116
Net assets, beginning of year	72,202	64,086
Net assets, end of year	$77,049	$72,202

Lecture 30.06
CLASS QUESTIONS
Please see the Class Questions and Class Solutions for this Lecture at the end of this Section.

Lecture 30.07
CLASS QUESTIONS
Please see the Class Questions and Class Solutions for this Lecture at the end of this Section.

CLASS QUESTIONS

Work through the below Class Questions while following along with the respective lectures. Once this is complete, you can begin independently practicing what you've learned by quizzing yourself on this course section in your Interactive Practice Questions (IPQ), which can be found in your online Student Dashboard. Your IPQ simulates the computer-based testing experience, and will also help you understand how concepts are applied to the exam. Each question includes answer explanations from expert CPAs that will help you determine why you answered a question correctly or incorrectly. This is key to your success on the CPA Exam.

Lecture 30.06

1. Candy Land, a nongovernmental not-for-profit organization, is preparing its year-end financial statements. Which of the following statements is required?

    a. Statement of changes in financial position.
    b. Statement of cash flows.
    c. Statement of changes in fund balance.
    d. Statement of revenue, expenses and changes in fund balance.

2. The Jackson Foundation, a private not-for-profit organization, had the following cash contributions and expenditures in 20X3:

    Unrestricted cash contributions of $500,000.
    Cash contributions of $200,000 restricted by the donor to the acquisition of property.
    Cash expenditures of $200,000 to acquire property with the donation in the above item.

    Jackson's statement of cash flows should include which of the following amounts?

	Operating activities	Investing activities	Financing activities
a.	$700,000	$(200,000)	$0
b.	$500,000	$0	$0
c.	$500,000	$(200,000)	$200,000
d.	$0	$500,000	$200,000

3. On December 30, 20X3, Leigh Museum, a not-for-profit organization, received a $7,000,000 donation of Day Co. shares with donor-stipulated requirements as follows:

    Shares valued at $5,000,000 are to be sold, with the proceeds used to erect a public viewing building.
    Shares valued at $2,000,000 are to be retained, with the dividends used to support current operations.

    As a consequence of the receipt of the Day shares, how much should Leigh report as temporarily restricted net assets on its 20X3 statement of financial position (balance sheet)?

    a. $0
    b. $2,000,000
    c. $5,000,000
    d. $7,000,000

Nonprofit Accounting   Section 30

4. The Jones family lost its home in a fire. On December 25, 20X3, a philanthropist sent money to the Amer Benevolent Society, a not-for-profit organization, to purchase furniture for the Jones family. During January 20X4, Amer purchased this furniture for the Jones family. How should Amer report the receipt of the money in its 20X3 financial statements?

   a. As an unrestricted contribution.
   b. As a temporarily restricted contribution.
   c. As a permanently restricted contribution.
   d. As a liability.

5. A not-for-profit organization receives $150 from a donor. The donor receives two tickets to a theater show and an acknowledgment in the theater program. The tickets have a fair market value of $100. What amount is recorded as contribution revenue?

   a. $0
   b. $ 50
   c. $100
   d. $150

6. Bryant Hospital, a nonprofit hospital affiliated with a religious group, reported the following information for the year ended December 31, 20X5:

Gross patient service revenue at the hospital's full established rates	$980,000
Bad debts expense	10,000
Contractual adjustments with third-party payors	100,000
Allowance for discounts to hospital employees	15,000

   On the hospital's statement of operations for the year ended December 31, 20X5, what amount should be reported as net patient service revenue?

   a. $865,000
   b. $880,000
   c. $855,000
   d. $955,000

7. Rosenthal Hospital, a nonprofit hospital affiliated with a private university, reported the following information for the year ended December 31, 20X5:

Cash contributions received from donors for capital additions to be acquired in 20X6	$150,000
Proceeds from sales at hospital gift shop and snack bar	75,000
Dividend revenue not restricted by donors or by law	25,000

   Using the information provided, what amount should be reported as "other operating and non-operating revenue and gains" on the hospital's statement of operations (activities) for the year ended December 31, 20X5?

   a. $ 25,000
   b. $ 75,000
   c. $100,000
   d. $250,000

©Roger CPA Review   Page 30-19

CLASS SOLUTIONS

1. (b) A not-for-profit organization is required to include a statement of financial position as of the reporting date, and statements of activities and of cash flows for the reporting period ending on that date whenever presenting a complete set of financial statements. Answer (a) is incorrect because a statement of changes in financial position, which would be similar to a statement of cash flows with a definition of funds that is different than cash and cash equivalents, is not required. Answer (c) is incorrect because a statement of changes in fund balance is not required. Answer (d) is incorrect because a statement of revenues, expenses, and changes in fund balance are not required.

2. (c) Unrestricted cash contributions of $500,000 are cash inflows from operating activities as they may be used for whatever purpose the board deems appropriate. Contributions that are designated by the donor for the funding of a long-term project, such as the $200,000 received that is restricted to the acquisition of property is considered an inflow from financing activities. When the funds are used for the acquisition of property, since property is a capital asset, the expenditure would be an outflow for investing activities.

3. (c) Since the shares valued at $5,000,000 were stipulated to be used for the erection of a public viewing building, they become unrestricted when used for that purpose and are, therefore, temporarily restricted. The shares valued at $2,000,000 are to be retained with no provision for their sale or other disposal. As a result, they are permanently restricted. Temporarily restricted funds would be $5,000,000.

4. (d) When the recipient of funds has little or no discretion as to how funds will be used, the funds are received by the NPO in the capacity of an agent. They are recognized as a liability, not as revenue, until such time as they are disbursed according to the donor's instructions.

5. (b) When a not-for-profit receives contributions and provides goods or services in exchange, the amount received in excess of the fair value of the goods or services is recognized as revenues. Of the $150 received, $100 was for the fair value of the tickets and $50 was contributions revenue.

6. (a) Net patient service revenue is the amount that the health care organization expects to collect subject to credit risk. Of the $980,000 billed at full rates, the hospital does not expect to collect the reductions due to contractual adjustments of $100,000 or the employee discounts of $15,000, resulting in $865,000 that the hospital expects to collect. This is subject to credit risk in that some patients or insurance companies may not be able to pay. The result is bad debt expense, on operating expense, of $10,000.

7. (c) On a hospital's statement of activities, other revenues and gains represent amounts received for reasons other than the performance of health care related services that is available to be used at the discretion of the board. It would not include contributions that are to be used for capital additions, as these are reported on the statement of changes in net assets, but not on the statement of operations (activities). However, the statement of operations would include revenues from gift and snack sales of $75,000 and dividend revenue that is not restricted of $25,000 for a total of $100,000.

Nonprofit Accounting — Section 30

Lecture 30.07
TASK-BASED SIMULATIONS

Task-Based Simulation 1

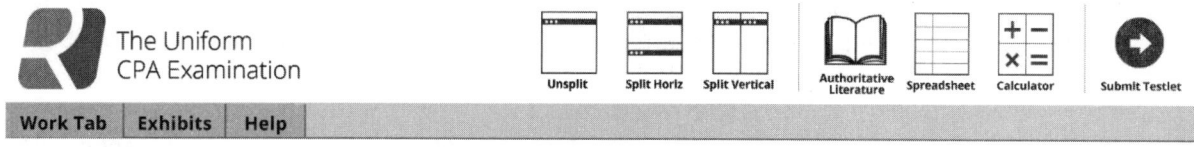

Situation:

Items 1 through 10 in the left-hand column represent various transactions pertaining to Philipp University, a private university, for the year ended December 31, 20X3. To the right of these transactions is a listing of how transactions could affect the **statement of activities** (List **A** effects) and the **statement of cash flows** (List **B** effects).

Required:

Indicate how each transaction should be reported by Philipp University on (1) the statement of activities and (2) the statement of cash flows prepared for the year ended December 31, 20X3. Philipp reports separate columns for the changes in unrestricted, temporarily restricted and permanently restricted net assets on its statement of activities. In addition, Philipp uses the direct method of reporting its cash flows from operating activities. Philipp has a policy of not restricting net assets related to plant. A List A or List B effect may be used once, more than once or not at all.

Transactions

1. A donor contributed $100,000 and stipulated that it be invested permanently.
2. Donors contributed $500,000 for the acquisition of equipment.
3. Depreciation expense of $750,000 was recorded for 20X3.
4. $3,000,000 was received, representing tuition for the spring, summer and fall semesters.
5. Investments of $100,000 were acquired with the cash received from the donor in transaction 1.
6. Interest and dividends of $8,000 were received from the investments acquired in transaction 5. The donor stipulated that earnings be used for student scholarships in 20X3.
7. $75,000 was received from donors in 20X3 who had pledged that amount in 20X2. The cash will be used to pay for a marketing campaign that aimed at increasing enrollment. The marketing cost was incurred in 20X3 and will be paid in 20X4.
8. $900,000 was paid to faculty for salaries incurred during the year.
9. $25,000 was given to the faculty for summer research grants. The grants came from donations made by alumni in 20X2.
10. $40,000 of donations were received from alumni who did **not** stipulate how their donations were to be used.

Statement of activities
List A effects

A. Increases unrestricted net assets net assets
B. Increases temporarily restricted
C. Increases permanently restricted net assets
D. Decreases unrestricted net assets
E. Decreases temporarily restricted net assets
F. Decreases permanently restricted net assets
G. Transaction not reported on the statement of activities

Statement of cash flows
List B effects

H. Increases cash flows from operating activities
I. Decreases cash flows from operating activities
J. Increases cash flows from investing activities
K. Decreases cash flows from investing activities
L. Increases cash flows from financing activities
M. Decreases cash flows from financing activities
N. Transaction not reported on the statement
O. Transaction reported in the schedule reconciling change in net assets to net cash provided from operating activities

Task-Based Simulation 2

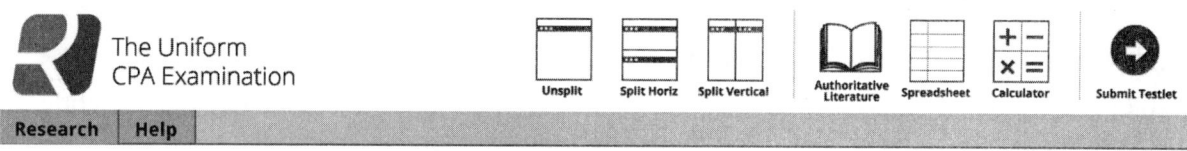

A not-for-profit client wishes to recognize pledges as revenue at the time the pledge is made, but is uncertain as to whether or not that is allowed. Identify the location in professional standards that indicates when contributions may be recognized as revenue.

Task-Based Simulation 3

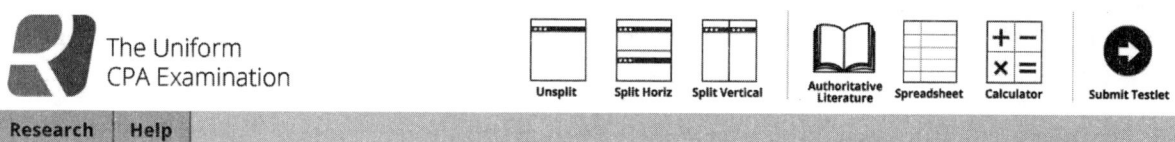

A not-for-profit entity received an investment as a contribution and wishes to determine how to recognize it. Identify the location in professional standards that indicates how and when to recognize an investment acquired by contribution.

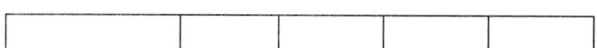

TASK-BASED SIMULATION SOLUTIONS

Task-Based Simulation Solution 1

1. (C,L) When a donor stipulates that some or all of a contribution is to be retained permanently, such as a requirement that it be invested permanently, the resources will be classified as permanently restricted net assets. Since they are restricted to be used for the purpose of acquiring permanent assets, the contribution is considered an inflow from financing activities.

2. (B,L) When contributions are restricted for a particular purpose or for a particular period of time, they are considered temporarily restricted net assets. When they are used for the intended purpose or retained for the requisite period, then become unrestricted. Since the resources are to be used to acquire equipment, a long-term asset, the contribution is considered an inflow from financing activities.

3. (D,O) All expenses, including depreciation, are considered reductions in unrestricted net assets. Since it is an expense that does not involve the use of cash, it is a reconciling item on the reconciliation of the change in net assets to cash flows from operating activities, as required to be included with the statement of cash flows.

4. (A,H) Amounts received for tuition are considered revenues and, in general, are increases in unrestricted net assets. They represent inflows of funds from the core operations of the college and are classified as inflows from operating activities.

5. (G,K) The purchase of securities represents the use of one permanently restricted asset, cash, to acquire another permanently restricted asset, investments. As a result, there is no change in permanently restricted net assets. The use of cash to acquire investments would be classified as an outflow for investing activities.

6. (B,H) Since the donor stipulated that interest and dividends be used for scholarships, those funds are considered restricted until such time as they are used for that purpose, when they become unrestricted. As a result, they are temporarily restricted funds and the receipt would represent an increase in temporarily restricted net assets. Interest and dividends received are considered cash inflows from operating activities.

7. (E,H) The amounts pledged from donors were recognized as revenues when received in 20X2, increasing temporarily restricted net assets at that time. In 20X3, the costs were actually incurred, and the funds became unrestricted, resulting in a decrease in temporarily restricted funds and an increase in unrestricted net assets. At the same time, the expense is recognized, which decreases unrestricted net assets resulting in no net change. The reclassification of the cash from temporarily restricted to unrestricted is considered an inflow of unrestricted cash and, as a result, an inflow from operating activities.

8. (D,I) All expenses are recognized as decreases in unrestricted net assets. The payment of expenses, including salaries, is an outflow from operating activities.

9. (E,I) When the donations were received in 20X2, they were recognized as an increase in temporarily restricted net assets. When they are used for their intended purpose, they are first reclassified to unrestricted, representing a decrease in temporarily restricted net assets. The increase in unrestricted net assets is offset by the decrease resulting from payment of the research grants, so there is no net change in unrestricted net assets. The payments of grants is considered a cash outflow from operating activities.

10. (A,H) Contributions received that are not restricted by external parties are considered unrestricted resources and result in an increase in unrestricted net assets. Contributions received are considered cash inflows from operating activities.

Task-Based Simulation Solution 2

| FASB ASC | 958 | 605 | 25 | 2 |

Task-Based Simulation Solution 3

| FASB ASC | 958 | 325 | 25 | 1 |

Section 31 - Business Combinations and Consolidations

Section 31 – Business Combinations and Consolidations

Corresponding Lectures

Watch the following course lectures with this section:

Lecture 31.01 – Business Combinations and Consolidations
Lecture 31.02 – Steps in Applying the Acquisition Method
Lecture 31.03 – Examples #1, #2 at date of Acquisition
Lecture 31.04 – Example #3 at Year End
Lecture 31.05 – Consolidations – Class Questions
Lecture 31.06 – Example #4 Noncontrolling Interest
Lecture 31.07 – Example #5 Noncontrolling Interest @ Year End
Lecture 31.08 – Intercompany Transactions
Lecture 31.09 – Consolidations – Class Questions
Lecture 31.10 – Consolidations – Class Question - TBS
Lecture 31.11 – Business Combinations under IFRS
Lecture 31.12 – Business Combinations under IFRS –
　　　　　　　　Class Question

EXAM NOTE: Please refer to the AICPA FAR Blueprint in the Introduction to find a listing of the representative tasks (and their associated skill levels—i.e., Remembering and Understanding, Application, and Analysis) that the candidate should be able to perform based on the knowledge obtained in this section.

Business Combinations and Consolidations
(ASC 805/810)

Lecture 31.01

BUSINESS COMBINATIONS

ASC 805 applies to all business combinations. The objective is to improve the relevance, representational faithfulness, and comparability of the information that a reporting entity provides in its financial reports about a business combination and its effects.

ASC 805, represents a conceptually more consistent method of consolidation and improves financial reporting by reflecting the **economic entity concept**. The method reflects the emphasis on the balance sheet rather than its traditional emphasis on the income statement. The new method recognizes all assets and liabilities of the acquired company and values them at *full fair value* (FASB ASC 820). Generally, this will result in higher consolidated assets and noncontrolling interests. The new approach will better reflect the investment made by the Acquirer, enhance financial statement comparability between companies, and provide more complete and relevant financial information.

When one corporation, the **Acquirer** (*the Parent*) acquires **Control** (a controlling financial interest) in another entity, the **Acquiree** (*the Subsidiary*), this creates a relationship requiring the preparation of consolidated financial statements at each balance sheet date. The Acquisition date is the date on which the acquirer obtains a controlling financial interest in the Acquiree.
- A controlling financial interest is most commonly obtained when one entity obtains a majority of the voting equity of another.
    o There are circumstances where an entity can own more than 50% of the voting equity of another entity and not have a controlling financial interest.
    o This would typically be when control is only temporary or when majority ownership does not provide the holder with control over the entity.

- A controlling financial interest may also be obtained as a result of the relationship between the entities.
    o The controlled entity would be considered a variable interest entity or VIE (FASB ASC 810).
    o The entity with control is considered the primary beneficiary of the VIE.

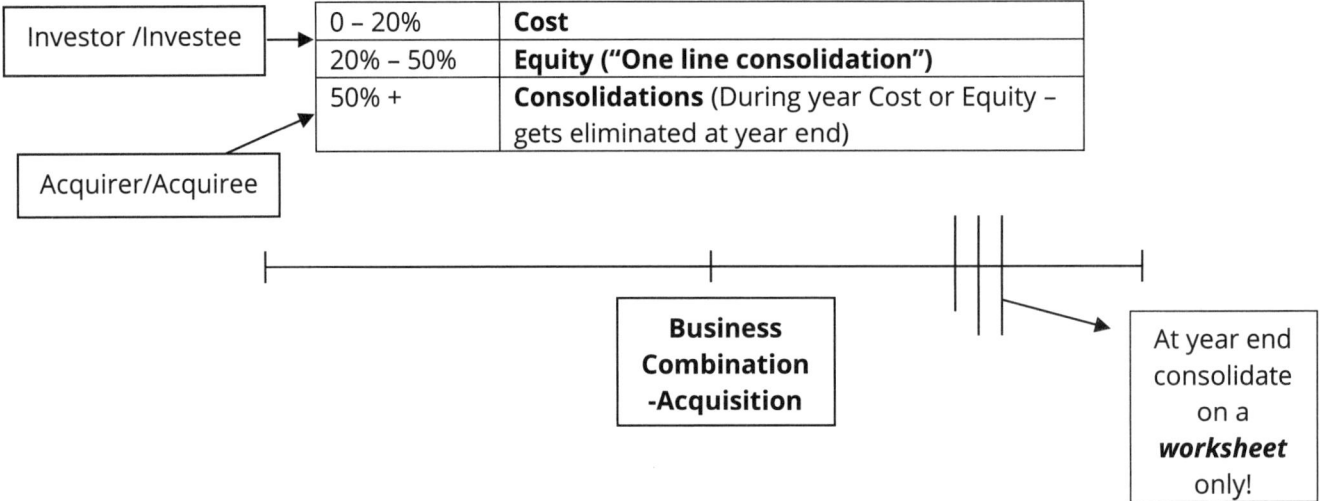

Lecture 31.02

Steps in Applying the Acquisition Method

ASC 805 - All consolidations must be performed using the **Acquisition** method (formally called the Purchase method). An acquisition is considered to be a financial transaction executed by the Acquirer, and the resulting entity is considered to be a continuation of the Acquirer. As a result, the assets and liabilities of the Acquiree are acquired at **fair values** (ASC 820) at the **acquisition date,** and **income** of the Acquiree is only included from the *date of acquisition on.*

There are 4 steps in applying the acquisition method.

1. **Identify the acquirer**

In a stock for assets transaction, the acquirer is the one giving the assets and acquiring the stock. In stock for stock transactions, however, various factors will be considered in determining which entity is the acquirer and which is the acquiree. Factors to consider may include:
- The entity that initiated the transaction.
- Representation in management and governance
- Relative voting rights

Identifying the acquirer can be very significant since the assets and liabilities of the acquirer remain at book value and those of the acquiree are reported at fair value.

2. **Determine the acquisition date**

The acquisition date is the date on which the acquirer obtains a controlling financial interest over the acquiree. In the case of an equity acquisition, it is the date on which the acquirer's holdings became a majority. In the case of a VIE, it may be the date on which a lease, a sale or purchase contract, or some other relationship was entered into.

The acquisition date is also referred to as the measurement date. It is the date as of which:
- Identifiable assets acquired and liabilities assumed are measured at fair value by the acquirer.
- The acquirer begins to recognize the revenues and expenses of the acquiree in the acquirer's consolidated financial statements.

Business Combinations and Consolidations					Section 31

3. Recognize and measure the identifiable assets acquired, liabilities assumed, and any *noncontrolling interest* (minority interest) in the acquiree

Identifiable assets, including those that are and are not included on the financial statements of the acquiree, and liabilities assumed are generally measured at fair value. The measurements are based on prescribed standards.
- For some items, specific guidelines have been established in authoritative accounting literature. For example:
    o The fair value of accounts receivable is its net realizable value.
    o The fair value of inventory is its replacement cost, subject to floor and ceiling limitations.
- For other items, there are no specific guidelines established in authoritative literature.
    o There are no authoritative guidelines for measuring the fair value of manufacturing equipment.
    o Such items are measured applying the general definition of fair value indicated in FASB ASC 820, Fair Value Measurement.

In some cases, the acquirer will not recognize assets or liabilities that are included in the financial statements of the acquiree. Examples may include:
- Any goodwill recognized on the financial statements of the acquiree.
- Prepaid rent or accrued rent resulting from recognizing operating lease payments on a straight-line basis.
- Deferred tax assets or liabilities, which will be measured by the acquirer on the basis of the differences between the newly recorded amounts and the tax bases of assets acquired and liabilities assumed.

In addition, the acquirer may recognize assets or liabilities that are not on the financial statements of the acquiree. Examples may include:
- An asset or liability related to an acquired operating lease with terms that are more or less favorable than current market terms, respectively.
- Intangibles, including internally developed intangibles, the costs of which were recognized as expense in the period incurred.

The acquirer recognizes all identifiable intangible assets at fair value at the date of acquisition. An intangible is considered identifiable if either:
- It represents a legal or contractual right; or
- It can be sold, transferred, licensed, or otherwise disposed of by itself.

Examples of identifiable intangibles that may be recognized by the acquirer include:
- **Marketing-related** *intangibles* – Trademarks, trade names, noncompetition agreements
- **Customer-related** *intangibles* – customer lists, customer contracts
- **Artistic-related** *intangibles* – plays, operas, books, magazines, pictures, videos, films, music
- **Contact-based** *intangibles* - licensing, royalty, advertising, lease and franchise agreements, construction permits
- **Technology-based** *intangibles* – computer software, mask works, trade secrets, recipes

The Private Company Council (PCC) of the FASB has established an alternative accounting approach that may be applied by nonpublic entities. When recognizing and measuring identifiable assets acquired, it allows them to disregard certain intangibles, effectively increasing the amount recognized as goodwill or decreasing the amount reported as a gain on bargain purchase.

In applying the alternative accounting approach, an entity **will not measure and recognize** the following items separate from goodwill:
- **Customer-related intangibles** that are not capable of being sold or licensed independently from other assets; and
- **Noncompetition agreements**.
- As is true of the other alternative accounting approaches, a nonpublic entity that wishes to adopt it is required to do so by making an election, doing so through disclosure, and will be required to disclose its application on an ongoing basis in the summary of significant accounting policies. In addition, this alternative accounting approach may only be elected if the entity is also electing to amortize goodwill.

In addition to measuring and recognizing identifiable assets acquired and liabilities assumed, the acquirer recognizes any noncontrolling interest in the acquiree at fair value. A noncontrolling interest results from the acquirer having a controlling financial interest that is not 100% of the voting equity of the acquiree.
- In the case of a stock acquisition, the noncontrolling interest would be the minority interest, the portion not owned by the acquirer.
- In the case of a VIE, it may be 100% of the ownership of the entity.

Since a noncontrolling interest may actually represent, in the case of a VIE, a majority of the equity ownership of an entity, it is not considered appropriate to refer to the unowned portion as the minority interest. It is, instead, required to be referred to as the noncontrolling interest (ASC 810).
- It is measured at its fair value as of the acquisition, or measurement, date.
- Fair value is considered to be market price of a single share multiplied by the number of shares on the acquisition date.

The noncontrolling interest is a component of stockholders' equity and is required to be reported in the **stockholders' equity section** of the balance sheet (ASC 810). The amount reported as the noncontrolling interest is periodically adjusted for its share of net income and other comprehensive income.
- Net income will include all revenues, expenses, gains, and losses of the parent and all subsidiaries, after adjusting for intercompany items.
  - An appropriate amount will be allocated to the noncontrolling interest on the income statement and will be closed to the noncontrolling interest account.
  - The remainder will be allocated to the parent and will be closed to retained earnings.
- Other comprehensive income will include all of the amounts recognized by the parent and all subsidiaries, after eliminating intercompany items.
  - An appropriate amount will be allocated to the noncontrolling interest on the statement of comprehensive income and will be closed to the noncontrolling interest account.
  - The remainder will be allocated to the parent and will be closed to accumulated other comprehensive income.

4. Recognize and measure Goodwill, or a Gain from a bargain purchase.

As indicated, when recording a business combination, assets and liabilities of the acquiree are recognized at fair value. The difference is the fair value of the underlying net assets.

Any noncontrolling interests are also recognized at fair value.

The acquirer will recognize consideration given, if any, at its fair value.

Business Combinations and Consolidations   Section 31

- Cash is, of course, reported at its face amount.
- Any assets transferred are included at fair value with any difference between fair value and book value treated as a gain or loss on disposal.
- Stock issued is recognized at fair value with a credit to common stock for any par or stated value and additional paid-in capital for the difference.

Most **costs incurred** in relation to the transaction will be **recognized as expense** when incurred. This includes any general expenses incurred; costs directly related to the acquisition, such as attorney or appraiser fees; and indirect costs, such as the costs of printing new stationery or developing new training manuals, finder fees.

One exception is the cost of issuing and registering debt and equity securities issued in the combination.
- Costs of issuing equity securities reduce additional paid-in capital.
- Costs of issuing debt securities are capitalized and amortized as debt issue costs.

Considering all of the factors involved in recognizing a business combination, and all of the different measurements, it would be very unusual for the entry recognizing the combination to balance.
- If the amount necessary to balance the entry is a debit, it will be recognized as **goodwill**.
    - It is measured as the excess of the consideration given over the fair value of the underlying net assets acquired.
    - The fact that the consideration is greater indicates that the company as a whole is worth more than the fair value of its net assets.

- If the amount necessary to balance the entry is a credit, it will be recognized as **gain on bargain purchase**.
    - It is measured as the excess of the fair value of the underlying net assets acquired over the consideration given.
    - The fact that the consideration is less indicates that the company may not have been a going concern and may not have had the ability to dispose of assets and settle liabilities at their fair values.

The acquisition is recorded in one of two ways. The acquirer can record the individual assets acquired and liabilities assumed or record the transaction as an investment. The acquirer will often record the individual assets acquired and liabilities assumed when there is no need to maintain separate records for the acquiree, either for internal purposes or for external reporting purposes.

When the acquirer records the individual assets and liabilities, the process will be as follows:
- Assets acquired and liabilities assumed, including some that may not have been recognized by the acquiree, are recognized at their fair values.
- Consideration is measured as follows:
    - Cash paid is recognized as a reduction to cash
    - Stock issued is recognized at its fair value with the par value credited to common stock and the remainder to additional paid-in capital.
    - If other assets are transferred, consideration will be the fair value and a gain or loss is recognized as if they were sold for their fair values.
    - Any previous investment, if accounted for at cost or under the equity method, is also included at fair value with a gain or loss recognized as if sold for that amount.

- Noncontrolling interest, if any, is recognized as a component of stockholders' equity at its fair value.
- Any remaining **debit** necessary to balance the entry is recorded as **Goodwill**.
- If a **credit** is necessary (paid less than net Fair Value for Acquiree) the bargain is recorded as a **GAIN** on the income statement.

Once the initial entry has been recorded, the acquirer will apply generally accepted accounting principles going forward and there is no special accounting required after the period of acquisition.

Lecture 31.03

Recording the Acquisition

When the acquirer records the transaction as an investment, recording the acquisition is quite straightforward. The Investment in acquiree is debited for the purchase price, meaning the total fair value of the consideration paid by the acquirer. Essentially, this is the balancing entry to offset the accounts being credited in the remainder of this entry. The book values of the acquiree accounts are ignored.
- Cash is credited for any amounts paid.
- Common stock is credited for the par value of any shares being issued by the acquirer.
- Additional paid-in capital is credited for the excess of the fair value of any shares being issued over their par value.

There is no entry to retained earnings, since the acquirer does not retroactively combine the income of the acquirer in a purchase. The Acquiree's income is included from the date of acquisition (prospective, not retroactive).

Preparing Consolidated Financial Statements

When the acquirer records the initial transaction as an investment, it will prepare consolidated financial statements each reporting period. Preparing consolidated financial statements involves a process under which:
- The investment is eliminated, as are the acquiree's (subsidiary's) equity accounts.
- Those assets and liabilities that were part of the original acquisition and are still on the books will be adjusted for differences between their book values and fair values on the acquisition date.
- The income statement effects of differences between book and fair values will be recognized in income to the extent that they apply to the current period and to retained earnings to the extent that they apply to prior periods.
- The effects of interentity transactions are eliminated.
- The noncontrolling interest will be recorded in equity based on the fair value on the date of acquisition adjusted for changes due to income or distribution since that date.

Pushdown Accounting

One of the more cumbersome aspects of preparing consolidated financial statements is keeping track of the differences between the fair values and the carrying values of the acquiree's assets and liabilities at the acquisition date. Each period, until all of those items have been disposed of or settled, an adjustment will be required to recognize that difference as well as any depreciation,

Business Combinations and Consolidations   Section 31

amortization, impairment, or other adjustment that would have been made to it since the date of acquisition.

GAAP provides an alternative in the form of pushdown accounting. When an acquiree decides to adopt pushdown accounting, it adjusts its assets and liabilities to the same amounts at which they will be reported by the acquirer (parent) and account for those assets and liabilities going forward on a basis similar to that which would be applied by the acquirer (parent). As a result, the consolidation process is simplified and the acquirer (parent) will only be required to eliminate inter-entity transactions, recognize the noncontrolling interest, and eliminate the investment account.

An acquiree is not required to adopt the pushdown basis of accounting but may decide to do so in any period in which there is a change in control event. If, for example, an investor with the ability to exercise significant influence over an investee acquires additional equity resulting in a controlling financial interest, the acquiree could adopt pushdown accounting in that period.
- An election to adopt pushdown accounting is irrevocable.
- If an entity does not elect to adopt pushdown accounting in the period of a change of control event, it may do so in a subsequent period and will account for the change as a change in accounting principle.

Examples of Consolidations on the Date of Acquisition
Class Example #1
Assume the following balance sheets are available for P Co. and S Co. at 12/31/X1:

Accounts	P Co.	S Co.
Cash	1000	100
A/R		
Inventory		
Equipment (PP&E)	8000	500
A/P		
Bonds Payable		
$1 CS	(1000)	(100)
APIC	(3000)	(100)
RE	(5000)	(400)

If P issues 150 shares of stock to acquire all of S, and the stock being issued has a market value of $6 per share, the entry to record the acquisition is:

```
Investment in S                         900
    Common stock                               150
    Additional paid-in capital                 750
```

If the purchase were for an equivalent amount of cash instead, the entry would be:

```
Investment in S                         900
    Cash                                       900
```

Combining Equity

When consolidated financial statements are prepared, the separate trial balances of the acquirer and acquiree are combined on a **worksheet** into a single set of numbers for presentation purposes. In the process, certain account balances must be eliminated or adjusted. This includes all accounts that treat the two companies as separate entities, since the presentation is designed to report them as a single entity. The consolidation process eliminates reciprocal items that are shown on both the acquirer's and acquiree's books. These eliminations are necessary to avoid double-counting the same items which would misstate the financial statements of the combined economic entity.

The concept of consolidated statements is that the resources of two or more companies are under the control of the acquirer. Consolidated statements are prepared as if the group of legal entities were one economic entity, based on the **economic entity concept.**

After an acquisition, the preparation of a consolidated financial statement requires substantial adjustments, since the investment has been recorded at the purchase price, not the underlying equity of the subsidiary.

The **entry to combine equity** includes all of the following elements:
- All of the equity accounts are debited to remove 100% of the acquiree account balances.
- Investment in acquiree is credited to remove the account.
- Investment is credited (for investments held prior to acquisition - Fair value of previously held equity interests in acquiree)
- Noncontrolling interest is credited (multiply the active market price on the acquisition date x the number of shares held by the noncontrolling parties)

If the fair value of net identifiable assets of the acquiree is *less than* the aggregate of the consideration transferred, plus the acquisition date fair value of previously held interests, plus the fair value of noncontrolling interest, **GOODWILL** is recognized.

If the fair value of net identifiable assets of the acquiree *exceeds* the aggregate of the consideration transferred, plus the acquisition date fair value of previously held interests, plus the fair value of the noncontrolling interest, then a bargain purchase occurs. A **GAIN** is recognized by the acquirer in the current period's income statement for the bargain purchase.

The calculation of Goodwill and Gain is as follows:
Fair value of consideration transferred (cost to the acquirer)
+ Fair value of previously held equity interests in acquiree
+ Fair value of noncontrolling interest
(-) Fair value of net identifiable assets of acquiree
Goodwill or Gain from bargain purchase

- **Goodwill** is defined as "an asset representing the future economic benefits that arises from other assets acquired in a business combination that are not individually identified and separately recognized."

Business Combinations and Consolidations — Section 31

In addition, the entry will usually require adjustments to Identifiable asset accounts whose fair value differed from book value on the date of the original acquisition, and an entry for goodwill for the remaining difference in the entry. The following approach is needed:

- Assets that were sold prior to the balance sheet date are ignored.
- Identifiable Assets still being held at the balance sheet date are adjusted for the difference between the fair value and book value **at the date of Acquisition**.
- The ID assets acquired, liabilities assumed and any noncontrolling interest are measured at fair value. Any **newly identified intangible assets** of the acquiree must also be recognized:
    - **Marketing-related** intangibles – trademarks, trade names, noncompetition agreements
    - **Customer-related** intangibles – customer lists, customer contracts
    - **Artistic-related** intangibles – plays, operas, books, magazines, pictures, videos, films, music
    - **Contact-based** intangibles – licensing, royalty, advertising, lease and franchise agreements, construction permits
    - **Technology-based** intangibles – computer software, mask works, trade secrets, recipes

- Any remaining **debit** necessary to balance the entry is recorded as **Goodwill**.
- If a **credit** is necessary (paid less than net Fair Value for Acquiree) the bargain purchase is recorded as a **GAIN** on the income statement.

    - Acquired assets and liabilities at **fair market value** (FMV). (Goodwill and FMV write-up)
        - Excess of FMV over BV considered FMV Increment (write up)
            - Land
            - PP&E
            - Inventory
            - Other Identifiable Assets (ID assets)

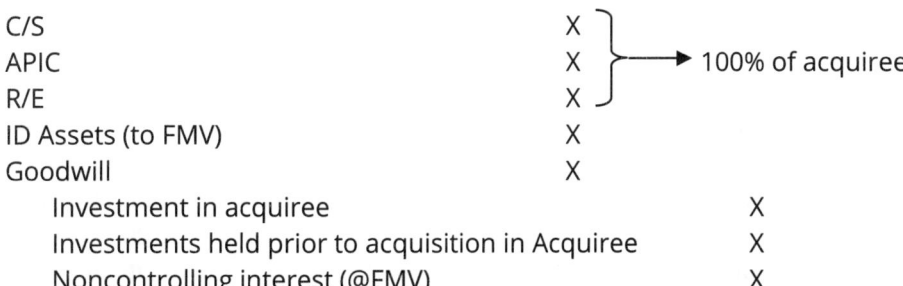

If an adjustment occurs to an asset which is **depreciable or amortizable**, an additional entry must be made to account for the depreciation or amortization between the purchase date and financial statement date. Intangible assets that do not have definite lives, such as **goodwill, will be tested for impairment** on an annual basis pursuant to FASB ASC 350.

Class Example #2

Assume that P Co. acquired all (100%) of the stock of S Co. in an acquisition on 12/31/X1 for a payment of $900 cash. At the time, the book value of S was $600, and all of the assets and liabilities had fair values equal to their book values, with the exception of equipment with a remaining life of 5 years and a fair value $100 higher than book value. The accounts of the two companies at 12/31/X1 are presented in a worksheet, along with the combining entry:

Everything acquired @ **FMV** of stock given or cash paid:

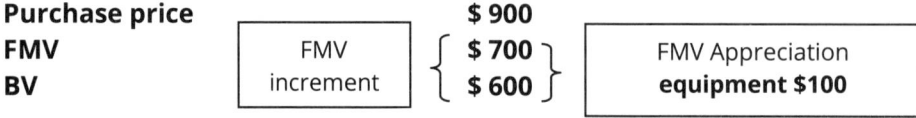

Accounts	P Co	S Co	Debits	Credits	Consol
Cash	100	100			200
Equipment	8000	500	100		8600
Inv in S	900			900	---
Goodwill			200		200
$1 CS	(1000)	(100)	100		(1000)
APIC	(3000)	(100)	100		(3000)
RE	(5000)	(400)	400		(5000)

To acquire Investment: (In books)

    Investment   900
        Cash   900

To consolidate: (On worksheet)

Goodwill is the balancing entry in the above: it represents the excess of the $900 investment over the $700 fair value of the net identifiable assets ($600 book value + $100 excess of fair value over book value of equipment = $700).

Lecture 31.04
Consolidations After the Date of Acquisition
Class Example #3
Acquire 100%, consolidate at year end

The following example assumes the acquirer used the equity method to account for the majority investment during the year.

Class Example

Let's look at a consolidation performed after the date of acquisition. Again, assume that P acquired all (100%) of S on 12/31/X1 for $900 cash, that equipment with a 5-year life had a fair value exceeding book value by $100 on 12/31/X1, and that goodwill, which came to $200 on 12/31/X1, is believed to be impaired as of 12/31/X2 and, as a result, only worth $195. Income during the year for P was $3,000 and S was $150. The investment is accounted for under the Equity method. Let's look at the consolidating worksheet that might appear one year later, on 12/31/X2:

Summary: Acquire 100% for $900 on 12/31/X1, and consolidate on 12/31/X2
- Income during the year:
    - P - $3000
    - S - $150
- Equipment useful life = 5 years
- Goodwill Impaired by $5
- Investment accounted for under the **equity method**.

To account for S's income under the equity method:

Investment	150	
Equity in earnings (I/S)		150

To Depreciate the Equipment (100/5 = $20):

Equity in earnings (I/S)	20	
Investment		20

To record Impairment of Goodwill:

Equity in earnings	5	
Investment		5

Investment	
900	
150	20
	5
1025	

To consolidate at year end:

C/S	100	
APIC	100	
R/E	550	
Equipment	80 (100-20)	
Goodwill	195 (200-5)	
Investment		**1025**

Accounts	P Co	S Co	Debits	Credits	Consol
Cash	3100	250			3350
Equipment	8000	500	80		8580
Inv in S	1025			1025	---
Goodwill			195		195
$1 CS	(1000)	(100)	100		(1000)
APIC	(3000)	(100)	100		(3000)
RE	(8125)	(550)	550		(8125)

In the earlier example, the retained earnings of P and S were $5,000 and $400, respectively. The retained earnings of both companies have changed, of course: P earned $3,000 from its separate operations, and S earned $150. P's bookkeeper has used the equity method of accounting, and has reported $125 equity in earnings of S. This is because the $150 income is reduced by depreciation on the $100 equipment excess over 5 years, for $20, and impairment of goodwill resulted in a $5 reduction in its carrying value from $200 to $195. Similarly, the net adjustments to the equipment and goodwill accounts are reduced by accumulated depreciation and impairment adjustments, respectively. In the above example, no separate accounts were presented for accumulated depreciation and impairment adjustments, so adjustments were made to the asset accounts directly.

Lecture 31.05

CLASS QUESTIONS

Please see the Class Questions and Class Solutions for this Lecture at the end of this Section.

Lecture 31.06

Noncontrolling interest (Minority Interest)

When one entity obtains a controlling financial interest in another entity, it may or may not entail the acquisition of the acquiree's equity securities, such as when a primary beneficiary has a controlling financial interest in a VIE. In addition, even when it does, the acquirer often acquires less than 100% of the acquiree's outstanding stock. The portion of the acquiree's equity that is held by parties or entities other than the acquirer is referred to as the **noncontrolling interest**.

The noncontrolling interest is considered a portion of shareholders; equity and is required to be reported in the shareholders' equity section of the balance sheet. It is originally recognized at fair value as of the date of acquisition:
- If the shares are traded in an active market, the per share market value will be multiplied by the number of shares owned by others.
- If the shares are not traded in an active market, an alternative method will be applied in determining fair value.

The noncontrolling interest is adjusted for:
- The noncontrolling interest's share of the acquiree's net income; and
- The noncontrolling interest's portion of distributions by the acquiree.

Business Combinations and Consolidations   Section 31

The consolidated income statement will include the revenues, expenses, gains, and losses of both the acquirer and the acquiree.
- The income statement effects of interentity transactions, including sales of merchandise, the performance of services, loans, leases, and the sale of other assets, are eliminated.
- The result is considered consolidated net income.
    - A portion, equal to the acquiree's unadjusted net income multiplied by the noncontrolling interest's percentage ownership in the acquiree, is allocated to, and recognized as an adjustment to the noncontrolling interest.
    - The remainder is allocated to the acquirer and recognized as an adjustment to retained earnings.

A similar approach is used in allocating other comprehensive income. The consolidated statement of other comprehensive income, or combined statement if the one-statement approach is used, will reflect all items of other comprehensive income for the period for both the acquirer and the acquiree, after eliminating interentity items, if any.
- A proportionate amount of those attributable to the noncontrolling interest's share is allocated to, and recognized as an adjustment to, the noncontrolling interest.
- The remainder is allocated to the acquirer and recognized as an adjustment to accumulated other comprehensive income.

Class Example #4:
Assume that P Co. acquired 90% (10% noncontrolling interest) of the stock of S Co. in an acquisition on 12/31/X1 for a payment of $900 cash. At the date of acquisition, S Co. had 100,000 shares of stock outstanding with a FMV of $8 per share. The book value of S was $600, and all of the assets and liabilities had fair values equal to their book values, with the exception of equipment with a remaining life of 5 years and a fair value $100 higher than book value. The accounts of the two companies at 12/31/X1 are presented in a worksheet, along with the combining entry:

The consolidating worksheet would appear as follows:

Purchase price		$ 900
FMV	FMV increment	$ 700
BV		$ 600

The FMV of the noncontrolling interest at the date of acquisition is 100,000 x $8 = $800,000 x 10% = $80,000.

The calculation of Goodwill or Gain is as follows:

Fair value of consideration transferred (cost to the acquirer)	$900,000
+ Fair value of previously held equity interests in acquiree	0
+ Fair value of noncontrolling interest	$ 80,000
(-) Fair value of net identifiable assets of acquiree	($700,000)
Goodwill or Gain from bargain purchase	**$280,000**

Accounts	P Co	S Co	Debits	Credits	Consol
Cash	100	100			200
Equipment	8000	500	100		8600
Inv in S	900			900	---
Goodwill			280		280
$1 CS	(1000)	(100)	100		(1000)
APIC	(3000)	(100)	100		(3000)
Noncontrol Int.				80	(80)
RE	(5000)	(400)	400		(5000)

Keep in mind that the income reported for 20X1 will be the **Acquirer's income only**, since purchases are accounted for prospectively, not retroactively. The acquiree's income (or 90% of it, in the case of a 90% purchase) is included from the date of purchase onward.

To acquire 90% of Investment: (Noncontrolling interest) (In books)

    Investment   900
        Cash   900

To consolidate: (On worksheet)

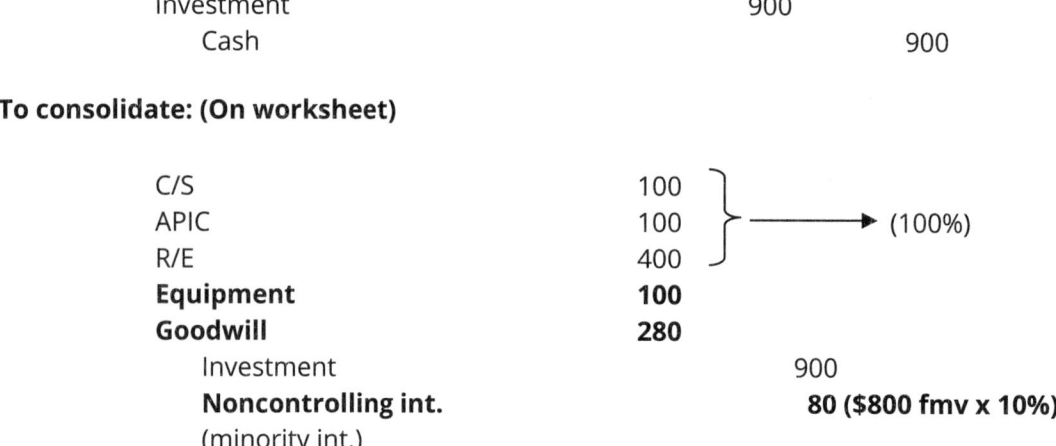

Lecture 31.07

Acquire 90%, consolidate at year end

When consolidated financial statements are prepared at year end or in subsequent years, the working paper eliminations are similar. The entries for intercompany transactions are the same as for a 100% acquisition. However, an important difference in the worksheet for the less than 100% acquisition is that the worksheet must reflect the noncontrolling interest in the acquiree. In the Income statement, consolidated net income is adjusted to disclose the net income or loss attributed to the noncontrolling interest. Comprehensive income is also adjusted to include the comprehensive income attributed to the noncontrolling interest.

Class Example #5:

Let's assume P Co. **Acquired 90% of S Co**. stock for $900 on 12/31/X1, at which time the acquiree's total stockholders' equity was $600 and the fair value of net identifiable assets was $700. Equipment with a 5-year life had a fair value exceeding book value by $100 on 12/31/X1, and that goodwill is believed to be impaired by $8 as of 12/31/X2. Income during the year for P was $3,000 and S was $150. S declared and paid dividends of $10 during the year. The investment is accounted for under the Equity method. At the date of acquisition, S Co. had 100,000 shares of stock outstanding with a FMV of $8 per share.

Summary: Acquire 90% for $900 on 12/31/X1, and consolidate on 12/31/X2
- Income during the year:
    - P - $3000
    - S - $150
- Dividends paid by S = $10
- Equipment useful life = 5 years
- Goodwill Impaired by $8
- Noncontrolling interest $80,000
- Investment accounted for under the **equity method**.

At 12/31/X2, the separate balances of P and S and the consolidating adjustments might appear as follows:

Accounts	P Co	S Co	Debits	Credits	Consol
Cash	3109	240			3349
Equipment	8000	500	80		8580
Inv in S	998			998	---
Goodwill			272		272
$1 CS	(1000)	(100)	100		(1000)
APIC	(3000)	(100)	100		(3000)
Noncontrol Int.				94	(94)
RE	(8107)	(540)	540		(8107)

Purchase price $ 900
FMV $ 700
BV $ 600

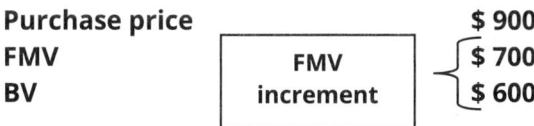

FMV increment

To account for S's income under the equity method:

Investment   135 (150 x 90%)
     Equity in earnings (I/S)   135

To account for S's Dividend paid under the equity method:

Cash   9 (10 x 90%)
     Investment   9

To Depreciate the Equipment (100/5 = $20):

Equity in earnings (I/S)	20	
Investment		20

To record Impairment of Goodwill:

			Investment	
Equity in earnings	8		900	
Investment		8	135	9
				20
				8
			998	

To consolidate at year end:

C/S	100
APIC	100
R/E	540 (400 + 150 -10)
PP&E	80 (100 – 20 dep)
Goodwill	272 (280-8 impairment)
Investment	**998**
Noncontrolling int.	**94** [80 + 15 (10% x $150 income) – 1 (10% x $10 div)]

Notice that the investment account was initially recorded at a cost of $900. It was then increased by 90% of the 150 of income ($135) and was reduced by the $9 dividend, the $20 (100/5yrs) of depreciation and the $8 impairment loss on goodwill, resulting in an ending balance of $998.

The change in the noncontrolling interest was attributed to a portion of net income ($15) and dividends ($1) of the acquiree being allocated to the noncontrolling interest (80+15-1=94)

Required disclosures on the **income statement** include the total consolidated Income and the income broken out between the Acquirer and Acquiree. For example:

Net Income	$ 3,150
Net income attributable to noncontrolling interest in acquiree	(15)
Net income attributable to acquirer	$ 3,135

Statement of Retained Earnings
- **COMBINE INCOME**
    - Acquirer – whole year
    - Acquiree – Date of Acquisition

Business Combinations and Consolidations   Section 31

Statement of Retained Earnings	
Beginning RE (Acquirer's only)	X
+/- Prior Period adjustment (0 of acquiree's earnings)	X
Adjusted beginning RE	X
+ **Net Income** - Acquirer (whole year)	X
- Acquiree (acq. date)	X
(Dividends) (Acquirer only)	X
Ending Retained earnings	X

Lecture 31.08

Intercompany Transactions

The process of consolidation results in the presentation of a single set of financial statements, which treats the Acquirer and Acquiree as a single entity. Since an entity cannot engage in business transactions with itself, adjustments will have to be made on the consolidating worksheet in order to eliminate the effects of **intercompany transactions**. There are four types of such transactions that commonly appear on the CPA exam:
- **Dividends paid** from the Acquiree to the Acquirer.
- **Sales of inventory** from one of the companies to the other.
- Sales of **property, plant, and equipment** from one to the other.
- Purchases by one of the **bonds** issued by the other.

In principle, an eliminating entry has a simple objective: to remove any evidence from the consolidated financial statements that the event occurred. If a transaction produced a receivable and payable, the elimination would involve debiting the payable and crediting the receivable. If a transaction produced a revenue and expense account, the elimination would involve debiting the revenue and crediting the expense.

There are, however, special complications associated with each of the 4 transactions cited above, since their effects often involve income on one side of the transaction but not on the other. These can be exceptionally complicated when the income is being reported by the acquiree in cases where the acquirer owns less than 100% of the acquiree. For the CPA exam, though, questions about intercompany transactions have consistently directed the candidate to ignore the noncontrolling interest (minority interest) problem. As a result, there is no need to make distinctions between **upstream** (acquiree-to-acquirer) and **downstream** (acquirer-to-acquiree) transactions.

Dividends paid by the acquiree to the acquirer must be completely eliminated in a consolidation, since an entity cannot pay dividends to itself. The manner in which the elimination entry is made depends on the accounts presented in the exam problem. Actually, there is no effect on the balance sheet to remove, since the equity accounts of the acquiree and the investment of the acquirer are eliminated in the combining of equity. The only exception is if a dividend has been declared but not yet paid, in which case an elimination of the receivable and payable may be needed:

      Dividends payable   100
            Dividends receivable   100

When there is a noncontrolling interest, dividends payable to the noncontrolling shareholders are not eliminated, since they are actual amounts owed to outside creditors. Additionally, since they represent the portion of the acquiree not owned by the acquirer, they won't be included in the combined equity of the consolidated entity anyway.

On rare exams, a consolidating worksheet will include the statement of retained earnings and income statement. When this has occurred, the acquirer has always used the cost method to account for the investment, reporting dividend income from the acquiree.

The eliminating entry is as follows:

Dividend income (I/S)	100	
Dividends paid (R/E)		100

When only a balance sheet is presented, this entry isn't needed, since both accounts are closed to retained earnings at year-end.

Dividends paid by the acquirer are not eliminated (except in the rare cases that the acquiree owns some stock in the acquirer, in which case that part is eliminated). As a result, once an acquisition has taken place, the consolidated statement of retained earnings will only report dividends paid by the acquirer. This is consistent with the fact that the equity accounts of the acquiree are eliminated in a consolidation.

Intercompany sales of inventory are the most common intercompany transactions. They have as many as three effects on the financial statements that may need to be eliminated:
- Sale vs. Purchase
- Receivable vs. Payable
- Profit in Ending Inventory

Let's assume that P Company has an item in inventory that was purchased from an outside suppler for $4, and that it is sold to S Company late in the year for $5. It remains in the ending inventory of the subsidiary at year-end, and the invoice has not yet been paid to the parent.

The elimination of the intercompany sale-purchase is as follows:

Sales	5	
Cost of sales		5

Remember that purchases are included in the computation of cost of sales, explaining the credit side of the entry. Keep in mind the above entry need not be made in an exam problem asking only for balance sheet effects, since both of the above accounts are closed into retained earnings at year-end.

The elimination of the intercompany receivable-payable is as follows:

Accounts payable	5	
Accounts receivable		5

The elimination of the intercompany profit in ending inventory ($5 - $4 = $1) is as follows:

    Cost of sales   1
        Inventory   1

Remember that ending inventory is included in the computation of cost of sales, explaining the debit side of the entry. If the problem only requires preparation of a balance sheet, the debit is made to retained earnings instead of cost of sales.

Of course, in most cases, the intercompany buyer will have paid for some or all of the goods purchased during the year, so the intercompany receivable-payable entry will be less than the intercompany sale-purchase entry. Also, some or all of the purchased goods will have been resold to outsiders before year-end, so the profit to be eliminated will not be the profit on all sales, only that on the purchased items still remaining at year-end.

When one of the companies in a consolidated group **sells a depreciable or amortizable asset to the other**, two eliminations will probably be needed:
1. Elimination of the gain on sale.
2. Elimination on the additional depreciation or amortization resulting from the markup of the asset.

Let's say P has equipment with a $50 cost and $20 accumulated depreciation on 1/1/X1, and sells it to S for $45. On the date of sale, the asset has an estimated remaining life of 3 years. In order to see the effects of the sale, look at the following comparison:

Account	Acquirer P	Acquiree S	Change
Equipment	50	45	(5)
Accumulated depreciation	(20)	(0)	20
Book value	30	45	15
20X1 depreciation	10	15	5

To eliminate the changes that resulted from the sale itself, the following entry is made:

    Gain on sale of equipment   15
    Equipment   5
        Accumulated depreciation   20

Notice that this entry returns the equipment to its $50 cost and $20 accumulated depreciation. If only a balance sheet is presented in the problem, the gain is debited to retained earnings instead.

Although not theoretically preferred, the following entry will correct the book value, and is permissible as an alternative:

    Gain on sale of equipment   15
        Equipment   15

After reducing the book value of the asset from $45 to $30, the depreciation over the subsequent year must be reduced in preparing financial statements for the year ended 12/31/X1:

Accumulated depreciation	5	
Depreciation expense		5

This reduces the depreciation from $15 to $10 for the year. In a balance sheet problem, the credit to depreciation expense is made to retained earnings instead.

Finally, **bonds issued** by one of the companies may be purchased by the other, and there are as many as three eliminations that may be needed:
- Investment in bonds vs. bonds payable
- Interest revenue vs. interest expense
- Accrued interest receivable vs. accrued interest payable

Let's assume that the acquiree issued an 8% bond at its $1,000 face value several years ago, and that the acquirer purchased the bond on the open market for $900 plus accrued interest on 12/31/X1. Also assume the bond pays interest annually on January 1.

To eliminate the bond itself, the following entry is made:

Bond payable	1000	
Investment in bond		900
Gain on retirement		100

Notice that the purchase of the bond of one company by the other is treated as an early retirement, as it would have been had a single entity bought its own bond on the open market.

Since annual interest of $1,000 x 8% = $80 is due tomorrow, the acquirer must have paid $80 accrued interest on the purchase date, and this must be eliminated as well:

Accrued interest payable	80	
Accrued interest receivable		80

Since the bond was purchased at the end of the year, no intercompany interest income has resulted, so there is no elimination. Had the bonds been held throughout the year, not merely acquired at year-end, interest revenue and interest expense would have been eliminated, though the different carrying values of the bond would have created complications that the exam has avoided testing.

Intercompany Transactions – Summary

- **Intercompany PP&E**

    ### Seller of PP&E
Cash or A/R	100	
Accumulated Depreciation	60	
PP&E		120
Gain		40

    ### Purchaser of PP&E
PP&E	100	
Cash or A/P		100

    ### To Fix on Worksheet at year end:
Gain	40	
PP&E	20	
Accumulated Depreciation		60

    ### To fix Over depreciation 40/10 = $4
Accumulated Depreciation	4	
Depreciation Expense		4

- **Intercompany Bonds**

    ### Issuer of bonds at Face/Par value
Cash	1000	
B/P		1000

    ### My subsidiary purchases the bonds from the outside investor for $980
Investment	1000	
Cash		980
Discount		20

    ### To Eliminate on the Worksheet at year end:
Bonds payable	1000	
Investment in Bonds		980 (1000-20 discount = 980 cv)
Gain on retirement		20

- **Intercompany inventory sales**

    ### Seller of Inventory
Cash	100	
Sales Revenue		100
COGS	80	
Inventory		80

    (note that intercompany profit is $20 or 20% of 100)

    ### Purchaser of Inventory
Inventory	100	
Cash		100

Assume the purchaser sells 90% of the inventory purchased for $200

Cash	200	
Sales Revenue		200
COGS	90	
Inventory		90

To Eliminate on the Worksheet at year end:

Sales Revenue	100	
Inventory (20% profit in ending)		2
COGS		98

If given a Worksheet, eliminate the following Entries: (Panic approach)

- Investment account = always zero at the end
- Eliminate 100% of acquiree's – C/S, APIC, R/E
- Set up noncontrolling interest (adjust for % of income and dividends)
- Dividend income if cost method or investment income if equity method
- Dividends paid by Acquiree
- Intercompany transactions (sales, COGS, unrealized inventory profits)
- Intercompany gains/losses on sale of PP&E
- Intercompany receivables/payables
- Bond investments
- Set up excess FMV of PP&E over BV
- Record goodwill
- Record depreciation on excess FMV of PP&E
- Record Impairments of goodwill

Some problems on the CPA exam involve the use of a **three-part worksheet**, consisting of an income statement section, a section for the statement of retained earnings, and a balance sheet section. When provided a three-part worksheet, the best approach is to:
1. Post all of the adjusting journal entries to the worksheet.
2. Complete the income statement section by:
   o Calculating the net balance for each income statement line item.
   o Total each column for the income statement section. The net amount in the final column will be net income.
3. Complete the statement of retained earnings section by:
   o Copying the totals from the income statement section on the net income line of the statement of retained earnings section.
   o Calculating the net balance for each line item in the section.
   o Total each column for the section. The net amount in the final column will be ending retained earnings.
4. Complete the balance sheet section by:
   o Copying the totals from the statement of retained earnings section on the retained earnings line of the balance sheet section.
   o Calculating the net balance for each line item in the section.
   o Total each column for the section.

The following **additional disclosures** are also required:
- The portion of consolidated net income and comprehensive income attributable to both the acquirer and the noncontrolling interest.
- The amounts attributable to the noncontrolling interest for each of the following:
  - income from continuing operations;
  - Discontinued operations; and
  - Components of other comprehensive income.
- A reconciliation of the annual change in reported amounts of noncontrolling interest, including separate disclosure of the following:
  - Consolidated net income attributable to noncontrolling interest;
  - Investments by and distributions to noncontrolling interest; and
  - Each component of comprehensive income.
- A footnote schedule showing the effects of transactions with the noncontrolling interest on the equity attributable to the noncontrolling interest.

Combined Financial Statements

Combining the financial positions and results of operations of related entities may be useful to financial statement users even though the requirements for the preparation of consolidated financial statements have not been met. Although consolidated financial statements may not be prepared when one entity does not have a controlling financial interest in another, it may be appropriate to prepare **combined financial statements**. Combined financial statements are often prepared, for example, for two or more entities that have common ownership, such as the unconsolidated subsidiaries of a parent.

Combined financial statements are very similar to consolidated financial statements in that the effects of interentity transactions are eliminated. They are different, however, in that:
- Amounts are not adjusted to fair values.
- The equity accounts are combined rather than being eliminated.

Variable Interest Entities (VIE)

Under **FASB ASC 810**, a reporting entity is required to include another entity in its consolidated financial statements when the reporting entity has a controlling financial interest in it. An entity can have a controlling financial interest in another entity without owning any equity in the other entity, in which case the controlled entity is referred to as a **variable interest entity, or VIE**. The reporting entity with a controlling financial interest is referred to as the ***primary beneficiary*** and is required to prepare consolidated financial statements that include the VIE.

A VIE relationship often occurs as a result of one of two common circumstances:
- An entity forms a separate entity for the purpose of holding certain assets or incurring liabilities. This may be done to keep items off of the balance sheet, referred to as *"off balance sheet financing"* a form of fraudulent financial reporting. It may also be done for legitimate business reasons, such as setting up a separate entity to acquire assets to be leased to the reporting entity while passing tax benefits to the owners.
- An entity enters into a relationship with another that occupies so many of the other entity's resources and becomes the focus of its operations, making the other entity essentially a division of the reporting entity.

The reporting entity will evaluate significant relationships with other entities to determine if it is the primary beneficiary of a VIE. The evaluation consists of 4 steps:
1. The natures of the entities and their relationship are evaluated to determine if there is a potential for a VIE, considering certain *exempt relationships* identified in ASC 810.
2. The potential VIE is evaluated to determine if it is self-sufficient or if there are indications that it is dependent on some form of additional subordinated financial support. Does the other entity have *one or more characteristics of a VIE*?
    - There may not be sufficient equity to sustain normal operations.
    - The equity holders may not have the normal characteristics of equity holders.
3. The reporting entity determines if it has a *variable interest in the potential VIE*, meaning that it will be affected if the value of the other entity's assets increase or decrease.
4. The reporting entity determines if it is the *primary beneficiary*, which is an entity with a variable interest in the potential VIE that both:
    - Has the **power** and authority to direct the operations and activities of the potential VIE that are most significant to its economic performance.
    - Participates in the VIE's profits and losses to an extent that is potentially significant to the VIE.

Certain relationships are *exempt* from applying the VIE provisions. For example, a for profit entity will generally not consolidate with a not-for-profit entity, a for profit entity will generally not consolidate with a governmental entity, and an entity will not consolidate with its entities representing pension trusts or other retirement benefits for its employees.

In addition, when the other entity qualifies as a business, it is not subject to the provisions associated with VIEs. This exemption does not apply, however, when the business, by its design, operates primarily for the benefit of the reporting entity.

If the relationship is not exempt, the entity will be evaluated to determine if it has either of the two more significant and common *characteristics of VIEs*.
- There is not sufficient equity at risk, which would be the case if the entity is unable to borrow on the basis of its own financial position and results of operations without additional subordinated financial support or if equity is not sufficient to cover what are referred to as expected losses, the expected value of potential performance that is below original expectations.
- The equity holders lack one or more of the characteristics of equity holders, such as the authority to make decisions affecting the entity, the requirement to absorb losses, and the right to benefit from residual profits.

If the entity has either of the characteristics of a VIE, the reporting entity determines if it has a *variable interest in the VIE*. A variable interest means the reporting entity will be affected as the value of the VIEs assets fluctuate. For example:
- A bank with a "with recourse" loan receivable that is secured by assets that have value in excess of the principal balance and that is supported by equity holders' personal guarantees would not have a variable interest. This is because, regardless of the value of the collateral, with recourse against the entity for any deficiency and the personal guarantee of the owners, the bank will receive the same amount of principal and interest.
- A bank with a shared appreciation mortgage, without recourse and without personal guarantees, on the other hand, would have a variable interest. If the value of the property increases, the bank will share in the appreciation because of the nature of the mortgage. If the value of the property drops dramatically, the bank bears the risk that the debtor will

abandon the property and, with neither recourse nor guarantees, the bank will lose the difference between the property's net realizable value and the principal balance.

When a reporting entity determines it is the primary beneficiary of a VIE, it is required to prepare consolidated financial statements treating the VIE as a subsidiary.
- If the entities are **not related**, the creation of the relationship will be treated as comparable to an acquisition and the same principles for recognizing the combination and for preparing consolidated financial statements will be followed.
    - Assets and liabilities of the VIE are reported at their *fair values*.
    - The VIE's equity accounts are eliminated.
    - The noncontrolling interest may represent 100% of the equity of the VIE.
- If the entities **are related**, the combination and subsequent consolidated financial statements will be prepared using *book values* rather than fair values.

Alternative Accounting Approach for Nonpublic Entities (Variable Interest Entities – VIE's)

Nonpublic companies often create separate entities for tax purposes that are subject to the provisions related to VIEs and often require the preparation of consolidated financial statements. The most common circumstance is when the owner of a closely-held entity acquires real estate, manufacturing equipment, or some other assets for the purpose of leasing them to the owned reporting entity.
- The assets are often acquired in a separate legal entity for liability protection purposes.
- The asset is leased to the other entity such that the payments are usually structured to cover the cash outflows incurred by the owner for mortgage payments and maintenance while providing the owners the tax benefits associated with deprecation.

This creates two problems for the closely-held entity. First, the analysis to determine whether or not the separate entity is a VIE, which is required to be performed, can be time consuming, confusing, and costly. In addition, the users of the financial statements, often limited to very few and frequently the ones who provided financing for the VIE, would prefer to have financial statements that are not consolidated and exclude the VIE.

As a result, the nonpublic entity is often required to present two sets of financial statements. One with the VIE consolidated so as to comply with GAAP and avoid a modified report. The second, presented as a supplementary schedule, excludes the VIE and reports financial position and results of operations applying lease accounting to the relationship.

In recognition of this, the **Private Company Council** of the **PCC** has established an alternative accounting approach for nonpublic entities. The alternative approach only applies when:
- A reporting entity and another entity are under common control.
- The reporting entity is the lessee and the other entity is the lessor in a lease involving the two entities.
- The lease is substantially the only relationship between the two entities.

When a nonpublic entity qualifies to apply the alternative accounting approach, it will not analyze the relationship to determine if it is the primary beneficiary of a VIE. It will, instead, account for the relationship by applying **lease accounting** and provide appropriate disclosure, including related party disclosures.

As is true of all Accounting Standards issued by the PCC, a nonpublic entity must elect to adopt it and disclose its adoption in the footnotes in the Summary of Significant Accounting Policies.

Lecture 31.09

CLASS QUESTIONS

Please see the Class Questions and Class Solutions for this Lecture at the end of this Section.

Lecture 31.10

CLASS QUESTIONS

Please see the Class Questions and Class Solutions for this Lecture at the end of this Section.

Lecture 31.11

BUSINESS COMBINATIONS UNDER IFRS

Requirements for business combinations are very similar under IFRS #3 and US GAAP (FASB ASC 805). Both require the application of the acquisition method, which involves:
- Identifying the acquirer;
- Determining the acquisition date;
- Measuring and recognizing identifiable assets acquired, liabilities assumed, and noncontrolling interests in the acquiree; and
- Recognizing goodwill or a gain on bargain purchase.

In general, procedures and measurements are performed similarly under US GAAP and IFRS. Both require the recognition and measurement of identifiable assets acquired and liabilities assumed at their acquisition date fair values. A potential difference occurs when measuring **noncontrolling interests**, if any. US GAAP always requires noncontrolling interests to be measured at their acquisition date fair values. IFRS, however, provides for an alternative method of measuring noncontrolling interests.
- Noncontrolling interests **may** always be recognized at acquisition date fair value.
- They may, however, be measured in an amount equal to a proportionate share of the recognized net asset of the acquiree when:
  - They represent present ownership interests; and
  - Holders are entitled to a proportionate share of the recognized net assets of the acquiree if it is liquidated.

Under both systems, goodwill is recognized when the recognized amount of the underlying net assets acquired is less than the total of:
- The fair value of any consideration given by the acquirer;
- The fair value of any retained investment in the acquiree that was held prior to the date of acquisition; and
- The amounts recognized as noncontrolling interests.

When the recognized amount of the acquired underlying net assets exceeds the total of these items, the difference, under both US GAAP and IFRS, is recognized as a gain on bargain purchase, included in income in the period of the combination.

Business Combinations and Consolidations   Section 31

For various reasons, the amount of goodwill or gain on bargain purchase may differ under US GAAP and IFRS. This occurs because of differences in how individual items are recognized. For example:
- Noncontrolling interests may be measured using an alternative approach under IFRS.
- IFRS requires the recognition of all contingent liabilities for which fair value can be reliably determined.
- IFRS does not recognize all deferred tax assets as required by US GAAP.

IFRS #10 provides guidelines for the preparation of consolidated financial statements. It requires a parent to prepare consolidated financial statements that include all entities over which the parent has control. Control is defined similarly to the definition of a primary beneficiary of a VIE under US GAAP. A parent is considered to have control over another entity when it participates in the variable returns of the entity, including rights to favorable returns and exposure to negative returns, and has power over the entity and the ability to use that power to impact the returns.

In certain circumstances, a parent may exclude a controlled entity from consolidated financial statements. Four conditions must be met in order to exclude such an entity:
- The entity is either a wholly-owned subsidiary or, if not wholly-owned, all voting and nonvoting owners are aware that it will not be included and have no objection to the exclusion;
- The entity has no publicly traded debt or equity instruments.
- The entity is not in the process of issuing debt or equity instruments to the public.
- A parent of the entity prepares consolidated financial statements in compliance with IFRS that are available to the public.

Similar to US GAAP, preparation of consolidated financial statements includes:
- Elimination of reciprocal inter-entity balances and the effects of inter-entity transactions.
- Reporting noncontrolling interests in the equity section of the statement of financial position.

Consolidated Financial Statements

US GAAP	IFRS
• Consolidation required when entity has controlling financial interest in other entity through equity or relationship	• Consolidation required when entity has control evidenced by power over investee, exposure to variable returns, and power to affect returns
• All subsidiaries must be consolidated in general purpose financial statements.	• Under certain restrictive situations a subsidiary may be exempt from consolidation.
• Noncontrolling interest measured at *fair value*.	• In certain restrictive circumstances a noncontrolling interest may be measured either at *fair value or the proportionate share* of the value of the identifiable assets and liabilities of the acquiree
• Control through relationship (VIE) reassessed on regular basis	• Consolidation reassessed only if change in circumstances

Section 31 Business Combinations and Consolidations

CLASS QUESTIONS

Work through the below Class Questions while following along with the respective lectures. Once this is complete, you can begin independently practicing what you've learned by quizzing yourself on this course section in your Interactive Practice Questions (IPQ), which can be found in your online Student Dashboard. Your IPQ simulates the computer-based testing experience, and will also help you understand how concepts are applied to the exam. Each question includes answer explanations from expert CPAs that will help you determine why you answered a question correctly or incorrectly. This is key to your success on the CPA Exam.

Lecture 31.05

1. In a business combination accounted for as an acquisition, the appraised values of the identifiable assets acquired exceeded the acquisition price. How should the excess appraised value be reported?

    a. As negative goodwill.
    b. As additional paid-in capital.
    c. As a reduction of the values assigned to certain assets and a gain for any unallocated portion.
    d. As a gain in net income for the period.

2. Which of the following expenses related to the business acquisition should be included, in total, in the determination of net income of the combined corporation for the period in which the expenses are incurred?

	Fees of finders and consultants	Registration fees for equity securities issued
a.	Yes	Yes
b.	Yes	No
c.	No	Yes
d.	No	No

Items 3 and 4 are based on the following:

On December 31, 20X9, Saxe Corporation was acquired by Poe Corporation. In the business combination, Poe issued 200,000 shares of its $10 par common stock, with a market price of $18 a share, for all of Saxe's common stock. The stockholders' equity section of each company's balance sheet immediately before the combination was

	Poe	Saxe
Common stock	3,000,000	$1,500,000
Additional paid-in capital	1,300,000	150,000
Retained earnings	2,500,000	850,000
	$6,800,000	$2,500,000

Business Combinations and Consolidations — Section 31

3. In the December 31, 20X9 consolidated balance sheet, additional paid-in capital should be reported at

   a. $950,000
   b. $1,300,000
   c. $1,450,000
   d. $2,900,000

4. In the December 31, 20X9 consolidated balance sheet, common stock should be reported at

   a. $3,000,000
   b. $3,500,000
   c. $4,000,000
   d. $5,000,000

Lecture 31.09

Items 5 through 9 are based on the following:

On January 1, 20X5, Polk Corp. and Strass Corp. had condensed balance sheets as follows:

	Polk	Strass
Current assets	$70,000	$20,000
Noncurrent assets	90,000	40,000
Total assets	$160,000	$60,000
Current liabilities	$30,000	$10,000
Long-term debt	50,000	--
Stockholders' equity	80,000	50,000
Total liabilities and stockholders' equity	$160,000	$60,000

On January 2, 20X5, Polk borrowed $60,000 and used the proceeds to purchase 90% of the outstanding common shares of Strass. This debt is payable in ten equal annual principal payments, plus interest, beginning December 30, 20X5. The excess cost of the investment over Strass' book value of acquired net assets should be allocated 60% to inventory and 40% to goodwill. On January 1, 20X5, the fair value of Polk shares held by noncontrolling parties was $10,000. On Polk's January 2, 20X5 consolidated balance sheet,

5. Current assets should be

   a. $90,000
   b. $99,000
   c. $100,000
   d. $102,000

6. Noncurrent assets should be

   a. $130,000
   b. $136,000
   c. $138,000
   d. $140,000

7. Current liabilities should be
   a. $50,000
   b. $46,000
   c. $40,000
   d. $30,000

8. Noncurrent liabilities should be
   a. $115,000
   b. $109,000
   c. $104,000
   d. $ 55,000

9. Stockholders' equity including noncontrolling interests should be
   a. $ 80,000
   b. $ 85,000
   c. $ 90,000
   d. $130,000

Items 10 through 12 are based on the following:

Selected information from the separate and consolidated balance sheets and income statements of Pard, Inc. and its subsidiary, Spin Co., as of December 31, 20X9, and for the year then ended is as follows:

	Pard	Spin	Consolidated
Balance sheet accounts			
Accounts receivable	$ 26,000	$ 19,000	$ 39,000
Inventory	30,000	25,000	52,000
Investment in Spin	67,000	---	---
Goodwill	---	---	30,000
Minority interest	---	---	10,000
Stockholders' equity	154,000	50,000	154,000
Income statement accounts			
Revenues	$200,000	$140,000	$308,000
Cost of goods sold	150,000	110,000	231,000
Gross profit	50,000	30,000	77,000
Equity in earnings of Spin	20,000	---	---
Net income	36,000	20,000	40,000

Business Combinations and Consolidations — Section 31

Additional information
- During 20X9, Pard sold goods to Spin at the same markup on cost that Pard uses for all sales. At December 31, 20X9, Spin had not paid for all of these goods and still held 37.5% of them in inventory.
- Pard acquired its interest in Spin on January 2, 20X9.

10. What was the amount of intercompany sales from Pard to Spin during 20X9?

    a. $ 3,000
    b. $ 6,000
    c. $29,000
    d. $32,000

11. At December 31, 20X9, what was the amount of Spin's payable to Pard for intercompany sales?

    a. $ 3,000
    b. $ 6,000
    c. $29,000
    d. $32,000

12. In Pard's consolidated balance sheet, what was the carrying amount of the inventory that Spin purchased from Pard?

    a. $ 3,000
    b. $ 6,000
    c. $ 9,000
    d. $12,000

Lecture 31.12

13. An Asset under IFRS is recognized as goodwill only when?

    a. When it is acquired by purchase.
    b. When it is internally generated or acquired by purchase.
    c. When it is clear that it exists and has value.
    d. When it has future economic benefits.

CLASS SOLUTIONS

1. (d) In recognizing a business combination, an acquirer will compare the fair value of the underlying net assets to the aggregate of the fair values of consideration transferred, previously held and retained investments in the acquiree, and any noncontrolling interests. When the fair value of the underlying net assets exceeds the total, the acquisition is considered a bargain purchase and the difference is recognized as a gain in the period of acquisition. Answer (a) is incorrect because it is not recognized as negative goodwill. Answer (b) is incorrect because it is not recognized as additional paid-in capital. Answer (c) is incorrect because it is not allocated among certain assets and recognized as a gain for the excess.

2. (b) Direct costs of a business combination, including finders' fees and consulting fees, are recognized as expenses in the period incurred. Costs of issuing securities in the combination, such as registration fees, reduce the amount recognized as proceeds from their issuance and are not recognized as expenses.

3. (d) Additional paid-in capital on consolidated financial statements is always equal to the parent's amount. Poe's APIC was $1,300,000 before the combination. It issued 200,000 shares with a fair value of $18 per share and a par of $10 per share. The difference of (200,000 x $8) $1,600,000 is recognized as APIC, increasing Poe's amount to $2,900,000.

4. (d) Common stock on consolidated financial statements is always equal to the parent's amount. Poe's CS was $3,000,000 before the combination. It issued 200,000 shares with a fair value of $18 per share and a par of $10 per share. The total par of the newly issued shares is $2,000,000, increasing Poe's amount to $5,000,000.

5. (d) Assets acquired in a business combination are recognized at their fair values. Strass's underlying net assets have a book value of $50,000 ($60,000 - $10,000). There is a minority interest with a fair value of $10,000, indicating that Polk paid $60,000 for the remaining $40,000. The difference of $20,000 is allocated 60%, or $12,000, to inventory, and 40%, or $8,000, to goodwill. Total current assets will equal the parent's amount plus the subsidiary's amount adjusted to fair value or $70,000 + $20,000 + $12,000) $102,000.

6. (c) Assets acquired in a business combination are recognized at their fair values. Strass's underlying net assets have a book value of $50,000 ($60,000 - $10,000). There is a minority interest with a fair value of $10,000, indicating that Polk paid $60,000 for the remaining $40,000. The difference of $20,000 is allocated 60%, or $12,000, to inventory, and 40%, or $8,000, to goodwill. Total noncurrent assets will equal the parent's amount plus the subsidiary's amount plus goodwill or $90,000 + $40,000 + $8,000 = $138,000.

7. (b) Total current liabilities will include the parent's amount plus the subsidiary's amount, adjusted to fair value if appropriate, plus any new current liabilities incurred in the combination. Polk borrowed $60,000 payable in 10 equal annual installments indicating a current portion of $6,000 and a noncurrent portion of $54,000. Total current liabilities is $30,000 + $10,000 + $6,000 = $46,000.

Business Combinations and Consolidations

8. (c) Total noncurrent liabilities will include the parent's amount plus the subsidiary's amount, adjusted to fair value if appropriate, plus any new noncurrent liabilities incurred in the combination. Polk borrowed $60,000 payable in 10 equal annual installments indicating a current portion of $6,000 and a noncurrent portion of $54,000. Total noncurrent liabilities is $50,000 + $0 + $54,000 = $104,000.

9. (c) Total stockholders' equity in consolidated financial statements consists of the parent's stockholders' equity plus any noncontrolling interest. The subsidiary's stockholders' equity accounts are eliminated on consolidation. The amount would be $80,000 + $10,000 = $90,000.

10. (d) Consolidated revenues equals the parent's amount plus the subsidiary's amount less intercompany sales. The total of the parent's and subsidiary's amounts is $340,000 and consolidated revenues is $308,000. The difference of $32,000 is intercompany sales.

11. (b) Accounts receivable and accounts payable will each equal the total of the parent's and the subsidiary's amounts for each less any intercompany reciprocal amounts. The total of Pard's and Spin's accounts receivable is $26,000 +_ $19,000 or $45,000 but consolidated accounts receivable is only $39,000. The $6,000 difference represents an intercompany account receivable and account payable.

12. (c) Since the amounts for Pard's and Spin's inventories are $30,000 and $25,000, respectively, for a total of $55,000, compared to a consolidated amount of $52,000, there is apparently intercompany profit in inventory of $3,000. Spin purchased inventory from Pard, who sells inventory at a markup of 1/3 of cost ($50,000 gross profit = 1/3 of $150,000 cost of sales). If the profit on the inventory purchased from Pard is $3,000, the cost or carrying value will be 3 times that amount or $9,000. In other words, sales were $12,000, cost of sales was $9,000, and the gross margin was $3,000.

13. (a) Similar to US GAAP, IFRS only allows for the recognition of goodwill as a result of a business combination in which the total of the fair values of consideration, noncontrolling interests, retained investments exceeds the fair value of the underlying net assets of the acquiree. Answer (b) is incorrect because costs incurred in to internally generate goodwill are recognized as expense in the period incurred. Answer (c) is incorrect because the only way that it can be clear that goodwill exists is as a result of a purchase when the acquirer pays more than the fair value of the share of the underlying net assets acquired in a purchase. Answer (d) is incorrect because the future benefits of goodwill are not determinable, resulting in the requirement that goodwill be evaluated for impairment at least annually.

Lecture 31.10
TASK-BASED SIMULATIONS

Task-Based Simulation 1

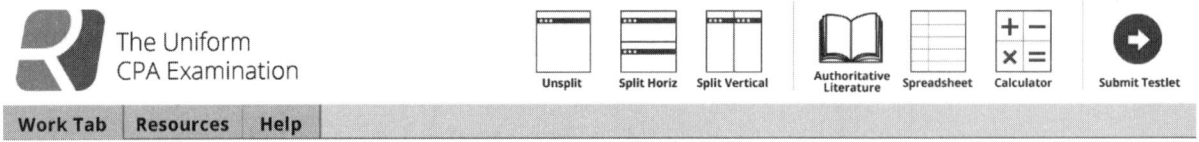

Situation:

Presented below are selected amounts from the separate unconsolidated financial statements of Poe Corp. and its 90%-owned subsidiary, Shaw Co., at December 31, 20X2.

Additional information follows:

	Poe	Shaw
Selected income statement amounts		
Sales	$710,000	$530,000
Cost of goods sold	490,000	370,000
Gain on sale of equipment	21,000	--
Earnings from investment in subsidiary	63,000	--
Interest expense	--	16,000
Depreciation	25,000	20,000
Selected balance sheet amounts		
Cash	$ 50,000	$ 15,000
Inventories	229,000	150,000
Equipment	440,000	360,000
Accumulated depreciation	(200,000)	(120,000)
Investment in Shaw	191,000	--
Investment in Shaw bonds	100,000	--
Discount on bonds	(9,000)	--
Bonds payable	--	(200,000)
Common stock	(100,000)	(10,000)
Additional paid-in capital	(250,000)	(40,000)
Retained earnings	(404,000)	(140,000)
Selected statement of retained earnings amounts		
Beginning balance, December 31, 20X1	$272,000	$100,000
Net income	212,000	70,000
Dividends paid	80,000	30,000

Business Combinations and Consolidations   Section 31

Additional information

- On January 2, 20X2, Poe, Inc. purchased 90% of Shaw Co.'s 100,000 outstanding common stock for cash of $155,000. On that date the fair value of the noncontrolling interest was $1.70 per share. On that date, Shaw's stockholders' equity equaled $150,000 and the fair values of Shaw's identifiable assets and liabilities equaled their carrying amounts. Poe has accounted for the purchase as an acquisition.
- On January 3, 20X2, Poe sold equipment with an original cost of $30,000 and a carrying value of $15,000 to Shaw for $36,000. The equipment had a remaining life of three years and was depreciated using the straight-line method by both companies.
- During 20X2, Poe sold merchandise to Shaw for $60,000, which included a profit of $20,000. At December 31, 20X2, half of this merchandise remained in Shaw's inventory.
- On December 31, 20X2, Poe paid $91,000 to purchase 50% of the outstanding bonds issued by Shaw. The bonds mature on December 31, 20X6, and were originally issued at par. The bonds pay interest annually on December 31 of each year, and the interest was paid to the prior investor immediately before Poe's purchase of the bonds.
- On September 4, 20X2, Shaw paid cash dividends of $30,000.
- On December 31, 20X2, Poe recorded its equity in Shaw's earnings.

Required:

Calculate the amounts that will appear on Poe's consolidated financial statement on December 31, 20X2.

1. Cash
2. Goodwill
3. Equipment
4. Common stock
5. Investment in Shaw
6. Dividends
7. Bonds payable
8. Noncontrolling interest

Section 31   Business Combinations and Consolidations

Task-Based Simulation 2

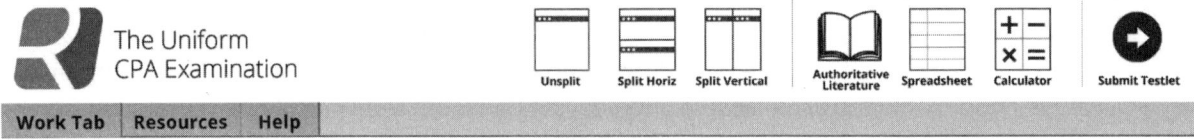

Situation:

On January 1, 20X1, Shaw purchases 100% of the stock of Poe in a transaction that was properly accounted for as a business combination.

Required:

Items 1 through 3 below represent transactions between Shaw and Poe during 20X1. Prepare the eliminating entries in general journal format for each of these transactions.

1. On January 3, 20X1, Shaw sold equipment with an original cost of $30,000 and a carrying value of $15,000 to Poe for $36,000. The equipment had a remaining life of three years and was depreciated using the straight-line method by both companies.

2. During 20X1, Shaw sold merchandise to Poe for $60,000, which included a profit of $20,000. At December 31, 20X1, half of this merchandise remained in Poe's inventory.

3. On December 31, 20X1, Shaw paid $91,000 to purchase 50% ($100,000) of the outstanding bonds issued by Poe. The bonds mature on December 31, 20X5, and were originally issued at par. The bonds pay interest annually on December 31 of each year, and the interest was paid to the prior investor immediately before Shaw's purchase of the bonds.

Business Combinations and Consolidations — Section 31

Task-Based Simulation 3

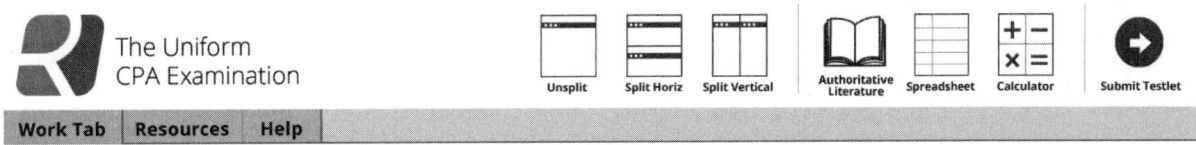

Situation:

On January 1, 20X0 Shaw acquires 90% of the stock in Poe in a transaction properly accounted for as a business combination. **Items 1 through 6** below refer to accounts that may or may not be included in Shaw and Poe's consolidated financial statements. The list below refers to the various possibilities of those amounts to be reported in Shaw's consolidated financial statements for the year ended December 31, 20X1. Both Shaw and Poe paid dividends to investors. Ignore income tax considerations.

Required:

Responses to be selected
- A. Sum of amounts on Shaw and Poe's separate unconsolidated financial statements
- B. Less than the sum of amounts on Shaw and Poe's separate unconsolidated financial statements but not the same as the amount on either
- C. Same as amount for Shaw only
- D. Same as amount for Poe only
- E. Eliminated entirely in consolidation
- F. Shown in consolidated financial statements but not in separate unconsolidated financial statements
- G. Neither in consolidated nor in separate unconsolidated financial statements

	(A)	(B)	(C)	(D)	(E)	(F)	(G)
1. Cash	○	○	○	○	○	○	○
2. Investment in subsidiary	○	○	○	○	○	○	○
3. Noncontrolling interest	○	○	○	○	○	○	○
4. Common stock	○	○	○	○	○	○	○
5. Beginning retained earnings	○	○	○	○	○	○	○
6. Dividends paid	○	○	○	○	○	○	○

Section 31 Business Combinations and Consolidations

Task-Based Simulation 4

  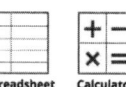

A client understands that a business combination recently entered into is required to be accounted for under the acquisition method. The client would like to understand what steps are required to be followed under that method. Identify the location in professional standards that indicates the steps that are required in applying the acquisition method.

Task-Based Simulation 5

 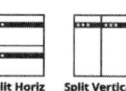 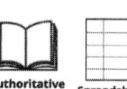 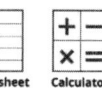

A company has entered into a business combination that has resulted in the recognition of a bargain purchase gain. As a result, it understands that it is required to perform a reassessment and wants to make certain that it is considering all aspects required. Identify the location in professional standards that indicates what items should be reassessed when a business combination results in a bargain purchase gain.

Business Combinations and Consolidations   Section 31

TASK-BASED SIMULATION SOLUTIONS

Task-Based Simulation Solution 1

Calculate the amounts that will appear on Poe's consolidated financial statement in December 31, 20X2.

1. Cash $ 65,000
2. Goodwill $ 22,000
3. Equipment $794,000
4. Common stock $100,000
5. Investment in Shaw $0
6. Dividends $ 80,000
7. Bonds payable $100,000
8. Noncontrolling interest $ 21,000

Explanation of solutions

1. Cash will be the total of Poe's and Shaw's amounts or $50,000 + $15,000 = $65,000

2. Goodwill is the difference between the total of the fair values of consideration given plus the fair value of noncontrolling interests and the fair value of underlying net assets. Poe paid consideration of $155,000 and the noncontrolling interest is 10,000 shares at $1.70 per share or $17,000 for a total of $172,000. The fair value of the underlying net assets is equal to the book value, which is Shaw's stockholders' equity of $150,000. The difference is goodwill of $22,000.

3. Consolidated equipment would equal the total of Poe's and Shaw's amounts, $440,000 + $360,000, or $800,000, adjusted for the effects of intercompany transactions. The only intercompany transaction is the sale on 1/3. Shaw is reporting equipment purchased at a cost of $36,000. If the intercompany sale had not occurred, the equipment would have been on Poe's books at its original $30,000 cost. The difference of $6,000 reduces the consolidated amount to $794,000.

4. Consolidated stockholders' equity consists of the parent's stockholders' equity accounts plus the noncontrolling interest. Common stock would consist of Poe's amount of $100,000.

5. The investment in Shaw account is eliminated in the consolidation process.

6. Consolidated stockholders' equity consists of the parent's stockholders' equity accounts plus the noncontrolling interest. Dividends would consist of Poe's amount of $80,000. Shaw's dividends of $30,000 include $27,000 paid to Poe and eliminated and $3,000 paid to the noncontrolling interest and reported as an adjustment directly to that account.

7. Consolidated bonds payable will equal the total of the amounts for Poe and Shaw less any intercompany holdings. Poe has no bonds outstanding and Shaw has $200,000 outstanding for a total of $200,000. Poe holds $100,000 of Shaw's bonds as an investment, which will be eliminated against bonds payable, resulting in a net amount of $100,000.

8. On January 2, the noncontrolling interest would have been recognized at its fair value of 10,000 shares at $1.70 per share or $17,000. It will be increased by the noncontrolling interest's 10% of Shaw's net income and reduced by 10% of Shaw's dividends. As a result, it will be $17,000 + $7,000 -0 $3,000 or $21,000.

Task-Based Simulation Solution 2

1.

Gain on equipment	21,000	
Accumulated depreciation		15,000
Equipment		6,000
Accumulated depreciation	7,000	
Depreciation expense		7,000

2.

Sales	60,000	
Cost of goods sold		50,000
Ending inventory		10,000

3.

Bonds payable	100,000	
Gain on retirement of bonds		9,000
Investment in bonds		91,000

Explanation of solutions

1. As a result of the intercompany sale, the following journal entries would have been made to record the sale and the subsequent depreciation:

SHAW			POE		
Cash	36,000		Equipment	36,000	
Accum dep	15,000		Cash		36,000
Equipment		30,000	Deprec exp	12,000	
Gain on sale		21,000	Accum dep		12,000

If the intercompany sale had not occurred, the only entry that would have been made would have been the recognition of depreciation expense by Shaw.

Deprec exp	5,000	
Accum depr		5,000

To eliminate the effect of the sale, the debit and credit to cash offset one another, there is a debit to equipment of $36,000 and a credit of $30,000 for a net debit of $6,000 to be reversed with a credit. The gain on sale has to be eliminated in the amount of $21,000, and the reduction to accumulated depreciation will be reversed. The elimination entry will be:

In addition, the excess depreciation recognized by Poe has to be eliminated. Poe recognized $12,000, 1/3 of the carrying value of $36,000, compared to Shaw's $5,000 based on 1/3 of its carrying value of $15,000.

2. To eliminate an intercompany sale, when all of the inventory has ultimately been sold to third parties, is a debit to sales and a credit to cost of sales for the gross amount of the sale. When some of the inventory remains on hand at the end of the period, any intercompany profit in ending inventory is eliminated with a credit to inventory, reducing the credit to cost of sales.
The intercompany sale is $60,000, all of which is eliminated, with a total profit of $20,000. Since one-half of the inventory remains on hand, $10,000 of the intercompany profit is included in inventory and has to be eliminated. The difference will be a reduction to cost of sales of $50,000.

3. When a parent buys the bonds of a subsidiary, it is accounted for as if the bonds were retired for their cost with a gain or loss on retirement recognized accordingly. If Poe had retired its bonds with a face and carrying value of $100,000 for $91,000, it would have recorded the following entry:

Bonds payable	100,000	
Cash		91,000
Gain on retirement		9,000

Instead, the following entry was recorded:

Invest in bonds	91,000	
Cash		91,000

The decrease to cash was properly recorded. The investment of $91,000 must be eliminated, bonds payable of $100,000 must be eliminated, and a gain on retirement of $9,000 needs to be recognized.

Task-Based Simulation Solution 3

	(A)	(B)	(C)	(D)	(E)	(F)	(G)
1. Cash	●	○	○	○	○	○	○
2. Investment in subsidiary	○	○	○	○	●	○	○
3. Noncontrolling interest	○	○	○	○	○	●	○
4. Common stock	○	○	●	○	○	○	○
5. Beginning retained earnings	○	○	●	○	○	○	○
6. Dividends paid	○	○	●	○	○	○	○

Explanation of solutions

1. (**A**) The amount reported as cash on consolidated financial statements is the total of the amounts reported by the parent and all consolidated subsidiaries.

2. (**E**) The amount reported by the parent as an investment in the subsidiary is eliminated along with the stockholders' equity accounts of the subsidiary.

3. (**F**) The noncontrolling interest represents the portion of a consolidated subsidiary that is owned by that subsidiary's own stockholders as opposed to the parent. It is not reported on the separate financial statements of the parent, which shows the subsidiary as an investment, reported as a single amount, or of the subsidiary, the stockholders' equity of which would consist of 100% without a noncontrolling interest.

4. (**C**) Consolidated stockholders' equity consists of the stockholders' equity accounts of the parent plus the noncontrolling interest. As a result, consolidated common stock will equal the Shaw's common stock amount.

5. (**C**) Consolidated stockholders' equity consists of the stockholders' equity accounts of the parent plus the noncontrolling interest. As a result, beginning retained earnings on the consolidated financial statements will be equal to Shaw's beginning retained earnings.

6. (**C**) Consolidated stockholders' equity consists of the stockholders' equity accounts of the parent plus the noncontrolling interest. As a result, dividends paid will include only those paid by the Shaw, the parent.

Task-Based Simulation Solution 4

| FASB ASC | 805 | 10 | 05 | 4 |

Task-Based Simulation Solution 5

| FASB ASC | 805 | 30 | 25 | 4 |

Section 32 - FAR Final Review

Section 32 – FAR Final Review
Corresponding Lecture

Watch the following course lecture with this section:

Lecture 32.01 - FAR Final Review

Lecture 32.01
YOU FINISHED YOUR FAR COURSE...NOW WHAT?
A quick guide to the final days leading up to, and following, the exam

I. FINAL REVIEW
Now is the time to make connections and solidify your understanding of the topics you found most challenging, and to review the most heavily tested topics on the exam.

- ❏ Reread your course notes and review bookmarked lectures.
- ❏ Review your Course Overview page in the Interactive Practice Questions (IPQ) software. Make sure to go through any unanswered questions and review any questions you have answered incorrectly or bookmarked for final review.
- ❏ A great way to gear up for the upcoming exam is by adding a Roger CPA Review Cram Courses to your studies. The Cram Course works very well as a final review, as it is designed to reinforce your understanding of the most heavily tested CPA Exam topics.
- ❏ Take at least one full practice exam using the CPA Exam Simulator in your IPQ. This will help you hone your test taking strategy, time management and self-discipline under exam-like conditions, while continuing to expose you to the material.

II. DAY OF THE EXAM
- ❏ Get a good night's rest before heading into your exam.
- ❏ Arrive to the Prometric testing center at least 60 minutes before your appointment so you have time to park, check-in, and use the restroom before your exam begins.
- ❏ Bring your Notice to Schedule (NTS) and two forms of acceptable identification (see Intro for more details).
- ❏ Proceed through check-in: store belongings, get fingerprinted, have photo taken, sign log book, get seated, write your Launch Code (from your NTS) on your noteboard.
- ❏ Don't stress. You've prepared for this; now, just breathe and power through!

III. DURING THE EXAM
- ❏ Remember your FAR Exam time strategy, and jot down the times at which you want to be at your benchmarks:
    - ○ FAR includes calculations
    - ○ Allocate 80 seconds per multiple choice question as a benchmark
    - ○ Allocate 15-25 minutes per task-based simulation, depending on complexity
    - ○ Plan to use no more than 10 minutes per research question
    - ○ Take the standard 15-minute break after the 3rd testlet – it does not count against your time
    - ○ (Remember that any other break will count against your time)

FAR: 4 Hour Exam					
Testlet 1	Testlet 2	Testlet 3	Break	Testlet 4	Testlet 5
33 MCQs	33 MCQs	2 TBSs		3 TBSs	3 TBSs
45 min	45 min	30 min		60 min	60 min

- You will be given 10 minutes to review the welcome screens and exam instructions. You should already be familiar with these screens after taking the AICPA Sample Test, and can bypass them during your exam.
- Once you begin testing, make sure to read each question carefully, paying close attention to the keywords that dictate the question's intention (e.g. *except, is greater than, must, never*).
- Take note if your questions are getting more difficult. That's a good sign! A progressively harder exam indicates that you are performing well.

IV. AFTER THE EXAM

- Remember, it is normal to not feel great after you're done with your exam. It's a tough exam and designed to challenge your confidence and competencies.
- Relax and celebrate! You've earned it.
- Your scores will be released within a couple of weeks (see Intro for table). GOOD LUCK!!!

Section 33 – Document Review Simulations (DRS) Appendix

Corresponding Lectures

Watch the following course lectures with this section:

Lecture 33.01 – DRS Introduction – Part 1
Lecture 33.02 – DRS Introduction – Part 2

Document Review Simulations (DRS) Appendix

Lecture 33.01

Lecture 33.02

DOCUMENT REVIEW SIMULATIONS OVERVIEW

In July of 2016, the CPA Exam introduced a new type of Task-based simulation known as Document Review Simulations (DRS). These problems have been added to the AUD, FAR and REG exams, and will be added to the BEC exam in conjunction with the overarching 2017 CPA Exam changes that will go into effect April 1, 2017.

What is a DRS?

DRS are designed to simulate tasks that the candidate will be required to perform as a newly licensed CPA (based on up to two years' experience as a CPA). Each DRS presents a document that has a series of highlighted phrases or sentences that the candidate will need to determine are correct or incorrect. To help make these conclusions, numerous supporting documents, or resources, such as legal letters, phone transcripts, financial statements, trial balances and authoritative literature will be included. The candidate will need to sort through these documents to determine what is, and what is not important to solving the problem.

Why is this happening?

The AICPA conducted a Practice Analysis from 2014-2015 in which one main finding was clear: firms are expecting newly licensed CPAs on their staff to perform at a higher level—and they aren't. So the AICPA is raising the bar with a revamped CPA Exam that more authentically tests candidates on the tasks and skill level that will be required of them as newly licensed CPAs. The introduction of DRS in July of 2016 was the first step in this larger initiative, with the overarching changes soon to follow in 2017.

What will DRS be testing?

Up until recently, the CPA Exam has only tested candidates on the skill levels *Remembering & Understanding* and *Application* (skill levels based on Bloom's Taxonomy of Educational Objectives). To meet industry demands for the CPA Exam to test at a higher skill level, the CPA Exam is pivoting to test the higher order skills *Analysis* and *Evaluation* (Evaluation in AUD only). As a direct correlation to this exam evolution, DRS problems are designed to test these higher order skills by requiring candidates to actually analyze and evaluate documents they would see in the work force.

HOW A DRS WORKS

As shown below, the DRS will present several tabs:
- **Document Review**: The main document for the candidate to review
- **Authoritative Literature**: Which is available on all Task-based simulations
- **Resources/Financial Statements**: A series of supporting documents which may, or may not help candidates complete the problem
- **Help**: Explanation of how to answer the problem

Notice the highlighted items within the main document. These represent the specific sentences or phrases that the candidate is required to analyze.

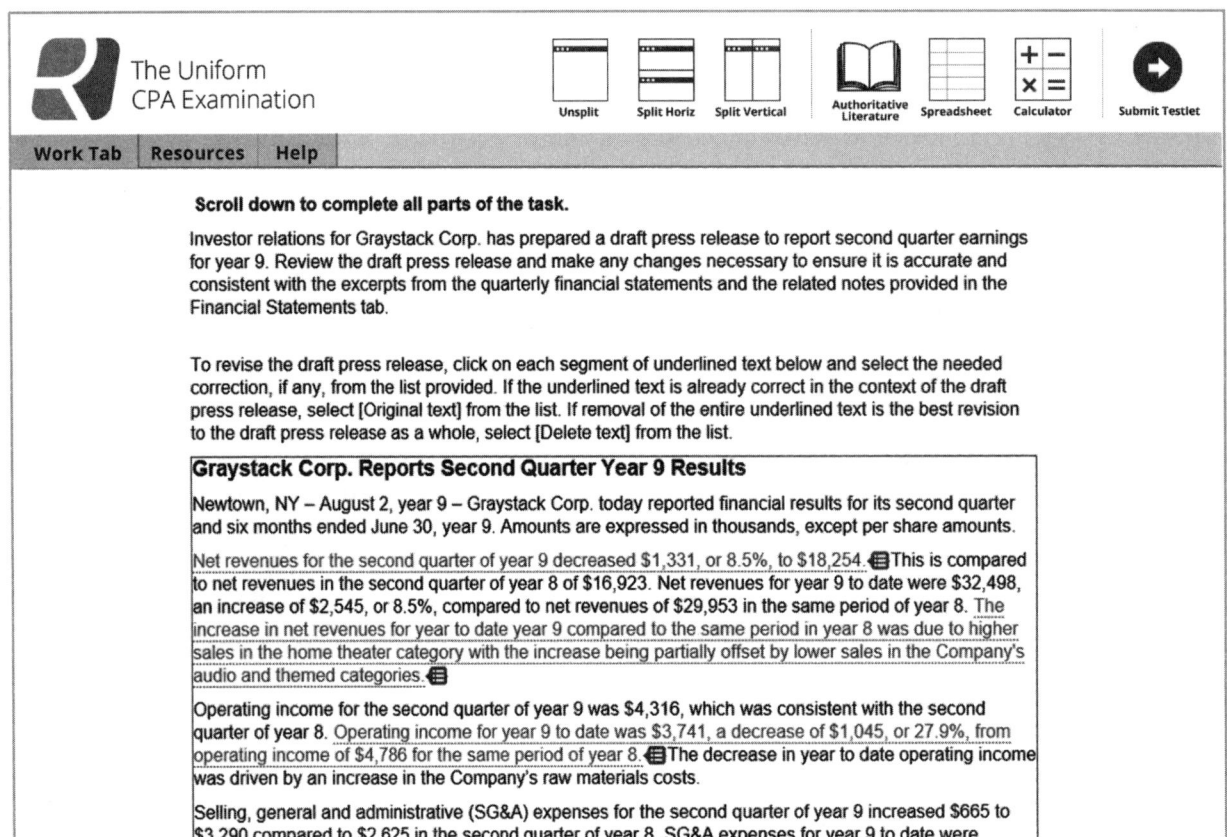

To address each item within the problem, click on the highlighted phrase to see answer options. Each item will include the option to leave original text, delete text, or edit the text using the provided edit choices.

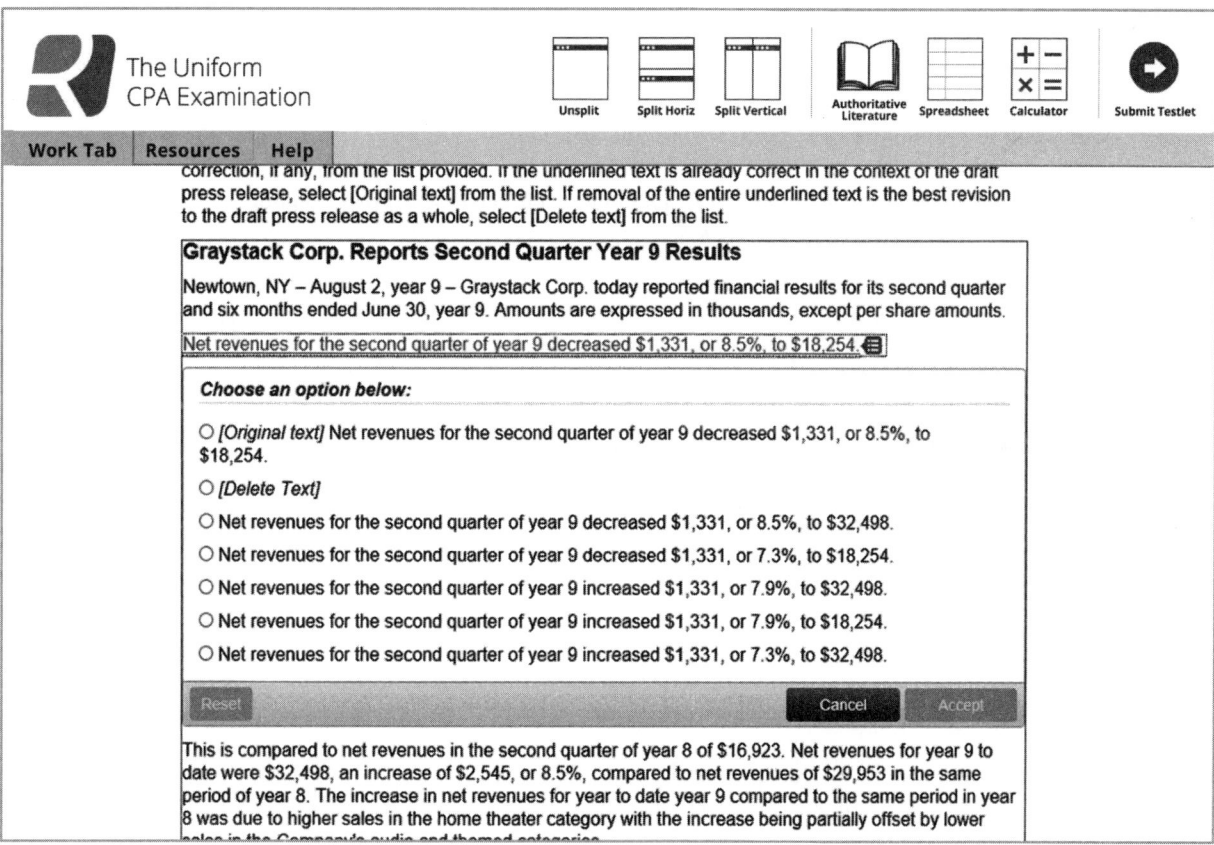

Once an item has been answered, a checkmark icon will appear next to the item in the document.

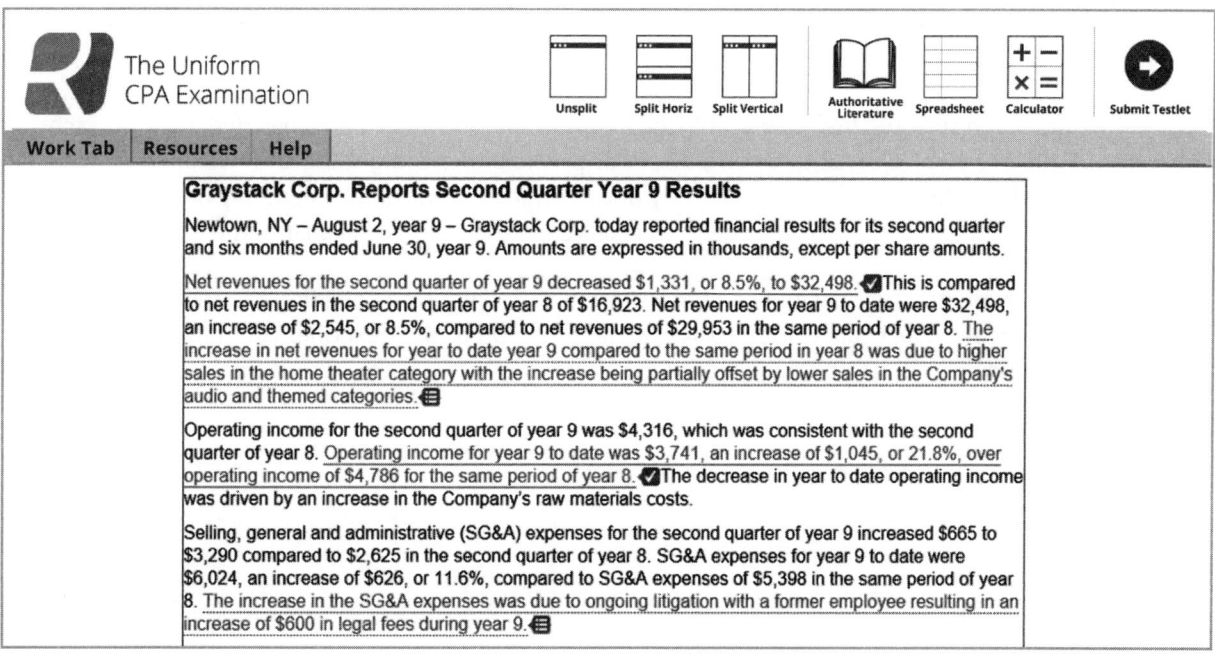

Approaching a FAR DRS

Step 1 – Get the lay of the land. YOU are the CPA – what is being asked of you? Skim over all the content in the Document Review tab to find out. You could be asked to do any of the following:
- Review the work of others – use your professional judgment, professional skepticism, and technical expertise to identify issues or correct errors.
- Plan the work of others.
- Analyze and choose the best course of action from various alternatives presented.
- Address a client's technical questions and requests.
- Draw on knowledge that is more extensively tested in a different exam section – detailed FAR knowledge may be expected for an AUD DRS, for instance.

Step 2 – Mentally note the gist of the DRS. "OK, this problem requires me to edit this company's d press release to make sure it is true to the financial information contained in the accompanying finan statements."

Step 3 – Note the DRS subquestions. Briefly note down each DRS subquestion on your scratch whiteboard – you bought a handheld whiteboard just for CPA Exam study, right? Use your own short For instance, you might write:
1. Net rev Δ (the triangles stand for delta, a common shorthand for change)
2. Reason for Δ net rev
3. Op income Δ
4. Reason for SG&A Δ
5. Stock warrants

Step 4 (Optional) – Choose an order of attack. Consider customizing the order in which you approach subquestions. It won't always be possible to tell, but if a few subquestions appear to be more time-consuming than others, consider moving them to the back of the queue. We don't know for sure, but we suspect each DRS subquestion is worth exactly as much as all the others – there are no bonus points for getting the most time-consuming ones right. Therefore, do the easiest ones first.

Here, the easier subquestions appear to be 1 and 3 above – change in net revenue or operating income is a simple calculation vs. thinking through **the reasons why** they changed.

Step 5 – Attack each subquestion one at a time. In either the default or custom order, work on each subquestion one at a time in order to be as efficient as possible to avoid getting overwhelmed. Remember that the necessary information for any one subquestion will almost certainly be contained across multiple documents. You may also need to research in the Authoritative Literature.

Try to focus strictly on one subquestion at a time, but if you find yourself spending too much time on any one subquestion, make a tactical decision to skip it and move on to the next one. You may even decide to leave that subquestion undone and only return to it after completing other TBSs in the TBS testlet containing the DRS.

Check off each subquestion on your list as you complete it.

Step 6 – Go through a process of elimination for each subquestion.

Each DRS subquestion is similar to a multiple-choice question. The process of elimination, therefore, is a great tactic to employ. You can first eliminate **documents** and then **answer choices**.
Read the subquestion and all its answer choices first. For instance, answering the subquestion with default text 'Net revenues for the second quarter of year 9 decreased $1,331, or 8.5%, to $18,254.' clearly will involve only the Consolidated Statements of Operations. Therefore, you can ignore pages 2 through 5 of the financial statements.

Next, as you focus on the relevant document(s), eliminate answer choices one by one. The Consolidated Statements of Operations make clear that Q2 net revenues **increased** from year 8 to year 9. That allows us to eliminate three answer choices easily:

- ~~Net revenues for the second quarter of year 9 decreased $1,331, or 8.5%, to $18,254.~~
- [Delete Text]
- ~~Net revenues for the second quarter of year 9 decreased $1,331, or 8.5%, to $32,498.~~
- ~~Net revenues for the second quarter of year 9 decreased $1,331, or 7.3%, to $18,254.~~
- Net revenues for the second quarter of year 9 increased $1,331, or 7.9%, to $32,498.
- Net revenues for the second quarter of year 9 increased $1,331, or 7.9%, to $18,254.
- Net revenues for the second quarter of year 9 increased $1,331, or 7.3%, to $32,498.

The clear winner from the three remaining is 'Net revenues for the second quarter of year 9 increased $1,331, or 7.9%, to $18,254.' because the year-over-year increase of $1,331 over Q2 year 8 revenue of $16,923 is a 7.9% increased.

Follow this process of elimination for each subquestion, first eliminating documents, then answer choices. Even in cases where you're not sure there is a clear 'winner' answer choice, you will at least have eliminated some clear losers and given yourself a fighting chance.

SAMPLE FAR DRS
Document Review

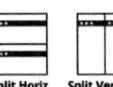

Scroll down to complete all parts of this task.

Investor relations for Graystack Corp. has prepared a draft press release to report second quarter earnings for year 9. Review the draft press release and make any changes necessary to ensure it is accurate and consistent with the excerpts from the quarterly financial statements and the related notes provided in the Financial Statements tab.

To revise the draft press release, click on each segment of underlined text below and select the needed correction, if any, from the list provided. If the underlined text is already correct in the context of the draft press release, select [Original text] from the list. If removal of the entire underlined text is the best revision to the draft press release as a whole, select [Delete text] from the list.

Graystack Corp. Reports Second Quarter Year 9 Results

Newtown, NY – August 2, year 9 – Graystack Corp. today reported financial results for its second quarter and six months ended June 30, year 9. Amounts are expressed in thousands, except per share amounts.

1.) <u>Net revenues for the second quarter of year 9 decreased $1,331, or 8.5%, to $18,254.</u> This is compared to net revenues in the second quarter of year 8 of $16,923. Net revenues for year 9 to date were $32,498, an increase of $2,545, or 8.5%, compared to net revenues of $29,953 in the same period of year 8. 2.) <u>The increase in net revenues for year to date year 9 compared to the same period in year 8 was due to higher sales in the home theater category with the increase being partially offset by lower sales in the Company's audio and themed categories.</u>

Operating income for the second quarter of year 9 was $4,316, which was consistent with the second quarter of year 8. 3.) <u>Operating income for year 9 to date was $3,741, a decrease of $1,045, or 27.9%, from operating income of $4,786 for the same period of year 8.</u> The decrease in year to date operating income was driven by an increase in the Company's raw materials costs. Selling, general and administrative (SG&A) expenses for the second quarter of year 9 increased $665 to $3,290 compared to $2,625 in the second quarter of year 8. SG&A expenses for year 9 to date were $6,024, an increase of $626, or 11.6%, compared to SG&A expenses of $5,398 in the same period of year 8. 4.) <u>The increase in the SG&A expenses was due to ongoing litigation with a former employee resulting in an increase of $600 in legal fees during year 9.</u>

Net income for the second quarter of year 9 was $3,232 or $0.13 basic net income per share compared to $3,587 for the second quarter of year 8 or $0.14 basic net income per share. Diluted net income per share for the second quarter of year 9 was $0.11 per share (year 8: $0.12). Net income for year 9 to date was $2,013 or $0.08 basic net income per share compared to a net income of $3,966 or $0.16 basic net income per share for the same period in year 8. Diluted net income per share for year 9 to date was $0.07 per share (year 8: $0.13). 5.) <u>If the warrants outstanding were exercised in full, diluted net income per share for year 9 to date would decrease to $0.06 per share.</u>

Resources
Financial Statements

GRAYSTACK CORP. AND SUBSIDIARIES
CONSOLIDATED STATEMENTS OF OPERATIONS
(Unaudited)
(In thousands, except earnings per share data)

	Three Months Ended June 30,		Six Months Ended June 30,	
	year 9	year 8	year 9	year 8
Net revenues:				
Net revenues	$18,254	$16,923	$32,498	$29,953
Costs and expenses:				
Cost of sales	9,625	8,999	20,774	17,927
Selling, general and administrative	3,290	2,625	6,024	5,398
Other operating costs and expenses	1,023	996	1,959	1,842
Total costs and expenses	13,938	12,620	28,757	25,167
Operating income	4,316	4,303	3,741	4,786
Interest, income, net	8	11	15	20
Unrealized (losses) gains on trading securities	(25)	249	(28)	511
Income before income taxes	4,299	4,563	3,728	5,317
Provision for income taxes	1,067	976	1,715	1,351
Net Income	$3,232	$3,587	$2,013	$3,966
Basic net income per share:	$0.13	$0.14	$0.08	$0.16
Diluted net income per share:	$0.11	$0.12	$0.07	$0.13
Weighted average shares outstanding:				
Basic	25,000	25,000	25,000	25,000
Diluted	30,000	30,000	30,000	30,000

The accompanying notes are an integral part of the interim consolidated financial statements.

GRAYSTACK CORP. AND SUBSIDIARIES
CONSOLIDATED BALANCE SHEETS
(In thousands, except earnings per share data)

	June 30, year 9 (unaudited)	December 31, year 8
ASSETS		
Current Assets:		
Cash	$ 10,843	$ 14,596
Restricted cash	20	20
Accounts receivables, net	7,366	5,128
Other receivables	237	385
Investments in trading securities	6,003	6,031
Inventory	9,382	8,946
Prepaid expenses and other current assets	14	18
Deferred tax assets	320	296
Total Current Assets	**34,185**	**35,420**
Property, plant, and equipment, net	2,062	2,102
Deferred tax assets	1,375	1,209
Other Assets	420	412
Total Assets	**$ 38,042**	**$ 39,143**
LIABILITIES AND SHAREHOLDERS' EQUITY		
Current liabilities:		
Short-term borrowings	$ 1,953	$ 2,850
Current maturities of long-term borrowings	102	102
Accounts payable	5,936	7,403
Accrued expenses	848	597
Income tax payable	398	378
Total current liabilities	**9,237**	**11,330**
Long-term borrowings	975	1,077
Deferred tax liabilities	111	89
Total liabilities	**10,323**	**12,496**
Shareholders' equity:		
Common shares - $.01 par value, 75,000 shares authorized, 50,000 shares issued, and 25,000 shares outstanding	250	250
Capital in excess of par value	13,598	13,598
Retained Earnings	26,371	25,299
Treasury shares, at cost, 25,000 shares	(12,500)	(12,500)
Total shareholders' equity	**27,719**	**26,647**
Total liabilities and shareholders' equity	**$ 38,042**	**$ 39,143**

The accompanying notes are an integral part of the interim consolidated financial statements

GRAYSTACK CORP. AND SUBSIDIARIES
CONSOLIDATED STATEMENTS OF CASH FLOWS
(Unaudited)
(In thousands)

	Six Months Ended June 30,	
	year 9	year 8
Cash flows from operating activities:		
Net income	$ 2,013	$ 3,966
Adjustments to reconcile net income to net cash (used) provided by operating activities:		
Depreciation and amortization	250	235
Deferred tax expenses	(168)	272
Unrealized (losses) gains on trading securities	28	(511)
Net changes in assets and liabilities:		
Accounts receivables, net	(2,238)	(1,695)
Other receivables	148	(57)
Inventory	(436)	(1,319)
Prepaid expenses and other current assets	4	7
Other assets	(8)	(24)
Accounts payable and accrued expenses	(1,216)	902
Income taxes payable	20	(41)
Net cash (used) provided by operating activities	**(1,603)**	**1,735**
Cash flow from investing activities:		
Additions to property and equipment	(210)	(324)
Cash flow from investing activities:	**(210)**	**(324)**
Cash flows from financing activities:		
Short-term borrowing	250	1,500
Repayments of short-term borrowing	(1,147)	(465)
Repayments of borrowings under long-term credit facility	(102)	(102)
Payment of cash dividends	(941)	(3,524)
Net cash used by financing activities	**(1,940)**	**(2,591)**
Net decrease in cash and cash equivalents	**(3,753)**	**(1,180)**
Cash and cash equivalents at beginning of period	**14,596**	**13,964**
Cash and cash equivalents at end of period	**$10,843**	**$12,784**
Cash paid during the period for:		
Interest	67	63
Income taxes	$ 1,567	$ 1,258

The accompanying notes are an integral part of the interim consolidated financial statements

Note 1 – BACKGROUND AND BASIS OF PRESENTATION

The unaudited interim consolidated financial statements include the accounts of Graystack Corp. ("Graystack", the "Company") an its subsidiaries and affiliates that the Company has a controlling financial interest in or is the primary beneficiary after elimination of intercompany accounts. The Company designs, sources, imports and markets a variety of electronic products. The unaudited interim consolidated financial statements reflect all normal and recurring adjustments that are, in the opinion of management, necessary for a fair presentation of the Company's financial statements. The preparation of the unaudited interim consolidated financial statements requires management to make estimates and assumptions that affect the amounts reported in the financial statements and accompanying notes; actual results could materially differ from those estimates. The unaudited interim consolidated financial statements have been prepared pursuant to the rules and regulations of the Securities and Exchange Commission and accordingly do not include all of the disclosures normally made in the Company's annual consolidated financial statements. While the Company believes that the disclosures presented are adequate to make the information not misleading, these unaudited interim consolidated financial statements should be read in conjunction with the consolidated financial statements and notes thereto for the year ended December 31, year 8, included in the Company's Annual Report on Form 10-K.

Due to the seasonal nature of the Company's business, the results of operations for the three and six month periods ended June 30, year 9 and the cash flows for the six-month period ended June 3, year 9, are not necessarily indicative of the results of operations or cash flows that may be expected for any other interim period or for the full year ended December 31, year 9.

DRS Appendix

Note 2 – NET INCOME PER SHARE

The following table sets forth the computation of basic and diluted net income per share (in thousands, except per share amounts):

	Three months ended June 30			Six months ended June 30	
	year 9	year 8		year 9	year 8
Numerator:					
Net income for basic and diluted net income per share	$3,232	$3,587		$2,013	$3,966
Denominator:					
Denominator for basic net income per share - weighted average shares	25,000	25,000		25,000	25,000
Warrants	5,000	5,000		5,000	5,000
Denominator for diluted net income per share - weighted average shares and assumed conversions	30,000	30,000		30,000	30,000
Basic net income per share	$0.13	$0.14		$0.08	$0.16
Diluted net income per share	$0.11	$0.12		$0.07	$0.13

NOTE 3 – SHAREHOLDERS' EQUITY

A summary of changes in shareholders' equity is presented below (in thousands):

	Common shares	Capital in excess of par value	Retained Earnings	Treasury shares	Total
Balance, December 31, year 8	250	13,598	25,299	(12,500)	26,647
Net income	-	-	2,013	-	2,013
Dividends paid	-	-	(941)	-	(941)
Balance, June 30, year 9	**250**	**13,598**	**26,371**	**(12,500)**	**27,719**

Outstanding capital stock at June 30, year 9, consisted of common stock only.

At June 30, year 9, the Company had approximately 5,000,000 warrants outstanding with exercise prices ranging from $.50 to $.60. The warrants are convertible in to 5,000 shares of the common stock of the Company.

NOTE 4 – INVENTORY

Inventory cost is determined using the first-in, first-out method. As of June 30, year 9, and December 31, year 8, inventories consisted of the following (in thousands):

	June 30 year 9	December 31 year 8
Finished goods	$7,500	$6,902
Raw materials	1,882	2,044
Inventory	**$9,382**	**$8,946**

NOTE 5 – ACCOUNTS RECEIVABLE

Accounts receivables represent amounts due from customers throughout the United States. The Company provides for any anticipated credit losses in the financial statements based on management's estimates and ongoing reviews of customer credit quality. The allowance for doubtful accounts balance as of June 30, year 9, was $820 (December 31, year 8: $390).

At the beginning of year 9, the Company discontinued its volume rebate program described below. During year 9, the Company launched a program that offers extended payment terms to long-term customers with high credit ratings and a history of timely payments. The program has resulted in an increase in sales over the prior year.

During the six-month period ended June 30, year 8, the Company provided major customers significant volume rebates. These volume rebates were accounted for on an accrual basis as a reduction to net revenues in the period in which the related revenues were recognized.

NOTE 6 – LEGAL PROCEEDINGS

In April, year 8, a former employee sued the Company alleging wrongful termination. The former employee is seeking damages of $10,000. Discovery is ongoing. Related to this lawsuit, the Company has incurred legal costs of $800 and $200 during the six months ended June 30, year 9 and year 8, respectively. The Company believes the lawsuit is without merit.

Items for Analysis

Net revenues for the second quarter of year 9 decreased $1,331, or 8.5%, to $18,254.

1. Choose an option below:

    - [Original text] Net revenues for the second quarter of year 9 decreased $1,331, or 8.5%, to $18,254.

    - [Delete Text]

    - Net revenues for the second quarter of year 9 decreased $1,331, or 8.5%, to $32,498.

    - Net revenues for the second quarter of year 9 decreased $1,331, or 7.3%, to $18,254.

    - Net revenues for the second quarter of year 9 increased $1,331, or 7.9%, to $32,498.

    - Net revenues for the second quarter of year 9 increased $1,331, or 7.9%, to $18,254.

The increase in net revenues for year to date year 9 compared to the same period in year 8 was due to higher sales in the home theater category with the increase being partially offset by lower sales in the Company's audio and themed categories.

2. Choose an option below:

    - [Original text] The increase in net revenues for year to date year 9 compared to the same period in year 8 was due to higher sales in the home theater category with the increase being partially offset by lower sales in the Company's audio and themed categories.

    - [Delete Text]

    - The increase in net revenues for year to date year 9 compared to the same period in year 8 was due to higher than normal sales volume rebates offered during year 8.

    - The increase in net revenues for year to date year 9 compared to the same period in year 8 was due to a significant customer going bankrupt during year 8 resulting in reduced sales in year 8.

    - The increase in net revenues for year to date year 9 compared to the same period in year 8 was due to the seasonal nature of the Company's business.

Operating income for year 9 to date was $3,741, a decrease of $1,045, or 27.9%, from operating income of $4,786 for the same period of year 8.

3. Choose an option below:

    - [Original text] Operating income for year 9 to date was $3,741, a decrease of $1,045, or 27.9%, from operating income of $4,786 for the same period of year 8.

    - [Delete Text]

    - Operating income for year 9 to date was $3,741, a decrease of $1,045, or 21.8%, from operating income of $4,786 for the same period of year 8.

    - Operating income for year 9 to date was $3,741, an increase of $1,045, or 21.8%, over operating income of $4,786 for the same period of year 8.

    - Operating income for year 9 to date was $3,741, an increase of $1,045, or 27.9%, over operating income of $4,786 for the same period of year 8.

The increase in the SG&A expenses was due to ongoing litigation with a former employee resulting in an increase of $600 in legal fees during year 9.

4. Choose an option below:

    - [Original text] The increase in the SG&A expenses was due to ongoing litigation with a former employee resulting in an increase of $600 in legal fees during year 9.

    - [Delete Text]

    - The increase in SG&A expenses was due to a $511 unrealized loss recorded in March, year 9 as a result of a decline in the fair value of trading securities.

    - The increase in SG&A expenses was due to an increase in the provision for income taxes during year 9.

    - The increase in SG&A expenses was due to the large increase in depreciation expense in year 9 on the acquisition of new property, plant and equipment in the fourth quarter of year 8.

If the warrants outstanding were exercised in full, diluted net income per share for year 9 to date would decrease to $0.06 per share.

5. Choose an option below:

    - [Original text] If the warrants outstanding were exercised in full, diluted net income per share for year 9 to date would decrease to $0.06 per share.

    - [Delete Text]

    - If the warrants outstanding were exercised in full, basic net income per share for year 9 to date would increase to $0.09 per share.

    - If the warrants outstanding were exercised in full, basic net income per share for year 9 to date would increase to $0.15 per share.

    - If the warrants outstanding were exercised in full, diluted net income per share for year 9 to date would decrease to $0.09 per share.

Solution to FAR DRS

Graystack Corp.

This question is asking the candidate to evaluate statements made in a press release regarding an entity's 2nd quarter financial statements. The press release includes 5 underlined sentences or phrases, which may be correct or may be in need of correction. The candidate need only address the underlined items.

To approach this type of problem, the candidate will generally find it most appropriate to deal with each issue in the order in which it is presented.

1. The first underlined item indicates "Net revenues for the second quarter of year 9 decreased $1,331, or 8.5% to $18,254." and, when clicked upon, the following choices appear:

    - *[Original text]* Net revenues for the second quarter of year 9 decreased $1,331, or 8.5% to $18,254.
    - *[Delete Text]*
    - Net revenues for the second quarter of year 9 decreased $1,331, or 8.5% to $32,498.
    - Net revenues for the second quarter of year 9 decreased $1,331, or 7.3% to $18,254.
    - Net revenues for the second quarter of year 9 increased $1,331, or 7.9% to $32,498.
    - Net revenues for the second quarter of year 9 increased $1,331, or 7.9% to $18,254.
    - Net revenues for the second quarter of year 9 increased $1,331, or 7.3% to $32,498.

    The information to answer this will be provided in Graystack's financial statements. By clicking on the tab for "Financial Statements", the candidate will find a statement entitled Consolidated Statements of Operations. This shows:

    - Revenues in the second quarter of year nine are reported at $18,254, compared to $16,923 in the corresponding quarter for year 8. This represents an increase, not a decrease, in revenues of the difference of $1,331.
    - An increase of $1,331, based on revenues of $16,923, represents an increase of $1,331/$16,923 or 7.9%.

    As a result, the correct response will be:

    - ***Net revenues for the second quarter of year 9 increased $1,331, or 7.9% to $18,254.***

2. The next underlined item indicates "The increase in net revenues for year to date year 9 compared to the same period in year 8 was due to higher sales in the home theater category with the increase being partially offset by lower sales in the Company's audio themed categories". The choices are:

    - *[Original text]* The increase in net revenues for year to date year 9 compared to the same period in year 8 was due to higher sales in the home theater category with the increase being partially offset by lower sales in the Company's audio themed categories.
    - *[Delete Text]*
    - The increase in net revenues for year to date year 9 compared to the same period in year 8 was due to higher than normal sales volume rebates offered during year 8.

- The increase in net revenues for year to date year 9 compared to the same period in year 8 was due to a significant customer going bankrupt during year 8 resulting in reduced sales in year 8.
- The increase in net revenues for year to date year 9 compared to the same period in year 8 was due to the seasonal nature of the Company's business.

The financial statements do not provide sufficient detail to be able to determine the cause for the increase in revenues. As a result, the candidate should address the notes to the financial statements. Upon scanning the footnotes, the candidate should be able to determine that Note 5 related to accounts receivable provides relevant information.

In the first sentence of the 2nd paragraph, it indicates "At the beginning of year 9, the Company discontinued its volume rebate program described below". In the 3rd paragraph it indicates "During the six-month period ending June 30, year 8, the Company provided major customers significant volume rebates. These volume rebates were accounted for on the accrual basis as a reduction to net revenues in the period in which the related revenues were recognized."

Since rebates, which reduce net revenues, were attributed to the first 6 months of year 8 and were discontinued as of the beginning of year 9, unless there was a reduction in sales volume in year 9, this alone would account for an increase in revenues.

As a result, the candidate should select:

- ***The increase in net revenues for year to date year 9 compared to the same period in year 8 was due to higher than normal sales volume rebates offered during year 8.***

As to the other choices:

- *[Original text]* The increase in net revenues for year to date year 9 compared to the same period in year 8 was due to higher sales in the home theater category with the increase being partially offset by lower sales in the Company's audio themed categories.

There is no information provided that indicates that there was an increase in home theater sales or a decrease in sales in the audio themed categories.

- The increase in net revenues for year to date year 9 compared to the same period in year 8 was due to a significant customer going bankrupt during year 8 resulting in reduced sales in year 8.

The bankruptcy of a major customer during year 8 would not only cause a decrease in sales in year 8, it could create an even greater decrease in year 9, assuming the customer may have had some recorded purchases in year 8, prior to the bankruptcy, and would have had no sales in year 9. Regardless, there is nothing in either the financial statements or the footnotes that indicates that a major customer declared bankruptcy during year 8.

- The increase in net revenues for year to date year 9 compared to the same period in year 8 was due to the seasonal nature of the Company's business.

The Company's seasonality would make some quarters' revenues within the same fiscal year to be disproportionately high and others to be disproportionately low, the same seasonal fluctuations would presumably occur each fiscal year and, as a result, would not justify the increase from one year to the next.

3. The next underlined item indicates "Operating income for year 9 to date was $3,741, a decrease of $1,045, or 27.9%, from operating income of $4,786 for the same period of year 8." The alternatives are:

- *[Original text]* Operating income for year 9 to date was $3,741, a decrease of $1,045, or 27.9%, from operating income of $4,786 for the same period of year 8.
- *[Delete Text]*
- Operating income for year 9 to date was $3,741, a decrease of $1,045, or 21.8%, from operating income of $4,786 for the same period of year 8.
- Operating income for year 9 to date was $3,741, an increase of $1,045, or 21.8%, over operating income of $4,786 for the same period of year 8.
- Operating income for year 9 to date was $3,741, an increase of $1,045, or 27.9%, over operating income of $4,786 for the same period of year 8.

By reviewing the income statement, it can be readily determined that operating income in year 8 was $4,786 and that it was only $3,741, representing a decrease, not an increase, of $1,045. The percentage difference can be determined by dividing the decrease by the amount for year 8, resulting in a decrease of $1,045/$4,786 or 21.8%.

As a result, the choice to be selected is:

- **Operating income for year 9 to date was $3,741, a decrease of $1,045, or 21.8%, from operating income of $4,786 for the same period of year 8.**

4. The next underlined item indicates "The increase in SG&A expenses was due to ongoing litigation with a former employee resulting in an increase of $600 in legal fees during year 9." The alternatives are:

- *[Original text]* The increase in SG&A expenses was due to ongoing litigation with a former employee resulting in an increase of $600 in legal fees during year 9.
- *[Delete Text]*
- The increase in SG&A expenses was due to a $511 unrealized loss recorded in March, year 9 as a result of a decline in the fair value of trading securities.
- The increase in SG&A expenses was due to an increase in the provision for income taxes during year 9.
- The increase in SG&A expenses was due to the large increase in depreciation expense in year 9 on the acquisition of new property, plant and equipment in the fourth quarter of year 8.

This item can best be solved by evaluating each alternative to determine which, if any, would result in an increase of $626 in SG&A expenses in the 2nd quarter of year 9 as compared to year 8.

- The 1st alternative is a possibility since the amount approximately corresponds to the increase, legal expenses would be included in SG&A expenses, and Note 6 – Legal Proceedings confirms that a case brought by a former employee has cost the company $800 in year 9 and $200 in year 8, a $600 difference.
- The 2nd alternative to delete the text will only be selected if none of the other choices fit. Since the 1st choice is a possibility, there clearly will be a selection. The candidate now needs to determine if there is a better alternative among those remaining.
- The 3rd alternative is not a possibility since an unrealized loss on trading securities is not reported in SG&A expenses. The candidate can note that, on the consolidated statements of operations, the loss is reported below operating income.

- The 4th alternative is not a possibility because the provision for income taxes is not included in SG&A expenses. The candidate can note that, on the consolidated statements of operations, the tax provision is reported below operating income.

- The 5th alternative is not a possibility because of the amount involved. Although depreciation is not reported separately on the consolidated statements of operations, the statement of cash flows indicates that depreciation and amortization in year 9 was $250, compared to $235 in year 8. This $15 increase does not reasonably account for an increase of over $600.

As a result, the best selection will be:

- *[Original text]* **The increase in SG&A expenses was due to ongoing litigation with a former employee resulting in an increase of $600 in legal fees during year 9**.

5. The next underlined item indicates "If the warrants outstanding were exercised in full, diluted net income per share for year 9 to date would decrease to $0.06 per share." The alternatives are:

    - *[Original text]* If the warrants outstanding were exercised in full, diluted net income per share for year 9 to date would decrease to $0.06 per share.
    - *[Delete Text]*
    - If the warrants outstanding were exercised in full, basic net income per share for year 9 to date would increase to $0.09 per share.
    - If the warrants outstanding were exercised in full, basic net income per share for year 9 to date would increase to $0.15 per share.
    - If the warrants outstanding were exercised in full, diluted net income per share for year 9 to date would decrease to $0.09 per share.

Since this item is asking about the effect on net income per share if warrants are exercised, the candidate should consider that the calculation of basic earnings per share is based on shares outstanding, which does not include the warrants, but diluted earnings per share is calculated based on the assumption that dilutive warrants are exercised. As a result, if the warrants were exercised, diluted net income per share would remain unchanged.

Basic earnings per share is equal to net income available to common stockholders divided by the weighted average shares outstanding, which would not include warrants.

The dilutive effect of options and warrants are reflected in diluted EPS. Two things the candidate should note:

- The facts of the problem do not provide enough information to apply the treasury stock method.
- Since the financial statements and notes reflect earnings per share information, unless directed otherwise, the candidate should assume that it is calculated correctly.

To determine the effect on basic earnings per share, the candidate will refer to Note 3, which indicates "At June 30, year 9, the Company had approximately 5,000,000 warrants outstanding with exercise prices ranging from $.50 to $.60. The warrants are convertible into 5,000,000 shares of the common stock of the Company." In addition, note 2 shows that 25,000 shares were used to calculate basic earnings per share and 30,000 shares were used to calculate diluted earnings per share, taking into account the 5,000,000 shares resulting from the presumed conversion of the warrants.

In calculating basic earnings per share, if all of the warrants were exercised, there would be no effect on net income, causing it to remain the same at $2,013. Shares, on the other hand, would increase from 25,000 to 30,000, resulting in a decrease in basic net income per share. Income of $2,013 would be divided by 30,000 shares, instead of the 25,000 previously used, giving basic net income per share of $0.07, the same as diluted net income per share.

The item to be selected will be:

- *[Delete Text]*